Personal Justice Denied

THE COMMISSION ON WARTIME RELOCATION AND INTERNMENT OF CIVILIANS

Joan Z. Bernstein, *Chair*

Daniel E. Lungren, *Vice-Chair*

Edward W. Brooke

Robert F. Drinan

Arthur S. Flemming

Arthur J. Goldberg

Ishmael V. Gromoff

William M. Marutani

Hugh B. Mitchell

Angus Macbeth, *Special Counsel*

Personal Justice Denied

Report of the Commission
on Wartime Relocation
and Internment of Civilians

With a New Foreword by Tetsuden Kashima

The Civil Liberties Public Education Fund
Washington, D.C., and San Francisco

University of Washington Press
Seattle and London

Personal Justice Denied was originally published in two volumes by the U.S. Government Printing Office in 1982 and 1983. The present volume was first published by The Civil Liberties Public Education Fund and the University of Washington Press in 1997.

Prologue © 1997 by The Civil Liberties Public Education Fund

Foreword by Tetsuden Kashima © 1997 by the University of Washington Press
Printed in the United States of America

Library of Congress Cataloging-in-Publication Data

United States. Commission on Wartime Relocation and Internment of Civilians.
    Personal justice denied / report of the Commission on Wartime Relocation and Internment of Civilians : with a new foreword by Tetsuden Kashima.
        p.   cm.
    Includes bibliographical references and index.
    ISBN 0–295–97558-X (alk. paper)
    1. Japanese Americans—Evacuation and relocation, 1942–1945.   2. Japanese Americans—Civil rights.   I. Title.
D769.8.A6U39   1996   96–13689
940.53′1503956073—dc20   CIP

The paper used in this publication meets the minimum requirements of American National Standard for Information Sciences—Permanence of Paper for Printed Library Materials, ANSI Z39.48–1984. ∞

The map on page 26 is reprinted from *Years of Infamy: The Untold Story of America's Concentration Camps*, by Michi Weglyn (University of Washington Press, 1996).

[I]t remained a fact that to loyal citizens this forced evacuation was a personal injustice, and Stimson fully appreciated their feelings.

—Henry L. Stimson and McGeorge Bundy,
On Active Service in Peace and War

Contents

Prologue by The Civil Liberties Public Education Fund   *ix*
Foreword by Tetsuden Kashima   *xv*
Introduction by Angus Macbeth, Special Counsel   *xxvii*
Summary   *1*

PART I. NISEI AND ISSEI
  1. Before Pearl Harbor   *27*
  2. Executive Order 9066   *47*
  3. Exclusion and Evacuation   *93*
  4. Economic Loss   *117*
  5. Assembly Centers   *135*
  6. Relocation Centers   *149*
  7. Loyalty: Leave and Segregation   *185*
  8. Ending the Exclusion   *213*
  9. Protest and Disaffection   *245*
  10. Military Service   *253*
  11. Hawaii   *261*
  12. Germans and German Americans   *283*
  13. After Camp   *295*
  Appendix: Latin Americans   *303*

PART II. THE ALEUTS
  War and Evacuation in Alaska   *317*

Notes to Parts I and II   *361*

PART III. RECOMMENDATIONS
  Recommendations   *455*

PART IV. PAPERS FOR THE COMMISSION
  Addendum to *Personal Justice Denied*   *471*

Index   *479*

Prologue

We often take our civil rights and civil liberties for granted. When we vote, we go to a polling place and privately vote our conscience, casting our ballot for a candidate or issue of choice. We are free to express our opinions on any controversial issue among friends, family, or others. We also can go to an after-hours grocery store to pick up something for a late-night snack. Moving about freely and expressing our opinions are not only socially acceptable, they are guaranteed under the Constitution and Bill of Rights.

But how would you respond if your civil liberties were taken away? How would you feel if the police arrested you because you were wearing a certain color shirt that was coincidentally the color worn by a local street gang? What if the minister at your neighborhood church were suddenly taken away for questioning because he was a respected leader in your community? What if vandals broke into your home, sprayed graffiti, and ransacked your property simply because of your race, gender, or religious affiliation? You would be angry and stunned! Yet these were exactly the outrages directed against an innocent group of American citizens and legal residents during a period of wartime hysteria. They happened during World War II, and could happen again, not just to citizens and permanent resident aliens of Japanese ancestry but to any other group, for an arbitrary reason, if we fail to learn the lessons of history.

That is why *Personal Justice Denied* is an important document for all Americans. We need to understand that our civil and constitutional rights, however precious and important they may be to us, are vulnerable to arbitrary intrusion from our own government, especially during times of crisis.

In many ways this publication was an extension of the Civil Rights Movement of the 1960s, which helped raise the nation's consciousness about the negative effects of racial prejudice and discrimination. In the sixties, nearly all segments of the country were struggling to understand the seeds of prejudice and hatred. For the Japanese American community, this period was also an opportunity to raise issues regarding its identity, culture, and experience in America. Through its own initiative and leadership, the community struggled to learn more about the wartime experience of Japanese Americans forced to leave their homes and businesses. Americans of Japanese ancestry struggled to understand issues of forced detention without due process, the rationale of military necessity and racial discrimination, and the emotional pain and suffering of those detained while their sons were serving in the military, defending the very rights their families were being denied.

The learning process was both enlightening and empowering. The lessons from this experience were important not just for one community but for the general population. In bringing this issue to the forefront of national attention, the Japanese American community sought to educate the American public about the violation of constitutional rights and the potential for abuse of power by the government and the military. They also appealed for redress for those directly affected.

In response to the advocacy for redress by a broad spectrum of the Japanese American community, Congress created the Commission on Wartime Relocation and Internment of Civilians (CWRIC) to review and analyze the official government contention, historically accepted, that the exclusion, forced removal, and detention of Americans of Japanese ancestry were justified by military necessity. The Commission was charged with issuing a report to Congress and with making appropriate recommendations based on its findings. One of the Commission's recommendations was to establish a program to educate the American public on the issues involved.

Based on CWRIC recommendations, the Congress adopted, and the President signed into law, Public Law 100-383 (The Civil Liberties Act of 1988), which created The Civil Liberties Public Education Fund (CLPEF). Specifically, the legislation mandates the CLPEF:

to sponsor research and public educational activities, and to publish and distribute the hearings, findings, and recommendations of the Commission, so that the events surrounding the evacuation, relocation, and internment of United States citizens and permanent resident aliens of Japanese ancestry will be remembered, and so that the causes and circumstances of this and similar events may be illuminated and understood.

Our collaboration with the University of Washington Press to publish the second edition of *Personal Justice Denied* partially fulfills the Congressional mandate. However, the CLPEF's interests were not limited to compliance with the mandate.

We collaborated on republishing this book because we believe it contributes to the advancement of knowledge about civil and human rights in general, as well as it illuminates the specific injustice aimed at Americans of Japanese ancestry. The wartime treatment of Japanese Americans was promulgated under Executive Order 9066, which was signed by President Franklin Roosevelt on February 19, 1942. After extensive hearings and deliberations, the Commission published its findings and conclusions in *Personal Justice Denied*, which stated:

> In sum, Executive Order 9066 was not justified by military necessity, and the decisions that followed from it—exclusion, detention, the ending of detention and the ending of exclusion—were not founded upon military considerations. The broad historical causes that shaped these decisions were race prejudice, war hysteria and a failure of political leadership. ("Recommendations," p. 459)

This conclusion and the supporting documentation contained in the publication are important in many respects. First, *Personal Justice Denied* was the catalyst for a series of historic public policies that addressed the violation of constitutional rights of a segment of its citizenry. Utilizing the findings and recommendations of the Commission on Wartime Relocation and Internment of Civilians, Congress, in its 100th session, deliberated upon and adopted House Resolution 442, which offered an apology to those whose constitutional rights were violated during World War II. Not only was this resolution adopted by Congress, but the legislation implementing it was signed into law by President Reagan at a ceremony in which he stated that "this is a great day for America." Civil rights attorneys used the testimony to the CWRIC as a basis to vacate U.S. Supreme Court convictions based on military necessity in the exclusion, forced removal, and detention of U.S. citizens during times of crisis.

Second, *Personal Justice Denied* is a record of injustices. It is

based on countless hours of testimony, and it documents human suffering and the waste of human resources. In 1983 dollars, the Commission
estimated that between $810 million and $2.0 billion was lost in income
and property ("Recommendations," p. 459). In the detention centers,
families lived in substandard housing, had inadequate nutrition and
health care, and had their livelihoods destroyed; many continued to
suffer psychologically long after their release. As their parents and
families were detained in the camps allegedly because of military necessity, young men volunteered or were drafted to defend their country in
the war. Others spent three years in the federal penitentiary after the
camps because of their resistance to the incarceration and their insistence that the camps were a violation of their constitutional rights.

Third, *Personal Justice Denied* is a case study of the violation of
constitutional rights of American citizens and of how to remedy those
violations when they occur. The story of the Commission is not simply
about redressing the past. It is a story about a free society's ability to
recognize the vulnerabilities and frailties of a democracy. The Commission's effort recognizes that from time to time in America's history
mistakes have been made, and that in the case of the detention of
Americans of Japanese ancestry, a clear violation of constitutional rights
occurred.

Fourth, *Personal Justice Denied* reminds us that this travesty of
justice could easily happen to any other group, especially at times when
certain groups are perceived to be unpopular: during periods of social
unrest, during political crises, during war, or during economic recession. Educating people about the incarceration of one group will help
prevent its happening to other minorities in our American democracy.

Personal Justice Denied was the foundation for these historic findings and conclusions. It provided a paper trail of compelling evidence
to document the serious violations of rights inflicted upon Japanese
American citizens and legal residents. With mountains of evidence and
detail, the book effectively refutes the rationale used to justify the
incarceration. It not only serves as an informative case study, it provides a framework for understanding how to deal with future attacks on
human rights.

The education of the American public regarding the exclusion,
forced removal, and detention of Americans of Japanese ancestry does
not begin, nor will it end, with this publication. There are now other
tools to educate the public on this shameful episode in American history. Some local school boards have adopted resolutions calling for
their schools to recognize February 19 as an official "Day of Remem-

brance." Museums sponsor exhibits capturing portions of the incarceration experience. State legislatures encourage textbook publishers to include in their textbooks more than just one sentence about the incarceration as a violation of human and civil rights and not an act of military necessity. Workshops are sponsored by community organizations to encourage the teaching of these valuable lessons. Still, ignorance persists. Many are not aware of the terrible story; others deny that the incarceration ever happened. The Civil Liberties Public Education Fund itself will sponsor a grants program aimed at educating the public in an effort to remind Americans that such events must never be allowed to happen again.

We hope that making *Personal Justice Denied* available to a wide audience will provide the foundation for a legacy that will be ingrained in American history and culture, and in the minds of the American people. We firmly believe that the lessons from the incarceration are as important as the lessons of the Revolutionary War, of slavery, of the Civil Rights Movement. We firmly believe that we should treat the Day of Remembrance as we do every other national holiday. We firmly believe that it should be common knowledge that the detention of Americans of Japanese ancestry during World War II was not an act of military necessity but an act of racial discrimination.

The republication of *Personal Justice Denied* is only one part of the education process. But we hope that in its new form, this important government document can stimulate other projects and further thought on the protection and strengthening of the civil rights of all Americans.

The Civil Liberties Public Education Fund
January 1997

Foreword

From December 7, 1941, through September 29, 1947,[1] the United States used its warpowers to incarcerate more than 110,000 American citizens and resident aliens. It confined most of them in barbed wire centers, under armed guard, where they were held for an unspecified time. This action was taken against Americans of Japanese ancestry and their parents—a group who had not committed any crimes or been accused of taking any action to warrant such adverse treatment.

Most other Americans were unaware of this facet of the wartime years. Among the Japanese Americans themselves, there was a noticeable reluctance from the mid-1940s through the 1950s to talk openly about their incarceration.[2] Then, in the 1960s, a noticeable change occurred, as first a few, then many, Japanese Americans became increasingly involved in various social and political movements. In 1967, for example, many Japanese Americans became involved at the national level in a movement to repeal Title II of the Internal Security Act of 1950. When it was repealed in 1971, the outcome offered proof to numerous Japanese Americans that a national social movement could be successful.[3] It was during this time that other Japanese Americans in

I am indebted to Judith Dollenmayer, Jack Herzig, Elsa Kudo, Dale Minami, Don Nakanishi, Shirley Shimada, Aiko Yoshinaga-Herzig, and other members of The Civil Liberties Public Education Fund Board for their comments and assistance.

the West Coast states started "pilgrimages" to the World War II incarceration sites and inaugurated a local "Day of Remembrance" to commemorate that experience.

Then, through the efforts of some vocal Nisei and Sansei (children and grandchildren of the original immigrants), the Japanese Americans started a grass-roots political and social campaign to redress the wrong committed against them by their government during World War II.[4] Initially formed at the local level, small groups—such as the Seattle-based Evacuation and Redress Committee—later became national organizations or worked with other existing Japanese American organizations.[5] The absence of a unified Japanese American community stance for a large-scale redress campaign, however, soon became evident. Roger Daniels estimates that one-third of the Japanese Americans were for a national campaign, a third were against it, and the last third were neutral.[6] There were various reasons for this situation. Some believed that revisiting such a painful past served little useful purpose; since what happened could not be undone, they argued, the past should be left buried so they could go on with their lives. Others said that even if this effort to obtain an apology and restitution was successful, no amount of money could compensate adequately for the lost years. They asked, "How does one put a price on such suffering?"

Nevertheless, proponents for a redress movement persevered. As time passed, awareness and support increased in the Japanese American community. Support by non–Japanese American individuals and organizations also served to strengthen the nascent movement. There was a growing and widespread awareness that the incarceration experience transcended the history of one minority group in America. The fact that almost two-thirds of the Japanese Americans so incarcerated were United States citizens and that almost all the remaining affected Japanese nationals were permanent residents made this an American issue. Farther north, as part of the wartime actions, the removal of the Aleuts and Pribilof Islanders from their homes, with the destruction of their communities and churches, was, as well, an American tragedy. As these injustices became known, various civil rights groups became interested in the issue as a possible instrument of public policy. Their interest coincided with the growing trend, beginning in the mid-1960s, for Americans to question their country's conduct in Vietnam, as well as its historical relationships with its minority groups—notably the Blacks, Chicanos, Native Americans, and Asian Americans.

Supporters of this redress movement also realized that there were ways and means by which the Japanese Americans' petition could be raised and heard in the government. Key legislators were in place who could become interested and instrumental in gaining the attention of the rest of the nation. Through their local and national organizations, Japanese Americans approached various political leaders for their support.[7] Eventually Senators Daniel K. Inouye, the late Spark Matsunaga, the late Samuel I. Hayakawa, and Ted Stevens agreed to co-sponsor Senate Bill 1647 (proposed on August 7, 1979); Representatives James Wright, Norman Mineta, Robert Matsui, and 114 others introduced House Resolution 5499 (on September 28, 1979). In response to these bills, Congress proposed the creation of the Commission on Wartime Relocation and Internment of Civilians (CWRIC), which President Jimmy Carter signed into law (Public Law 96-317) on July 31, 1980.

Commission on Wartime Relocation and Internment of Civilians

The CWRIC had three charges: First, to "review the facts and circumstances surrounding Executive Order Numbered 9066 [signed by President Franklin D. Roosevelt, EO 9066 was used to exclude and incarcerate the vast majority of persons of Japanese ancestry] . . . and the impact of such Executive Order on American citizens and permanent resident aliens." Second, to "review directives of United States military forces requiring the relocation and, and in some cases, detention in internment camps of American citizens, including Aleut civilians, and permanent resident aliens of the Aleutian and Pribilof Islands"; and, third, "to recommend appropriate remedies."

The CWRIC Commissioners held twenty days of public hearings from July to December of 1981, in ten locations, mainly on the East and West Coasts.[8] They heard testimony from over 750 witnesses, most of whom were formerly incarcerated Japanese Americans and Aleuts or Pribilof Islanders, but who included as well former internees brought up from Peru, noted scholars, and a few apologists of the incarceration or internment experience. The Commission and its staff also perused extensively the available government archival materials, investigated other sources such as the Franklin D. Roosevelt Library, and examined numerous secondary source materials. It issued its report, *Personal Justice Denied*, on February 24, 1983; its *Recommendations* appeared on June 16, 1983. Both reports are included in this volume.

Also in 1983, the CWRIC issued a third publication, *Papers for the Commission*, with limited distribution. In it was an Addendum to

Personal Justice Denied by Special Counsel Angus Macbeth. Here, he specifically addressed the intercepted Japanese diplomatic cables—code-named MAGIC—and their lack of influence on the U.S. government's decision to remove and incarcerate the Japanese Americans from the West Coast. This addendum and remarks by Commissioner Daniel Lungren are also included in this volume (see Part IV).

Personal Justice Denied constitutes an impressive report, centering on the treatment during World War II of persons of Japanese ancestry from the contiguous 48 states, the territories of Hawaii and Alaska, and various Latin American countries, as well as 976 Aleuts and Pribilof Islanders.[9] One salient feature of this report is that its conclusion is neither unique nor startling: "The promulgation of Executive Order 9066 was not justified by military necessity, and the decisions which followed from it—detention, ending detention and ending exclusion—were not driven by analysis of military conditions. The broad historical causes which shaped these decisions were race prejudice, war hysteria and a failure of political leadership"[10]

Much earlier, even during the war years, numerous Japanese Americans argued that their wholesale expulsion from their homes and subsequent incarceration were unjust. Other individuals also condemned the action as a travesty of justice and inimical to basic democratic rights and American values. Outstanding legal scholar Eugene V. Rostow, for example, in 1945 challenged the legality of the incarceration, calling it "a disaster."[11] Later, many who had advocated or assisted in the expulsion and incarceration began to question their wartime actions. For example, Earl Warren, who as the Attorney General of California had urged the removal and incarceration; William O. Douglas, Justice of the Supreme Court, who had joined the majority opinion to validate the mass incarceration; and Milton Eisenhower, the first Director of the War Relocation Authority—all in varying ways in later decades publicly questioned the propriety of their previous positions.[12]

If its conclusion is not unique, then what makes this a significant volume? There are three reasons why this report is so remarkable. The first resides in its imprimatur, or to put it another way, its impeccable credentials. This volume represents the findings of an official government agency of the United States of America. The second rests on its solidity. The report represents a tremendous amount of research and study, the distillation of a mountain of information leading to a solid conclusion and recommendations. And the final reason has to do with its influence. It immediately affected American social policy and actions and continues to influence subsequent writings and scholarship on the incarceration. Let us examine each of these points.

Imprimatur

For more than forty years, most writers and students of the wartime incarceration, although never a large group, condemned the actions of the United States government. There were some important works that examined critically the actions of the United States government during the War. Carey McWilliams, Dorothy Thomas and Richard Nishimoto, Morton Grodzins, Jacobus tenBroek with Edward Barnhart and Floyd Matson, and Charles Allen, to name a few, wrote influential books during this period.[13] Yet their criticisms of the government's actions remained almost buried and unrecognized. Most textbooks up to the 1980s did not mention the Japanese American incarceration. When they did so, the perspective taken was that during World War II the government did "evacuate" persons of Japanese ancestry and place them in "relocation" centers because of a military necessity.[14] By implication then, all Japanese Americans were considered to be "dangerous." The contrary view, that this group did not constitute such a dire threat, was never given the same emphasis in such influential sources.

Why the contrary view received so little attention is in part a reflection of life in the United States during those times. Expressing opposition toward the government was much more difficult from the 1940s to the mid-1960s than it was to become later. Soon after World War II and the post-war adjustment phase, America entered into the Korean War. Senator Joseph McCarthy's anti-Communism/infiltration crusade and the start of the Cold War reflected—or resulted in—a national attitude that discouraged criticism of the government. This attitude continued until the late 1960s and early 1970s, when the social climate dramatically changed. Then, in a time of social upheaval and protest, individuals could be more outspoken and could more freely voice their opinions. It was in this changed atmosphere that the CWRIC was conceived and *Personal Justice Denied* issued.

The vital point here is that the CWRIC report represents the government's own findings. The same entity that initiated and justified the incarceration forty years earlier now concluded that it had erred in its basic assertions. The Commission not only declared that there was no military necessity, it recommended a public apology and monetary restitution to those affected by EO 9066. The Commission's findings rightfully became front- and editorial-page material because they drastically altered an official position held for some four decades. In one volume, the United States government publicly repudiated the rationale of those who had conceived the expulsion and carried out the incarceration.

Solidity

Personal Justice Denied is also significant as sound scholarship. It is based on eighteen months of investigation by the Commission members and their impressive staff.[15] They listened and talked to numerous witnesses, examined publications and resources from a vast number of governmental and non-governmental files resting in the National and other archives. This effort resulted in an exhaustive study whose basic facts have been overwhelmingly accepted. No other volume on the wartime incarceration experience has had the benefit of drawing from such an extensive array of materials, investigatory skill, and assistance from witnesses and other scholars.[16]

As a highly readable work of scholarship, the CWRIC report succinctly condensed important aspects of this tremendously difficult time. Few persons have challenged its data and presentation.[17] Moreover, it is eminently interesting, skillfully interweaving gripping stories of human suffering and political intrigue.

Influence

The third reason for the significance of *Personal Justice Denied* has to do with its impact. Rarely has a government report had such far-reaching repercussions in so many areas affecting social policies and actions. Let us take only four areas of influence to illustrate this: economics, law, international affairs, and the academic arena.

There is little doubt that this CWRIC report and recommendations were crucial to effecting the passage of the presidential apology and monetary restitution bills in Congress. Implementing the recommendations was by no means an easy task.[18] Eventually, however, Congress sent to the President for his signature House Bill 442—numbered in honor of the famed Nisei 442nd Regimental Combat Team—which allotted more than 1.2 billion dollars to a fund from which each surviving Japanese American affected by EO 9066 would receive $20,000,[19] with additional sums for the Aleuts and Pribilof Islanders. As part of its recommendations, the Civil Liberties Public Education Fund was to be created from the unused moneys allocated for the survivors. This latter fund was dedicated to support research and to undertake a public educational program to be administrated and directed by a Board of Directors. The CWRIC report was not the sole reason for this turn of events, yet its straightforward, unequivocal conclusion and the unanimous stance[20] taken by the CWRIC members helped to preclude the introduction of other interpretations or positions.

The report had an impact on the law as well. During World War II, the Supreme Court found constitutional the curfew and exclusion orders enforced against persons of Japanese ancestry. Three major cases of those who resisted the curfew and exclusion orders involve Gordon Hirabayashi, Fred Korematsu, and Minoru Yasui. Legal scholar Peter Irons, in 1981, uncovered internal Justice Department documents written during the war years charging that high-ranking officers knowingly suppressed vital evidence and misrepresented facts in parts of their presentations of these cases to the Supreme Court.[21] Irons presented his findings to the Commission and to the individuals and civil rights attorneys who worked to overturn the original convictions of these three persons. Later, when these cases were re-opened through a *writ of error coram nobis,* the evidence that Peter Irons and Aiko Yoshinaga-Herzig[22] had discovered, along with that in *Personal Justice Denied* and *Recommendations,* was entered directly into the legal debate. For example, in *Korematsu v United States* the Court took judicial notice of certain conclusions of the CWRIC that credible evidence contradicted the assertions of the Commander of the Western Defense Command that military necessity justified the exclusion and detention of all persons of Japanese ancestry.[23]

In the international arena, during World War II, Canada also excluded and/or incarcerated almost all of its residents who were of Japanese ancestry. One phase of the Japanese Canadian redress movement ended successfully in 1988 when Prime Minister Brian Mulroney issued an "Acknowledgment" and ordered an individual payment of $21,000 to those survivors affected by Canada's exclusion order. Numerous Japanese Canadians who worked on their redress campaign point to two factors that positively influenced their government's actions toward the Japanese Canadians: the first was the upcoming general election, and the second was the passage of the redress bill in the United

States. Many Japanese Canadians believe that their own redress efforts would have been greatly hampered if Japanese Americans had failed to win redress.

Finally, based on its present influence, *Personal Justice Denied* will undoubtedly have an impact on all future scholarship done on the incarceration experience. It has already become a bench mark that present writers cannot ignore, since almost everything written on the incarceration after 1983 refers to this report. It has also sparked additional academic and media interest in the Japanese American World War II experiences; since its release, numerous books have been issued detailing previously unknown and unexamined facets of the wartime experience. It would be fair to state that many more studies will be forthcoming and that the CWRIC report will be one important standard by which newer volumes will be judged and appreciated.

The entire redress movement, in which *Personal Justice Denied* has played such a key role, has also helped to heal the social wound opened a half century ago. As President George Bush wrote in his 1990 letter of apology to each recipient of a redress payment: "A monetary sum and words alone cannot restore lost years or erase painful memories; neither can they fully convey our Nation's resolve to rectify injustice and to uphold the rights of individuals. We can never fully right the wrongs of the past. But we can take a clear stand for justice and recognize that serious injustices were done to Japanese Americans during World War II." Behind these few words, the United States helped to rectify its grievous wartime error; *Personal Justice Denied* was an important factor in this process.

Tetsuden Kashima
University of Washington

NOTES

1. Yoshiaki Fukuda, *Yokuru Seikatsu Rokunen* (Okayama: Tamashima Kappansho, 1957), translated as *My Six Years of Internment: An Issei's Struggle for Justice* (San Francisco: Konko Church of San Francisco, 1990).

2. Tetsuden Kashima, "Japanese American Internees Return, 1945–1955: Readjustment and Social Amnesia," *Phylon* 41(2):107–15, 1980.

3. See Raymond Okamura, "Campaign to Repeal the Emergency Detention Act: Background and History," *Amerasia Journal* 2:72–94, 1974; and Don T. Nakanishi, "Surviving Democracy's 'Mistake': Japanese Americans and the

Enduring Legacy of Executive Order 9066," *Amerasia Journal* 19(1):7–35, 1992. I am indebted to Don Nakanishi for this point.

4. One person stands out in the memory of many Japanese Americans as an early and influential voice for a redress movement. Due credit should be given to the late Edison Uno, San Francisco, California.

5. Space limitation precludes a listing of all the organizations that worked on the campaign for redress. Organizations at the national level include the Japanese American Citizens League, the National Council for Japanese American Redress, and the National Coalition for Redress and Reparations.

6. Roger Daniels, *Asian Americans: Chinese and Japanese in the United States since 1850*, p. 334 (Seattle: University of Washington Press, 1988). See also Roger Daniels, Sandra Taylor, and Harry Kitano, eds., *Japanese Americans: From Relocation to Redress* (Seattle: University of Washington Press, 1996 [originally published 1986]); and Yasuko Iwai Takezawa, *Breaking the Silence: Redress and Japanese American Ethnicity*, pp. 33–42 (Ithaca, NY: Cornell University Press, 1995).

7. Congressman Mike Lowry, Washington State, was the first to introduce a bill into the United States Congress advocating direct monetary restitution to the Japanese Americans incarcerated during World War II. In 1979 he introduced H.R. 5977, which provided for a governmental apology, $15,000, and $15 for each day of an individual's internment. This bill was not passed.

8. The nine CWRIC Commissioners were Joan Bernstein, Chair, former general counsel of the Department of Health and Human Services; former Senator Edward Brooke; former Congressman Father Robert Drinan; Arthur Flemming, U.S. Commission on Civil Rights; Former Supreme Court Justice Arthur Goldberg; Father Ishmael Gromoff; Congressman Daniel Lungren; Judge William Marutani; and former Senator Hugh Mitchell. Hearings or major meetings were held twice in Washington, D.C., and once each in the following cities: Alaska (Anchorage, St. Paul, Unalaska), California (Los Angeles, San Francisco), Boston, Chicago, New York, and Seattle.

9. *Personal Justice Denied* also included new materials at that time rarely found in other publications. This new material included, for example, the shipment to the United States of Japanese, German, and other Axis countries' nationals from Latin American countries. Most of these Japanese came from Peru, and although their story is included in the report, theirs is a continuing story as they seek acceptable redress from the United States government. See C. Harvey Gardiner, *Pawns in a Triangle of Hate: The Peruvian Japanese and the United States* (Seattle: University of Washington Press, 1981); and Seiichi Higashide, *Namida no Adios* (Tokyo: Sairyusha, 1985), translated as *Adios to Tears, The Memoirs of a Japanese-Peruvian Internee in U.S. Concentration Camps* (Honolulu: E & E Kudo, 1993). On the removal of the Aleutians and Pribilof Islanders, see Dean Kohlhoff, *When the Wind Was a River: Aleut Evacuation in World War II* (Seattle: University of Washington Press, 1995).

10. *Personal Justice Denied*, p. 18.

11. Eugene V. Rostow, "The Japanese-American Cases—A Disaster," *Yale Law Journal* 45(1945):489–533; and "Our Worst Wartime Mistake," *Harper's* (September 1945), pp. 193–201.

12. Warren wrote: "I have since deeply regretted the removal order and my own testimony advocating it, because it was not in keeping with our American concept of freedom and the rights of citizens," in *The Memoirs of Chief Justice Earl Warren*, p. 149 (Garden City, New York: Doubleday and Co., 1977). See also Morse Saito, "Warren 'Regrets' His Role in 1942 Evacuation," *Hokubei Mainichi* newspaper, San Francisco, #8336, p.1, June 3, 1974; William O. Douglas, *The Court Years, 1939–1975*, pp. 279–80 (New York: Random House, 1980); and Milton S. Eisenhower, *The President Is Calling*, p. 125 (New York: Doubleday and Company, 1974).

13. It would be difficult to mention all the important early books. See, for example, Carey McWilliams, *Prejudice—Japanese-Americans: Symbol of Racial Intolerance* (Boston: Little, Brown, and Company, 1944); Dorothy S. Thomas and Richard Nishimoto, *The Spoilage* (Berkeley: University of California Press, 1946); Morton Grodzins, *Americans Betrayed: Politics and the Japanese Evacuation* (Chicago: University of Chicago Press, 1949); Jacobus tenBroek, Edward N. Barnhart, and Floyd W. Matson, *Prejudice, War and the Constitution* (Berkeley: University of California Press, 1954); and Charles Allen, *Concentration Camp, U.S.A* (New York: Marzani and Munsell, 1966). Later influential books include Roger Daniels, *Concentration Camps USA: Japanese Americans and World War* (New York: Holt, Rinehart and Winston, 1972), and Michi Weglyn, *Years of Infamy: The Untold Story of America's Concentration Camps* (Seattle: University of Washington Press, 1996 [originally published in 1976]).

14. See U.S. Commission on Civil Rights, "Asian Americans and Pacific Peoples: A Case of Mistaken Identity," p. 33, February 1975. Recent middle- and high-school texts now mention the Japanese American experience; one text even mentions *Personal Justice Denied* but offers an ambiguous interpretation: "Historians today agree that the relocation order grew out of more than military necessity. The Order also reflected anti-Japanese racism. According to the Commission [CWRIC], the relocation order had been a grave injustice, motivated by prejudice and war hysteria. The issue remains unsettled." In Ernest R. May and Winthrop D. Jordan, *The American People: A History from 1877*, p. 404 (Evanston, IL: McDougal, Littell, and Co., 1986). See also L. Joanne Buggery, Gerald A. Danzer, Charles Mitsakos, and C. Frederick Risinger, *America! America!*, 2d ed., p. 635 (Glenview, IL: Scott, Foresman, and Company, 1987); and Norman K. Risjord and Terry L. Haywoode, *A History of the United States from 1877*, p. 220 (New York: Holt, Rinehart, and Winston, 1979).

15. The writing of *Personal Justice Denied* was primarily the work of Special Counsel Angus Macbeth, senior editor Judith Dollenmayer, and editor Kate Beardsley, with the approval of the nine CWRIC Commissioners. Under the leadership of Joan Z. Bernstein, Chair, and in close consultation with the staff, the Commissioners then formulated the Recommendations to the President and the Congress.

16. The "Papers of the U.S. Commission on Wartime Relocation and Internment of Civilians, Part 1: Numerical File Archives," which includes almost all the documents used by the CWRIC in its *Personal Justice Denied*, is available at various university libraries and may be purchased from the

University Publications of America. I am indebted to Don Nakanishi for this information.

17. Some former government officials and individuals express disagreement with the Report's conclusion and its recommendations. John. J. McCloy, then Assistant Secretary of War, and Karl Bendetsen, then Major, U.S. Army, participated in the decision to incarcerate persons of Japanese ancestry. Both continue to defend their actions. See Daniels, Taylor, and Kitano, eds., *Japanese Americans*, pp. 213–16.

18. Accounts are now available on the difficulty of the entire process. See, for example, Daniels, Taylor, and Kitano, eds., *Japanese Americans*, and Yasuko I. Takezawa, *Breaking the Silence*.

19. In order to qualify for the monetary payment, the Japanese American must have been alive on August 10, 1988, when President Reagan signed the redress bill. If he or she then died, the money would first go to the surviving spouse; if there were no spouse, the children would be entitled to it.

20. All nine CWRIC Commissioners agreed unanimously to the Report's conclusions. As for the Recommendations, Daniel Lungren was the lone dissenter, who felt that a monetary restitution should not be offered.

21. See Peter Irons, ed., *Justice Delayed: The Record of the Japanese American Internment Cases*, p. 4 (Middletown, CT: Wesleyan University Press, 1989). Gordon Hirabayashi, Fred Korematsu, and Minoru Yasui's cases were re-heard after the release of the CWRIC Report and Recommendations. Another legal battle during this time centered around a class-action redress suit brought by William Hohri. See William Hohri, *Repairing America: An Account of the Movement for Japanese American Redress* (Pullman: Washington State University Press, 1988).

22. Aiko Yoshinaga-Herzig was a CWRIC senior researcher.

23. See *Korematsu v United States*, 584 F. Supp. 1406 (1984). The Court continued by quoting *Personal Justice Denied:* the "broad historical causes which shaped these decisions [exclusion and detention] were race prejudice, war hysteria and a failure of political leadership" (1416–1417). I am indebted to Dale Minami for this information. It is also cited in *Hirabayashi v United States*, Opinion of the Court of Appeals, U.S. Court of Appeals for the Ninth Circuit, 828 F. 2d 591 (9th Cir. 1987), September 24, 1987 (footnote 9, in Peter Irons, *Justice Delayed*, pp. 386–410).

Introduction

The Commission's report is rooted in both its hearings and in archival research. Between July and December 1981, the Commission held 20 days of hearings and took testimony from more than 750 witnesses: Japanese Americans and Aleuts who had lived through the events of World War II, former government officials, public figures, interested citizens, and other professionals who have studied the subjects of the Commission's inquiry. Between July 1981 and December 1982, the Commission staff collected and reviewed materials from government and university archives and read and analyzed the relevant historical writing.

The account of decisions made by officials of the federal government is primarily drawn from contemporaneous memoranda, writings and transcribed conversations with a lesser reliance on memoirs and testimony before the Commission.

The account of public events outside the federal government as well as those chapters which deal with background before Pearl Harbor or events in Hawaii or the First World War experience of German Americans, cited for comparison, rely more heavily on secondary sources. For instance, while many of the working papers at the University of California which analyzed press attitudes in the first months of the war

xxviii   PERSONAL JUSTICE DENIED

were reviewed by the staff, no effort was made to collect and reread the entire range of press coverage and comment.

The account of the experiences of Japanese Americans and Aleuts relies heavily on the personal testimony given in the Commission hearings, although substantial support is also provided by contemporaneous government reports. It has been suggested that some of these accounts suffer from the fading of memories over forty years; but it is difficult to give greater weight to accounts by a captive population which may well have believed that fully candid statements accessible to a hostile public or government were not in its best interest. The Commission proceeded carefully to develop out of the testimony a fair, accurate account of the experiences of exclusion, evacuation and detention.

The Commission has not attempted to change the words and phrases commonly used to describe these events at the time they happened. This leaves one open to the charge of shielding unpleasant truths behind euphemisms. For instance, "evacuee" is frequently used in the text; *Webster's Third International Dictionary* defines an evacuee as one "who is removed from his house or community in time of war or pressing danger as a protective measure." In light of the Commission's conclusion that removal was not militarily necessary, "excludee" might be a better term than "evacuee." The Commission has largely left the words and phrases as they were, however, in an effort to mirror accurately the history of the time and to avoid the confusion and controversy a new terminology might provoke. We leave it to each reader to decide for himself how far the language of the period confirms an observation of George Orwell: "In our time, political speech and writing are largely the defense of the indefensible. . . . Thus political language has to consist largely of euphemism, question-begging and sheer cloudy vagueness."

* * *

As Special Counsel to the Commission, I wish to extend deep thanks to all the consultants, volunteers and members of the staff of the Commission throughout its existence. They have borne the burden of a difficult and sensitive task with unfailing diligence and patience. They deserve the entire credit for the additions to knowledge and understanding which the Commission's report provides: Paul T. Bannai, Mark Baribeau, Kate C. Beardsley, Donald R. Brown, Jeanette Chow, Michelle Ducharme, Donna H. Fujioka, Aiko Herzig-Yoshinaga, Jack Herzig, Helen Hessler, Toro Hirose, Stuart J. Ishimaru, Gregory G. King, Key K. Kobayashi, Donna Komure, Barbara Kraft,

Alex M. Lichtenstein, Karen L. Madden, Teresa M. Myers, Robin J. Patterson, Ardith Pugh, Mitziko Sawada, Nancy J. Schaub, Lois Schiffer, Maria Josephy Schoolman, Katrina A. Shores, Charles Smith, Fumie Tateoka, Tom Taketa, Terry Wilkerson, Lois J. Wilzewske, Cheryl Yamamoto and Kiyo Yamada.

I owe a special debt to two members of the staff who have borne more than their fair share of the Commission's labor: Aiko Herzig-Yoshinaga, who in large part found and organized and remembered the vast array of primary documents from which the report was written, and Terry Wilkerson, whose calm and unfailing professionalism in handling a manuscript that sometimes resembled a jig-saw puzzle was crucial in allowing us to produce a printable manuscript.

The immense job of locating relevant material could not have been completed without the very substantial assistance of a great many people in archival libraries and government departments to whom the Commission wishes to express its gratitude. Without their help the report could not have been finished.

National Archives: Margaret E. Branson, George Chelow, Edwin R. Coffee, Sylvan Dubow, Angela M. Fernandez, Cynthia Ghee, Terri Hammett, Jerry Hess, Joseph Howerton, Cynthia D. Jackson, Charles Johnson, Bill Lewis, William Lind, Mary Walton Livingston, Naida Loescher, Michael McReynolds, Michael Miller, Ellie Malamud, James Paulauskas, Fred Pernell, John Pontius, Edward J. Reese, William Roth, Aloha South, John E. Taylor, John Van Dereedt, Ted Weir and Harold Williams.

Department of Justice, Immigration and Naturalization Service, Federal Bureau of Investigation: William Haynes, Madelyn Johnson, Jean Kornblut, Russell Powell, Jane Scott.

Department of Defense: Dean Allard, Alfred Beck, Bernard Cavalcanti and Hannah Zeidlik.

New Executive Office Building and White House Libraries: Judith Grosberg, Sharon Kissel, Bridget Reischer, Peter Sidney, Diane Talbert and Robert Updegrove.

Federal Reserve Bank, San Francisco: Patricia Rey.

Library of Congress: Peter Sheridan.

Franklin Delano Roosevelt Library: Robert Parks, Susan Bosanko.

University of California at Berkeley: Bancroft Library Staff.

Yale University, Sterling Library: Judith Schiff.

In addition, a number of people in private life with particular knowledge or interest in the subject of the Commission's inquiry were especially helpful: Lydia Black, Peter H. Irons, Lael Morgan, David

Musto, Raymond Y. Okamura, Thomas M. Powers, Kenneth A. Ringle and Michi N. Weglyn.

Roger Daniels and Bill Hosokawa undertook to read the historical part of the report in draft form and offered innumerable useful suggestions. They bear no responsibility for the content or conclusions of the report in its final form. The Commission staff undertook the research and review of documents and testimony from which the report was written, and any errors or omissions are the responsibility of the staff.

Great contributions to the editing and production of the report were made by Judith Dollenmayer.

Last, but by no means least, I wish to thank my wife, JoAnn, for her understanding and support throughout the time which I have devoted to the Commission's work.

—Angus Macbeth
Special Counsel

Washington, D.C.
December, 1982

Personal Justice Denied

Summary

The Commission on Wartime Relocation and Internment of Civilians was established by act of Congress in 1980 and directed to

1. review the facts and circumstances surrounding Executive Order Numbered 9066, issued February 19, 1942, and the impact of such Executive Order on American citizens and permanent resident aliens;

2. review directives of United States military forces requiring the relocation and, in some cases, detention in internment camps of American citizens, including Aleut civilians, and permanent resident aliens of the Aleutian and Pribilof Islands; and

3. recommend appropriate remedies.

In fulfilling this mandate, the Commission held 20 days of hearings in cities across the country, particularly on the West Coast, hearing testimony from more than 750 witnesses: evacuees, former government officials, public figures, interested citizens, and historians and other professionals who have studied the subjects of Commission inquiry. An extensive effort was made to locate and to review the records of government action and to analyze other sources of information including contemporary writings, personal accounts and historical analyses.

By presenting this report to Congress, the Commission fulfills the instruction to submit a written report of its findings. Like the body of the report, this summary is divided into two parts. The first describes

1

actions taken pursuant to Executive Order 9066, particularly the treatment of American citizens of Japanese descent and resident aliens of Japanese nationality. The second covers the treatment of Aleuts from the Aleutian and Pribilof Islands.

PART I: NISEI AND ISSEI*

On February 19, 1942, ten weeks after the Pearl Harbor attack, President Franklin D. Roosevelt signed Executive Order 9066, which gave to the Secretary of War and the military commanders to whom he delegated authority, the power to exclude any and all persons, citizens and aliens, from designated areas in order to provide security against sabotage, espionage and fifth column activity. Shortly thereafter, all American citizens of Japanese descent were prohibited from living, working or traveling on the West Coast of the United States. The same prohibition applied to the generation of Japanese immigrants who, pursuant to federal law and despite long residence in the United States, were not permitted to become American citizens. Initially, this exclusion was to be carried out by "voluntary" relocation. That policy inevitably failed, and these American citizens and their alien parents were removed by the Army, first to "assembly centers"—temporary quarters at racetracks and fairgrounds—and then to "relocation centers"—bleak barrack camps mostly in desolate areas of the West. The camps were surrounded by barbed wire and guarded by military police. Departure was permitted only after a loyalty review on terms set, in consultation with the military, by the War Relocation Authority, the civilian agency that ran the camps. Many of those removed from the West Coast were eventually allowed to leave the camps to join the Army, go to college outside the West Coast or to whatever private employment was available. For a larger number, however, the war years were spent behind barbed wire; and for those who were released, the prohibition against returning to their homes and occupations on the West Coast was not lifted until December 1944.

This policy of exclusion, removal and detention was executed against

---

*The first generation of ethnic Japanese born in the United States are *Nisei;* the *Issei* are the immigrant generation from Japan; and those who returned to Japan as children for education are *Kibei*.

120,000 people without individual review, and exclusion was continued virtually without regard for their demonstrated loyalty to the United States. Congress was fully aware of and supported the policy of removal and detention; it sanctioned the exclusion by enacting a statute which made criminal the violation of orders issued pursuant to Executive Order 9066. The United States Supreme Court held the exclusion constitutionally permissible in the context of war, but struck down the incarceration of admittedly loyal American citizens on the ground that it was not based on statutory authority.

All this was done despite the fact that not a single documented act of espionage, sabotage or fifth column activity was committed by an American citizen of Japanese ancestry or by a resident Japanese alien on the West Coast.

No mass exclusion or detention, in any part of the country, was ordered against American citizens of German or Italian descent. Official actions against enemy aliens of other nationalities were much more individualized and selective than those imposed on the ethnic Japanese.

The exclusion, removal and detention inflicted tremendous human cost. There was the obvious cost of homes and businesses sold or abandoned under circumstances of great distress, as well as injury to careers and professional advancement. But, most important, there was the loss of liberty and the personal stigma of suspected disloyalty for thousands of people who knew themselves to be devoted to their country's cause and to its ideals but whose repeated protestations of loyalty were discounted—only to be demonstrated beyond any doubt by the record of Nisei soldiers, who returned from the battlefields of Europe as the most decorated and distinguished combat unit of World War II, and by the thousands of other Nisei who served against the enemy in the Pacific, mostly in military intelligence. The wounds of the exclusion and detention have healed in some respects, but the scars of that experience remain, painfully real in the minds of those who lived through the suffering and deprivation of the camps.

The personal injustice of excluding, removing and detaining loyal American citizens is manifest. Such events are extraordinary and unique in American history. For every citizen and for American public life, they pose haunting questions about our country and its past. It has been the Commission's task to examine the central decisions of this history—the decision to exclude, the decision to detain, the decision to release from detention and the decision to end exclusion. The Commission has analyzed both how and why those decisions were made, and what their consequences were. And in order to illuminate those events, the mainland experience was compared to the treatment of Japanese Americans in Hawaii and to the experience of other Americans of enemy alien descent, particularly German Americans.

The Decision to Exclude

The Context of the Decision. First, the exclusion and removal were attacks on the ethnic Japanese which followed a long and ugly history of West Coast anti-Japanese agitation and legislation. Antipathy and hostility toward the ethnic Japanese was a major factor of the public life of the West Coast states for more than forty years before Pearl Harbor. Under pressure from California, immigration from Japan had been severely restricted in 1908 and entirely prohibited in 1924. Japanese immigrants were barred from American citizenship, although their children born here were citizens by birth. California and the other western states prohibited Japanese immigrants from owning land. In part the hostility was economic, emerging in various white American groups who began to feel competition, particularly in agriculture, the principal occupation of the immigrants. The anti-Japanese agitation also fed on racial stereotypes and fears: the "yellow peril" of an unknown Asian culture achieving substantial influence on the Pacific Coast or of a Japanese population alleged to be growing far faster than the white population. This agitation and hostility persisted, even though the ethnic Japanese never exceeded three percent of the population of California, the state of greatest concentration.

The ethnic Japanese, small in number and with no political voice—the citizen generation was just reaching voting age in 1940—had become a convenient target for political demagogues, and over the years all the major parties indulged in anti-Japanese rhetoric and programs. Political bullying was supported by organized interest groups who adopted anti-Japanese agitation as a consistent part of their program: the Native Sons and Daughters of the Golden West, the Joint Immigration Committee, the American Legion, the California State Federation of Labor and the California State Grange.

This agitation attacked a number of ethnic Japanese cultural traits or patterns which were woven into a bogus theory that the ethnic Japanese could not or would not assimilate or become "American." Dual citizenship, Shinto, Japanese language schools, and the education of many ethnic Japanese children in Japan were all used as evidence. But as a matter of fact, Japan's laws on dual citizenship went no further than those of many European countries in claiming the allegiance of the children of its nationals born abroad. Only a small number of ethnic

Japanese subscribed to Shinto, which in some forms included veneration of the Emperor. The language schools were not unlike those of other first-generation immigrants, and the return of some children to Japan for education was as much a reaction to hostile discrimination and an uncertain future as it was a commitment to the mores, much less the political doctrines, of Japan. Nevertheless, in 1942 these popular misconceptions infected the views of a great many West Coast people who viewed the ethnic Japanese as alien and unassimilated.

Second, Japanese armies in the Pacific won a rapid, startling string of victories against the United States and its allies in the first months of World War II. On the same day as the attack on Pearl Harbor, the Japanese struck the Malay Peninsula, Hong Kong, Wake and Midway Islands and attacked the Philippines. The next day the Japanese Army invaded Thailand. On December 13 Guam fell; on December 24 and 25 the Japanese captured Wake Island and occupied Hong Kong. Manila was evacuated on December 27, and the American army retreated to the Bataan Peninsula. After three months the troops isolated in the Philippines were forced to surrender unconditionally—the worst American defeat since the Civil War. In January and February 1942, the military position of the United States in the Pacific was perilous. There was fear of Japanese attacks on the West Coast.

Next, contrary to the facts, there was a widespread belief, supported by a statement by Frank Knox, Secretary of the Navy, that the Pearl Harbor attack had been aided by sabotage and fifth column activity by ethnic Japanese in Hawaii. Shortly after Pearl Harbor the government knew that this was not true, but took no effective measures to disabuse public belief that disloyalty had contributed to massive American losses on December 7, 1941. Thus the country was unfairly led to believe that both American citizens of Japanese descent and resident Japanese aliens threatened American security.

Fourth, as anti-Japanese organizations began to speak out and rumors from Hawaii spread, West Coast politicians quickly took up the familiar anti-Japanese cry. The Congressional delegations in Washington organized themselves and pressed the War and Justice Departments and the President for stern measures to control the ethnic Japanese—moving quickly from control of aliens to evacuation and removal of citizens. In California, Governor Olson, Attorney General Warren, Mayor Bowron of Los Angeles and many local authorities joined the clamor. These opinions were not informed by any knowledge of actual military risks, rather they were stoked by virulent agitation which encountered little opposition. Only a few churchmen and academicians were prepared to defend the ethnic Japanese. There was little or no political risk in claiming that it was "better to be safe than sorry" and, as many did, that the best way for ethnic Japanese to prove their loyalty was to volunteer to enter detention. The press amplified the unreflective emotional excitement of the hour. Through late January and early February 1942, the rising clamor from the West Coast was heard within the federal government as its demands became more draconian.

Making and Justifying the Decision. The exclusion of the ethnic Japanese from the West Coast was recommended to the Secretary of War, Henry L. Stimson, by Lieutenant General John L. DeWitt, Commanding General of the Western Defense Command with responsibility for West Coast security. President Roosevelt relied on Secretary Stimson's recommendations in issuing Executive Order 9066.

The justification given for the measure was military necessity. The claim of military necessity is most clearly set out in three places: General DeWitt's February 14, 1942, recommendation to Secretary Stimson for exclusion; General DeWitt's *Final Report: Japanese Evacuation from the West Coast, 1942;* and the government's brief in the Supreme Court defending the Executive Order in *Hirabayashi* v. *United States.* General DeWitt's February 1942 recommendation presented the following rationale for the exclusion:

> In the war in which we are now engaged racial affinities are not severed by migration. The Japanese race is an enemy race and while many second and third generation Japanese born on United States soil, possessed of United States citizenship, have become "Americanized," the racial strains are undiluted. To conclude otherwise is to expect that children born of white parents on Japanese soil sever all racial affinity and become loyal Japanese subjects, ready to fight and, if necessary, to die for Japan in a war against the nation of their parents. That Japan is allied with Germany and Italy in this struggle is no ground for assuming that any Japanese, barred from assimilation by convention as he is, though born and raised in the United States, will not turn against this nation when the final test of loyalty comes. It, therefore, follows that along the vital Pacific Coast over 112,000 potential enemies, of Japanese extraction, are at large today. There are indications that these were organized and ready for concerted action at a favorable opportunity. The very fact that no sabotage has taken place to date is a disturbing and confirming indication that such action will be taken.

There are two unfounded justifications for exclusion expressed here: first, that ethnicity ultimately determines loyalty; second, that "indications" suggest that ethnic Japanese "are organized and ready for concerted action"—the best argument for this being the fact that it hadn't happened.

The first evaluation is not a military one but one for sociologists or historians. It runs counter to a basic premise on which the American nation of immigrants is built—that loyalty to the United States is a matter of individual choice and not determined by ties to an ancestral country. In the case of German Americans, the First World War demonstrated that race did not determine loyalty, and no negative assumption was made with regard to citizens of German or Italian descent during the Second World War. The second judgment was, by the General's own admission, unsupported by any evidence. General DeWitt's recommendation clearly does not provide a credible rationale, based on military expertise, for the necessity of exclusion.

In his 1943 *Final Report*, General DeWitt cited a number of factors in support of the exclusion decision: signaling from shore to enemy submarines; arms and contraband found by the FBI during raids on ethnic Japanese homes and businesses; dangers to the ethnic Japanese from vigilantes; concentration of ethnic Japanese around or near militarily sensitive areas; the number of Japanese ethnic organizations on the coast which might shelter pro-Japanese attitudes or activities such as Emperor-worshipping Shinto; and the presence of the Kibei, who had spent some time in Japan.

The first two items point to demonstrable military danger. But the reports of shore-to-ship signaling were investigated by the Federal Communications Commission, the agency with relevant expertise, and no identifiable cases of such signaling were substantiated. The FBI did confiscate arms and contraband from some ethnic Japanese, but most were items normally in the possession of any law-abiding civilian, and the FBI concluded that these searches had uncovered no dangerous persons that "we could not otherwise know about." Thus neither of these "facts" militarily justified exclusion.

There had been some acts of violence against ethnic Japanese on the West Coast and feeling against them ran high, but "protective custody" is not an acceptable rationale for exclusion. Protection against vigilantes is a civilian matter that would involve the military only in extreme cases. But there is no evidence that such extremity had been reached on the West Coast in early 1942. Moreover, "protective custody" could never justify exclusion and detention for months and years.

General DeWitt's remaining points are repeated in the *Hirabayashi* brief, which also emphasizes dual nationality, Japanese language schools and the high percentage of aliens (who, by law, had been barred from acquiring American citizenship) in the ethnic population. These facts represent broad social judgments of little or no military significance in themselves. None supports the claim of disloyalty to the United States and all were entirely legal. If the same standards were applied to other ethnic groups, as Morton Grodzins, an early analyst of the exclusion decision, applied it to ethnic Italians on the West Coast, an equally compelling and meaningless case for "disloyalty" could be made. In short, these social and cultural patterns were not evidence of any threat to West Coast military security.

In sum, the record does not permit the conclusion that military necessity warranted the exclusion of ethnic Japanese from the West Coast.

The Conditions Which Permitted the Decision. Having concluded that no military necessity supported the exclusion, the Commission has attempted to determine how the decision came to be made.

First, General DeWitt apparently believed what he told Secretary Stimson: ethnicity determined loyalty. Moreover, he believed that the ethnic Japanese were so alien to the thought processes of white Americans that it was impossible to distinguish the loyal from the disloyal. On this basis he believed them to be potential enemies among whom loyalty could not be determined.

Second, the FBI and members of Naval Intelligence who had relevant intelligence responsibility were ignored when they stated that nothing more than careful watching of suspicious individuals or individual reviews of loyalty were called for by existing circumstances. In addition, the opinions of the Army General Staff that no sustained Japanese attack on the West Coast was possible were ignored.

Third, General DeWitt relied heavily on civilian politicians rather than informed military judgments in reaching his conclusions as to what actions were necessary, and civilian politicians largely repeated the prejudiced, unfounded themes of anti-Japanese factions and interest groups on the West Coast.

Fourth, no effective measures were taken by President Roosevelt to calm the West Coast public and refute the rumors of sabotage and fifth column activity at Pearl Harbor.

Fifth, General DeWitt was temperamentally disposed to exaggerate the measures necessary to maintain security and placed security far ahead of any concern for the liberty of citizens.

Sixth, Secretary Stimson and John J. McCloy, Assistant Secretary of War, both of whose views on race differed from those of General

DeWitt, failed to insist on a clear military justification for the measures General DeWitt wished to undertake.

Seventh, Attorney General Francis Biddle, while contending that exclusion was unnecessary, did not argue to the President that failure to make out a case of military necessity on the facts would render the exclusion constitutionally impermissible or that the Constitution prohibited exclusion on the basis of ethnicity given the facts on the West Coast.

Eighth, those representing the interests of civil rights and civil liberties in Congress, the press and other public forums were silent or indeed supported exclusion. Thus there was no effective opposition to the measures vociferously sought by numerous West Coast interest groups, politicians and journalists.

Finally, President Roosevelt, without raising the question to the level of Cabinet discussion or requiring any careful or thorough review of the situation, and despite the Attorney General's arguments and other information before him, agreed with Secretary Stimson that the exclusion should be carried out.

The Decision to Detain

With the signing of Executive Order 9066, the course of the President and the War Department was set: American citizens and alien residents of Japanese ancestry would be compelled to leave the West Coast on the basis of wartime military necessity. For the War Department and the Western Defense Command, the problem became primarily one of method and operation, not basic policy. General DeWitt first tried "voluntary" resettlement: the ethnic Japanese were to move outside restricted military zones of the West Coast but otherwise were free to go wherever they chose. From a military standpoint this policy was bizarre, and it was utterly impractical. If the ethnic Japanese had been excluded because they were potential saboteurs and spies, any such danger was not extinguished by leaving them at large in the interior where there were, of course, innumerable dams, power lines, bridges and war industries to be disrupted or spied upon. Conceivably sabotage in the interior could be synchronized with a Japanese raid or invasion for a powerful fifth column effect. This raises serious doubts as to how grave the War Department believed the supposed threat to be. Indeed, the implications were not lost on the citizens and politicians of the interior western states, who objected in the belief that people who threatened wartime security in California were equally dangerous in Wyoming and Idaho.

The War Relocation Authority (WRA), the civilian agency created by the President to supervise the relocation and initially directed by Milton Eisenhower, proceeded on the premise that the vast majority of evacuees were law-abiding and loyal, and that, once off the West Coast, they should be returned quickly to conditions approximating normal life. This view was strenuously opposed by the people and politicians of the mountain states. In April 1942, Milton Eisenhower met with the governors and officials of the mountain states. They objected to California using the interior states as a "dumping ground" for a California "problem." They argued that people in their states were so bitter over the voluntary evacuation that unguarded evacuees would face physical danger. They wanted guarantees that the government would forbid evacuees to acquire land and that it would remove them at the end of the war. Again and again, detention camps for evacuees were urged. The consensus was that a plan for reception centers was acceptable so long as the evacuees remained under guard within the centers.

In the circumstances, Milton Eisenhower decided that the plan to move the evacuees into private employment would be abandoned, at least temporarily. The War Relocation Authority dropped resettlement and adopted confinement. Notwithstanding WRA's belief that evacuees should be returned to normal productive life, it had, in effect, become their jailer. The politicians of the interior states had achieved the program of detention.

The evacuees were to be held in camps behind barbed wire and released only with government approval. For this course of action no military justification was proffered. Instead, the WRA contended that these steps were necessary for the benefit of evacuees and that controls on their departure were designed to assure they would not be mistreated by other Americans on leaving the camps.

It follows from the conclusion that there was no justification in military necessity for the exclusion, that there was no basis for the detention.

The Effect of the Exclusion and Detention

The history of the relocation camps and the assembly centers that preceded them is one of suffering and deprivation visited on people against whom no charges were, or could have been, brought. The Commission hearing record is full of poignant, searing testimony that recounts the economic and personal losses and injury caused by the

exclusion and the deprivations of detention. No summary can do this
testimony justice.

Families could take to the assembly centers and the camps only
what they could carry. Camp living conditions were Spartan. People
were housed in tar-papered barrack rooms of no more than 20 by 24
feet. Each room housed a family, regardless of family size. Construction
was often shoddy. Privacy was practically impossible and furnishings
were minimal. Eating and bathing were in mass facilities. Under continuing pressure from those who blindly held to the belief that evacuees
harbored disloyal intentions, the wages paid for work at the camps
were kept to the minimal level of $12 a month for unskilled labor,
rising to $19 a month for professional employees. Mass living prevented
normal family communication and activities. Heads of families, no
longer providing food and shelter, found their authority to lead and to
discipline diminished.

The normal functions of community life continued but almost
always under a handicap—doctors were in short supply; schools which
taught typing had no typewriters and worked from hand-me-down
school books; there were not enough jobs.

The camp experience carried a stigma that no other Americans
suffered. The evacuees themselves expressed the indignity of their
conditions with particular power:

> On May 16, 1942, my mother, two sisters, niece, nephew, and I
> left . . . by train. Father joined us later. Brother left earlier by
> bus. We took whatever we could carry. So much we left behind,
> but the most valuable thing I lost was my freedom.

* * *

> Henry went to the Control Station to register the family. He came
> home with twenty tags, all numbered 10710, tags to be attached
> to each piece of baggage, and one to hang from our coat lapels.
> From then on, we were known as Family #10710.

The government's efforts to "Americanize" the children in the
camps were bitterly ironic:

> An oft-repeated ritual in relocation camp schools . . . was the
> salute to the flag followed by the singing of "My country, 'tis of
> thee, sweet land of liberty"—a ceremony Caucasian teachers found
> embarrassingly awkward if not cruelly poignant in the austere
> prison-camp setting.

* * *

In some ways, I suppose, my life was not too different from a lot of kids in America between the years 1942 and 1945. I spent a good part of my time playing with my brothers and friends, learned to shoot marbles, watched sandlot baseball and envied the older kids who wore Boy Scout uniforms. We shared with the rest of America the same movies, screen heroes and listened to the same heart-rending songs of the forties. We imported much of America into the camps because, after all, we were Americans. Through imitation of my brothers, who attended grade school within the camp, I learned the salute to the flag by the time I was five years old. I was learning, as best one could learn in Manzanar, what it meant to live in America. But, I was also learning the sometimes bitter price one has to pay for it.

After the war, through the Japanese American Evacuation Claims Act, the government attempted to compensate for the losses of real and personal property; inevitably that effort did not secure full or fair compensation. There were many kinds of injury the Evacuation Claims Act made no attempt to compensate: the stigma placed on people who fell under the exclusion and relocation orders; the deprivation of liberty suffered during detention; the psychological impact of exclusion and relocation; the breakdown of family structure; the loss of earnings or profits; physical injury or illness during detention.

The Decision to End Detention

By October 1942, the government held over 100,000 evacuees in relocation camps. After the tide of war turned with the American victory at Midway in June 1942, the possibility of serious Japanese attack was no longer credible; detention and exclusion became increasingly difficult to defend. Nevertheless, other than an ineffective leave program run by the War Relocation Authority, the government had no plans to remedy the situation and no means of distinguishing the loyal from the disloyal. Total control of these civilians in the presumed interest of state security was rapidly becoming the accepted norm.

Determining the basis on which detention would be ended required the government to focus on the justification for controlling the ethnic Japanese. If the government took the position that race determined loyalty or that it was impossible to distinguish the loyal from the disloyal because "Japanese" patterns of thought and behavior were too alien to white Americans, there would be little incentive to end detention. If the government maintained the position that distinguishing the loyal from the disloyal was possible and that exclusion and detention were required only by the necessity of acting quickly under the threat of Japanese attack in early 1942, then a program to release those considered loyal should have been instituted in the spring of 1942 when people were confined in the assembly centers.

Neither position totally prevailed. General DeWitt and the Western Defense Command took the first position and opposed any review that would determine loyalty or threaten continued exclusion from the West Coast. Thus, there was no loyalty review during the assembly center period. Secretary Stimson and Assistant Secretary McCloy took the second view, but did not act on it until the end of 1942 and then only in a limited manner. At the end of 1942, over General DeWitt's opposition, Secretary Stimson, Assistant Secretary McCloy and General George C. Marshall, Chief of Staff, decided to establish a volunteer combat team of Nisei soldiers. The volunteers were to come from those who had passed a loyalty review. To avoid the obvious unfairness of allowing only those joining the military to establish their loyalty and leave the camps, the War Department joined WRA in expanding the loyalty review program to all adult evacuees.

This program was significant, but remained a compromise. It provided an opportunity to demonstrate loyalty to the United States on the battlefields; despite the human sacrifice involved, this was of immense practical importance in obtaining postwar acceptance for the ethnic Japanese. It opened the gates of the camps for some and began some reestablishment of normal life. But, with no apparent rationale or justification, it did not end exclusion of the loyal from the West Coast. The review program did not extend the presumption of loyalty to American citizens of Japanese descent, who were subject to an investigation and review not applied to other ethnic groups.

Equally important, although the loyalty review program was the first major government decision in which the interests of evacuees prevailed, the program was conducted so insensitively, with such lack of understanding of the evacuees' circumstances, that it became one of the most divisive and wrenching episodes of the camp detention.

After almost a year of what the evacuees considered utterly unjust treatment at the hands of the government, the loyalty review program began with filling out a questionnaire which posed two questions requiring declarations of complete loyalty to the United States. Thus, the questionnaire demanded a personal expression of position from each evacuee—a choice between faith in one's future in America and outrage at present injustice. Understandably most evacuees probably had deeply ambiguous feelings about a government whose rhetorical values of liberty and equality they wished to believe, but who found their present treatment in painful contradiction to those values. The loyalty questionnaire left little room to express that ambiguity. Indeed, it provided an effective point of protest and organization against the government, from which more and more evacuees felt alienated. The questionnaire finally addressed the central question of loyalty that underlay the exclusion policy, a question which had been the predominant political and personal issue for the ethnic Japanese over the past year; answering it required confronting the conflicting emotions aroused by their relation to the government. Evacuee testimony shows the intensity of conflicting emotions:

> I answered both questions number 27 and 28 [the loyalty questions] in the negative, not because of disloyalty but due to the disgusting and shabby treatment given us. A few months after completing the questionnaire, U.S. Army officers appeared at our camp and gave us an interview to confirm our answers to the questions 27 and 28, and followed up with a question that in essence asked: "Are you going to give up or renounce your U.S. citizenship?" to which I promptly replied in the affirmative as a rebellious move. Sometime after the interview, a form letter from the Immigration and Naturalization Service arrived saying if I wanted to renounce my U.S. citizenship, sign the form letter and return. Well, I kept the Immigration and Naturalization Service waiting.

*   *   *

> Well, I am one of those that said "no, no" on it, one of the "no, no" boys, and it is not that I was proud about it, it was just that our legal rights were violated and I wanted to fight back. However, I didn't want to take this sitting down. I was really angry. It just got me so damned mad. Whatever we do, there was no help from outside, and it seems to me that we are a race that doesn't count. So therefore, this was one of the reasons for the "no, no" answer.

Personal responses to the questionnaire inescapably became public acts open to community debate and scrutiny within the closed world of the camps. This made difficult choices excruciating:

> After I volunteered for the [military] service, some people that I knew refused to speak to me. Some older people later questioned my father for letting me volunteer, but he told them that I was old enough to make up my own mind.

*   *   *

The resulting infighting, beatings, and verbal abuses left families torn apart, parents against children, brothers against sisters, relatives against relatives, and friends against friends. So bitter was all this that even to this day, there are many amongst us who do not speak about that period for fear that the same harsh feelings might arise up again to the surface.

The loyalty review program was a point of decision and division for those in the camps. The avowedly loyal were eligible for release; those who were unwilling to profess loyalty or whom the government distrusted were segregated from the main body of evacuees into the Tule Lake camp, which rapidly became a center of disaffection and protest against the government and its policies—the unhappy refuge of evacuees consumed by anger and despair.

The Decision to End Exclusion

The loyalty review should logically have led to the conclusion that no justification existed for excluding loyal American citizens from the West Coast. Secretary Stimson, Assistant Secretary McCloy and General Marshall reached this position in the spring of 1943. Nevertheless, the exclusion was not ended until December 1944. No plausible reason connected to any wartime security has been offered for this eighteen to twenty month delay in allowing the ethnic Japanese to return to their homes, jobs and businesses on the West Coast, despite the fact that the delay meant, as a practical matter, that confinement in the relocation camps continued for the great majority of evacuees for another year and a half.

Between May 1943 and May 1944, War Department officials did not make public their opinion that exclusion of loyal ethnic Japanese from the West Coast no longer had any military justification. If the President was unaware of this view, the plausible explanation is that Secretary Stimson and Assistant Secretary McCloy were unwilling, or believed themselves unable, to face down political opposition on the West Coast. General DeWitt repeatedly expressed opposition until he left the Western Defense Command in the fall of 1943, as did West Coast anti-Japanese factions and politicians.

In May 1944 Secretary Stimson put before President Roosevelt and the Cabinet his position that the exclusion no longer had a military justification. But the President was unwilling to act to end the exclusion until the first Cabinet meeting following the Presidential election of November 1944. The inescapable conclusion from this factual pattern is that the delay was motivated by political considerations.

By the participants' own accounts, there is no rational explanation for maintaining the exclusion of loyal ethnic Japanese from the West

Coast for the eighteen months after May 1943—except political pressure and fear. Certainly there was no justification arising out of military necessity.

The Comparisons

To either side of the Commission's account of the exclusion, removal and detention, there is a version argued by various witnesses that makes a radically different analysis of the events. Some contend that, forty years later, we cannot recreate the atmosphere and events of 1942 and that the extreme measures taken then were solely to protect the nation's safety when there was no reasonable alternative. Others see in these events only the animus of racial hatred directed toward people whose skin was not white. Events in Hawaii in World War II and the historical treatment of Germans and German Americans shows that neither analysis is satisfactory.

Hawaii. When Japan attacked Pearl Harbor, nearly 158,000 persons of Japanese ancestry lived in Hawaii—more than 35 percent of the population. Surely, if there were dangers from espionage, sabotage and fifth column activity by American citizens and resident aliens of Japanese ancestry, danger would be greatest in Hawaii, and one would anticipate that the most swift and severe measures would be taken there. But nothing of the sort happened. Less than 2,000 ethnic Japanese in Hawaii were taken into custody during the war—barely one percent of the population of Japanese descent. Many factors contributed to this reaction.

Hawaii was more ethnically mixed and racially tolerant than the West Coast. Race relations in Hawaii before the war were not infected with the same virulent antagonism of 75 years of agitation. While anti-Asian feeling existed in the territory, it did not represent the longtime views of well-organized groups as it did on the West Coast and, without statehood, xenophobia had no effective voice in the Congress.

The larger population of ethnic Japanese in Hawaii was also a factor. It is one thing to vent frustration and historical prejudice on a scant two percent of the population; it is very different to disrupt a local economy and tear a social fabric by locking up more than one-third of a territory's people. And in Hawaii the half-measure of exclusion from military areas would have been meaningless.

In large social terms, the Army had much greater control of day-to-day events in Hawaii. Martial law was declared in December 1941, suspending the writ of habeas corpus, so that through the critical first months of the war, the military's recognized power to deal with any emergency was far greater than on the West Coast.

Individuals were also significant in the Hawaiian equation. The War Department gave great discretion to the commanding general of each defense area and this brought to bear very different attitudes toward persons of Japanese ancestry in Hawaii and on the West Coast. The commanding general in Hawaii, Delos Emmons, restrained plans to take radical measures, raising practical problems of labor shortages and transportation until the pressure to evacuate the Hawaiian Islands subsided. General Emmons does not appear to have been a man of dogmatic racial views; he appears to have argued quietly but consistently for treating the ethnic Japanese as loyal to the United States, absent evidence to the contrary.

This policy was clearly much more congruent with basic American law and values. It was also a much sounder policy in practice. The remarkably high rate of enlistment in the Army in Hawaii is in sharp contrast to the doubt and alienation that marred the recruitment of Army volunteers in the relocation camps. The wartime experience in Hawaii left behind neither the extensive economic losses and injury suffered on the mainland nor the psychological burden of the direct experience of unjust exclusion and detention.

The German Americans. The German American experience in the First World War was far less traumatic and damaging than that of the ethnic Japanese in the Second World War, but it underscores the power of war fears and war hysteria to produce irrational but emotionally powerful reactions to people whose ethnicity links them to the enemy.

There were obvious differences between the position of people of German descent in the United States in 1917 and the ethnic Japanese at the start of the Second World War. In 1917, more than 8,000,000 people in the United States had been born in Germany or had one or both parents born there. Although German Americans were not massively represented politically, their numbers gave them notable political strength and support from political spokesmen outside the ethnic group.

The history of the First World War bears a suggestive resemblance to the events of 1942: rumors in the press of sabotage and espionage, use of a stereotype of the German as an unassimilable and rapacious Hun, followed by an effort to suppress those institutions—the language, the press and the churches—that were most palpably foreign and perceived as the seedbed of Kaiserism. There were numerous examples of official and quasi-governmental harassment and fruitless investigation of German Americans and resident German aliens. This history is made even more disturbing by the absence of an extensive history of anti-German agitation before the war.

* * *

The promulgation of Executive Order 9066 was not justified by military necessity, and the decisions which followed from it—detention, ending detention and ending exclusion—were not driven by analysis of military conditions. The broad historical causes which shaped these decisions were race prejudice, war hysteria and a failure of political leadership. Widespread ignorance of Japanese Americans contributed to a policy conceived in haste and executed in an atmosphere of fear and anger at Japan. A grave injustice was done to American citizens and resident aliens of Japanese ancestry who, without individual review or any probative evidence against them, were excluded, removed and detained by the United States during World War II.

In memoirs and other statements after the war, many of those involved in the exclusion, removal and detention passed judgment on those events. While believing in the context of the time that evacuation was a legitimate exercise of the war powers, Henry L. Stimson recognized that "to loyal citizens this forced evacuation was a personal injustice." In his autobiography, Francis Biddle reiterated his beliefs at the time: "the program was ill-advised, unnecessary and unnecessarily cruel." Justice William O. Douglas, who joined the majority opinion in *Korematsu* which held the evacuation constitutionally permissible, found that the evacuation case "was ever on my conscience." Milton Eisenhower described the evacuation to the relocation camps as "an inhuman mistake." Chief Justice Earl Warren, who had urged evacuation as Attorney General of California, stated, "I have since deeply regretted the removal order and my own testimony advocating it, because it was not in keeping with our American concept of freedom and the rights of citizens." Justice Tom C. Clark, who had been liaison between the Justice Department and the Western Defense Command, concluded, "Looking back on it today [the evacuation] was, of course, a mistake."

PART II: THE ALEUTS

During the struggle for naval supremacy in the Pacific in World War II, the Aleutian Islands were strategically valuable to both the United

States and Japan. Beginning in March 1942, United States military intelligence repeatedly warned Alaska defense commanders that Japanese aggression into the Aleutian Islands was imminent. In June 1942, the Japanese attacked and held the two westernmost Aleutians, Kiska and Attu. These islands remained in Japanese hands until July and August 1943. During the Japanese offensive in June 1942, American military commanders in Alaska ordered the evacuation of the Aleuts from many islands to places of relative safety. The government placed the evacuees in camps in southeast Alaska where they remained in deplorable conditions until being allowed to return to their islands in 1944 and 1945.

The Evacuation

The military had anticipated a possible Japanese attack for some time before June 1942. The question of what should be done to provide security for the Aleuts lay primarily with the civilians who reported to the Secretary of the Interior: the Office of Indian Affairs, the Fish and Wildlife Service and the territorial governor. They were unable to agree upon a course of action—evacuation and relocation to avoid the risks of war, or leaving the Aleuts on their islands on the ground that subsistence on the islands would disrupt Aleut life less than relocation. The civilian authorities were engaged in consulting with the military and the Aleuts when the Japanese attacked.

At this point the military hurriedly stepped in and commenced evacuation in the midst of a rapidly developing military situation. On June 3, 1942, the Japanese bombed the strategic American base at Dutch Harbor in the Aleutians; as part of the response a U.S. ship evacuated most of the island of Atka, burning the Aleut village to prevent its use by Japanese troops, and Navy planes picked up the rest of the islanders a few days later.

In anticipation of a possible attack, the Pribilof Islands were also evacuated by the Navy in early June. In early July, the Aleut villages of Nikolski on Umnak Island, and Makushin, Biorka, Chernofski, Kashega and Unalaska on Unalaska Island, and Akutan on Akutan Island were evacuated in a sweep eastward from Atka to Akutan.

At that point, the Navy decided that no further evacuation of Aleut villages east of Akutan Island was needed. Eight hundred seventy-six Aleuts had been evacuated from Aleut villages west of Unimak Island, including the Pribilofs. Except in Unalaska the entire population of each village was evacuated, including at least 30 non-Aleuts. All of the Aleuts were relocated to southeastern Alaska except 50 persons who were either evacuated to the Seattle area or hospitalized in the Indian Hospital at Tacoma, Washington.

The evacuation of the Aleuts had a rational basis as a precaution to ensure their safety. The Aleuts were evacuated from an active theatre of war; indeed, 42 were taken prisoner on Attu by the Japanese. It was clearly the military's belief that evacuation of non-military personnel was advisable. The families of military personnel were evacuated first, and when Aleut communities were evacuated the white teachers and government employees on the islands were evacuated with them. Exceptions to total evacuation appear to have been made only for people directly employed in war-related work.

The Aleuts' Camps

Aleuts were subjected to deplorable conditions following the evacuation. Typical housing was an abandoned gold mine or fish cannery buildings which were inadequate in both accommodation and sanitation. Lack of medical care contributed to extensive disease and death.

Conditions at the Funter Bay cannery in southeastern Alaska, where 300 Aleuts were placed, provide a graphic impression of one of the worst camps. Many buildings had not been occupied for a dozen years and were used only for storage. They were inadequate, particularly for winter use. The majority of evacuees were forced to live in two dormitory-style buildings in groups of six to thirteen people in areas nine to ten feet square. Until fall, many Aleuts were forced to sleep in relays because of lack of space. The quarters were as rundown as they were cramped. As one contemporary account reported:

> The only buildings that are capable of fixing is the two large places where the natives are sleeping. All other houses are absolutely gone from rot. It will be almost impossible to put toilet and bath into any of them except this one we are using as a mess hall and it leaks in thirty places. . . . No brooms, soap or mops or brushes to keep the place suitable for pigs to stay in.

People fell through rotten wooden floors. One toilet on the beach just above the low water mark served ninety percent of the evacuees. Clothes were laundered on the ground or sidewalks.

Health conditions at Funter Bay were described in 1943 by a doctor from the Territorial Department of Health who inspected the camp:

> As we entered the first bunkhouse the odor of human excreta and waste was so pungent that I could hardly make the grade. . . . The buildings were in total darkness except for a few candles here

and there [which] I considered distinct fire hazards. . . . [A] mother
and as many as three or four children were found in several beds
and two or three children in one bunk. . . . The garbage cans
were overflowing, human excreta was found next to the doors of
the cabins and the drainage boxes into which dishwater and kitchen
waste was to be placed were filthy beyond description. . . . I
realize that during the first two days we saw the community at its
worst. I know that there were very few adults who were well. . . .
The water supply is discolored, contaminated and unattractive.
. . . [F]acilities for boiling and cooling the water are not readily
available. . . . I noticed some lack of the teaching of basic public
health fundamentals. Work with such a small group of people who
had been wards of the government for a long period of time should
have brought better results. It is strange that they could have
reverted from a state of thrift and cleanliness on the Islands to the
present state of filth, despair, and complete lack of civic pride. I
realize, too, that at the time I saw them the community was largely
made up of women and children whose husbands were not with
them. With proper facilities for leadership, guidance and stimulation . . . the situation could have been quite different.

In the fall of 1942, the only fulltime medical care at Funter Bay
was provided by two nurses who served both the cannery camp and a
camp at a mine across Funter Bay. Doctors were only temporarily
assigned to the camp, often remaining for only a few days or weeks.
The infirmary at the mining camp was a three-room bungalow; at the
cannery, it was a room twenty feet square. Medical supplies were
scarce.

Epidemics raged throughout the Aleuts' stay in southeastern Alaska;
they suffered from influenza, measles, and pneumonia along with tuberculosis. Twenty-five died at Funter Bay in 1943 alone, and it is
estimated that probably ten percent of the evacuated Aleuts died during their two or three year stay in southeastern Alaska.

To these inadequate conditions was added the isolation of the camp
sites, where climatic and geographic conditions were very unlike the
Aleutians. No employment meant debilitating idleness. It was prompted
in part by government efforts to keep the Pribilovians, at least, together
so that they might be returned to harvest the fur seals, an enterprise
economically valuable to the government. Indeed a group of Pribilovians were taken back to their islands in the middle of the evacuation
period for the purpose of seal harvesting.

The standard of care which the government owes to those within
its care was clearly violated by this treatment, which brought great
suffering and loss of life to the Aleuts.

Return to the Islands

The Aleuts were only slowly returned to their islands. The Pribilovians were able to get back to the Pribilofs by the late spring of 1944, nine months after the Japanese had been driven out of the Aleutian chain. The return to the Aleutians themselves did not take place for another year. Some of this delay may be fairly attributed to transport shortage and problems of supplying the islands with housing and food so that normal life could resume. But the government's record, especially in the Aleutians, reflects an indifference and lack of urgency that lengthened the long delay in taking the Aleuts home. Some Aleuts were not permitted to return to their homes; to this day, Attuans continue to be excluded from their ancestral lands.

The Aleuts returned to communities which had been vandalized and looted by the military forces. Rehabilitation assessments were made for each village; the reports on Unalaska are typical:

All buildings were damaged due to lack of normal care and upkeep. . . . The furnishings, clothing and personal effects, remaining in the homes showed, with few exceptions, evidence of weather damage and damage by rats. Inspection of contents revealed extensive evidence of widespread wanton destruction of property and vandalism. Contents of closed packing boxes, trunks and cupboards had been ransacked. Clothing had been scattered over floors, trampled and fouled. Dishes, furniture, stoves, radios, phonographs, books, and other items had been broken or damaged. Many items listed on inventories furnished by the occupants of the houses were entirely missing. . . . It appears that armed forces personnel and civilians alike have been responsible for this vandalism and that it occurred over a period of many months.

Perhaps the greatest loss to personal property occurred at the time the Army conducted its clean up of the village in June of 1943. Large numbers of soldiers were in the area at that time removing rubbish and outbuildings and many houses were entered unofficially and souvenirs and other articles were taken.

When they first returned to the islands, many Aleuts were forced to camp because their former homes (those that still stood) had not yet been repaired and many were now uninhabitable. The Aleuts rebuilt their homes themselves. They were "paid" with free groceries until their homes were repaired; food, building and repair supplies were procured locally, mostly from military surplus.

The Aleuts suffered material losses from the government's occupation of the islands for which they were never fully recompensed, in cash or in kind. Devout followers of the Russian Orthodox faith, Aleuts treasured the religious icons from czarist Russia and other family heirlooms that were their most significant spiritual as well as material losses. They cannot be replaced. In addition, possessions such as houses, furniture, boats, and fishing gear were either never replaced or replaced by markedly inferior goods.

In sum, despite the fact that the Aleutians were a theatre of war from which evacuation was a sound policy, there was no justification for the manner in which the Aleuts were treated in the camps in southeastern Alaska, nor for failing to compensate them fully for their material losses.

Part I

Nisei and Issei

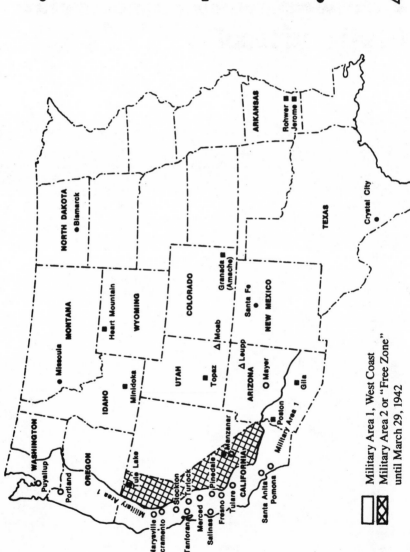

KEY

○ **ASSEMBLY CENTERS**
Puyallup, Wash.
Portland, Ore.
Marysville, Calif.
Sacramento, Calif.
Tanforan, Calif.
Stockton, Calif.
Turlock, Calif.
Merced, Calif.
Pinedale, Calif.
Salinas, Calif.
Fresno, Calif.
Tulare, Calif.
Santa Anita, Calif.
Pomona, Calif.
Mayer, Ariz.

■ **RELOCATION CENTERS**
Manzanar, Calif.
Tule Lake, Calif.
Poston, Ariz.
Gila, Ariz.
Minidoka, Ida.
Heart Mountain, Wyo.
Granada, Colo.
Topaz, Utah
Rohwer, Ark.
Jerome, Ark.

● **JUSTICE DEPARTMENT INTERNMENT CAMPS**
Santa Fe, N. Mex.
Bismarck, N. Dak.
Crystal City, Tex.
Missoula, Mont.

△ **CITIZEN ISOLATION CAMPS**
Moab, Utah
Leupp, Ariz.

☐ Military Area 1, West Coast
⊠ Military Area 2 or "Free Zone"
  until March 29, 1942

1

Before Pearl Harbor

On December 7, 1941, Japan attacked and crippled the American fleet at Pearl Harbor. Ten weeks later, on February 19, 1942, President Roosevelt signed Executive Order 9066 under which the War Department excluded from the West Coast everyone of Japanese ancestry—both American citizens and their alien parents who, despite long residence in the United States, were barred by federal law from becoming American citizens. Driven from their homes and farms and businesses, very few had any choice but to go to "relocation centers"— Spartan, barrack-like camps in the inhospitable deserts and mountains of the interior.*

---

*There is a continuing controversy over the contention that the camps were "concentration camps" and that any other term is a euphemism. The government documents of the time frequently use the term "concentration camps," but after World War II, with full realization of the atrocities committed by the Nazis in the death camps of Europe, that phrase came to have a very different meaning. The American relocation centers were bleak and bare, and life in them had many hardships, but they were not extermination camps, nor did the American government embrace a policy of torture or liquidation of the ethnic Japanese. To use the phrase "concentration camps" summons up images and ideas which are inaccurate and unfair. The Commission has used "relocation centers" and "relocation camps," the usual term used during the war, not to gloss over the hardships of the camps, but in an effort to find an historically fair and accurate phrase.

This was done out of fear—fear of sabotage, of espionage, of fifth column activity. There was no evidence that any individual American citizen was actively disloyal to his country. Nevertheless, the World War II history of Americans of Japanese ancestry was far different from that of German Americans, Italian Americans or any other ethnic group. It is the bitter history of an original mistake, a failure of America's faith in its citizens' devotion to their country's cause and their right to liberty, when there was no evidence or proof of wrongdoing. It is a history which deeply seared and scarred the lives of Japanese Americans. How did it happen?

War inflamed many passions in the country. On the West Coast it rekindled the fears and prejudices of long years of anti-Asian agitation carried on by organized interest groups. Decades of discrimination against immigrants from Japan and public hostility toward Americans of Japanese descent fueled outraged shock at the Pearl Harbor attack and impotent anger against the Japanese as they swept through the Philippines and down the Malay Peninsula to Singapore. Reports of American battlefield deaths lit sparks in one community after another up and down the West Coast, where fear of invasion was very real. In significant measure, the evacuation decision was ignited by the fire of those emotions, especially in California.

The hostile reception and treatment of Japanese immigrants on the West Coast are the historical prelude to the exclusion and evacuation. Federal immigration and naturalization laws, frequently sponsored and backed by westerners, demonstrate this public hostility to Asians, particularly the Japanese. Laws which prohibited the ownership of land by Japanese resident aliens and imposed segregation in the schools tell the same story in the western states. Public perceptions and misconceptions about the Japanese in this country were affected by myths and stereotypes—the fear of "the yellow peril" and antagonistic misunderstanding of the cultural patterns of the Japanese in America. Resentment of effective economic competition also inflamed public feeling and, combined with differences of language and culture, left the small minority of Japanese Americans on the West Coast comparatively isolated—a ready target at a time of fear and anxiety.

IMMIGRATION AND LEGALIZED DISCRIMINATION

Discrimination in American immigration laws started with the Naturalization Act of 1790, which provided for naturalization of "any alien, being a free white person."[1] Following revision of the statute after the Civil War, the act was read to prohibit any Chinese immigrant from becoming an American citizen.[2] It was generally assumed that the prohibition would extend to the Japanese as well and, in 1922, the Supreme Court interpreted the statute to prohibit the naturalization of any Oriental.[3] Although immigrants from Asia could not become American citizens, their children born on American soil became citizens by birth.[4] The Fourteenth Amendment to the Constitution assured to everyone born in the United States the rights and privileges of citizenship without regard to the status of one's parents.

The Chinese began immigrating into this country under these adverse conditions in the middle of the nineteenth century, several decades before significant Japanese immigration began. California was at the center of American discrimination against the Chinese and, later, against the Japanese. By 1870 approximately ten percent of California's population was Chinese. A great many of the Chinese immigrants were railroad laborers; when the transcontinental line had been completed in 1869 they were discharged wherever they happened to be. This left almost 10,000 unemployed Chinese in a depressed labor market, and anti-Chinese sentiment became widespread and vocal throughout the west. The financial recession of the 1870's was blamed on "cheap Mongolian labor," and protests were directed against the Chinese and their employers. The San Francisco labor movement prospered by using anti-Chinese agitation as an organizing tool. The Chinese threat, first characterized as unfair labor competition, eventually included claims of racial impurity and injury to western civilization. The press and political parties pandered to these anti-Chinese attitudes. After 1871, both the Republican and Democratic parties in California had anti-Chinese planks in their platforms. Moreover, an independent workingmen's party organized in California around populism and anti-Chinese measures.[5]

Pressures mounted for the federal government to prohibit Chinese immigration.[6] Under that pressure, Congress passed a Chinese exclusion bill in 1880 which President Hayes vetoed. In 1882, President Arthur vetoed a similar bill; however, as a compromise he signed into law a ten-year suspension of Chinese immigration.[7] The Chinese Exclusion Act of 1882 was renewed in 1892 and made permanent in 1902.[8] Immigration and naturalization of the Chinese was not permitted until 1943, when the United States was allied with China in the Second World War.[9]

Significant Japanese immigration into the United States did not start until the late nineteenth century. In 1853, Commodore Matthew

Perry led an expedition to Japan to establish trade relations, and the next year he negotiated a treaty which opened Japan to American commerce.[10] Relations between the two countries developed quickly. Direct shipping between San Francisco and Japan was begun in 1855; diplomatic relations were established in 1860, but by 1880 the total Japanese population in this country was only 148 persons.[11]

Several factors increased Japanese immigration significantly in the following decades. Adverse economic conditions at home were an impetus to emigration in this instance as in many other movements to the United States. During the last half of the nineteenth century, Japan's economy industrialized rapidly, with attendant dislocations. By 1884 the disruption was significant, and led Japan to grant passports for contract labor in Hawaii where there was a demand for cheap labor and, in 1886, to legalize emigration.[12] Between 1885 and 1894, the years during which large-scale contract labor immigration continued, over 25,000 Japanese went to Hawaii.[13] Many subsequently emigrated to the American mainland.[14]

As reports of better economic conditions in the United States were carried back to Japan, more immigrants were drawn to this country. In addition, the Chinese Exclusion Act of 1882 was perceived to leave room for cheap agricultural labor, which allowed immigration and recruitment of Japanese from both Hawaii and Japan.[15] The Alaska gold rush of 1897–99 drained the Pacific northwest of labor needed to link Seattle and Tacoma with the east by railroad, so Japanese laborers were sought.[16] By 1890 there were 2,039 Japanese immigrants and native-born American citizens of Japanese ancestry in the United States; by 1900 there were 24,326; between 1901 and 1908, a time of unrestricted immigration, 127,000 Japanese entered the United States.[17]

What were the characteristics of the immigrants? Their predisposition to the United States was probably more than economic, since the United States and its institutions were deeply admired by the Japanese—in Japanese government textbooks, Benjamin Franklin and Abraham Lincoln were models to be emulated.[18] The vast majority were young adult males from the agricultural class—ambitious young men of limited means.[19] The Japanese emphasis on small-scale individual enterprise served the immigrants well in the United States. In many cases, their knowledge of intensive cultivation, new to the west—including knowledge of soils, fertilizers, skill in land reclamation, irrigation and drainage—enabled them to cultivate and develop marginal lands successfully and to pioneer the production of new crops. Many were fishermen who eventually revolutionized the fishing industry.[20]

Their occupations were overwhelmingly manual but their hard work, thrift, respect for education and social stability were a firm foundation for a better economic future.[21]

The Japanese who emigrated to the mainland United States settled on the West Coast, primarily in California. In 1900 41% of the ethnic group and, in 1940, 70% had made their homes in California.[22] Numerically, they remained a tiny minority, making up only 2.1% of California's population at the time of greatest concentration, and in 1940 comprising only 1.6% of the population of California, most heavily concentrated in and around Los Angeles.[23]

The California of 1900 to 1920 was highly heterogeneous, based on expansive resources, space and an expanding economy. A state largely populated by citizen newcomers, California society was unintegrated, unstable, mobile and loosely organized. The state was made up of culturally insulated and isolated communities. Without a general sense of community or purpose, many outsiders, such as the "Okies" of the Depression years, were regarded as inferior.[24]

The Japanese immigrants were excluded from political life by the prohibition against naturalization and were effectively barred from participation in social and economic affairs. As with many new immigrant groups, they brought with them customs and mores which also tended to set them apart in the early years after arrival. There was a sustaining pride in the Japanese people and its culture, which honored traditional social values and cohesive group relationships, with particular deference to those in positions of authority and status within the family and the community.[25] There were also the obvious differences of language and religion. These factors promoted internal solidarity within the Japanese community and, combined with the hostile nativism of California, placed the Issei* in comparative isolation in the public and economic life of the West Coast.

The Japanese were a major focus of California politics in the fifty years before World War II. Their small numbers, their political impotence and the racial feelings of many Californians frequently combined with resentment at the immigrants' willingness to labor for low pay to make them a convenient target for demagogues or agitators.

---

*The *Issei* are the immigrant generation from Japan; the first generation born in the United States are *Nisei*, the second generation born here, *Sansei*. Those who returned to Japan for education are termed *Kibei* and the entire ethnic Japanese group in America are *Nikkei*.

Following early incidents in the 1890's, anti-Japanese activity commenced in earnest in 1900. On May 7, 1900, local labor groups called a major anti-Japanese protest in San Francisco. Political, economic, and social arguments were made.[26] Mayor James Duval Phelan of San Francisco expressed the prevalent feelings:

> The Japanese are starting the same tide of immigration which we thought we had checked twenty years ago. . . . The Chinese and Japanese are not bona fide citizens. They are not the stuff of which American citizens can be made. . . . Personally we have nothing against Japanese, but as they will not assimilate with us and their social life is so different from ours, let them keep at a respectful distance.[27]

In the same year, the American Federation of Labor adopted a resolution asking Congress to re-enact the Chinese exclusion law and include all "Mongolian" labor. Also in 1900, both the Democrats and the Populists of California adopted expressly anti-Japanese planks in their platforms; similarly, the Republican position proposed effective restriction on "cheap foreign labor." In November 1901, a Chinese Exclusion Convention met in San Francisco. Designed to instruct Congress to extend the Chinese Exclusion Act, the convention determined not to seek Japanese exclusion only because the request would dissipate its message. Contemporary accounts of that convention show a growing hostility in California toward Japanese immigrants.[28]

After Japan's striking victory over Russia in 1904–05, fear of Japanese territorial advances fueled the anti-Japanese immigration forces—movies, novels and newspapers reiterated accusations that Japanese in America were merely agents of the Emperor.[29] In February 1905, *The San Francisco Chronicle* began a series of anti-Japanese articles, the first entitled "The Japanese Invasion, the Problem of the Hour." Although the motivation for these articles is unclear, they evoked strong responses; some San Francisco clergy and the Japanese residents themselves objected, but the public in general supported the paper's views. In early March, both houses of the California legislature passed anti-Japanese resolutions.[30]

Then in May 1905, delegates from 67 organizations met in San Francisco to form what became the Japanese Exclusion League (Asiatic Exclusion League), led primarily by labor groups. Ironically, many of the League's leaders themselves had emigrated from Europe. The League's motivations were racial and economic; its purpose, Japanese exclusion; its methods, legislation, boycott, school segregation and propaganda.[31] By 1908, the League had over 100,000 members and

238 affiliated groups, mostly labor unions.[32] The League's presence helped to catalyze anti-Japanese activity, despite the failure of its proposals. In the words of Roger Daniels, one of the foremost historians of Japanese Americans: "From the day of the League's formation, May 14, 1905, until after the end of the Second World War, there was in California an organized anti-Japanese movement that would eventually draw support from all segments of the state's population."[33]

The next aim of the anti-Japanese activists, including the League, was to segregate schoolchildren of Japanese ancestry. In May 1905, the San Francisco School Board announced a policy of removing Japanese students to the one Oriental school so that "our children should not be placed in any position where their youthful impressions may be affected by association with pupils of the Mongolian race." On December 11, 1906, under increasing public pressure spurred by a coalition of labor and politicians, the school board issued an order which barred Asian children, including Japanese, from white primary schools. To put the problem in perspective, only 93 Japanese students, 25 of them born in the United States, were then in the San Francisco public schools.[34]

School segregation in San Francisco made discrimination against the Japanese an issue of international diplomacy. The school board's order caused serious embarrassment to President Theodore Roosevelt, who learned of it through reports from Tokyo. Concerned about maintaining sound diplomatic relations with Japan, which had just demonstrated its military power by resoundingly defeating Russia in the Russo-Japanese War, Roosevelt began negotiations with California. After consultation, the President agreed that if the San Francisco School Board rescinded its order and if California refrained from passing more anti-Japanese legislation, he would negotiate with Japan to restrict immigration in a manner which did not injure that country's pride. Roosevelt also sent a message to Congress opposing school segregation and supporting naturalization of the Japanese. Public opposition greeted his views. Roosevelt did not press the naturalization legislation, and his message was regarded as an effort to placate Japan in the face of the school board order.[35]

To carry out President Roosevelt's part of the bargain with Japan, Secretary of State Elihu Root drafted, and Congress passed, legislation generally authorizing immigration restriction from such intermediate points as Hawaii. On March 14, 1907, the President issued an Executive Order barring further Japanese immigration from Hawaii, Mexico and Canada.[36]

In 1907 the two countries entered into the "Gentlemen's Agreement" under which Japan agreed not to issue more workers' passports valid for the continental United States, and to restrict issuance to "laborers who have already been in America and to the parents, wives and children of laborers already resident there." This agreement sharply curtailed, but did not eliminate, Japanese immigration. Between 1908 and 1924, many Japanese men resident in the United States brought to this country the brides of arranged marriages,[37] creating an inaccurate public impression that Japan had deceived the United States in implementing the agreement. Resentment was expressed as early as 1910, when campaign platforms of the Republican, Democratic and Socialist parties all included exclusionist planks.[38]

The next phase of anti-Japanese activity, again centered in California, was an effort to prohibit land ownership by Japanese immigrants, a particularly harsh measure in light of the fact that a very high percentage of the immigrants were farmers. In 1913, the Democrats and the Progressives, led by the Governor of California and supported by some farmers who feared economic competition, pressed the California legislature to enact such a law. President Wilson lobbied against passage, as did major businesses interested in good relations with Japan. After extensive politicking, however, the state legislature passed the Alien Land Law of 1913 (the Webb-Heney Act), which barred future land purchases by aliens ineligible for citizenship and forbade such aliens to acquire leases for periods longer than three years.[39] The law was a particularly outrageous discriminatory measure aimed at the Japanese, but it did not end anti-Japanese agitation because it was easily avoided and largely ineffectual. Immigrant Japanese who had citizen children could vest ownership in the children with a parent as guardian; for those without children, a bare majority of stock could be transferred to a citizen as ostensible owner.[40] Such groups as the Anti-Jap Laundry League attacked the legislation.

After the First World War, anti-Japanese activity in the United States intensified. Over the next several years, it had two foci—a more restrictive alien land law in California, and total prohibition of immigration from Japan. Four major organizations, reflecting the views of labor, "patriots" and farmers, supported and led this anti-Japanese movement: The Native Sons (and Native Daughters) of the Golden West; the American Legion; the California State Federation of Labor and the California State Grange.[41] The old Asiatic Exclusion League was reorganized into the California Joint Immigration Committee.[42] Small businessmen also opposed continued Japanese immigration,[43] and the California Real Estate Association opposed land ownership by Japanese aliens.[44] Big business, including the Chamber of Commerce, opposed a prohibition on immigration as a possible interference with trade,[45] and large-scale agriculture, interested in access to cheap labor, took the same position.

The breadth of the anti-Japanese groups, and their unity, were indeed effective. All united in adopting a five-point plan:

1. Cancellation of the "Gentlemen's Agreement;"

2. Prohibition against the entry of "Picture Brides;"

3. Rigorous prohibition against further immigration from Japan;

4. Confirmation of the policy that Asians should be forever barred from American citizenship; and

5. Amendment of the federal Constitution to provide that no child born in the United States should become an American citizen unless both parents were of a race eligible for citizenship.[46]

In 1920 the groups in California succeeded in passing an initiative which further restricted Japanese landholding in California. The Los Angeles County Asiatic Association urged Californians to vote yes on Proposition One to "Save California—Stop Absorption of State's Best Acreage by Japanese Through Leases and Evasions of Law."[47] This measure was an attempt to shore up the Alien Land Act of 1913. The 1920 law prohibited any further transfer of land to Japanese nationals, forbade them to lease land, barred any corporation in which Japanese held a majority of stock from lease or purchase of land, and prohibited immigrant parents from serving as guardians for their minor citizen children.[48]

This law also proved largely ineffectual. The provision barring Japanese parents from acting as guardians for their children was ruled unconstitutional.[49] Because there were many citizen children by 1920, avoiding the other new restrictions was not difficult. Nevertheless, the law had some effect: in combination with the prohibition on immigration, it reduced the number of acres held in California by persons of Japanese ancestry.[50] Similar anti-Japanese sentiment led to the enactment of parallel anti-alien land legislation in Arizona, Washington and Oregon,[51] even though by 1920 only 4,151 Japanese lived in Oregon and owned only 2,185 acres of land.[52]

From 1908 to 1924, while the Gentlemen's Agreement was in

effect, 159,675 Japanese immigrated into the continental United States.[53] Many immigrants, however, returned to Japan with their children. The 1910 census shows 72,157 persons of Japanese ancestry in the continental United States; the 1920 census shows 111,010 and the 1930 census shows 138,834.[54] Nevertheless, in large part because the Gentlemen's Agreement had been represented to California as an exclusion act,[55] many wrongly believed that Japan had breached the Agreement.[56] This mistaken view as well as the political and perceived economic interests of the anti-Japanese groups aided the drive to end all Japanese immigration. In 1920, the exclusionists formed the Japanese Exclusion League of California, organized under V. S. McClatchy and State Senator Inman to seek passage of exclusion legislation.[57] McClatchy was once publisher of *The Sacramento Bee* and a director of the Associated Press; from 1920 to 1932 he represented the California Joint Immigration Committee. Publicly adept, McClatchy was an untiring and successful advocate of Japanese exclusion—not on the basis of prejudice, he claimed, but because the Japanese were superior workers and thus an economic threat.[58] In 1924, at the culmination of isolationist trends in the United States and particularly of the anti-Japanese movement, the federal immigration law was changed expressly to exclude the Japanese.[59]

After 1924, there were no major successful legislative initiatives against the ethnic Japanese until after Pearl Harbor, but anti-Japanese activity continued. For instance, there were repeated efforts to pass statutes banning aliens not eligible for citizenship from employment in the government and on public works projects,[60] and in 1938 the California legislature defeated a bill which would have removed the Issei from the tuna-fishing industry in San Diego and San Pedro.[61] The Joint Immigration Committee worked to insure that the exclusion law was not amended, aided in the passage of alien land laws in the interior states and influenced the deletion of passages favorable to Japanese in textbooks used in California and Hawaii.[62] Anti-Japanese agitation and sentiment continued to be part of the public life of the West Coast.

THE ROOTS OF PREJUDICE—MYTHS, STEREOTYPES AND FEARS

Stereotypes and fears mixed with economic self-interest, often growing out of and contributing to racial antipathy, were the seedbed for the politics of prejudice which bred discriminatory laws.

"The Yellow Peril"

Underlying anti-Japanese sentiment in the United States was fear of the "yellow peril." The origin of the term is obscure, but in its earliest forms the abstraction imagined a wave of "coolie" immigration, fed by a high birthrate and famine conditions in China, which would engulf the whites of California and the Pacific Coast.[63] This notion stirred both fear and hatred, although at its peak in 1907 Japanese immigration was less than 3% of immigration to the United States, and in California the Japanese never reached 3% of the state's population.[64]

This creature of propaganda was first turned upon the Chinese and later the Japanese. American confusion between the Japanese and the Chinese, and increasing Japanese immigration on the West Coast, often led the public to view both groups as a single racial threat.

The unexpected military victories of the Japanese over the Russians in 1904-05 added fuel to the fire. After the Russo-Japanese War, rumors circulated in California that Japan would organize the wealth and manpower of China to provide and equip armies that would revive the power of Genghis Khan and create a real "yellow peril"—hordes of Asians overpowering and subjugating a scattered white population strung out along the immense Pacific Coast. Fear of possible war with Japan, a now-powerful country, exacerbated these anxieties. Much anti-Japanese activity in the United States, including the Alien Land Law of 1920 and the Oriental Exclusion Act of 1924, provoked strong protest from Japan and fostered fears of war. As Japan grew more aggressive and hostile after 1931, anxiety revived. Japan's invasion of Manchuria, its desertion of the League of Nations, its abandonment of agreements on naval limitation, the further invasion of China, and the bombing of the American gunboat *Panay* on the Yangtze River in 1937 fed public concern about war with Japan and, aided by the press, revived fear of the yellow peril.[65]

Popular writing, the movies, and the Hearst newspapers in particular, promoted the fear.[66] "Patria," produced by Hearst's International Film Service Corp. in 1917, and "Shadows of the West," circulated by the American Legion, both portrayed Japanese immigrants as sneaky, treacherous agents of a militaristic Japan seeking to control the West Coast.[67] Two novels written by the respected Peter B. Kyne and Wallace Irwin about dangers of Japanese land ownership were serialized in the *Saturday Evening Post* and Hearst's *Cosmopolitan*.[68] Pseudoscientific literature began to discuss the inferiority of Eastern and Southern European stock as well as the "yellow people."[69] Madison Grant's 1917 work *The Passing of the Great Race* argued that immigration was "mongrelizing" America; Lothrop Stoddard published *The*

Rising Tide of Color Against White World Supremacy in 1920; Stoddard and Grant together were influential in expounding the new racism.[70]

Purported espionage by those of Japanese ancestry in the United States was advanced as one threat from the yellow peril. Allegations that persons of Japanese descent were a "secret army" for Japan and the Emperor were constantly repeated by anti-Japanese agitators.

The "Japanese Birthrate"

Fears of Japanese expansionism and the "yellow peril" were fed by wild overestimation of the birthrate among persons of Japanese ancestry in the continental United States. When the 1920 Alien Land Law was being considered, Governor William Stephens of California asserted that the greatest danger to white Californians came from the high birthrate of the Japanese. A state report sought to demonstrate that the Japanese birthrate was three times that of white citizens of the state. The report failed, however, to take account of the fact that the pattern of Japanese immigration led to older husbands bringing to the United States young brides who, married only a few years at the time of the survey, were at the peak of their fertility. To compare that sample to the birthrate among all women of childbearing age in California was misleading. In fact, the long-range birthrate of the immigrant generation fell below that of the contemporary European immigrant groups and only slightly above that of native whites during the 1920's and 1930's. By 1940 the birthrate among Japanese Americans in every state on the West Coast was lower than the birthrate of the general population. The "high Japanese birthrate" was a myth.[71]

Education, Religion and Associations

The Issei left behind a country characterized by pride, strong moral convictions, and community cohesiveness. Many cultural patterns were transplanted into Japanese community life in the United States. Although the Issei were criticized for being clannish, early discrimination reinforced the typically separate living patterns of non-English-speaking immigrants and delayed their cultural assimilation. The Issei responded by trying to raise their children in a two-culture environment. What resulted was a general acceptance among Nisei of some traditional Japanese mores, and continuing criticism from anti-Japanese groups that the immigrants and their families were unassimilable and pro-Japan.

Many Issei wished to prepare their children for life in either country, fearing that future discriminatory laws would prevent them from continuing to live in the United States. Dual citizenship, pursued actively or passively, was one contingency measure. Japan, as well as several European countries, had traditionally followed the principle of *jus sanguinis*, meaning that the children of Japanese nationals, regardless of country of birth, were citizens of Japan. Expatriation and citizenship acts passed in Japan in 1916 and 1924 modified the *jus sanguinis* principle, however, so that after 1924 ethnic Japanese born in the United States had to be registered promptly with the Japanese consul in order to obtain dual citizenship. The Japanese Association, established on the West Coast to promote Japanese immigrants' interests, encouraged Issei to expatriate their Nisei children and worked to terminate dual citizenships. By the 1930's, only twenty percent of the Nisei held dual citizenship.[72]

Next to parental authority, education was the strongest molder of values. To preserve their cultural heritage and to ensure their children's success in the Japanese community, or, if necessary, in Japan, Issei stressed the learning of the Japanese language.[73] Such language instruction was not unusual among first-generation immigrant groups. A large segment of the Nisei attended Japanese language school despite the generation gap which developed between Issei and Nisei as the young Japanese Americans came to identify more closely with American values. These classes were held after school, which made for a very long day of "education," drawing resentment from many Nisei and resulting in few ever truly mastering Japanese.[74] The education program of the schools was diverse but the lessons typically embodied and taught respect for parents and elders, self-reliance, obligation, hard work and other virtues believed to be inherently Japanese.[75] The language schools also supplied a stage for Japanese folklore, plays, songs, novels, and movies, all emphasizing Japanese ethics that in many instances paralleled the "Puritan work ethic." Although the schools were much Americanized over time, their approach depended on the teacher and the local community, and some schools stressed Japanese nationalism and loyalty. Senator Daniel Inouye recounted his experience in one such school in 1939:

> Day after day, the [Buddhist] priest who taught us ethics and Japanese history hammered away at the divine prerogatives of the Emperor . . . He would tilt his menacing crew-cut skull at us and solemnly proclaim, "You must remember that only a trick of fate has brought you so far from your homeland, but there must be no question of your loyalty. When Japan calls, you must know that it is Japanese blood that flows in your veins."[76]

Eventually, Inouye was thrown out of the school in a dispute about religion. Inouye's own career is ample proof that even such emotional instruction often had negligible effect. Nevertheless, the language schools and the much-stereotyped and exaggerated code of the *samurai* were viewed by many on the West Coast as threats to the American social system.

A smaller number of children were sent to Japan for formal education. These Kibei lived with relatives in Japan and returned with an education designed to be the key to their success in a Japanese community excluded from mainstream America. The length of time spent in Japan varied a great deal, as did the age at which children were sent; in consequence, the impact of the education varied considerably. A number of those who spent many of their formative years in Japan found it somewhat difficult to identify and to communicate with their American-educated peers, Nisei or Caucasian,[77] although they had not become fully Japanese either. With such variation within the group, calculating the total number of Kibei is not very illuminating, but by 1940 several thousand Nisei had had substantial education in Japan.[78]

The Buddhist church was also an educational influence for the Nisei. Although theologically different, Buddhism and Christianity shared many ethical similarities, including values of honesty, charity and hard work. But Buddhism was distrusted and largely misunderstood by Caucasians,[79] and even officials of Japan opposed the vigorous introduction of Buddhist missionaries into America.[80] Moreover, the Issei believed that joining Christian churches would open more doors for them in terms of employment and social acceptance.[81] By the 1930's half the Nisei were Christians[82] and, just before the war, in Seattle's ethnic Japanese community, Christians outnumbered those subscribing to Oriental religions.[83]

The Shinto religion had very few followers and was less understood in America than Buddhism.[84] Village Shinto in Japan overlapped Buddhism; state Shinto developed later and was less a religion than a patriotic worship of the emperor used initially to overthrow the Japanese feudal system. This cult was dominated by highly nationalistic fervor but its influence among Japanese in America was small, perhaps because its peak of influence came only after most of the Issei generation had left for the United States and reached adulthood. In fact, criticism of some of the ultra-nationalistic aspects of Japanese life in the 1930's led to the banning in Japan of some publications by Japanese Americans.[85]

Excluded from politics and many social functions of the white-dominated social structure on the West Coast, Issei formed a multiplicity of ethnic organizations and associations. Initially associations were established mainly for social purposes and were called *kenjinkai*, since members of each association were from the same *ken* or province of Japan. These developed and perpetuated an inner community within the entire Japanese community. The kenjinkais were mainly significant to the immigrant generation and the Nisei showed little interest in them. Other Issei associations sprang up as well. By 1905, in San Francisco alone, fifteen ken societies; seven religious organizations; and associations for tailors, cobblers, restauranteurs, barbers and houseworkers; a students' club; and a residence for women were established.[86] Politically strongest were the Japanese Associations, established in response to increased anti-Japanese activity. The most important function of the Association was to serve as a legal adviser and lobbyist. Critics among the white majority in California claimed the Association was under the direct influence of Japan, and suspicion of the Association and its leaders grew, peaking at the the start of the war.[87]

Nisei, seeking to assert their citizenship rights and to champion the rights of Japanese Americans and Japanese immigrants, formed two independent organizations immediately after World War I: The American Loyalty League in San Francisco and the Progressive Citizens' League in Seattle. These groups had little influence until the late 1920's, when many Nisei reached adulthood. The two merged into a national organization, the Japanese American Citizens League (JACL). The League was too young and poorly organized to achieve much success in improving the social and economic stature of the Nisei before the war, but it did provide an association separate from the Issei.[88]

All of these cultural patterns—dual citizenship; the language schools and education in Japan; foreign religion, particularly Shinto; and ethnic organizations, particularly groups of Issei veterans who had served in Japan—became targets for the anti-Japanese faction on the West Coast. They were viewed as proof that the ethnic Japanese would not or could not assimilate to "American" life and represented an alien threat to the dominant white society. It bore a kinship to the know-nothing nativism that sprang up on the East Coast during the European immigrations of the nineteenth century. The ethnic institutions were also wrongly viewed as mechanisms through which the Japanese government could influence and control the Issei and Nisei. Unfortunately, there was little informed American opinion to counter these exaggerated, alarmist views.

ECONOMIC STATUS

The relative economic status of the Nikkei affected anti-Japanese agitation in the United States as did general economic conditions. Frequently, anti-Japanese activity increased during periods of recession if competition from the ethnic Japanese was perceived as an economic threat.[89] This makes an understanding of the economic position of the Nikkei important to comprehending both the prewar and wartime history.

Since most of the Japanese who immigrated to the United States had worked in agriculture in Japan, farming was by far the predominant occupation among the Issei.[90] Other early immigrants found work as manual laborers for railroads, lumber companies, canneries or mines.[91] Initially, the Japanese concentrated in railroads, sugar beets and hop-harvesting. Both types of agricultural work paid by the piece, so meager incomes could be increased by hard work. The Japanese later moved into a wide range of farming activities, growing and cultivating citrus fruits, vineyards, berries and vegetables.[92] When these immigrants first arrived, many worked for $1 a day while other workers were earning up to $1.65 for the same work.[93] They took lower wages to obtain work; even low pay in the United States was higher than what they would have been able to earn in Japan.[94]

About half the Japanese in California were engaged in agriculture. Often, a Japanese immigrant would begin as a migrant laborer for a year or two, then settle in one place to harvest for a single farmer. The next step was sharecropping. After that, the worker would rent land, either paying cash or, for the first year or two, clearing the land in lieu of rent. The goal was ownership.[95] Land tenure statistics for California illustrate the pattern:[96]

TABLE 1: Japanese American Land Tenure in California

	Shared Crop (in acres)	Leased (in acres)	Owned (in acres)
1904	19,572½	35,258½	2,422
1909	59,001½	80,232	16,449½
1919	....	383,287	74,769

By 1910, 39,000 persons of Japanese ancestry were engaged in agriculture; of these, 6,000 were independent, mostly tenant, farmers.[97]

The skills of the Issei as intensive farmers were rewarded. In 1917, for example, the average production per acre among all California farmers was less than $42; for the average Issei it was $141.[98] In 1920, the market value of the crops produced by California Issei was $67 million, or over 10% of the total California value. They were able to develop marginal areas effectively. In part because of the alien land laws, the Japanese selected quick-growth crops which required minimal capital investment; for instance, in southern California, they concentrated on truck farming rather than citrus growing.[99]

In Oregon by 1940 the Nikkei grew an estimated $2.7 million worth of produce. In Washington in that year, they raised more than $4 million of produce. They also commenced farming in states where they had come to work on the railroads: Utah, Wyoming, Montana, Nebraska, Idaho, Colorado and Nevada.[100]

After World War I, total acreage under Japanese cultivation declined. By 1941, the value of all crops from Nikkei farms in California was $32 million (compared to the World War I high of $55 million). The decline was brought about by reduced Japanese acreage as well as plummeting crop values during the Depression.[101] Nevertheless, the Nikkei were important to the California agricultural economy; they were expected to produce 30-40% of the state's truck crops in 1942.[102]

Because of hostility and discrimination by whites, the Japanese entered agricultural produce distribution, primarily in Los Angeles, where they came to dominate the fruit and vegetable supply system by 1940.[103] The Japanese also entered produce marketing in Fresno, Sacramento, Seattle and Salt Lake City; in San Francisco, however, they were excluded from produce marketing.[104]

The Nikkei were also shopkeepers, primarily serving their own community. A detailed study of the Nikkei in Los Angeles (about one-third of the Japanese in the United States) shortly before World War II determined that most of those in business operated small enterprises with low capital investment that survived because of the unpaid labor of family members.[105] Before World War II, the Nisei were gradually moving into clerical work, seeking the security of jobs over the status of independent enterprise.[106] Other occupations of Nikkei before World War II included fishing, fish cannery work, housework and gardening.

Few were professionals.[107] This was so despite remarkable educational achievements. In 1940, the median education for all people of Japanese descent 25 years old and older was 8.6 years, compared with 9.9 years for Californians and 8.6 years for the entire United States population. But these numbers included the Issei, who typically had few years of schooling; for Nisei 25 years old and older, the 1940 median education was 12.2 years in California.[108] Continuing discrimination made finding a job difficult for college-educated Nisei and prevented a great many from entering higher professional, white collar or skilled occupations.[109] By 1940, only 960 persons of Japanese ancestry were employed as professionals in California, and the main source of white collar employment was federal civil service.[110]

The estimated median income for the Nikkei in California in 1940 was $622. This compares with a median income for the entire United States labor force of $627 and for California of $852 in the same year. In 1940, the Nikkei had high rates of employment: 96.7 percent of those in the labor force were employed, compared to 85.6 percent for the entire California population.[111] This higher rate may, however, include a substantial percentage of low-paid family workers.

Economic advancement for the immigrants was built on hard work, frugality and willingness to save and invest. Individual effort was aided by stable family structure and by ethnic organizations such as credit associations. Very few Japanese went on relief during the Depression. But such self-improvement frequently brought resentment from economic competitors, so that laborers and later independent farmers grew antagonistic to the Nikkei as their economic self-interest was affected.[112] V. S. McClatchy was particularly direct in expressing these views, arguing that Japanese immigration should be cut off because the immigrants were superior workers against whom West Coast whites could not compete.

RACE RELATIONS IN THE UNITED STATES

The status and treatment of Issei and Nisei is best understood against the background of the country's history on racial questions, posed most often between blacks and whites.[113] In 1940, racial segregation by law was still widespread and racial discrimination by custom and practice was found everywhere, largely accepted as part of American life. The Supreme Court still construed the constitutional promise of equal protection of the law for all Americans regardless of race, creed or color to require only that the states or the federal government provide equal though segregated facilities for the separate races. The supposed test of equality, however, was rarely met. "Scientific" studies, based in part on intelligence testing widely used by the military during World War I and in part on views of evolution, kept alive the theory that blacks were inferior and that there was a hierarchy of capability and attainment among the races. Whatever the reasons or motives, much of the country believed in fundamental racial differences and practiced those beliefs through some form of discrimination or segregation.

While racial discrimination was most deeply entrenched in the south, the problem was national. By 1940, blacks were no longer so heavily concentrated in the south. In the early 1900's mechanization of agricultural production in the south destroyed the paternal debt-perpetuating sharecropping system and displaced many blacks. During World War I, they had begun migration to the north and midwest, some gaining employment in war industries. Since immigration was restricted by law shortly after World War I, continued growth of industry, particularly during the prosperous 1920's, drew upon increasing black migration for unskilled labor. Although the Depression interrupted the process, the trend was fixed. Consequently, race relations were no longer seen as simply a southern problem. 1942 opened with race riots in Detroit, after an attempt to open a housing project for blacks in a white neighborhood.[114]

Particularly in the south, blacks, by law, learned in segregated schools, worked at segregated jobs and went home to segregated neighborhoods. They were effectively barred from voting and political activity by poll taxes, literacy tests, and a system of carefully maintained Jim Crow laws and practices. Elsewhere the color line was imposed by custom, but it was found almost everywhere. Blacks were effectively banned from most unions. In 1940 professional baseball was still a segregated sport. The federal government did virtually nothing to interfere with these state systems and social customs. When America entered World War II, blacks and whites did not mix in the armed forces; blacks served in segregated units throughout the war. The federal government accepted the predominant racial views and prejudices of the American people. And, for all its economic liberalism, the New Deal had done very little to advance equal treatment of the races.

By the time of Pearl Harbor, small signs of change could be discerned. In 1938, the Supreme Court had held that Missouri could not refuse to provide a law school for the black people of the state.[115] The case was the first on the long road to school desegregation, but *Brown v. Board of Education* was still sixteen years away. And only when a group led by A. Philip Randolph threatened to march on Washington did President Roosevelt establish a Fair Employment Practices Commission in January 1941 to police the practices of contractors with the federal government.

The inconsistent impulses of the nation's attitude toward blacks at the time the United States entered World War II is effectively captured in a diary entry of Henry L. Stimson, the Secretary of War. He recounted his effort to dissuade Archibald MacLeish, then working in the government's Office of Facts and Figures, from giving a speech decrying Army discrimination against blacks. Stimson's account combines an appreciation of the injustice of past treatment of blacks and the need for racial justice in the United States with the rarely-challenged assumption of the society that racial differences will persist and that whites retain inherent racial advantages. These were views born not of animus but of a recognition of what Stimson and many, many others believed was a realistic appraisal of the facts of life.

> I gave [MacLeish] my life history, so to speak, on the subject because I have come in contact with this race problem in many different ways during my life. I told him how I had been brought up in an abolitionist family; my father fought in the Civil War, and all my instincts were in favor of justice to the Negro. But I pointed out how this crime of our forefathers had produced a problem which was almost impossible of solution in this country and that I myself could see no theoretical or logical solution for it at war times like these, but that we should merely exercise the utmost patience and care in individual cases. I told him of my experience and study of the incompetency of colored troops except under white officers, and the disastrous consequence to the country and themselves which they were opening if they went into battle otherwise, although we were doing our best to train colored officers. I pointed out that what these foolish leaders of the colored race are seeking is at the bottom social equality, and I pointed out the basic impossibility of social equality because of the impossibility of race mixture by marriage. He listened in silence and thanked me, but I am not sure how far he is convinced.[116]

2

Executive Order 9066

At dawn on December 7, 1941, Japan began bombing American ships and planes at Pearl Harbor. The attack took our forces by surprise. Japanese aircraft carriers and warships had left the Kurile Islands for Pearl Harbor on November 26, 1941, and Washington had sent a war warning message indicating the possibility of attack upon Pearl Harbor, the Philippines, Thailand or the Malay Peninsula. Nevertheless, the Navy and Army were unprepared and unsuspecting. After a few hours of bombing, Japan had killed or wounded over 3,500 Americans. Two battleships were destroyed, four others sunk or run aground; a number of other vessels were destroyed or badly damaged. One hundred forty-nine American airplanes had been destroyed. Japan lost only 29 planes and pilots.[1]

That night President Roosevelt informed his Cabinet and Congressional leaders that he would seek a declaration of war.[2] On December 8 the President addressed a joint session of Congress and expressed the nation's outraged shock at the damage which the Japanese had done on that day of infamy. The declaration of war passed with one dissenting vote.[3] Germany and Italy followed Japan into the war on December 11.

At home in the first weeks of war the division between isolationists and America Firsters, and supporters of the western democracies, was set aside, and the country united in its determination to defeat the Axis powers. Abroad, the first weeks of war sounded a steady drumbeat

47

of defeat, particularly as the Allies retreated before Japanese forces in the Far East. On the same day as Pearl Harbor, the Japanese struck the Malay Peninsula, Hong Kong, Wake and Midway Islands, and attacked the Philippines, destroying substantial numbers of American aircraft on the ground near Manila. The next day Thailand was invaded and within days two British battleships were sunk off Malaysia. On December 13 Guam fell, and on Christmas the Japanese captured Wake Island and occupied Hong Kong. In the previous seventeen days, Japan had made nine amphibious landings in the Philippines. General Douglas MacArthur, commanding Army forces in the islands, evacuated Manila on December 27, withdrew to the Bataan Peninsula, and set up headquarters on Corregidor. With Japan controlling all sea and air approaches to Bataan and Corregidor, after three months the troops isolated there were forced to surrender unconditionally in the worst American defeat since the Civil War. On February 27 the battle of the Java Sea resulted in another American naval defeat with the loss of thirteen Allied ships.[4] In January and February 1942, the military position of the United States in the Pacific was bleak indeed. Reports of American battlefield deaths gave painful personal emphasis to the war news.*

Pearl Harbor was a surprise. The outbreak of war was not. In December 1941 the United States was not in the state of war-readiness which those who anticipated conflict with the Axis would have wished, but it was by no means unaware of the intentions of Japan and Germany. The President had worked for some time for Lend-Lease and other measures to support the western democracies and prepare for war. In

---

*Some have argued that mistreatment of American soldiers by the Japanese Army—for instance, the atrocities of the Bataan Death March—justifies or excuses the exclusion and detention of American citizens of Japanese ancestry and resident Japanese aliens. The Commission firmly rejects this contention. There is no excuse for inflicting injury on American citizens or resident aliens for acts for which they bear no responsibility. The conduct of Japan and her military forces is irrelevant to the issues which the Commission is considering. Congressman Coffee made the point eloquently on December 8, 1941: "It is my fervent hope and prayer that residents of the United States of Japanese extraction will not be made the victim of pogroms directed by self-proclaimed patriots and by hysterical self-anointed heroes. . . . Let us not make a mockery of our Bill of Rights by mistreating these folks. Let us rather regard them with understanding, remembering they are the victims of a Japanese war machine, with the making of the international policies of which they had nothing to do." *Congressional Record*, 77th Cong., 1st Sess. (Dec. 8, 1941), p. A5554.

1940, he had broadened the political base of his Cabinet, bringing in as Secretary of the Navy Frank Knox, the publisher of the Chicago *Daily News* who had been Alfred M. Landon's vice-presidential candidate in 1936. Roosevelt drafted as Secretary of War one of the most distinguished Republican public servants of his time, Henry L. Stimson, who had served as Secretary of War under Taft and Secretary of State under Hoover. Stimson, who brought with him the standing and prestige of half a century of active service to his country, carried a particularly impressive weight of principled tradition. He brought into the War Department other, younger easterners, many of whom were fellow lawyers and Republicans. John J. McCloy came from a prominent New York law firm to become first a Special Assistant and then Assistant Secretary for War, and after the outbreak of war he was the civilian aide to Stimson responsible for Japanese American questions.[5] Roosevelt later named Francis Biddle, a Philadelphian who was a firm defender of civil rights, as Attorney General when Robert Jackson was appointed to the Supreme Court.

Ten weeks after the outbreak of war, on February 19, 1942, President Roosevelt signed Executive Order 9066 which gave to the Secretary of War and the military commanders to whom he delegated authority, the power to exclude any persons from designated areas in order to secure national defense objectives against sabotage and espionage. The order was used, as the President, his responsible Cabinet officers and the West Coast Congressional delegation knew it would be, to exclude persons of Japanese ancestry, both American citizens and resident aliens, from the West Coast. Over the following months more than 100,000 people were ordered to leave their homes and farms and businesses. "Voluntary" resettlement of people who had been branded as potentially disloyal by the War Department and who were recognizable by their facial features was not feasible. Not surprisingly, the politicians and citizens of Wyoming or Idaho believed that their war industries, railroad lines and hydroelectric dams deserved as much protection from possible sabotage as did those on the Pacific Coast, and they opposed accepting the ethnic Japanese. Most of the evacuees were reduced to abandoning their homes and livelihoods and being transported by the government to "relocation centers" in desolate interior regions of the west.

As the Executive Order made plain, these actions were based upon "military necessity." The government has never fundamentally reviewed whether this massive eviction of an entire ethnic group was justified. In three cases the Supreme Court reviewed the Executive

Order in the context of convictions for violations of military orders issued pursuant to it, but the Court chose not to review the factual basis for military decisions in wartime, accepting without close scrutiny the government's representation that exclusion and evacuation were militarily necessary. Forty years later, the nation is sufficiently concerned about the rights and liberties of its citizens and residents, that it has undertaken to examine the facts and pose to itself the question of whether, in the heat of the moment, beset by defeat and fearful of the future, it justly took the proper course for its own protection, or made an original mistake of very substantial proportion. "Peace hath her victories/No less renowned than war."

Was a policy of exclusion militarily justified as a *precautionary* measure? This is a core initial question because the government has conceded at every point that there was no evidence of actual sabotage, espionage or fifth column activity among people of Japanese descent on the West Coast in February 1942. The Commanding General of the Western Defense Command, John L. DeWitt, put the point plainly, conceding in his recommendation to the War Department "[t]he very fact that no sabotage has taken place to date."[6] The Justice Department, defending the exclusion before the Supreme Court, made no claim that there was identifiable subversive activity.[7] The Congress, in passing the Japanese-American Evacuation Claims Act in 1948, reiterated the point:

> [D]espite the hardships visited upon this unfortunate racial group by an act of the Government brought about by the then prevailing military necessity, there was recorded during the recent war not one act of sabotage or espionage attributable to those who were the victims of the forced relocation.[8]

Finally, the two witnesses before the Commission who were most involved in the evacuation decision, John J. McCloy and Karl R. Bendetsen, who was first liaison between the War Department and the Western Defense Command and later General DeWitt's chief aide for the evacuation, testified that the decision was not taken on the basis of actual incidents of espionage, sabotage or fifth column activity.[9]

One may begin, then, by examining the competent estimates of possible future danger from the ethnic Japanese, citizen and alien, on the West Coast in early 1942. This is not to suggest that a well-grounded suspicion is or should be sufficient to require an American citizen or resident alien to give up his house and farm or business to move hundreds of miles inland, bearing the stigma of being a potential danger to his fellow citizens—nor that such suspicion would justify condemnation of a racial group rather than individual review—but it does address the analysis that should be made by the War Department charged with our continental defenses.

INTELLIGENCE

The intelligence services have the task of alerting and informing the President, the military and those charged with maintaining security about whether, where and when disruptive acts directed by an enemy may be expected. Intelligence work consists predominantly of analytical estimate, not demonstrably comprehensive knowledge—there may always be another, undiscovered ring of spies or a completely covert plan of sabotage. Caution and prudence require that intelligence agencies throw the net of suspicion wide, and take measures to protect vital information or militarily important installations. At the same time, if intelligence is to serve the ends of a society which places central value on personal liberty, even in time of war, it must not be overwhelmed by rumors and flights of fancy which grip a fearful, jittery public. Above all, effective intelligence work demands sound judgment which is immune to the paranoia that treats everyone as a hostile suspect until his loyalty is proven. In 1942, what credible threat did Japan pose to the internal peace and security of the United States?

It was common wisdom that the Nazi invasions of Norway and Western Europe had been aided by agents and sympathizers within the country under attack—the so-called fifth column—and that the same approach should be anticipated from Japan.[10] For this reason intelligence was developed on Axis saboteurs and potential fifth columnists as well as espionage agents. This work had been assigned to the Federal Bureau of Investigation and the Navy Department but not to the War Department.[11] The President had developed his own informal intelligence system through John Franklin Carter, a journalist, who helped Roosevelt obtain information and estimates by exploiting sources outside the government. None of these organizations operated with the thoroughness of, say, the modern CIA, but they were the best and calmest eyes and ears the government had.

Each of these sources saw only a very limited security risk from the ethnic Japanese; none recommended a mass exclusion or detention of all people of Japanese ancestry.

On November 7, 1941, John Franklin Carter forwarded to the

President a report on the West Coast situation by Curtis B. Munson, a well-to-do Chicago businessman who had gathered intelligence for Carter under the guise of being a government official.[12] Carter summarized five points in the report, which may be all the President read;[13] the War Department also reviewed the report at Roosevelt's request.[14] Regarding sabotage and espionage, Munson wrote:

> There will be no armed uprising of Japanese. There will undoubtedly be some sabotage financed by Japan and executed largely by imported agents or agents already imported. There will be the odd case of fanatical sabotage by some Japanese "crackpot". In each Naval District there are about 250 to 300 suspects under surveillance. It is easy to get on the suspect list, merely a speech in favor of Japan at some banquet, being sufficient to land one there. The Intelligence Services are generous with the title of suspect and are taking no chances. Privately, they believe that only 50 or 60 in each district can be classed as really dangerous. The Japanese are hampered as saboteurs because of their easily recognized physical appearance. It will be hard for them to get near anything to blow up *if it is guarded*. There is far more danger from Communists and people of the Bridges type on the Coast than there is from Japanese. The Japanese here is almost exclusively a farmer, a fisherman or a small business man. He has no entree to plants or intricate machinery.
>
> The Japanese, if undisturbed and disloyal, should be well equipped for obvious physical espionage. A great part of this work was probably completed and forwarded to Tokio years ago, such as soundings and photography of every inch of the Coast. . . . An experienced Captain in Navy Intelligence, who has from time to time and over a period of years intercepted information Tokio bound, said he would certainly hate to be a Japanese coordinator of information in Tokio. He stated that the mass of useless information was unbelievable. This would be fine for a fifth column in Belgium or Holland with the German army ready to march in over the border, but though the local Japanese could spare a man who intimately knew the country for each Japanese invasion squad, there would at least have to be a terrific American Naval disaster before his brown brothers would need his services. The dangerous part of their espionage is that they would be very effective as far as movement of supplies, movement of troops and movement of ships out of harbor mouths and over railroads is concerned. They occupy only rarely positions where they can get to confidential papers or in plants. They are usually, when rarely so placed, a subject of perpetual watch and suspicion by their fellow workers. They would have to buy most of this type of information from white people. . . .
>
> Japan will commit some sabotage largely depending on imported Japanese as they are afraid of and do not trust the Nesei [sic].

There will be no wholehearted response from Japanese in the United States. They may get some helpers from certain Kibei. They will be in a position to pick up information on troop, supply and ship movements from local Japanese.

For the most part the local Japanese are loyal to the United States or, at worst, hope that by remaining quiet they can avoid concentration camps or irresponsible mobs. We do not believe that they would be at least any more disloyal than any other racial group in the United States with whom we went to war.[15]

Munson sent three or four more reports to Carter between December and February, including a long review of the situation in Hawaii; he did not change his estimate of the West Coast situation.[16] Most of these reports found their way to Roosevelt's desk. After Pearl Harbor, where Japan received no aid from fifth column activity or sabotage, Munson pointedly noted that "[a]n attack is the proof of the pudding,"[17] and remained firmly persuaded that the number of people on the West Coast who could reasonably be suspected of a menacing degree of loyalty to the enemy was small—and not demonstrably greater among the ethnic Japanese than other racial groups. In addition, the physical characteristics of the Japanese which made them readily identifiable made it more difficult for them to engage in sabotage unnoticed or to do any espionage beyond collecting public information open to anyone.

Although Munson was an amateur at intelligence, he talked at length to professionals such as the FBI agent in charge in Honolulu and the people in Naval Intelligence in southern California. He was also in touch with British Intelligence in California and reported that they shared his principal views. The British intelligence officer made one point, repeated by other professionals, which gave savage irony to the exclusion program: "It must be kept in mind when considering the 'Security' to be derived from the mass evacuation of all Japanese, that the Japanese in all probability employed many more 'whites' than 'Japanese' for carrying out their work and this 'white' danger is not eliminated by the evacuation of the Japanese."[18]

Munson had also come to respect the views of Lieutenant Commander K. D. Ringle of the Office of Naval Intelligence in southern California.[19] Ringle had spent much time doing intelligence work in both Japan and southern California[20] where he had assisted in breaking a major Japanese spy ring through a surreptitious entry[21] and developed an effective system of Nisei informants (which he shared with the FBI). When Ringle wanted the membership list of the "Black Dragon" society, a super-patriotic Japanese group, for example, the society's original books for the western half of the United States were delivered to him three days later.[22]

In late January 1942, Ringle estimated that the large majority of ethnic Japanese in the United States were at least passively loyal to this country. There were both citizens and aliens who could act as saboteurs or espionage agents, but he estimated the number to be 3% of the total—or 3,500 in the entire United States who were identifiable individually. Many Nisei leaders had voluntarily contributed valuable anti-subversive information to federal agencies, said Ringle, and if discrimination, firings and personal attacks became prevalent, *that* conduct would most directly incite sabotage and riots.[23] Ringle saw no need for mass action against people of Japanese ancestry. It is difficult to judge how far one should go in equating Ringle's views with those of Naval Intelligence, since there is no single statement of their position, but he claimed that Naval Intelligence sympathized with his opinions.[24]

The third major source of intelligence was the FBI, which assessed any danger to internal security and had plans ready in case of war. Immediately after Pearl Harbor, President Roosevelt signed Proclamation 2525 pursuant to the Alien Enemy Act of 1798, as amended, which gave the government the authority to detain enemy aliens and confiscate enemy property wherever found. The Proclamation permitted immediate and summary apprehension of "alien enemies deemed dangerous to the public health or safety of the United States by the Attorney General or Secretary of War." On December 8, similar proclamations were issued for the summary apprehension of suspect Germans and Italians.[25]

The FBI had already drawn up lists of those to be arrested—aliens "with something in their record showing an allegiance to the enemy." Three categories of suspects had been developed: "A" category—aliens who led cultural or assistance organizations; "B"—slightly less suspicious aliens; and "C"—members of, or those who donated to, ethnic groups, Japanese language teachers and Buddhist clergy.[26] People in the "A," "B," and "C" categories were promptly arrested in early December.[27] Throughout the initial roundup, Attorney General Biddle was concerned that arrests be orderly. He did not want citizens taking matters into their own hands or directing hostility toward American citizens on the basis of descent, and on December 10 issued a press release stating these themes loudly and clearly.[28] The Attorney General was also firm from the beginning that citizens would not be arrested or apprehended unless there were probable cause to believe that a crime had been committed—the usual standard for arrest. Such arrests were not to occur until the FBI was ready to initiate criminal charges,[29] and the same standards applied to those of German, Italian and Japanese nationality or descent.

By December 10, 1942, FBI Director J. Edgar Hoover reported that "practically all" whom he initially planned to arrest had been taken into custody: 1,291 Japanese (367 in Hawaii, 924 in the continental United States); 857 Germans; 147 Italians.[30] In fact, however, the government continued to apprehend enemy aliens. By February 16, 1942, the Department of Justice held 2,192 Japanese; 1,393 Germans; and 264 Italians[31] and arrests continued even after that date. Many arrested in the early sweeps were Issei leaders of the Japanese American community and its organizations.[32]

FBI views on the need for mass exclusion from the West Coast were provided at the Attorney General's request shortly before the Executive Order was signed, and must be read in that context. Hoover did not believe that demands for mass evacuation were based on factual analysis. Although he doubted Nisei loyalty in case of invasion and grasped the obvious point that people excluded from the West Coast could not commit sabotage there, he pointed out that the cry for evacuation came from political pressure. The historical experience of the FBI showed that Japan had used Occidentals for its espionage[33]— which Ringle had learned from his clandestine raid on the Japanese consulate.[34] Hoover balanced his own opinions by sharing with the Attorney General his West Coast field offices' views of evacuation, which varied from noncommittal in Los Angeles to dismissive in San Francisco to vehemently favorable in San Diego and Seattle.[35] Nevertheless, Hoover's own opinion, and thus the Bureau's, was that the case to justify mass evacuation for security reasons had not been made.

These mainland intelligence views were blurred by sensational and inaccurate reports from Hawaii. On December 9, 1941, Secretary of the Navy Knox went to Hawaii to make the first brief examination of the reasons for American losses at Pearl Harbor. He returned to the mainland on December 15 and told the press, "I think the most effective Fifth Column work of the entire war was done in Hawaii with the possible exception of Norway."[36] This laid major blame for the Pearl Harbor defeat at the door of the ethnic Japanese in the United States. Knox's statement was not only unfounded: it ignored the fact that Japanese Americans in large numbers had immediately come to the defense of the islands at the time of the attack.[37]

The Secretary raised the matter again at the Cabinet meeting of

December 19, when Attorney General Biddle noted that "Knox told me, which was not what Hoover had thought, that there was a great deal of very active, fifth column work going on both from the shores and from the sampans" in the Pearl Harbor attack.[38]* John Franklin Carter also disputed Knox in a memo to Roosevelt.[39] Nor were his views supported by General Short,[40] who had been in command at the time of the Pearl Harbor attack, and they were contradicted a few days later by the new Commanding General in Hawaii, Delos Emmons, who stated in a broadcast to the islands that there had been very few acts of sabotage at the time of the attack.[41] The basis of Knox's statement has never been clear; he may have relied on rumors which had not yet been checked, or he may have confused prewar espionage by Japanese agents with fifth column activity.[42] Nevertheless, because military news from Hawaii was carefully censored and the Secretary appeared to speak from firsthand knowledge, Knox's statement carried considerable weight. His accompanying recommendation for the removal of all Japanese, regardless of citizenship, from Oahu is one of the first calls for mass racial exclusion. The alarm Knox had rung gave immediate credence to the view that ethnic Japanese on the mainland were a palpable threat and danger. The damage was remarkable. When Knox's official report came out on December 16, there was no reference to fifth column activities; it described espionage by Japanese consular officers and praised the Japanese Americans who had manned machine guns against the enemy. Nevertheless, the story ran in major West Coast papers headlined "Fifth Column Treachery Told," "Fifth Column Prepared Attack" and "Secretary of Navy Blames 5th Column for Raid."[43] Nothing was promptly done at the highest level of the government to repudiate Knox's initial statement or publicly to affirm the loyalty of the ethnic Japanese, even though Munson (through Carter) emphasized

---

*Hoover did not believe that fifth column activities were prevalent in Hawaii, having heard from the FBI's special agent in charge in Honolulu as early as December 8, that General Short had reported absolutely no sabotage during the attack and, on December 17, he advised the Attorney General that it was believed that the great majority of the population of foreign extraction in the islands was law-abiding. Hoover directly questioned Knox's opinion, but did not do so publicly, and it is unknown whether his views were heard outside the Justice Department. Memo, Hoover to Tolson, Tamm and Ladd, Dec. 8, 1941; Memo, Hoover to Attorney General, Dec. 17, 1941. FBI (CWRIC 5786–89; 5830).

Knox's inaccuracy and urged that such a statement be made by the President or Vice President.[44]

Much calmer (though opaque) views were reported by the first official inquiry into the Pearl Harbor disaster. The Roberts Commission, appointed by the President and chaired by Supreme Court Justice Owen J. Roberts,[45] issued a report on January 23, 1942, which never mentioned sabotage, espionage or fifth column activity in its conclusion. Regarding such activity, the body of the report says in part:

> There were, prior to December 7, 1941, Japanese spies on the island of Oahu. Some were Japanese consular agents and other [sic] were persons having no open relations with the Japanese foreign service. These spies collected and, through various channels transmitted, information to the Japanese Empire respecting the military and naval establishments and dispositions on the island. . . .
>
> It was believed that the center of Japanese espionage in Hawaii was the Japanese consulate at Honolulu. It has been discovered that the Japanese consul sent to and received from Tokyo in his own and other names many messages on commercial radio circuits. This activity greatly increased toward December 7, 1941. The contents of these messages, if it could have been learned, might have furnished valuable information. In view of the peaceful relations with Japan, and the consequent restrictions on the activities of the investigating agencies, they were unable prior to December 7 to obtain and examine messages transmitted through commercial channels by the Japanese consul, or by persons acting for him.
>
> It is now apparent that through their intelligence service the Japanese had complete information.[46]

Testimony at secret hearings lay behind the conclusions. General Short, in command of the Army on Hawaii at the time of Pearl Harbor, had misinterpreted the warning message of late November as an alert against sabotage[47] and so should have been particularly conscious of it; Short testified that "I do not believe since I came here that there has been any act of sabotage of any importance at all, but the FBI and my intelligence outfit know of a lot of these people and knew they probably would watch the opportunity to carry out something."[48]

Robert L. Shivers, the FBI's Special Agent in Charge in Hawaii (and a man Munson thought highly of)[49] testified that Japanese espionage before Pearl Harbor "centered in the Japanese consulate;" he held responsible the 234 consular representatives who had not been prosecuted in 1941 for failure to register as foreign agents.[50] These men were arrested immediately after Pearl Harbor and kept in custody. Shivers offered documentary proof to support his views, and testified that there were no acts of sabotage in Hawaii during the Pearl Harbor raid.[51]

Despite such telling testimony, the Roberts Report did not use language designed to allay the unease spread by Knox. In fact the Report tended to have the opposite effect; in March a House Committee stated that public agitation in favor of evacuation dated from publication of the Roberts Report.[52] Predictions which the Commission heard in Hawaii may have caused this silence. Besides Roberts, the Commissioners were high-ranking military officers who, at Secretary Stimson's direction, used the Commission's inquiry to look into the future defense of the islands.[53] They asked intelligence staff in Hawaii about the prospects for future sabotage or fifth column activity and received conflicting advice.

Shivers asserted that "just as soon as Japan achieves some temporary decisive victory, the old spirit will begin to bubble forth" and that:

[If] there should be an out-and-out attack on this island by the Japanese Navy, reinforced by their air arm, I think you could expect 95% of the alien Japanese to glory in that attack and to do anything they could to further the efforts of the Japanese forces.

You would find some second- and third-generation Japanese, who are American citizens but who hold dual citizenship, and you would find some of those who would join forces with the Japanese attackers for this and other reasons. Some of them may think they have suffered discrimination, economic, social, and otherwise, and there would probably be a few of them who would do it.[54]

He also thought the Japanese community in the United States and Hawaii was highly organized, and so in theory had the ability to assist the Axis. Finally, Shivers believed only individuals, not the Japanese in the United States collectively, would become potential saboteurs.[55]

Angus Taylor, the United States Attorney for Hawaii, a man of vehement and strident views, not directly engaged in intelligence work, testified that in the event of subsequent Japanese attack, even the third-generation citizens would "immediately turn over to their own race."[56]

The Intelligence Officer of the 14th Naval District, Irving Mayfield, believed that the Japanese system of spies and saboteurs would not rest on race or ethnicity.[57] This point had, of course, been made repeatedly by Hoover, Munson and Ringle. The professionals largely agreed that the Japanese did not rely on Issei and Nisei for espionage, and there was no reason to believe they would for sabotage. In a 1943 memorandum, Mayfield set out the logic of his position: it had to be

the operating premise of counterespionage that Japan's spying operation might be made up of only ethnic Japanese, only non-ethnic Japanese or a combination of the two. A solely ethnic Japanese group
might be able to rely on people of known loyalty to Japan with close
ties to that country, but American suspicion of such people and the
possibility that they might be detained in time of war might well lead
Japan to rely entirely on people who were not ethnic Japanese. Var-
iations of these extremes were equally possible:

> For purposes of security, the vital core of the organization might
> be composed of non-Japanese. . . . On the other hand, the nucleus
> of the organization may be composed of Japanese, who will make
> use of non-Japanese as the need and opportunity arises. This group
> might even have available a non-Japanese whose sole function
> would be to assume direction of the espionage organization in case
> the members of the original core are immobilized or rendered
> ineffective by security or counter-espionage measures.[58]

Mayfield's thorough approach to the problem exposed the flimsy reasoning behind the policy of exclusion—without evidence, there was
no sound basis for expecting the Japanese to employ any particular
ethnic group as spies or saboteurs. This proved true; in Hawaii one of
the few alien residents brought to trial for war-related crimes was
Bernard Julius Otto Kuehn, a German national in the pay of Japan,[59]
and on the mainland the few people convicted of being illegal agents
of Japan were predominantly not ethnic Japanese.[60]

But these views did not reach the topmost level of the War Department. Secretary Stimson recorded in his diary a long evening with
Justice Roberts after his return from Hawaii, noting Roberts' expressed
fear that the Japanese in the islands posed a major security risk through
espionage, sabotage and fifth column activity.[61] Roberts also visited
General DeWitt and one may assume that he presented similar views
to the General.[62]

Thus, in the early months of war, the intelligence services largely
agreed that Japan had quietly collected massive amounts of useful
information over recent years, in Hawaii and on the mainland, a great
deal of it entirely legally, and that the threat of sabotage and fifth
column activity during attack was limited and controllable. Significantly, the intelligence experts never focused exclusively on ethnic
Japanese in the United States: logically the Japanese would not depend
solely on the Issei and Nisei, and experience showed that they did not
trust the Nisei, employing Occidentals for espionage.

The prophecy about who might conduct future espionage and

sabotage was based on a number of factors. No significant sabotage or fifth column activity had helped destroy Pearl Harbor. Insofar as the Japanese would rely on the Issei or other Axis aliens' assistance, those who were at all suspect had been interned by the Department of Justice. Insofar as the Japanese would rely on the Nisei, there was no knowledge or evidence of organized or individual Nisei spying or disruption. Ringle and Munson did not believe there would be any greater disloyalty from them than from any other American ethnic group; Taylor, and perhaps Shivers in Hawaii, dissented. The course recommended by Hoover (Ringle and Munson suggested similar approaches[63]) was one of surveillance but not arrest or detention without evidence to back up individualized suspicion. Hoover recommended registering all enemy aliens in the United States; also, to protect against fifth columnists, he wanted specific authority (either suspension of the writ of habeas corpus or a "so-called syndicalism law") to permit the apprehension of any citizen or alien "as to whom there may be reasonable cause to believe that such person has been or is engaging in giving aid or comfort to the enemies of the United States;" and he backed Department of Justice evaluation of lists of suspect citizens to determine who should be taken into custody under any such extreme authority.[64]

These restrained views did not prevail. Those with intelligence knowledge were few, and they rarely spoke as a body. Navy Intelligence, for instance, felt it had enough on its hands without contradicting or challenging the Army. Whatever its intelligence officers thought, the Navy was intent on moving the ethnic Japanese away from its installations at Terminal Island near Los Angeles and Bainbridge Island in Puget Sound, and Secretary Knox's support of stern measures against the ethnic Japanese seemed unlikely to change.[65] Few voices were raised inside the War Department, which was responsible for security on the West Coast. Stronger political forces outside the intelligence services wanted evacuation. Intelligence opinions were disregarded or drowned out.

THE GOVERNMENT'S INITIAL REACTIONS TO WAR

Action on the West Coast after Pearl Harbor lay immediately with those dealing with the "enemy alien problem." This initially led the Army down the road toward the Executive Order. The government accepted that, in time of war, aliens of enemy nationality could be controlled and interned without the need for any justification beyond their status. Internment began immediately after December 7 and, as FBI figures show, its weight fell disproportionately on the Japanese— against whom it was particularly effective since the ineligibility of Issei for citizenship and the status of the ethnic Japanese as comparatively recent immigrants allowed the government to round up most leaders of the Japanese American community.

The government took other actions which affected the business life of the ethnic Japanese.[66] Earlier in 1941 the fixed deposits (similar to savings certificates) which many ethnic Japanese maintained in the Japanese banks which had branches on the West Coast were in effect frozen when commercial relations with Japan were curtailed.[67] At the time of Pearl Harbor, all Japanese branch banks were immediately closed and taken over by the state bank superintendent or the Alien Property Custodian who called in all outstanding loans.[68] In addition, approximately $27.5 million of business enterprises and real estate owned by Japanese aliens was taken over by the Alien Property Custodian.[69] Finally, the Treasury froze the dollar deposits of both citizens and aliens who had been dealing with Japan before the war, releasing only small monthly payments to the account holders.[70] Cumulatively, these measures affected not only most Issei and people in the import-export business but a very large proportion of the Japanese American community.

Other steps were taken as well. Congress passed and the President implemented a plan for censorship, primarily of the mail.[71] Military officials began to consider transferring American soldiers of Japanese ancestry away from the West Coast.[72]

Although many of these government measures were applied equally to all aliens of enemy nationality, even in the early days after Pearl Harbor, the military on the West Coast tended to single out ethnic Japanese for harsher treatment. The Nisei reacted to these gathering clouds by actions to persuade the country of their loyalty. In the San Joaquin Valley, they enlisted as air raid wardens and helped guard the water supply at Parlier against possible sabotage. In Seattle, the creator of the Joe Palooka comic strip was persuaded to introduce some Nisei GIs into the cartoon as loyal Americans. Other communities drew up pledges of loyalty.[73] The Japanese Association of Fresno wired Congressman Gearhart offering its services against Japan, and the Congressman placed the message in the *Congressional Record*.[74] But these efforts did not turn the rising tide of suspicion which became more apparent with the development through December and January of two programs run cooperatively by the Justice Department and the War Department through the Western Defense Command: the seizure of contraband from enemy aliens and the establishment of prohibited areas.

As part of the Presidential Proclamations issued immediately after Pearl Harbor, Roosevelt ordered confiscation of cameras, weapons, radio transmitters, and other instruments of possible espionage and sabotage belonging to enemy aliens. The War Department was concerned at the slow pace of the Justice Department's implementation of the proclamations, including the portions relating to search and seizure.[75] The Army was particularly concerned that alien Japanese inside the United States were making radio transmissions to Japanese ships offshore.

In time, and clearly under pressure from the Army, the FBI and Department of Justice cooperated to develop plans for search and seizure in enemy alien homes. At first, search warrants were not issued without probable cause.[76] When the Attorney General insisted that probable cause in the usual constitutional sense be found, DeWitt pressed the proposition that merely being an enemy alien was sufficient to constitute probable cause. The Justice Department at first rejected the idea.[77] The FBI was not convinced that the perceived problem was real; Hoover suggested that the Army submit any specific evidence of disloyalty to the FBI.[78] Later Hoover pointed out to Biddle that reports in the San Francisco area about radios and weapons were often unfounded; in some instances only low-frequency shortwave radios had been found, and the guns were small-caliber weapons such as any person, especially a farmer, might possess.[79] DeWitt continued to stress the need for searches and arrests, including those of citizens, without warrants.[80] In early January, the Justice Department reached an accommodation with the Western Defense Command. All enemy aliens were to deposit prohibited articles with the local police within a few days, and merely being an enemy alien would be sufficient cause for a search.[81]

The Justice Department, firm that mass raids should not be conducted,[82] gave in to multiple spot searches without a warrant.[83] The compromise was important for government policy toward Japanese Americans because the Justice Department was the crucial bulwark of civil liberties and due process; yet, under military pressure, Justice was gradually giving way to the Army's fear of espionage and sabotage.

This change of policy came despite reports from the Federal Communications Commission (FCC), which monitored all broadcasts, that illegal transmitter operation was minimal. At the turn of the year, V. Ford Greaves of the FCC in California guessed that, including the records in Washington, "there would not be more than ten to twenty-five cases of reasonably probable illegal operation of radio sending sets on the entire Pacific Coast."[84] Checking FCC records on the West Coast and in Washington, Greaves found that there were "no active cases on file indicating the possession of radio transmitters by alien enemies. Several active cases have been closed during the past few months through court action."[85] In short, the Army's fears were groundless. In mid-January one reason became apparent: FCC staff on the West Coast reported that the military was woefully deficient in radio intelligence work, to the point where the Army and Navy were reporting each other's broadcasts as Japanese.[86]

Similar discord arose between the Justice and War Departments over Justice's power, exercised upon War Department request, to prohibit enemy aliens from entering designated areas of military significance. As on the contraband issue, General DeWitt pressed for broad powers in terms of both geographic area and affected persons. The Army wanted the military commander in each theatre of operations to be able to designate restricted areas;[87] the Justice Department wanted exclusive authority to name areas where civilian restrictions would apply, although it agreed to designate any area specified by the military.[88] By early January the Justice Department was prepared to make any designations DeWitt wanted, on its understanding that areas would be limited and carefully drawn. Although there was some confusion on this point,[89] the Army appears not to have been contemplating a mass exclusion from large areas.

At this point, on January 4, designation of restricted areas appeared to be a device to exclude only aliens, not citizens.[90] However, as early as January 8, some military officers began to consider broadening the definition of "enemy aliens." Major Carter Garver, Acting Assistant Adjutant General of the Army, wrote to General DeWitt:

> Upon being consulted in this connection, Admiral C. S. Freeman, Commandant 13th Naval District, recommended that all enemy aliens be evacuated from the states of Washington and Oregon; that all American [sic] born of Japanese racial origin who cannot show actual severance of all allegiance to the Japanese government be classified as enemy aliens, and lastly that no pass or temporary permit to enter these states be issued to enemy aliens. He based this recommendation on the fact that communications and industry in these states are so vital to the operations of the Naval District

that any hostile activities in the two states will be a serious embarrassment. This view is also held by this headquarters.

The reputed operations of Axis spies and Fifth Columnists in Europe and the known activities of such elements during the recent Japanese attack on Hawaii clearly indicate the danger of temporizing with such a menace. It is deemed to be a certainty that any hostile operations against the Northwestern Sector will be characterized by a similar treacherous activity. From what is known of the Japanese character and mentality it is also considered dangerous to rely on the loyalty of native born persons of Japanese blood unless such loyalty can be affirmatively demonstrated.[91]

Inaccurate reports from Hawaii and incongruous notions of Japanese racial characteristics were causing these military officers to consider extending their exclusion of aliens from restricted military areas to include American citizens of Japanese ancestry.

The West Coast had been declared a theatre of operations—but never placed under martial law—and, in the normal course, great discretion was given the commanding general with field responsibility. Exercising that discretion and directly confronting the issue of military security was Lieutenant General John L. DeWitt, a lifelong Army man who was, in 1942, in command of the Western Defense Command (WDC). DeWitt's approach was routinely to believe almost any threat to security or military control; not an analyst or careful thinker who sought balanced judgments of the risks before him, DeWitt did little to calm the fears of West Coast people.

Major General Joseph W. Stilwell, who in the first month of the war served under DeWitt in charge of southern California, recorded in his diary that the San Francisco headquarters of the WDC continually gave credence to every rumor that came in. No cool mind sifted fact from fiction; indeed, there was a willingness to believe the sky was falling at every news report: "Common sense is thrown to the winds and any absurdity is believed." Stilwell summed up his view of DeWitt's G-2, the Army intelligence branch, very succinctly:

> The [Fourth] Army G-2 is just another amateur, like all the rest of the staff. RULE: the higher the headquarters, the more important is calm. Nothing should go out unconfirmed. Nothing is ever as bad as it seems at first.[92]

WDC's alarmism may have come partly from its inferior intelligence and information-gathering ability. In a February 1 memo to Biddle, J. Edgar Hoover severely criticized the intelligence capability of the Army on the West Coast, finding it untrained, disorganized, incapable and citing instances where "[h]ysteria and lack of judgment" were evident in the Military Intelligence Division.[93] Hoover had earlier sarcastically dismissed the Western Defense Command's gullible, intemperate approach to internal security problems, noting "that although the situation was critical, there was no sense in the Army losing their heads as they did in the Booneville Dam affair, where the power lines were sabotaged by cattle scratching their backs on the wires, or the 'arrows of fire' near Seattle, which was only a farmer burning brush as he had done for years."[94] The FCC found the same ramshackle operation when helping the Army on radio interception: "I have never seen an organization that was so hopeless to cope with radio intelligence requirements. . . . The personnel is unskilled and untrained. . . . They know nothing about signal identification, wave propagation and other technical subjects, so essential to radio intelligence procedure. . . . As a matter of fact, the Army air stations have been reported by the Signal Corps station as Jap enemy stations."[95] Abysmal intelligence capability was not conducive to any rational approach to military problems such as sabotage or espionage.

General DeWitt appears not to have consulted the intelligence services to correct his views or ask factual analysis. For instance, ignoring FCC evidence, he reported to Stimson on February 3 that "regular communications are going out from Japanese spies in those regions [California cities and Puget Sound] to submarines off the coast assisting in the attacks by the latter which have been made upon practically every ship that has gone out."[96] One finds no extended examination of Munson's views, which were shared with the Western Defense Command,[97] and no interest was shown in consulting Ringle who twice traveled to San Francisco in vain attempts to see Colonel Bendetsen.[98]

Given the speed with which the disgraced General Short and Admiral Kimmel were forced out of the military after Pearl Harbor,[99] it is not surprising that the Commanding General on the West Coast would take a very cautious, even nervous, approach to any threat of attack or disruption; as DeWitt himself put it, he was "not going to be a second General Short."[100] But DeWitt's views had another aspect. His opinions are remarkable even for the racially divided America of 1940. In January 1942 he personally gave James Rowe, the Assistant Attorney General, his views on sabotage and espionage: "I have little confidence that the enemy aliens are law abiding or loyal in any sense of the word. Some of them, yes; many, no. Particularly the Japanese, I have no confidence in their loyalty whatsoever. I am speaking now of the native born Japanese—117,000—and 42,000 in California alone."[101]

Five weeks later, recommending to Stimson the exclusion of Nisei from the West Coast, DeWitt was direct indeed:

In the war in which we are now engaged racial affinities are not severed by migration. The Japanese race is an enemy race and while many second and third generation Japanese born on United States soil, possessed of United States citizenship, have become "Americanized," the racial strains are undiluted. To conclude otherwise is to expect that children born of white parents on Japanese soil sever all racial affinity and become loyal Japanese subjects, ready to fight and, if necessary, to die for Japan in a war against the nation of their parents. That Japan is allied with Germany and Italy in this struggle is no ground for assuming that any Japanese, barred from assimilation by convention as he is, though born and raised in the United States, will not turn against this nation when the final test of loyalty comes. It, therefore, follows that along the vital Pacific Coast over 112,000 potential enemies, of Japanese extraction, are at large today.[102]

A year later before a Congressional committee, discussing his exclusionary policy, DeWitt reiterated his views:

Gen. DeWitt: . . . I have the mission of defending this coast and securing vital installations. The danger of the Japanese was, and is now,—if they are permitted to come back—espionage and sabotage. It makes no difference whether he is an American citizen, he is still a Japanese. American citizenship does not necessarily determine loyalty.

Mr. Bates: You draw a distinction then between Japanese and Italians and Germans? We have a great number of Italians and Germans and we think they are fine citizens. There may be exceptions.

Gen. DeWitt: You needn't worry about the Italians at all except in certain cases. Also, the same for the Germans except in individual cases. But we must worry about the Japanese all the time until he is wiped off the map. Sabotage and espionage will make problems as long as he is allowed in this area—problems which I don't want to have to worry about.[103]

The General made the point again the next day in an off-the-record press conference. DeWitt condensed his opinion of a policy he had opposed, allowing American soldiers of Japanese ancestry into the excluded areas, by telling the reporters that "a Jap is a Jap."[104]

These declarations came at important moments when the General could fairly be expected to speak his mind. Those who had agitated against the Japanese in the forty years before the war could not have given the racial argument more blood-chilling bluntness.

Under General DeWitt's guidance from the Presidio, the War Department moved toward the momentous exclusion of American citizens from the West Coast without any thoughtful, thorough analysis of the problems, if any, of sabotage and espionage on the West Coast or of realistic solutions to those problems. In part there was an easy elision between excluding Issei and Nisei. The legal basis for excluding aliens was essentially unquestioned; no rigorous analysis of military necessity was needed because there were no recognized interests or rights to weigh against the interest in military security that was served by moving enemy aliens. The very word "Japanese," sometimes used to denote nationality and at other times to indicate ethnicity, allowed obvious ambiguities in discussing citizens and resident aliens. The War Department came toward the problem with a few major facts: the Japanese were winning an incredible string of victories in the Far East; the West Coast was lightly armed and defended, but now appeared far more vulnerable to Japanese raid or attack than it had been before Pearl Harbor—although General Staff estimates were that the Japanese could not make a sustained invasion on the West Coast. But after the surprise of Pearl Harbor, laymen, at least, doubted the reliability of military predictions: it was better to be safe than sorry.[105] And laymen had a great deal to say about what the Army should do on the West Coast.

THE STORM OF WEST COAST REACTION

It was the voices of organized interests, politicians and the press on the West Coast that DeWitt heard most clearly—and the War Department too. The first weeks after Pearl Harbor saw no extensive attacks on the ethnic Japanese, but through January and early February the storm gathered and broke. The latent anti-Japanese virus of the West Coast was brought to life by the fear and anger engendered by Pearl Harbor, stories of sabotage in Hawaii and Japan's victories in Asia. Among private groups the lead was typically taken by people with a long history of anti-Japanese agitation and by those who feared economic competition. It is difficult forty years later to recreate the fear and uncertainty about the country's safety which was generally felt after Pearl Harbor; it is equally impossible to convey in a few pages the virulence and breadth of anti-Japanese feeling which erupted on the West Coast in January and February of 1942.[106]

On January 2 the Joint Immigration Committee sent a manifesto to California newspapers which summed up the historical catalogue of charges against the ethnic Japanese. It put them in the new context of reported fifth column activity in Hawaii and the Philippines and a war that turned the Japanese into a problem for the nation, not California alone. Repeating the fundamental claim that the ethnic Japanese are "totally unassimilable," the manifesto declared that "those born in this country are American citizens by right of birth, but they are also Japanese citizens, liable . . . to be called to bear arms for their Emperor, either in front of, or behind, enemy lines." Japanese language schools were attacked as "a blind to cover instruction similar to that received by a young student in Japan—that his is a superior race, the divinity of the Japanese Emperor, the loyalty that every Japanese, wherever born, or residing, owes his Emperor and Japan."[107] In these attacks the Joint Immigration Committee had the support of the Native Sons and Daughters of the Golden West and the California Department of the American Legion, which in January began to demand that "all Japanese who are known to hold dual citizenship . . . be placed in concentration camps."[108] By early February, Earl Warren, then Attorney General of California, and U.S. Webb, a former Attorney General and co-author of the Alien Land Law, were actively advising the Joint Immigration Committee how to persuade the federal government that all ethnic Japanese should be removed from the West Coast.[109]

The Native Sons and Daughters of the Golden West saw the war as a fulfillment of everything they had feared and fought. In the January 1942 issue of *The Grizzly Bear*, the organization's publication, the editor emphasized the consequences of ignoring past predictions:

> Had the warnings been heeded—had the federal and state authorities been "on the alert" and rigidly enforced the Exclusion Law and the Alien Land Law; had the Jap propaganda agencies in this country been silenced; had the legislation been enacted . . . denying citizenship to offspring of all aliens ineligible to citizenship; had the Japs been prohibited from colonizing in strategic locations; had not Jap-dollars been so eagerly sought by White landowners and businessmen; had a dull ear been turned to the honeyed words of the Japs and the pro-Japs; had the yellow-Jap and the white-Jap "fifth columnists" been disposed of within the law; had Japan been denied the privilege of using California as a breeding ground for dual-citizens (nisei);—the treacherous Japs probably would not have attacked Pearl Harbor December 7, 1941, and this country would not today be at war with Japan.[110]

Through the first few weeks of 1942, local units of the Native Sons passed resolutions demanding removal of the ethnic Japanese from the coast.[111]

The American Legion first demanded the removal of enemy aliens, but by late January and early February the cry for removal of all ethnic Japanese had spread through Washington and Oregon. The Portland post of the Legion appealed for help in securing "the removal from the Pacific Coast areas of all Japanese, both alien and native-born, to points at least 300 miles inland,"[112] and resolved that "this is no time for namby-pamby pussyfooting, fear of hurting the feelings of our enemies; that it is not the time for consideration of minute constitutional rights of those enemies but that it is time for vigorous, whole-hearted and concerted action. . . ."[113] At least 38 Legion posts in Washington passed resolutions urging evacuation.[114]

These traditional voices of anti-Japanese agitation were joined by economic competitors of the Nikkei. The Grower-Shipper Vegetable Association was beginning to find a voice in January, although its bluntest statement can be found in a *Saturday Evening Post* article in May:

> We're charged with wanting to get rid of the Japs for selfish reasons. We might as well be honest. We do. It's a question of whether the white man lives on the Pacific Coast or the brown man. They came into this valley to work, and they stayed to take over. . . . If all the Japs were removed tomorrow, we'd never miss them in two weeks, because the white farmers can take over and produce everything the Jap grows. And we don't want them back when the war ends, either.[115]

Through January and early February, the Western Growers Protective Association, the Grower-Shippers, and the California Farm Bureau Federation all demanded stern measures against the ethnic Japanese. All assured the newspapers and politicians to whom they wrote that the removal of the ethnic Japanese would in no way harm or diminish agricultural production.[116]

This wave of self-assured demands for a firm solution to the "Japanese problem" encountered no vigorous, widespread defense of the Issei and Nissei. Those concerned with civil liberties and civil rights were silent. For instance, a poll of the Northern California Civil Liberties Union in the spring of 1942 showed a majority in favor of the evacuation orders.[117]

West Coast politicians were not slow to demand action against ethnic Japanese. Fletcher Bowron, reform mayor of Los Angeles, went to Washington in mid-January to discuss with Attorney General Biddle the general protection of Los Angeles as well as the removal of all ethnic Japanese from Terminal Island in Los Angeles Harbor. By February 5, in a radio address, the Mayor was unequivocally supporting mass evacuation. In the meantime, all Nisei had been removed from the city payrolls. The Los Angeles County Board of Supervisors fired all its Nisei employees and adopted a resolution urging the federal government to transport all Japanese aliens from the coast.[118] Following Los Angeles, 16 other California counties passed formal resolutions urging evacuation; Imperial County required the fingerprinting, registration and abandoning of farming by all enemy aliens; San Francisco demanded suppression of all Japanese language newspapers. Portland, Oregon, revoked the licenses of all Japanese nationals doing business in the city.[119] The California State Personnel Board ordered all "descendants" of enemy aliens barred from civil service positions, and Governor Olson authorized the State Department of Agriculture to revoke the produce-handling licenses of enemy aliens. Attorney General Warren found these measures unlawful, but he sympathized with their basic aim, laboring to persuade federal officials that the military should remove ethnic Japanese from what Warren thought sensitive areas on the West Coast.[120]

In Washington, most West Coast Congressmen and Senators began to express similar views, Congressman Leland Ford of Los Angeles taking the early lead. On January 16, 1942, he wrote the Secretaries of War and Navy and the FBI Director informing them that his California mail was running heavily in favor of evacuation and internment:

> I know that there will be some complications in connection with a matter like this, particularly where there are native born Japanese, who are citizens. My suggestions in connection with this are as follows:
> 1. That these native born Japanese either are or are not loyal to the United States.
> 2. That all Japanese, whether citizens or not, be placed in inland concentration camps. As justification for this, I submit that if an American born Japanese, who is a citizen, is really patriotic and wishes to make his contribution to the safety and welfare of this country, right here is his opportunity to do so, namely, that by permitting himself to be placed in a concentration camp, he would be making his sacrifice and he should be willing to do it if he is patriotic and is working for us. As against his sacrifice, millions of other native born citizens are willing to lay down their lives, which is a far greater sacrifice, of course, than being placed in a concentration camp.[121]

On January 27, Congressmen Alfred J. Elliott and John Z. Anderson met with officials of the Justice Department to press for evacuation.[122] On January 30, House members from the Pacific Coast urged the President to give the War Department "immediate and complete control over all alien enemies, as well as United States citizens holding dual citizenship in any enemy country, with full power and authority to require and direct the cooperation and assistance of all other agencies of government in exercising such control and in effecting evacuation, resettlement or internment." The War Department in turn was urged to develop and consummate "as soon as possible . . . complete evacuation and resettlement or internment" of all enemy aliens and dual citizens.[123]

This clamor for swift, comprehensive measures against the ethnic Japanese both reflected and was stimulated by the press. In December the West Coast press had been comparatively tolerant on the issue of the Nikkei, but by January more strident commentators were heard. John B. Hughes, who had a regular Mutual Broadcasting Company program, began a month-long series from Los Angeles which steadily attacked the ethnic Japanese, spreading rumors of espionage and fifth column activity and even suggesting that Japanese dominance of produce production was part of a master war plan.[124]

Nurtured by fear and anger at Japanese victories in the Far East and by eagerness to strike at the enemy with whom the Nisei were now identified, calls for radical government action began to fill letters to the editor and newspaper commentary. Private employers threw many ethnic Japanese out of their jobs, while many others refused to deal with them commercially.[125] Old stereotypes of the "yellow peril" and other forms of anti-Japanese agitation provided a ready body of lore to bolster this pseudo-patriotic cause. By the end of January the clamor for exclusion fired by race hatred and war hysteria was prominent in California newspapers. Henry McLemore, a Hearst syndicated columnist, published a vicious diatribe:

> The only Japanese apprehended have been the ones the FBI actually had something on. The rest of them, so help me, are free as birds. There isn't an airport in California that isn't flanked by Japanese farms. There is hardly an air field where the same situation doesn't exist. . . .
>
> I know this is the melting pot of the world and all men are created equal and there must be no such thing as race or creed hatred, but do those things go when a country is fighting for its life? Not in my book. No country has ever won a war because of courtesy and I trust and pray we won't be the first because of the lovely, gracious spirit. . . .
>
> I am for immediate removal of every Japanese on the West Coast to a point deep in the interior. I don't mean a nice part of

the interior either. Herd 'em up, pack 'em off and give 'em the inside room in the badlands. Let 'em be pinched, hurt, hungry and dead up against it . . .

Personally, I hate the Japanese. And that goes for all of them.[126]

By the end of January the western Congressional delegation and many voices in the press and organized interest groups were pressing for evacuation or internment of aliens and citizens. The Presidio at San Francisco listened, and by January 31, General DeWitt had embraced the Representatives' view that all enemy aliens and dual citizens should be evacuated and interned; action should be taken at the earliest possible date "even if they [the aliens and dual citizens] were temporarily inconvenienced."[127]

FEBRUARY 1942

The struggle within the government over the "Japanese problem" crystallized by February 1. DeWitt was now expressing prevailing opinion on the West Coast. War Department headquarters in Washington was undecided. DeWitt was no longer satisfied with the Justice Department program for excluding enemy aliens from carefully-drawn prohibited areas, although it was now moving forward rapidly on the basis of recommendations from the Western Defense Command and the War Department. In a series of press releases between January 31 and February 7, the Attorney General announced 84 prohibited areas in California, 7 in Washington, 24 in Oregon, and 18 in Arizona—135 zones around airports, dams, powerplants, pumping stations, harbor areas and military installations. In most cases the areas were small, usually circles of 1,000 feet or rectangles of several city blocks. The Justice Department also announced "restricted" areas for enemy aliens, including an extensive part of the California coast in which the movement of enemy aliens was very carefully controlled. But the Justice Department balked at quarantining extensive populated areas such as all of Seattle and Portland.[128]

The Justice Department was unpersuaded of the military need for a mass movement of aliens or citizens away from the coast, and it opposed General DeWitt on those grounds. On February 3, J. Edgar Hoover sent the Attorney General his analysis of the fervor for mass exclusion:

The necessity for mass evacuation is based primarily upon public and political pressure rather than on factual data. Public hysteria and in some instances, the comments of the press and radio announcers, have resulted in a tremendous amount of pressure being brought to bear on Governor Olson and Earl Warren, Attorney General of the State, and on the military authorities. . . .

Local officials, press and citizens have started widespread movement demanding complete evacuation of all Japanese, citizen and alien alike. [129]

Both on their reading of the facts from Hoover and by philosophical inclination, top Justice Department officials—Biddle, James Rowe and Edward Ennis, who ran the Alien Enemy Control Unit—opposed the exclusion. The only major Justice Department figure not against it was Tom C. Clark, later a Supreme Court Justice, who was West Coast liaison with the Western Defense Command; he was clearly ready to go along with some form of mass evacuation. [130]

Nevertheless, despite the urging of aides such as Ennis, the Attorney General was not prepared to argue that a mass exclusion was illegal or unconstitutional under the war powers of the Constitution if the War Department insisted on it as a matter of wartime necessity based on military judgment. [131] It would have been acceptable to the Justice Department at that point to have excluded all citizens and aliens from designated areas, such as the vicinity of aircraft plants, and then to allow back only those the Army permitted. [132] These views were no doubt confirmed by a memorandum prepared for Biddle by Benjamin Cohen, Oscar Cox and Joseph Rauh, liberal and respected Washington lawyers, who opined that everyone of Japanese ancestry, both alien and citizen, could constitutionally be excluded from sensitive military areas without excluding people of German or Italian stock from similar areas; although they argued for limited measures, they did not contend that the facts of the West Coast situation failed to justify exclusion. [133]

On February 1, the Justice Department drafted a press release to issue jointly with the War Department in order to calm public fears about sabotage and espionage, and to let the public know that the government was working on the "Japanese problem." The draft set out the extensive steps being taken to control any problem from enemy aliens:

The Army has surveyed and recommended 88 prohibited areas in California. Further areas have been studied by the Army and are being recommended in California, Washington, Oregon and the other West Coast states. The Attorney General designated these areas immediately upon the recommendation of the War Department to be evacuated of all alien enemies, Japanese, German and Italians. . . .

All alien enemies in the Western Defense Command will be registered between Feb. 2nd and February 7th. They will be identified, photographed, fingerprinted and their residence and employment recorded. These steps will insure compliance with control over alien enemies exercised in the restricted areas.

The draft release tried to calm groundless fears of sabotage and to address the situation of Nisei citizens:

The Federal Bureau of Investigation has charge of the investigation of the [sic] subversive activities. To date there has been no substantial evidence of planned sabotage by any alien. The FBI and the other agencies of the Federal Government are, however, very much alive to the possibility of acts of sabotage, particularly in case of a possible attack on our shores by the enemy. . . .

The government is fully aware of the problems presented by dual nationalities, particularly among the Japanese. Appropriate governmental agencies are now dealing with the problem. The Department of War and the Department of Justice are in agreement that the present military situation does not at this time require the removal of American citizens of the Japanese race.[134]

As General Gullion, the Provost Marshal General, described it, the meeting to discuss the press release between Stimson, McCloy and Bendetsen from the War Department and Biddle, Hoover and Rowe from Justice was heated indeed:

[The Justice officials] said there is too much hysteria about this thing; said these Western Congressmen are just nuts about it and the people getting hysterical and there is no evidence whatsoever of any reason for disturbing citizens, and the Department of Justice, Rowe started it and Biddle finished it—The Department of Justice will having [sic] nothing whatsoever to do with any interference with citizens, whether they are Japanese or not. They made me a little sore and I said, well listen Mr. Biddle, do you mean to tell me that if the Army, the men on the ground, determine it is a military necessity to move citizens, Jap citizens, that you won't help me. He didn't give a direct answer, he said the Department of Justice would be through if we interfered with citizens and write [sic] of habeas corpus, etc.[135]

The sticking point in the press release was the final statement that the removal of Nisei was unnecessary. Secretary Stimson and Assistant Secretary McCloy wanted DeWitt to consider the draft before they responded. Later that day Bendetsen and Gullion read the release over the phone to DeWitt. Gullion said he knew DeWitt now believed mass evacuation of Japanese Americans, including citizens, was essential, although Justice officials believed that DeWitt earlier had opposed mass evacuation. Gullion reported the position he had outlined to the Attorney General at the meeting: "I suggested that General DeWitt has told me that he has travelled up and down the West Coast, he has visited all these sectors, he has talked to all the Governors and other local civil authorities and he has come to this conclusion, it is my understanding that General DeWitt does favor mass evacuation. . . ."[136]

This, of course, was not a persuasive military justification for moving 100,000 people, but despite numerous conversations with DeWitt it was all that Gullion and Bendetsen could report. This was probably accurate: DeWitt favored moving the Japanese American community on the basis of his own opinions and those of the politicians he had consulted amid the flood of anti-Japanese rhetoric on the West Coast. Both the Governor of California and the Mayor of Los Angeles met with DeWitt, who was apparently interested primarily in their recommendations for action rather than in communicating what the military situation required.[137] The General reiterated his conclusory views about exclusion in the call about the press release: protection against sabotage "only can be made positive by removing those people who are aliens and who are Japs of American citizenship. . . ."[138] Gullion told DeWitt that he should put in writing his views and the justification for them, so his arguments could persuade McCloy and the Justice Department. DeWitt promised a memorandum for McCloy in the next few days.

The instructions to DeWitt were sound, for Secretary Stimson and McCloy were not yet persuaded.[139] In his diary for February 3, 1942, Stimson wrote that DeWitt was anxiously clamoring for evacuation of Japanese from the areas around San Diego, Los Angeles, San Francisco and Puget Sound, where important airplane factories and shipyards were located:

> If we base our evacuations upon the ground of removing enemy aliens, it will not get rid of the Nisei who are the second generation naturalized Japanese, and as I said, the more dangerous ones. If on the other hand we evacuate everybody including citizens, we must base it as far as I can see upon solely the protection of specified plants. We cannot discriminate among our citizens on the ground of racial origin. We talked the matter over for quite a while and then postponed it in order to hear further from General DeWitt who has not yet outlined all of the places that he wishes protected.[140]

McCloy also hesitated. On February 3, 1942, DeWitt and McCloy spoke by phone, DeWitt reading to McCloy the memorandum he had promised Gullion on the first. It was another installment in the General's talks with the politicians. DeWitt urged deleting the line in the press release stating that the military situation did not require removal of American citizens of Japanese race. The reason? DeWitt had conferred with California Governor Olson the day before and agreed that all male adult Nisei should leave the California combat zone. The General's military reasoning on this sweeping proposition defies paraphrase:

> [T]o protect the Japanese of American birth from suspicion and arrest, they should also have to carry identification cards to prove that they are not enemy aliens, as the enemy alien by not carrying identification card on his person could claim to be an American Japanese. In other words, all Japanese look alike and those charged with the enforcement of the regulation of excluding alien enemies from restricted areas will not be able to distinguish between them. The same applies in practically the same way to alien Germans and alien Italians but due to the large number of Japanese in the State of California (approximately 93,000), larger than any other State in the Union, and the very definite war consciousness of the people of California, as far as pertains to the Japanese participation in the war, the question of the alien Japanese and all Japanese presents a problem in control, separate and distinct from that of the German and Italian.
>
> The general consensus of opinion as agreed to by all present at this conference was that, due to the above facts, the removal of all male adult Japanese, that is over 18 years of age, whether native or American born, alien enemy or Japanese, from that area of California defined as a combat zone [should be achieved].[141]

Governor Olson wanted to achieve this by "voluntary" evacuation and General DeWitt thought this excellent.* Not surprisingly, McCloy was baffled, suggesting that dangerous people would not voluntarily leave a sensitive military area. DeWitt, who described himself as sitting on the sidelines during the conference in Olson's office, replied that he didn't know how Olson would handle that, but that if something weren't done soon the public would take matters into its own hands because "Out here, Mr. Secretary, a Jap is a Jap to these people now." It is remarkable that McCloy did not press DeWitt in this conversation for some military justification for moving the Nisei, but perhaps DeWitt's

---

*Olson's central role in devising this program is corroborated by one of the group of Nisei with whom he met on February 6 to explain the plan and to whom Olson stated that "he has been asked by the Federal authorities to recommend" the best procedure to handle "this complicated Japanese situation." (Letter, Ken Matsumoto to Ringle, Feb. 7, 1942 [CWRIC 19547]).

assurance that the Governor thought only 20,000 would have to move (and voluntarily) may have veiled the importance of what was afoot. In any event, McCloy was most concerned about the legality of any government action. He favored the procedure of designating restricted zones and letting people back in by permit; he would allow in "[e]veryone but the Japs." The dictates of military necessity were not part of the dialogue; McCloy, like the Justice Department, was satisfied with a legalistic procedure which only masked exclusion on the basis of ethnicity.[142]

Public pressure, of course, continued. FBI officials reported that the Los Angeles newspapers were carrying reports that Attorney General Warren of California and "approximately one hundred sheriffs and district attorneys throughout the State of California have recommended and demanded that all Japanese aliens be moved from all territories of the State of California."[143] But public opinion was not uniform. Archibald MacLeish of the Office of Facts and Figures summarized for McCloy a California opinion poll which showed that "the situation in California is serious; that it is loaded with potential dynamite; but that it is not as desperate as some people are said to believe. . . . We can be pretty definite in saying that a majority of people think that the Government (chiefly the FBI) has the situation in hand." Between 23 and 43 percent of the population felt further action was needed. The report suggested that these people "tend to cluster in the low income, poorly educated groups, and they are the ones who are most suspicious of local Japanese in general."[144]

After the discussion of February 3, events moved quickly. On the 4th, McCloy met with Gullion, Rowe, Ennis and Ennis's assistant, Burling, to discuss possible legislation that might be drawn up to remove both citizens and aliens from parts of the West Coast.[145] On the same day Bendetsen outlined his views and concluded that the enemy alien problem was primarily a Japanese problem, encompassing both aliens and citizens. He recommended the designation of military areas surrounding all vital installations in the Western Defense Command; all persons who did not have express permission to enter and remain would be excluded. He rejected mass evacuation as unjustified by military necessity and expected his recommendation to involve moving approximately 30,000 people. Bendetsen's position rested on his belief that "by far the vast majority of those who have studied the Oriental assert that a substantial majority of Nisei bear allegiance to Japan, are well controlled and disciplined by the enemy, and at the proper time will engage in organized sabotage, particularly, should a raid along the Pacific Coast be attempted by the Japanese."[146] It is unknown who these Oriental experts were, but Bendetsen, the one westerner close to War Department decision makers in Washington, may merely have repeated prejudices common on the West Coast.

On February 5, Rowe and McCloy discussed the alien problem by telephone[147] and Gullion gave McCloy his views of what steps should be taken about the "Japanese problem." This discussion shows that by early February the focus was shifting from military necessity to operations, from the question of "whether" to "how." The War Department draft proposal began:

> The War Department recommends the following steps be taken in connection with the "alien enemy-potential saboteur" problem on the West Coast and elsewhere in the United States:
>
> Step 1
>
> The establishment of military areas surrounding all vital national defense installations within the United States as designated by the appropriate Commanding Generals and approved by the War Department. From these areas will be excluded all persons, whether aliens or citizens, who are deemed dangerous as potential saboteurs, espionage agents and fifth columnists by the administering military authorities.
>
> Step 2
>
> The continuation, vigorously, of the alien enemy apprehension and internment program.[148]

This approach still covered narrow geographic areas but it affected aliens and citizens alike. Doubts of the necessity for evacuation were drowning in details of how to accomplish it.

Then on February 7, Biddle had lunch with the President and communicated his views about mass evacuation:

> I discussed at length with him the Japanese stating exactly what we had done, that we believe mass evacuation at this time inadvisable, that the F.B.I. was not staffed to perform it; that this was an Army job not, in our opinion, advisable; that there were no reasons for mass evacuation and that I thought the Army should be directed to prepare a detailed plan of evacuation in case of an emergency caused by an air raid or attempted landing on the West Coast. I emphasized the danger of the hysteria, which we were beginning to control, moving east and affecting the Italian and German population in Boston and New York. Generally he approved being fully aware of the dreadful risk of Fifth Column retaliation in case of a raid.[149]

By the time he made his decision, therefore, Roosevelt knew Biddle's views,[150] but it is important to note that, while the Attorney General did not believe evacuation was necessary, he did not tell the President that evacuation would fail to pass constitutional muster on the facts.

Stimson's diary entry for February 10, 1942, reiterates his previous view that "The second generation Japanese [Nisei] can only be evacuated either as part of a total evacuation, giving access to the areas only by permits, or by frankly trying to put them out on the ground that their racial characteristics are such that we cannot understand or trust even the citizen Japanese. This latter is the fact but I am afraid it will make a tremendous hole in our constitutional system to apply it." His concern was heightened by his view that Japan might try to invade the United States; the Secretary mused on Homer Lea's predictions twenty-five years earlier in *The Valor of Ignorance* that in the Pacific geopolitical forces were shifting so that Japan was capable of invading a lightly populated and defended West Coast and holding the Pacific slope to the crest of the Sierras: "In those days [Lea's] book seemed fantastic. Now the things that he prophesied seem quite possible."[151]

At this point Stimson's mind was still not made up, at least about the scope of evacuation, and he still wanted from DeWitt a specific recommendation based on a careful review of military necessity.[152] There is no indication that Stimson received such a memo immediately, but he must have been persuaded that the case had been or would be made, for the next day his diary notes:

> I then had a conference in regard to the west coast situation with McCloy and General Clark who has been out there. This is a stiff proposition. General DeWitt is asking for some very drastic steps, to wit: the moving and relocating of some 120,000 people including citizens of Japanese descent. This is one of those jobs that is so big that, if we resolved on it, it just wouldn't be done; so I directed them to pick out and begin with the most vital places of army and navy production and take them on in that order as quickly as possible. . . .
>
> I tried to get an interview with the President over these various matters but was unable to do so. I then arranged for a telephone call which finally came through about one thirty.
>
> I took up with him the west coast matter first and told him the situation and fortunately found that he was very vigorous about it and told me to go ahead on the line that I had myself thought the best.[153]

Stimson may not have had in mind the massive evacuation of all citizens and aliens of Japanese descent; his description of what he supported resembled most the designation of military areas and entry into them by permit, which would be denied to Japanese citizens and aliens.

The first ten days of February had not yet produced a better rationale for evacuation from General DeWitt than his fundamental racial mistrust of the ethnic Japanese. Now, perhaps by dint of repetition or exposure to the anti-Japanese view of West Coast interest groups and politicians, mistrust had taken hold at the top of the War Department. Clamor from the press and politicians was relentless. Incessant West Coast demands for evacuation were countered by no one of stature who knew the Pacific Coast.

On February 12, Walter Lippmann, a prominent, intellectually respected syndicated columnist, wrote of his serious concern about a Japanese raid on the United States and potential sabotage. Because Lippmann thought saboteurs would be native-born Nisei as well as aliens, the procedure he recommended which "ought to be used for all persons in a zone which the military authorities regard as open to enemy attack" was to compel everyone to prove that he had a good reason to be there. "Under this system all persons are in principle treated alike."[154] He recommended that the West Coast be made a combat zone open only to those with a reason to be present. This was the plan being discussed in the War Department; Lippmann had talked over the issue with Attorney General Warren, who had spoken extensively to federal officials, and there is no reason to believe Lippmann formed an opinion without knowing the basic issues the government was looking at.[155] Lippmann's article was taken as a recommendation to exclude all ethnic Japanese from the West Coast, and from the strident right Westbrook Pegler popularized the suggestion a few days later:

> Do you get what [Lippmann] says? . . . the enemy has been scouting our coast. . . . The Japs ashore are communicating with the enemy offshore and . . . on the basis of "what is known to be taking place" there are signs that a well-organized blow is being withheld only until it can do the most damage. . . .
>
> We are so dumb and considerate of the minute constitutional rights and even of the political feelings and influence of people whom we have every reason to anticipate with preventive action!

Pegler put his central point very simply: "The Japanese in California should be under armed guard to the last man and woman right now and to hell with *habeas corpus* until the danger is over."[156] The entire spectrum of press opinion was uniting to advocate exclusion.

At the same time, Manchester Boddy, liberal editor and publisher of the *Los Angeles Daily News* who had earlier written a book on the ethnic Japanese in America,[157] sent first a telegram, then a letter, to Attorney General Biddle warning that the "alien Japanese situation [is] deteriorating rapidly." To forestall irresponsible citizen action, Boddy suggested prompt evacuation of alien Japanese who "have anticipated evacuation and are in state of readiness," and placement into a concentration camp now, with consideration of their ultimate disposition later. Boddy found "no distinction in public mind regarding Japanese aliens and their dual citizenship children" and therefore expressly assumed that aliens and citizens would both be moved.[158]

Fear of violence against Japanese Americans had grown markedly among law enforcement officials in California.

At a conference of California district attorneys and sheriffs on February 2, it was announced that various civic and agricultural groups were actively fostering extra-legal action against the Japanese. Subsequently the sheriff of Merced County reported "rumblings of vigilante activity"; the chief of police of Huntington Beach described anti-Japanese feeling as "at fever heat"; the police chief at Watsonville announced that "racial hatred is mounting higher and higher" and that Filipinos were "arming themselves and going out looking for an argument with Japanese"; and Oxnard's police chief reported that "it has been planned by local Filipinos and some so-called '200 percent Americans' to declare a local 'war' against local Japanese, during the next blackout."[159]

Pressure for government action was also increasing in Congress. On February 13 Congressman Clarence Lea, the senior West Coast Representative, wrote to President Roosevelt on behalf of the members of Congress from California, Oregon and Washington:

We recommend the immediate evacuation of all persons of Japanese lineage and all others, aliens and citizens alike, whose presence shall be deemed dangerous or inimical to the defense of the United States from all strategic areas.

In defining said strategic areas we recommend that such areas include all military installations, war industries, water and power plant installations, oil fields and refineries, transportation and other essential facilities as well as adequate protective areas adjacent thereto.

We further recommend that such areas be enlarged as expeditiously as possible until they shall encompass the entire strategic area of the states of California, Oregon and Washington, and Territory of Alaska.

We make these recommendations in order that no citizen, located in a strategic area, may cloak his disloyalty or subversive activity under the mantle of his citizenship alone and further to guarantee protection to all loyal persons, alien and citizen alike, whose safety may be endangered by some wanton act of sabotage.[160]

Roosevelt forwarded the letter to Secretary Stimson, [161] although the views of the West Coast delegation were well known to the War Department, which had already briefed the Congressmen.[162]

At this late date of February 14 General DeWitt finally sent to the Secretary of War his final recommendation on the "Evacuation of Japanese and Other Subversive Persons from the Pacific Coast." Having estimated that the West Coast was open to air and naval attacks as well as sabotage, but without suggesting that a Japanese raid or invasion would land troops on the West Coast, the General set out his military justification for requesting the power to exclude ethnic Japanese:

> The area lying to the west of Cascade and Sierra Nevada Mountains in Washington, Oregon and California, is highly critical not only because the lines of communication and supply to the Pacific theater pass through it, but also because of the vital industrial production therein, particularly aircraft. In the war in which we are now engaged racial affinities are not severed by migration. The Japanese race is an enemy race and while many second and third generation Japanese born on United States soil, possessed of United States citizenship, have become "Americanized," the racial strains are undiluted. To conclude otherwise is to expect that children born of white parents on Japanese soil sever all racial affinity and become loyal Japanese subjects, ready to fight and, if necessary, to die for Japan in a war against the nation of their parents. That Japan is allied with Germany and Italy in this struggle is no ground for assuming that any Japanese, barred from assimilation by convention as he is, though born and raised in the United States, will not turn against this nation, when the final test of loyalty comes. It, therefore, follows that along the vital Pacific Coast over 112,000 potential enemies, of Japanese extraction, are at large today. There are indications that these are organized and ready for concerted action at a favorable opportunity. The very fact that no sabotage has taken place to date is a disturbing and confirming indication that such action will be taken.[163]

The only justification for exclusion here, beyond DeWitt's belief that ethnicity ultimately determines loyalty, is the unsupported conclusion that "indications" show that the Japanese "are organized and ready for concerted action." The General's best argument for the truth of this was the fact that it hadn't happened yet. It would be hard to concoct a more vicious, less professional piece of military reasoning. Perhaps DeWitt's final recommendation came too late to shock McCloy and Stimson into demanding sound military arguments for what was now rolling forward. Perhaps the poverty of DeWitt's position also explains the growing emphasis on the danger of vigilantism, which argued that the Nisei now must be moved for their own protection.

In the face of still-swelling demands for evacuation and the recommendation of his Secretary of War, Roosevelt was not likely to reconsider his decision. Nevertheless, on February 17 Attorney General Biddle sent a memorandum to the President in the guise of a briefing paper for a press conference. Biddle opposed evacuation once again, elaborating the arguments he had made to Stimson:[164]

For several weeks there have been increasing demands for evacuation of all Japanese, aliens and citizens alike, from the West Coast states. A great many of the West Coast people distrust the Japanese, various special interests would welcome their removal from good farm land and the elimination of their competition, some of the local California radio and press have demanded evacuation, the West Coast Congressional Delegation are asking the same thing and finally, Walter Lippman [sic] and Westbrook Pegler recently have taken up the evacuation cry on the ground that attack on the West Coast and widespread sabotage is imminent. My last advice from the War Department is that there is no evidence of imminent attack and from the F.B.I. that there is no evidence of planned sabotage.

I have designated as a prohibited area every area recommended to me by the Secretary of War, through whom the Navy recommendations are also made. . . .

We are proceeding as fast as possible. To evacuate the 93,000 Japanese in California over night would materially disrupt agricultural production in which they play a large part and the farm labor now is so limited that they could not be quickly replaced. Their hurried evacuation would require thousands of troops, tie up transportation and raise very difficult questions of resettlement. Under the Constitution 60,000 of these Japanese are American citizens. If complete confusion and lowering of morale is to be avoided, so large a job must be done after careful planning. The Army has not yet advised me of its conclusion in the matter.

There is no dispute between the War, Navy, and Justice Departments. The practical and legal limits of this Department's authority which is restricted to alien enemies are clearly understood. The Army is considering what further steps it wishes to recommend.

It is extremely dangerous for the columnists, acting as "Armchair Strategists and Junior G-Men," to suggest that an attack on the West Coast and planned sabotage is imminent when the military authorities and the F.B.I. have indicated that this is not the fact. It comes close to shouting FIRE! in the theater; and if race riots

occur, these writers will bear a heavy responsibility. Either Lippman [sic] has information which the War Department and the
F.B.I. apparently do not have, or is acting with dangerous irre-
sponsibility.[165]

No minds were changed, and by this time the Attorney General
was taking coarse and threatening abuse for his unwillingness to join
the stampede to mass evacuation. Seven months later, Congressman
Ford recalled speaking to Biddle at this point:

> I phoned the Attorney General's office and told them to stop
> fucking around. I gave them twenty four hours notice that unless
> they would issue a mass evacuation notice I would drag the whole
> matter out on the floor of the House and of the Senate and give
> the bastards everything we could with both barrels. I told them
> they had given us the run around long enough . . . and that if
> they would not take immediate action, we would clean the god
> damned office out in one sweep. I cussed at the Attorney General
> and his staff himself just like I'm cussing to you now and he knew
> damn well I meant business.[166]

On February 17 Stimson recorded meeting with War Department
officials to outline a proposed executive order; General Gullion undertook to have the order drafted that night: "War Department orders
will fill in the application of this Presidential order. These were outlined
and Gullion is also to draft them." Further, Stimson said, "It will
involve the tremendous task of moving between fifty and one hundred
thousand people from their homes and finding temporary support and
sustenance for them in the meanwhile, and ultimately locating them
in new places away from the coast."[167] In short, whatever his views
during discussion with the President a few days before, Stimson now
contemplated a mass move.

On February 18, 1942, Stimson met about the executive order
with Biddle, Ennis, Rowe, and Tom Clark of the Department of Justice;
and Robert Patterson, Under Secretary of War; McCloy; Gullion; and
Bendetsen from the War Department. Stimson wrote:

> Biddle, McCloy and Gullion had done a good piece of work in
> breaking down the issues between the Departments the night
> before, and a draft of a presidential executive order had been
> drawn by Biddle based upon that conference and the preceding
> conference I had had yesterday. We went over them. I made a
> few suggestions and then approved it. This marks a long step
> forward towards a solution of a very dangerous and vexing prob-
> lem. But I have no illusions as to the magnitude of the task that
> lies before us and the wails which will go up in relation to some
> of the actions which will be taken under it.[168]

The Attorney General remembered the tenor of the meeting somewhat differently, but, writing in his autobiography, agreed about the result:

> Rowe and Ennis argued strongly against [the Executive Order].But the decision had been made by the President. It was, he said, a matter of military judgment. I did not think I should oppose it any further. The Department of Justice, as I had made it clear to him from the beginning, was opposed to and would have nothing to do with the evacuation.[169]

In Los Angeles on the night of February 19, the United Citizens Federation, representing a wide range of pro-Nisei interests, held its first meeting of more than a thousand people. Plans were laid to persuade the press, the politicians and the government that their attacks upon the ethnic Japanese were unfounded.[170] It was too late.

Earlier in the day, President Roosevelt had signed Executive Order 9066. The Order directed the Secretary of War and military commanders designated by him, whenever it was deemed necessary or desirable, to prescribe military areas "with respect to which, the right of any person to enter, remain in, or leave shall be subject to whatever restrictions the Secretary of War or the appropriate Military Commander may impose in his discretion."[171] There was no direct mention of American citizens of Japanese descent, but unquestionably the Order was directed squarely at those Americans. A few months later, when there was talk of the War Department using the Executive Order to move Germans and Italians on the East Coast, the President wrote Stimson that he considered enemy alien control to be "primarily a civilian matter except of course in the case of the Japanese mass evacuation on the Pacific Coast."[172]

The next day, to underscore the government's new-found unity on this decision, Attorney General Biddle sent to the President's personal attention a memorandum justifying the Executive Order and its broad grant of powers to the military. Biddle's note paraphrased liberally from the memorandum he had received earlier from Cohen, Cox and Rauh:

> This authority gives very broad powers to the Secretary of War and the Military Commanders. These powers are broad enough to permit them to exclude any particular individual from military areas. They could also evacuate groups of persons based on a reasonable classification. The order is not limited to aliens but includes citizens so that it can be exercised with respect to Japanese, irrespective of their citizenship.
>
> The decision of safety of the nation in time of war is necessarily

for the Military authorities. Authority over the movement of persons, whether citizens or noncitizens, may be exercised in time of war. . . . This authority is no more than declaratory of the power of the President, in time of war, with reference to all areas, sea or land.

The President is authorized in acting under his general war powers without further legislation. The exercise of the power can meet the specific situation and, of course, cannot be considered as any punitive measure against any particular nationalities. It is rather a precautionary measure to protect the national safety. It is not based on any legal theory but on the facts that the unrestricted movement of certain racial classes, whether American citizens or aliens, in specified defense areas may lead to serious disturbances. These disturbances cannot be controlled by police protection and have the threat of injury to our war effort. A condition and not a theory confronts the nation.[173]

After the decision, there was no further dissent at the highest levels of the federal government. The War Department stood behind the facts and the Justice Department stood behind the law which were the foundation of the Executive Order.

JUSTIFYING THE DECISION

Any account which relies on finding documents forty years after a decision may reasonably be questioned when it concludes that little or nothing in the record factually supports the reasons given at the time to justify the decision. For that reason, the two major justifications of the exclusion composed during the war by the War Department and the Justice Department must be considered: General DeWitt's *Final Report: Japanese Evacuation from the West Coast, 1942*, which he forwarded to the Secretary of War in June 1943, and the Justice Department's brief in *Hirabayashi* v. *United States*, filed in the Supreme Court in May 1943.*

---

*The House Select Committee Investigating National Defense Migration, commonly known as the Tolan Committee, was the first official body to examine the exclusion, holding hearings on the West Coast in late February and March 1942. It chose to treat the exclusion as a *fait accompli*, but in its reports it noticeably failed to offer an effective defense of the exclusion. In the context of the Germans and Italians, it emphasized "the fundamental fact that place of birth and technical noncitizenship alone provide no decisive criteria for assessing the alinement [sic] of loyalties in this world-wide conflict." The

DeWitt's *Final Report* bases the War Department decision on a number of factors: signaling from shore to enemy submarines; arms and contraband found by the FBI during raids on Nikkei homes and businesses; danger to evacuees from vigilantes; concentration of the ethnic Japanese population around or near militarily sensitive areas; the number of Japanese ethnic organizations on the coast which might shelter pro-Japanese attitudes or activities such as Emperor-worshipping Shinto; the presence of the Kibei, who had recent ties to Japan. "It was, perforce, a combination of factors and circumstances with which the Commanding General had to deal. Here was a relatively homogenous, unassimilated element bearing a close relationship through ties of race, religion, language, custom and indoctrination to the enemy."[174]*

Two items in DeWitt's list stand out as demonstrable indications of military danger: shore-to-ship signaling and the discovery of arms and contraband. Reading the *Final Report* while preparing to defend the exclusion in the Supreme Court, Justice Department attorneys

---

Committee did not doubt that fifth column elements were present among Germans and Italians as well as Japanese but concluded, "Surely some more workable method exists for determining the loyalty and reliability of these people than the uprooting of 50 trustworthy persons to remove one dangerous individual." Moreover, in comparing German and Italian aliens to Japanese aliens, the Committee found only two significant differences: the Japanese tended to live in separate communities and an unusually high proportion were engaged in agriculture and produce distribution. Neither has any obvious military significance. Given this line of reasoning it is not surprising that in its March report, the Committee reported "[a] profound sense of certain injustices and constitutional doubts attending the evacuation of the Japanese," and in its May report stated, "The Nation must decide and Congress must gravely consider, as a matter of national policy, the extent to which citizenship, in and of itself, is a guaranty of equal rights and privileges during time of war." Report of the Select Committee Investigating National Defense Migration, House of Representatives, 77th Cong., 2d Sess., House Report No. 1911, pp. 15, 21–22, 25; Fourth Interim Report of the Select Committee Investigating National Defense Migration, 77th Cong., 2d Sess., House Report No. 2124, pp. 11, 25.

*DeWitt also referred to three "striking illustrations" of the need for evacuation—shellings by the Japanese of Goleta, California, and Astoria, Oregon, and a bombing of Brookings, Oregon. All three incidents took place *after* the Executive Order was signed. Moreover, the military importance of these episodes was clearly negligible. (Grodzins, *Americans Betrayed*, pp. 294–95.)

were drawn to the signaling contention. It was investigated by the FCC and found to be so utterly unsubstantiated that, in its brief to the Supreme Court, the Justice Department was careful not to rely on DeWitt's *Final Report* as a factual basis for the military decision it had to defend.[175] There simply had not been any identifiable shore-to-ship signalling.

The Justice Department had dismissed the arms and contraband argument earlier. By May 1942 the FBI had seized 2,592 guns of various kinds; 199,000 rounds of ammunition; 1,652 sticks of dynamite; 1,458 radio receivers; 2,014 cameras and numerous other items which the alien Japanese had been ordered to surrender in January. But numbers alone meant little; a truckload of guns and ammunition had been picked up in a raid on a sporting goods store and another large supply of material was found in the warehouse of a general store owner. The Department of Justice concluded that it all had negligible significance:

> We have not, however, uncovered through these searches any dangerous persons that we could not otherwise know about. We have not found among all the sticks of dynamite and gun powder any evidence that any of it was to be used in bombs.
>
> We have not found a single machine gun nor have we found any gun in any circumstances indicating that it was to be used in a manner helpful to our enemies. We have not found a camera which we have reason to believe was for use in espionage.[176]

To the government's official military historian of the evacuation, Stetson Conn, this was the most damaging tangible evidence against the evacuees, and he clearly believed it was insubstantial.[177]

The argument that the exclusion served to protect the Nikkei against vigilantism had wide currency. The violence against ethnic Japanese on the West Coast cannot be dismissed lightly. Between Pearl Harbor and February 15, 5 murders and 25 other serious crimes— rapes, assaults, shootings, property damage, robbery or extortion— were reported against ethnic Japanese.[178] This was no lynch mob on the loose, but it was serious and, in fact, more violence against ethnic Japanese followed the signing of the Executive Order. tenBroek describes it succinctly:

> During March an attempt was made to burn down a Japanese-owned hotel at Sultana. On April 13 at Del Ray five evacuees were involved in a brawl with the local constable—following which a crowd of white residents, some armed with shotguns, threatened violence to a nearby camp of Japanese Americans. On succeeding nights the windows of four Japanese stores were smashed, and similar incidents occurred in Fresno. In northern Tulare County,

a group known as the "Bald Eagles"—described by one observer as a "a guerrilla army of nearly 1,000 farmers"—armed themselves for the announced purpose of "guarding" the Japanese in case of emergency. A similar organization was formed in the southeast part of the county, where a large number of evacuees were concentrated.[179]

Protecting ethnic Japanese from vigilantes is a justification for the exclusion which has been repeatedly emphasized over the years. Stim-son's autobiography relied on it as a principal reason:

> What critics ignored was the situation that led to the evacuation. Japanese raids on the west coast seemed not only possible but probable in the first months of the war, and it was quite impossible to be sure that the raiders would not receive important help from individuals of Japanese origin. More than that, anti-Japanese feeling on the west coast had reached a level which endangered the lives of all such individuals; incidents of extra-legal violence were increasingly frequent.[180]

McCloy emphasized the same point in his testimony before the Commission[181] and it appears in his papers in 1942 as a subsidiary reason for exclusion.[182] Tom Clark, writing long after the war, gave protection against vigilantism as the reason he was willing to support the exclusion.[183]

This explanation sounds lame indeed today. It was not publicly advanced at the time to justify the exclusion and, had protection been on official minds, a much different post-evacuation program would have been required. McCloy himself supplied the most telling rebuttal of the contention in a 1943 letter to General DeWitt:

> That there is serious animosity on the West Coast against all evacuated Japanese I do not doubt, but that does not necessarily mean that we should trim our sails accordingly. . . . The Army, as I see it, is not responsible for the general public peace of the Western Defense Command. That responsibility still rests with the civil authorities. There may, as you suggest, be incidents, but these can be effectively discouraged by prompt action by law enforcement agencies, with the cooperation of the military if they even [sic] assume really threatening proportions.[184]

That is the simple, straightforward answer to the argument of protection against vigilantes—keeping the peace is a civil matter that would involve the military only in extreme situations. Even then, public officials would be duty-bound to protect the innocent, not to order them from their homes for months or years under the rubric of a military measure designed to maintain public peace.

DeWitt's analysis in the *Final Report* of Japanese population concentration and Japanese organizations is lifted, virtually verbatim, from testimony by Earl Warren before a Congressional committee after the Executive Order was promulgated. The pattern of land purchases near "military" areas means very little when one realizes that sensitive military installations included aircraft plants, oilfields, dams, isolated areas of the coast and powerlines as well as forts or Navy bases. The fact that a number of Japanese ethnic organizations shared the same post office box seems equally meaningless. A similar "analysis" of Italians and Italian Americans who lived under dual citizenship laws more strict than the Japanese in claiming the allegiance of children born to Italian citizens,[185] would have produced an equally alarming and meaningless pattern. Morton Grodzins has neatly set out the usual indices of probable Japanese disloyalty in terms of the Italians:

> Because of their concentration in the fishing industry, Italians if anything were located in more strategic coastal locations than the Japanese. This was especially true of the San Francisco Bay area and adjoining counties.
> The Italians had their full quota of language schools and their own churches. They and their children made numerous trips to their home country. The Italian consuls were active and important members of the community, and Fascist propaganda was reflected in a vernacular press which supported Mussolini's domestic and foreign policies. If naturalization were any indication of acculturation, then the single fact that more than half the foreign-born Italians had not become citizens of the United States demonstrated a low degree of Americanization. Educational achievement rates of children of Italian ancestry were lower, and their delinquency rates were higher, in comparison with those of Japanese ancestry. Italians in California had contributed funds to the Italian relief agencies following the conquests of Ethiopia and Albania.[186]

For good measure, one might add the spectre of the Mafia as a well-organized force willing to resort to any illegal means to achieve its ends. For "evidence" of this sort to be credible, one must be predisposed to believe that a well-organized conspiracy is in progress. The development of such views is hindered when the alleged conspirators are well-known, familiar neighbors. It is equally important to recognize that the military would not usually be expected to have expertise about these social and cultural patterns; on such issues, if anyone's judgment deserves deference it would be that of sociologists, not generals.

The Justice Department did no better than the War Department in producing a factual record to support the evacuation decision. It made a virtue of necessity:

> The record in this case does not contain any comprehensive ac-

count of the facts which gave rise to the exclusion and curfew measures here involved. These facts, which should be considered in determining the constitutionality of the Act [prohibiting violation of military orders issued under the Executive Order], embrace the general military, political, economic, and social conditions under which the challenged orders were issued. These historical facts . . . are of the type that are traditionally susceptible of judicial notice in considering constitutional questions, and in particular, many of these facts appear in official documents, such as the contemporary Tolan Committee's reports, which are peculiarly within the realm of judicial notice.[187]

The first point the *Hirabayashi* brief made about reasons to conclude that the ethnic Japanese might be disloyal, reviewed the discriminatory history of the immigration and alien land laws as well as economic discrimination in the west. The passage concludes by suggesting that such hostile treatment might well have caused an absence of loyalty to the United States—in other words, the resident Japanese *ought* to be disloyal. Next, the high percentage of aliens in the community was stressed (though the relevance of this to a case involving an American citizen is by no means clear). The remaining points repeat the tired catalogue of West Coast anti-Japanese propaganda; the headings of the brief tell the story: *Dual Nationality, Shintoism, Education of American-born Children in Japan, Japanese Language Schools on the West Coast, Japanese Organizations* and, finally, *Possibility of Civil Disorder*.[188] The argument cites a vast array of general articles and books, refers liberally to Congressional committee hearings and quotes newspaper articles. This matches the Department's position that the facts of the case should be determined on judicial notice—in other words, everyone knew that the Japanese were likely to be disloyal, so all the government needed to show was that opinion's respectability and near-universality. No particular facts were needed. And no particular facts of probative force were supplied.

Unhappily, on the West Coast and across most of the country in February 1942, these baseless canards made respectable opinion. The old prejudicial propaganda of the anti-Japanese faction, unopposed, had won the day. As a Joint Immigration Committee official put it in early February, "This is our time to get things done that we have been trying to get done for a quarter of a century."[189] The War Department and the President, through the press and politicians with the aid of General DeWitt, had been sold a bill of goods. In accepting the vicious views of California's ugly past, they came to believe that the Issei and Nisei represented a threat to the security of the coast. Perhaps only later did John J. McCloy, an easterner with little experience of the west before Pearl Harbor,[190] discover whose program he had been carrying out on the Pacific Coast after the War Department had failed to scrutinize General DeWitt's demands closely and critically. It was certainly with an air of disgust that McCloy wrote to General DeWitt's successor, introducing California after his transfer from Hawaii:

> The situation in California is not the same [as in Hawaii]. You have no doubt become aware of the existence of active and powerful minority groups in California whose main interest in the war seems to take the form of a desire for permanent exclusion of all Japanese, loyal or disloyal, citizen or alien, from the West Coast or, at least, from California. . . . This means that considerations other than of mere military necessity enter into any proposal for removal of the present restrictions.[191]

The program could not be ended on the basis of "mere military necessity," largely because it did not begin that way.

3

Exclusion and Evacuation

With the signing of Executive Order 9066, the course of the President
and the War Department was set. American citizens of Japanese ancestry would be required to move from the West Coast on the basis
of wartime military necessity, and the way was open to move any other
group the military thought necessary. For the War Department and
the Western Defense Command (WDC), the problem now became
primarily one of method and operation, not basic policy. General DeWitt
first tried "voluntary" resettlement: the Issei and Nisei were to move
outside restricted military zones on the West Coast but were free to
go wherever they chose. From a military standpoint, this policy was
bizarre and utterly impractical besides. If the Issei and Nisei were
being excluded because they threatened sabotage and espionage, it is
difficult to understand why they would be left at large in the interior
where there were, of course, innumerable dams, power lines, bridges
and war industries to be spied upon or disrupted. For that matter,
sabotage in the interior could be synchronized with a Japanese raid or
invasion for a powerful fifth column effect. If this was of little concern
to General DeWitt once the perceived problem was removed beyond
the boundaries of his command, it raises substantial doubts about how
gravely the War Department regarded the threat. The implications
were not lost on the citizens and politicians of the interior western
states; they believed that people who were a threat to wartime security
in California were equally dangerous in Wyoming and Idaho.

For the Issei and Nisei, "voluntary" relocation was largely impractical. Quick sale of a going business or a farm with crops in the ground could not be expected at a fair price. Most businesses that relied on the ethnic trade in the Little Tokyos of the West Coast could not be sold for anything close to market value. The absence of fathers and husbands in internment camps and the lack of liquidity after funds were frozen made matters more difficult. It was not easy to leave, and the prospect of a deeply hostile reception in some unknown town or city was a powerful deterrent to moving.

Inevitably the government ordered mandatory mass evacuation controlled by the Army; first to assembly centers—temporary staging areas, typically at fairgrounds and racetracks—and from there to relocation centers—bleak, barbed-wire camps in the interior. Mass evacuation went forward in one locality after another up and down the coast, on short notice, with a drill sergeant's thoroughness and lack of sentimentality. As the Executive Order required, government agencies made an effort, only partially successful, to protect the property and economic interests of the people removed to the camps; but their loss of liberty brought enormous economic losses.

Even in time of war, the President and the military departments do not make law alone. War actions must be implemented through Congress, and the courts may review orders and directions of the President about the disposition of the civilian population. Finally, in a democratic society with a free press, public opinion will be heard and weighed. In the months immediately following Executive Order 9066, none of these political estates came to the aid of the Nisei or their alien parents. The Congress promptly passed, without debate on questions of civil rights and civil liberties, a criminal statute prohibiting violation of military orders issued under the Executive Order. The district courts rejected Nisei pleas and arguments, both on habeas corpus petitions and on the review of criminal convictions for violating General DeWitt's curfew and exclusion orders. Public opinion on the West Coast and in the country at large did nothing to temper its violently anti-Japanese rage of early February. Only a handful of citizens and organizations—a few churchmen, a small part of organized labor, a few others—spoke out for the rights and interests of the Nisei.

Few in numbers, bereft of friends, probably fearful that the next outburst of war hysteria would bring mob violence and vigilantism that law enforcement officials would do little to control, left only to choose a resistance which would have proven the very disloyalty they denied—the Nisei and Issei had little alternative but to go. Each carried a personal burden of rage or resignation or despair to the assembly centers and camps which the government had hastily built to protect 130 million Americans against 60,000 of their fellow citizens and their resident alien parents.

CONGRESS ACTS

The Executive Order gave the military the power to issue orders; it could not impose sanctions for failure to obey them. The Administration quickly turned to Congress to obtain that authority. By February 22, the War Department was sending draft legislation to the Justice Department. General DeWitt wanted mandatory imprisonment and a felony sanction because "you have greater liberty to enforce a felony than you have to enforce a misdemeanor, viz. You can shoot a man to prevent the commission of a felony."[1] On March 9, 1942, Secretary Stimson sent the proposed legislation to Congress. The bill was introduced immediately by Senator Robert Reynolds of North Carolina, Chairman of the Senate Committee on Military Affairs, and by Representative John M. Costello of California.[2]

The Executive Order was what the West Coast Congressional delegation had demanded of the President and the War Department. Congressman John H. Tolan of California, who chaired the House Select Committee which examined the evacuation from prohibited military areas, characterized the order as "the recommendation in almost the same words of the Pacific coast delegation."[3] With such regional support and military backing, there were only two circumstances under which one might have expected Congressional opposition: if Tolan's Committee, which held hearings on the West Coast in late February, immediately after the Executive Order was signed, had returned to Washington prepared to argue against the Executive Order; or if, given the fact that there was no evidence of actual sabotage or espionage, members concerned with civil rights and civil liberties had protested.

Members of the Tolan Committee did not openly abandon support of the Executive Order after their West Coast hearings. They went out persuaded that espionage and fifth column activity by Issei and Nisei in Hawaii had been central to the success of the Japanese attack. Censorship in Hawaii meant that the only authoritative news from the islands was official. With regard to sabotage and fifth column activity,

activity, that version of events was still largely made up of two pieces: Secretary Knox's firmly-stated December views that local sabotage had substantially aided the attack, and the Roberts Commission's silence about fifth column activity.[4] Thus there was no effective answer to be made when Tolan challenged pro-Nisei witnesses:

> We had our FBI in Honolulu, yet they had probably the greatest, the most perfect system of espionage and sabotage ever in the history of war, native-born Japanese. On the only roadway to the shipping harbor there were hundreds and hundreds of automobiles clogging the street, don't you see.[5]

Not privy to the facts in Hawaii, advocates of Japanese American loyalty such as the Japanese American Citizens League, were frequently reduced to arguing lamely that the mainland Nisei were different from, and more reliable than, the residents of Hawaii.[6] This view of Pearl Harbor goes a long way toward explaining the argument, repeated by the Congressmen, that the lack of sabotage only showed that enemy loyalists were waiting for a raid or invasion to trigger organized activity.[7]

The Nisei spoke in their own defense; a few academics, churchmen and labor leaders supported them.[8] Even much of this testimony, assuming that a mass evacuation was a *fait accompli*, addressed secondary issues such as treatment during evacuation. Traditional anti-Japanese voices such as the California Joint Immigration Committee testified firmly in favor of the Executive Order, reciting again the historical catalogue of anti-Japanese charges.[9]

Earl Warren, then Attorney General of California and preparing to run for governor, joined the anti-Japanese side of the argument. One of the first witnesses, Warren presented extensive views to the Committee; he candidly admitted that California had made no sabotage or espionage investigation of its own and that he had no evidence of sabotage or espionage.[10] In place of evidence Warren offered extensive documentation about Nikkei cultural patterns, ethnic organizations and the opinions of California law enforcement officers; his testimony was illustrated by maps vividly portraying Nikkei land ownership. This was nothing but demagoguery:

> I do not mean to suggest that it should be thought that all of these Japanese who are adjacent to strategic points are knowing parties to some vast conspiracy to destroy our State by sudden and mass sabotage. Undoubtedly, the presence of many of these persons in their present locations is mere coincidence, but it would seem equally beyond doubt that the presence of others is not coinci-

dence. It would seem difficult, for example, to explain the situation in Santa Barbara County by coincidence alone.

In the northern end of that county is Camp Cook where, I am informed, the only armored division on the Pacific coast will be located. The only practical entrance to Camp Cook is on the secondary road through the town of Lompoc. The maps show this entrance is flanked with Japanese property, and it is impossible to move a single man or a piece of equipment in or out of Camp Cook without having it pass under the scrutiny of numerous Japanese. I have been informed that the destruction of the bridges along the road to Camp Cook would effectually bottle up that establishment for an indefinite time, exit to the south being impossible because of extremely high mountains and to the north because of a number of washes with vertical banks 50 to 60 feet deep. There are numerous Japanese close to these bridges.

Immediately north of Camp Cook is a stretch of open beach ideally suited for landing purposes, extending for 15 or 20 miles, on which almost the only inhabitants are Japanese.

Throughout the Santa Maria Valley and including the cities of Santa Maria and Guadalupe every utility, airfield, bridge, telephone, and power line or other facility of importance is flanked by Japanese, and they even surround the oil fields in this area. Only a few miles south, however, is the Santa Ynez Valley, an area equally as productive agriculturally as the Santa Maria Valley and with lands equally available for purchase and lease, but without any strategic installations whatever. There are no Japanese in the Santa Ynez Valley.

Similarly, along the coastal plain of Santa Barbara County from Gaviota south, the entire plain, though narrow, is subject to intensive cultivation. Yet the only Japanese in this area are located immediately adjacent to such widely separated points as the El Capitan oil field, Elwood oil field, Summerland oil field, Santa Barbara Airport, and Santa Barbara Lighthouse and Harbor entrance, and there are no Japanese on the equally attractive lands between these points.

Such a distribution of the Japanese population appears to manifest something more than coincidence. But, in any case, it is certainly evident that the Japanese population of California is, as a whole, ideally situated, with reference to points of strategic importance, to carry into execution a tremendous program of sabotage on a mass scale should any considerable number of them be inclined to do so.[11]

As late as February 8, Warren had advised the state personnel board that it could not bar Nisei employees on the basis that they were children of enemy alien parentage; such action was a violation of constitutionally protected liberties.[12] This earlier stance must have given his performance before the Tolan Committee special force and effect.*

At bottom, Warren's presentation had no probative value, and calm reflection would probably have led many to question whether people planning to blow up dams or bridges would have purchased the surrounding land rather than masking their intentions more thoroughly. But these were not weeks of calm reflection. The overpowering mass of Warren's data—maps and letters and lists from all over California—gripped the imagination and turned the discussion to fruitless argument about whether land was bought before or after a powerline or plant was built; no one focused on whether there was reason to believe that this "evidence" meant anything at all. A similar "analysis" of ethnic Italian land ownership would probably have produced an equally alarming and meaningless pattern, and, as Governor Olson testified to the Committee, there were many Italian language schools which frequently inculcated Fascist values.[13] Of course, no such comparison was made; even Olson's shocked revelation failed to attract the attention of the Committee. The fact that the first witness called by the Tolan Committee was Mayor Rossi of San Francisco and that a great deal of time was devoted to extolling the unquestionable Americanism of the DiMaggio brothers (although their father and mother were aliens), clearly brings home the advantages which numbers, political voices and comparative assimilation provided in 1942's hour of crisis.[14] Helpful, too, was the absence of an organized anti-Italian faction and the patronizing ethnic stereotype of being, as President Roosevelt remarked, nothing but a lot of opera singers.[15]

In late February and early March, the Tolan Committee assumed that Secretary Knox knew what he was talking about and that the President was acting on informed opinion. The views of anti-Japanese witnesses added substance and confirmed what was already known or suspected. Although the Committee was eager to see that the property

---

*It was certainly persuasive with the Western Defense Command. In DeWitt's *Final Report,* much of Warren's presentation to the Tolan Committee was repeated virtually verbatim, without attribution. Warren's arguments, presented after the signing of the Executive Order, became the central justifications presented by DeWitt for issuing the Executive Order (Compare *Final Report,* pp. 9-10, to Tolan Committee, p. 10974). This quick reorganization of history does little to enhance the reputation of the Western Defense Command for candor and independent analysis, although Warren may well have presented his views to DeWitt earlier in February.

of aliens was safeguarded by the government and wanted the Army to be concerned about hardship cases in an evacuation, it returned to Washington unwilling to challenge the need for Executive Order 9066 and the evacuation. Only in reports issued over the next few months did the Committee begin to raise serious questions about the policy underlying exclusion and removal.[16]

There was no civil liberty opposition in Congress to making criminal any violation of the Executive Order. There were, of course, few Nisei of voting age and they had no voice in Congress. No one publicly questioned the military necessity of the action or its intrusion into the freedom of American citizens. Such debate as there was focused on the inclusive wording of the bill.

The language of the bill was loose indeed. Senator Danaher wondered how a person would know what conduct constituted a violation of the act, an essential requirement for a criminal statute.[17] Senator Taft spoke briefly against the bill, although he did not vote against it:

I think this is probably the "sloppiest" criminal law I have ever read or seen anywhere. I certainly think the Senate should not pass it. I do not want to object, because the purpose of it is understood. . . .

[The bill] does not say who shall prescribe the restrictions. It does not say how anyone shall know that the restrictions are applicable to that particular zone. It does not appear that there is any authority given to anyone to prescribe any restriction. . . .

I have no doubt an act of that kind would be enforced in war time. I have no doubt that in peacetime no man could ever be convicted under it, because the court would find that it was so indefinite and so uncertain that it could not be enforced under the Constitution.[18]

The debate was no more pointed or cogent in the House, where there seemed to be some suggestion that the bill applied to aliens rather than citizens.[19] The bill passed without serious objection or debate, and was signed into law by the President on March 21, 1942.[20]

This ratification of Executive Branch actions under Executive Order 9066 was particularly important; another independent branch of government now stood formally behind the exclusion and evacuation, and the Supreme Court gave great weight to the Congressional action in upholding the imposition of a curfew and the evacuation itself.[21]*

---

*The Administration also considered introducing other legislation which would have affected Japanese Americans. For example, Secretary Stimson wrote to the Director of the Bureau of Budget on February 24 about legislation

IMPLEMENTING THE EXECUTIVE ORDER

Executive Order 9066 empowered the Secretary of War or his delegate to designate military areas to which entry of any or all persons would be barred whenever such action was deemed militarily necessary or desirable.[22] On February 20, 1942, Secretary Stimson wrote to General DeWitt delegating authority to implement the Executive Order within the Western Defense Command and setting forth a number of specific requests and instructions: American citizens of Japanese descent, Japanese and German aliens, and any persons suspected of being potentially dangerous were to be excluded from designated military areas; everyone of Italian descent was to be omitted from any plan of exclusion, at least for the time being, because they were "potentially less dangerous, as a whole." DeWitt was to consider redesignating the Justice Department's prohibited areas as military areas, excluding Japanese and German aliens from those areas by February 24 and excluding actually suspicious persons "as soon as practicable;" full advantage was to be taken of voluntary exodus; people were to be removed gradually to avoid unnecessary hardship and dislocation of business and industry "so far as is consistent with national safety;" accommodations were to be made before the exodus, with proper provision for housing, food, transportation and medical care. Finally, evacuation plans were to provide protection of evacuees' property.[23]

Over the next month DeWitt began to implement Stimson's instructions. On March 2, he issued Public Proclamation No. 1, announcing as a matter of military necessity the creation of Military Areas No. 1 and No. 2. Military Area 1 was the western half of Washington, Oregon, and California and the southern half of Arizona; all portions of those states not included in Military Area No. 1 were in Military Area No. 2. A number of zones were established as well; Zones A-1 through A-99 were primarily within Military Area No. 1; Zone B was

---

to amend the Nationality Act of 1940. The proposed amendments would have permitted those who did not speak English to apply for citizenship; at the same time, it would have provided a process for cancelling citizenship for those whose conduct established allegiance to a foreign government. (Memo, Stimson to Smith, Feb. 24, 1942 [CWRIC 2809]). In effect, the legislation would have allowed naturalization of aliens from enemy countries in Europe and the cancellation of citizenship of some persons, particularly ethnic Japanese—a step never before provided, but one which the anti-Japanese faction on the West Coast had pushed in the past and would continue to urge.

the remainder of Military Area No. 1. The Proclamation further noted that in the future people might be excluded from Military Area No. 1 and from Zones A-2 to A-99, and that the designation of Military Area No. 2 did not contemplate restrictions or prohibitions except with respect to the Zones designated. The Proclamation clearly foreshadowed extensive future exclusions. It also provided that any Japanese, German, or Italian alien, and any person (citizen) of Japanese ancestry residing in Military Area No. 1 who changed his residence, was required to file a form with the post office. Finally, the Proclamation expressly continued the prohibited and restricted areas designated by the Attorney General.[24] A curfew regulation requiring all enemy aliens and persons of Japanese ancestry to be in their homes between 8 p.m. and 6 a.m. was added by proclamation on March 24, 1942.[25]

In the press statement accompanying his first public proclamation, DeWitt announced that Japanese—both aliens and citizens—would be evacuated first (suspicious persons were, of course, being apprehended daily); only after the Japanese had been excluded would German and Italian aliens be evacuated. In addition, some German and Italian aliens would be altogether exempt from evacuation.[26]

At this point "voluntary" resettlement outside the designated zones was contemplated; excluded people were free to go where they chose beyond the prohibited areas. "Voluntary" evacuation actually began before Executive Order 9066. Enemy aliens had been excluded from areas designated by the Department of Justice as early as December 1941, and many had moved out of the prohibited areas voluntarily. The Army had an interest in attempting to continue that system; Bendetsen noted that many aliens ordered to move after Pearl Harbor had found new places for themselves, stressing that the Army should not advertise that it would provide food and housing for those it displaced because numerous aliens might rush to take advantage of a free living. He also thought the Army should not be responsible for resettlement, since its job "is to kill Japanese not to save Japanese;" devoting resources to resettlement would make the Army's primary task—that of winning the war—more difficult.[27]

In Seattle, optimism marked the voluntary evacuation program. Local FBI agents informed J. Edgar Hoover in late February that Japanese aliens were prepared to evacuate, and that the Japanese American Citizens League, through the Maryknoll Mission, was attempting to secure facilities and employment for the Seattle Japanese community—both citizens and aliens—in St. Louis, Missouri.[28] The Seattle Chapter of the JACL passed and published a resolution that its members would make every effort to cooperate with the government to facilitate evacuation measures.[29]

More sober minds saw that the voluntary program could not work. As early as February 21, the Tolan Committee was beginning to receive complaints from areas to which the evacuees were moving;[30] fears of sabotage and destruction were spreading inland.[31] Both Earl Warren and Richard Neustadt, the regional director of the Federal Security Agency, saw that only an evacuation and relocation program run by the government could work.[32]

The reaction from the interior was direct and forceful. On February 21, 1942, Governor Carville of Nevada wrote to General DeWitt that permitting unsupervised enemy aliens to go to all parts of the country, particularly to Nevada, would be conducive to sabotage and subversive activities:

> I have made the statement here that enemy aliens would be accepted in the State of Nevada under proper supervision. This would apply to concentration camps as well as to those who might be allowed to farm or do such other things as they could do in helping out. This is the attitude that I am going to maintain in this State and I do not desire that Nevada be made a dumping ground for enemy aliens to be going anywhere they might see fit to travel.[33]

Governor Ralph L. Carr of Colorado was characterized by many contemporaries as the one mountain state governor receptive to relocation of the Issei and Nisei in his state.[34] His radio address of February 28, 1942, gives a vivid impression of how high feelings ran about these unwanted people:

> If those who command the armed forces of our Nation say that it is necessary to remove any persons from the Pacific coast and call upon Colorado to do her part in this war by furnishing temporary quarters for those individuals, we stand ready to carry out that order. If any enemy aliens must be transferred as a war measure, then we of Colorado are big enough and patriotic enough to do our duty. We announce to the world that 1,118,000 red-blooded citizens of this State are able to take care of 3,500 or any number of enemies, if that be the task which is allotted to us. . . .
>
> The people of Colorado are giving their sons, are offering their possessions, are surrendering their rights and privileges to the end that this war may be fought to victory and permanent peace. If it is our duty to receive disloyal persons, we shall welcome the performance of that task.
>
> This statement must not be construed as an invitation, however. Only because the needs of our Nation dictate it, do we even consider such an arrangement. In making the transfers, we can feel assured

that governmental agencies will take every precaution to protect our people, our defense projects, and our property from the same menace which demands their removal from those sections.[35]

The government was also beginning to realize the hardship which the "voluntary" program brought upon evacuees. For instance, Secretary Knox forwarded to the Attorney General a report that the situation of the Japanese in southern California was critical because they were being forced to move with no provision for housing or means of livelihood.[36] McCloy, still in favor of the voluntary program, wrote Harry Hopkins at the White House that "[o]ne of the drawbacks they have is the loss of their property. A number of forced sales are taking place and, until the last minute, they hate to leave their land or their shop."[37]

Inevitably, the "voluntary" evacuation failed. The Army recognized this in Public Proclamation No. 4 on March 27, which prohibited persons of Japanese ancestry in Military Area No. 1 from changing their residence without instruction or approval from the Army. The Western Defense Command explained that the Proclamation was "to ensure an orderly, supervised, and thoroughly controlled evacuation with adequate provision for the protection . . . of the evacuees as well as their property." The evacuees were to be shielded from intense public hostility by this approach.[38] Full government control had arrived.

The change-of-address cards required by Public Proclamation No. 1 show the number of people who voluntarily relocated before March 29. In the three weeks following March 2, only 2,005 reported moving out of Military Area No. 1; since approximately 107,500 persons of Japanese descent lived there, these statistics alone showed that voluntary migration would not achieve evacuation. Public Proclamation No. 4 was issued on March 27 effective at midnight March 29. In the interval the Wartime Civil Control Administration received a rush of approximately 2,500 cards showing moves out of Military Areas No. 1 and 2.[39] The statistics in General DeWitt's *Final Report* are not altogether consistent: they show that from March 12 to June 30, 1942, 10,312 persons reported their "voluntary" intention to move out of Military Area No. 1. But a *net* total[40] of less than half that number— 4,889—left the area as part of the "voluntary" program. Of these voluntary migrants, 1,963 went to Colorado; 1,519 to Utah; 305 to Idaho; 208 to eastern Washington; 115 to eastern Oregon; and the remainder to other states.[41] The *Final Report* surmises that this net total "probably accounts for 90 percent of the total number of Japanese . . . who voluntarily left the West Coast area for inland points."[42]

While the voluntary program was failing, government officials and others began to propose programs designed for the evacuees. On February 20, 1942, Carey McWilliams, then a California state official and later editor of *The Nation*, sent a telegram to Biddle recommending that the President establish an Alien Control Authority run by representatives of federal agencies. The agency would register, license, settle, maintain and reemploy the evacuees, and conserve alien property. Ennis forwarded the suggestion to McCloy, who thought it had merit.[43] During the first week of March 1942, the Commissioner of Indian Affairs in the Interior Department, John Collier, proposed what he considered to be a constructive program for the evacuees, including useful work, education, health care and other services to be provided to them, as well as a plan for rehabilitation after the war. Collier said that the Department of the Interior would be interested in working on such a program if it were a meaningful one.[44] The Tolan Committee filed an interim report which showed great prescience about future problems and considerable concern for the fate of the evacuees.[45]

Whatever their individual merit, these proposals reflect genuinely sympathetic interest in the evacuees. Unfortunately, much of the thought and care that went into these programs was lost in the rush to evacuate and relocate.

MANDATORY EVACUATION

Once the decision was made that evacuation was no longer voluntary, a plan for compulsory evacuation was needed.* The core of this plan

---

*There is a continuing controversy over whether the Census Bureau breached the confidentiality of census information in order to aid other government agencies in locating ethnic Japanese. John Toland, in his recent book *Infamy: Pearl Harbor and Its Aftermath* (Garden City, NY: Doubleday & Co., Inc., 1982), pp. 269, 284–85, recounts an episode on November 26, 1941, in which Henry Field, an anthropologist working as an aide to President Roosevelt, was called to the office of Grace Tully, Roosevelt's secretary:

> She told Field that the President was ordering him to produce, in the shortest time possible, the full names and addresses of each American-born and foreign-born Japanese listed by locality within each state. Field

was that evacuation and relocation could not be accomplished simultaneously.[46] Therefore, sites had to be found for both temporary quarters and longer-term settlement.

During the period of the voluntary evacuation program, the Army had begun a search for appropriate camp facilities, both temporary and permanent.[47] Regarding the criteria for selection of assembly centers, General DeWitt later wrote:

> Assembly Center site selection was a task of relative simplicity. As time was of the essence, it will be apparent that the choice was limited by four rather fundamental requirements which virtually pointed out the selections ultimately made. First, it was necessary to find places with some adaptable pre-existing facilities suitable for the establishment of shelter, and the many needed

---

was completely bewildered and didn't know how to begin. She explained it was to be done by using the 1930 and 1940 censuses.

Within one week, Field is said to have delivered to Grace Tully the names and addresses of all the ethnic Japanese in the United States.

Calvert Dedrick, a Census Bureau employee who became a consultant to the Western Defense Command in late February 1942, testified to the Commission that to his knowledge the Census Bureau provided the Western Defense Command with detailed tabulations of the location of the ethnic Japanese population but did not provide the names or addresses of individuals. (Testimony, Dedrick, Washington, DC, Nov. 3, 1981, pp. 170–90.) The Census Bureau undertook an internal investigation after the publication of Toland's book and concluded that the account to Toland was not accurate and that names and addresses had not been released. (Bureau of the Census "Statement on Census Bureau Actions at the Outset of World War II as Reported in *Infamy: Pearl Harbor and Its Aftermath,* by John Toland," Oct. 1982 [CWRIC 2929–34].) A brief statement by the Census Bureau of its activities in connection with the evacuation, written in 1946, also states that names and individual identifications were not provided to the Western Defense Command. (Roger Daniels, "The Bureau of the Census and the Relocation of the Japanese Americans: A Note and a Document," *Amerasia Journal,* vol. 9, no. 1, 1982, pp. 101–05.) In his interview for the Earl Warren Oral History Project, Tom Clark mentioned the Census Bureau data in passing:

> The Census Bureau moved out its raw files. . . .They would lay out on tables various city blocks where the Japanese lived and they would tell me how many were living in each block. (Earl Warren Oral History Project, *Japanese American Relocation Reviewed,* vol. 1, Interview of Tom C. Clark, p. 9.)

There is no direct evidence or testimony to the effect that the Western Defense Command was in possession of the names and addresses of individual ethnic Japanese, as collected by the Census Bureau, at the time that mandatory evacuation was carried out, but Field's story raises questions.

community services. Second, power, light, and water had to be within immediate availability as there was no time for a long pre-development period. Third, the distance from the Center of the main elements of evacuee population served had to be short, the connecting road and rail net good, and the potential capacity sufficient to accept the adjacent evacuee group. Finally, it was essential that there be some area within the enclosure for recreation and allied activities as the necessary confinement would otherwise have been completely demoralizing. The sudden expansion of our military and naval establishments further limited the choice.[48]

Site selection did not proceed perfectly smoothly, however. After Owens Valley in California was selected as a center, Congressman Ford of California, who had been prominent in urging the evacuation, objected. In a conversation with Gullion, DeWitt discussed Ford's objection: "Well, they are going to Owens Valley, and that's all. I don't care anything about the howl of these Congressmen or anybody else."[49] The attitude was typical of DeWitt who, given authority, did not hesitate to use it; but Ford continued to press his position, meeting with Justice Department officials and planning to meet with Bendetsen and possibly others.[50] He was not successful, since Stimson stood behind DeWitt, but it gave fair warning that many interested politicians who had pushed to establish the evacuation program and exclude the Nikkei from the West Coast retained a vital interest. As the months went by the War Department in Washington was to learn what DeWitt may have known all along: exclusion fulfilled the program of powerful organized interests in California, and no part of it would be given up without a fight.

In March work began at the first two permanent relocation centers, Manzanar in the Owens River Valley and the Northern Colorado Indian Reservation in Arizona; the sites served as both assembly and relocation centers.[51] The other assembly centers were selected with dispatch. The *Final Report* explains:

> After an intensive survey the selections were made. Except at Portland, Oregon, Pinedale and Sacramento, California and Mayer, Arizona, large fairgrounds or racetracks were selected. As the Arizona requirements were small, an abandoned Civilian Conservation Corps camp at Mayer was employed. In Portland the Pacific International Live Stock Exposition facilities were adapted to the purpose. At Pinedale the place chosen made use of the facilities remaining on a former mill site where mill employees had previously resided. At Sacramento an area was employed where a migrant camp had once operated and advantage was taken of nearby utilities.[52]

A major step toward systematizing evacuation at this time was the establishment of the War Relocation Authority (WRA), a civilian agency, to supervise the evacuees after they left Army assembly centers. The War Department was eager to be out of the resettlement business, and discussed with the Attorney General and the Budget Bureau the mechanism for setting up a permanent organization to take over the job. Milton Eisenhower, a candidate fully acceptable to the War Department, was chosen to head the agency; McCloy took him to San Francisco to meet DeWitt before the Executive Order setting up the WRA was promulgated.[53] By March 17, plans for the independent authority responsible for the Japanese Americans were completed; the next day Roosevelt signed Executive Order 9102 to establish the War Relocation Authority,[54] appointed Eisenhower Director,[55] and allocated $5,500,000 for the WRA.[56]

WRA was established "to provide for the removal from designated areas of persons whose removal is necessary in the interest of national security. . . ." The Director was given wide discretion; the Executive Order did not expressly provide for relocation camps, and it gave the Director authority to "[p]rovide, insofar as feasible and desirable, for the employment of such persons at useful work in industry, commerce, agriculture, on public projects, prescribe the terms and conditions of such public employment, and safeguard the public interest in the private employment of such persons."[57] In short, the WRA's job would be to take over the supervision of the evacuees from the Army's assembly centers. With that final destination put in the hands of a civilian agency, the Army was ready to push firmly ahead with its part of the evacuation.

Once Public Proclamation No. 4 took effect on March 29, and persons of Japanese ancestry were barred from moving out of Military Area No. 1, systematic mandatory evacuation began. Both the evacuation and the operation of the assembly centers were under the authority of the Army, by agreement with the War Relocation Authority. Evacuation was under military supervision. The centers themselves were operated by the Wartime Civil Control Administration (WCCA), the civilian branch of the Western Defense Command. Ninety-nine geographic exclusion areas were established in Military Area No. 1; an additional nine were specified later. The California portion of Military Area No. 2 was declared a prohibited area in June.[58] Areas regarded as militarily sensitive were evacuated first. The order of evacuation was kept secret "so that the information would not reach any affected person within the area." Once announced, each evacuation plan gave seven days from the date of posting the order until the movement of evacuees.[59]

The small-scale evacuation of Terminal Island was a precursor of the mass evacuation of the West Coast and provides a vivid impression of the hardship brought by evacuation. Roughly six miles long and a half-mile wide, Terminal Island marks the boundaries of Los Angeles Harbor and the Cerritos Channel. Lying directly across the harbor from San Pedro, the island was reached in 1941 by ferry or a small drawbridge.

The Japanese community on the island was isolated, primarily occupied in fishing and canning. A half-dozen canneries, each with its own employee housing, were located on the island.[60] In 1942 the Japanese population of Terminal Island was approximately 3,500, of whom half were American-born.[61] Most of the businesses which served the island were owned or operated by Issei or Nisei. The island economy supported restaurants, groceries, barbershops, beauty shops and poolhalls in addition to three physicians and two dentists.[62]

On February 10, 1942, the Department of Justice posted a warning that all Japanese aliens had to leave the island by the following Monday. The next day, a Presidential order placed Terminal Island under the jurisdiction of the Navy. By the 15th, Secretary of the Navy Knox had directed that the Terminal Island residents be notified that their dwellings would be condemned, effective in about 30 days.[63] Even this pace was too slow: on February 25 the Navy informed the Terminal Islanders that they had 48 hours to leave the island. Many were unprepared for such a precipitous move.

The FBI had previously removed individuals who were considered dangerous aliens on December 7, 1941, and followed this by "daily dawn raids . . . removing several hundred more aliens."[64] As a consequence, the heads of many families were gone and mainly older women and minor children were left.[65] With the new edict, these women and children, who were unaccustomed to handling business transactions, were forced to make quick financial decisions. With little time or experience, there was no opportunity to effect a reasonable disposition.

Dr. Yoshihiko Fujikawa, a resident of Terminal Island, described the scene prior to evacuation:

> It was during these 48 hours that I witnessed unscrupulous vultures in the form of human beings taking advantage of bewildered housewives whose husbands had been rounded up by the F.B.I. within 48 hours after Pearl Harbor. They were offered pittances

for practically new furniture and appliances: refrigerators, radio consoles, etc., as well as cars, and many were falling prey to these people.[66]

The day after evacuation, Terminal Island was littered with abandoned household goods and equipment.[67] Henry Murakami's loss was typical. He had become a fisherman after graduating from high school. After gaining experience he leased a boat from Van Camp Seafood Company and went out on his own, saving money to increase and to improve his equipment:

> By the time World War II had started, I was now the owner of 3 sets of purse seine nets. These nets were hard to get and the approximate costs of these nets in 1941 were:
>
> | | |
> |---|---:|
> | set of nets for Tuna | $10,000 |
> | set of nets for Mackerel | $7,500 |
> | set of nets for Sardines | $5,000 |
>
> When Pearl Harbor was attacked we were stopped from going out to fish and told to remain in our fishing camp.[68]

In early February, along with every alien male on Terminal Island who held a fisherman's license, Murakami was arrested and sent to Bismarck, North Dakota. His equipment lay abandoned, accessible for the taking.

The first exclusion order under the Army program was issued for Bainbridge Island near Seattle in Puget Sound, an area the Navy regarded as highly sensitive. It is illustrative of the Army's evacuation process. The order was issued on March 24, 1942, for an evacuation a week later[69] that was carried out under the direction of Bendetsen, who had been promoted to colonel and put in charge of the evacuation by DeWitt as head of the WCCA, which operated in conjunction with other federal agencies.[70]

Tom G. Rathbone, field supervisor for the U.S. Employment Service, filed a report after the Bainbridge Island evacuation, with suggestions for improvement which give a clear picture of the government's approach. A meeting to outline evacuation procedures was called on March 23; representatives of a number of federal agencies were present. After setting up offices on the island, the government group "reported to Center at 8:00 a.m. . . . for the purpose of conducting a complete registration of the forty-five families of persons of Japanese ancestry who were residents of the Island." Rathbone suggested that more complete instructions from Army authorities would clarify many problems, including what articles could be taken, climate at the assembly centers and timing of evacuation. He also suggested better planning so that the evacuees would not be required to return repeatedly to the center: "such planning would have to contemplate the ability to answer the type of question [sic] which occur and the ability to give accurate and definite information which would enable the evacuee to close out his business and be prepared to report at the designated point with necessary baggage, etc." Further, Rathbone noted that disposition of evacuees' property following relocation caused the most serious hardship and prompted the most questions. He reported:

> We received tentative information late Friday afternoon to the effect that it was presumed that the Government would pay the transportation costs of such personal belongings and equipment to the point of relocation upon proper notice. When this word was given to the evacuees, many complained bitterly because they had not been given such information prior to that time and had, therefore, sold, at considerable loss, many such properties which they would have retained had they known that it would be shipped to them upon relocation. Saturday morning we receive additional word through the Federal Reserve Bank that the question had not been answered and that probably no such transportation costs would be paid. Between the time on Friday afternoon and Saturday morning some Japanese had arranged to repossess belongings which they had already sold and were in a greater turmoil than ever upon getting the latter information. To my knowledge, there still is no answer to this question, but it should be definitely decided before the next evacuation is attempted.[71]

After the Bainbridge evacuation, exclusion orders were issued for each of the other 98 exclusion areas in Military Area No. 1 and areas "were evacuated in the order indicated by the Civilian Exclusion Order number with but a few exceptions."[72] (A typical order, with map and instructions attached, appears after page 111.)

Later evacuations were better organized, but difficulties persisted. The handling of evacuee property presented a major problem for the government; one to which considerable, only partially successful effort was addressed. Congressman Tolan had sent a telegram to Attorney General Biddle on February 28, first urging the appointment of an Alien Property Custodian at the same time as an evacuation order was issued and the appointment of a coordinator for other enemy alien problems; Tolan did not address the problems of property protection or relocation assistance for citizens.[73] When McCloy informed Harry Hopkins of evacuees' property problems, he asked that a property custodian be appointed.[74] Hopkins replied that aliens' property could already be protected through the Treasury Department; as to the property of citizens, if McCloy would draw up documents for the President to sign, Hopkins thought a custodian for citizens' property was a good idea.[75] The War Department drew up the papers,[76] but the custodial plan did not go through; instead the Treasury Department directed the Federal Reserve Board to assist evacuees in disposing of their property—"not a custodianship matter at all but a sort of free banking service."[77] For years to come, problems of property disposal and protection continued to haunt the evacuees and the federal government.

A minor but illuminating problem occurred when the Navy language school, which had Japanese personnel, realized it would have to relocate from Monterey to a place inland. The Navy was not pleased, but DeWitt prevailed once more, showing that he would enforce his authority to the letter without regard to the consequences for other government agencies or services.[78] There were no cases that merited making exceptions.

On May 23, 1942, Bendetsen spoke to the Commonwealth Club of San Francisco and reported that evacuation would be nearly completed by the end of May.[79] By June 6, all Japanese Americans had been evacuated from Military Area No. 1 to the assembly centers.[80] On June 8, 1942, DeWitt issued Public Proclamation No. 7, which provided "should there be any areas remaining in Military Area No. 1 from which Japanese have not been excluded, the exclusion of all Japanese from these areas is provided for in this proclamation."[81] By that proclamation, any ethnic Japanese remaining in the area and not exempt were ordered to report in person to the nearest assembly center.

In early June, the next stage of the evacuation occurred when, by Public Proclamation No. 6, DeWitt ordered the exclusion of Japanese aliens and American citizens of Japanese ancestry from the California portion of Military Area No. 2 on the grounds of military necessity.[82] Earlier the voluntary evacuees had been encouraged to move inland with no suggestion that Military Area No. 2 in California or any other state would be cleared of ethnic Japanese.[83] Indeed, in late April, Bendetsen was still resisting the politicians and agricultural interests who were pushing for expansion of the exclusion zone beyond Military Area No. 1.[84] The exclusion from the California portion of Military Area No. 2 appears to have been decided without any additional evidence of threat or danger in the area. The *Final Report* lamely explains this change:

> Military Area No. 2 in California was evacuated because (1) geographically and strategically the eastern boundary of the State of California approximates the easterly limit of Military Area No. 1 in Washington and Oregon . . . and because (2) the natural forests

FIGURE A: An Exclusion Order

Headquarters
Western Defense Command
and Fourth Army
Presidio of San Francisco, California
April 30, 1942

Civilian Exclusion Order No. 27

1. Pursuant to the provisions of Public Proclamations Nos. 1 and 2, this Headquarters, dated March 2, 1942, and March 16, 1942, respectively, it is hereby ordered that from and after 12 o'clock noon, P.W.T., of Thursday, May 7, 1942, all persons of Japanese ancestry, both alien and non-alien, be excluded from that portion of Military Area No. 1 described as follows:

All of that portion of the County of Alameda, State of California, within that boundary beginning at the point at which the southerly limits of the City of Berkeley meet San Francisco Bay; thence easterly and following the southerly limits of said city to College Avenue; thence southerly on College Avenue to Broadway; thence southerly on Broadway to the southerly limits of the City of Oakland; thence following the limits of said city westerly and northerly, and following the shoreline of San Francisco Bay to the point of beginning.

2. A responsible member of each family, and each individual living alone, in the above described area will report between the hours of 8:00 A. M. and 5:00 P. M., Friday, May 1, 1942, or during the same hours on Saturday, May 2, 1942, to the Civil Control Station located at:

530 Eighteenth Street
Oakland, California.

3. Any person subject to this order who fails to comply with any of its provisions or with the provisions of published instructions pertaining hereto or who is found in the above area after 12 o'clock noon, P.W.T., of Thursday, May 7, 1942, will be liable to the criminal penalties provided by Public Law No. 503, 77th Congress, approved March 21, 1942 entitled "An Act to Provide a Penalty for Violation of Restrictions or Orders with Respect to Persons Entering, Remaining in, Leaving, or Committing any Act in Military Areas or Zones," and alien Japanese will be subject to immediate apprehension and internment.

4. All persons within the bounds of an established Assembly Center pursuant to instructions from this Headquarters are excepted from the provisions of this order while those persons are in such Assembly Center.

J. L. DEWITT
Lieutenant General, U. S. Army
Commanding

Source: J. L. DeWitt, *Final Report: Japanese Evacuation from the West Coast, 1942* (1943), p. 97.

FIGURE B: Map of a Prohibited Area

PROHIBITED AREA
EXCLUSION ORDER NO. 27
Western Defense Command and Fourth Army

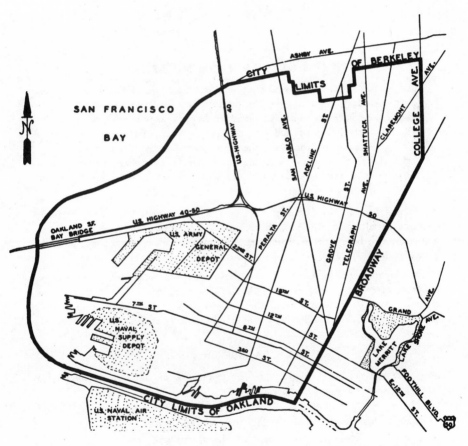

C. E. Order 27

This Map is prepared for the convenience of the public; see the Civilian Exclusion Order for the full and correct description.

Source: J. L. DeWitt, *Final Report: Japanese Evacuation from the West Coast, 1942* (1943), p. 98.

FIGURE C: Instructions to Evacuees

WESTERN DEFENSE COMMAND AND FOURTH ARMY
WARTIME CIVIL CONTROL ADMINISTRATION
Presidio of San Francisco, California

INSTRUCTIONS

TO ALL PERSONS OF

JAPANESE

ANCESTRY

LIVING IN THE FOLLOWING AREA:

All of that portion of the County of Alameda, State of California, within that boundary beginning at the point at which the southerly limits of the City of Berkeley meet San Francisco Bay; thence easterly and following the southerly limits of said city to College Avenue; thence southerly on College Avenue to Broadway; thence southerly on Broadway to the southerly limits of the City of Oakland; thence following the limits of said city westerly and northerly, and following the shoreline of San Francisco Bay to the point of beginning.

Pursuant to the provisions of Civilian Exclusion Order No. 27, this Headquarters, dated April 30, 1942, all persons of Japanese ancestry, both alien and non-alien, will be evacuated from the above area by 12 o'clock noon, P.W.T., Thursday May 7, 1942.

No Japanese person living in the above area will be permitted to change residence after 12 o'clock noon, P.W.T., Thursday, April 30, 1942, without obtaining special permission from the representative of the Commanding General, Northern California Sector, at the Civil Control Station located at:

530 Eighteenth Street,
Oakland, California.

Such permits will only be granted for the purpose of uniting members of a family, or in cases of grave emergency.

The Civil Control Station is equipped to assist the Japanese population affected by this evacuation in the following ways:

1. Give advice and instructions on the evacuation.

2. Provide services with respect to the management, leasing, sale, storage or other disposition of most kinds of property, such as real estate, business and professional equipment, household goods, boats, automobiles and livestock.

3. Provide temporary residence elsewhere for all Japanese in family groups.

4. Transport persons and a limited amount of clothing and equipment to their new residence.

THE FOLLOWING INSTRUCTIONS MUST BE OBSERVED:

1. A responsible member of each family, preferably the head of the family, or the person in whose name most of the property is held, and each individual living alone, will report to the Civil Control Station to receive further instructions. This must be done between 8:00 A. M. and 5:00 P. M. on Friday, May 1, 1942, or between 8:00 A. M. and 5:00 P. M. on Saturday, May 2, 1942.

2. Evacuees must carry with them on departure for the Assembly Center, the following property:

    (a) Bedding and linens (no mattress) for each member of the family;

    (b) Toilet articles for each member of the family;

    (c) Extra clothing for each member of the family;

    (d) Sufficient knives, forks, spoons, plates, bowls and cups for each member of the family;

    (e) Essential personal effects for each member of the family.

All items carried will be securely packaged, tied and plainly marked with the name of the owner and numbered in accordance with instructions obtained at the Civil Control Station. The size and number of packages is limited to that which can be carried by the individual or family group.

3. No pets of any kind will be permitted.

4. No personal items and no household goods will be shipped to the Assembly Center.

5. The United States Government through its agencies will provide for the storage at the sole risk of the owner of the more substantial household items, such as iceboxes, washing machines, pianos and other heavy furniture. Cooking utensils and other small items will be accepted for storage if crated, packed and plainly marked with the name and address of the owner. Only one name and address will be used by a given family.

6. Each family, and individual living alone will be furnished transportation to the Assembly Center or will be authorized to travel by private automobile in a supervised group. All instructions pertaining to the movement will be obtained at the Civil Control Station.

Go to the Civil Control Station between the hours of 8:00 A. M. and 5:00 P. M., Friday, May 1, 1942, or between the hours of 8:00 A. M. and 5:00 P. M., Saturday, May 2, 1942, to receive further instructions.

J. L. DeWitt
Lieutenant General, U. S. Army
Commanding

April 30, 1942

See Civilian Exclusion Order No. 27.

Source: J. L. DeWitt, *Final Report: Japanese Evacuation from the West Coast, 1942* (1943), pp. 99–100.

and mountain barriers, from which it was determined to exclude all Japanese, lie in Military Area No. 2 in California, although these lie in Military Area No. 1 of Washington and Oregon.[85]

It is hard to believe that this is a candid analysis of the decision. The eastern boundary of California lies more than 100 miles east of Military Area No. 1 at the Oregon border. If there had been a general decision to exclude the ethnic Japanese from forests and mountains, why had they been allowed to resettle in Military Area No. 2? Morton Grodzins carefully analyzed this second exclusion decision and made a persuasive case that it was another example of the Western Defense Command adopting an utterly unsound military rationale to carry out the program of politicians, agriculturalists and agitators in eastern California who were intent on removing all ethnic Japanese from the state.[86]

Whatever the motivation, there were two obvious results: the "voluntary" evacuees who had resettled in eastern California were uprooted a second time, and, by August 18, 1942, everyone of Japanese descent had been expelled from the entire state of California except for those under guard at the Tule Lake and Manzanar camps and a small handful under constant supervision in hospitals and prisons.[87] California's anti-Japanese faction had triumphed.

PUBLIC OPINION AND PROTEST

From March 28 to April 7, as the program evolved from voluntary to mandatory evacuation, the Office of Facts and Figures in the Office for Emergency Management polled public opinion about aliens in the population. Germans were considered the most dangerous alien group in the United States by 46 percent of those interviewed; the Japanese, by 35 percent. There was virtual consensus that the government had done the right thing in moving Japanese aliens away from the coast; 59 percent of the interviewees also favored moving American citizens of Japanese ancestry. The answers reflected clear educational and geographic differences. Relatively uneducated respondents were more likely to consider the Japanese the most dangerous alien group, and they were also disposed to advocate harsher treatment of the Japanese who were moved away from the coast. The east considered the Germans most dangerous, the west the Japanese. People in the south, in particular, were prone to treat Japanese harshly. The Pacific Coast public led all other regions in believing the evacuees should be paid less than prevailing wages.[88]

Despite the strong endorsement of public opinion, protest against the mass evacuation continued through a small but steady stream of letters and public statements and through litigation which contested the enforcement of the curfew and exclusion orders.

Protest was most common among church figures and academics. The Federal Council of Churches and the Home Missions Council had already made known their views that the evacuation of American citizens of Japanese ancestry was wasting a national resource.[89] Mrs. Roosevelt sent along to McCloy the objections of Virginia Swanson, a Baptist missionary.[90] Eric C. Bellquist, a professor of political science at Berkeley, presented to the Tolan Committee a lengthy and remarkably well-informed analysis which forcefully dissented from the policy of exclusion and evacuation.[91] A few days later, Monroe Deutsch, Provost of the University of California, sent a telegram to Justice Felix Frankfurter protesting evacuation of people, including the Japanese, identified only as members of a group. To Deutsch this struck "an unprecedented blow at all our American principles."[92] He did not receive any support in that quarter; an exchange between Frankfurter and McCloy concluded with the Justice assuring the Assistant Secretary that he was handling a delicate matter with both wisdom and appropriate hard-headedness.[93]

The second stream of protest came through court challenges to the curfew and evacuation. Although the Japanese American Citizens League firmly opposed test litigation,[94] several individuals either brought lawsuits challenging the government's actions or failed to obey requirements, thereby challenging the legality of curfew and evacuation.

On April 13, 1942, Mary Ventura, an American citizen of Japanese ancestry married to a Filipino, filed a habeas corpus petition in the federal district court in the State of Washington to challenge the curfew and other restrictions imposed on her. The court denied the petition on the ground that, because Mrs. Ventura had not violated the curfew and was not in custody, she was not entitled to the remedy of habeas corpus which provides release from custody. But, in addition, the judge discussed the reasons why he would be likely to deny her petition on the merits:

> The question here should be viewed with common sense consideration of the situation that confronts this nation now—that confronts this coast today. These are critical days. To strain some technical right of petitioning wife to defeat the military needs in

this vital area during this extraordinary time could mean perhaps that the "constitution, laws, institutions" of this country to which her petition alleges she is "loyal and devoted" would be for a time destroyed here on Puget Sound by an invading army. . . .

The petitioners allege that the wife "has no dual citizenship," that she is in no "manner a citizen or subject of the Empire of Japan." But how many in this court room doubt that in Tokyo they consider all of Japanese ancestry though born in the United States to be citizens or subjects of the Japanese Imperial Government? How many here believe that if our enemies should manage to send a suicide squadron of parachutists to Puget Sound that the Enemy High Command would not hope for assistance from many such American-born Japanese?

I do not believe the Constitution of the United States is so unfitted for survival that it unyieldingly prevents the President and the Military, pursuant to law enacted by the Congress, from restricting the movement of civilians such as petitioner, regardless of how actually loyal they perhaps may be, in critical military areas desperately essential for national defense.

Aside from any rights involved it seems to me that if petitioner is as loyal and devoted as her petition avers she would be glad to conform to the precautions which Congress, the President, the armed forces, deem requisite to preserve the Constitution, laws and institutions for her and all Americans, born here or naturalized.[95]

Habeas petitions should have been a particularly attractive vehicle for testing the military orders, since the Nisei would not have to come into court under arrest in violation of the law as written, but even the great writ was no help in the crisis of 1942; obviously the War Department would not be put through a critical review of its decision by this judge.[96]

The Nisei received no greater measure of relief in the criminal test cases. Minoru Yasui was a member of the Oregon bar and reserve officer in the Army who was working for the Consulate General of Japan in Chicago at the time of Pearl Harbor. He immediately resigned his consular position and sought to go on active duty with the Army, which would not accept him. In March he decided to violate the curfew regulations in order to test their constitutionality and was indicted by a grand jury. Yasui moved to dismiss the indictment on the ground that the curfew order was unconstitutional as applied to American citizens. The district judge agreed, but found that Yasui by his work for the consulate had renounced his citizenship, and proceeded to convict him as an alien of violating the curfew order.[97] Although satisfied with the result, the Justice Department did not support this outlandish theory.

Gordon Hirabayashi, an American-born university student in Seattle who was a Quaker and conscientious objector to military service, declined to report to the WCCA evacuation center. Hirabayashi was arrested for violating the curfew and failing to report and was convicted on May 16, 1942.[98] His case and Yasui's were decided by the Supreme Court on June 21, 1943; the Court restored Yasui's citizenship, but upheld the convictions for violation of the curfew regulations.[99]

Other arrests resulted in convictions and sentences or in guilty pleas and suspended sentences conditional upon compliance with the curfew or evacuation orders.[100] Perhaps the clearest irony in the court challenges was that of Lincoln Kanai, a citizen who failed to leave San Francisco after the evacuation proclamation. While released following his arrest Kanai left the area, then presented a habeas petition to the federal district court in Wisconsin. The judge held that he would not substitute his judgment for that of the generals regarding the proper extent of military areas. Kanai was brought back to San Francisco to stand trial; he pled guilty, and on August 27, 1942, was sentenced to six months' imprisonment.[101]

This was an extreme example of General DeWitt's unbending policy of making no exceptions to strict enforcement of the exclusion and evacuation in order to help the government's legal posture. Apart from his personal inclinations, DeWitt had been advised that "If we should consent to the exemption in [one] particular case, we have opened up the whole subject of the evacuation of citizen Japanese. We would be extremely unfair to those who have cooperated by voluntary movement and to those in similar circumstances, who have been evacuated to Santa Anita and Manzanar." He responded, "*No exemptions of Japanese.*"[102]

It was not until later in 1943, after the Supreme Court decisions in *Hirabayashi* and *Yasui*, that district courts critically examined claims of military necessity as the basis for exclusion. Two orders individually excluding Maximilian Ebel and Olga Schueller, naturalized American citizens of German descent, from the Eastern Defense Command were struck down by the courts.[103] In these cases the military was put to its proof as to both the military importance of the eastern seaboard and the threat posed by the excluded person. The evidence about the East Coast is probably on a par with what could have been produced on the West Coast:

The evidence introduced through officers of Military Intelligence showed that the Eastern Military Area since the beginning of hostilities and up to the present date is known as a "sensitive area" (an area in which are located large concentrations of war-time installations or activities and also an area in which observation can be made and information valuable to the enemy can readily be obtained); that the area is open to offensive action and maneuvers; that it is exposed to direct attack by air and because of the tremendous amount of war installations and utilities exposed to sabotage. The evidence further showed that the area covering less than 14% of the land area of the United States includes about 40% of the population and over 60% of all plants manufacturing tools. There is also contained in this area a major portion of war-time installations and naval activities. It is the seat of the federal government and installations of management over communications. There are vast freight movements of supplies and equipment passing over its transportation lines; ship movements of men and supplies with their convoys and naval activities are easily discernible in this area.[104]

The government's evidence was clearly focused on the persons to be excluded as it had never been in the Nisei cases. Ebel, for instance, had served in the German Army in World War I, was president of the Boston branch of the Kyffhaeuser Bund from at least 1939 to January 1942, when the group was disbanded. "This Bund was one of the foremost international German societies in America in its encouragement of the military spirit and keeping alive the love of Germany in the hearts of former German soldiers and civilians."[105]

The courts did not in any way dispute the legal standards established in *Hirabayashi*. Nevertheless, in testing whether, under the war powers, there was military danger on the East Coast in 1943 sufficient to justify depriving citizens of the right to live and conduct business where they chose, the courts concluded that they had to determine whether the degree of restriction bore a reasonable relation to the degree of danger. In both cases the restriction was found excessive and the exclusion order struck down.

Surely an impartial judge would have reached the same conclusion on the West Coast in 1942 had the military been put to its proof against Nisei with unquestionable records of loyalty to the United States. How could a conscientious objector like Hirabayashi seriously be considered a threat to the security of Seattle? But in the spring of 1942 on the West Coast, not even the courts of the United States were places of calm and dispassionate justice.

4

Economic Loss

Exclusion from the West Coast imposed very substantial economic losses on the Nikkei. The complete picture of those losses is a mosaic of thousands of personal histories of individual families. Owners and operators of farms and businesses either sold their income-producing assets under distress-sale circumstances on very short notice or attempted, with or without government help, to place their property in the custody of people remaining on the Coast. The effectiveness of these measures varied greatly in protecting evacuees' economic interests. Homes had to be sold or left without the personal attention that owners would devote to them. Businesses lost their good will, their reputation, their customers. Professionals had their careers disrupted. Not only did many suffer major losses during evacuation, but their economic circumstances deteriorated further while they were in camp. The years of exclusion were frequently punctuated by financial troubles: trying to look after property without being on the scene when difficulties arose; lacking a source of income to meet tax, mortgage and insurance payments. Goods were lost or stolen. Income and earning capacity were reduced to almost nothing during the long detention in relocation centers, and after the war life had to be started anew on meager resources. War disrupted the economic well-being of thousands of Americans, but the distinct situation of the Nikkei—unable to rely on family or, often, on close friends to tend their affairs—involved demonstrably greater hardship, anxiety and loss than other Americans suffered. Forty years after the events, a detailed reckoning of Nikkei losses and suffering is difficult, as the postwar effort to calculate these losses and to make partial recompense for them shows.

CALCULATING AND COMPENSATING FOR LOSS

In 1948 Congress passed the Japanese-American Evacuation Claims Act[1] which gave persons of Japanese ancestry the right to claim from the government "damage to or loss of real or personal property," not compensated by insurance, which occurred as "a reasonable and natural consequence of the evacuation or exclusion."[2] The Act was amended over the years but remained the central vehicle by which the federal government attempted to compensate for the economic losses due to exclusion and evacuation. There were many kinds of injury the Evacuation Claims Act made no attempt to compensate: the stigma placed on people who fell under the evacuation and relocation orders; the deprivation of liberty suffered during detention in the assembly and relocation centers; the psychological impact of evacuation and relocation; the loss of earnings or profits; physical injury or death during detention; and losses from resettlement outside the camps. The legislative history reflects that such claims were considered too speculative.[3]

Twenty-six thousand, five hundred sixty-eight claims totaling $148 million were filed under the Act; the total amount distributed by the government was approximately $37 million.[4] It is difficult to estimate the extent of property losses which were not fully compensated under the Evacuation Claims Act, for the evidence is suggestive rather than comprehensive or complete.

First, by the time the claims were adjudicated, most of the essential financial records from the time of the evacuation were no longer available. When the Evacuation Claims Act was set in motion in 1948, the Department of Justice discovered that the Internal Revenue Service had already destroyed most of the 1939 to 1942 income tax returns of evacuees—the most comprehensive set of federal financial records.[5] Nor was the situation better among the evacuees themselves. The Japanese American Citizens League emphasized this problem in testifying in favor of amending the Evacuation Claims Act in 1954:

> It was the exception and not the rule when minute and detailed records and documents were retained. In the stress and tension

of 1942, when one could only take to camp what could be hand carried, when one did not know how long he would be detained or whether he would ever be allowed to return, it would be unreasonable to expect that emotion-charged men and women would have chosen to pack books and records instead of the food, the medicines, and the clothing which they took with them to war relocation centers.

The whole community was moved, and so books and records could not be left with neighbors or even with friends.

And, today 12 years later, with all the great changes that have taken place particularly on the west coast, it is almost impossible to secure even remotely accurate appraisals and evaluations of the homes, the businesses, the farms and the properties of more than a decade ago, a decade of war and upheaval.

To add further difficulties, under Federal and State codes, most of the Government records of 1942—which might have been of value as cross-references—have been destroyed pursuant to law.[6]

Thus the best evidence of economic losses no longer existed by 1954. The passage of another twenty-eight years, coupled with the deaths of many Issei and witnesses, has only added to the difficulty.

One study of property and income losses due to evacuation was done shortly after World War II, Broom and Riemer's *Removal and Return*. It focused on Los Angeles and the authors estimated that each evacuated adult had a median property loss of $1,000 and an income loss of $2,500[7]—which would have resulted in approximately $77 million in claims payments under the Evacuation Claims Act, rather than the approximately $37 million actually paid. The Broom and Riemer estimates are conservative. Replacement costs of 1941 were used to estimate personal property losses. Estimates of real property losses were not presented separately and it is not clear how they were calculated. In addition, Broom and Riemer did not distinguish between income losses imputable to property and that part of income imputable to labor and management components.[8] In 1954 the JACL characterized this study as authoritative to the Congressional subcommittee considering amendments to the Act[9] and it is certainly the most thorough analytical work that is even roughly contemporaneous with the evacuation.

A second suggestive study by Lon Hatamiya, "The Economic Effects of the Second World War Upon Japanese Americans in California," relies on Broom and Reimer's work but develops other data in analyzing the income of the ethnic Japanese in California. Hatamiya points out that Broom was already dealing with recollections which were five years old and that the study was limited to Los Angeles, but his analysis supports Broom on income figures and thus suggests the general soundness of Broom's property loss figures. Hatamiya estimates the 1940 median annual income of Japanese (alien and citizen) at $622.[10] Broom had estimated the mean as $671–694.[11] Hatamiya argues that since median figures are often less than mean figures, there is no major discrepancy between these numbers. Hatamiya does not attempt to estimate property losses directly.

For years, writers and commentators have cited an estimate by the Federal Reserve Bank of San Francisco that evacuee property losses ran to $400 million.[12] The Commission has inquired of the Federal Reserve, which can find no basis in its records for such an estimate, and the Commission can identify no known source for the number. In short, the $400-million figure appears to be unsubstantiated.

Consideration of how claims were disposed of under the Evacuation Claims Act allows one to judge further the fairness of its results. The program moved very slowly in its first years, when the Attorney General was required to adjudicate each claim presented to him. In 1949 and 1950, only 232 claims were adjudicated out of more than 26,000 filed.[13] In 1951 the formal adjudication requirement was removed from the Act for claims settled for the lesser of $2,500 or 75% of their value.[14] A rush of settlements followed: by the end of 1955 approximately 22,000 claims had been settled.[15] These limitations must have operated as a forceful incentive to reduce claims in order to get a quick resolution and cash payment. In 1956, with a small number of large claims remaining (approximately 2,000 claims for $55 million), the Act was again changed to allow the Attorney General to settle for up to $100,000 and to permit contested cases to go to the Court of Claims. Thereafter, almost all claims were compromised and settled— only 15 cases were taken to the Court of Claims.[16]

Regardless of the low level of litigation, the settlement procedure was tilted in favor of the government. It was not until 1956 that the Act was amended to provide for appeal past the Attorney General to the Court of Claims.[17] Before 1956, decisions of the Attorney General were final and, in approaching settlement, the Justice Department's attitude, not surprisingly, balanced protecting the interests of the United States with trying to give claimants such liberality as the Act provided.[18] In practice, the Department tried to reach the same result trial might have produced.[19] "Where the problem is created by failure to supply information, the amount should be on the low side."[20] Moreover, no matter was too small for careful consideration by Justice Department officers, and the rulings were published in a volume of "Precedent

Decisions" to guide all future similar cases. For instance, a $7.50 claim for Japanese phonograph records destroyed by the claimant because it was rumored that anyone with Japanese records would be arrested, was not allowed since the loss did not spring from the evacuation but was caused by "the general hysteria among an alien people arising out of the state of war;"[21] but a $3.00 claim for the cost of advertising a car for sale at the time of evacuation was thoroughly reviewed and allowed.[22] Thus the difficulty of providing persuasive evidence of claimants' losses, the evidentiary standards followed by the Justice Department and a compromise authority which encouraged the reduction of many claims, would tend to result in settlements well below the actual value of losses.[23] Recently released from camps, struggling to survive and to reestablish their lives, the claimants badly needed financial resources to sustain themselves; this too played a part.

One cannot readily appraise how much below truly fair compensation were settlements under the Act, but evacuees' testimony before the Commission drew a picture of economic hardship and suffering that could not be fairly compensated by an amount close to $37 million.

THE IMPACT OF EVACUATION

Evacuees repeatedly pointed out that they had had little time in which to settle their affairs:

> We had about two weeks, I recall, to do something. Either lease the property or sell everything.[24]

> While in Modesto, the final notice for evacuation came with a four day notice.[25]

> We were given eight days to liquidate our possessions.[26]

> I remember how agonizing was my despair to be given only about six days in which to dispose of our property and personal possessions.[27]

Testimony emphasized that the governmental safeguards were never entirely successful; they began late, and information about the programs was never widely disseminated among evacuees; the evacuees also distrusted even a quasi-governmental body. The protection and management of the property and personalty many evacuees left behind was inadequate. Businessmen were forced to dispose of their inventory and business at distress prices. It was difficult for evacuees to get reasonable prices in a hostile marketplace. Individuals sold their personal belongings in a buyer's market, realizing only a fraction of their worth.

The makeshift warehouses which evacuees used—homes, garages and other structures—were vandalized; the goods frequently stolen or destroyed. Often those who had agreed to serve as caretakers for the evacuees' property mulcted them in various ways. Some who had found tenants for their property discovered, to their sorrow and financial loss, that the promised rent never appeared or that tenants did not continue the previous land use; many disposed of evacuees' property as their own, or simply abandoned it.

The evacuees' losses mounted as their exclusion from the West Coast lengthened. Some evacuees became aware of the destruction of their property while they were still in relocation centers; others only discovered the full extent of their losses upon their return home. The loss of time, of potential and of property were to many of the evacuees irreparable blows—financial blows from which many never wholly recovered.

AGRICULTURE AND FISHING

The greatest impact of the mass exclusion and evacuation was felt in agriculture, where the Nikkei's economic contribution was concentrated. In 1940, 45% of those gainfully employed among the 112,353 persons of Japanese descent living in the three Pacific Coastal states were engaged in growing crops. Another 18% were employed in wholesaling, retailing, and transporting food products. Census figures show that nearly two-thirds of the work force directly depended upon agriculture and that in the three West Coast states, the value of the 6,118 farms operated by Nikkei was $72,600,000 with an estimated $6 million worth of equipment in use.[28]

These farms represented 2.2% of the number and value of all farms in the three West Coast states, but only .4% of all land in farms, and 1.5% of all crop land harvested. The average farm was roughly 42 acres; 84% were in California.[29] These figures give a misleading indication of the importance of Nikkei farming. The average value per acre of all farms in 1940 was $37.94; that of Nikkei farms was $279.96. Three out of every four acres of evacuee farm land were under cultivation, while only one out of every four acres of total farm land was planted in crops.[30] Fruit, truck and specialty crops predominated. Much of their acreage was planted and harvested two or more times a year.[31] In California the Nikkei dominated the wholesale and retail distribution of fruits and vegetables. In Los Angeles County $16 million of the annual $25 million flower market business was in Nikkei hands.[32]

When the Japanese arrived in the United States they were at the bottom of the economic ladder. Gradually they saved money and were able to rent or indirectly purchase cheap land. By working hard, living frugally and with family cooperation, they were able to increase their acreage. The impact of evacuation is made more poignant by the fact that it cut short the life and strength of the immigrants, frequently destroying the fruit of years of effort to overcome grindingly adverse Depression conditions. Mary Tsukamoto described the yearly economic cycle many farmers followed, especially those around Florin, California:

> This was important, to have time to bring in their crops. The money that they had borrowed from the stores and shipping companies was a tremendous burden. They had to depend on the crop and the harvest to pay for their debts before they could be free again. Each year this was the pattern.
>
> They had struggled hard through the Depression to come out of it, gradually some of them were beginning to pay off their mortgages. Many people still had mortgages to pay.[33]

Others also spoke of just beginning to recover from the effects of the Depression at the time they were forced to leave the West Coast. The west's expanding economy had enabled many to purchase new equipment or lease additional land and, in general, to raise their standard of living. Henry Sakai's father had been a successful businessman:

> He farmed during the Depression, and then he lost it all. [I]t was too late to start over again. . . .[34]

Clarence Nishizu told of the gains his father and family had made after the Depression in which:

> [the] farmer receive[d] 25¢ for a lug of tomatoes all packed, neatly selected as to size and color. I had to stay on the farm and help on the farm. I had to go through those days we were too poor to have tractors—we had only proud horses and mules. However, toward the end of the thirties, I began to get [a] foothold . . . I had two tractors, several trucks and pickups and was just beginning to make headway by using machinery in farming. I [had] just bought a new K5 Internatkon Truck and a used 1941 Chevrolet Sedan for $650.00 and loaded it on the new truck in Springfield,

Ohio and arrived home on December 5, 1941. Two days later, Pearl Harbor was bombed and the war started.[35]

One evacuee had followed in his father's footsteps as a commercial fisherman working the coastal waters off Monterey. He described their struggle to keep their boat:

> We built one of the first purse seiners . . . in 1929 just prior to the Great Depression of the 30's. My father retired and I struggled during those years to keep the finance company from repossessing our boat as not only our family but twelve crew members and their families depended on the continuing operation of the boat. Because of the changes in the industry, I sold the boat in 1935 and began to charter various vessels. The purse-seine net was my investment in the business and at that time valued around $8,000. Today the same net would cost in the neighborhood of $50,000. . . . Every cent I owned was invested in my fishing equipment, and I had to store it in the family garage knowing it would deteriorate and be worthless within a few years.[36]

For many evacuees the most immediate, painful loss was their profit from what promised to be a bumper crop in 1942. The parents of Jack Fujimoto lost the proceeds from an abundant crop of cucumbers and berries which they were unable to harvest before evacuation in May. Instead, the caretaker benefitted from the hard work of this couple who had tilled the soil without much success until then. The Fujimotos never heard from the caretaker.[37]

Hiroshi Kamei recounted:

> My family's greatest economic loss was loss of standing crops. We had several acres of celery just about ready for harvest. . . . Several weeks after our evacuation, the price of celery jumped up to about $5 or $6 a crate.[38]

Another described how he had worked on his farm until he was evacuated, but his crop had been harvested by strangers and he himself received no return for his labor and time.[39]

The white growers and shippers who expanded in the wake of the evacuation did very well in 1942. The managing secretary of the Western Growers Protective Association summed up matters at the end of the year:

> A very great dislocation of our industry occurred when the Japanese were evacuated from Military Zones one and two in the Pacific Coast Areas, and although as shipping groups these dislocations were not so severe the feeding of the cities in close proximity to large Japanese truck farm holdings was considerable and shortages in many commodities developed and prices skyrocketed to almost unheard of values. This, coupled with increased

buying power in practically every district of the United States, also brought to the growers and shippers most satisfactory prices on almost every commodity shipped from California and Arizona. . . .[40]

For many families who owned nurseries, evacuation occurred near one of the richest days in the flower business—Mother's Day, which accounts for one-fifth of the annual sale of flowers. With the Mother's Day crop about to be harvested, evacuation upon short notice caused obvious financial hardship:

> The hardest thing to lose was the full 1942 Mother's Day crop of flowers which [had been] in process from Christmas time.[41]

> When No. 9066 evacuation came, most of the nurseries, with Mother's Day crop before them, were left with very precarious arrangements, or abandoned.[42]

Many evacuees who had been in the flower and nursery business told similar stories. Heizo Oshima described the voluntary evacuation of one community of Japanese families in floriculture around Richmond, El Cerrito and San Pablo:

> The evacuation of the Japanese in the Richmond and El Cerrito area came earlier than the Executive Order 9066. The Issei in this area were ordered to leave in February of '42 because they were posed as a threat to the Standard Oil plant in Richmond. . . . Nisei children remained behind to tend the nurseries. . . . The Japanese in this community were very frightened and confused by the order to evacuate the Issei.[43]

The Nisei children left in charge of the nurseries were untrained and unaccustomed to handling financial details of the family business. They were at a distinct disadvantage when they had to sell in a market of rock bottom prices. Mary Ishizuka told of the heavy loss suffered by her father, who in 1942 had one of the largest nurseries in southern California:

> He had 20 acres of choice land on Wilshire and Sepulveda. He had very choice customers [such] as Will Rogers and Shirley Temple's parents . . . because he had specimen trees. . . . But wealth and standing did not save my father from being arrested . . . on the night of December 7, 1941. When . . . 9066 mandated that all Japanese were to evacuate, we were faced with the awesome task of what to do. And my mother on her own without father, father taken to Missoula, was not able to consult him. We didn't know what to do. You cannot get rid of large nurseries—nursery stock—at this short notice. So what did she do but she gave all of the nursery stock to the U. S. Government, the Veterans Hospital which was adjoining the nursery. It was written up in the

local newspaper along with the story of our evacuation. Itemized piece by piece the dollar amount . . . totalled $100,000 in 1942.[44]

The loss of hard-earned farm machinery was also very bitter; a Los Angeles witness told his family's story:

> The loss, not only in property, but also potential harvest was considerable and all-important to our family. What I remember most was my father who had just purchased a Fordson Tractor for about $750 a few months prior to the notice.
>
> Imagine his delight, after a lifetime of farming with nothing but a horse, plow, shovel and his bare hands, to finally be able to use such a device. He finally had begun to achieve some success. A dream was really coming true.
>
> He had much to look forward to. Then came the notice, and his prize tractor was sold for a measley $75.[45]

The exclusion and evacuation seriously disrupted the agricultural economy of California and led the government to exhort those suspected of disloyalty to produce food for war needs until the final moment when they were thrown off their land. The Secretary of Agriculture had established farm production goals for 1942, and the Japanese farmers of California had been expected to produce over 40% of all truck crops.[46] It was sufficiently critical to the government that the evacuees produce as much as possible, that continued crop production became a measure of loyalty.[47] Tom C. Clark, Chief of the Civilian Staff, Western Defense Command, declared on March 10, 1942:

> There can be no doubt that all persons who wish to show their loyalty to this country should continue farming operation to the fullest extent.[48]

Three days later Clark was no longer equating crop production with evacuee loyalty. Crop neglect or damage had been elevated to an act of sabotage:

> [I]t would be most helpful if you would advise the Japanese [in Hood River County] that they are merely damaging themselves when they fail to take care of their orchards. In addition to this, any failure to do so might be considered as sabotage and subject them to severe penalties.[49]

Witnesses recalled the government's insistence that they continue to farm (with evacuation imminent) or be charged with sabotage:

> With the beginning of the war, we not only had to terminate our basket business, but we lost all financial investments in the asparagus farm as well. However, we were forced to continue farming with no financial gain because the government stated that any neglect on our part would be considered an act of sabotage.[50]

A gentleman . . . wanted to harvest a small strawberry crop.

He wanted 24 hours. He came to me [a U.S. Employment Service Employee assigned to the Federal Reserve Bank] and asked if I could get some kind of time deferral. I could not. So another frustration, he plowed his crop under. The following day I found out that the FBI had picked him up and he had been jailed because he had committed an act of sabotage.[51]

Shigeo Wakamatsu told how the Issei truck farmers of the Puyallup Valley in Washington responded to the regulation to continue crop production:

By the middle of May, when the valley folks were sent to the assembly center, the telephone peas were waist high and strung, the pole beans were staked, early radishes and green onions were ready for the market, strawberries were starting to ripen and the lettuce had been transplanted.

Not much is known how the crops fared in the harvest nor what prices were obtained, but the Issei farmers went into camp with their heads held high, knowing that they had done everything that was possible to help our nation face its first summer of World War II.[52]

SMALL BUSINESSES

Next to agriculture, major occupations of evacuees were in small shops and businesses. Shops, hotels, restaurants and other service-oriented businesses were common. Witnesses told how they were forced by circumstances to accept low prices or abandon property or, with a mixture of desperation and hope, to place the property in insecure storage.

Seattle evacuees had two hundred hotels which were typically run as family enterprises.[53] Shokichi Tokita's father had purchased a hotel in a prime downtown Seattle location after his health had been threatened by his original profession as a sign painter. As a painter the elder Tokita had been acclaimed by the Seattle Art Museum as one of the ten best artists in the Pacific Northwest. He made an equal success of his hotel:

They did very well . . . saving over $16,000 over a five or six year period before the war. This was all lost in the evacuation.[54]

One evacuee with extensive property holdings was forced to sell his forty-five room hotel for $2,500 to a buyer who was able to make only a $500 down payment; the balance was sent to the evacuee in camp two months later. The hotel owner's loss was accentuated by the fact that he was denied the profits which would have accrued to him in a defense boom town such as Seattle became during World War II.[55]

A former interviewer with the U.S. Employment Service who had been assigned to the Federal Reserve Bank cited a number of loss cases; one woman had owned a twenty-six room hotel:

> She came to me and said she was offered $500 and no more and that she had three days in which to dispose of the property.
> Three days later, she came to me in tears, frustrated and frightened. She told me that she had to sell it for the $500.[56]

Other instances of women who had built up businesses and lost the fruit of years of labor were described. Widowed at age 32 with four young children to raise, one had used the proceeds of her deceased husband's insurance policy to buy a hotel in Stockton, California. Her son testified:

> The hotel was a successful venture for [her] and then the war . . . [and] my mother was forced to sell the hotel for a piddling [amount] the day before we left.[57]

She had purchased the hotel for $8,000; it had been a home for her and her children. Now it was gone.

One Issei woman described taking over her husband's insurance business after he was confined to a tuberculosis sanitarium. She built up the business to the point where she had an average monthly income of $300 to $400 to support herself and her children. She found herself, her family and her northern California clients torn from their homes. Many of her clients had no way to continue paying their policy premiums, nor could she effectively service their policies.[58]

The owner of an Oakland Oriental art and dry goods store was unable to dispose of his merchandise in the few weeks given him prior to his evacuation. No one wanted to purchase "Japanese products." He had to store an inventory worth more than $50,000 in a Japanese Methodist Church which had been converted into a warehouse.[59]

The Yoshida family, owners and operators of the Western Goldfish Hatchery and Western Aquarium Manufacturing Company, gave away their goldfish because they required constant care and feeding. Unable to find someone to purchase the goldfish within the three weeks before their evacuation, the Yoshidas had no other recourse. The hatchery comprised six large fish hatching ponds on an acre of land; they stored the aquarium inventory and personal property in the business sales office.[60]

Anti-Japanese sentiment caused financial problems for the owners of many stores and restaurants. For example, at the Sukiyaki Restaurant in Salem, Oregon, FBI visits heightened anti-Japanese feeling. Vandals struck the restaurant and customers ceased to patronize it, afraid of being viewed as unpatriotic.[61] In short, the small businessman fared no better than the farmer.

WHITE COLLAR WORKERS

The smaller numbers of salaried workers and professionals also testified eloquently to the economic impact of evacuation; their losses were less tangible, but no less real than those of farmers and entrepreneurs. Doctors, dentists and architects lost their homes, their practices, their equipment and a lucrative period of their careers.[62]

Many businessmen and professionals couldn't collect outstanding accounts and lost their accumulated charge account receipts.[63] Mrs. Mutsu Homma gave an example of the financial predicament of many evacuee professionals:

[Dr. Homma] after 10 years of dental practice in West Los Angeles and several months of working on people preparing to leave for relocation camps, had more than $20,000 uncollected bills.[64]

The salaried worker in some instances found that the curfew restricted his movements and prevented him from doing his job, or else he lost his chance for economic advancement.[65]

AUTOMOBILES

Cars and trucks were in demand during the evacuation period by both the Army and the civilian population of the West Coast. In this post-Depression period of a growing economy the automobile was a proud symbol of economic advancement. The auto's importance to the way of life and economic well-being of evacuees can be seen in the frequency and detail of car sales described by witnesses:

We had a 1939 car which I recall we sold for $100 and a brand new Ford pickup truck for $100.[66]

In 1941 we purchased a new Chevrolet which the Army took and reimbursed us in the amount of $300.[67]

One man wanted to buy our pickup truck. My father had just
spent about $125 for a set of new tires and tubes and a brand new
battery. So, he asked for $125. The man "bought" our pickup for
$25.[68]

Evacuees were permitted to dispose of their vehicles by private
sale. The other option was to place the cars in government storage,
but the deterioration likely to result from long-term storage encouraged
evacuees to sell. General DeWitt's *Final Report* states that the majority
of cars in storage were "voluntarily" sold to the Army.[69]

Cars driven to the assembly centers were automatically placed in
the custody of the Federal Reserve Bank. The vehicles were then
valued by two disinterested appraisers and the possibility of resale to
the Army or the civilian sector was considered. Those which qualified
for Army purchase were quickly bought up by the government. The
new 1942 models were sold only to auto dealers, so they would have
stock; factories were being converted to wartime production.

Originally 1,905 vehicles were placed in the custody of the Federal
Reserve Bank; 1,469 were voluntarily sold to the Army and 319 were
released according to evacuee instructions. The remaining 117 remained in storage under Bank control.

In late fall 1942, the joint military authorities decided to requi-
sition these vehicles "in consideration of national interest during wartime, and in the interests of the evacuees themselves."[70] Justifying this
move, General DeWitt explained that only those vehicles in open
storage whose owners had refused to sell were requisitioned.[71]

PROPERTY DISPOSAL

It came to the attention of the Tolan Committee early in its West Coast
hearings that frightened, bewildered Japanese were being preyed upon
by second-hand dealers and real estate profiteers. On February 28,
the Committee cabled Attorney General Biddle recommending that
an Alien Property Custodian be appointed.[72]

Before any such action was taken, however, evacuation was under
way. Spot prohibited zones had been cleared of Japanese by order of
the Department of Justice; the Navy had evacuated Terminal Island;
and the Western Defense Command had urged a number of West
Coast residents of Japanese ancestry to leave the military area voluntarily. Whatever their good intentions, the military's primary con-

cern was to remove evacuees from the designated areas, not to look after their property.

In early March, the Federal Reserve Bank of San Francisco was given responsibility for handling the urban property problems of the evacuees; an Alien Property Custodian was appointed on March 11; and on March 15 the Farm Security Administration assumed responsibility for assisting with farm problems. Each agency retained its obligation until the WRA assumed total responsibility in August 1942.[73] By this time, many abuses had already been committed. The Tolan Committee gave a succinct example of what it discovered was going on:

> A typical practice was the following: Japanese would be visited by individuals representing themselves as F.B.I. agents and advised that an order of immediate evacuation was forthcoming. A few hours later, a different set of individuals would call on the Japanese so forewarned and offer to buy up their household and other equipment. Under these conditions the Japanese would accept offers at a fraction of the worth of their possessions. Refrigerators were thus reported to have been sold for as low as $5.[74]

Property and business losses also arose from confusion among government agencies. The military's delay in providing reasonable and adequate property protection and its failure to provide warehouses or other secure structures contributed to initial evacuee losses. Confusion existed among the Federal Reserve Bank of San Francisco, the Farm Security Administration and the Office of the Alien Property Custodian. Not only did each agency have different policies; there was also confusion within each about how to implement its program. Dillon S. Myer decried the result:

> The loss of hundreds of property leases and the disappearance of a number of equities in land and buildings which had been built up over the major portion of a lifetime were among the most regrettable and least justifiable of all the many costs of the wartime evacuation.[75]

In general people were encouraged to take care of their own goods and their own affairs.[76] Given the immense difficulties of protecting the diverse economic interests of 100,000 people, it is not surprising that despite the government's offer of aid it relied primarily on the evacuees to care for their own interests. Conversely, it is not surprising that, facing the distrust expressed in the government's exclusion policy, most evacuees wanted to do what they could for themselves. Approximately 11% of their farms were transferred to non-Japanese (there was a transfer of 3% to ethnic Japanese, probably the result of settlement of business affairs in anticipation of exclusion).[77]

Evacuees were vulnerable to opportunists. Droves of people came to purchase goods and to take advantage of the availability of household furnishings, farm equipment, autos and merchandise at bargain prices.

> Our house was in from Garden Grove Boulevard about 200 yards on a dirt driveway and on the day before the posted evacuation date, there was a line up of cars in our driveway extending about another 200 yards in both directions along Garden Grove Boulevard, waiting their turn to come to our house. . . .[78]

> Swarms of people came daily to our home to see what they could buy. A grand piano for $50, pieces of furniture, $50. . . . One man offered $500 for the house.[79]

> It is difficult to describe the feeling of despair and humiliation experienced by all of us as we watched the Caucasians coming to look over our possessions and offering such nominal amounts knowing we had no recourse but to accept whatever they were offering because we did not know what the future held for us.[80]

> People who were like vultures swooped down on us going through our belongings offering us a fraction of their value. When we complained to them of the low price they would respond by saying, "you can't take it with you so take it or leave it". . . . I was trying to sell a recently purchased $150 mangle. One of these people came by and offered me $10.00. When I complained he said he would do me a favor and give me $15.00.[81]

The evacuees were angered by the response of their former friends and neighbors; some attempted to strike back however they could. Joe Yamamoto vented his feelings by

> putting an ad in our local paper stating that I wanted to dispose of a car, a 1941, which had three brand new tires with it. These were premium items in those days. I gave an address that was fictitious. They could go chase around the block for a few times.[82]

Another evacuee related how he tried to destroy his house when he abandoned his property and his business after evacuation notices were posted on February 19, 1942:

> I went for my last look at our hard work. . . . Why did this thing happen to me now? I went to the storage shed to get the gasoline tank and pour the gasoline on my house, but my wife. . . . said don't do it, maybe somebody can use this house; we are civilized people, not savages.[83]

ORAL CONTRACTS AND CARETAKERS

The evacuees were unprotected and vulnerable. The prevalent use of oral contracts created difficulties for many. The practice of regarding a person's word as binding, a carryover from Meiji Japan reinforced by dealing primarily within their own ethnic group, made it difficult for many evacuees to document when, where, how and to what extent financial loss occurred. Their verbal agreements with caretakers frequently brought theft, fraud or misappropriation.

Kimiyo Okamoto followed the prevalent practice of evacuees in all walks of life and entrusted his property to a friend:

> Prior to the evacuation we had a successful hotel business in Sacramento. Because of the time that was allotted to us, we were not able to sell our hotel . . . One of the trusted guests offered to manage our hotel. He was inexperienced, but we had no other choice.[84]

Another Seattle witness asked Caucasian friends to take over the property and financial management of their apartment house. Unfortunately, they returned from camp to discover the property faced foreclosure due to three years' tax arrearage.[85]

The daughter of concessionaires at Venice and Ocean Park Piers and small carnivals throughout California spoke of the problems created by FBI detention of her father. In desperation, her mother gave the carnival equipment—truck, trailer, games—to one employee and turned over the beach concessions to another who had agreed to act as caretaker until the evacuees returned. When the family did return, neither the business nor the employee could be found.[86]

When the part-owner of a movie business was picked up by the FBI, his business was hurriedly entrusted to the man who had handled his business insurance. The eager caretaker visited the owners while they were in camp to secure power-of-attorney from them so he could handle corporate affairs. Having gained power-of-attorney, the caretaker moved to gain corporate ownership on the basis that all Japanese members of the corporation were "enemy aliens."[87]

In sum, economic losses from the evacuation were substantial, and they touched every group of Nikkei. The loss of liberty and the stigma of the accusation of disloyalty may leave more lasting scars, but the loss of worldly goods and livelihood imposed immediate hardships that anyone can comprehend. Moreover, it was the loss of so much one had worked for, the accumulated substance of a lifetime—gone just when the future seemed most bleak and threatening.

5

Assembly Centers

On May 16,1942, my mother, two sisters, niece, nephew, and I left . . . by train. Father joined us later. Brother left earlier by bus. We took whatever we could carry. So much we left behind, but the most valuable thing I lost was my freedom.[1]

On March 31, 1942, the evacuation began. Until August 7, 1942, groups left their homes for assembly centers, directed by one of the 108 "Civilian Exclusion Orders."[2] About 92,000 people were evacuated to the centers,[3] where they remained for an average of about 100 days.[4] Some 70% were citizens of the United States.[5]

Elaborate preparations had preceded their departure. Once a notice of evacuation had been posted, a representative of each family would visit a control center where the family was registered and issued a number, told when and where to report, and what could be taken along.[6] The numbering process was particularly offensive:

I lost my identity. At that time, I didn't even have a Social Security number, but the WRA gave me an I.D. number. That was my identification. I lost my privacy and dignity.[7]

Henry went to the Control Station to register the family. He came home with twenty tags, all numbered 10710, tags to be attached to each piece of baggage, and one to hang from our coat lapels. From then on, we were known as Family #10710.[8]

Baggage restrictions posed an immediate problem, for many evacuees did not know where they would be going. They could take only what they could carry,[9] a directive that required much anguished sorting of a lifetime's possessions.

On departure day, the evacuees, wearing tags and carrying their baggage, gathered in groups of about 500 at an appointed spot. Although some were allowed to take their cars, traveling in convoys to the centers, most made the trip by bus or train. The Wartime Civil Control Administration (WCCA) had made an effort to foresee problems during the journey. Ideally, each group was to travel with at least one doctor and a nurse, as well as medical supplies and food. One of every four seats was to be vacant to hold hand luggage. The buses were to stop as needed, and those who might need medical care would be clustered in one bus with the nurse.[10]

Despite such plans, many evacuees experienced the trips differently. In some cases, there was no food on long trips.[11] Sometimes train windows were blacked out, aggravating the evacuee's feelings of uncertainty.[12] The sight of armed guards patrolling the trains and busses was not reassuring.[13] Grace Nakamura recalled her trip:

> On May 16, 1942 at 9:30 a.m., we departed . . . for an unknown destination. To this day, I can remember vividly the plight of the elderly, some on stretchers, orphans herded onto the train by caretakers, and especially a young couple with 4 pre-school children. The mother had two frightened toddlers hanging on to her coat. In her arms, she carried two crying babies. The father had diapers and other baby paraphernalia strapped to his back. In his hands he struggled with duffle bag and suitcase. The shades were drawn on the train for our entire trip. Military police patrolled the aisles.[14]

At the end of the trip lay the assembly center. Evacuees often recall two images of their arrival: walking to the camp between a cordon of armed guards, and first seeing the barbed wire and searchlights, the menacing symbols of a prison. Leonard Abrams was with a Field Artillery Battalion that guarded Santa Anita:

> We were put on full alert one day, issued full belts of live ammunition, and went to Santa Anita Race Track . . . There we formed part of a cordon of troops leading into the grounds; busses kept on arriving and many people walked along . . . many weeping or simply dazed, or bewildered by our formidable ranks.[15]

William Kochiyama recalled his entry into Tanforan:

> At the entrance . . . stood two lines of troops with rifles and fixed bayonets pointed at the evacuees as they walked between the soldiers to the prison compound. Overwhelmed with bitterness and blind with rage, I screamed every obscenity I knew at the armed guards daring them to shoot me.[16]

For many evacuees, arrival at the assembly center brought the first vivid realization of their condition. They were under guard and considered dangerous.

Once inside the gates, some evacuees were searched, finger-printed, interrogated, and inoculated; [17] then they were assigned to quarters. Red Cross representatives who visited the centers described some evacuees' reactions soon after arrival:

> Many families with sons in the United States Army and married daughters living in Japan are said to feel terrific conflict. Many who consider themselves good Americans now feel they have been classed with the Japanese. . . . There is a great financial insecurity. Many families have lost heavily in the sale of property. . . . Savings are dipped into for the purchase of coupon books to be used at the center store, and with the depletion of savings comes a mounting sense of insecurity and anxiety as to what will be done when the money is gone. . . . Doubtless the greatest insecurity is that about post-war conditions. Many wonder if they will ever be accepted in Caucasian communities. [18]

HOUSING AND FACILITIES

All sixteen assembly centers were in California, except Puyallup in Washington, Portland in Oregon and Mayer in Arizona. The WCCA had tried, not always successfully, to place people in centers close to their homes. [19] Table 1 (page 138) summarizes basic information about the centers. [20]

Design and construction of the centers varied; most were located at fairgrounds or racetracks. In Portland's Pacific International Livestock Exposition Pavilion, all of the evacuees could be housed under one roof because the pavilion covered eleven acres. Puyallup had four areas; the first three were originally parking lots, the fourth was the fairground itself. [21] Existing facilities usually housed everything except living quarters, and the WCCA sometimes added new buildings. [22]

The WCCA reported that generally it had constructed living quarters for the evacuees, although in a few places existing facilities were used. The basic community unit was usually a "block," a group of units housing 600 to 800 people. Each block had showers, lavatories and toilets. Where possible each block had its own messhall, though some larger groups were fed at a single place. [23]

WCCA policy was to allot a space of 200 square feet per couple.

TABLE 1: Assembly Centers, 1942

Assembly Center	Maximum Population		Dates Occupied	
	Number	Date 1942	From 1942	To 1942
Puyallup	7,390	July 25	April 28	Sept. 12
Portland	3,676	June 6	May 2	Sept. 10
Marysville	2,451	June 2	May 8	June 29
Sacramento	4,739	May 30	May 6	June 26
Tanforan	7,816	July 25	April 28	Oct. 13
Stockton	4,271	May 21	May 10	Oct. 17
Turlock	3,661	June 2	April 30	Aug. 12
Salinas	3,586	June 23	April 27	July 4
Merced	4,508	June 3	May 6	Sept. 15
Pinedale	4,792	June 29	May 7	July 23
Fresno	5,120	Sept. 4	May 6	Oct. 30
Tulare	4,978	Aug. 11	April 20	Sept. 4
Santa Anita	18,719	Aug. 23	March 27	Oct. 27
Pomona	5,434	July 20	May 7	Aug. 24
Mayer	245	May 25	May 7	June 2
Manzanar[1]	9,837		March 21	June 2

[1] Transferred to WRA for use as a relocation camp.

Family groups inside the centers were to be kept together and families would share space with others only if it were unavoidable. To meet these needs, units would be remodeled if necessary, and each was to be furnished with cots, mattresses, blankets and pillows. Each was to have electrical outlets.[24] But the speed of evacuation and the shortages of labor and lumber[25] meant that living arrangements did not always conform to WCCA policy. At Tanforan, for example, a single dormitory housed 400 bachelors.[26]

During the Commission's hearings, evacuees described typical living arrangements that were far below the WCCA's Spartan standards:

> **Pinedale.** The hastily built camp consisted of tar paper roofed barracks with gaping cracks that let in insects, dirt from the . . . dust storms . . . no toilet facilities except smelly outhouses, and community bathrooms with overhead pipes with holes punched in to serve as showers. The furniture was camp cots with dirty straw mattresses.[27]

> **Manzanar.** [The barracks were] nothing but a 20 by 25 foot of barrack with roof, sides of pine wood and covered with thin tar

paper . . . no attic, no insulation. But the July heat separated the pine floor and exposed cracks to a quarter of an inch. Through this a cold wind would blow in or during the heat of the day dusty sand would come in through the cracks. To heat, one pot bellied wood stove in the center of the barracks.[28]

Puyallup (Camp Harmony). This was temporary housing, and the room in which I was confined was a makeshift barracks from a horse stable. Between the floorboards we saw weeds coming up. The room had only one bed and no other furniture. We were given a sack to fill up with hay from a stack outside the barracks to make our mattresses.[29]

Portland. The assembly center was the Portland stockyard. It was filthy, smelly, and dirty. There was roughly two thousand people packed in one large building. No beds were provided, so they gave us gunny sacks to fill with straw, that was our bed.[30]

Santa Anita. We were confined to horse stables. The horse stables were whitewashed. In the hot summers, the legs of the cots were sinking through the asphalt. We were given mattress covers and told to stuff straw in them. The toilet facilities were terrible. They were communal. There were no partitions. Toilet paper was rationed by family members. We had to, to bathe, go to the horse showers. The horses all took showers in there, re-gardless of sex, but with human beings, they built a partition . . . The women complained that the men were climbing over the top to view the women taking showers. [When the women com-plained] one of the officials said, are you sure you women are not climbing the walls to look at the men. . . .[31]

It had extra guard towers with a searchlight panoraming the camp, and it was very difficult to sleep because the light kept coming into our window . . . I wasn't in a stable area, . . . [but] everyone who was in a stable area claimed that they were housed in the stall that housed the great Sea Biscuit.[32]

Despite these problems, the Red Cross representative who visited the centers at the Army's request concluded, taking into account his own experience in housing large numbers of refugees, that as a whole the evacuees were "comfortably and adequately sheltered:"

Generally, the sites selected were satisfactory with the possible exception of Puyallup, where lack of adequate drainage and sewage disposal facilities created a serious problem. . . . In studying the housing facilities in these centers, it is necessary to keep in mind that the job was without precedent, and that the sites were se-lected and buildings completed in record-breaking time in the face of such handicaps as material and labor shortages and trans-portation difficulties.[33]

Evacuees immediately began to improve their quarters. One man salvaged two crates that he redesigned into an armchair with a reclining back. For a hammer he used a rock.[34] Scrap lumber piles left over from construction provided some wood, and government carpenters still at work lost building materials regularly.[35] Victory gardens were planted beside the barracks, and Tanforan evacuees even built a miniature aquatic park with bridge, promenade and islands.[36]

One of the most severe discomforts of the assembly centers was the lack of privacy. Overcrowding continued despite WCCA planning. Eight-person families were placed in 20 by 20 foot rooms, six persons in 12 by 20 foot rooms, and four persons in 8 by 20 foot rooms. Peggy Mitchell described seven of her family in one compartment;[37] Kazuko Ige told of nine to a room.[38] Many smaller families had to share a single room.[39] James Goto and his wife lived with three other married couples; they were separated by sheets hung on wires across the room.[40] Nor did the partitions between apartments provide much privacy, for many did not extend up to the roof, and conversations on the other side were necessarily overheard.[41] Nor were latrines properly partitioned. Elaine Yoneda finally approached the Service Division Director to get toilet partitions and shower curtains and was told that existing arrangements conformed to Army specifications. Six weeks later, after much protest, partitions and curtains were installed.[42]

The weather often made conditions more oppressive. On hot days, overcrowding and sewage problems made the heat seem unbearable.[43] At Pinedale Center, temperatures soared to 110°[44] and evacuees were given salt tablets.[45] Puyallup had its own problem:

> We fought a daily battle with the carnivorous Puyallup mud. The ground was a vast ocean of mud, and whenever it threatened to dry and cake up, the rains came and softened it into slippery ooze.[46]

FAMILY SEPARATION

Many families arrived at the assembly centers incomplete. In some cases, family members, usually the father, had earlier been taken into custody by the FBI.[47] Peter Ota, 16, and his 13-year-old sister travelled without either parent. His father had been detained and his mother was in a tuberculosis sanitorium, where he was allowed to visit her only once in four and a half months.[48] The Kurima family was forced to institutionalize a mentally retarded son who had always been able to live at home.[49] The Shio family was separated from their father who, because he had cancer, was not interned although he was directed to move out of the evacuated area.[50]

Another source of family separation was the WCCA policy defining who was "Japanese." Many individuals of mixed parentage had some Japanese ancestors; others were Caucasian but married to someone of Japanese ancestry. Many of these people went to the assembly centers but had a particularly difficult time because they were not fully accepted into the community. Those who were allowed to leave often did so.[51]

Some families were separated after they reached the centers. A seventeen-year-old who sneaked away from Santa Anita to go to the movies one night was apprehended. He was sent to a different camp and did not see his family again for three years.[52]

Family separation probably occurred most often among those who lived in different homes. Grown children were sent to centers different from their parents if they lived in another community. There were, of course, no visiting privileges save for exceptional circumstances.

FOOD, SANITATION, CLOTHING AND MEDICAL CARE

> [W]e stood two hours three times a day with pails in our hands like beggars to receive our meals. There was no hot water, no washing or bathing. It took about two months before we lived half way civilized.[53]

The assembly centers had been organized to feed the evacuees in large messhalls.[54] At Santa Anita, for example, one evacuee recalls three large messhalls where meals were served in three shifts of 2,000 each.[55] Where shift feeding was instituted, a system of regulatory badges prevented evacuees from attending the same meal at various messhalls.[56] Lining up and waiting to eat is a memory shared by many:

> We stood in line with a tin cup and plate to be fed. I can still vividly recall my 85-year-old grandmother gravely standing in line with her tin cup and plate.[57]

The community feeding weakened family ties. At first families tried to stay together;[58] some even obtained food from the messhall and brought it back to their quarters in order to eat together. In time, however, children began to eat with their friends.[59]

All who testified agreed that their food left much to be desired. One remembered his first meal at Tanforan: two slices of discolored cold cuts, overcooked Swiss chard and a slice of moldy bread.[60] Another recalls: "breakfast consisted of toast, coffee, occasionally eggs or bacon. Then it was an ice cream scoop of rice, a cold sardine, a weeny, or sauerkraut."[61] A third recollected: "For the first few months our diet . . . consisted of brined liver—salted liver. Huge liver. Brown and bluish in color ..[that].. would bounce if dropped. . . . Then there was rice and for dessert, maybe half a can of peach or a pear, tea and coffee. Mornings were better with one egg, oatmeal, tea or coffee."[62] In time the kitchens were taken over by evacuees,[63] and culinary style improved, but basic problems of quality remained.

The Red Cross reported that, given the inherent limitations of mass feeding, menus "showed no serious shortages in nutritive values,"[64] although several evacuees testified that food was a problem. Many evacuees testified that there was enough milk only for babies and the elderly, which contradicts the WCCA report that "per capita consumption of milk by the population was higher than before evacuation and that it was also higher than that of the American population as a whole."[65] At some centers, the problem was aggravated by a prohibition on importing food into the center.[66]

The WCCA had the same food allowance prescribed for the Army— 50 cents per person per day. The assembly centers actually spent less than that—an average of 39 cents per person per day.[67] The outside community pressed the government to cut expenses even more.

Food became controversial at Santa Anita, where a camp staff member was apparently stealing food. A letterwriting campaign began[68] and, at one point, a confrontation with the guards was narrowly avoided when evacuees tried to halt the car of a Caucasian mess steward whom they believed was purloining food. Following an investigation, the guilty staff member was dismissed.[69]

Primitive sanitation arrangements are vividly remembered. Shower, washroom, toilet and laundry facilities were overcrowded. "We lined up for mail, for checks, for meals, for showers, for washrooms, for laundry tubs, for toilets, for clinic service, for movies. We lined up for everything."[70] The distance to the lavatories, more than 100 yards in some parts of Puyallup, posed a problem for the elderly and families with small children. Chamber pots became a highly valued commodity.[71] At some centers sewage disposal was a problem as well.[72] "The plumbing was temporary and the kids played in the shower water that overflowed from the plumbing."[73] To minimize health risks, WCCA established a system of block monitors to inspect evacuee quarters[74] and each barrack was inspected often by the assembly center housing supervisor.[75]

Securing everyday necessities was difficult. Most evacuees had brought their own clothing but a few, either because of poverty or because they had not anticipated the climate, did not own appropriate clothes. In these cases, upon application, the WCCA provided a clothing allowance of between $25 and $42.19 a year depending on age and sex.[76] The centers had canteens, though often there was nothing to buy.[77] Everything else was ordered from mail order houses.[78]

Perhaps the greatest problem in the assembly centers was inadequate medical facilities and care. Usually the medical problems were not life-threatening, but most brought added fear, pain and inconvenience.[79] Medical care was under the jurisdiction of the Public Health Service, which recruited evacuee doctors and nurses to staff infirmaries.[80] An evacuee physician in each center was designated as chief medical officer and dealt directly with the management.[81] Upon arrival, these recruits found minimal equipment and supplies.[82] At Pinedale, dental chairs were made out of crates and the only instruments were forceps and a few syringes.[83] At Fresno, the hospital was a large room with cots; the only supplies were mineral oil, iodine, aspirin, Kaopectate, alcohol and sulfa ointment.[84] Yoshiye Togasaki, a San Francisco doctor, went early to Manzanar to prepare for the incoming evacuees:

> The nurse and I had to set up the medical services and program until additional staff arrived. At this time only one barrack was available for medical "clinic" living quarters. Construction was going on, open trenches, gutters, etc. The usual camp structure of bath facilities and kitchen were centralized but still unroofed. Equipment sent in for medical care was the usual packaged unit for a military emergency hospital. To obtain necessary supplies such as vaccines for children, laboratory materials for tests, special medication for pregnant women, I had to depend on the generous contributions of a few friends until the government could set up its usual channels. Problems of formula preparation, since barracks had no water, no stove, only a single electric light in the center of a room, created much hardship for the mothers who had to care for newborn infants and children.
>
> In three weeks time we were faced with children ill with measles, chickenpox, whooping cough, diarrhea. The only place we had for care were barracks without heat, no stove, no water. In due time the Military Emergency Hospital Unit [equipment] arrived as did medical staff among the evacuees. For me, it was a matter of 14–16 hours per day of struggle and frustration.[85]

Some of the doctors who had not brought their instruments were sent home to retrieve them[86] and all relied, to some extent, on donated supplies.[87] There were shortages of personnel as well. At Fresno, two doctors had to care for 2,500 people.[88] At Manzanar, high school students were trained as technicians and nurses' aides.[89]

With a few exceptions, medical staff treated the normal range of illnesses and injuries. There were, however, some special challenges. At Fresno an outbreak of food poisoning affected over 200 people. At Puyallup, there was a similar incident.[90] At Santa Anita, hospital records show that about 75% of the illnesses came from occupants of the horse stalls.[91] More serious illnesses were treated at nearby hospitals outside the camps and the Army reported that it paid for these services. Some evacuees, however, recall paying for themselves.[92]

LIFE IN THE CENTERS

Because the WCCA had planned only short stays in the assembly centers, they paid little attention to how evacuees would spend their time. As the move to permanent centers was further postponed the WCCA and the evacuees together tried to restore a semblance of normal life.

The educational program got off to a slow start but progressed rapidly at most centers. The Red Cross reported that:

> Because removal of Japanese families to the assembly centers occurred near the end of the school term and because it was contemplated that the centers would be only temporary, there was no provision in the original plan for schools or educational work.[93]

The WCCA appointed a director of education at each center. Rudimentary classrooms were staffed by evacuee teachers, mostly college graduates, a number of whom were certified.[94] They were paid $16 a month.[95] At Manzanar, Frances Kitagawa began a preschool and kindergarten in May with 65 children. Three or four months later, it was reorganized and expanded by the WRA.[96] At Tanforan, schools opened late[97] but were well attended; of 7,800 evacuees, 3,650 were students and 100 teachers. Merced had 110 students; Tulare 300.[98] At Santa Anita, there was no organized education.[99]

The curriculum varied, but all the traditional subjects were taught in elementary and high schools, and adult education offered English, knitting and sewing, American history, music and art. Progress reports were issued and work was exhibited regularly. Lack of textbooks and supplies was a constant problem. Textbooks came principally from the state and county schools the children had attended; supplies arrived from outside, the gifts of interested groups and individuals.[100]

Recreation was organized cooperatively between WCCA and the evacuees. Scout troops, musical groups, and arts and crafts classes were formed. Sports teams and leagues for baseball and basketball began. A calisthenics class at Stockton drew 350. Donations helped remedy equipment shortages.[101] Movies were shown regularly at many centers. At Tanforan, the mess card served as an entrance pass; different nights were reserved for different messhall groups.[102] Some centers opened libraries to which both evacuees and outside donors contributed.[103] Virtually all had some playground area and some had more elaborate facilities; one had a pitch-and-putt golf course.

Holidays were cause for elaborate celebrations. Sachi Kajiwara described her preparation for the Fourth of July at Tanforan:

> I worked as a recreation leader in our block for a group of 7-10 year old girls. Perhaps one of the highlights was the yards and yards of paper chains we (my 7-10 year old girls) made from cut up strips of newspaper which we colored red, white, and blue for the big Fourth of July dance aboard the ship (recreation hall) dubbed the S.S.-6.
>
> These paper chains were the decoration that festooned the walls of the Recreation Hall. It was our Independence Day celebration, though we were behind barbed wire, military police all around us, and we could see the big sign of "South San Francisco" on the hill just outside of the Tanforan Assembly Center.[104]

Some recreation was more *ad hoc*. At Tanforan, the camp police raided several gambling games.[105] *Goh* and *Shogi*, Japanese games akin to chess, were popular among the Issei, who ran frequent tournaments and matches.[106] Knitting was a great pastime among the women.[107]

The evacuees were predominantly Buddhist or Protestant. WCCA's policy allowed evacuees to hold religious services within the centers and to request any necessary assistance from outside religious leaders. The center manager arranged for services and designated facilities. Caucasian religious workers were not allowed to live in the centers and could visit only by invitation.[108] The services themselves were monitored for fear they might be used for propaganda or incitement. The use of Japanese was generally prohibited and written publications had to be cleared.[109] The prohibition on speaking Japanese created particular problems for the Buddhists, who had few English-speaking priests; their services had to be restructured and service books rewritten.[110]

Control of publications extended to the mimeographed center newspapers as well. There were fifteen of these, written in English under the "guidance" of WCCA public relations representatives, who confined news items to those of "actual interest" to the evacuees.[111]

At some centers, evacuees began to organize a government. At Tanforan, for example, the evacuees elected a Center Advisory Council. In August, however, the Army ended these efforts with an order dissolving all self-government bodies.[112]

Even though no evacuee was required to work, the WCCA had planned that assembly center operations should be carried out principally by the evacuees.[113] There was "the standard round of jobs, from doctor to janitor."[114] Evacuees also assisted WCCA administrators. For example, Yayoi Ono was a secretary to the public relations officer; her husband was chief of personnel who oversaw movement to the "permanent" relocation centers.[115] Over 27,000 evacuees—more than 30% of them— worked in center administration.[116]

The appropriate payment for these services was a matter of some difficulty. At first there was no pay. Eventually evacuees were nominally compensated for work actually done, and given subsistence, shelter and a small money allowance. General DeWitt established the following wage schedule: unskilled work, $8.00 per month; skilled, $12.00 per month; professional and technical, $16.00 per month. Subsistence, shelter and hospitalization, medical and dental care were to be furnished without cost.[117] These low wages and allowances were a source of continuing dissatisfaction among evacuees.

Two centers experimented with establishing enterprises for the war effort. Manzanar evacuees tried to devise practical methods of rooting guayule rubber cuttings, planting more than 230,000 seedlings. The project was successful in exploring the potential of guayule rubber, but met market resistance. Santa Anita's camouflage net project produced enough to offset the cost of food for the whole camp.[118] Limited to American citizens, the project attracted more than 800 evacuees. The camouflage net factory was the site of the only strike in the assembly centers, a sit-down protest over working conditions, including insufficient food.[119] At Marysville, in May 1942, a group of evacuees was given leave to thin sugar beets.[120] This situation was exceptional; from most assembly centers, there was no leave.

SECURITY

> Day and night . . . camp police walked their beats within the center. They were on the lookout for contraband and for suspicious actions.[121]

Two groups were responsible for security at the centers. Military police patrolled the perimeters and monitored entries and exits. The internal police were responsible for security inside the centers; most were deputized to handle violations of local and state laws. The FBI had jurisdiction over suspected subversive activities and violations of federal laws.[122]

The Army police guarding the perimeters aroused substantial concern; armed with machine guns, they appeared menacing. In some cases, they propositioned and otherwise harassed female evacuees.[123] In general, however, they were rather remote from the life of the centers, entering only at the director's request, but this is not to suggest that they had no effect on the centers. As the Red Cross described it:

> The high fences and the presence of the military police definitely signify the loss of freedom and independence. Although there is general group acceptance or rather compliance with evacuation, many individuals reject it.[124]

The internal police caused more hardship. Internal security measures varied among centers, but curfews and rollcalls were common. At Puyallup, curfew was at 10 p.m.[125] At Tanforan, rollcall was held twice a day, at 6:45 a.m. and 6:45 p.m.[126]

Most centers held inspections as well, designed to search out and seize contraband. The definition of "contraband" changed as time went on. Flashlights and shortwave radios that could be used for signalling were always contraband.[127] Hot plates and other electrical appliances were usually contraband, although exceptions were sometimes granted.[128] Alcoholic beverages were forbidden.[129] "Potentially dangerous" items were also prohibited; in addition to weapons, the "potentially dangerous" category sometimes included knives, scissors, chisels and saws.[130] At Tulare, inspection sometimes occurred at night.[131] At Tanforan, one was conducted by the Army, which placed each "section" under armed guard while searching.[132] At Puyallup, evacuees were told to remain in their quarters during the search.[133]

Santa Anita evacuees vividly recall the "riot" of August 4, 1942. The uproar began with a routine search for contraband, particularly electrical hot plates, which had, in some cases, been authorized. Some of the searchers became over-zealous and abusive. When the evacuees failed for several hours to reach the chief of internal security, rumors began to spread and crowds formed. The searchers were harassed, although none was injured.[134] At this point, the military police were called in with tanks and machine guns, ending the "riot."[135] The "over-zealous" officers were later replaced.

Visits to the centers were tightly controlled. Visitors bringing gifts watched packages being opened; melons, cakes and pies were cut in half to ensure that none contained weapons or contraband.[136] At some centers, evacuees might talk to visitors only through a wire fence.[137] Others designated special visiting areas. At Tanforan, a room at the top of the grandstand was reserved for receiving visitors during certain hours.[138] At Pomona, the arrangement was similar.[139] At Santa Anita, each family was allowed only one visitor's permit a week, and visits were limited to 30 minutes.[140]

Evacuees endured the frustrations and inconveniences of the assembly centers for the most part peacefully and stoically. They believed these centers were temporary and most hoped for better treatment at the next stop on their journey—the relocation center.

6

The Relocation Centers

Near the end of May 1942, the first evacuees began to arrive at the relocation centers.[1] Most came directly from the WCCA assembly centers, although a few arrived from other places, as shown in Figure A. Evacuees had been assured that the WRA centers would be more suitable for residence and more permanent than the hastily established assembly centers. They also believed that at the new camps some of the most repressive aspects of the assembly centers, particularly the guard towers and barbed wire, would be eliminated.[2] All things considered, they were prepared for an orderly, cooperative move.

By June 30, over 27,000 people were living at three relocation centers: Manzanar, Poston and Tule Lake.[3] Three months later, all the centers except Jerome had opened, and 90,000 people had been transferred.[4] By November 1, transfers had been completed and, at the end of the year, the centers had the highest population they would ever have—106,770 people.[5] Over 175 groups of about 500 each had moved, generally aboard one of 171 special trains, to a center in one of six western states or Arkansas.[6]

The train trips, particularly the longer ones, were often uncomfortable. Even on trips of several days, sleeping berths were provided only for infants, invalids and others who were physically incapacitated.[7] Most evacuees sat up during the entire trip,[8] and mothers with small children who were allowed berths were separated from their husbands.[9] Ventilation was poor because the military had ordered that the

FIGURE A: The Evacuated People

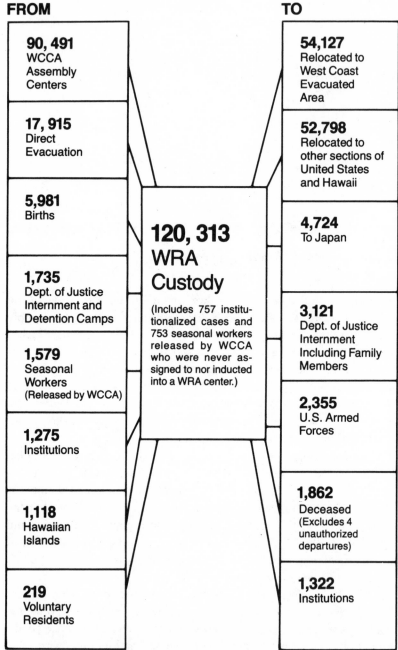

FROM

90, 491
WCCA
Assembly
Centers

17, 915
Direct
Evacuation

5,981
Births

1,735
Dept. of Justice
Internment and
Detention Camps

1,579
Seasonal
Workers
(Released by WCCA)

1,275
Institutions

1,118
Hawaiian
Islands

219
Voluntary
Residents

**120, 313
WRA
Custody**

(Includes 757 institu-
tionalized cases and
753 seasonal workers
released by WCCA
who were never as-
signed to nor inducted
into a WRA center.)

TO

54,127
Relocated to
West Coast
Evacuated
Area

52,798
Relocated to
other sections of
United States
and Hawaii

4,724
To Japan

3,121
Dept. of Justice
Internment
Including Family
Members

2,355
U.S. Armed
Forces

1,862
Deceased
(Excludes 4
unauthorized
departures)

1,322
Institutions

Source: U.S. Department of the Interior, WRA, *The Evacuated People: A Quantitative Description* (1946), p. 8.

shades be drawn.[10] The toilets sometimes flooded, soaking suitcases and belongings on the floor.[11] The trips were slow because the trains were old, and sometimes they were shunted to sidings while higher-priority trains passed. Delays could be as long as ten hours.[12] Although the WCCA reported that it had made provision for meals on the trains,[13] these arrangements were not always satisfactory.[14] Medical care was sometimes poor; although the WCCA had ordered that trains be stopped and ailing evacuees hospitalized along the route,[15] two evacuees testified about separate incidents of infants dying during the journeys.[16]

The military guards harassed some evacuees.[17] Two testified about their experiences:

> When we finally reached our destination, four of us men were ordered by the military personnel carrying guns to follow them. We were directed to unload the pile of evacuees' belongings from the boxcars to the semi-trailer truck to be transported to the concentration camp. During the interim, after filling one trailer-truck and waiting for the next to arrive, we were hot and sweaty and sitting, trying to conserve our energy, when one of the military guards standing with his gun, suggested that one of us should get a drink of water at the nearby water faucet and try and make a run for it so he could get some target practice.[18]

The second evacuee reported:

> At Parker, Arizona, we were transferred to buses. With baggage and carryalls hanging from my arm, I was contemplating what I could leave behind, since my husband was not allowed to come to my aid. A soldier said, "Let me help you, put your arm out." He proceeded to pile everything on my arm. And to my horror, he placed my two-month-old baby on top of the stack. He then pushed me with the butt of the gun and told me to get off the train, knowing when I stepped off the train my baby would fall to the ground. I refused. But he kept prodding and ordering me to move. I will always be thankful [that] a lieutenant checking the cars came upon us. He took the baby down, gave her to me, and then ordered the soldier to carry all our belongings to the bus and see that I was seated and then report back to him.[19]

At the end of these long train and bus rides were the new centers and the "intake" procedure, which usually took about two hours.[20] Leighton described the process at Poston:

> They begin to file out of the bus, clutching tightly to children and bundles. Military Police escorts anxiously help and guides direct them in English and Japanese. They are sent into the mess halls where girls hand them ice water, salt tablets and wet towels. In the back are cots where those who faint can be stretched out, and the cots are usually occupied. At long tables sit interviewers sug-

gesting enlistment in the War Relocation Work Corps. . . . Men and women, still sweating, holding on to children and bundles, try to think. . . . Interviewers ask some questions about former occupations so that cooks and other types of workers much needed in the camp can be quickly secured. Finally, fingerprints are made and the evacuees troop out across an open space and into another hall for housing allotment, registration and a cursory physical examination. . . . In the end, the evacuees are loaded onto trucks along with their hand baggage and driven to their new quarters. . . .

"Intake" was a focus of interest and solicitude on the part of the administrative staff. The Project Director said it was one of the things he would remember longest out of the whole experience at Poston. He thought the people looked lost, not knowing what to do or what to think.[21]

It was not an auspicious introduction to the War Relocation Authority.

THE WAR RELOCATION AUTHORITY

When evacuees stepped off the buses and began the "intake" procedures, they left Army jurisdiction and came into the custody of a new agency, the War Relocation Authority (WRA). Three months before, the WRA had been created on March 18, 1942, by Executive Order 9102, to

formulate and effectuate a program for the removal, from [designated areas] of the persons or classes of persons designated . . . and for their relocation, maintenance, and supervision.

To carry out this function, the Director was to

provide for the relocation of such persons in appropriate places, provide for their needs in such manner as may be appropriate, supervise their activities . . . provide . . . for employment . . . prescribe the terms and conditions of such employment.[22]

On the same day, President Roosevelt had appointed as the WRA's first director Milton Eisenhower, brother of the general, who had previously served as an official in the Department of Agriculture. By his own account, Eisenhower knew little about the West Coast ethnic Japanese, the deliberations that had preceded the decision to evacuate them, or future plans for the evacuees.[23] He faced a mammoth task— building an agency to direct and supervise the lives of over 100,000 people and, at the same time, deciding what to do with them. He quickly concluded that the evacuation would eventually be viewed as "avoidable injustice."[24]

Eisenhower faced an initial decision that would shape the rest of the WRA program—would the evacuees be resettled and placed in new homes and jobs, or would they be detained, confined and supervised for the duration of the war? He had been given almost no guidance on this crucial matter. Beyond the fact that the military would deliver the evacuees to the WRA and thereafter wished no further part in the "Japanese problem," nothing had been decided.

The Tolan Committee had reported this major deficiency in planning in March:

> To date the committee has been unable to secure from anyone charged with responsibility a clear-cut statement of the status of the Japanese evacuees, alien or citizen, after they pass through the reception center.[25]

They also offered some guidance. The Committee was firmly opposed to incarcerating the evacuees for reasons that proved remarkably prophetic:

> The incarceration of the Japanese for the duration of the war can only end in wholesale deportation. The maintenance of all Japanese, alien and citizen, in enforced idleness will prove not only a costly waste of the taxpayers' money, but it automatically implies deportation, since we cannot expect this group to be loyal to our Government or sympathetic to our way of life thereafter.
> Serious constitutional questions are raised by the forced detention of citizens against whom no individual charges are lodged.[26]

Instead, they favored a loyalty review at the assembly centers:

> Presumably, the loyalty and dependability of all Japanese, alien and citizen alike, would be examined at the reception center. This would be followed by arrangements for job placement outside of the prohibited areas of all persons certified.[27]

Only when this process failed to resolve all questions did the Committee envision the creation of resettlement communities.

Eisenhower and his lieutenants started from premises much like those of the Tolan report; they believed that the vast majority of evacuees were law-abiding and loyal and that, once out of the combat zone, they should be returned quickly to conditions approximating normal life. Believing WRA's goal should be to achieve this rehabilitative measure, they immediately devised a plan to move evacuees to the intermountain states.[28] The government would operate "reception centers" and some evacuees would work within them, developing the land and farming. Many more, however, would work outside the centers, in private employment—manufacturing, farming or creating new self-supporting communities.[29]

Mike Masaoka, National Secretary of the Japanese American Citizens League (JACL), soon approached Eisenhower with a lengthy letter setting out recommendations and suggestions for policies the WRA should follow. This effort was grounded on the basic position the JACL had taken on exclusion and evacuation:

> We have not contested the right of the military to order this movement, even though it meant leaving all that we hold dear and sacred, because we believe that cooperation on our part will mean a reciprocal cooperation on the part of the government.

Among the letter's many specific recommendations was the plea that the government permit Japanese Americans to have as much contact as possible with white Americans to avoid isolation and segregation.[30]

The WRA's own plans were in sympathy with such an approach, but the government's experience with voluntary relocation suggested that the WRA would only be successful if it could enlist the help of the interior state governors.[31] WRA arranged a meeting for officials of the ten western states for April 7 in Salt Lake City, the day after Masaoka had sent Eisenhower his appeal for a cooperative relationship with the government. From the federal side, the two principal representatives were Bendetsen and Eisenhower; from the states came five governors and a host of other officials, as well as a few farmers who were anxious to employ evacuees for harvesting.

Bendetsen made the first presentation, describing the evacuation and the WDC's reasons for it. He argued that, although some evacuees might be disloyal, once they were removed from the West Coast, the danger would be minimal. There were two real problems, as he saw it: possible fifth column activity in the event of an invasion and the possibility of confusing the Japanese Americans with the enemy; both problems were peculiar to the West Coast. Eisenhower then described his planned program. He assured state participants that security precautions would be taken. Evacuees would not be permitted to own land against the wishes of the state, and the WRA would insure that evacuees did not become permanent residents. He played down the portions of the plan involving private employment.

The governors of the mountain states fully grasped the politics of the situation, and they were unimpressed by both Bendetsen's sophistry and Eisenhower's social engineering. They opposed any evacuee land purchase or settlement in their states and wanted guarantees that the government would forbid evacuees to buy land and that it would remove them at the end of the war. They objected to California using the interior states as a "dumping ground" for a California "problem." People in their states were so bitter over the voluntary evacuation, they said, that unguarded evacuees would face physical danger.

Governor Herbert Maw of Utah put forth a plan whereby the states would run the relocation program with federal financing. Each state would be given a quota of evacuees for which it "would hire the state guards, and would set up camps of Japanese and would work them under general policies and plans specified by the Federal government." The evacuees could not be allowed to roam at large, said Maw, citing strategic works in Utah. Accusing the WRA of being too concerned about the constitutional rights of Japanese American citizens, he suggested that the Constitution could be changed.

The Governor of Idaho agreed with Maw and advocated rounding up and supervising all those who had already entered his state. Idaho, he said, had as many strategic works as California. The Governor of Wyoming wanted evacuees put in "concentration camps." With few exceptions, the other officials present echoed these sentiments. Only Governor Carr of Colorado took a moderate position. The voices of those hoping to use the evacuees for agricultural labor were drowned out.[32]

Bendetsen and Eisenhower were unable or unwilling to face down this united political opposition. Bendetsen briefly attempted to defend the War Department's actions. Eisenhower closed the meeting: the consensus was that the plan for reception centers was acceptable, as long as the evacuees remained under guard within the centers.[33] As he left Salt Lake City, Eisenhower had no doubt that "the plan to move the evacuees into private employment had to be abandoned— at least temporarily."[34] Bendetsen, too, had received the same message. As he described it several weeks later: "You can't move people across the street! The premise is that who you consider to be so dangerous, that you can't permit him to stay at point 'A'—point 'B' will not accept."[35]

Before it had begun, Eisenhower and the WRA thus abandoned resettlement and adopted confinement. West Coast politicians had achieved their program of exclusion; politicians of the interior states had achieved their program of detention. Without giving up its belief that evacuees should be brought back to normal productive life, WRA had, in effect, become their jailer, contending that confinement was for the benefit of the evacuees and that the controls on their departure were designed to prevent mistreatment by other Americans.[36]

WRA had to move quickly in finding centers to house 120,000 people and in developing policies and procedures for handling the evacuees soon to come under its jurisdiction. The President had stressed the need for immediate action;[37] both the War Department and the WRA were anxious to remove the evacuees from the primitive, make-shift assembly centers.

Selecting the sites for the relocation centers proved complicated. Two sites had been chosen by military authorities before the WRA was born.[38] Eight more locations were needed—designed to be "areas where the evacuees might settle down to a more stable kind of life until plans could be developed for their permanent relocation in com-munities outside the evacuated areas."[39] Site selection required the War Department and the WRA to agree, although each had different interests.[40] The WRA retained the portion of its early plan that called for large-scale agricultural programs in which evacuees would clear, develop and cultivate the land. Thus, the centers had to be on federal land so that improvements would become a public benefit. The Army, now face-to-face with the actual movement of people, no longer ad-vocated freedom of movement outside the Western Defense Com-mand. It became concerned about security and insisted that sites be located at a safe distance from "strategic installations," a term that included power lines and reservoirs. The Army also wanted each camp to have a population of at least 5,000 so that the number of guards could be minimized. To be habitable, the centers had to have suitable transportation, power and water facilities.[41] By June 5, after consid-ering 300 proposed sites[42] and negotiating with many potentially af-fected state and local government officials, the WRA chose the final eight sites.[43]

More than any other single factor, the requirement for large tracts of land virtually guaranteed that the sites would be inhospitable. As Roger Daniels explained it: "That these areas were still vacant land in 1942, land that the ever-voracious pioneers and developers had either passed by or abandoned, speaks volumes about their attractiveness."[44]

The sites were indeed unattractive. Manzanar and Poston, se-lected by the Army, were in the desert. Although both could eventually produce crops, extensive irrigation would be needed,[45] and Poston's climate was particularly harsh. Six other sites were also arid desert. Gila River, near Phoenix,[46] suffered almost as severely from the heat.[47] Minidoka and Heart Mountain, the two northernmost centers, were known for hard winters and severe dust storms. Tule Lake was the most developed site; located in a dry lake bed, much of it was ready

for planting.[48] Topaz was covered in greasewood brush.[49] Granada was
little better, although there was some provision for irrigation.[50] The
last two centers—Rohwer and Jerome in Arkansas—were entirely different. Located in swampland, the sites were heavily wooded, with
severe drainage problems.[51] Table 2 lists the location and capacity of
each center.

TABLE 2[52]: Relocation Centers

Name	Location	Capacity (in persons)
Central Utah (Topaz)	West-central Utah	10,000
Colorado River (Poston)		
Unit 1	Western Arizona	10,000
Unit 2	Western Arizona	5,000
Unit 3	Western Arizona	5,000
Gila River (Rivers)		
Butte Camp	Central Arizona	10,000
Canal Camp	Central Arizona	5,000
Granada (Amache)	Southeastern Colorado	8,000
Heart Mountain	Northwestern Wyoming	12,000
Jerome (Denson)	Southeastern Arkansas	10,000
Manzanar	East-central California	10,000
Minidoka (Hunt)	South-central Idaho	10,000
Rohwer	Southeastern Arkansas	10,000
Tule Lake (Newell)	North-central California	16,000

Having selected the sites, the WRA's second job was to develop
the policies and procedures that would control the lives of evacuees.
This was begun almost immediately, with help from the JACL. In his
April 6 letter to Eisenhower, Masaoka set forth a long list of recommendations for regulating life in the camps and stressed, among other
things, the importance of respecting the citizenship of the Nisei, protecting the health of elderly Issei, providing educational opportunities,
and recognizing that the evacuees were "American" in their outlook
and wanted to make a contribution to the war effort.[53] The first set of
policies issued May 29 were labelled by the Director "tentative, still
fairly crude, and subject to immediate change." Further, they did not
reach the centers until three weeks after the first groups had arrived.
They were not clarified until August, when over half the evacuee
population had been transferred to the centers. Given the limited time
available and the novelty of WRA's task as both jailer and advocate for
the evacuees, it is not surprising that the agency was not fully pre-

pared.[54] Still, the fact that WRA was not able to provide dependable answers to basic questions about how the centers would be managed probably fed the disaffection that increasingly characterized reactions to the relocation centers.

The confluence of diverse political interests had again conspired against the evacuees. The new centers at which they were arriving were barely an improvement over the assembly centers they had left. The increased freedom and possible resettlement they had anticipated had been reversed in favor of confinement. And the rules that would govern their lives were uncertain or non-existent.

LIFE IN CAMP

Housing and Facilities

Except at Manzanar, which was built as an assembly center and transferred to the WRA for use as a relocation center, all the relocation camps were built from scratch. Thus, the design and facilities were relatively standard. By agreement with the WRA, the camps were built by the War Department according to its own specifications.[55] Barbed-wire fences, watchtowers, and armed guards surrounded the residential and administrative areas of most camps.[56]

The military police and administrative personnel had separate quarters, more spacious and better furnished. At most centers, evacuees built the administrative housing, which had not been included in the original construction contracts. At Topaz, Gladys Bell and her family, who were with the administrative staff, had an entire four-room barrack complete with piano.[57] At Manzanar, staff houses were painted and had residential cooling systems, refrigerators, indoor toilets and baths.[58]

Arrangements for the evacuees were not comparable. The basic organizational unit was once again the "block," consisting of about 12 to 14 barracks, a mess hall, baths, showers, toilets, a laundry and a recreation hall.[59] Each barrack was about 20 by 100 to 120 feet, divided into four or six rooms, each from 20 by 16 to 20 by 25 feet.[60] Each room housed at least one family, even if the family was very large. Even at the end of 1942, in 928 cases, two families shared a 20 by 25-foot room.[61]

Construction was of the kind used to house soldiers overseas—the so-called "theatre of operations" type,[62] modified somewhat to accommodate women and children.[63] The barracks were built of planks nailed to studs and covered with tarpaper.[64] In some places the green wood warped quickly, cracking walls and floors.[65] Congressman Leland Ford said of the Manzanar barracks that "on dusty days, one might just as well be outside as inside."[66] "So much of our work was done sloppily," Dean Meeker testified of Heart Mountain:

> I can remember the foreman's comment when he found cracks in the building. He said, "Well, I guess those Japs will be stuffing their underwear in there to keep the wind out."
>
> In my defense, I will say I applied a bit more diligence and care to my work when I realized people would actually have to survive a Wyoming winter in this housing. We all knew that there was no way anyone accustomed to California weather could possibly survive a Wyoming winter in those barracks. If they were from California, they probably didn't even own the proper clothing for a winter in Cody.[67]

No inside walls or ceilings were included in the original plans. As part of a winterization program, however, evacuee construction crews eventually added firboard ceilings and inside walls in many of the centers.[68]

A visiting reporter from *The San Francisco Chronicle* described quarters at Tule Lake:

> Room size—about 15 by 25, considered too big for two reporters. Condition—dirty.
>
> Contents—two Army cots, each with two Army blankets, one pillow, some sheets and pillow cases (these came as a courtesy from the management), and a coal-burning stove (no coal). There were no dishes, rugs, curtains, or housekeeping equipment of any kind. (We had in addition one sawhorse and three pieces of wood, which the management did not explain.)[69]

The furnishings at other camps were similar. At Minidoka, arriving evacuees found two stacked canvas cots, a pot-bellied stove and a light bulb hanging from the ceiling;[70] at Topaz, cots, two blankets, a pot-bellied stove and some cotton mattresses.[71] Rooms had no running water, which had to be carried from community facilities.[72] Running back and forth from the laundry room to rinse and launder soiled diapers was a particular inconvenience.[73]

For some evacuees the camps were an improvement over the assembly centers.

> At least there were flush toilets in the community bathrooms and we were given two rooms instead of one.[74]
>
> The buildings were the same type of barracks, although they had flooring.[75]

. Our new homes were better insulated from the dust and storm and noise than those at the assembly center.[76]

Others, however, found not even the minimal comforts that had been planned for them. An unrealistic schedule combined with wartime shortages of labor and materials meant that the WRA had difficulty meeting its construction schedule.[77] In most cases, the barracks were completed, but at some centers evacuees lived without electric light, adequate toilets or laundry facilities.[78]

When we first arrived at Minidoka, everyone was forced to use outhouses since the sewer system had not been built. For about a year, the residents had to brave the cold and the stench of these accommodations.[79]

Mess halls planned for about 300 people had to handle 600 or 900 for short periods.[80] Three months after the project opened, Manzanar still lacked equipment for 16 of 36 messhalls.[81] At Gila:

There were 7,700 people crowded into space designed for 5,000. They were housed in messhalls, recreation halls, and even latrines. As many as 25 persons lived in a space intended for four.[82]

As at the assembly centers, one result was that evacuees were often denied privacy in even the most intimate aspects of their lives.

Apartment is shared by married couple, age around 50 years, and our family of four, one girl just nine and one ten years old, my husband is out during the day on a job. . . . The heat is terrific and the lady in our apartment is very sensitive to heat, so whenever her washing and ironing is done she is always taking naps—makes it hard for children to run in and out—for fear it may disturb her. She is an understanding person, but still there is time she wished she could have slept just another ten minutes.[83]

Even when families had separate quarters, the partitions between rooms failed to give much privacy. Gladys Bell described the situation at Topaz:

[T]he evacuees . . . had only one room, unless there were around ten in the family. Their rooms had a pot-bellied stove, a single electric light hanging from the ceiling, an Army cot for each person and a blanket for the bed. Each barrack had six rooms with only three flues. This meant that a hole had to be cut through the wall of one room for the stovepipe to join the chimney of the next room. The hole was large so that the wall would not burn. As a result, everything said and some things whispered were easily heard by people living in the next room. Sometimes the family would be a couple with four children living next to an older couple, perhaps of a different religion, older ideas and with a difference in all ways of life—such as music.[84]

Despite these wretched conditions the evacuees again began to rebuild their lives. Several evacuees recall "foraging for bits of wallboard and wood"[85] and dodging guards to get materials from the scrap lumber piles to build shelves and furniture.[86] Even the refuse of better times was treasured in camp:

> To a friend who became engaged, we gave nails—many of them bent—precious nails preserved in fruit wrappings, snitched from our fathers' meager supply or found by sifting through the sand in the windbreak where scrap lumber was piled.[87]

Eventually, rooms were partitioned and shelves, tables, chairs and other furniture appeared.[88] Paint and cloth for curtains and spreads came from mail order houses at evacuee expense.[89] Flowers bloomed and rock gardens emerged;[90] trees and shrubs were planted. Many evacuees grew victory gardens.[91] One described the change:

> [W]hen we entered camp, it was a barren desert. When we left camp, it was a garden that had been built up without tools, it was green around the camp with vegetation, flowers, and also with artificial lakes, and that's how we left it.[92]

The success of evacuees' efforts to improve their surroundings, however, was always tempered by the harsh climate. In the western camps, particularly Heart Mountain, Poston, Topaz[93] and Minidoka, dust was a principal problem. Monica Sone described her first day at Minidoka:

> [W]e were given a rousing welcome by a dust storm. . . . We felt as if we were standing in a gigantic sand-mixing machine as the sixty-mile gale lifted the loose earth up into the sky, obliterating everything. Sand filled our mouths and nostrils and stung our faces and hands like a thousand darting needles. Henry and Father pushed on ahead while Mother, Sumi and I followed, hanging onto their jackets, banging suitcases into each other. At last we staggered into our room, gasping and blinded. We sat on our suitcases to rest, peeling off our jackets and scarves. The window panes rattled madly, and the dust poured through the cracks like smoke. Now and then when the wind subsided, I saw other evacuees, hanging on to their suitcases, heads bent against the stinging dust. The wind whipped their scarves and towels from their heads and zipped them out of sight.[94]

In desert camps, the evacuees met severe extremes of temperature as well. In winter it reached 35 degrees below zero[95] and summers brought temperatures as high as 115°.[96] Because the desert did not cool off at night, evacuees would splash water on their cots to be cool enough to sleep.[97] Rattlesnakes and desert wildlife added danger to discomfort.[98]

The Arkansas camps had equally unpleasant weather. Winters were cold and snowy while summers were unbearably hot and humid, heavy with chiggers and clouds of mosquitos:[99]

> When the rains came in Rohwer, we could not leave our quarters. The water stagnated at the front steps. . . . The mosquitos that festered there were horrible, and the authorities never had enough quinine for sickness . . . Rohwer was a living nightmare.[100]

Necessities: Food, Clothing and Health

The WRA walked a fine line in providing for evacuees' basic needs. On the one hand was their genuine sympathy for the excluded people. On the other was a well-founded apprehension that the press and the politicians would seek out and denounce any evidence that evacuees were being treated generously.[101] WRA's compromise was to strive for a system that would provide a healthy but Spartan environment. They did not always succeed, and it was usually the evacuees who suffered when they failed.

The meal system was institutional—food served in messhalls at designated times. Lines were long and tables crowded. Special arrangements were made for infants, the sick or elderly, but, as in most institutions, they were developed from necessity, not convenience. There were formula kitchens for the babies, to which their mothers brought them at designated times; some mothers walked many "blocks" as often as six times a day to get their infants fed when the camps first opened.[102] Others bought hot plates to make formula, but without running water this system was almost as unsatisfactory.[103] The arrangements for those on restricted diets were difficult. The diet kitchens were often located in the administration complex, far from the residential area; the sick and the elderly had to walk as much as a mile three times a day to get their special food.[104]

Food quality and quantity varied among centers, generally improving in the later months as evacuees began to produce it themselves. The WRA's expressed policy was that evacuees were entitled to the same treatment as other American citizens: WRA was to provide an adequate diet; foods rationed to the public would be available to evacuees in the same quantities.[105] The reality, however, was very different. Weiners, dry fish, rice, macaroni and pickled vegetables are among the foods evacuees recall eating most frequently.[106] Meatless days were regular at some centers—two or three times a week,[107] and many items were unavailable. Continuing dairy shortages meant that, at most centers, fluid milk was served only to those with special needs,[108] while at others, there was watery skim milk.[109] In fact, no really appetizing meals could be produced regularly under a requirement that feeding the evacuees could not cost more than rations for the Army, which were set at 50 cents per person per day.[110] Actual costs per evacuee were approximately 45 cents per person per day;[111] sometimes they fell as low as 31 cents.[112]

In January 1943, after accusations that evacuees were being coddled, the WRA adopted new policies which showed that their fear of adverse publicity had overcome any humanitarian impulse. "At no time would evacuees' food have higher specifications than or exceed in quantity what the civil population may obtain in the open market." Centers were ordered to submit their planned menus for each 30-day period to Washington for advance approval to make sure that the public was adequately informed of WRA feeding policies and procedures.[113] Perhaps the best that can be said of the meal system is that no one starved.

No one froze either. As winter approached, many evacuees were unprepared, either because they had brought no warm clothing due to baggage limitations or because they did not own such clothing, never having needed it at home. In response, the WRA provided monthly clothing allowances and distributed surplus clothing. Each employed evacuee and his or her dependents were supposed to receive from $2 to $3.75 each month,[114] depending on the evacuee's age and the climate of the center. The system, however, did not work well because the shorthanded WRA assigned it to an inexperienced, overworked staff, which was unable to handle the additional workload,[115] and delays continually frustrated evacuees at the mercy of the WRA for their survival. The surplus distribution became the principal source of warm clothing during the first winter, when need was greatest. The clothes were old GI peajackets and uniforms, sizes 38 to 44. However unattractive, they were warm and a source of great amusement.[116]

The adequacy of health care in the camps has been a matter of continuing debate. No issue was raised more frequently during the testimony. The WRA itself readily acknowledged some of the system's larger flaws. The hospitals that had been planned were behind schedule; some were not completed until the end of 1942.[117] Equipment shortages were constant and many supplies, including medicines, were unavailable.[118] Evacuees were forced back on their own resources, bringing their own equipment from home or making it from materials found in camp.[119]

By far the biggest problem, however, was too few medical personnel, particularly nurses.[120] The result was overworked doctors and nurses and delays in treatment.[121] At Jerome, for example, only seven doctors were on hand to care for 10,000 people in October of 1942.[122] The only medical profession filled to capacity in the camps was dentists; there were so many at some centers that not all could practice.[123] By 1943, the situation in most centers had grown worse as medical personnel left to resettle. By the last half of 1943, not only were personnel few, but hospital bed usage rose as older evacuees whose families had resettled fell back on hospital rather than family care.[124] The shortage of nurses was handled in part by training evacuees as aides.[125] Some felt that their training was inadequate:[126]

> In Topaz, I took three weeks of instruction from one of the five Registered Nurses assigned to Topaz and went on duty as a Nurse's Aide. I didn't even know the names of the instruments—I felt terribly inadequate to take care of some very sick people.[127]

As a result of nationwide medical personnel shortages, some staff physicians were not the best. At Manzanar, for example, a Caucasian doctor set strict limits on work by the evacuee doctors in his charge, limiting the efficiency of the medical program for some time.[128] At Tule Lake, the elderly physician in charge was not aware of and would not allow newer medical procedures. After a great deal of protest from the evacuees, he departed.[129]

Caring for people with special medical needs was particularly difficult. In a situation where running water was a luxury and normal conveniences virtually absent, it was very difficult to provide special care. Tuberculosis might well mean separation from one's family to outside facilities for the duration of the evacuation.[130] Retarded children who could have been cared for by their families at home had to be institutionalized.[131] Serious illnesses, such as mental breakdowns, meant removal to state hospitals.[132]

There were, however, some positive aspects to the system. Most of the centers stressed preventive health care and set up immunization programs as soon as possible.[133] The camp hospitals were nearby, although reaching them might be a problem with no transportation but walking.[134] Care was free, and evacuees had time to attend to their health.

Any real measure of the system's effectiveness would require a statistical evaluation of the center's health records compared to the records of a comparable group outside the centers. No such studies exist. The WRA noted few problems. Epidemics of chicken pox and respiratory tract infections were mentioned,[135] as were problems "de-

veloped in connection with the water supply at some centers."[136] In
the Arkansas centers, there was malaria, which abated after a mosquito
eradication campaign, better public education and more screening.[137]
The WRA asserted that evacuees' physical health remained satisfactory,[138] and, in a 1946 comparison of death rates in the camps to deaths
in the U.S. population as a whole, they found that death rates in the
camps were lower than those in the general population.[139]

Testimony before the Commission, however, suggests a different
story. The evacuees recall more than one problem caused by inadequate sewage disposal. Epidemics of dysentery were reported at Topaz,[140] Minidoka,[141] and Jerome,[142] and a typhoid epidemic occurred
at Minidoka.[143]

Evacuees testified about polio and tuberculosis as well.[144] The
polio problem was apparently quite severe at Granada during the latter
part of 1943. Some organized activities were cancelled,[145] and WRA
stopped giving passes to nearby towns.[146] At Poston, Rita Cates found
140 cases of tuberculosis in 8 months.[147] Several evacuees testified
about situations in which inadequate care led to death or disability that
might have been avoided.[148]

Employment

One of the many unresolved issues for arriving evacuees was the
extent to which they would be required to support themselves. Were
they in fact prisoners for whom the state had an obligation to provide
continuing minimal help? Or were they simply to be regarded as people
who had moved, responsible for themselves, for whom WRA would
provide initial help and encouragement? Eisenhower's original plan
tended toward the latter view. The WRA would, in the main, help
provide or locate opportunities for the evacuees, not regard them as
indefinite dependents. Once the decision had been made that evacuees
were to be confined, however, WRA expectations had to change. Evacuees confined to government camps would definitely have limited
career opportunities. Still, the WRA was not prepared to regard evacuees as wards of the state. The WRA, determined to strive for communities that would be as self-sufficient as possible,[149] wanted to avoid
creating a permanently dependent population like the Indians. They
believed that prolonged idleness would deepen the evacuees' feelings
of frustration and isolation. Further, the war effort demanded that all
labor be used, and WRA believed constructive work would rehabilitate
evacuees in the eyes of their countrymen.[150] Therefore, the WRA
approach to employment (as to many other issues) became a compro-

mise—expecting and encouraging evacuees to work while denying them freedom of choice or incentives to perform. Needless to say, the result satisfied no one.

The first plan to emerge from these conflicting objectives was the notion of an evacuee work corps. Each working-age evacuee would be given an opportunity to join the corps. Enlistment was voluntary but the evacuee had to enlist to be eligible for work. The corps was to develop land, build irrigation structures, produce food and turn out war-related manufactured items. [151]

By May 29, the WRA had refined its plan. Each center would be a "partnership enterprise." WRA would furnish the essentials of living and try to develop work opportunities. Evacuee members of the work corps were to work toward providing their own living requirements, developing the center's land, and producing surplus goods for sale. At the end of the year, any profits (the surplus of earnings over maintenance costs) would be distributed to work-corps members. Meanwhile, evacuees would receive cash advances. Eligible residents who chose not to join the corps would be charged $20 a month for themselves and each dependent to cover subsistence costs. [152]

This plan set the amount of "cash advances," which eventually became "wages." On March 23, before any policy had been adopted, a Hearst newspaper ran a story alleging that evacuees "will be paid much more than the American soldiers fighting the country's battles overseas." The evacuees, it reported, would get $50 to $94 a month, while the soldier's base pay was $21 a month. This misleading story led to a Congressional investigation and attendant publicity that put great pressure on Eisenhower. Eventually he agreed that evacuee pay would not, under any circumstances, exceed the base pay of a soldier; the scale adopted was $12 a month for unskilled labor, $16 for skilled labor, and $19 for professional employees. [153] Congress and the press had delivered a message parallel to that of the mountain states governors: the WRA might look on its work as returning to normal life a group against whom there were no charges and most of whom were concededly loyal to the United States, but a great many members of Congress and the press saw WRA as warden of a dangerous group whose subversive potential required stern control. As a result, most of WRA's constructive programs were defeated by measures of compulsion or deprivation.

Despite elaborate planning, neither the work corps nor the "partnership" idea ever got off the ground. The evacuees decisively rejected the work corps by refusing to sign up in large numbers. The partnership notion, with or without the work corps, was flawed. Some centers had greater potential than others; the accounting system would have been extremely complex, and the whole scheme was subject to allegations of "unfair competition" from local interests. By August 1942, it was dropped. The only element that remained was the schedule of "cash advances," now known as "wages."[154]

The new policy adopted in August remained substantially unchanged throughout the WRA program. Its principal elements were:

- Evacuees in centers would receive food, shelter, medical care and education without charge.
- Evacuees working at the centers would be paid $12, $16 or $19 a month.
- Unemployment compensation payments, at rates ranging from $1.50 to $4.75 a month, would be paid to each employable evacuee (and each dependent) who was out of work through no fault of his own.[155]

The wage scale immediately became controversial and remained so. Public opinion dictated that wages should be low. Evacuees demanded a higher scale; they saw themselves as victims of a misguided, hysterical war reaction and utterly undeserving of treatment different from that of other Americans.

Moreover, the system caused severe financial hardship. Evacuees could not afford to meet even their minimal needs inside the centers. Sometimes the barest essentials in the Sears catalogue, such as shoes for the children, were out of reach. Meeting their outside obligations, such as mortgage payments, was impossible unless they already had savings or income-producing property. And it was insulting. A WRA librarian received $167 a month, while her evacuee staff received $16 a month.[156] Despite the agitation, the system was never changed. By the time it might have been, the WRA was encouraging evacuees to leave the centers and did not want to create an incentive to stay.

Opportunities for work were also the subject of continuing debate and change. The WRA had promised jobs for those who wanted to work, but meager opportunities led to overstaffing and encouraged slack work habits. When the WRA decided to tighten up in 1943, eliminating many jobs and much of the unemployment roll, there was considerable protest. Labor grievances were widespread and motivation was a real problem. Many evacuees saw no reason to devote their best efforts to a system which displayed so little trust in them and held out such demeaning rewards.[157]

Despite these problems, the employment program was not a total failure. The centers were staffed almost completely by evacuees, and some agricultural efforts and war industries succeeded moderately.

At all centers, workers were most needed in operations—food preparation,[158] winterization,[159] health and sanitation, security[160] and the like.[161] Feeding the community was most labor-intensive.[162] Among those who testified about their employment, by far the largest group worked in center operations.

Although the centers never met WRA expectations for agriculture, some did produce considerable amounts of food. Begun at Tule Lake and Gila River, vegetable production later became substantial at other centers as well.[163] By the end of 1943, WRA estimated that the centers were producing 85 percent of their own vegetables and that 2.5 million pounds had been sold.[164] In addition to vegetables, all of the centers eventually raised hogs.[165] "The hogs ate everything we left and ultimately we ate the hogs."[166] Most raised poultry as well. Four had beef herds, and Gila River ran a dairy.[167]

The first industry in operation was the camouflage net project at Manzanar. From June to December 1942, nearly 500 citizen evacuees garnished nets with colored fabric in summer, winter and desert patterns. Near the end of 1942, net factories operating under contract began production at Gila River and Poston. They set up an incentive system that allowed workers to make extra money by high production. Not surprisingly, the incentive system was resented by those to whom no incentives were offered.[168]

During 1943, two other war-related industries were established: a silk-screen poster shop at Heart Mountain and a model warship facility at Gila River, both preparing Navy orders.[169] In 1943 sawmills began at two centers.[170] Several other industries began to produce goods for internal consumption. By the end of 1942, sewing projects to renovate and repair work clothes; woodworking establishments to produce furniture; and projects to produce bean sprouts and soy sauce were under way.[171] In 1943, others were added.[172] Susumu Togasaki described the growth of small-scale enterprise through the birth of his *tofu* (bean curd) factory:

> We began manufacturing with a meat grinder and a washing machine. I recruited my friends and acquaintances (Messrs. Yamaguchi, Shimizu, Asakawa, Harada, Tsuruoka, and Mrs. Umezawa). There was some controversy regarding our spending too much money. So we instituted an invoice system with the administration. We invoiced all the tofu and bean sprouts delivered to the mess halls in the three camps. We also contra-accounted the re-

ceipt of raw materials, and the salaries of the members of the tofu factory. We showed a profit at the end of the first month.

Our invoices were later to be a problem. The administration made inquiries in various cities regarding the prices of bean sprouts and tofu. They apparently felt our paper profits were too high. However, complaints were voiced by civilians in the cities that our prices were too low.

Once the tofu and bean sprout operations were running smoothly, our group looked for other projects. In response to the unavailability of fresh flowers for funerals, weddings, and gatherings, we decided to manufacture artificial flowers. We purchased crepe paper and wire on a retail basis from Phoenix. We soon realized the crepe paper prices were exorbitant, and wrote to the manufacturer. We began buying enough crepe paper to be awarded the sole distributorship for the Pacific Southwest. My friends later sold crepe paper to the retail stores in the Phoenix area. We also started a greeting card manufacturing business, using linoleum block prints. The cards were designed and executed by artists among the internees.

The majority of the people working these operations were paid $19.00 per month. The administration felt some of the people should be paid less, since that was a supervisorial wage rate. I argued that each person on our staff was exercising independent judgment. Thus the salary levels were justified and continued. [173]

Finally, "community enterprises" provided goods and services to the evacuees beyond the WRA subsistence items—stores, hairdressers, newspapers, theaters and the like. Most of these were begun under WRA auspices; the plan, however, was to transform them into consumer cooperatives. [174] Many centers did in fact establish such cooperatives, [175] purchasing goods on credit from wholesalers. Those not set up as cooperatives were organized as trusts. [176] By the end of 1942, there were 116 such enterprises doing over $700,000 worth of business a month. [177]

From Day to Day

Life begins each day with a siren blast at 7:00 a.m., with breakfast served cafeteria style. Work begins at 8:00 for the adults, school at 8:30 or 9:00 for the children. [178]

Camp life was highly regimented and it was rushing to the wash basin to beat the other groups, rushing to the mess hall for breakfast, lunch and dinner. When a human being is placed in captivity, survival is the key. We develop a very negative attitude toward authority. We spent countless hours to defy or beat the system. Our minds started to function like any POW or convicted criminal. [179]

Living in a relocation camp meant waiting, not just waiting for food and facilities, but waiting to see what would happen next. There was no way to prepare for the future—to plan for retirement or to choose a career path. There was little reason to work, except to pass the time or to fill immediate community needs. Choices were denied, from the choice of where to live to the choice of what to eat. Merely surviving was physically and psychically draining. Getting to the messhall on time; finding an empty shower; keeping the diapers clean; coping with the heat, the cold, insects or snakes were major tasks. Holding the family together without privacy or authority required a full commitment. Yet the camps were busy places. Most of those who could work, did so, and both WRA and the evacuees clearly tried to create the illusion of a normal community with normal pastimes. Nowhere was this more evident than in their efforts to set up community activities.

Yet the same contradictions within WRA applied here as in other aspects of living. How could they provide enough without being accused of providing too much? How could they permit evacuees to control their communities without compromising their responsibilities as jailers? The illusion that the captive population controlled their own lives could not be sustained. Once again, compromise satisfied no one.

Education. When the evacuees arrived at the relocation centers, the education program was little more than a promise that schools would be the first order of business. [180] School buildings and equipment had not been part of the original construction, so classes were held in barrack-like recreation halls. [181] The WRA described conditions as schools opened somewhat later than usual between 1942 and January 1943:

> With no exceptions, schools at the centers opened in unpartitioned barracks meant for other purposes and generally bare of furniture. Sometimes the teacher had a desk and chair; more often she had only a chair. In the first few weeks many of the children had no desks or chairs and for the most part were obliged to sit on the floor—or stand up all day. Linoleum laying and additional wall insulation were accomplished in these makeshift schoolrooms some time after the opening of school. At some centers cold waves struck before winterization could be started.
>
> By the [end of 1942] . . . it was no longer necessary for many pupils to sit on the floor, but seating was frequently of a rudimentary character. Text books and other supplies were gradually arriving. Laboratory and shop equipment and facilities, however, were still lacking. No center had been able to obtain its full quota of teachers. [182]

At Minidoka, the "washroom became the biology and chemistry laboratory."[183] At Tule Lake, students in the typing class never saw a typewriter: "We drew circles on a sheet of paper, lettered the circles, and practiced by pressing our fingers over the circles."[184] The shortage of textbooks and supplies was mitigated, though never resolved. States donated old textbooks[185] and other donations came through the American Friends Service Committee.[186]

Recruiting and training teachers was a constant problem. Few evacuees were certified, because teaching opportunities before the war were few for those of Japanese ancestry. It was difficult to recruit outside teachers because of the centers' harsh living conditions,[187] and staff turnover was high.[188] Thus, many evacuees with two or more years of college became "assistant teachers" who in some cases assumed a full teaching load.[189] Although an evacuee certification program was established at each center, the shortage continued, particularly as the resettlement effort quickened.[190] One evacuee described his chemistry class:

> I recall sitting in classrooms without books and listening to the instructor talking about technical matters that we could not study in depth. The lack of qualified evacuee teachers, the shortage of trained teachers was awful. I remember having to read a chapter a week in chemistry and discovering at the end of a semester that we had finished one full year's course. There was a total loss of scheduling with no experiments, demonstrations or laboratory work.[191]

Despite these problems, education began at four different levels: nursery school, elementary school, high school, and adult education.[192] Limited vocational education was added.[193] School clubs and extracurricular activities began.[194]

The curriculum, set in consultation with state education authorities, was consistent with the recognized standards of the state in which the center was located,[195] although some evacuees recall a dearth of science, language, math and other college preparatory courses.[196] All schools except Tule Lake were accredited. The children of families leaving the centers could usually transfer to outside schools without losing credit,[197] although some evacuees testified that some of their camp credits were not accepted.[198]

Education was a high priority in the centers, but adverse conditions took a toll. Many evacuees believed that deficiencies in the educational program have handicapped them ever since,[199] both because the physical environment was poor and because evacuees' attitudes toward the centers colored their attitudes about education.

The education program, ironically, emphasized "Americanization" and inculcation of the country's values. The centers certainly provided a new context for the precepts of the Founding Fathers:

> An oft-repeated ritual in relocation camp schools . . . was the salute to the flag followed by the singing of "My country, 'tis of thee, sweet land of liberty"—a ceremony Caucasian teachers found embarrassingly awkward if not cruelly poignant in the austere prison-camp setting.[200]

The life of children is, of course, in many ways oblivious of the fears and angers of adults, but experiences of childhood teach their own lessons, and the half-free, half-prison world of the camps left its mark:

> In some ways, I suppose, my life was not too different from a lot of kids in America between the years 1942 and 1945. I spent a good part of my time playing with my brothers and friends, learned to shoot marbles, watched sandlot baseball and envied the older kids who wore Boy Scout uniforms. We shared with the rest of America the same movies, screen heroes and listened to the same heartrending songs of the forties. We imported much of America into the camps because, after all, we were Americans. Through imitation of my brothers, who attended grade school within the camp, I learned the salute to the flag by the time I was five years old. I was learning, as best one could learn in Manzanar, what it meant to live in America. But I was also learning the sometimes bitter price one has to pay for it.[201]

Recreation. In the early months, the recreation halls often had to be used for other purposes, equipment was minimal, and professionals to organize the program were few. By the winter of 1942, however, conditions were improving. Church groups loaned or gave equipment,[202] and supervisors were on the job in all centers but one.[203]

Athletics were a major recreation. While the preferences of Issei and Nisei differed in most cases, baseball was a common denominator. At some centers, there were as many as 100 teams active at one time, ranging from children to Issei in their sixties.[204] Basketball and touch football were popular as well. Indoor sports were limited to those that took little space—primarily ping-pong, judo, boxing[205] and badminton.[206] *Sumo* wrestling bouts were given for those interested in the traditional sports of Japan.[207] By the end of 1943, evacuees were sometimes allowed to leave the grounds, so that hiking and swimming became popular pastimes.[208]

The evacuees also diverted themselves with dancing, plays, concerts, and games—cards, chess, checkers, *Goh*, *Shogi* and *Mah-jongg*.[209] Some activities were underwritten by outside groups—an art competition in 1943, for example, was sponsored by Massachusetts Quakers.[210] There were numerous art or craft exhibitions[211] and films that came to each messhall.[212] At Manzanar, an outdoor walk-in theatre was eventually built, where evacuees could see most current films.[213] Although there were few instruments, there was a good deal of music. Dancing classes at Topaz, for example, included tap, ballet, toe and Oriental, and there were two orchestras.[214]

Most of the centers had libraries. By 1943, the Manzanar library had a staff of sixteen and five branches including a main library, a small fiction branch, a high school and elementary branch and a teacher's library.[215] By the end of 1943, most of the libraries had Japanese language sections as well.[216]

Holidays remained important, as they had been in the assembly centers. At Topaz, for example, Arbor Day was celebrated by distributing small shrubs to each block; at Christmas, there were decorated trees, special food, and presents donated by the American Friends Society;[217] New Year's was celebrated[218] traditionally with *mochi*, a kind of rice cake; at Easter, a large outdoor ceremony was planned; and the Buddhists held a parade and folk dances to celebrate the anniversary of the birth of Buddha.[219]

The WRA encouraged the establishment of local chapters of national organizations.[220] By the end of 1942, most centers had chapters of the American Red Cross, YMCA, YWCA, Boy Scouts and Girl Scouts.[221] There were scrap metal drives, bond sales, Red Cross drives and blood donations.[222] Ultimately, these organizations, particularly the YMCA and YWCA, were active in helping evacuees to resettle.[223]

Not all recreation, of course, was organized. At Topaz, women created beautiful designs in seashells collected around the campground, once the bottom of an ancient lake. Many of the men did woodworking. At other centers doll-making, sewing, crochet, calligraphy and flower-arranging were popular.[224]

Religion. The WRA's policy was to allow complete freedom of worship, except for barring State Shinto on the grounds that it involved Emperor worship.[225] A building—generally the recreation hall—was provided for services, and evacuees were permitted to invite outside pastors if they wished.[226] Pianos and organs were loaned or donated.[227] Originally, the WRA was willing to allow churches to be built,[228] but later reversed this plan because of materials shortages.[229] The WRA did not pay ministers,[230] so they were financed by their congregations or the national churches.[231] Unlike the assembly centers, here the use of Japanese was permitted.[232]

Newspapers. All centers had community newspapers, published in English with a Japanese language section. They were supervised by the WRA center information officer but the editors and staff were evacuees. *The San Francisco Chronicle* reported that there was no censorship at Tule Lake and that the content was "innocuous,"[233] though one must question whether censorship would be necessary where the seat of power was so obvious and the effective paths of protest so few. Most papers published two or three times a week, although some were weekly and Poston's came out daily.[234] Most were underwritten by the WRA; at Manzanar, Minidoka and Heart Mountain, papers were printed and managed by the community enterprise associations.[235] The papers were intended to keep the evacuees informed about the center and outside. Camp administration used them for announcements, and resettlement news appeared frequently once it was under way.[236]

Government. From the beginning, it was clear that a channel of communication between camp administrators and evacuees would be needed. WRA planned a system of community government to meet this need and also to function like a municipal government adopting ordinances and policies on internal matters.[237] The form was to be an elected community council of representatives from each block. For legal and policy reasons, however, WRA held a veto over the legislative activities of the governments and adopted policies describing how they would be structured.[238] Because of these restrictions, particularly one barring Issei from holding elective office, many evacuees regarded the system as a sham, further evidence that they were not trusted, and an example of bad faith by the WRA.[239]

Despite these problems, most centers eventually did have some sort of government. By the end of 1942, eight centers had temporary community councils. Eventually, all the centers had councils except Manzanar, which continued to function through its system of elected block managers.[240]

At some centers, block managers were the real channels of communication. Generally appointed by the project director (except at Manzanar, where block managers were elected) and usually a respected Issei, the block manager had three specific responsibilities: to ensure that evacuees had necessities; to supervise maintenance of grounds and structures; and to transmit official WRA announcements and regulations.[241] They were paid the going wage of $16 a month.[242] Many of these individuals enjoyed a measure of patriarchal respect that gave them authority[243] within the community and allowed them to lead when the community councils could not.

Security. The typical relocation center was surrounded by barbed-wire fences punctuated with guard towers.[244] At Topaz, the evacuees themselves built the fences and towers after they arrived.[245] By agreement between the Army and the WRA, the Army assumed responsibility for guarding the perimeter,[246] controlling traffic in and out of the centers and, within the Western Defense Command, inspecting parcels for contraband.[247]

> I worked at the camp post office alongside American soldiers who were to inspect packages for contraband. Although not all could be described as such, most were callous, destructive in their inspection of mail order packages, and insensitive. Clothing was cut with their knives and intimate articles (including condoms, etc.) were held up for all to see, causing great embarrassment to the recipients.[248]

The military police were solely for external guarding unless they were called in by the project director to handle an emergency.[249] Even so, they created problems in several instances. A WRA investigation of Manzanar in the summer of 1942 reported:

> The guards have been instructed to shoot anyone who attempts to leave the Center without a permit, and who refuses to halt when ordered to do so. The guards are armed with guns that are effective at a range of up to 500 yards. I asked Lt. Buckner if a guard ordered a Japanese who was out of bounds to halt and the Jap did not do so, would the guard actually shoot him. Lt. Buckner's reply was that he only hoped the guard would bother to ask him to halt. He explained that the guards were finding guard service very monotonous, and that nothing would suit them better than to have a little excitement, such as shooting a Jap.
>
> Some time ago, a Japanese [Nisei] was shot for being outside of a Center. . . . The guard said that he ordered the Japanese to halt—that the Japanese started to run away from him, so he shot him. The Japanese was seriously injured, but recovered. He said that he was collecting scrap lumber to make shelves in his house, and that he did not hear the guard say halt. The guard's story does not appear to be accurate, inasmuch as the Japanese was wounded in the front and not in the back.[250]

There were shootings at other centers as well. At Topaz, an elderly evacuee thought to be escaping was killed.[251] Mine Okubo described the incident:

> A few weeks later the Wakasa case stirred up the center. An elderly resident was shot and killed within the center area inside the fence, by a guard in one of the watchtowers. Particulars and facts of the matter were never satisfactorily disclosed to the residents. The anti-administration leaders again started to howl and the rest of the residents shouted for protection against soldiers with guns.

As a result, the guards were later removed to the rim of the outer project area and firearms were banned.[252]

At Gila River, a guard shot and wounded a mentally deranged evacuee.[253] At Tule Lake, after segregation, an evacuee in an altercation with a guard was shot and killed.[254]

Even when the guards were not shooting, their presence had a lasting impact. As George Takei described it:

> I was too young to understand, but I do remember the barbed wire fence from which my parents warned me to stay away. I remember the sight of high guard towers. I remember soldiers carrying rifles, and I remember being afraid.[255]

Internal security was the center manager's job. Generally, he would appoint an internal security officer to supervise a police force composed largely of evacuees. The internal security forces were to make all arrests. Misdemeanors were handled at the center, and felony suspects were turned over to outside authorities. The FBI was called if intelligence or investigation of subversive activities was needed.[256]

Generally, the crime record at the centers compared favorably with that of an average American community of similar size. A 1944 survey of comparative crime rates indicated that the law was being broken about a third as often in relocation centers as in an ordinary city.[257]

Tensions and Crisis

> Two-thirds—the younger, American-born and American-citizen Nisei—are becoming increasingly bitter, resentful and even sullen.
>
> The camp is a mare's nest of rumors, of suspicion and distrust. Many of the Japanese feel that the Government has not kept all its promises—and the Government certainly hasn't—and they wait apprehensively for the next blow to fall.[258]

Discontent over camp living conditions was inevitable. Housing and food were poor. Suspicion that staff was stealing and selling food was widespread.[259] Wages and clothing allowances were delayed. For many older residents, there were no jobs. WRA had promised that household goods would be brought to evacuees as soon as they arrived; months later, none had come. There were continual shortages of equipment and material for education and recreation. WRA had promised that one of its first jobs would be to build schools and furnish school equipment, but priority often went instead to improving quarters for WRA personnel.[260]

Fear, uncertainty and the monotony of enforced idleness aggravated tension. At the older centers, WRA policies had not been set when evacuees arrived, and there were no answers to many of their questions.[261] They feared the future—not only what would happen after the war, but also whether there would be enough food or quality medical care at the centers.[262] Many had lost income and property, which left them few resources to fall back on. They feared the "outside." Relations with outside communities were poor, and evacuees knew that some towns had passed resolutions against the free movement of evacuees. Local communities and politicians had investigated the camps for evidence of "coddling."[263]

Evacuees feared and resented the changes forced by life in the centers, particularly the breakdown of family authority, created in part by a situation in which children no longer depended so heavily on their parents. Family separation was common, and mass living discouraged normal communication and family activity.[264] Perhaps most difficult, the position of the head of the family had been weakened. No longer the breadwinner providing food and shelter, he had been supplanted by the government; his authority over the family and his ability to lead and discipline were diminished. Children unsettlingly found their parents as helpless as they.[265]

At the root of it all, evacuees resented being prisoners against whom no crime was charged and for whom there was no recourse. Armed guards patrolled their community and searched their packages. No evacuee could have a camera. Even beer was prohibited. For a long time, no evacuee could leave the center, except for emergency reasons, and then only in the company of someone who was not of Japanese ancestry.[266] Evacuee positions were subordinate to WRA personnel, regardless of ability, and wages were low.[267] At some centers, project officials actively tried to maintain class and role distinctions, forbidding WRA personnel and evacuees to eat in the same messhall, for example.[268]

Not all hostility was directed at the WRA; tensions among evacuees also began to surface. Conflicts between Issei and Nisei arose. Most difficult was coping with the WRA-mandated "self-government," which specified that only citizens could serve on community councils. Parallel organizations, like competing block manager groups made up largely of Issei, heightened conflicts.[269]

There were also conflicts between early and later arrivals. Early arrivals tended to be young, aggressive people who had volunteered to open the centers. They were accused of having taken the best jobs,[270] often the level of administration just below WRA staff. Charges of corruption, incompetence and, most divisive, collaboration began to grow.[271]

The same kinds of problems developed between JACL leaders, who were often favored by center administrators,[272] and other evacuees, particularly the Kibei, who were denied some of the rights (such as student leave) that other evacuees received.[273] Some JACL leaders blamed the Issei and Kibei for camp disturbances and charged them with being "disloyal."[274] In fact, Masaoka volunteered to Myer that JACL leaders might identify the "known agitators" at the camps so that the WRA could separate them from the rest of the evacuees.[275] Some evacuees felt that the JACL had sold out the cause of Japanese Americans.[276]

As tension grew, anyone perceived as close to the administration became suspect as an *inu* or dog.[277] At Manzanar, a group called the Black Dragons surfaced, a handful of profascist enthusiasts for Imperial Japan. Among other activities, the Black Dragons instigated rock-throwing at the camouflage-net workers[278] and beat those they considered *inu*. Other gangs, too, were involved in beatings. As the leave program got under way, draining the centers of many of the most constructively aggressive young men,[279] the gangs grew.

Other signs of disaffection were emotional meetings and a petition in favor of better living and working conditions.[280] Karl Yoneda testified:

[We] formed the Manzanar Citizens Federation on July 20, 1942. Some of the topics we discussed were: improved camp conditions, education of citizens for leadership, participation in the war efforts and postwar preparations.[281]

Finally came the crises at Poston and Manzanar. Although these were the only two major confrontations (except at Tule Lake after the segregation), beatings and hostilities continued.[282]

Incidents at Poston and Manzanar. At Poston on November 1, 1942, an evacuee who had cooperated with the WRA and was suspected of being an "informer" was beaten by a group of unidentified men. Evacuee police arrested two men on suspicion and held them at the FBI's request while the beating was investigated. After the two had been detained two days, a group of older evacuees asked their release; the request was refused. The next day, a crowd of about 1,000 demanded the release of the prisoners as did the community council. When their request was refused, the council resigned. Although one suspect was released after the FBI investigation, the other was held to be tried in the county court.[283]

The evacuees formed a leadership committee which decreed a general strike[284] and organized pickets surrounding the center's jail to prevent removal of the detained man. On November 23, an agreement was finally reached in which the prisoner was released to custody of two evacuee lawyers pending trial, and the emergency leaders agreed to help stop the beatings and try to establish better rapport with the administration.[285]

On December 5, 1942, at Manzanar, a suspected "informer" was assaulted by six masked men. From the hospital he said he could identify one of the attackers, who was arrested and jailed outside the center. The next day a mass meeting was held to protest the arrest. The crowd decided to try to negotiate with the project director, appointing a committee of five. Meanwhile, the project director had asked military police to stand by. At first the director refused to negotiate. Later he agreed to do so and thought he had reached a compromise: the suspect would be returned and tried at the center and evacuees would cooperate on various future matters. Under the agreement, the suspect was returned to the center jail.[286]

Later that day, the crowd reassembled.[287] They demanded the suspect's release and made plans to get ten or eleven other suspected "informers."[288] At this point, the project director called in the military police. When the crowd refused to disperse, the MPs threw tear gas. The crowd formed again as soon as the gas had blown away. When a person in the crowd started an empty car and headed it toward a machine gun, the MPs opened fire. Two evacuees were killed and nine wounded.[289]

> I ran and became one of the curious spectators. The MP fired shots into the defenseless crowd. A classmate, Jimmy Ito, was shot and killed. It was a terrifying experience.[290]

The suspected "informers," a group who had cooperated with WRA administrators, were removed for safety to the military police barracks and later to an abandoned CCC camp, from which they resettled.[291] Those whom the authorities believed to have been implicated in the mass demonstrations were sent either to Justice Department internment camps (if aliens) or to a WRA isolation camp at Moab, Utah (if citizens). Eventually the WRA isolation camp and its inhabitants, now including dissidents from other centers as well, were moved to Leupp, Arizona. From Leupp, some eventually returned to relocation centers or to internment camps; most, however, were removed to Tule Lake after segregation, when Leupp was closed.[292]

The allegations of "informer" and "collaborator" that underlie the incidents at Poston and Manzanar touch nerves still sensitive today. The same is true of the controversy over whether the WRA's community analysts operated in good faith. In early 1943, the WRA had established a Community Analysis Section designed to "assist in the problems of administering the relocation centers, in the interests of both administrators and evacuees."[293] The analysts, many of whom were sociologists and anthropologists, observed and interviewed WRA staff and evacuees, then made recommendations to improve the WRA program, yielding a substantial literature of over 100 reports. The Commission heard some testimony, particularly that of Dr. Peter Suzuki,[294] alleging that some of the analysts were not objective reporters and problem-solvers, but informers for the WRA who suppressed important information. Dr. Edward Spicer, formerly head of the community analysts, offered a rebuttal of the Suzuki charges.[295]

The role of the analysts and the question of whether cooperation with or resistance to the WRA, passive or active, was the better course for evacuees, remain matters of intense, sometimes bitter controversy among those who lived in the camps. There is no "right" answer to the evacuees' dilemma; nor do isolated examples of informing prove or disprove WRA's intentions. In both cases, the facts are almost impossible to determine. For the Commission to delve into these matters, attempting to settle old scores, would be inappropriate.

Leave

It was an opportunity for the farmers and *hakujins* [white folk] out there because they were looking for cheap labor. Here was this source, in this camp, for cheap labor and they said why not? We saw it as an opportunity to get to go to the store and to buy stuff to bring back to the family.[296]

Even as Eisenhower decided in April 1942 that the WRA would plan primarily in terms of confining the evacuees, the process that would secure their release was beginning. Before the first evacuees reached the relocation centers, the WDC had begun to release a few for one of two purposes: to continue their college education or to harvest crops.

The evacuation meant that some 3,500 Japanese Americans would be prohibited from attending colleges and universities on the West Coast—an incalculable loss to both the nation and the ethnic Japanese community.[297] First to recognize and confront the problem was a group from the University of California at Berkeley led by Robert Gordon Sproul, then president of the university. Sproul and his colleagues set out to transfer as many students as possible to universities in the interior.[298] Milton Eisenhower, also concerned about the problem, had contacted Clarence Pickett, a prominent Quaker leader. Pickett recruited a group of educators, industrialists and cultural leaders to form the National Student Relocation Council, which then set about transferring students to other institutions.[299]

Even with such impressive support, numerous kinds of resistance to the program had to be overcome. Many institutions refused to accept evacuee students because the university was involved in war-related research.[300] The students themselves were sometimes harassed:

At my first opportunity, in March, 1943, I left camp to attend school in Milwaukee, Wisconsin. On my way to Milwaukee, I was harassed by MPs checking for my ID number and pass many times. I even got spat upon by some of the passengers on the train.

When I arrived in Milwaukee, I discovered that the engineering school had misrepresented themselves and only wanted my money. Then I moved to Chicago, Illinois and with the help of American Friends Service Committee, found a job in a box factory. I worked there for three months.

Then I tried to enroll in a school of engineering at the University of Illinois, but when I told them I was an evacuee from camp, they refused my admission. I told them of my WRA clearance, but my protests went unheeded. Finally, I was accepted at the University of Michigan in Ann Arbor, because I listed my Chicago address and did not mention internment.[301]

The federal government never supported these students, except to subsidize travel. The majority were aided by private philanthropy, most of it organized by various Christian groups.[302] Several evacuees mentioned the efforts of the American Friends Service Committee;[303] others depended on their parents' meager savings.[304]

Nevertheless, some 250 students had left to attend one of 143 colleges and universities by autumn 1942.[305] Eventually, the program placed about 4,300 students.[306]

The second escape from the camps was the seasonal leave program for farm labor. As early as the beginning of April 1942, the WDC was receiving requests to release evacuees for seasonal farm labor and trying to construct a policy.[307] By early summer, the agricultural producers had become increasingly concerned that, without help, the crops, particularly sugar beets, would be lost. At the beginning of May, they petitioned the White House for help, and the agricultural leave program began.[308]

The first group of 15 evacuees was released on May 21 from the Portland Assembly Center to help thin beets in eastern Oregon.[309] The program had a number of requirements. Governors at the state level; sheriffs, prosecuting attorneys, commissioners and judges at the county level, were required to pledge in writing that labor was needed and that workers' safety would be guaranteed; employers were required to furnish transportation and had to pay prevailing wages; evacuees could not be hired in place of available local labor. The U.S. Employment Service in the affected counties agreed to provide housing in the area of employment at no cost to evacuees. By the end of June, 1,500 workers had been recruited under the program. Incidents were few and minor. Because the evacuees were efficient and well-liked, "labor pirating" by prospective employers occurred. Contracts between employers and evacuee groups helped correct the problem. In September the demand for seasonal workers from the centers increased enormously; by mid-October, 10,000 evacuees were on seasonal leave, and the demand well exceeded the supply.[310] When the harvest ended, the Nisei were credited with having saved the sugar beet crops of several western states.[311]

Although the WRA tried to ensure that employers made clear the conditions in which evacuees would be working,[312] they were not always successful.

[W]hen we arrived there, we were met by a farmer supervisor who led us to a large horse barn, one-third of which was filled with hay. He told us this was where we were going to sleep.[313]

Our living quarters was a shack without running water, heated by a coal stove, and we had to bathe in a ditch that was on the farm.[314]

Despite the guarantees, some evacuees on agricultural work leave also encountered hostility from communities in which they worked and travelled. One evacuee was arrested and beaten by police while travelling back to Poston.[315] Another describes how local toughs made teenage evacuees crawl through the city park.[316] A survey of Manzanar returnees taken in Fall 1942 showed that the majority believed the public was "not yet ready to accept an Oriental as a U.S. citizen."[317]

Still, overall, the program was judged a success. For the farmers, crops were saved. For the evacuees, it was a chance to get out of the camp and to make more than camp wages, which was particularly important for the many evacuees in increasing financial distress.[318]

The success of the student and agricultural leave programs contributed to the decision to attempt resettlement on a larger scale. Perhaps even more important was the appointment of a new director. On June 17, 1942, Eisenhower resigned;[319] the President appointed a new Director of WRA, Dillon Myer, who saw the program through to its conclusion. Myer felt strongly that the evacuees should be released and resettled, which led him to make resettlement a WRA priority.[320]

Myer did not, however, simply return to the position that the evacuees were free to leave the camps when and how they chose. On July 20, the WRA issued a carefully circumscribed relocation policy statement, which permitted relocation by Nisei who had never studied in Japan and who had a definite offer of employment outside the camps. The clearance process, which involved the WRA, FBI and other federal intelligence agencies, was lengthy, and often job offers were cancelled because clearance took so long. As a result, few evacuees were able to relocate.[321]

In late July, the WRA established a staff committee to work out a more comprehensive policy. Importantly, one possibility considered was an all-out program permitting any evacuee to leave a center at his or her own discretion. While this would have been ideal from a civil liberties standpoint, the lack of public understanding and the earlier experience of the voluntary evacuees made such a drastic policy seem impractical both to WRA and to the Justice Department.[322]

The new rules, which became effective on October 1, 1942,[323] over WDC objections,[324] stopped far short of opening the center gates. They allowed both Issei and Nisei to apply and provided three kinds of leave: short-term leave for up to 30 days (for example, for medical purposes); work group leave (for seasonal employment); and indefinite leave for employment, education or indefinite residence outside the relocation area. To obtain indefinite leave, which was in fact relocation, a person had to show that he had a means of support and that no evidence in his files (either at the center or after a check by the FBI) showed that he might endanger national security. He needed to show his presence was likely to be acceptable where he planned to live, and to agree to inform WRA of any change of address. Special provisions applied to aliens of enemy nationality who were issued leave permits.

In his autobiography, Myer states that when these relocation regulations were issued, key WRA staff members were convinced that such a leave policy was essential for a number of reasons: discriminatory segregation would discourage loyalty; "wide and enforced deviation from normal cultural and living patterns might very well have lasting and unfavorable effects upon individuals, particularly children and young people;" the WRA had an obligation to the evacuees and to the people of the United States to restore loyal citizens and law-abiding aliens to "a normal useful American life" with all possible speed; confinement in centers bred suspicion of evacuees; and continued confinement would help foster a new set of reservations similar to Indian reservations.[325] This was the voice of that side of WRA which saw itself as the advocate of Japanese American interests, but, as usual, that voice did not speak clearly. The program conveyed the message that all Japanese were supposed to be under armed guard unless the government permitted otherwise, and even those released were granted only "indefinite leave." At least in theory, the government retained its control.

In mid-November 1942, WRA reorganized to reflect its increasing emphasis on resettlement. It brought most of its functions into the Washington office and established a series of field offices to expedite the relocation process. Seven district offices had already opened in the west; established at first to supervise the seasonal work program, they began now to promote indefinite leave. Midwestern field offices were also established, beginning on January 4, 1943, with an office in Chicago. By 1943, 42 field offices were scattered throughout the country. Myer described their important job:

> In the early months these offices were primarily concerned with creating favorable community acceptance and in finding suitable jobs for evacuees and in working closely with community resettlement committees. The officers gave talks to business, professional, social, civic, church and fraternal groups. They met with employers individually and in groups, enlisted the aid of unions, and spoke to employees in plants where the employment of Japanese was contemplated. They supplied news to the press and carried on a public relations job in general.[326]

Organizing support among community groups and citizens to form local resettlement committees was also a WRA task during the fall of 1942.[327] Church organizations in particular were involved,[328] as was the Pacific Coast Committee on American Principles and Fair Play, organized in 1942.[329]

By the end of 1942, the WRA was firmly committed to a program of leave and resettlement. Manpower demands were growing, and the agricultural and student leave programs had gone well. Conditions in the camps were deteriorating. The evacuees were becoming increasingly disaffected and the original plans for large-scale agriculture and industry within the centers had been largely abandoned. Although the indefinite leave programs had not been particularly successful in resettling large numbers, the WRA was committed to getting evacuees out of the camps and into the war effort.

7

Loyalty: Leave and Segregation

By October 1942, the government was holding over 100,000 evacuees in relocation centers. Evacuation had been an emergency measure, but politics and the chimera of a threat to military security had sentenced the evacuees to indefinite confinement. They were still detained although no individual charges had been, or could have been, made against them. Supported by neither statute nor explicit executive order, the legal basis for confining evacuees was plainly suspect. The human toll the camps were taking was enormous—physical hardship, growing anger toward the United States and deteriorating morale. The tide of war turned with the American victory at the battle of Midway in June 1942 and as the possibility of Japanese attack grew more remote, the military necessity for detention and exclusion became increasingly difficult to defend. Nevertheless, other than the WRA's ineffective leave program, the government had no plans to remedy the situation and no means of distinguishing the loyal from the disloyal—if it were inclined to do so. Total control of these civilians in the presumed interest of state security was rapidly becoming the accepted norm.

How would the government deal with this new status quo in the fall of 1942? Having bowed to political pressure in deciding to control and detain the ethnic Japanese, what standard or test or presumption was to be established to return the evacuees to liberty? Or would the government embrace the proposition that, in wartime, total control of suspect groups of civilians is justified and legally permissible?

185

Commentators have characterized the exclusion and detention of the ethnic Japanese as a triumph of military over civilian authority.[1] As our account of the decisions to evacuate and detain makes clear, this view is accurate to a limited degree since the military was carrying out a program largely conceived and promoted by civilian groups and politicians. The friction between military and civilian interests is more clearly seen in the decision of whether and how to end the detention. Some in the Western Defense Command argued that there was a military interest in restricting the release of the evacuees to those who posed no conceivable military threat and, ultimately, that the Army should prepare through planning and intelligence work to control large groups of suspect civilians in any future war. The security of the state should be paramount. The civilians at the top of the War Department understood their responsibility differently; returning the loyal evacuees to normal life outside a detention camp should be the touchstone of government policy and, since exclusion and detention rested on a military justification, the War Department had to play an active role in that effort. The WRA shared this view and had more liberal opinions on the indicia of loyalty. It is a bitter irony that the loyalty review program, which the WRA and the War Department established as the predicate for release from the camps—the first major governmental decision in which the interests of the evacuees prevailed—was carried out without sufficient sensitivity or knowledge of the evacuees. Designed to hasten their release, the program instead became one of the most divisive, wrenching episodes of the captivity.

McCLOY AND THE NISEI COMBAT TEAM

The government decision makers closest to the evacuees increasingly believed that wholesale confinement was not justified or acceptable. Dillon Myer strongly held this view and was already looking for ways to achieve large-scale resettlement. Milton Eisenhower had never been comfortable with the program. Now in the fall of 1942 John J. McCloy also adopted this view as the matter was raised with him in the context of whether evacuees should be permitted to serve in the Army.

Once the decision to evacuate was made and the WRA had taken custody of the evacuees, Stimson and McCloy had largely left the treatment of Japanese Americans to others. The Nisei in the Army, their only immediate concern, were few because the Selective Service had stopped induction at about the time of the evacuation.[2] In February, making the decision to evacuate, Stimson and McCloy had relied heavily on DeWitt, ignoring the contrary views of the FBI and failing to seek other opinions. Since then McCloy had begun to study the matter and to hear that most evacuees were loyal, that they wanted to get out of the camps and prove their loyalty, and that they could assist the war effort.[3] He was persuaded by what he heard and believed it should be applied to War Department decisions.

Allowing the Nisei to serve would reverse a policy which had evolved over the previous year. On December 7, 1941, about 5,000 young Nisei from Hawaii and the mainland were in the Army, the majority having been drafted.[4] Immediately after Pearl Harbor, the Selective Service delegated discretion for the induction of Japanese Americans to local draft boards. Some Nisei volunteers were accepted, but the induction of others was delayed.[5] During the late winter and early spring of 1942, local draft boards became increasingly reluctant to draft Nisei. The center of discriminatory practice was again the West Coast. A War Department order of March 30, 1942, discontinued the induction of Nisei on the West Coast.[6] Enlisted Japanese Americans found themselves in a precarious situation. The personal attitude of their commanding officer was decisive; some Nisei stayed in service, while others were discharged without explanation.[7]

No clear-cut Selective Service policy was established to evaluate the status of draft-age Japanese Americans until June 17, 1942, when the War Department announced that it would not, aside from exceptional cases, "accept for service with the armed forces Japanese or persons of Japanese extraction, regardless of citizenship status or other factors."[8] In July, a War Department Board convened to examine Nisei induction, and "no immediate change in War Department policy was made except for selected individuals procurred [sic] for special purposes."[9] On September 14, the Selective Service adopted regulations prohibiting Nisei induction, and classifying registrants of Japanese ancestry IV-C, the status of enemy aliens. Previously, many draft-age Nisei had been reclassified from I-A to IV-F, unsuitable for military service.[10]

McCloy had favored using Nisei in the military since at least May 1942.[11] By fall, opinions supporting his position were beginning to trickle in. Delos Emmons, the commander in Hawaii, was particularly persuasive, arguing that the Nisei would make "grand soldiers."[12] His opinion was substantiated by the excellent performance of the all-Nisei Hawaii National Guard group then in training at Camp McCoy.[13] Nisei in the Military Intelligence Service Language School were doing equally well. Moreover, departmental officials involved in recruiting reported that large numbers of Nisei were embittered by the denial of their right to serve.[14] These voices inside the War Department were joined by some influential voices outside. Dillon Myer pressed the point with McCloy throughout the fall;[15] in November, the JACL passed a resolution requesting that the Selective Service be reinstituted.[16]

Perhaps because of the enlistment issue, McCloy was also beginning to ponder the plight of evacuees, locked up indefinitely in the unhealthy atmosphere of the camps. McCloy was not entirely sure of the ultimate loyalty of each ethnic Japanese, but he did not express the belief that all evacuees were inherently dangerous; it was clear to him that the evacuees could not be held in "pens" forever and that they should be released as soon as that was possible and safe.[17] In fact, it was impossible to consider a Nisei combat team apart from the exclusion and detention issue. Any discussion of whether the Nisei belonged in the armed forces inevitably questioned whether they could be trusted to bear arms—in other words, whether they were loyal. And the question of loyalty inevitably focused on the presumption of probable disloyalty which was inherent in the exclusion.

There were other reasons to link the combat team to the general issue of release from detention. Recruiting for a combat team without loosening other restrictions would open the War Department to the charge that the Nisei were being used as "cannon fodder."[18] It would be unfair to deny individuals barred from military service the opportunity to participate in the war effort in some other way, and it would be illogical to argue that loyalty should be tested only for those who might serve in the Army.[19] Discussions began to focus on the combat team as a way to get evacuees out of the camps and to rehabilitate them in the eyes of the public. McCloy's assistant, Colonel Scobey, explained bluntly that the need was "to assist the release of these people from the centers, to expedite the WRA mission."[20]

McCloy himself was convinced that change was needed, but his advocacy alone did not make policy. A War Department study, commissioned earlier in 1942 and approved on September 14, recommended that "the military potential of the United States citizens of Japanese ancestry be considered as negative because of the universal distrust in which they are held."[21] Thus, by the end of September, the career military opposed McCloy.

On October 2, Elmer Davis, Director of the Office of War Information (OWI), and Milton Eisenhower, now Davis's deputy, raised the issue with the President. In order to establish the legitimate interest of the OWI, Davis characterized the issue as one of war propaganda and asked the President to intervene and authorize the enlistment of Japanese Americans. His memorandum also reflected the debate's humanitarian overtones:

> Loyal American citizens of Japanese descent should be permitted, after individual test, to enlist in the Army and Navy. It would hardly be fair to evacuate people and then impose normal draft procedures, but voluntary enlistment would help a lot.
>
> This matter is of great interest to OWI. Japanese propaganda to the Philippines, Burma, and elsewhere insists that this is a racial war. We can combat this effectively with counter propaganda only if our deeds permit us to tell the truth. Moreover, as citizens ourselves who believe deeply in the things for which we fight, we cannot help but be disturbed by the insistent public misunderstanding of the Nisei. . . .[22]

As Davis and Eisenhower no doubt expected, the memorandum was referred to Secretary Stimson for comment. McCloy set out to persuade Stimson and General Marshall of the wisdom of his position. Dismissing the War Department study as too narrow, McCloy made three major points: almost everyone agreed that most Nisei were loyal; citizens had a fundamental right to serve their country; and enlistment would have an important psychological effect internationally.[23] Stimson took little convincing and sent Marshall a handwritten note which read in its entirety:

> I am inclined strongly to agree with the view of McCloy and Davis. I don't think you can permanently proscribe a lot of American citizens because of their racial origin. We have gone to the full limit in evacuating them. That's enough.[24]

Meanwhile, the careerists were reviewing their previous findings. Their September recommendations against Nisei combat service had not been unanimous and, with indications that their civilian leadership was tending in the other direction, they revised their conclusions. On December 16, the general staff sent Marshall a memorandum advocating an all-Nisei combat team.[25]

The new recommendations were approved by Marshall on January 1, 1943.[26] In testimony before the Commission, McCloy recalled: "I encountered opposition from everybody except those on my immediate staff and General Marshall. I went to General Marshall who then ordered the unit formed."[27]

On January 2, 1943, a committee was convened by Deputy Chief of Staff McNarney and told that some evacuees might be released. The committee's job was to "determine by what means Japanese-Americans of the Nisei class may be released from war relocation centers, and, if released, what disposition may be made of them."[28] A week later, the committee reported back, recommending the procedure that ultimately prevailed.

A questionnaire for Japanese Americans would be devised to reveal "tendencies of loyalty or disloyalty to the United States,"[29] including questions about the background and affiliations of the Nisei, and also soliciting a pledge of loyalty to the United States. Teams of Army personnel would supervise execution of the forms at the relocation centers. Copies of the questionnaires for males within the age limits for military service would be sent to military intelligence to decide who should be inducted. The remaining questionnaires would go to the Provost Marshal General's office which would check with the FBI and Naval Intelligence and evaluate the answers given. Then the questionnaires would be shipped to the Western Defense Command for investigation.

The second phase of the program would be handled by a Joint Board, including representatives of the Navy, WRA, military intelligence and the Provost Marshal General, which would decide whether the individual might be released from the relocation center and whether he might be employed in a plant important to the war effort.[30] The Board's mission was subsequently amended to make the Board's determination on release advisory to the WRA, which retained final authority.[31] The Joint Board retained power to decide whether an individual would be allowed to work in a war production facility.

The Joint Board was conceived as a way to avoid multiple investigations. Individuals who had been investigated and released by the WRA were being reinvestigated by the Army sector commander after they reached their destination. This inefficient process also handicapped the arriving evacuee by branding him suspicious. The Board would now make the only investigation.[32]

The WRA had not been involved in the War Department's planning.[33] Upon learning of the forthcoming registration, early in January, the WRA proposed that the process be enlarged to cover all persons over 17 years of age, including the Issei. This step, they believed, would expedite the existing leave clearance process which took so long that promised jobs were sometimes gone before the evacuee was released. By asking everyone to fill out the form, the WRA reasoned, much of the investigative work could be done before the evacuee was actually ready to leave. The WRA thus prepared a companion questionnaire, titled "Application for Leave Clearance," to be filled out by the Issei and Nisei females.[34] The entire review program was vehemently but unsuccessfully opposed by DeWitt and the Western Defense Command, who remained firmly persuaded that the loyal could not be distinguished from the disloyal.[35] The War Department rejected these views and prepared to go forward with the WRA on the broad program of loyalty review and release.

Secretary Stimson announced the new policy on the combat team:

> It is the inherent right of every citizen, regardless of ancestry, to bear arms in the Nation's battle. When obstacles to the free expression of that right are imposed by emergency considerations, those barriers should be removed as soon as humanly possible. Loyalty to country is a voice that must be heard, and I am now able to give active proof that this basic American belief is not a casualty of war.[36]

There was also a letter from the President, released the following week, approving the combat team. With a fine disregard for past treatment of the Nisei, Roosevelt proclaimed:

> No loyal citizen of the United States should be denied the democratic right to exercise the responsibilities of his citizenship, regardless of his ancestry. The principle on which this country was founded and by which it has always been governed is that Americanism is a matter of the mind and heart; Americanism is not, and never was, a matter of race or ancestry. A good American is one who is loyal to this country and to our creed of liberty and democracy. Every loyal American citizen should be given the opportunity to serve this country wherever his skills will make the greatest contribution—whether it be in the ranks of our armed forces, war production, agriculture, government service, or other work essential to the war effort.[37]

The first significant steps to end detention had been taken.

REGISTRATION

By February 6, ten teams of Army officers, enlisted men and WRA staff, trained for this assignment, were on the way to the relocation centers.[38] The questionnaires they carried sought background information, but also asked two prospective questions. Question 27 asked draft-age males: "Are you willing to serve in the armed forces of the United States on combat duty, wherever ordered?" For others, including the Issei and women, it asked whether they would be willing to join the WACs or the Army Nurse Corps. Question 28 was the loyalty question:

> Will you swear unqualified allegiance to the United States of America and faithfully defend the United States from any or all attack by foreign or domestic forces, and forswear any form of allegiance or obedience to the Japanese emperor, or any other foreign government, power or organization?[39]

The registration teams arriving at the centers during the first weeks of February 1943 found a hostile audience. In the past year, evacuees had endured the evacuation, the assembly centers and the relocation camps. Living conditions were poor, their lives outside the centers had disintegrated, and the government had broken many promises. Congressmen in Washington continued to agitate for stripping the Nisei of citizenship. Disturbances at Poston and Manzanar during the two previous months showed tensions that existed to some degree at all the camps. It was not surprising that many were ready to question any government action that might affect their future,[40] and there was considerable sentiment for putting the claims of family ahead of those of country.

It became rapidly apparent that the government had not thought through the implications of the loyalty review program. Not only was the program forced on the evacuees with no notice and with few answers to important questions, but the documents themselves were flawed. The evacuees did not know how their responses would be used.[41] Particularly critical to the Issei was Question 28 on loyalty. The question was both unfair and unanswerable because it called upon the Issei to renounce their Japanese nationality, although they were barred by law from becoming United States citizens. To answer it affirmatively, they argued, would have made them "men without a country."[42] On the other hand, answering it negatively might well bring separation from one's family and attract suspicion to oneself as a security risk. The WRA quickly corrected the question to avoid forcing Issei to make such a Hobson's choice,[43] but suspicion and distrust lingered. There was confusion about the program and its basic intent. The document for Issei and women was titled "Application for Leave Clearance." Did this mean, asked many, that they would be forced to leave the center? They had lost their homes and property; with no assets were they now to be abandoned by the government in hostile communities? One evacuee described this dilemma:

> One can understand a situation of the head of a household, his livelihood taken away, having to face the possibility of earning a

living for his family in some strange city. The temptation to declare a "no," "no" position [to Questions 27 and 28] just to maintain the dependent life style in the camps was very strong indeed. In such cases the issue is survival, not loyalty.[44]

The Issei were also bitter about their own treatment and that of their citizen children. As a Naval Intelligence report stated, Issei opposition to enlistment was based less on reluctance to see their sons fighting Japan than on losing faith in America:

[T]he parents have made quite an issue of the fact that the citizen Japanese and the alien Japanese received identical treatment. This indicates, they say, the American Government does not recognize the nisei [sic] as full citizens.[45]

The Nisei too doubted the government's good faith and were wary of the program. The same Army and country confining them and their families behind barbed wire now asked Japanese Americans to volunteer to fight for principles of liberty, justice and equal protection under the law. To some, the segregated combat unit, although signifying the restoration of some of their rights as citizens, also continued discrimination.[46] While German and Italian Americans were drafted by normal procedures through the Selective Service System, Japanese Americans were stigmatized by their classification as enemy aliens.

Others had different problems with Question 27. A "yes" answer might be interpreted as volunteering.[47] A number of those who were loyal would stop short of enlisting in the military. With dependents at home and perhaps relatives in Japan who might suffer reprisals if they were known to have enlisted, some could not easily say "yes" to Question 27.

Finally, many were obligated to care for aging parents who were becoming more dependent and fearful in the camps' isolated confinement. If they were separated on the basis of differing answers, who would tend the Issei? Some felt they had to comply with parents who demanded that they maintain family solidarity.[48]

My father was no longer willing to venture out from camp to a society from which he had been expelled and whose business was demolished. [To him, it was clear that] the questionnaire was to be used to force him out of the camp. . . . The other, the bind that I was in, was to try and make a resolution in which I would pay homage and honor my parents so that I would not break up the family and yet try to figure out how to give expression to my own future.[49]

The Nisei, too, had problems with Question 28, the loyalty question. Some saw it as a trick question: "forswearing" their allegiance to the Japanese Emperor required admitting that they had once had such an allegiance.[50]

> Not only had our government disregarded our citizenship but put us behind barbed wire, but now was asking these same citizens to foreswear [sic] allegiance to the Emperor of Japan and to swear allegiance to the United States as if at one time all of us had sworn allegiance to the Japanese Emperor.[51]

Then, there was the insult of being asked to fill out another questionnaire which implicitly doubted one's loyalty. To many, their earlier compliance with the orders to evacuate and to be confined in the relocation centers had sufficiently shown their loyalty.[52]

Still, despite reservations, most answered that they were loyal. Some retained their faith in the United States; some felt that, whatever happened, their future lay here; some simply wanted to leave camp.

> [M]y family all wrote "yes, yes." There is a Japanese saying, "umi-no-oya-yori mo sodate no oya," meaning, "your adoptive parents are your real parents."[53]

> [I]n my case I registered "yes, yes" because I felt that this is the only country I have.[54]

In those centers where good relations between government authorities and evacuees had fostered a sense of trust in the government, a higher proportion of evacuees were willing to state their loyalty. Minidoka, for example, had the highest number of positive responses. There, the project director consulted with a number of Issei leaders before any meetings on the loyalty questionnaire. Some of the Issei participated in the meetings, and thorough discussion followed.[55]

At the other extreme was Tule Lake. There, discussion was cursory and no time was allowed for discussion from the floor. When registration was to begin, many evacuees were unwilling to fill out questionnaires. After the administration announced that registration was compulsory, there were still refusals and resistance. Gangs formed to prevent others from registering and, eventually, a group of resisters were removed from the center. Finally, the community council and Issei planning board resigned.[56] Frank Kageta described his experience at Tule Lake:

> The most tragic, as well as traumatic, event that happened during my stay in Tule Lake that still remains with me is the questionnaire with the loyalty oath that was required of all of us to answer. I have never even mentioned this to my children. This, as you may know, was a controversial document that affected each of us 17 years of age or older, in one way or another. We were forced into

concentration camps by the government, and then we were being forced into taking a loyalty oath. Furthermore, at this point there was no indication as to what the consequences would be for refusing. We had area block meetings on the issue. Rumors were numerous and sinister. We voted, at that time, as a block, not to sign the loyalty oath. Soon after we voted not to sign this document, based solely on rumors, I was pointedly accused by my peers as having been seen going to the administration office to sign the questionnaire. Our family got together after this ugly incident and told them that I had not gone to sign the loyalty oath.[57]

Registration at Tule Lake was never completed;[58] approximately 3,000 ultimately refused to register.[59]

Despite the turmoil, the WRA judged the program a success. The agency acquired the background data to expedite leave clearance, and 1,208 volunteers for the Army had been recruited.[60] Although this was a small proportion of the 10,000 eligible that the War Department had estimated,[61] and fell short of the 3,000 that it had expected to recruit,[62] the WRA judged that those who had volunteered represented "the cream of the draft-age group."[63] By WRA's count, 77,957 residents had been eligible to register, of whom 68,018 (87%) had answered the loyalty question with an unqualified "yes." Of the remaining 9,939, about 5,300 had answered "no," and the rest had failed to register, failed to answer the loyalty question, or qualified their loyalty in some way. Relatively few were unwilling to profess their loyalty. Still, government planners were disturbed to find that over 20 percent of the Nisei males were in the negative category. Of the approximately 21,000 Nisei males eligible to register, about 4,600 answered the loyalty question with a "no," a qualified answer or no reply.[64]

Although the Western Defense Command interpreted the results as a vindication of its position that there were many disloyal evacuees,[65] other observers looked behind the responses for reasons. Certainly some evacuees wanted to go to Japan and serve that country.[66] But, for many, the reasons for answering "no" had little to do with loyalty. As Dillon Myer explained it, the negative answers meant many things. They were the answers of people unhappy at the way they had been treated, enraged at the government, and discouraged about their future in the United States.[67] Testimony before the Commission supports Myer's conclusion—the loyalty questionnaire demanded a personal expression of position from each evacuee, a choice between faith in the future in America and outrage at present injustice. Most evacuees probably had deeply-ambiguous feelings about a government in whose rhetorical values of liberty and equality they wanted to believe, but who found their present treatment a painful contradiction of those values. The loyalty questionnaire left little room to express that ambiguity. Indeed, it provided an effective point of protest and organization against the government, from which an increasing number of evacuees felt alienated. The questionnaire finally raised the central question underlying exclusion policy, the loyalty issue which had dominated the political and personal lives of the Nikkei for the past year. Questions 27 and 28 forced evacuees to confront the conflicting emotions aroused by their relation to the government:

> I answered both questions number 27 and 28 in the negative, not because of disloyalty but due to the disgusting and shabby treatment given us. A few months after completing the questionnaire, U.S. Army officers appeared at our camp and gave us an interview to confirm our answers to the questions, and followed up with a question that in essence was asking: "Are you going to give up or renounce your U.S. citizenship?" to which I promptly replied in the affirmative as a rebellious move. Sometime after the interview, a form letter from the Immigration and Naturalization Service arrived saying if I wanted to renounce my U.S. citizenship, sign the form letter and return. Well, I kept the Immigration and Naturalization Service waiting.[68]

> Well, I am one of those that said "no, no" on them, one of the "no, no" boys, and it is not that I was proud about it, it was just that our legal rights were violated and I wanted to fight back. However, I didn't want to take this sitting down. I was really angry. It just got me so damned mad. Whatever we do, there was no help from outside, and it seems to me that we are a race that doesn't count. So, therefore, this was one of the reasons for the "no, no" answer.[69]

Personal responses to the questionnaire inescapably became public acts open to community debate and scrutiny within the closed world of the camps. This made difficult choices excruciating.

> After I volunteered for the service, some people that I knew refused to speak to me. Some older people later questioned my father for letting me volunteer, but he told them that I was old enough to make up my own mind.[70]

> [T]he resulting infighting, beatings, and verbal abuses left families torn apart, parents against children, brothers against sisters, relatives against relatives, and friends against friends. So bitter was all this that even to this day, there are many amongst us who do not speak about that period for fear that the same harsh feelings might arise up again to the surface.[71]

Because of the incarcerations, here I was, a 19-year-old, having to make a decision that would affect the welfare of the whole family. If I signed, "no, no," I would throw away my citizenship and force my sisters and brother to do the same. Being the oldest son and being brought up in the Japanese tradition, it was up to me to take care of my parents, sisters, and brother. It was about a mile to the administration building. I can still remember vividly. Every step I took, I questioned myself, shall I sign it "no, no," or "no, yes?" The walk seemed like it took hours and then when I got there, a colonel asked me the first question and I cursed him and answered, "no." To me, he represented the powers that put me in this predicament. I answered "yes" to the second question. In my 57 years, I have never had to make such a difficult decision as that.[72]

The response to the call for Army volunteers in Hawaii, where there was no substantial exclusion or detention, underscores the effects of the exclusion program. There, nearly 10,000 Nisei volunteered—one third of those of draft age, although the Hawaiian quota had been set at only 1,500.[73]

The registration process, conceived by the War Department and WRA as a dramatic step toward freedom, had become for many evacuees their bitterest experience in the camps.

LOYALTY REVIEW

With the ambiguous results of the loyalty questionnaire in hand, the government began to decide who should leave the camps. The WRA's leave policies had been in effect for several months. It was now ready to modify these. The War Department was not content to leave this matter to the WRA. Despite the continuing protestations that evacuees were a matter for the civilian WRA, the War Department plan of January 1943 called for the formation of a Japanese American Joint Board (JAJB)—a largely military body—which would also have a hand in deciding whom to release. While the WRA would retain ultimate authority, the JAJB would recommend individual releases.

In devising a release policy after a year of war the justification for the evacuation and detention—military necessity—required reexamination. Logic suggests that the appropriate course would have been to have recognized that no threat to security existed in 1943 (whether or not it ever had), and to have thrown open the gates of the camps. No one, however, advocated this position. It would have created a public relations problem and perhaps raised doubt about the original decision to evacuate—both unpalatable. Two choices remained: one, to determine that the security risk still outweighed the right to individual liberty and, thus, to release as few people as possible. This was, in essence, the view of the WDC, which had never conceded the validity of the loyalty program. The other alternative was to find a compromise to balance the claims of security and liberty in individual cases. This was the position adopted by the JAJB and WRA. But, lacking common assumptions or precedent to guide their task, and having differing views on the matter, the two agencies found actual decisions about leave confusing, inconsistent and a cause of friction.

The Western Defense Command

On January 14, DeWitt first learned of the loyalty review program. For months, he had argued that the War Department's responsibility on Japanese American issues had ended with the exclusion from the West Coast; now the loyalty review program undermined DeWitt's fundamental premise that the loyal could not be separated from the disloyal. Rejection of that premise implied that the War Department was reversing DeWitt and his policy. Worse still from DeWitt's point of view, it would be difficult to sustain the exclusion of certified loyal evacuees from the Western Defense Command. DeWitt and Bendetsen turned to defeating the plan. They failed, but they did not change their minds. DeWitt and his associates remained firm in their belief that the evacuees were a risk to security. As long as they believed that the loyal could not be separated from the disloyal, they would find all ethnic Japanese suspect. Far from rethinking their position, they worked to substantiate it through a project designed to demonstrate "danger" from the ethnic Japanese.

The WDC research project began in 1942 to remedy the dearth of information on individual evacuees.[74] It was designed too to collect adverse information on as many ethnic Japanese as possible. The project's approach was to collect masses of material on the Japanese American community—newspapers, immigration records, magazines and pamphlets of evacuee organizations—and to use it to identify dangerous organizations and individuals. For example, four Japanese language newspapers were analyzed from 1937 to 1942; information thus gained about organizations and their members were noted in individual files. Upon deciding that an organization was suspect, for example, because it had sent money to Japan to support the Russo-Japanese War, the WDC would identify all members of the organization and label them suspicious as well. From there, it might implicate their close relatives. The idea was to investigate an entire population and to evaluate individuals not by their statements or illegal acts but primarily by their affiliations and travel patterns. From records of entirely legal prewar activities, the WDC tried to evaluate an individual's potential risk to military security. The task was mammoth, the method crude and, by the WDC's own admission, fraught with error. After two and a half years, shortly after General Emmons took over the Western Defense Command, the research project remained incomplete but was halted due to insufficient manpower.

The most notable feature of the WDC project was the extraordinarily large effort it devoted to extracting a minimum of useful information. There is no indication that it uncovered evidence of criminal activity, much less espionage or sabotage. The entire project was based on dubious assumptions. The finding that 40% of adult Nisei had been to Japan at some time is important only if one accepts the assumption that those who went to Japan were potentially dangerous;[75] that there were 29,704 accounts of fixed deposits (similar to savings certificates) in Japanese banks is irrelevant unless fixed deposits are linked to security risk.[76] The connection WDC attempted to make between carefully researched material and security risk was simply not credible.

Nevertheless the WDC did not abandon its fundamental premise that individuals could be judged by the organizations and programs in which they participated. Rather, they concluded that more time and planning should be devoted to the task. The WDC urged that the military be better prepared for the next crisis and recommended, in its postwar analysis of the program,

> That there be created a peacetime unit within the Federal government charged with the continued study and research relative to all organizations with foreign connections within the United States. This unit should be small, but composed of highly trained personnel who will have access to all intelligence information. In wartime this personnel should form the nucleus of a central organization that would make security determinations.
>
> That complete planning be instituted by the War Department as to necessary civilian controls in the event of a future war, upon the assumption that the next war will involve a large portion of our civilian population from the outset. The planning should include types of controls, the mechanics of putting the control into force, the methods of notification, and the means of enforcement.[77]

The WDC did not flinch from the conclusion that they were urging abandonment in wartime of the normal protections of American constitutional government. In the view of the WDC, the review and control of civilians who presented some security question might well require other methods:

One of the most fundamental parts of the problem is that Americans, having been trained under our Common Law system of courts and juries, are strongly imbued with the idea that determinations by courts and juries are not only reasonably accurate but also that they completely solve a specific problem, and that a problem, having once been decided by a jury, cannot be reopened under the double jeopardy theory of our law. This unquestionably is the reason so many people felt that hearing or screening boards could easily have examined the records of the members of the Japanese population and satisfactorily separated the sheep from the goats. At the same time, they would be quite undisturbed by the fact that possibly some who should have been goats were labelled as sheep. It is a real question whether in wartime we can afford to protect our peace and security by these quite slipshod determinations. Ordinarily in peacetime, if a criminal, who has committed a theft or some crime of violence, has been acquitted, there is little likelihood that the public as a whole will be penalized for this inaccurate judgement of the court or jury, for such a criminal will only again commit a crime probably affecting one member of society; but in the case of one committing espionage or sabotage, the effect upon the population as a whole is quite different. The furnishing of a vital piece of information to the enemy may affect thousands of lives, rather than just one individual. . . . So the question has to be asked whether our Common Law system of trial by jury for an individual crime is sufficiently satisfactory in the situation under discussion here.

Another phase of our court system that works well enough in the eyes of the majority in peacetime, but which has to be reexamined in time of war, is the theory that the jury can only be composed of people who have formed no opinion about the trial at issue, for otherwise a jury member either will be removed for cause or pre-emptorily [sic] challenged by either side. . . .

The theory that any reasonably honest and intelligent person is capable of passing judgment upon many complex factors is certainly open to severe question in the case of making determinations in the interest of the peace and security of the country in time of war.[78]

The WDC went the additional step of suggesting a citizen education program to condition the public to accept such deprivations of due process in a future war.

In essence, the WDC was willing to advocate military control of civilians in wartime unfettered by normal constitutional restraints. Having prejudged the loyalty of Japanese Americans on the flimsiest evidence, they also believed the United States should begin a continuing program of domestic intelligence-gathering to make judgments about which civilians should be "controlled" in future wars. The interests of state security would predominate over the civil liberties of suspect citizens, even if there were no basis for criminal charges against them. This would truly exalt military authority in war over every traditional protection of American government.

The Japanese American Joint Board

The JAJB, composed almost entirely of representatives of the military intelligence agencies, had tremendous difficulties from the start in administering the loyalty review. Indeed, in attacking the loyalty program, General DeWitt had pointed out one omission in planning symptomatic of JAJB's entire effort. If the Joint Board were presented with an individual on whom it had no information, asked DeWitt, would it presume loyalty and recommend release of that individual, or presume disloyalty and recommend continued confinement?[79]

Under normal circumstances, asking such a question about United States citizens would be absurd, but the question was important now. Whatever the original intent, the fact of exclusion and detention worked as a presumption against Nisei loyalty and innocence. If the Joint Board presumed innocence, then the government would be reversing its previous position, implicitly admitting that its earlier assumption of potential danger had been wrong. As DeWitt put it:

> If the presumption is favorable to loyalty then the federal government would seem to be embarrassing its original position that evacuation was a military necessity. This follows because it was the fundamental premise that Japanese loyalties were unknown or doubtful.[80]

If, on the other hand, the Joint Board were to remain consistent and presume probable danger, the procedure would become unworkable. As DeWitt expressed it:

> If the presumption is unfavorable to loyalty then the chances of determining the loyalty of any substantial segment will probably be low. This is because there is a great dearth of positive information on the majority of Nisei. There are two reasons for this: (1) Only the Japanese themselves know the answers and (2) the Nisei Japanese are mostly too young to have any records. . . . The resultant inability to establish the loyalty of any substantial segment of Nisei may unnecessarily embarrass the government. . . .[81]

In fact, the problem was even more difficult than DeWitt thought.

Proving loyalty would be impossible in any circumstances. Unlike proving disloyalty, which involves showing only one disloyal act, proving loyalty would require exploring a person's entire life to show the absence of disloyal acts. Undertaking such a task for even a small group, let alone tens of thousands, would be hopelessly expensive and time-consuming.

That the JAJB never answered this fundamental question speaks volumes about its effort. Rather than face the hard questions, it floundered, trying various systems to determine the "dangerousness" of each evacuee. A point system failed as did a system of assigning cases to individual members of the Board. Finally, an ever-changing system was adopted that would bring an adverse recommendation if any one of a number of "factors" were present. The "factors" included whether the person was Kibei; whether he refused to register; whether he was a leader in any organization controlled or dominated by aliens; and whether he had substantial fixed deposits in Japan.[82] By adopting this approach, the JAJB was spared having to find an illegal or even disloyal act as the basis of recommending continued confinement. Instead, individual characteristics and legal acts became cause for a finding of "dangerousness."

After about a year of making such determinations as well as doing its other work of clearing laborers for vital war plants (an equally uncertain venture), the JAJB was finally terminated. It had handled nearly 39,000 cases and made over 25,000 recommendations for leave clearance.[83] Of 12,600 recommendations against release, the WDC reported that the WRA ignored half and released the people anyway.[84] That no espionage or sabotage occurred among this group of over 6,000 released despite JAJB objection suggests the doubtful value of the JAJB's work. Clearly, it erred on the side of security, once again to the detriment of evacuees.

The WRA

Compared to the WDC or the JAJB, the WRA pursued a liberal course, although its policies continued to compromise individual civil liberties. At the beginning of 1943 WRA policy was a two-step process: the evacuee needed both "leave clearance"—which required a finding that he was not a danger to national security—and a "leave permit"—which would be issued if WRA was satisfied with the resettlement arrangements he had made.[85] The policy's central disadvantage was the extended time it took to process individual evacuees.

With the results of the mass registration in hand, WRA moved to simplify and expedite the procedure. Rather than requiring clearance from Washington, it allowed project directors to grant leave to those considered unquestionably loyal.[86] In March 1943, a financial aid system was instituted. Although the grants were minimal—about $25.00 per person plus transportation costs, they did provide some assistance.[87] A leave clearance review was established in the summer of 1943 for those who had some adverse information in their file. Principally these were cases in which Question 28 had not been answered with an unqualified "yes;" where repatriation or expatriation had been asked, or there was an adverse report from an intelligence agency or the JAJB.[88] Using this system, 16,000 evacuees left the centers on indefinite leave during 1943 in addition to 5,000 seasonal farm workers and a number of students.[89] Not one case of espionage or sabotage was reported among these evacuees.[90]

In early 1944, two changes in leave regulations were made, again to encourage resettlement. Agricultural work leaves were restricted in order to encourage indefinite leaves. Indefinite leave for a four-month trial period was made available, with no return to centers allowed during that time. Return was permitted only during the two months following the initial four.[91] Before December 1944, 18,500 more evacuees left the centers on indefinite leave.[92]

Despite the government's cautious leave decisions, WRA continued to have political problems with relocation. In April, Mayor Fiorello LaGuardia of New York objected to Under Secretary Fortas about the number of Japanese Americans who could come into the city. Fortas told LaGuardia that barring relocatees from New York would immediately become a nationwide issue and would be vigorously opposed by organizations throughout the country which were interested in humane, decent handling of these people. In addition, a prohibition would adversely affect the fate of American citizens, including New Yorkers, interned in Japan; it would also be used by the Japanese in anti-American racial propaganda.[93] LaGuardia raised the old cry to haunt every government resettlement effort since the exclusion decision: "If it was necessary to evacuate them from their homes originally and put them in a concentration camp, what justification is there for turning them loose in Eastern cities at this time? If Washington, Oregon, and California do not want them, what right has the Federal government in placing them in New York?"[94]

Continuing public hostility was reflected in WRA policies. In February 1944, Dillon Myer wrote the Attorney General explaining WRA's leave regulations; he stressed that the WRA had considered permitting people with leave clearance to leave the centers at any time, instead of requiring them to show some means of support and a good chance of community acceptance:

> We decided, however, that it was not administratively wise to take that course. The enemies of the relocation program could easily distort such an action on our part and picture it as a dangerous relaxation of controls in disregard of the national interest in time of war.
>
> If the Supreme Court should hold that detention of such an evacuee under such circumstances is invalid, the very fact of the Court's decision would serve to provide public justification for such a change in the program. I believe, therefore, that communities generally throughout the Nation would continue to be willing to receive evacuees after such a Court decision, whereas the storm that might attend an administrative change of the Regulations in this respect might very well seriously retard the relocation program.
>
> This is one case where I strongly believe that it is more desirable to have the change made as a result of a Court decision than a result of unforced administrative action.[95]

The Executive now hoped that the Supreme Court would kill the monster it had created.

LEAVING THE CAMPS

Most evacuees found beginning a new life difficult; many were unenthusiastic about the prospect. A mid-1943 WRA survey gave the reasons: uncertainty about public reaction; lack of funds or information about conditions; fear of inability to support oneself and family; and fear of failing to find adequate housing.[96] Many had come to view the camps as refuges and would prefer to stay where their most basic needs would be supplied.[97] The young were most willing to leave. Seven of every ten individuals leaving the camps in 1943 and 1944 were between 15 and 35. Many were women. Those who came from the northwest were more willing to resettle than the Californians.[98] Those who left found that, while their experience was fundamentally peaceful, it was not without incident and hardship.[99] Some faced housing discrimination[100] and cramped quarters.[101]

> [W]e could not get housing. It is critical for anyone, but for Japanese and someone with a child—we have walked miles and miles

every day, dragging Linda here and there, snatching a few hours for a nap here, carrying her there, looking for a place to stay.[102]

Seeking work, many found discrimination against Japanese Americans[103] and ended up working at menial or low-paying jobs,[104] depriving the country of skills needed during the war.[105]

The uncertain period of resettlement was not easy for my family. My older sisters worked at low paying jobs. For four years, we lived in a one bedroom apartment that housed five of us.[106]

In a few places, there were incidents. In New York City, for example, the establishment of a hostel in Brooklyn met local resistance that was eventually overcome.[107] May Ichida described her experience in Cleveland:

Our two sons were immediately placed in public schools and the experience of being a resettled person was compounded with jeering remarks and fights.[108]

The WRA made some effort to help evacuees resettle, as did several church groups.[109] The WRA opened field offices in key eastern and midwestern cities designed to create community acceptance and find jobs that evacuees might fill. They worked with resettlement committees set up by concerned individuals and groups, particularly the churches.[110] By mid-1943, church groups were running hostels for short-term living space in four midwestern cities.[111]

Although the evacuees moved to many cities, particularly Denver and Salt Lake City,[112] Chicago became the center of resettlement. There was less discrimination there, integration into the larger Caucasian community was easier, and jobs were plentiful. As word of conditions in Chicago filtered back to the camps, the midwest became a favored area. When the exclusion ended, Chicago was the only resettlement community from which there was no mass exodus to the West Coast.[113]

The evacuees leaving in 1943 and 1944 took all manner of jobs. A few had enough capital to begin their own businesses,[114] although not all were successful.

[W]e relocated to Brigham City, Utah, and worked at the Brigham City Laundry and Dry Cleaning Company. Because my uncle wanted to get back to farming which was his profession, we moved to American Fork, Utah, in 1946, to try farming one more time. That summer we planted onions, cabbage and celery. As it turned out, this was a fiasco. In the fall, while we were still harvesting the crops, heavy frost came early and destroyed the cabbage crop, destroyed the celery crop. If it was not for the onions, we would have come out of there poverty-stricken. The summer's hard labor

was all for naught. By Christmas 1946, we were back at Brigham
City, my uncle and mother going back to laundry jobs. Mother
and I lived in a one bedroom apartment in the heart of the city
above the J.C. Penney Company, rat infested, roach infested. We
lived like a poverty-stricken downtrodden ghetto dweller. Mother
cooked on a two burner kerosene stove. I had the bedroom and
mother slept on the couch.[115]

Most went to work for others. Seabrook Farms in New Jersey, the
largest single employer of ethnic Japanese, took 1,500 workers into
farming and processing food.[116] Several evacuees recalled the long
hours, camp-like conditions, and hostility from surrounding communities that marked Seabrook.[117]

Most who went to the larger cities were employed in industry,
although white-collar work was also available.[118] Departing from prewar patterns, most evacuees did not work in jobs serving the ethnic
Japanese community. Following WRA advice, many resettlers avoided
associating exclusively with each other, working instead to become
integrated into the larger communities.[119]

The loyalty program was partly responsible for allowing many to
leave the camps and resettle in the interior. For the many more left
in camp, the questionnaire was less benign. Now it would become a
tool to distinguish the loyal from the disloyal before moving all the
disloyal to Tule Lake.

SEGREGATION

The idea of separating evacuees into groups arose almost at once after
evacuation. The WDC, still protesting that it wanted nothing further
to do with the evacuees, interfered again. By August 1942, General
DeWitt was convinced that Nisei should be separated from Kibei and
advocated stripping the Kibei of their citizenship, interning and ex-
patriating them (along with the Issei) to Japan as rapidly as possible.[120]
DeWitt pressed his point with Chief of Staff Marshall in four letters
from September 8 through November 23; the Kibei were subverting
otherwise loyal Nisei and should be segregated.[121] By the end of October, McCloy had come to believe the idea was worth considering,[122]
and in November he wrote both DeWitt and WRA that he too favored
segregation,[123] although he was unwilling to impose his view on WRA.

By mid-December, DeWitt had developed a plan for the segregation. In extraordinary detail, his plan envisioned a surprise move in which designated evacuees would be gathered, put aboard trains and moved to the Poston camp, where evacuees not to be segregated would then be removed. The people to be segregated would include those who wished repatriation; parolees from detention or internment camps; those with "bad" records during their confinement in assembly centers or relocation camps; others whom the intelligence services thought dangerous; and immediate families of segregants. The plan anticipated about 5,600 segregants.[124]

As the War Department view of segregation evolved, WRA was also considering the idea. WRA objected to DeWitt's early proposals because they suggested segregating by category. As Myer explained it:

The War Relocation Authority, after full consideration, rejected the idea of segregating entire categories of the population. We felt, and still feel, that while we should probably look with particular care at the individuals who fall into certain specific categories, the arbitrary removal of an entire class would be unjust, unwise, and seriously damaging to evacuee morale. The evacuation process itself was such a categorical segregation involving, as has been acknowledged, many injustices to individuals. The evacuation was justified by military urgency, but military necessity could not justify segregation on a categorical basis as proposed to the Authority. The disloyal of the group were now in safe custody under military guard.

Moreover, there were practical considerations. Removal of the Issei en masse would have disrupted the majority of the families. There are in the centers some 40,000 American citizens under 20 years of age, most of whom are sons and daughters of aliens. At the time of evacuation General DeWitt had repeatedly reassured the evacuees that family composition would not be disturbed; in fact, the Western Defense Command put itself to great trouble to unite families during and immediately following evacuation to assembly centers. Removal of the Kibei, likewise, would have penalized many loyal citizens. In this connection, it is relevant that a large proportion of the evacuees recruited for the special Army school at Camp Savage, Minnesota, and for the Navy language school at the University of Colorado are Kibei.[125]

WRA rejected the December plan for different reasons. It called for secrecy, military control, cancellation of normal activities, and it raised the probability of rioting and bloodshed—all entirely at odds with the semblance of normality that WRA hoped to achieve.[126] Three steps already under way would, WRA hoped, eliminate a need to segregate: the indefinite leave program; Justice Department custody for aliens whom WRA believed should be interned; and an isolation center at Leupp for troublemakers.[127]

During Spring 1943, however, pressure grew to segregate. Senator Chandler's Senate Committee recommended segregation, which McCloy publicly (and Secretary Stimson privately) endorsed. The JACL favored it, and in May WRA project directors unanimously approved segregation.[128] Remarking that he still felt relocation was "the only civilized way" of separating the evacuees, Myer finally agreed.[129]

Tule Lake was chosen as the segregation center because it was a large facility and already housed many potential segregants. Five groups would be segregated:

- those who had applied for expatriation or repatriation to Japan and not withdrawn their application before July 1, 1943;
- those who answered "no" to the loyalty question or refused to answer it during registration and had not changed their answers;
- those who were denied leave clearance due to some accumulation of adverse evidence in their records;
- aliens from Department of Justice internment camps whom that agency recommended for detention; and
- family members of segregants who chose to remain with the family.[130]

On July 15, 1943, the WRA announced the policy of segregating persons who "by their acts have indicated that their loyalties lie with Japan during the present hostilities or that their loyalties do not lie with the United States."[131]

Next came a series of rehearings for individuals selected because of a "wrong" loyalty answer. Despite the consequences, most evacuees stuck by their original statements and the rehearing process registered mostly grief, disappointment and anger. Numerous Issei professed "disloyalty" as a way of getting back to California or of avoiding release. Many Kibei chose Tule Lake out of frustration with official distrust of their group. Others had no choice; they were family members—elderly, children or handicapped—who could not leave their relatives. A number of evacuees already at Tule Lake embraced disloyalty to avoid moving again.[132]

Between mid-September and mid-October, thirty-three trips transferred 6,289 people from Tule Lake and 8,559 to Tule Lake from other centers; later transfers moved 249 more residents out and 3,614 additional segregants in. Six thousand old Tuleans stayed. Meanwhile, Tule Lake was being transformed. A double eight-foot fence was erected, the guard increased to a battalion, and six tanks lined up conspicuously.[133]

Tule Lake now had a more diverse population than any other

center. People had come from all over California, Hawaii, Washington and Oregon. They were disproportionately rural people and unmarried farm laborers.[134] Of 18,422 evacuees at Tule Lake between September 1943 and May 1944, 68 percent were citizens. Most were there because they had requested repatriation or expatriation (39 percent), answered the loyalty questionnaire unsatisfactorily (26 percent) or were family of someone who was segregated (31 percent).[135]

The arriving group immediately found themselves at a disadvantage. There was not enough housing, so segregants were squeezed into quarters that did not give them even the usual small space, or they occupied makeshift dormitories in recreation halls. Improvements by former occupants were gone, for they had taken most of their handiwork on leaving. Remaining furniture and shelves had been appropriated by other residents before the segregants arrived; even plasterboard and wood had been ripped from the walls to make crates. The "old Tuleans" had taken all the best jobs, too. Finally, many transferees found the facilities, the food and the environment inferior to their "home" projects.[136]

Tule Lake's population and restrictive policies guaranteed conflict there. The first incident was a labor dispute when on October 7 the administration fired 43 coal workers. No one would take the vacant positions. On October 12, the administration reinstated the workers and made other concessions. Three days later an accident touched off a strike when a truck carrying a work crew to the project farm overturned, killing one worker and injuring several. Dissident leaders used the incident to begin a strike of agricultural workers for more safety precautions. The next week a committee presented demands to the project director including a demand for "resegregation"—separating those who preferred the Japanese way of life from those at Tule Lake for other reasons. The committee also requested physical improvements and staff changes. The work stoppage among the farm workers was not resolved. On October 28, the administration announced it was firing the farm employees and bringing in a group of "loyal" evacuees from other camps. Compounding the insult, food from evacuee warehouses was requisitioned to feed the new farm workers.[137]

On November 1, while Myer was visiting the camp, a large group gathered and the committee demanded to talk to him. During their discussion, another group of evacuees had visited the hospital and ended up beating the chief medical officer. Eventually, Myer addressed the full group and the gathering dispersed.[138]

Several days later, on November 4, the explosion came. A gang moved into the administrative area to prevent the removal of food for volunteer farm workers from other centers. They fought with the internal security force and a staff member was injured. When the rioters moved toward the project director's house, the military guard was called in.[139]

Tokio Yamane described this incident from an evacuee's point of view:

It was on November 4th, 1943, as I recall, that the Tule Lake Food Warehouse Disturbances occurred. A Mr. Kobayashi, a Japanese American on security patrol, discovered several WRA Caucasian personnel stealing food from the Internee Food Warehouse during the night and loading the food on their own truck which was parked alongside the warehouse. Mr. Kobayashi, who had the authority of a warder, remonstrated with the WRA personnel because they were taking the internees' food. Mr. Kobayashi was attacked by the Caucasian WRA personnel and a scuffle ensued.

As the scuffle was going on, the Organization for the Betterment of Camp Conditions, made up of representatives of the numerous internee blocks, was holding a meeting. As soon as news of this incident was brought to the Organization, Rev. Kai and Mr. Kuratomi, the heads of the Organization, asked Mr. Koji Todorogi and me, who were attending the meeting, to go to the scene and try to restore calm and keep the situation under control by bringing back the internees who had gathered at the scene of the incident.

As Mr. Koji Todorogi and I were heading toward the warehouse area, several Caucasian WRA personnel suddenly appeared out of the darkness and attacked the two of us, without any provocation on our part, with pistols, rifles, and bats, and finally took us to the WRA office.

As the two of us were being interrogated, Mr. Kobayashi, the warder, was brought in by another group of Caucasians. During his interrogation Mr. Kobayashi was hit on the head with such force that blood gushed out and the baseball bat actually broke in two. I was a witness to this brutal attack and remember it very vividly.

From about 9 P.M. that evening until daybreak, we were forced to stand with our backs against the office wall with our hands over our heads and we were continuously kicked and abused as we were ordered to confess being the instigators of the disturbance. We denied these accusations but our protestations of innocence were completely ignored by our tormentors. The beatings continued all night long and at day break the three of us were turned over to the Military Police and we were thrown into the stockade for confinement.

As if the camp authorities had been expecting this incident to happen, the Military Police Detachment immediately entered the detainee compound with tanks, machine guns, and tear gas, and started their repressive measures to cow the detainees, and to overwhelm the youth organization which was made up of unarmed and defenseless teenagers. The repressive measures and the martial law instituted by the camp authorities took the following forms:

1. The MP tanks and jeeps constantly patrolled the area in a show of force designed to harass and frighten the detainees.

2. Unannounced and frequent inspections of the detainees' barracks in search of alleged contraband such as kitchen paring knives, sewing scissors, carpenters' and gardeners' tools.

3. Firing of tear gas at small groups of unarmed internees assembling at bath houses and bathrooms to get water for washing, or standing at the coal pile to get coal or kindling for heating, or standing at the shower area waiting to bathe, or at the laundry area to do their laundry. These repressive measures lasted two or three months and resulted in nightmarish fear, particularly among the very young and the very old detainees.[140]

Leaders of the demonstration were isolated in a detention center that became known as "the stockade."[141]

The Army retained control of Tule Lake until January 15, 1944. The period was one of "turmoil, idleness, impoverishment, and uncertainty."[142]

I was thirteen years old when we were at Tule Lake, California. The most upsetting experience happened to me when martial law was declared throughout the camp because of a food riot. We were told that the military police would come to search each one of our families in the barracks. The two MPs looked formidable as they walked in with guns at their side and asked roughly if we had any weapons, liquor or cameras. To be forced to let the MPs in our small humble quarters seemed like such invasion of personal privacy that the emotional effect of that search still haunts me.[143]

The partial strike continued and the stockade's population grew. Although there were no more major outbursts, the distinction sharpened between "loyal and disloyal," and suspicion of collaborators and informers flourished.

The loyalty program pushed evacuees in opposite directions. Some had been released and were heading toward a more normal, productive life. To those who expressed their anger and frustration, however, the loyalty program brought a more repressive, violent and frustrating period at Tule Lake. The loyalty program is rightly remembered as one of the most divisive events in the camp. It broke apart the community of evacuees by forcing each to a clear choice—a choice that could be made only by guesswork about a very uncertain future. It was a choice that was hard to hedge, and it divided families and friends philosophically, emotionally and, finally, physically, as some went east to make new lives and others were taken off to the grimmer confinement of Tule Lake.

8

Ending the Exclusion

Historical writing about the exclusion, evacuation and detention of the ethnic Japanese has two great set pieces—analysis of events which led to Executive Order 9066, and life in the relocation camps.[1] In large measure, these events were accessible to historians from the moment they took place; equally important events have remained obscure—most significantly, the end of the exclusion from the West Coast. Examining how exclusion ended brings one full circle to a deeper understanding of the forces and ideas behind Executive Order 9066.

The ending of the exclusion should logically depend on its beginning: when the circumstances that justified exclusion no longer exist, exclusion itself should cease. Three separate justifications for exclusion suggested two distinct sets of circumstances in which it would end. Through the first six months of 1943, a long struggle was waged in the War Department to determine which of these theories and programs would prevail.

General DeWitt and the Western Defense Command embraced at one time or another two theories for exclusion. The first, which DeWitt relied on in his final recommendation to Stimson urging exclusion, was that loyalty was determined by ethnicity.[2] For that reason the ethnic Japanese would ultimately be loyal to Japan. The second theory employed the stereotype of the "inscrutable Oriental;" it was adopted by the Western Defense Command in its supplement to the *Final Report,* the fully developed apologia for evacuation. The ethnic

213

Japanese were so alien to the patterns of American thought and behavior, this theory suggested, that it was impossible to distinguish the loyal from the disloyal.[3] For the Western Defense Command, both theories justified the exclusion of Nisei and Issei from the West Coast for the duration of the war; in the first case, because they were presumptively dangerous and ultimately enemies and, in the second, because no one could distinguish enemy from friend.

The third theory held that loyalty was a matter of individual choice and that the loyal could be distinguished from the disloyal, but urgency required exclusion because it was impossible to conduct individual loyalty reviews in early 1942, under imminent threat of Japanese raids or sabotage. The War Department in Washington, particularly McCloy and Stimson, held this view.[4] Its logical conclusion was that no good reason existed to exclude from the West Coast at least those Issei and Nisei who cleared a loyalty review. At root, this theory held that the ethnic Japanese were a greater threat to security than ethnic Germans and Italians, and it did not extend the presumption of loyalty to American citizens of Japanese descent; but it also saw limits to the danger they were believed to present—and made government responsible for reviewing loyalty and reassessing the military position so as to return people to normal life as soon as possible.

The intensity of the argument between the Western Defense Command and the War Department over how and when to end the exclusion demonstrated the truth of what the Tolan Committee suspected as early as March 1942: there had been no common understanding of the basis of the original decision to exclude nor of how to treat loyal ethnic Japanese after exclusion.[5] As McCloy told Bendetsen in April 1943: "We never thought about it."[6] In early 1943, debate over ending exclusion ranged over a number of issues: starting a loyalty review in connection with raising the volunteer combat unit (which the Western Defense Command recognized as logically leading to the end of exclusion for the loyal); the question of the conditions under which Nisei soldiers and other classes of ethnic Japanese who presented no obvious security risk could return to the West Coast; the language for General DeWitt's *Final Report* justifying the evacuation; and, finally, the conditions under which the War Department would revoke the exclusion orders.

The War Department recognized by early 1943 that military necessity could not justify the exclusion from the West Coast of loyal American citizens or resident aliens of Japanese ancestry, but it was unwilling to force a revision of the exclusion orders or to make public the opinions which Stimson, Marshall and McCloy then held. Only in May 1944 did Stimson recommend to President Roosevelt and the Cabinet the ending of exclusion, and only after the 1944 election did the President act on the recommendation. Just as the exclusion was born of political pressure, it was continued out of political considerations long after those who first believed it to be militarily justified had abandoned that position.

THE WESTERN DEFENSE COMMAND VS. THE WAR DEPARTMENT

On January 14, 1943, the same day that McCloy received word that the project for raising the Nisei combat unit was launched, General DeWitt first became aware of the full dimensions of the project, including the plan for a review and determination of loyalty. His reaction was immediate and candid. DeWitt telephoned his old ally General Gullion, the Provost Marshal General, and expressed his concern, reminding him that "[t]here isn't such a thing as a loyal Japanese and it is just impossible to determine their loyalty by investigation—it just can't be done."[7] DeWitt got the lay of the land at the War Department, then cabled General Marshall asking an opportunity to comment before the plan was put into operation.[8]

Between January 14 and 27, when DeWitt dispatched formal comments to Marshall, DeWitt and his aides (including Bendetsen) honed their arguments.* By the time the comments were prepared, they believed the loyalty review program would undermine total exclusion—first, by adopting a rationale for exclusion which included individual review of loyalty and, second, by permitting the loyal to return to the West Coast. Both actions would expose the War Department

---

*Although it is difficult to distinguish the voices of DeWitt and Bendetsen in the documents, it is clear their points of view differed. DeWitt was strident and assured; he never hesitated to make racist remarks and never expressed doubts about the wisdom of his position. Even after the War Department had endorsed the loyalty questionnaire, DeWitt continued to assert that loyalty could not be determined. Bendetsen was hesitant. Although the written documents are undoubtedly the work of both men, final responsibility for positions of the Western Defense Command was DeWitt's, and we have attributed them to the Commanding General.

and the Western Defense Command to bitter criticism. The first issue immediately drew everyone to reexamine the original decision to evacuate. It had always been DeWitt's view, expressed often and publicly, that the loyal could not be separated from the disloyal. The loyalty review program, established to do exactly that, was, by its very existence, a repudiation of DeWitt. As DeWitt described it to McCloy:

> I feel that I wouldn't be loyal to you or honest to you if I didn't say that it is a sign of weakness and an admission of an original mistake. Otherwise—we wouldn't have evacuated these people at all if we could determine their loyalty.[9]

While DeWitt was unwavering in believing the evacuation decision sound, Bendetsen was sufficiently disturbed by the War Department's position that he apparently began to question the original decision. Discussing the issue with Captain John Hall, one of McCloy's assistants, Bendetsen remarked:

> Of course [the difficulty of determining loyalty] is probably true of white people, isn't it? You know that old proverb about "not being able to look into the heart of another"? And "not even daring to look into your own" . . . well maybe there's something in that.[10]

Both DeWitt and Bendetsen must have realized that their contention that loyal could not be separated from disloyal was unlikely to prevail at the War Department strictly on the merits; the loyalty program was too far along for that. Instead, they argued that the public would react badly to the Army's shift of position and the Department would look foolish for changing its mind. Bendetsen mentioned this several times in conversation with War Department staff:

> [T]he record shows that (1) that it was a concentration of a large number of persons of Japanese ancestry in strategic areas near war plants and all that. And that it could not be permitted. And (2) That you couldn't determine loyalty and therefore you had to take the wheat with the chaff. Not that there wasn't time, but that you just couldn't. So that's what the original record shows. So whatever you do, I think you ought to bear that pretty closely in mind. That's what the record shows out here where the main record was made . . . in the Press and the Periodicals.
>
> *   *   *
>
> I'm scared to death principally because of the public relations part of it. That's it, to put it in a nutshell.[11]

DeWitt was somewhat more circumspect but raised essentially the same issues in his formal comments.[12]

The War Department hierarchy, however, was not persuaded.

Regardless of what DeWitt had said, for McCloy the issue was one of timing. His view had never been that loyal could not be separated from disloyal, but that they could not have been distinguished *fast enough*. Now, McCloy argued, the Department was moving to determine loyalty, as it had always planned to do.[13] But Bendetsen and DeWitt believed this would also expose the Department to criticism. If the plan had always been to determine loyalty, why had it not been done earlier, when evacuees were still in the assembly centers? If loyalty review had only been postponed, then the government had unnecessarily prolonged the confinement of 100,000 people and wasted $80 million building relocation centers. Bendetsen and Braun, drafting comments for DeWitt, explored this point:

> *Braun:* You had them under control [in the assembly centers] but you had not yet moved them inland—you had not yet spent any 80 million dollars—you had accomplished the main thing as to time and space. And at that point, if you could determine loyalty, it should then have been done.
>
> *Bendetsen:* And that will have to be answered.
>
> *Braun:* It will have to be answered.
>
> *Bendetsen:* . . . [T]he answer may be that you could have, but that's not such a hot public relations answer.
>
> *Braun:* I've just been talking that over . . . and I said "If you fellows were to say to me tomorrow,—that is the big rub, what were we going to do about it?—because we're going thru with this anyway," the best thing I had thought of up to this moment was for us to be completely honest and say "well maybe we could, though we didn't think so at the time."
>
> *Bendetsen:* Right. We still don't think so [at the Western Defense Command].
>
> *Braun:* No but I'm talking now about suppose we were told "you gotta' do it" and "how are we going to do it?" That's the only answer I could think of that would make any sense.
>
> *Bendetsen:* Didn't think so then but we do now. Maybe our ideas on the Oriental have been all cock-eyed.
>
> *Braun:* We've got more information now than we had . . . and than we thought we could get.
>
> *Bendetsen:* That's right. Maybe he isn't inscrutable.[14]

There is no record of how Stimson and McCloy would have explained why they had waited so long to separate loyal from disloyal. It may be that with the other massive problems of fighting the war, this question had occupied little or none of their attention; there is no evidence that, when they addressed it, they believed that detention camps, at least for the loyal, could be justified. As Stimson said: "We have gone to the full limit in evacuating them."[15]

The second and more vexing problem for DeWitt was the possible effect of the loyalty program on the evacuated area. The plan itself was silent on this point, but a Nisei certified loyal by the government could hardly be considered too dangerous to return to the West Coast. If exclusion of the loyal were to end, DeWitt's judgment would be publicly reversed and, particularly on the West Coast, the War Department might look very foolish for spending millions of dollars on relocation camps and uprooting the lives of thousands of people. It would, as Bendetsen put it, be "confess[ing] an original mistake of terrifically horrible proportions." Bendetsen was not prepared to make the confession:

> Even if the decision was wrong I wouldn't make it a practice gallop. Even in that case. I would find it very hard to justify the expenditure of 80 million dollars to build Relocation Centers, merely for the purpose of releasing them again. That, I would find difficult to do.[16]

If, on the other hand, the exclusion policy were not ended, then the loyalty review plan would be logically inconsistent. Bendetsen discussed this with Captain Hall, McCloy's assistant:

> *Bendetsen:* How could you keep him out of the evacuated zone, if you said he was [loyal enough] to work in a war plant?
> *Hall:* [The program is] . . . going to be limited to the areas outside of the evacuated area.
> *Bendetsen:* How can you be consistent—do one and say that he can't come in the other?
> *Hall:* Simply sensitivity of the West Coast to enemy attack. The reasons justifying the original evacuation still exist in certain degree.
> *Bendetsen:* No, I don't see how they do . . . [t]he plan says that you assume that one of the reasons for evacuation was that there was no time to determine loyalty. One of the primary reasons. So that now that you decide that you can determine loyalty you've erased that reason, haven't you?
> *Hall:* Well not necessarily. As far as the loyalty of this fellow is concerned, we feel that he is completely loyal. But because of certain military considerations—partly responsible for the evacuation, we feel at least for the present he should not go back into the evacuated area.
> *Bendetsen:* Kind of beats the devil around the bush, doesn't it?[17]

In fact, in January, McCloy was not prepared to press this point with the Western Defense Command. When McCloy first discussed the loyalty program with DeWitt on January 14, he assured the General that it would not affect exclusion from the West Coast.[18] McCloy did not explain why he took this position. There are various possible explanations: he may have believed that continuing military necessity required the exclusion of the loyal; the War Department may not have wished or been able to overcome political opposition on the West Coast; or McCloy may not have wanted to invite charges that the Department had wasted money building relocation camps. Only military necessity would provide a defensible explanation and, a few months later, McCloy made clear that he could not find military reasons for excluding people the government found loyal.

McCloy's assistant, Captain Hall, in discussing the matter with Bendetsen, attempted to argue for such a course and merely succeeded in demonstrating how hopeless the task was:

> *Bendetsen:* . . . when you come out with a plan and say that you can determine loyalty for working in a warplant around high-explosives . . . you can hardly say that "well he can" [sic] go back to San Francisco . . . it will be difficult to say that he can't" and when you do that you confess a very original, horrible mistake.
>
> *Hall:* . . . confess an original horrible mistake. [What about] the possibility of Fifth Column activity of landing of parachute troops dressed as civilians, the possibility of confusion. I think those are still very real factors. . . .
>
> *Bendetsen:* Suppose you drop white troops dressed as civilians. You don't evacuate all the white folks. That's no point. Suppose white people drop dressed as civilians. You don't evacuate all the white people.
>
> *Hall:* Your danger on the West Coast is . . . Japanese.
>
> *Bendetsen:* Well your danger on the East Coast is from Germans and Italians, who are white.
>
> *Hall:* Yes but there are too many of them out here.
>
> *Bendetsen:* Too many what?
>
> *Hall:* Far more assimilated than the Japanese population ever have been.
>
> *Bendetsen:* You mean too many white people on the East Coast. That's not a point, because the enemy could drop white soldiers dressed as civilians, and [who] could speak English. That . . .
>
> *Hall:* But that would be on the East Coast.
>
> *Bendetsen:* Well, they could do it on either coast.
>
> *Hall:* Not so easily on the West Coast.
>
> *Bendetsen:* I'm just trying to give you my reaction to the point.
>
> *Hall:* There is a logicality there, there's no doubt about it. But I think it might be wise to take this as a first step, perhaps looking toward (if this works all right) toward eventual return to the evacuated area providing the military situation warrants it.
>
> *Bendetsen:* Well I think that's certainly true, when the peace comes. That's when I think the military situation would warrant it with consistency.[19]

For the moment, the debate on lifting the exclusion order did not move beyond McCloy's position of January 14; loyalty would be determined and loyal evacuees released, but exclusion would not be terminated. But the argument could not and did not end, simply shifting to other issues, first to the question of exceptions to the universal ban of ethnic Japanese from the West Coast.

During the early months of 1943 DeWitt fought an unrelenting war of attrition with McCloy, who tried to persuade the General to introduce some humane common sense by allowing some return to the West Coast. DeWitt opposed every such effort. For instance, at the WRA's urging,[20] McCloy suggested that loyalty to the United States would be a better standard than race for dealing with "mixed marriage" cases because, as part of the War Department's effort to solve the "Japanese problem," he wanted to recognize the loyalty of individuals rather than to presume the disloyalty of the entire group. DeWitt did not accept the suggestion.[21]

The breaking point came over the issue of letting Nisei soldiers on furlough into the excluded area. DeWitt fought for months to prevent or encumber such entries, but McCloy drew the line at this and was supported by Stimson and Marshall.[22] If a Jap was a Jap to DeWitt, a GI was a GI to McCloy. The War Department ordered that Nisei soldiers be allowed onto the West Coast with a minimum of interference and control.

This argument clarified the connection between loyalty and exclusion and forced a conscious reassessment of the military justification for exclusion. On April 8, 1943, McCloy set out the disagreements between the War Department and the Western Defense Command in a frank letter to General DeWitt. He first addressed the circumstances that had changed since early 1942:

> The threat of Japanese attack is far from what it was. We are better organized to meet such an attack if it occurred. And we know a great deal more about our Japanese population. Furthermore, the War Department has established a combat team for volunteer American citizens of Japanese ancestry. This program has been indorsed by the President who looks upon it as "a natural and logical step toward the reinstitution of the Selective Service procedures, which were temporarily disrupted by the evacuation from the West Coast." Similarly, the War Department has initiated a process for loyalty investigations of all Japanese Americans to determine their eligibility for work in plants and facilities vital to the war effort. In other words, in the face of manpower difficulties, the policy of the national Government, as well as that of the War

Department, is presently looking toward the restoration to all loyal persons of Japanese ancestry of all their normal rights and privileges, to the end that they may be able to make their maximum contribution to the war effort. The very "entering wedge" which you appear to dread is precisely what must be accomplished.

McCloy next assailed the corrupt policy he believed the Army acceded to on the West Coast:

That there is serious animosity on the West Coast against all evacuated Japanese I do not doubt, but that does not necessarily mean that we should trim our sails accordingly. The longer California luxuriates in the total absence of the Japanese the more difficult it will be to restore them to the economy of California. They have a place in California as well as in any other state as long as military considerations do not intervene. I cannot help but feel that social considerations rather than military ones determine the total exclusion policy. The Army, as I see it, is not responsible for the general public peace of the Western Defense Command. That responsibility still rests with the civil authorities. There may, as you suggest, be incidents, but these can be effectively discouraged by prompt action by law enforcement agencies, with the cooperation of the military if they even assume really threatening proportions. I certainly deplore any policy which prohibits an American soldier from entering areas in the United States for fear of the consequences which may attend such entry.[23]

McCloy concluded by urging on DeWitt the policy of gradual resettlement onto the Pacific Coast that had been debated all that spring. McCloy suggested allowing the reentry of screened individuals in four broad categories: wives, parents, brothers and sisters of soldiers; wives of Caucasians; individuals whose employment on the coast would aid the war effort; and veterans of the First World War and their families.

On April 13, 1943, DeWitt appeared before a House Committee looking into the effect of large military facilities on local communities; he used the occasion to answer McCloy publicly. Asked whether he had any problems he would like to discuss, DeWitt fired both barrels:

I haven't any except one—that is the development of a false sentiment on the part of certain individuals and some organizations to get the Japanese back on the West Coast. I don't want any of them here. They are a dangerous element. There is no way to determine their loyalty. The West Coast contains too many vital installations essential to the defense of the country to allow any Japanese on this coast. There is a feeling developing, I think, in certain sections of the country, that the Japanese should be allowed to return. I am opposing it with every proper means at my disposal.[24]

DeWitt did resist pointing the finger directly at McCloy and Stimson in public. Asked whether "the element responsible for bringing them back [was] the same one that wants them put in the Army," the General replied that he didn't know what element the Congressman was referring to. Congressmen Izac, who had earlier claimed credit for getting the evacuation ordered, and Mott opposed any such change of policy and told the General they would watch the situation.[25]

The next day, for good measure, DeWitt once more aired his differences with the War Department over allowing Nisei soldiers on the West Coast. At an off-the-record news conference he told sympathetic reporters:

> As I told the War Department, the Japanese Government finding out we are bringing these men in, it is the ideal place to infiltrate men in uniform. . . . [A] Jap is a Jap. The War Department says a Jap-American soldier is not a Jap; he is American. Well, all right. I said, I have the Jap situation to take care of and I'm going to do it . . .[26]

Of course, DeWitt mixed this with avowals of being a loyal soldier who did not oppose his superiors, but his conduct could not have been more clearly calculated to sabotage any War Department effort to achieve quiet, gradual resettlement of evacuees on the West Coast.

These episodes occurred while General DeWitt was preparing his *Final Report* on the Japanese evacuation. The document was to be both the Army's official explanation of the reasons for the exclusion and evacuation and its account of this massive movement of people. The *Final Report* was to be formally submitted to Secretary Stimson, but there was an understanding that a draft would be reviewed and discussed with McCloy beforehand. McCloy was surprised when it came to him in printed form in mid-April, and livid after reading the first few chapters. He found it "too self-glorifying and too self-serving for the type of document that I think should be perpetuated,"[27] but two statements particularly angered McCloy: first, that it was impossible to determine the loyalty of the ethnic Japanese and that this impossibility, not urgency, was the "military necessity" on which exclusion rested; second, that the ethnic Japanese should not be allowed to return to the West Coast until after the war, regardless of the improved military situation.[28]

McCloy plainly considered the printed report DeWitt's attempt to talk past his War Department superiors to politicians and the public. Because DeWitt's gambit put the War Department in a most uncomfortable political position, a major negotiation between DeWitt and McCloy over the *Report's* final language followed. First, Bendetsen

McCloy over the *Report's* final language followed. First, Bendetsen was called to Washington to work on revisions and get McCloy's views and objections firsthand.[29] He was then sent to DeWitt, who was in Alaska, to discuss the changes McCloy wanted, though the General would not be compelled to make them.[30] At first the General was adamant in opposing any changes,[31] but after Bendetsen's visit to Alaska DeWitt not only accepted McCloy's suggestions but set out to destroy every copy of the April version.[32] One can only speculate on what persuaded DeWitt, but it may have been Bendetsen's memorandum on the War Department's position about excluding loyal ethnic Japanese from the West Coast:

> After an extended discussion, Mr. McCloy stated his conclusion to be that there no longer existed any military necessity for the continued exclusion of all Japanese from the evacuated zone. He stated that the War Department, of its own motion, would not take any action to direct or require the revision or revocation of present restrictions in this regard. He did say, however, that if the question were to be presented officially to the Secretary of War by the White House or by any other official federal agency having a legitimate interest whether from the viewpoint of the War Department there is longer any military objection to the return of those Japanese "whose loyalty had been determined," the answer had to be, "No."[33]

McCloy told Bendetsen that these views were shared by Stimson and Marshall.[34] Persistence by DeWitt might have resulted in a public break with the War Department over exclusion. DeWitt was obviously unwilling to press this far, and McCloy seemed remarkably determined not to let their differences become a matter of public debate. This is demonstrated by three incidents. After DeWitt's appearance before the House subcommittee, Secretary Ickes wrote in sarcastic outrage about press reports of the General's testimony, but McCloy replied merely that DeWitt had been inaccurately quoted and did not disclose his disagreement with the General.[35]*

Next, in late May, McCloy would not spread the public impression that DeWitt was being relieved of his command and kicked upstairs, as he was in Fall 1943, because of his stand on the exclusion policy. The Assistant Secretary urged that DeWitt be kept on the West Coast

---

*The press had used DeWitt's off-the-record remark that "a Jap is a Jap." Ickes repeated this in his letter to McCloy and the Assistant Secretary, no doubt unaware of the press conference, denied that the General had made the remark.

a short time longer to avoid this inference,[36] and later he vetoed a draft announcement by General Emmons, DeWitt's successor, identifying the exclusion policy as DeWitt's rather than the War Department's.[37]

Finally, McCloy and Stimson faced the problem of answering a long letter from Dillon Myer of the WRA about plans for getting evacuees out of the relocation centers. The letter fairly, though indirectly, asked the War Department's justification for continued exclusion from the West Coast.[38] Stimson, in a letter apparently drafted by McCloy,[39] commented only on the WRA's administrative problems and avoided discussing the military justification for continuing exclusion, a matter plainly within the War Department's competence.[40]

This was extraordinary: the War Department no longer believed that military necessity justified excluding loyal ethnic Japanese from the West Coast, but it was unwilling to reverse its orders. What is more, officials of the first rank consciously withheld their views from others both in and outside the government although the context fairly demanded some expression of opinion. Probably they feared a political firestorm—the War Department was reluctant, or perhaps felt itself unable, to face down strong political objection to returning Issei and Nisei, regardless of loyalty, to the West Coast.

In the first half of 1943, anti-Japanese forces on the West Coast, reacting to the leave program and loyalty review, were stirring again. The first prominent group to act was the California American Legion which, in January, began to pass resolutions urging deportation of all ethnic Japanese, both citizens and aliens.[41] Soon grand juries, local governments, and state legislatures joined the crusade, while numerous civic groups were created expressly to voice anti-Japanese sentiment.[42]

The issue reached Washington in the form of a resolution to transfer the WRA to Army control, accompanied by allegations that evacuees were being "pampered" and "coddled."[43] The resolution was referred to a Senate subcommittee headed by Senator A. B. Chandler of Kentucky, who, seeing an opportunity for headlines, determined to hold hearings and visit four camps himself. His tour featured a number of sensational announcements. Chandler thought 60 percent of the residents at one center were disloyal, adding that "in my mind there is no question that thousands of these fellows were armed and prepared to help Japanese troops invade the West Coast right after Pearl Harbor."[44] In May the committee released its report, with conclusions that had little to do with the Senator's previous announcements but recommended that the draft be resumed, that disloyals be segregated, and that loyal ethnic Japanese be privately employed.[45]

The committee had nevertheless again aroused people around the country on the "Japanese problem." Seeing the agitation in California, other states and local governments began to consider restrictive legislation. Arizona passed a bill curtailing the liberties of released evacuees and Arkansas made it illegal for ethnic Japanese to own land there.[46]

General DeWitt's remarks before the House Naval Affairs Committee in April had set the newspapers to editorializing against the ethnic Japanese once again. *The San Francisco Chronicle* put its view simply in the caption, "DeWitt Is Right," and, waving aside "the ethical factors, the constitutional factors, the question of the Bill of Rights," went on to announce that the return of ethnic Japanese cleared by the loyalty review would mean riots. *The Los Angeles Times* summarized its view of the possible end of exclusion in three words, "Stupid and Dangerous," and concluded its lengthy editorial by underscoring the political consequences:

> How much of the recent smashing defeat for reelection of former Governor Olson of California was due to his suggestion that the Japs be recalled for agricultural work cannot be estimated, but it was undoubtedly considerable. There are worse things than food shortages.
>
> As a race, the Japanese have made for themselves a record for conscienceless treachery unsurpassed in history. Whatever small theoretical advantages there might be in releasing those under restraint in this country would be enormously outweighed by the risks involved.[47]

In April 1943, when the Western Defense Command announced that Nisei soldiers on furlough would be allowed to return to the coast and rumors circulated that General DeWitt might be relieved,[48] anti-Japanese forces renewed their assault by urging the Dies Committee on Un-American Activities to investigate. Even before the Committee began its work, Representative J. Parnell Thomas visited Los Angeles and, without touring a single camp, began to issue press releases about the evacuees. He accused the WRA of pampering and overfeeding them and declared that there had been an organized division of the Japanese Army on the West Coast before Pearl Harbor. He called for halting the "WRA policy of releasing disloyal Japs" until the Dies Committee had completed its report.[49]

Even the Pacific Coast Committee on American Principles and Fair Play, a group of prominent citizens under honorary chairman Dr.

Robert Gordon Sproul, President of the University of California, expressly took no position on the issue of whether persons of Japanese ancestry should return to the Pacific Coast at that time, even though the group had issued a statement in June favoring an "opportunity for loyal Americans of Japanese ancestry to resettle in the manner, which, in the judgment of the federal government, is best designed to meet the manpower shortage."[50]

Dies Committee hearings began on June 8, starting with the anti-evacuee group. The most sensational witness was H.H. Townshend, a former WRA employee who claimed, among other things, that evacuees cached food in the desert and that over 1,000 Japanese soldiers lived in the Poston Center.[51] Throughout the hearings, committee staff made other observations to the press, for example, that WRA was releasing spies and saboteurs.[52]

This time the WRA decided to fight back. Demanding to testify, the agency prepared a strong statement in which the Committee was accused of seeking publicity by making and soliciting "sensational statements based on half-truths, exaggerations, and falsehoods."[53] One WRA document rebutted the Townshend testimony, pinpointing 42 lies or misleading statements. In his autobiography, Myer recounts the reaction of Committee Chairman Costello to this document. After reviewing it, the Chairman opened the session:

> Mr. Myer we have reviewed your document on the Townshend testimony in which you say there were 42 lies or half-truths, but we find only 39.

Myer agreed to "settle for 39."[54]

Once again, the final committee report of September 1943 was extremely mild, advocating segregation, a new board to investigate evacuees to be released, and an "Americanization" program in the camps. For the first time the government had taken on the anti-Japanese groups, and it had won. Not only were the Committee's recommendations consistent with WRA policy and planning, but, every bit as important, the Committee was denounced by the national press for its prejudice and procedure.[55]

The tide had turned. The rest of the country no longer shared the West Coast view. A *Washington Post* editorial responding to General DeWitt's succinct analysis that "a Jap is a Jap," put the matter in simple terms:

> The general should be told that American democracy and the Constitution of the United States are too vital to be ignored and flouted by any military zealot. The panic of Pearl Harbor is now

past. There has been ample time for the investigation of these people and the determination of their loyalty to this country on an individual basis. Whatever excuse there once was for evacuating and holding them indiscriminately no longer exists.[56]

President Roosevelt may have helped a little during the summer by responding to a Senate request for Administration views on returning ethnic Japanese to the West Coast; the President announced that while there were no present plans to end exclusion, its continuation depended only on military considerations.[57] It is unknown whether Roosevelt had in hand the War Department's opinion at that time on the military necessity for continuing exclusion, but the President's statement certainly suggested that the government did not foresee exclusion for the rest of the war.

As his support at the top of the government ebbed, General DeWitt did not stop trying to maintain complete exclusion. Alerted in early July by Governor Warren that two ethnic Japanese were reported to be on a fishing trip near Dinuba, California, DeWitt not only mounted a thorough investigation but also wrote the Governor about his fears of the future:

I am fully aware that persons released from the War Relocation Authority Camps may in considerable numbers attempt to return to the prohibited zones, perhaps as a trial effort to learn the official reaction to their presence. It is only through the mutual efforts of the military authorities and the Federal and State law enforcement officers that such plans will be defeated.[58]

Given such constant effort to defeat any humane, orderly return of ethnic Japanese to the West Coast, it was a palpable relief to McCloy when, in Fall 1943, DeWitt and Bendetsen left the Western Defense Command and General Delos Emmons took command at the Presidio.[59] Emmons did not immediately urge that the exclusion be revoked, but he began to review individual hardship cases more leniently, and cautiously prepared for ending exclusion before the war was over.[60]

WAITING FOR THE ELECTION

At the end of 1943, Attorney General Biddle returned to the fray. He wrote the President about a group of Californians and the Hearst press, who continued to make trouble for people of Japanese ancestry, stressing that:

The important thing is to secure the reabsorption of about 95,000 Japanese, of whom two-thirds are citizens and who give every indication of being loyal to the United States, into normal American life. The present practice of keeping loyal American citizens in concentration camps on the basis of race for longer than is absolutely necessary is dangerous and repugnant to the principles of our Government. It is also necessary to act now so that the agitation against these citizens does not continue after the war.

Biddle, aware of the political problems from public hostility to resettlement on the West Coast, recommended that the WRA be made part of a permanent cabinet agency, most likely the Interior Department, to give it a more effective voice with the public and within the government. "Care should be taken to make it clear that any change of administration is not a reflection upon the WRA relocation policy or administration. . . ."[61]

On January 5, 1944, President Roosevelt directed that an Executive Order be prepared placing "the whole of WRA under the Interior,"[62] and on February 16, the President signed Executive Order 9423, transferring authority over WRA to the Department of the Interior; the authority of the Director went to the Secretary of the Interior, who retained Dillon Myer as operating head of the program.[63] Harold Ickes, already a champion of the evacuees, was now their spokesman.

In the spring of 1944, the War Department finally proposed to the President that the exclusion be ended. Secretary Stimson took the issue to the Cabinet on May 26, 1944. Attorney General Biddle noted:

The Secretary of War raised the question of whether it was appropriate for the War Department, at this time, to cancel the Japanese Exclusion Orders and let the Japs go home. War, Interior, and Justice had all agreed that this could be done without danger to defense considerations but doubted the wisdom of doing it at this time before the election.[64]

The fact that "military necessity" no longer justified exclusion was repeated often during the following months. In June, Secretary Ickes bluntly urged the President to decide the issue:

[T]he continued retention of these innocent people in the relocation centers would be a blot upon the history of this country.[65]

Edward Stettinius, Jr., the Under Secretary of State, summarized the matter for the President: "The question appears to be largely a political one, the reaction in California, on which I am sure you will probably wish to reach your own decision."[66]

Roosevelt expressed his views to Ickes and Stettinius on June 12, 1944:

The more I think of this problem of suddenly ending the orders excluding Japanese Americans from the West Coast the more I think it would be a mistake to do anything drastic or sudden.

As I said at Cabinet, I think the whole problem, for the sake of internal quiet, should be handled gradually, i.e., I am thinking of two methods:

a. Seeing, with great discretion, how many Japanese families would be acceptable to public opinion in definite localities on the West Coast.

b. Seeking to extend greatly the distribution of other families in many parts of the United States. I have been talking to a number of people from the Coast and they are all in agreement that the Coast would be willing to receive back a portion of the Japanese who were formerly there—nothing sudden and not in too great quantities at any one time.

Also, in talking to people from the Middle West, the East and the South, I am sure that there would be no bitterness if they were distributed—one or two families to each county as a start. Dissemination and distribution constitute a great method of avoiding public outcry.

Why not proceed seriously along the above line—for a while at least?[67]

Whatever the military, legal or moral virtues of the evacuees' cause, the President would not do anything precipitous to upset the West Coast. There would be an election in November.

In 1942 political pressures for exclusion came from the West Coast and, somewhat transformed, wound through the War Department to the President. In 1944 the President was plainly leading his subordinates by responding to political demands for which they could no longer find military justification. Even the Western Defense Command was prepared to abandon the military rationale. The new Commanding General, C. H. Bonesteel, wrote McCloy on July 3, 1944:

My study of the existing situation leads me to a belief that the great improvement in the military situation on the West Coast indicates that there is no longer a military necessity for the mass exclusion of the Japanese from the West Coast as a whole. There is still a definite necessity for the exclusion of certain individuals.[68]

Moreover, after a July courtesy visit to Roosevelt in San Diego, Bonesteel reported to McCloy that the President's plans for scattering the Nikkei population lacked realism:

The solution envisaged by the President would be entirely satisfactory if the Japanese excludees would conform. However, although a few thousand will do so, it is my opinion and the opinion of all of those who are closely connected with the problem that the great majority of the Japanese will insist on going back to the areas from which they were originally removed. There is more than a question of obstinacy involved, for if one or two families should be located in a single white community, they would be isolated from their own people and would particularly be deprived of the religious, social and cultural contacts to which they are accustomed and which the Japanese particularly treasure. In addition, it must be appreciated that the economic factor is an important one. For example, a Japanese dentist or merchant will have great difficulty in establishing himself in a white community.

I think that we must base our action on the fact that a major portion of the excludees will wish to return to their original homes and that if they are not returned a very large number of them will bring legal action to accomplish it.[69]

Now that sobriety and sympathetic common sense were the order of the day at the Presidio, the hollowness of the existing policy was discussed more openly. McCloy began one meeting with the old Justice Department adversaries of exclusion by remarking to J. L. Burling that

it was curious how the two major cases in which the Army had interfered with civilians had started out for serious military reasons and had ended being required by wholly non-military considerations. For example, the Japanese were evacuated back in the dark days before Midway when an attack on the Pacific Coast was feared. Now the exclusion is being continued by the President for social reasons.[70]

Finally, and importantly, in September 1944 even the Navy came around. Admiral E. J. King, the Commander-in-Chief, United States Fleet, concurred that "the military situation no longer justifies the mass exclusion of persons of Japanese ancestry from the Western Defense Command."[71]

Through 1944, the new guard at Western Defense Command had been reexamining the mass exclusion orders. During the spring, General Emmons suggested that the size of the prohibited area be reduced, and that the War Department end the exclusion of individuals not actually or potentially dangerous.[72] This position reversed DeWitt and brought the WDC into line with the War Department. Despite the lack of movement on this broad proposition, Emmons began issuing Certificates of Exemption from the exclusion orders; these allowed people who had passed security investigations to return permanently to the West Coast. Other individual exemptions were granted as well: for travel and temporary residence on business; for a serious illness within the immediate family; for travel to relocation centers and public institutions inside the exclusion zone (at WRA's request); or for induction into the armed forces. Applications were extremely low at first; by April 1, 1944, 40 had been filed; by August 1 there were 235 and 515 by September 15. By the end of 1944, 1,485 ethnic Japanese were residing in the Western Defense Command by special exemption. Most were spouses of Caucasian residents.[73] In a very quiet way, General Emmons had begun the return of the Nikkei to the West Coast.

Emmons and Bonesteel were also concerned about lawsuits brought by the ethnic Japanese.[74] Three cases were central: *Shiramizu v. Bonesteel*, *Ochikubo v. Bonesteel*, and *Ex parte Endo*. In *Shiramizu*, the Nisei widow of a sergeant in the 100th Battalion who had died of combat wounds and against whom there was no evidence of disloyalty, challenged the continued exclusion of such Japanese from the Western Defense Command, and sought to restrain interference with her return to California.[75] Ochikubo, a dentist, sought similar relief.[76] In *Endo*, pending for some time in the courts and under review in the Supreme Court, Mitsuye Endo, a concededly loyal American citizen, had been granted leave clearance by the WRA, but was not permitted to reenter the Western Defense Command.[77]

The government's lawyers, including the Judge Advocate of the Western Defense Command, no longer believed that the exclusion policy could be justified to a judge.[78] They knew it would be difficult to prevail on the two available grounds: the present possibility of espionage and sabotage, and the unrest which resettlement would cause— the so-called "social resistance defense."[79] To avoid a court ruling on these questions, the government considered granting special exemptions to the plaintiffs. But exemptions might signal that anyone who sued would receive an exemption, thereby forcing a flood of uncontrolled reentries.

When the government offered Mrs. Shiramizu an exemption, more than a personal interest was at stake; "she had brought legal action in order to restore the rights of her race which she felt had been improperly taken away."[80] Nevertheless, the Department of Justice recommended that the exemptions be granted and that the cases of Mrs. Shiramizu and Dr. Ochikubo be rendered moot. The government needed time to develop some administrative method for dealing with its increasingly untenable position.[81] In Ochikubo's case an exemption was not granted because he had been denied leave clearance by the Japanese American Joint Board,[82] but the government was still able to prevail because the court determined that Dr. Ochikubo was unlikely to face immediate use of force if he returned; therefore an injunction against the use of force was not appropriate.[83] These cases showed the government that it had to develop promptly a plan for orderly return to the West Coast or the courts might well permit a less controlled return.

The War Department now assumed that the exclusion would end soon, and the Western Defense Command focused on maintaining the power to exclude individuals and assure an orderly return. On August 8, 1944, General Bonesteel sent General Marshall a long, detailed memorandum outlining reasons to terminate mass exclusion and institute an individual exclusion program. Recognizing that public opinion against the ethnic Japanese might lead to unrest, Bonesteel thought it could be confined if dangerous individuals were excluded. A number of important groups stood ready to assist the returning Nisei, he noted, because they "feel strongly that the Japanese who are citizens are entitled to their rights as such."[84] The memorandum brought no response.

On September 19, 1944, Bonesteel wrote a rather alarmed followup memorandum. More requests for travel and residence permits in the prohibited area, and more publicity about changes in the exclusion program suggested by the settlement of suits such as *Shiramizu*, led Bonesteel to fear forced change by the courts if mass exclusion were not lifted.[85] Two days later another Bonesteel memorandum repeated that prompt action was essential and outlined the West Coast publicity given to *Shiramizu* and *Ochikubo*; again he insisted "[i]t would be most unfortunate if the return of Japanese Americans should be accomplished abruptly and without adequate controls."[86]

Bonesteel wrote again on October 24, this time to McCloy, whom he asked for a personal meeting. A week later McCloy at last began to address the matter, revealing why the Department had been lethargic:

> [F]rom what I can judge to be the sense of those who will have the ultimate decision on most of these questions, there is a disposition not to crowd action too closely upon the heels of the election. As many of the considerations will have to be dealt with on high political rather than military levels, I am inclined to think we shall have a greater opportunity for constructive plans at a date somewhat later than November 6th.[87]

THE END OF EXCLUSION

The presidential election brought matters to a head. At the first Cabinet meeting after the election, on November 10, it was decided to lift the exclusion. On November 13, a meeting in the Attorney General's office discussed how to implement that decision, talking of plans and a tentative date for lifting the order.[88] Clearly, impending decisions in the Supreme Court cases, which would address the legality of exclusion and detention, were spectres harrying the decision makers.

On November 20, 1944, Attorney General Biddle wrote McCloy that rumors of the proposed releases are "about the West Coast" and he emphasized "utmost secrecy."[89] The President didn't drop his guard on the subject. At a press conference on November 21 he was directly asked about ending the exclusion:

Q. Mr. President, there is a great deal of renewed controversy on the Pacific Coast about the matter of allowing the return of these Japanese who were evacuated in 1942. Do you think that the danger of espionage or sabotage has sufficiently diminished so that there can be a relaxation of the restrictions that have been in effect for the last two years?

The President: In most of the cases. That doesn't mean all of them. And, of course, we have been trying to—I am now talking about. . . . Japanese Americans. I am not talking about the Japanese themselves. A good deal of progress has been made in scattering them through the country, and that is going on almost every day. I have forgotten what the figures are. There are about roughly a hundred—a hundred thousand Japanese-origin citizens in this country. And it is felt by a great many lawyers that under the Constitution they can't be kept locked up in concentration camps. And a good many of them, as I remember it—you had better check with the Secretary of Interior on this—somewhere around 20 or 25 percent of all those citizens have re-placed themselves, and in a great many parts of the country.

And the example that I always cite, to take a unit, is the size of the county, whether it's in the Hudson River valley or in western "Joe-gia" (Georgia) which we all know, in one of those counties, probably half a dozen or a dozen families could be scattered around on the farms and worked into the community. After all, they are American citizens, and we all know that American citizens have certain privileges. And they wouldn't—what's my favorite word?— discombobolate—(Laughter)—the existing population of those particular counties very much. After all—what?—75 thousand families scattered all around the United States is not going to upset anybody. . . . And, of course we are actuated by the—in part by the very wonderful record that the Japanese in that battalion in Italy have been making in the war. It is one of the outstanding battalions we have.

Q. But, sir, the discussion on the West Coast is more about the relaxation of the military restrictions in that prohibited area, as to whether they should be allowed in the areas from which they have been excluded. It isn't about allowing them to go elsewhere in the country. I was wondering if you felt that the danger of espionage had sufficiently diminished so that the military restrictions that were passed could be lifted?

The President: That I couldn't tell you, because I don't know.[90]

Thus, the government entered December with the decision made but not publicly announced.

By December 9, the government was establishing policies and procedures for the "final phase of the program" and preparing press statements to be issued when exclusion was lifted. The statement noted that the WRA would extend its relocation program to cover the entire country, but lifting the order did not mean that a hasty mass movement would return all evacuees to the West Coast. "One of the major WRA aims, from the beginning, has been to encourage the widest possible dispersal of evacuees throughout the Nation, and this will continue as a prime objective during the final phase of the program." By December 1944, 35,000 of the 110,000 persons originally evacuated had relocated outside the Western Defense Command area. The statement also noted that WRA would work toward early shutdown of the relocation centers, with all to be closed within a year.[91]

As an essential part of ending exclusion, the Departments of War and Justice began to develop lists of individual evacuees. Separately enumerated were Japanese aliens under segregation parole orders prohibiting them from leaving Tule Lake Segregation Center; ordinary parolees at Tule Lake who might be excluded from military areas; Japanese aliens paroled under Immigration Service safeguards that forbade their return to the Coast; and individuals under ordinary parole outside Tule Lake who might be excluded from the West Coast. The Justice Department believed that being on parole was not a sufficient basis for exclusion.[92] On December 9 the Western Defense Command delivered to the Chief of Staff a list of persons it thought had to be excluded from critical areas of the WDC and detained in a camp similar to Tule Lake.[93] The list consisted of 4,963 persons, of whom 3,066 were in the Tule Lake Segregation Center; others were in a number of other camps; 510 were unaccounted for.[94] The Army suggested to Dillon Myer that the number might grow to approximately 5,500.[95] The standards by which excludees were selected were:

- Refusal to register on the Selective Service questionnaire.
- Refusal to serve in the United States armed forces.
- Refusal, without qualification, to swear allegiance to the United States.
- Voluntary submittal of a written statement of loyalty to Japan.
- Agents or operatives of Japan.

- Voluntary request of revocation of American citizenship.[96]

Finally, after extensive preparation, the termination plan was presented to Roosevelt for concurrence. On December 13, 1944, Secretary Stimson told the President, yet again, that continued mass exclusion was no longer a matter of military necessity—the loyal had been separated from the disloyal and the morale of Japanese American soldiers was suffering because of continued exclusion. Stimson worried about sabotage and espionage, but was persuaded that return of most Japanese to the West Coast should nonetheless be carried out. He set forth safeguards to assure that return would be gradual and that efforts would continue to relocate those of Japanese descent in other parts of the country. An individual exclusion program would be instituted. The Department of Justice would ultimately take responsibility for detention and for determining who should be released. Because it would be announced that only persons cleared by the military authorities would be permitted to return, Stimson was confident that any civil unrest could be handled. Finally, Stimson noted that a system to permit orderly return was much preferable to an unfavorable court decision that might require sudden, unplanned return.[97] In a cover memorandum to Roosevelt's secretary, Stimson noted that he wanted to be sure the President had no objection, but that he was not asking Roosevelt to make the decision.[98] The President did not object to the announcement.[99]

Implementation remained. On December 15, Colonel William Ryan of the Western Defense Command sent Dillon Myer the so-called "white list" of 95,975 names of those who would not be excluded. He noted that an additional 19,956 persons under age 14 were in the same category (totaling over 115,000).[100] On December 16, 1944, the Solicitor General sent copies of correspondence about the rescission of exclusion and a copy of Public Proclamation Number 21 to Chief Justice Stone, presumably in the hope of mooting any decision in the *Endo* case.[101]

Finally, on December 17, 1944, Public Proclamation Number 21 was issued. General DeWitt's mass exclusion orders were rescinded, and individual exclusions from "sensitive" areas of the Western Defense Command took their place. Even in the proclamation the federal government worked to protect its political position on the West Coast by stressing the care it took before restoring the ethnic Japanese to their full rights:

The people of the states situated within the Western Defense Command, are assured that the records of all persons of Japanese

> ancestry have been carefully examined and only those persons
> who have been cleared by military authority have been permitted
> to return. They should be accorded the same treatment and al-
> lowed to enjoy the same privileges accorded other law abiding
> American citizens or residents.[102]

An accompanying press release rehearsed the history of the exclusion
order, then stated that persons of Japanese ancestry had their loyalty
investigated "probably more thoroughly than any other segment of our
population."[103] Another press release stressed that "[t]hose persons
who will be permitted to return have been cleared by Army authorities."[104]

Secretary Ickes marked the occasion by sending appropriate thanks
to the entire staff of the War Relocation Authority:

> Behind you is a record of accomplishment of which you may all
> be proud. You have efficiently and devotedly carried out one of
> the most difficult and trying jobs that has been entrusted to an
> agency of Government. You, and particularly Mr. Dillon Myer,
> the Director of the War Relocation Authority, have been subjected
> to a good deal of abuse from persons who could not or would not
> understand the problem with which you were dealing. But in spite
> of this, you have carried through a carefully devised program with
> regard not only for the conditions imposed by military authority,
> but also for the human values concerned.[105]

THE SUPREME COURT RULINGS

Immediately after the announcement the Supreme Court handed down
opinions in both *Korematsu* and *Ex parte Endo*.[106] In *Korematsu*, a
divided court upheld the criminal conviction of Fred Korematsu for
failing to report to an assembly center in May 1942 pursuant to the
plan through which he would be excluded from California and sent to
a relocation center. Justice Hugo Black wrote a short opinion for the
majority which is remarkable in its treatment of both the facts and the
law. The Court did not undertake any careful review of the facts of
the situation on the West Coast in early 1942. It avoided this task by
choosing to give great deference to the military judgment on which
the decision was based. This approach of deferring to the military
judgment rather than looking closely at the record which the government had been able to pull together was the only plausible course for
the Court to follow if it were to conclude that exclusion was consti-

tutionally permissible. If the Court had looked hard, it would have found that there was nothing there—no facts particularly within military competence which could be rationally related to the extraordinary action taken. Justice Murphy's vehement dissent made that plain as he dissected and destroyed General DeWitt's *Final Report.* It is the inevitable conclusion which the Commission has also reached after extensive study of a very substantial body of facts. It was also the conclusion of those who carefully studied the opinion, the briefs and the record immediately after *Korematsu* was decided. Eugene Rostow wrote the seminal article about the cases in 1945 and dealt pointedly with the issue of factual proof of "military necessity." Rostow believed a convincing and substantial factual case had to be made before civil rights could be permissibly invaded as they were here, but he concluded that one did not have to insist upon that rule of proof to conclude that the Japanese American cases were wrongly decided:

> No matter how narrowly the rule of proof is formulated, it could not have been satisfied in either the *Hirabayashi* or the *Korematsu* cases. Not only was there insufficient evidence in those cases to satisfy a reasonably prudent judge or a reasonably prudent general: there was no evidence whatever by which a court might test the responsibility of General DeWitt's action, either under the statute of March 21, 1942, or on more general considerations. True, in the *Hirabayashi* case the Court carefully identified certain of General DeWitt's proclamations as "findings," which established the conformity of his actions to the standard of the statute—the protection of military resources against the risk of sabotage and espionage. But the military proclamations record conclusions, not evidence. And in both cases the record is bare of testimony on either side about the policy of the curfew or the exclusion orders. There was every reason to have regarded this omission as a fatal defect, and to have remanded in each case for a trial on the justification of the discriminatory curfew and of the exclusion orders.
>
> Such an inquiry would have been illuminating. General DeWitt's Final Report and his testimony before committees of the Congress clearly indicated that his motivation was ignorant race prejudice, not facts to support the hypothesis that there was a greater risk of sabotage among the Japanese than among residents of German, Italian, or any other ethnic affiliation. The most significant comment on the quality of the General's report is contained in the government's brief in *Korematsu* v. *United States.* There the Solicitor General said that the report was relied upon "for statistics and other details concerning the actual evacuation and the events that took place subsequent thereto. We have specifically recited in this brief the facts relating to the justification for the evacuation,

of which we ask the Court to take judicial notice, and we rely upon the Final Report only to the extent that it relates such facts." Yet the Final Report embodied the basic decision under review and stated the reasons why it was actually undertaken. General DeWitt's Final Recommendation to the Secretary of War, dated February 14, 1942, included in the Final Report, was the closest approximation we have in these cases to an authoritative determination of fact.[107]

We have already analyzed the conclusory beliefs about ethnicity determining loyalty which are central to DeWitt's final recommendation, and have pointed out the weakness of the government's case when it was put to its proof on the facts in cases such as *Ebel* and *Schueller*.

No one reading the Supreme Court's opinion today with knowledge of the exclusion, evacuation and detention can conclude that the majority opinion displays any close knowledge of the reasoning used by the government in the momentous historical events under review. The only concrete item pointed out to show disloyalty among evacuees was the fact that approximately 5,000 American citizens in the relocation camps had refused to swear unqualified allegiance to the United States, a fact that is meaningless without understanding conditions within the camps.

What of the law on which the case was based? There are two principles in contention in the majority opinion; the presumption against invidious racial discrimination which requires that racial classifications be given strict scrutiny, and the deference to military judgment in wartime based on the war powers of the Constitution and expressed in the banal aphorism that the power to wage war is the power to wage war successfully. In this case, of course, the Court found that military interests prevailed over the presumption against racial discrimination.

Today the decision in *Korematsu* lies overruled in the court of history. First, the Supreme Court, a little more than a year later in *Duncan* v. *Kahanamoku*, reviewed the imposition of martial law in Hawaii and struck it down, making adamantly clear that the principles and practices of American government are permeated by the belief that loyal citizens in loyal territory are to be governed by civil rather than military authority, and that when the military assumes civil functions in such circumstances it will receive no deference from the courts in reviewing its actions.[108] *Korematsu* fits the *Duncan* pattern—the exclusion of the Nikkei not only invaded the recognized province of civil government, it was based on cultural and social facts in which the military had no training or expertise. General DeWitt had assumed the role of omniscient sociologist and anthropologist. *Duncan* makes clear that no deference will be given to military judgments of that nature.

The other legal leg of the opinion, the failure to strike down an invidious racial discrimination, stands isolated in the law—the Japanese American cases have never been followed and are routinely cited as the only modern examples of invidious racial discrimination which the Supreme Court has not stricken down. Typically, Justice Powell wrote in 1980:

> Under this Court's established doctrine, a racial classification is suspect and subject to strict judicial scrutiny. . . . Only two of this Court's modern cases have held the use of racial classifications to be constitutional. See *Korematsu* v. *United States*, 323 U.S. 214 (1944); *Hirabayashi* v. *United States*, 320 U.S. 81 (1943). Indeed, the failure of legislative action to survive strict scrutiny has led some to wonder whether our review of racial classifications has been strict in theory, but fatal in fact.[109]

Moreover, the law has evolved in the last forty years and the equal protection of the laws, once applicable only to the states by the language of the Fourteenth Amendment, has now been applied through the due process clause of the Fifth Amendment to actions of the federal government.[110] Thus the constitutional protection against federal discrimination has been strengthened. *Korematsu* is a curiosity, not a precedent on questions of racial discrimination.

Finally, insofar as *Korematsu* relied on the inherent authority of an executive order from the Commander in Chief and not on a program articulated and defined by statute, that precedent has been overruled by the decision of the Court in the steel seizure case.[111]

Korematsu has not been overruled—we have not been so unfortunate that a repetition of the facts has occurred to give the Court that opportunity—but each part of the decision, questions of both factual review and legal principles, has been discredited or abandoned.

The result in the companion case of *Ex parte Endo* was very different. The Court unanimously reversed *Endo* and ruled that an admittedly loyal American citizen could not be held in a relocation camp against her will. But even this ruling was on the narrow ground that no statute or even an explicit executive order supported this course of conduct. The Supreme Court does not reach constitutional issues unnecessarily, but the tone of Justice Douglas's writing in *Endo* was nonetheless crabbed and confined. Even this very substantial and important victory for the evacuees did not come with an air of generosity or largeness of spirit.[112]

GOING HOME

Resettlement now moved forward, although the government continued to develop lists of individual excludees, with the WRA and the War Department disputing how many were on the lists and whether new persons could be added. For example, Dillon Myer was concerned that the Western Defense Command continued to exclude those who had been granted leave clearance by WRA, most Buddhist priests, and other previously unlisted persons.[113] The Eastern Defense Command was anxious about accepting people of Japanese descent excluded from the West Coast.[114] Governor Wallgren, newly-elected in the State of Washington, continued to favor mass exclusion; he was "extremely antagonistic toward the Japanese and . . . positive in his assertion that a mistake had been made, from the point of view of the war effort, in allowing any to return and that this mistake should be remedied."[115] But generally the Army was pleased with the course of events on the West Coast. General Pratt, now in charge of the WDC, wrote, "The first reactions to the change in the policy with reference to control of Japanese Americans has been even more favorable than I hoped. While I anticipate that this favorable reaction will continue and will be a strong factor in preventing the development of unfavorable agitation, we should be prepared in case any untoward incident occurs."[116]

Whether and how quickly to close the relocation centers was another concern. Proclamation No. 21 indicated that the centers would be closed within a year. WRA believed that such an announcement was essential to assure that people in the centers would move out, and that evacuees in the camps would not become a dependent group like the American Indians. The public and some government officials, however, expressed concern that some persons of Japanese ancestry would be left homeless and without livelihoods if the centers were permanently closed.[117] On the other side, Congressman May suggested introducing legislation to have the centers closed by June 30, 1945. Secretary Ickes, sensitive to the need to provide for relocatees, opposed the bill.[118] Indeed, all centers but Tule Lake were closed by January 1946. Tule Lake was kept open to permit the Justice Department to complete its hearings on detainees there.[119]

The end of mass exclusion did not spell the end of hardship for the evacuees. Throughout 1945, evacuees returned to the West Coast, not only from the camps but also from interior states where they had been resettled. For many, leaving the camps was as traumatic as entering them. However unpleasant their lives in camp, it was preferable to an unknown, possibly hostile reception on the West Coast. By January 1945, only one of every six Issei had left.[120] Now they would have to be persuaded to leave.[121] Suicides, especially among elderly bachelors, were reported.[122] Many were frightened, particularly of reintegrating with whites after the segregated life of the camps.[123] Some came to resettlement lacking self-esteem, and perhaps identifying with the stereotypes that had been projected upon them.[124] Some felt shame when they were let out of camp.[125] A great many felt the burden of starting over, at an older age and for a second time.[126] After encouraging everyone to leave and scheduling closing dates for each camp, the WRA finally gave the remaining evacuees train fare to the point of their evacuation, and made them leave.[127]

They returned by the trainload to Los Angeles, San Francisco and Seattle. Often elderly and infirm or burdened with heavy family responsibility, the last evacuees to leave "piled into temporary shelters, hotels, converted Army barracks, and public housing."[128] Each person was given an allowance of $25.[129] Very few could come back to their prewar holdings. Only about 25 percent of the prewar farm operators, for example, retained property.[130]

Many testified that their stored possessions had been lost or stolen.[131] Sometimes taxes had not been paid, and special measures to keep property from tax sales were required.[132] Others found their homes or farms ill-cared-for, overgrown with weeds, badly tended or destroyed.[133] Furnishings, farm equipment and machinery were lost or stolen.[134] One person reported finding strangers living in his former home.[135]

Almost uniformly, those who did not return to homes they owned testified that housing was extremely hard to find because of postwar shortages and discrimination against Japanese Americans.[136] The WRA concluded that "no other problem has provided so widespread an obstacle to satisfactory adjustment."[137] Families lived in a single room, sometimes with a common bathroom or kitchen down the hall, or they lived in hotels or churches.[138] Some, particularly women, took room-and-board jobs—low-skilled and low-paying work—in order to have a place to live.[139] Indeed, it was not uncommon that almost every family member had to work in order to make ends meet.[140] John Saito's experience typifies much of the testimony:

> My father first came back to Los Angeles in July of 1945, and worked as a dishwasher at a skid row restaurant on 5th Street. I came back to Los Angeles after my father and stayed at his hotel room in the skid row area. There was only one room, and only

one bed, he worked the graveyard shift and I went to school during the day, therefore, we managed to use the same bed at different hours of the day. My mother was still in Idaho working as a cook at a farm labor camp. My older brother was still overseas with the 442nd Regimental Combat Team. My mother had scrimped and saved her salary as a cook for over three years, and finally had enough money for a down payment on a house. We purchased the house in 1946, and tried to move in only to find two Caucasian men sitting on the front steps with a court injunction prohibiting us from moving in because of a restrictive convenant. If we moved in, we would be subject to $1,000 fine and/or one year in the County Jail. We were in a financial bind because we could not afford both mortgage and rental payments. We had to sell our house during a period of a housing shortage.[141]

Housing was not the only problem—during the first six months of 1945, violence was relatively common. One of the first incidents occurred on January 8, when someone tried to dynamite and burn an evacuee's fruit packing shed. About thirty incidents followed, mostly shots fired into evacuee homes.[142] Boycotts of evacuee produce were threatened.[143] General harassment, such as signs announcing "No Japs allowed, no Japs welcome," was widespread.[144]

Although jobs on the West Coast were relatively plentiful, much employment discrimination blocked evacuees,[145] and many had to take menial jobs.[146] Although they had little difficulty finding work as farm laborers,[147] the number who ran their own establishments was much lower than it had been before the war. Only a fourth as many were farming now, which meant severely curtailed opportunities for wholesale and retail operations.[148] So the majority moved into other fields, scattered among many different jobs. Others were compelled to take welfare payments.[149] Almost all worked long and hard to restore their former status. The Issei were particularly burdened, for many would otherwise have retired; but now they had to work.[150]

Another matter of great concern during this period was reuniting families. In many cases the younger, more employable members had relocated to the east during 1943 and 1944. Their parents were likely to return to the West Coast on leaving the camps. Thus the resettlement process was marked by much second-time resettling, as children came from the east to join their parents or vice versa.[151]

Despite the many problems faced by the returning evacuees, most were successful in rebuilding their lives. The political leadership, both federal and state, was working to expedite their return. The West Coast was experiencing tremendous postwar growth and the ethnic

Japanese were becoming just one of many minority groups. Equally important were the groups working for justice for the ethnic Japanese. Many were church people, particularly Quakers and liberals, who worked with the Army and WRA. They offered temporary shelter, provided moral support, sponsored public talks about the Nisei military record and tried to counteract anti-Japanese movements.[152] At long last the Nikkei captivity was over; the arduous task of creating new lives had begun.

9

Protest and Disaffection

The loyalty questionnaire brought each evacuee a choice: would he believe the country's rhetoric and hope for his own future in the United States, or protest the squalid injustice of camp life and the betrayal of American promises? Rage and protest were deeply human reactions to circumstances that often allowed no dignified response. But, inside the camp, bitterness offered little on which to build a new and satisfying life. As 1944 began, the energetic and optimistic were rapidly relocating, leaving behind in camp the old and hostile. Tule Lake was a nightmare of strikes and Army occupation, for any progress toward ending the exclusion had not touched these evacuees. They had lost almost everything, even modest control of their own lives. And their deepening sense of loss and frustration had virtually no outlet.

When the government forced choices upon them, by restoring the draft and making it possible to renounce citizenship, many evacuees, particularly those swayed by strong leaders, reacted with predictable outrage. They would reject decisively the country that had rejected them. Even those whose character forbade angry outbursts could vent their anger in a quiet way—by asking to go to Japan. Draft resistance and renunciation illuminated the darkest shadows of exclusion and detention, showing losses as painful as losing home or business: the loss of confidence in American society and its moral values. Resistance and renunciation were all the more poignant because they often seemed the only way to maintain one's dignity and self-respect.

THE DRAFT

In December 1943, the government announced that Selective Service would begin to induct Nisei. The idea of drafting the Nisei was not new. It had been discussed at least as early as October 1942, when Elmer Davis argued to the President that "it would hardly be fair to evacuate people and then impose normal draft procedures."[1] At that time, Davis's view had prevailed. Now the War Department was changing its mind, which Secretary Stimson attributed to the fine record of Nisei volunteers.[2] The need for manpower and the small number of volunteers from the camps were undoubtedly factors as well.[3] Supporting the decision as a return to normal nondiscriminatory citizenship were the JACL and WRA, which had long been on record supporting the draft.[4]

Not until January 14, 1944, however, did Selective Service local board regulations permit Nisei eligibility for the draft, subject to War Department acceptability, principally a review of loyalty.[5] Acceptable registrants were reclassified I-A, the status of other eligible citizens. Many of the 2,800 Nisei inductees from the camps welcomed the draft. It reinstated their rights, offered a means to evade their parents' objection to voluntary enlistment and produced a job as well as escape from the debilitating idleness and confinement of camp. The draft successfully solicited replacements for the 100th Battalion and the 442nd Regimental Combat Team.

For others, however, the draft was yet another humiliation. The government that had already behaved so shabbily now was forcing its prisoners to fight the war. About 300 refused to report for physicals or induction[6] on the grounds that their citizenship rights should be fully restored before they were compelled to serve in the armed forces. The most organized resistance came from Heart Mountain, although Poston had a greater number of refusals.[7] In early 1944, *Rocky Shimpo*, a Denver newspaper, ran a series of articles against the draft, and at Heart Mountain, a "Fair Play Committee" took over the resistance. Although the newspaper was silenced, the Committee dissolved and its leaders sent to Tule Lake, their work had effect: sixty-three Nisei at Heart Mountain resisted the draft, fifty-one of whom said they would serve if their citizenship rights were restored.[8] The resisters argued that their cases were test cases to clarify their citizenship rights. They were tried, convicted, and sentenced to three years in federal prison; appeals failed.[9]

Three hundred fifteen young men refused to be inducted. Of

these, 263 were convicted. The rest were released, or volunteered, or were in process at the time these statistics were compiled.[10] In 1947, a Presidential pardon was granted to those who had been convicted.[11]

RENUNCIATION

> I think this was a program in the Department of Justice which failed.   —Edward Ennis[12]

By mid-1944, relations between the administration and the evacuees were at a low ebb. Evacuees had been confined for two years and their loyalty had been questioned while their sons were drafted. The mood was particularly bleak at Tule Lake. The first six months of 1944 were highly emotional as the accommodationists struggled for power in camp with more extreme pro-Japan forces. The extremists had poor conditions on their side. Although the Army fully withdrew from the camp in May, the stockade—the prison within a prison—established after the November "riot" remained. Sanitation was primitive and food inadequate. Mail was censored and visitors prohibited.[13] Tokio Yamane described conditions in the stockade's "bull pen:"

> Prisoners in the stockade lived in wooden buildings which, although flimsy, still offered some protection from the severe winters of Tule Lake. However, prisoners in the "bull pen" were housed outdoors in tents without heat and with no protection against the bitter cold. The bunks were placed directly on the cold ground, and the prisoners had only one or two blankets and no extra clothing to ward off the winter chill. And, for the first time in our lives, those of us confined to the "bull pen" experienced a life and death struggle for survival, the unbearable pain from our unattended and infected wounds, and the penetrating December cold of Tule Lake, a God Forsaken concentration camp lying near the Oregon border, and I shall never forget that horrible experience.[14]

Appeals to the Spanish consul, acting as intermediary for the government of Japan, had been largely unsuccessful.[15] Although the stockade was quickly abolished after ACLU Attorney Wayne Collins threatened suit in August 1944,[16] in June, after eight months of existence, it appeared permanent.

Outside the camps, repercussions from the "riot" of the previous November continued. The old idea of stripping the Nisei of their citizenship revived. Under Congressional pressure, Attorney General

Biddle finally agreed to compromise; he would support a new option—a statute permitting voluntary renunciation of citizenship.[17] A bill was passed and signed into law on July 1, 1944,[18] designed primarily to get the extremist group who demanded return to Japan out of Tule Lake and into Justice Department internment camps.[19]

After conferences between WRA and the Department of Justice, a procedure to effect renunciation was announced in October 1944.[20] The evacuee would make a written request to the Justice Department, followed by a hearing. After the hearing and a formal renunciation, the Attorney General would grant approval.[21]

At Tule Lake, the new renunciation process began just as the strongly militant pro-Japan faction emerged in camp. From the beginning of Tule Lake's existence as a segregation center, some evacuees (dubbed "resegregationists") had asked for a camp composed solely of people who preferred Japan and the Japanese way of life.[22] By mid-1944, this group generally dominated the camp, and the WRA seemed unwilling or unable to restore balance to the community. In July a moderate evacuee had been murdered, and the resegregationists were implicated. There had also been a wave of beatings of people who were suspected *inu*—dogs, who collaborated with the authorities.[23] Few were willing to risk falling victim to this terrorist activity.[24] The resegregationists had also begun a series of "Japanese" activities—language schools, lectures and athletics,[25] which attracted a wide following.[26] Soon morning outdoor exercises were added, which gradually grew militaristic, complete with uniforms bearing emblems of the rising sun.[27] Taeko Okamura described her childhood experience of this time at Tule Lake:

> My sister and I were enrolled in a Japanese school in preparation for our eventual expatriation to Japan. Our teachers were generally pro-Japan and taught us not only how to read and write in Japanese but also to be proud as Japanese. Their goals were to teach us to be good Japanese so that we would not be embarrassed when we got to Japan.
>
> We were often asked to wear red or white headbands and do marching exercises. We were awakened early, hurriedly got dressed and gathered at one end of the block where a leader led us in traditional Japanese calisthenics. As the sun rose, we bowed our heads to the east. This was to show our respect to the Emperor. We were also led in the clean-up of our block area before breakfast.
>
> Our block was located on the southwest corner of the camp grounds. The double barbed wire fence was just beyond the next barrack from our compartment. A guard tower with uniformed men and weapons were in view at all times. Search lights were

beamed onto the camp grounds at night. Uniformed men with weapons driving around in jeeps was a common sight. As a result of this experience, I used to be afraid of any white adult male for a very long time.

Demonstrations in protest of one thing or other were frequent. We very often locked ourselves in our room to avoid participating in these demonstrations. Physical violence and verbal abuses were common at these demonstrations where feelings ran high. And whenever a large demonstration took place, we could always expect the camp authorities to send out soldiers to search our rooms for contraband. These searches were very thorough and everything was ransacked.

Life in Tule Lake Segregation Camp for children was not very pleasant. There was very little to do for entertainment. Toys were scarce. We often played hopscotch using the coal pieces from the pile in front of the bathroom area. Coal was fed into the furnace by a man to make hot water. Our mothers gave us outdated Wards or Sears catalogues so we could cut out the models to use as paper dolls. We also spent a great deal of time looking for tiny shells which our mothers bleached and made into necklaces and pins.[28]

Other witnesses recalled similar experiences:

It was almost mandatory for all Japanese students to attend Japanese Language School. The pressure of academic excellence was stressed.[29]

The militant group were the Kibei and they had control of the people by strong arm tactics. They had military marching exercises and attempted to make everybody get out and march around the camp.[30]

Now the resegregationists added renunciation of citizenship to their program.

As soon as official procedures for renunciation were established, strong pressure was applied by the extremists. The resegregationists stepped up militaristic activity, began to spread news of Japanese victories,[31] and circulated rumors that those who did not renounce would be drafted or ineligible for repatriation. Despite these tactics, however, by mid-December only about 600 people had filed their applications.[32]

On December 17, however, two announcements turned the tide in favor of renunciation: the WDC's rescission of the mass exclusion order and WRA's decision to close the camps within a year.[33] To the segregees, alienated and distrustful, this meant destruction of the refuge of the camps and the synthetic world they had created there.[34] Communications from campmates who had left for the West Coast and news reports then convinced the evacuees that their old neighborhoods were more hostile and dangerous than before evacuation.[35] Renunciation seemed the best way to escape resettlement.[36] The December 27 Justice Department roundup and removal to internment camps of a number of the first group of renunciants seemed to confirm this.[37] Renunciation also seemed a way to keep the family together. Many believed that disloyal Issei would be deported after the war; by renouncing, the Nisei could join them.[38] Thus strengthened, resegregationists intensified their coercive tactics,[39] including threats to beat up families unless the Nisei renounced,[40] and WRA continued to allow resegregationists to terrorize the camp. Finally, renunciation was one more way to express resentment. As Edward Ennis described it, renunciants were "obviously a lot of people who were deprived of their liberty and put into camps. This was a perfectly honest expression of what they felt. They just threw back their citizenship at us."[41]

By January, renunciation had become a mass movement, as 3,400 applied in that month alone.[42] Over a thousand applied in February. In March, after four more transfers to internment camps, the WRA finally decided to crack down. They decreed that Japanese nationalistic activities were unlawful and began to step into the internal affairs of the camp.[43] At this point, the fervor declined. But by then over 5,000 citizens, including more than 70 percent of the Tule Lake Nisei, had renounced their citizenship.[44]

In the late spring of 1945, thousands of renunciants began to regret their decisions. The success of the Nisei combat team was beginning to turn the tide of public opinion, and relocation went more smoothly. Japan was on the verge of defeat. The Justice Department had decided to use Tule Lake to hold many renunciants while their Issei parents were resettled.[45]

The Justice Department, unmoved by the plight of Nisei who wanted to regain their citizenship and leave camp with the rest of their families, announced on October 8 that it would begin to send renunciants to Japan.[46] To fight the deportation, a group of renunciants again called upon Wayne Collins, who filed in federal courts to release the renunciants and void the renunciations. The suits charged that these were not free acts and that the government had knowingly allowed the resegregationists to carry out their violent, seditious campaign.[47] When the judge stayed the deportation, the Justice Department began individual hearings to determine whether internees should be released. All but 449 were allowed to relocate.[48] On June 30, 1947, the court ruled that none could be held, and remaining renunciants went free. In 1948, the same court ruled that all renunciations were invalid.[49]

In 1950, however, the later judgment was overturned by the Ninth Circuit Court of Appeals, which decided that the District Court's finding of mass coercion was incorrect; coercion had to be shown in each case.[50] Collins continued the fight, filing over 10,000 affidavits on behalf of the renunciants. Not until 1968 was the last of these finally processed.[51]

REPATRIATION AND EXPATRIATION

While the stories of draft resisters and renunciants dramatically reveal the angry disillusion of the camps, a brief account of aliens or citizens who filed for repatriation or expatriation to Japan shows with equal force the disaffection caused by evacuation and prolonged detention. During 1942, the year in which those who felt instinctively loyal to Japan could have been expected to ask to go there, relatively few applications were made. By the end of 1942, the WRA had only 2,255 applications from a possible group of about 120,000.[52] About 58 percent of these came from aliens; another 23 percent were citizens under 18, many of whom were probably dependents of aliens.[53] In short, very few adult American citizens had made an independent effort to express allegiance to Japan by leaving the United States.

By the end of 1943, the situation had changed remarkably. There were 9,028 applications on file, an increase of 6,673.[54] Furthermore, by more than two to one, applications came from American citizens. What prompted this surge of feeling against the United States? The loyalty registration was clearly one factor. Over 40 percent of the new applications had been filed during approximately ten weeks of registration.[55] They came from all camps, but Granada and Minidoka, which had little problem with registration, produced fewest applications.[56] Clearly, a request to leave for Japan had become one of the few outlets whereby imprisoned evacuees could vent their anger about the loyalty questionnaire, and perhaps escape it entirely.[57]

In 1944, the numbers jumped again. The WRA records 19,014 applications in December 1944, an increase of 9,986 over the previous year. Over 75 percent of these came from Tule Lake,[58] where filing an application made one less likely to face "inu" taunts from resegregationists.[59] By the end of 1945, over 20,000 requests had been made through the WCCA and WRA—over 16 percent of the total number of evacuees.

Most of the applicants never left for Japan. Only 4,724 travelled directly to Japan from the WRA centers[60] and, nationwide, only about 8,000 left.[61] When the exclusion order was lifted, many repatriate and expatriate applicants were free to resettle; more were released after their renunciation hearings. Apparently neither the government nor the evacuees actively attempted to follow up after the war.

No other statistics chronicle so clearly as these the decline of evacuees' faith in the United States. In the assembly and relocation centers, applications to go to Japan had been one of the few nonviolent ways to protest degrading treatment. During three years of rising humiliation, 20,000 people chose this means to express their pain, outrage and alienation, in one of the saddest testaments to the injustice of exclusion and detention. The cold statistics fail, even so, to convey the scars of mind and soul that many carried with them from the camps.

10

Military Service

Since their words would not have been believed, especially in wartime, [Japanese Americans] communicated by action and behavior. "We are good Americans," they said. "We are good neighbors. We are useful and productive citizens. We love America and are willing to die for her." These messages were communicated by the industry of workers and businessmen and farmers, by their service to the communities in which they live, by their behavior as good citizens, and by the war record of the 442nd. *It was a form of communication for which there is no verbal or symbolic substitute.*

—*S. I. Hayakawa*[1]

Following the attack on Pearl Harbor, the War Department stopped taking Japanese Americans into the military, and many already in service were released. Almost from the beginning, two institutions were exempt: the Military Intelligence Service Language School (MISLS) and the 100th Battalion. By early 1943, when Nisei volunteers were again accepted, a new Nisei unit was formed, the 442nd Regimental Combat Team. Many Nisei also contributed in other capacities throughout the war.

Approximately 33,000 Nisei served in the military during World War II.[2] Although many had come from the camps where their families were still detained, Nisei service was extraordinarily heroic. At war's end, their valor and the public tributes heaped upon them did much to hasten the acceptance of ethnic Japanese released from the camps:

the question of loyalty had been most powerfully answered by a battlefield record of courage and sacrifice.

THE MILITARY INTELLIGENCE SERVICE
LANGUAGE SCHOOL

In the spring of 1941, a few alert Army intelligence officers realized that, if war came, the Army would need Japanese language interpreters and translators. After much delay, Lieut. Col. John Weckerling and Capt. Kai Rasmussen won approval to start a small school for training persons with some background in Japanese. On November 1, 1941, the school opened at Crissy Field in San Francisco with four Nisei instructors and 60 students, 58 of whom were Japanese Americans.[3] The attack on Pearl Harbor confirmed the value of the program. During the spring of 1942, while evacuation was proceeding, the school was enlarged and transferred to Camp Savage in Minnesota.[4] Meanwhile, the first group had completed training, and 35 of its graduates went to the Pacific—half to Guadalcanal and half to the Aleutian Islands.[5]

The school, now renamed the Military Intelligence Service Language School (MISLS) and officially part of the War Department, began its first class at Camp Savage in June 1942 with 200 students.[6] By the end of 1942, more than 100 Nisei had left for the Pacific.[7] By Fall 1944, over 1,600 had graduated.[8] When the school closed in 1946, after being moved once more to Fort Snelling, Minnesota, it had trained 6,000 men. Of these, 3,700 served in combat areas before the Japanese surrender. Ironically, the often-mistrusted Kibei—Japanese Americans who had received formal education in Japan—proved most qualified for the interpreter's task; most Nisei had too little facility with Japanese to be useful.[9] As Mark Murakami pointed out:

> [On] the one hand the Japanese Americans were condemned for having the linguistic and cultural knowledge of Japanese, and on the other hand the knowledge they had was capitalized on and used as a secret weapon by the Army and Naval Intelligence.[10]

At the beginning, MISLS graduates were poorly used in the Pacific. A few ended up fighting rather than using their rare language talent. Others were sent to remote, inactive outposts or were ineffectively employed by the Army.[11] As the war went on, however, the situation improved as the Army learned how to use this valuable specialized resource.

Many of the linguists worked in teams, translating captured documents at intelligence centers around the Pacific. Large groups, for example, were posted in Australia, New Delhi and Hawaii.[12] Their assignments included battle plans, defense maps, tactical orders, intercepted messages and diaries. From these, American commanders could anticipate enemy action, evaluate strengths and weaknesses, avoid surprise, and strike unexpectedly.[13] The Nisei's first major accomplishment was translation of a document picked up on Guadalcanal; it completely listed Imperial Navy ships with their call signs and code names, and did the same for the Japanese Navy's air squadrons and bases.[14] Among other accomplishments was translation of the entire Japanese naval battle plan for the Philippines as well as plans for defending the island.[15]

In addition to rear-echelon duties, language school graduates took part in combat, adding to their other duties interrogating enemy prisoners and persuading enemy soldiers to surrender. The first Nisei to help the Allies in actual combat through his language ability was Richard Sakakida, who translated a captured set of Japanese plans for a landing on Bataan early in the war; American tanks were able to move up and ambush the invaders as they arrived.[16] One early group of linguists in a combat zone went to the Aleutian Islands.[17] The linguists took part in every landing in the bitter island-hopping campaign through New Guinea, the Marianas, the Philippines and Okinawa, and participated in surrender ceremonies in Tokyo Bay.[18] Nisei linguists served with about 130 different Army and Navy units, with the Marine Corps, and they were loaned to combat forces from Australia, New Zealand, England and China.[19] Arthur Morimitsu's experiences make clear the range of demands on the linguists:

> This unit later joined other units to form the Mars Task Force, a commando unit. The mission was to cut off the enemy supply and reinforcements miles behind enemy lines along the Burma Road.
>
> We served as interpreters, questioned prisoners, translated the captured documents. We also worked as mule skinners, volunteered for patrol duty with advanced units and brought down dead and wounded soldiers from the battlefields.
>
> After we completed our duties with the Mars Task Force, I was sent back to New Delhi, India, assigned to the OSS, Office of Strategic Services, as head of a detachment of Nisei MIS to interrogate Japanese prisoners in preparation for the invasion of Japan.[20]

After the surrender, MISLS shifted to civil matters, and its graduates helped to occupy and reconstruct Japan. They interpreted for military government teams, located and repatriated imprisoned Americans, and interpreted at the war crimes trials.[21] Despite their importance—General Willoughby, MacArthur's chief of intelligence, has said that the work of the Nisei MIS shortened the Pacific war by two years[22]—these accomplishments got little publicity; most were classified information during the war. Instead, the highly-publicized exploits of the 100th Battalion and 442nd Regimental Combat Team in Europe first helped to show where Nisei loyalty clearly lay.

THE 100TH BATTALION

The 100th Battalion began as part of the Hawaii National Guard. As evacuation plans were formulated on the mainland, the War Department also debated the best way to handle ethnic Japanese in Hawaii.[23] On February 1, 1942, Hawaiian Commander Lieut. General Delos Emmons learned to his dismay that the War Department wanted to release the Nisei from active duty. He needed the manpower and had been impressed with the desire of many Hawaiian Nisei to prove their loyalty. After much discussion, Emmons recommended that a special Nisei Battalion be formed and removed to the mainland; General Marshall concurred. By June 5, 1942, 1,432 men—soon to be known as the 100th Battalion—had sailed.[24] The battalion went to Camp McCoy, Wisconsin, for training and later to Camp Shelby in Mississippi. Over a year later, the group finally was ordered to North Africa, arriving on September 2, 1943.[25]

From North Africa, the 100th immediately went north to Italy, promptly going into combat at Salerno on September 26.[26] From then until March 1944, the 100th plunged into the bloody campaign which moved the Allies slowly up the Italian peninsula. The 100th suffered heavy casualties; 78 men were killed and 239 wounded or injured in the first month and a half alone.[27] By the time the 100th finally pulled out, its effective strength was down to 521 men.[28] The battalion had earned 900 Purple Hearts and the nickname "Purple Heart Battalion."[29] As Warren Fencl, who fought near the 100th, said of it:

> The only time they ever had a desertion was from the hospital to get back to the front.[30]

After a brief rest, the 100th was sent into the offensive from the Anzio beachhead, where it soon joined the other Nisei unit, the 442nd Regimental Combat Team.

THE 442ND REGIMENTAL COMBAT TEAM

While the 100th Battalion fought its way through Italy, the 442nd Regimental Combat Team had been formed and trained in Camp Shelby. Composed of volunteers from Hawaii and the mainland, many of whom came directly from relocation centers, the team trained from October 1943 to February 1944. Small groups left regularly to replace men from the 100th. On June 2, the 442nd landed at Naples and moved immediately to the beaches of Anzio. When the 442nd arrived, the 100th had already pushed toward Rome and engaged in heavy fighting. On June 15, the two came together and the 100th formally became part of the 442nd.[31]

The 442nd fought through Belvedere, Luciana, and Livorno during the first half of the summer, finally pulling back for rest in late July. On July 27, Lieut. General Mark W. Clark, Commander of the Fifth Army, awarded the 100th a Presidential Unit Citation and commended the other units for their performance during the month, saying:[32]

> You are always thinking of your country before yourselves. You have never complained through your long periods in the line. You have written a brilliant chapter in the history of the fighting men in America. You are always ready to close with the enemy, and you have always defeated him. The 34th Division is proud of you, the Fifth Army is proud of you, and the whole United States is proud of you.[33]

On August 15, the 442nd went back into combat. Their first objective, to cross the Arno River, was accomplished early in September. Once again, the cost was great, for the unit's casualties totalled 1,272— more than one-fourth of its total strength.[34]

From the Arno the 442nd moved to France to join the attack on the Vosges Mountains.[35] Its first assignment was to take the town of Bruyeres, which was won after three days of bitter fighting. Describing the encounter, the Seventh Army reported:

> Bruyeres will long be remembered, for it was the most viciously fought-for town we had encountered in our long march against the Germans. The enemy defended it house by house, giving up a yard only when it became so untenable they could no longer hope to hold it.[36]

In the same month the 442nd encountered its bloodiest battle— rescue of the "Lost Battalion."[37] Deep in the Vosges and meeting heavy German resistance, the 442nd was ordered to find and bring back a Texan battalion trapped nine miles away. For six days, the 442nd fought enemy infantry, artillery and tanks through forests and mountain ridges until it reached the Lost Battalion, suffering 800 casualties in a single week.[38] They then pushed on for ten more days to take the ridge that was the Lost Battalion's original objective.[39] From Bruyeres through the Vosges, the combat team had been cut to less than half its original strength. The casualty list numbered 2,000, of whom 140 had been killed.[40] After another month of fighting, the 442nd finally came out of the line to rest.[41] Sam Ozaki described arriving to join the 442nd after this engagement:

> The four others went overseas with the original 442nd. I joined them later as a replacement. I remember November 1944, when the replacements joined the 442nd, after they had pulled back from the Battle of Bruyeres, the lost battalion. I went looking for my buddies. I found one, Ted. Harry had been in a hospital, had been sent back to a hospital with a wound. The two others had been killed in action, saving the lost battalion.[42]

After a relatively quiet winter of 1944-45 in the south of France, the 442nd moved back to Italy in March 1945. During its first assignment, to take a line of ridges, Pfc. Sadao Munemori took over his squad from a wounded leader. After destroying machine guns twenty feet ahead, he saw an enemy grenade fall into a nearby shellhole and dove on top of it, dying while saving his comrades. For this heroism Munemori received posthumously the Congressional Medal of Honor.[43] The 442nd now advanced into the rugged and heavily fortified Apennines. In a surprise attack following a secret all-night ascent through the mountains, the 442nd took their assigned peaks, thereby cracking the German defensive line.[44] A diversionary move had turned into a full-scale offensive;[45] from there, the unit continued northward until, on April 25, German resistance broke. By May 2, the war in Italy was over and, by May 9, the Germans had surrendered.[46]

In seven major campaigns, the 442nd took 9,486 casualties—more than 300 percent of its original infantry strength, including 600 killed. More than 18,000 men served with the unit.[47] Commenting on the painful loss of many fellow Nisei in the European theater, Masato Nakagawa admitted that "it was a high price to pay," but "[i]t was to prove our loyalty which was by no means an easy [task]."[48] The 442nd was one of the war's most decorated combat teams, receiving seven Presidential Distinguished Unit Citations and earning 18,143 individual decorations—including one Congressional Medal of Honor, 47 Distinguished Service Crosses, 350 Silver Stars, 810 Bronze Stars and more than 3,600 Purple Hearts. As President Truman told members of the 442nd as he fastened the Presidential Unit banner to their regimental colors, these Nisei fought "not only the enemy, but prejudice."[49]

OTHER NISEI SERVICE

Although the 442nd's exploits are the most celebrated Nisei contribution to the war, many others played effective roles. FBI-trained Nisei operatives in the prewar Philippines kept the Japanese population under surveillance. Others escaped the Army's segregation policy and served in other combat units. One Nisei even became an Air Force gunner and flew bombing missions over Tokyo. A small group served with Merrill's Marauders in Burma and a few were involved in the surrender of China.[50]

Numerous others served in less glamorous but equally critical jobs. There were Nisei medics, mechanics and clerks in the Quartermaster Corps and Nisei women in the WACs. Nisei and Issei served as language instructors, employees in the Army Map Service, and behind the scenes in the Office of Strategic Services (OSS) and Office of War Information (OWI).[51] In the latter groups were primarily younger Issei who had fled Japan after World War I to avoid political persecution. At OWI and OSS, some made broadcasts to Japan, while others wrote propaganda leaflets urging Japanese troops to surrender or pamphlets dropped over Japan to weaken civilian morale.[52]

IMPACT OF THE NISEI MILITARY RECORD

Although the exploits of the 442nd and 100th Battalion were publicized during the war, returning veterans still faced harassment and discrimination. Night riders warned Mary Masuda, whose brother had earned a posthumous Distinguished Service Cross, not to return to her home. A barber refused to give Captain Daniel Inouye a haircut.[53] Mitsuo Usui's story is one that probably typifies the experiences of many returning veterans:

> Coming home, I was boarding a bus on Olympic Boulevard. A lady sitting in the front row of the bus, saw me and said, "Damn Jap." Here I was a proud American soldier, just coming back with

my new uniform and new paratrooper boots, with all my campaign medals and awards, proudly displayed on my chest, and this? The bus driver upon hearing this remark, stopped the bus and said, "Lady, apologize to this American soldier or get off my bus"— She got off the bus.

Embarrassed by the situation, I turned around to thank the bus driver. He said that's okay, buddy, everything is going to be okay from now on out. Encouraged by his comment, I thanked him and as I was turning away, I noticed a discharge pin on his lapel.[54]

Men who had served with Nisei brought home stories of their heroism, and War Department officials praised the valuable service of the 442nd.[55] The WRA sponsored speaking tours by returning veterans and officers who had served with them.[56] On July 15, 1946, the men of the 442nd were received on the White House lawn by President Truman, who spoke eloquently of their bravery.[57] In a few cases, military service led directly to community acceptance. In August 1946, *The Houston Press* ran a story about Sergeant George Otsuka, who had helped rescue the Lost Battalion, a Texas outfit, and was now being told to "keep away" from a farm he planned to purchase. Public response to the story was strong, and Sergeant Otsuka had no further trouble moving to his farm.[58] Even on the West Coast, it was difficult to continue abusing veterans with an excellent record.

The Nisei had indeed distinguished themselves. As the acerbic and distinguished General Joseph Stilwell said of Japanese Americans:

They bought an awful hunk of America with their blood. . . . you're damn right those Nisei boys have a place in the American heart, now and forever. We cannot allow a single injustice to be done to the Nisei without defeating the purposes for which we fought.[59]

11

Hawaii

When Japan attacked Pearl Harbor, nearly 158,000 persons of Japanese ancestry lived in Hawaii—more than 35 percent of the population. Surely, if there were dangers from espionage, sabotage and fifth column activity by American citizens and resident aliens of Japanese ancestry, danger would be greatest in Hawaii, and one would anticipate that the most swift and severe measures of control would be taken there. Nothing of the sort happened.

Less than 2,000 Nikkei in Hawaii were taken into custody during the war—barely one percent of the population of Japanese descent. Many factors contributed to this reaction, so fundamentally different from the government's alarmed activity on the West Coast.

Hawaii was more ethnically mixed and racially tolerant than the West Coast. Race relations in Hawaii before the war were not infected with the virulent antagonisms of 75 years of anti-Asian agitation. Anti-Asian feeling certainly existed in the territory—for instance, there had been an attempt to suppress Japanese language schools,[1] but it did not represent the longtime views of well-organized groups as it did on the West Coast and, without statehood, xenophobia had no effective voice in the Congress. In Hawaii, the spirit of *aloha* prevailed, and white supremacy never gained legal recognition.[2]

The larger population of ethnic Japanese in Hawaii mattered, too. It is one thing to act the bully in venting frustration and historical prejudice on a scant two percent of the population; it is very different to disrupt a local economy and tear a social fabric by locking up more than one-third of the territory's people. And, of course, in Hawaii the half-measure of exclusion from military areas would have been meaningless.

Finally, in large social terms, the Army had much greater control of day-to-day events in Hawaii. Martial law was declared in December 1941, suspending the writ of habeas corpus, so that through the critical first months of war, the military's recognized power to deal with any emergency was far greater than on the West Coast.

Individuals were also significant in the Hawaiian equation. The War Department gave great discretion to the commanding general of each defense area and this brought to bear in Hawaii and on the West Coast very different attitudes toward persons of Japanese ancestry. General DeWitt fixedly distrusted those of Japanese descent and fought even minor modification of the exclusion orders. General Delos Emmons, who became commanding general in Hawaii shortly after Pearl Harbor had retired General Short in disgrace, took a very different view. Emmons restrained plans to take radical measures with the local population, raising practical problems of labor shortages and transportation until the pressure to evacuate the Hawaiian Islands had subsided. Emmons does not appear to have been a man of dogmatic racial views; in rather practical terms, he appears to have argued quietly but consistently for treating the Issei and Nisei as loyal to the United States, unless evidence to the contrary appeared. He urged the use of Nisei in the Army's combat forces; his military intelligence officers scoffed at the Western Defense Command's view that the loyal could not be distinguished from the disloyal;[3] and he firmly rejected the anti-Japanese stance of the United States Attorney in Hawaii, emphasizing to the War Department that it was not backed by any evidence of espionage or sabotage. A few months after succeeding DeWitt as commanding general on the West Coast, Emmons suggested to the War Department that the size of the prohibited area be reduced and that it end the exclusion of persons not actually or potentially dangerous; in addition, Certificates of Exemption from the exclusion orders were issued so that a program of gradual return to the West Coast was set in motion.

JAPANESE IMMIGRATION TO HAWAII

The first Japanese arrived as contract laborers in 1868. Of the original 149 laborers, 92 stayed after their contracts expired and disappeared into Hawaiian society. Japanese did not come again to Hawaii until 1885, when economic and social unrest in Japan's swiftly industrializing economy attracted the Japanese government to exporting contract laborers.[4]

Between 1885 and 1894, 28,691 Japanese contract laborers migrated to Hawaii, and most stayed on after completing their contracts. In 1899, Hawaii was annexed to the United States but not yet a territory. Planters, fearing that the mainland ban on contract labor would be extended to Hawaii, brought in 26,103 contract laborers. The following year contract labor was outlawed by the Organic Act establishing the Territory of Hawaii. Japanese businessmen also emigrated to Hawaii in the 1890's and eventually became leaders of the emerging Japanese community. The official number of immigrants from Japan to Hawaii was high between 1900 and 1910, but a substantial proportion, mostly young single males, moved on to the mainland until this migration was ended by the "Gentlemen's Agreement" of 1907–08. By 1910, one-fourth of those of Japanese ancestry in Hawaii were native-born. A press, language schools and other elements of Japanese culture emerged in the islands.[5]

In 1940, nearly three-quarters of the ethnic Japanese population of Hawaii was native-born. (In contrast, Californians of Japanese descent comprised less than 2 percent of the state's population, and 64 percent were American-born.)[6] Despite white fears that Hawaii would be taken over by the Nikkei, race relations were far better than on the mainland. By the outbreak of World War II, Nisei were becoming integrated into the Hawaiian economy, earning places in the municipal and territorial government, becoming schoolteachers and administrators, practicing law and medicine, and working in businesses owned by old line *haole* (white) families.[7]

WAR BREAKS OUT

Following the Pearl Harbor attack, control of Hawaii was immediately turned over to the military, and steps were taken at once to control people who were believed to present real risks to wartime operations. The territorial governor invoked the Hawaii Defense Act, suspended the writ of habeas corpus, and, through Hawaii's Organic Act, placed the territory under martial law "during the emergency and until the danger of invasion is removed." He relinquished all powers normally exercised by the governor and by judicial officers and employees of the Territory to the commanding general of the Hawaiian Department.[8] Enemy agents and "suspicious characters" were immediately rounded up by Army Intelligence; by December 10, 449 Japanese, German and Italian nationals were interned, along with 43 American citizens.[9]

Sabotage at the time of Pearl Harbor would have been easy, since the city's utilities as well as the storage tanks of private oil companies were concentrated in a limited area and were not adequately protected. After the attack, rumors of sabotage and fifth column activities abounded. People reported cars zig-zagging along highways or parking across roads to block traffic, shots being fired from ambush or from cars, guiding swaths cut in sugarcane or pineapple fields to point out important installations, and signals to enemy planes. After investigation, Naval Intelligence, the FBI and Military Intelligence all agreed that no sabotage in fact took place.[10] At the time a quite different public impression was created. We have already described the background and impact of the reports made by Secretary Knox following his brief trip to Hawaii in mid-December and the more extensive investigation of the Roberts Commission.[11] It is sufficient here to emphasize that the Roberts Commission heard conflicting opinions from the intelligence services about the security danger, if any, posed by the ethnic Japanese in the islands. The Roberts Commission did not attempt to sift or evaluate these opinions and make a judgment of future threats. It simply reported that "There were, prior to December 7, 1941, Japanese spies on the island of Oahu. Some were Japanese consular agents and other [sic] were persons having no open relations with the Japanese foreign service."[12] The report did not assert that sabotage or fifth column activity had been carried on to aid the Japanese attack; nor did it make clear whether espionage had been carried on only by Japanese nationals or also by other aliens or American citizens of any particular ethnic background, but it was widely understood at the time to mean that Japanese Americans had aided the attack. On his return to Washington, Justice Roberts personally conveyed to Secretary Stimson his fear that ethnic Japanese in the islands posed a major risk of espionage, sabotage and fifth column activity.[13] These official reports, although based on the divided opinions of intelligence officers, on rumors rife in the islands, and on the Niihau Incident,[14] created doubts about the ultimate loyalty of the Japanese Americans—doubts treated very differently in Washington and in Honolulu.

At the December 19 Cabinet meeting, Knox recommended that the Secretary of War remove all Japanese aliens in the Hawaiian Islands and intern them on an island other than Oahu.[15] The unpublished recommendations of Roberts and his fellow Commissioners may have taken the same line. Such informal high-level advice combined with anti-Japanese clamor from the West Coast to move Washington toward stern measures to control the Hawaiian population of Japanese descent.

In Honolulu the atmosphere was easier. On December 21st, in his first radio address to the public as military governor and commander of the Hawaiian Department, General Emmons stated that "there is no intention or desire on the part of the federal authorities to operate mass concentration camps. No person, be he citizen or alien, need worry, provided he is not connected with subversive elements." Without mentioning the Japanese or any other ethnic group by name in his entire speech, Emmons assured the Hawaiian public:

[T]here have been very few cases of actual sabotage. . . . Additional investigations and apprehensions will be made and possibly additional suspects will be placed in custodial detention. . . .

While we have been subjected to a serious attack by a ruthless and treacherous enemy, we must remember that this is America and we must do things the American Way. We must distinguish between loyalty and disloyalty among our people.[16]

These conflicting views were reflected in the Army's treatment of the Nisei already in military service and those seeking to serve. When war broke out, around 2,000 Nisei were serving with two infantry regiments of the Army in Hawaii.[17] Japanese American soldiers from these regiments helped to defend Pearl Harbor, making a commendable showing. But post-Pearl Harbor rumors fed mistrust, and the reliability of Japanese American soldiers was questioned by military commanders, concerned whether Nisei and future Japanese invaders would be distinguishable.[18] As a consequence, the Nisei were placed in a segregated unit called the Hawaiian Provisional Infantry Battalion and assigned limited roles in defense of the islands. Pressure from civilians and soldiers brought in from the mainland caused the eventual transfer of the Hawaiian Nisei battalion and Japanese American National Guardsmen to Camp McCoy in Wisconsin, in June 1942, with the expectation that they would serve as a combat unit on another front.[19] This battalion was redesignated the 100th Infantry Battalion.

After Pearl Harbor, draft-age Nisei particularly sought to prove their loyalty to the United States. They resented being distrusted and contributed actively to the war effort by purchasing war bonds, donating to blood banks, and volunteering for civil defense organizations. This included service in the Hawaii Territorial Guard, established on December 7 to employ the islands' manpower. The Guard was composed largely of draft-age men of Japanese ancestry enrolled in Honolulu high schools and ROTC at the University of Hawaii.[20] Opposition to Japanese Americans guarding public utilities and vital waterfronts, however, caused the dismissal in mid-January 1942 of the 317 Nisei members of the Guard, without explanation, on orders from Washington.[21] The excluded Nisei university students of the Hawaii Territorial Guard petitioned General Emmons to be allowed a productive role in the war effort, and in February they were assigned to a regiment of engineers as a 160-man auxiliary unit called the Varsity Victory Volunteers.[22]

Suspicion and trust in the Nisei competed for the dominant position in government policy during the next year, while Hawaii's day-to-day affairs were conducted under a regime of military authority unknown on the mainland.

MILITARY RULE

After the declaration of martial law, Hawaii's civilians were ruled by military order and proclamation. By the end of the war, the territorial governor had declared 151 "defense act rules," the territorial director of civilian defense had issued over 100 "directives," and numerous other regulations had come from miscellaneous government executives. In addition, 181 "old series" general orders were issued by the military governor (the Commanding General of the Hawaiian Department) before March 10, 1943; 70 "new series" orders between March 1943 and October 1944; 12 "security orders" and 12 "special orders" from the Office of Internal Security after October 1944. Many orders were worded to cover the territory, but in practice, they applied only to Oahu unless reissued by authorities on each island.[23]

Some orders were specifically directed at enemy aliens. No Japanese alien could travel by air, change residence or occupation, or "otherwise travel or move from place to place" without the approval of the Provost Marshal General. Nor could Japanese buy or sell liquor, be at large during the blackout, assemble in groups exceeding ten persons, or be employed in restricted areas without permission. On December 8, aliens were required to turn in firearms, explosives, cameras, shortwave receivers and numerous other items.[24] Two months later, all American citizens of Japanese, German and Italian ancestry were ordered to turn in firearms, explosives, ammunition and weapons.[25]

Beginning December 7, the Army imposed a curfew applicable to all residents, shut down bars and banned liquor sales, closed schools, rationed gasoline, barred food sales in order to make a complete island inventory, and supplanted the civil courts with provost courts.[26] The summoning of grand juries and trial by jury were prohibited, and criminal law was administered entirely by the military.

Within two hours after the Pearl Harbor attack, censorship was instituted to prevent information of military value from leaving the islands. Mail was examined and censored, and censors listened to all inter-island and trans-Pacific telephone calls. Only conversations conducted in English were allowed. Film developing was limited to those with permits, and photographs in violation of regulations were withheld from the owners until the end of the war. All radio scripts were censored in advance, although after March 10, 1943, voluntary censorship replaced Army censorship of newspapers. Publication of Japanese vernacular newspapers was temporarily suspended and foreign language broadcasts halted. Censorship in Hawaii finally ended on August 15, 1945.[27]

The registration and fingerprinting of all civilians on Oahu over the age of six was ordered on December 27, 1941, and in March 1942 the order was extended to include the other islands as well. Residents of Hawaii were required to carry identification cards at all times. Citizens found without cards were fined $5 or $10 in police courts; aliens were fined $25 to $50 in provost courts.[28]

Hoarding immediately after Pearl Harbor threatened the currency supply. To prevent large amounts of cash from becoming available to foreign agents or invaders, after January 1942 no person was permitted to hold more than $200 in cash and no business more than $500 except to meet payrolls. New currency, good only in Hawaii, was issued, replacing regular currency from July 1942 to October 1944.[29]

Under martial law, Hawaii's civil courts were replaced by a military commission which tried offenses punishable by more than a $5,000 fine and five years' imprisonment, and by several provost courts, each with a single judge, which heard lesser cases.[30] On December 16, 1941, the civil courts were permitted to function in certain uncontested civil matters, and on January 27, 1942, they were further allowed to entertain certain civil cases acting as agents of the military governor. Jury trials, summoning grand juries, and issuing writs of habeas corpus, however, continued to be prohibited.[31]

On July 23, 1942, United States District Judge Ingram M. Stainback, a vocal critic of martial law, was appointed territorial governor, replacing Joseph B. Poindexter, whom Interior Secretary Ickes felt had not been aggressive enough in resisting the Army's encroachment on civilian authority.[32] On August 31, civil court jurisdiction was extended to jury trials, and four days later the Army issued an order listing the criminal offenses against the government or related to the war effort over which the civil courts had no authority.[33] By mid-fall, the Departments of War, Justice and Interior "had agreed upon a restoration of an appreciable number of civil rights to the civil administration, but . . . [Judge Advocate] General Green had 'interpreted' all of these vital matters out by an order that he had issued subsequently."[34] On December 10, Secretary Ickes announced that civilian rule would be restored to Hawaii as soon as possible, and nineteen days later the President approved a plan for restoration.

Civilian government was substantially returned to Hawaii on March 10, 1943. Martial law and the suspension of habeas corpus were still in effect, however, and the military kept control of labor and certain other matters. The civil courts were given jurisdiction over all violations of criminal and civil laws except cases involving military personnel, civil suits against them for acts or omissions in the line of duty, and criminal prosecutions for civilian violations of military orders.

Presidential Proclamation No. 2627 formally ended martial law in Hawaii on October 24, 1944. The territory was designated a "military area," and a series of security orders and special orders replaced general orders issued by the military, with all civilian violations of these orders heard in the U.S. District Court. Few or no changes were made in orders controlling the activities of enemy aliens, entry to restricted areas, censorship, labor control or the curfew.[35]

THE QUESTION OF EVACUATION

The issue of evacuating Issei and Nisei from Hawaii is only partially understood from a literal reading of memoranda between the War Department in Washington and General Emmons in Hawaii. First, the West Coast evacuation was locally popular; in Hawaii the impetus for evacuation or control of the ethnic Japanese came from Washington. The uproar in California echoed from Washington to Honolulu. Second, one can only conclude from his writing that General Emmons saw little or no military necessity for action against Issei and Nisei not rounded up in the first days after Pearl Harbor. General Emmons did not directly oppose the evacuation of Issei and Nisei from Hawaii, however. Perhaps he preferred wearing down the War Department by attrition rather than by a sharply focused resolution of opposing views; perhaps his views of the danger of sabotage or fifth column activity adjusted quickly to the changing fortunes of the Americans in the Pacific war. Emmons emphasized the practical problems of any evacuation and proposed using the program for the not-strictly-military goal of increasing war productivity in Hawaii by removing unproductive people from the territory.

Just as General DeWitt largely succeeded in preventing the War Department from humanizing and relaxing the exclusion program in the Western Defense Command when the policy was reviewed in the winter of 1942–43, so Emmons effectively scuttled the Hawaiian evacuation program that Washington sought to pursue in 1942.

The question of evacuation from Hawaii was raised by Secretary Knox's request to evacuate Oahu and the War Department's inquiry to General Emmons on January 10, 1942, asking his views on the subject. Emmons responded that such a move would be highly dangerous and impracticable. Large quantities of building materials would be needed at a time when construction and shipping were already taxed to the limit; many additional troops to guard the islands would be required, when the Hawaii garrison had less than half the troops it needed for missions already assigned. Moreover, Emmons felt, a mass evacuation of the ethnic Japanese, citizens and aliens, who provided most of the island's skilled labor (including a great many Army employees), would severely disrupt Oahu. Over ninety percent of the carpenters, nearly all the transportation workers, and a high percentage of agricultural workers were of Japanese ancestry. They were "absolutely essential" to rebuild defenses destroyed by the Pearl Harbor attack unless they were replaced by equivalent labor from the mainland. If the War Department decided to evacuate any or all Japanese, urged Emmons, such a move should be to the continental United States.[36]

In early February, General Emmons's view was again solicited. He agreed with the desirability of evacuating to the mainland as many Japanese Americans and aliens as possible, at the earliest date practical; but he did not want to evacuate more than a few hundred until some 20,000 white civilian women and children had been removed. Although all ethnic Japanese against whom there were specific grounds for suspicion were already in custody, the commander of the Hawaiian Department informed the War Department that it would probably be necessary to evacuate 100,000 Japanese from Hawaii to ensure removing all the potentially disloyal.[37] This was hardly a practical program when transportation and shipping were in very short supply.

On February 9, the War Department ordered General Emmons to suspend all ethnic Japanese civilians employed by the Army. Emmons now returned to the argument that the Japanese were an irreplaceable labor force in Hawaii and that "the Japanese question" was both "delicate and dangerous" and "should be handled by those in direct contact with the situation."[38] In other words, he did not want to follow the Department's anti-Japanese program. The War Department rescinded its order.

In mid-February 1942, the War Plans Division recommended that General Emmons "be authorized to evacuate all enemy aliens and all citizens of Japanese extraction selected by him with their families, subject to the availability of shipping and facilities for their internment or surveillance on the mainland"; it was discussing numbers in the 100,000 range.[39] Washington was moving toward a program of complete control of the Issei and Nisei population of Hawaii since, at the same time, the Army suggested that the Joint Chiefs discuss establishing a "concentration camp" on Molokai or preferably on the mainland because it was "essential that the most dangerous group, approximately 20,000 persons . . . be evacuated as soon as possible," and that "eventually all Japanese residents will be concentrated in one locality and kept under continuous surveillance."[40] On March 13, after Secretary Stimson and the Joint Chiefs of Staff agreed that an ethnic Japanese evacuation to Molokai, although desirable, was impractical, the President reluctantly approved a mass evacuation of ethnic Japanese to the mainland "on the basis . . . that evacuation would necessarily be a slow process and that what was intended, first, was to get rid of about 20,000 potentially dangerous Japanese."[41]

Despite consensus in Washington, it soon became apparent to officials that the military authorities in Hawaii did not agree. On his visit to the Territory, Assistant Secretary McCloy learned that the Army and Navy in Hawaii were opposed to any large-scale evacuation to the mainland or to Molokai and, at the March 23 War Council meeting, he reported that they preferred to "treat the Japanese in Hawaii as citizens of an occupied foreign country"—a reference that seems to imply little more than the martial law already imposed.[42] And in a marked departure from the War Department's 20,000-person figure, on March 27 General Emmons made a "present estimate" of 1,500 men and 50 women as the number of dangerous Japanese aliens and citizens, while conceding that "circumstances may arise at any time making it advisable to raise this estimate to much larger figures."[43]

McCloy concurred with the Commanding General that, although desirable, evacuating many Japanese from the Hawaiian Islands was simply impractical due to shipping and labor problems Emmons had cited; providing suitable facilities for relocated Japanese would also be difficult, and there would be "political repercussions on the West Coast and in the United States generally to the introduction of 150,000 more Japanese." The General, moreover, opposed a substantial movement of Japanese before receiving his requested complement of troops and munitions.[44]

To McCloy's legal mind, removal of the Issei and Nisei from Hawaii presented troublesome problems. Unlike exclusion from the West Coast, it was difficult to characterize such a program as simply barring people from sensitive military areas. Here American citizens would have to be transported several thousand miles from their homes, across the Pacific, and through evacuated areas of the Western Defense Command into the interior. Moreover, in this case the ultimate destination of detention camps was faced as the reality. At this point McCloy did not oppose the Hawaiian evacuation, but he was uneasy about it, stating in a memorandum to Eisenhower that "[t]here are also some grave legal difficulties in placing American citizens, even of Japanese ancestry, in concentration camps."[45] Stimson was somewhat more blunt in his diary:

> As the thing stands at present, a number of them have been arrested in Hawaii without very much evidence of disloyalty, have been shipped to the United States, and are interned there. McCloy and I are both agreed that this was contrary to law; that while we have a perfect right to move them away from defenses for the purpose of protecting our war effort, that does not carry with it the right to imprison them without convincing evidence.[46]

Stimson briefed the President on the "really difficult constitutional question" of "the President's own attempt to imprison by internment some of the leaders of the Japanese in Hawaii against whom we however have nothing but very grave suspicions." Moreover, the Hawaiian Japanese interned on the mainland had applied for writs of habeas corpus. There were, however, very practical limits to the concern at the top of the War Department for this problem. Stimson and McCloy gave an unassailable lawyer's answer to the "Japanese problem" on

Hawaii; Stimson informed President Roosevelt that they were sending the American citizens "back to Hawaii which is under a state of martial law and where we can do what we please with them."[47]

On April 20, Secretary Knox renewed his plea for "taking all of the Japs out of Oahu and putting them in a concentration camp on some other island" because he was "gravely concerned about security in Oahu."[48] The President supported Knox's solution at the April 24 Cabinet meeting,[49] and four days later Stimson, Knox, McCloy, Admirals Wilson, Wilkinson, Bloch and several others met to discuss evacuating the Japanese from Hawaii. "Everybody was agreed on the danger" but not on the solution and, Secretary Stimson surmised, "We shall probably send a bunch of perhaps eight or ten or twelve thousand of them to the United States and even without internment try to keep them away from the islands."[50] Later in the summer, General Marshall and Admiral King told the President they supported such a plan limited to 15,000 people, thus bringing top professional military opposition to Knox's call for evacuation.[51]

Meanwhile, the War Department had received support for its views in a report from the Department of Justice warning of conditions in Hawaii, but a counter-report from Emmons to McCloy discounted this document as "so fantastic it hardly needs refuting." General Emmons was particularly troubled by the statements of Angus Taylor, Acting United States Attorney in Hawaii:

> The feeling that an invasion is imminent is not the belief of most of the responsible people. . . .
>
> There have been no known acts of sabotage committed in Hawaii.
>
> I talked with Mr. Taylor at great length several weeks ago at which time he promised to furnish evidence of subversive or disloyal acts on the part of Japanese residents to me personally or to my G-2. Since that time he has, on several occasions, furnished information about individuals and groups which turned out to be based on rumors or imagination. He has furnished absolutely no information of value.
>
> Mr. Taylor is a conscientious, but highly emotional, violently anti-Japanese lawyer who distrusts the FBI, Naval Intelligence and the Army Intelligence. . . . I do not believe that he is sufficiently informed on the Japanese question to express an official opinion. . . .
>
> As you well know, the Japanese element of the population in Hawaii constitutes one of our most serious problems but, in my judgment, there is no reason for you to change the opinions formed on your recent visit.[52]

The view Emmons and McCloy shared reverses the positions taken by the War and Justice Departments on the mainland and underscores that personal judgment was as important as institutional predisposition in the decisions of 1942.

In May, McCloy advised Emmons to make an alternative evacuation plan, and on June 20 the Hawaii commander proposed a voluntary evacuation to the mainland of not only internees' families, but also persons who were more a drain than a benefit to Hawaii's economy and war effort. By July 1, again assessing the local situation, the Hawaiian Department had determined that most of the Japanese population was "highly satisfactory" and therefore urged evacuating only 5,000 persons.[53] On July 17, 1942, the President authorized resettlement on the mainland of up to 15,000 persons, in family groups, who were "considered as potentially dangerous to national security."[54]

In October, while Knox was still writing the President that sterner, more thorough measures were urgently needed for the ethnic Japanese population in Hawaii,[55] Emmons came forward with another evacuation plan. It was essentially the same plan he had offered in June; now, though, evacuation would be compulsory not voluntary, with priority to those who sapped Hawaii's resources, not to those considered "dangerous." Emmons proposed to send out 300 Japanese every two weeks if berths were available, and more if space permitted.[56]

On October 12, Stimson designated General Emmons as a military commander under Executive Order 9066, giving him the authority to exclude individuals from military areas within his command—not an essential authority, since the writ of habeas corpus was suspended in Hawaii, but for "good public relations" and to add "another barrel" to Emmons's gun.[57]

By this time the War Department's conviction that evacuation was militarily necessary was ebbing, but Secretary Knox and President Roosevelt remained uneasy. They still believed that "a very large number of Japanese sympathizers, if not actual Japanese agents, [are] still at large in the population of Oahu, who, in the event of an attack upon these islands, would unquestionably cooperate with our enemies."[58] Secretary Stimson tried to reassure the President:

> [A]ll persons of Japanese ancestry resident in the Hawaiian Islands who are known to be hostile to the United States have been placed under restraint in internment camps either in the islands or on the mainland. In addition, many others suspected of subversive tendencies have been so interned.
> . . . It is intended to move approximately five thousand during

the next six months as shipping facilities become available. This, General Emmons believes, will greatly simplify his problem, and considering the labor needs in the islands, is about all that he has indicated any desire to move although he has been given authority to move up to fifteen thousand.[59]

Stimson's letter, General Emmons wrote him, accurately portrayed the Hawaiian situation, but Emmons wanted to clarify the definition of future evacuees:

> This group will comprise those residents who might be potentially dangerous in the event of a crisis, yet they have committed no suspicious acts. It is impossible to determine whether or not they are loyal.
>
> In general the evacuation will remove persons who are least desirable in the territory and who are contributing nothing to the war effort.[60]

In other words, the field commander now saw less military justification for any evacuation.

The President responded strongly to Stimson's letter:

> I think that General Emmons should be told that the only consideration is that of the safety of the Islands and that the labor situation is not only a secondary matter but should not be given any consideration whatsoever. . . .
>
> Military and naval safety is absolutely paramount.[61]

Despite the President's opinion, Emmons's plan selectively to evacuate Japanese residents of Hawaii remained unchanged, for the Hawaiian Department did not consider the situation dangerous. The move to the mainland was "primarily for the purpose of removing nonproductive and undesirable Japanese and their families from the Islands" and "largely a token evacuation to satisfy certain interests which have strongly advocated movement of Japanese from the Hawaiian Islands."[62]

THE EVACUATION

Negotiation over the terms of evacuation went on and on, plainly inconsistent with any pressing military necessity. A year after Pearl Harbor, only 59 families had been evacuated from Hawaii. By design or accident, General Emmons had succeeded in reducing Washington's evacuation program to negligible numbers.

Following the early internees, the first two units of evacuees were transferred to the mainland in July and December 1942; 42 percent were under the age of 19. Of the 59 families evacuated, 26 were headed by aliens, 20 of whom were already interned on the mainland, with 17 requesting repatriation. The remaining 33 families were headed by Americans interned on Sand Island, none of whom asked expatriation. The first installment was hardly a roll call of dangerous persons; nevertheless, evacuation planning continued. By December 1, 1942, projections for the total number of additional Japanese available and on evacuation order were:[63]

Aliens	
Repatriates	225
Relief	150
"Voluntary"	50
Citizens	
"Voluntary"	350
Non-Internees	
Fishermen	2000
Kibei	475
Total	3250

By mid-December 1942, the WRA had ascertained that:

During the next twelve months the maximum number of evacuees could be approximately 5,000; but I believe the actual number will be no more than 3,000, and probably much less than that. The maximum shipment will be 150 every two weeks, unless the Western Defense Command succeeds in having the minimum single shipment raised to 500. There are many reasons for such a small evacuation, but the most tangible one is the lack of transportation. . . . I was assured . . . that no evacuees would be sent, other than repatriates, who would not be eligible for indefinite leave from our Centers. . . .

After essential war construction has tapered off, the tempo of the evacuation can be increased if transportation is available. It is extremely important that no Hawaiian Japanese be repatriated, at least for six months after they leave the Islands, nor should they be permitted to talk to other Japanese being repatriated, because most of the strategic and secret defense work in the islands has been constructed by Japanese. . . .

Influential white . . . individuals fear that it may not be long before the Japanese-Americans will have economic and political control of the Territory of Hawaii. Men like J.A. Balch, Chairman of the Board of Directors of the Mutual Telephone Company of Honolulu, and Angus Taylor, U.S. Attorney, feel that this is the time to rid the Islands permanently of this dangerous Japanese influence.[64]

On August 25, 1942, the first party of island Japanese, about 40 families, left Hawaii in exchange for Americans in Japan.[65] Since any Japanese alien might be exchanged for an American held by Japan, the War Department tried to use internment and detention to assure that no one recently familiar with Hawaii's defenses was returned to Japan; the Department favored repatriation from the mainland, not Hawaii.[66] On March 30, 1943, the Secretary of War wrote the Secretary of State:

> There are . . . 783 Japanese nationals now in the United States who have been evacuated from Hawaii to the mainland prior to January 11, 1943. All these you may treat as available for repatriation subject to the right now exercised by intelligence agencies to object to any particular alien. . . .
>
> [T]here are approximately 261 other Japanese nationals who have been evacuated from Hawaii to the mainland since January 11, 1943, and from time to time that number will probably be increased. If there are any in this category whose repatriation you particularly desire to effect, I suggest you furnish me their names and such other identifying data as may be available and I will undertake to give you a final decision in each case.[67]

At the end of February 1943, Dillon Myer of the WRA requested that further evacuation from Hawaii be suspended. At the Jerome Relocation Center, Hawaiians were "unwilling workers, and half of them had answered 'no' to the loyalty question number 28 in the selective service registration form." In the director's words, "They definitely are not the kind of people who should be scattered among the West Coast evacuees." Also, the space they hoped to use for the Hawaiians had not become available; and the removal of people likely to be repatriated plus evacuees shifting from project to project was obstructing proper relocation center administration.[68]

By March "everyone had agreed that this movement should cease, and on 2 April 1943 the War Department instructed General Emmons to suspend evacuation to the mainland until and unless the number of his internees exceeded the capacity of the Hawaiian Department's own facilities for internment, which never happened."[69]

Beginning in February 1942 and continuing through December 1943, between 700 and 900 Hawaiian Japanese were removed to Department of Justice internment camps on the mainland. Families were left behind.[70] Both aliens and Nisei departed, until it was determined that on the mainland the Justice Department had no authority to detain those who were citizens and therefore could not be classified as enemy aliens. In August 1942, the first group of Nisei were returned to confinement in Hawaii.[71] Between November 12, 1942, and March 3, 1943, about 1,200 Japanese American aliens and citizens were evacuated from Hawaii, including approximately 474 adult males. A large proportion of the group was families of men previously interned.[72] By the end of the war, a total of 1,875 Hawaiian residents of Japanese ancestry had been removed to the mainland; 1,118 to WRA camps and the remainder to Department of Justice internment camps. One hundred forty of those originally assigned to WRA camps were later transferred to Justice Department camps (some voluntarily to join their families), and 99 persons originally interned entered WRA camps on their parole or release.[73]

Divergent policies toward ethnic Japanese in Hawaii and those on the mainland began to create administrative problems in 1945. Many Hawaiians who "voluntarily" evacuated to the mainland in 1943 agreed to do so partly as a matter of patriotic cooperation with the military authorities. But by mid-February 1945, reports had reached evacuees on the mainland that some who had not accepted voluntary evacuation, staying in Hawaii, had been released from detention and allowed to return home. The voluntary evacuees—still not permitted to go back to Hawaii—naturally felt that cooperation with the Army had plunged them into a worse situation. They were anxious to return. Secretary Ickes felt that "relocation in non-restricted parts of the United States . . . at best is a temporary expedient."[74] The War Department soon established a board of officers to review the case of each Hawaiian evacuee to determine whether return would be permitted, and, if so, to assign that person a travel priority group. Travel preference was given to persons with children in the armed forces, to the aged, the infirm, and others in special circumstances.[75]

The first group of ten evacuees and their families returned to Hawaii in July 1945. Nearly 1,500 evacuees eventually came home, some bringing children born on the mainland. With them came 206 West Coast Japanese, most of whom were former residents of the islands or those who had met and married islanders in camp. Only 241 Hawaiians elected to remain on the mainland, and only 248 Hawaiian Japanese chose wartime repatriation to Japan.[76]

THE INTERNEES

Out of nearly 158,000 ethnic Japanese in Hawaii, less than 2,000 were taken into custody during the war. Approximately one-third were American citizens, mostly Kibei. Several hundred ethnic Japanese were released after investigation, and several thousand more were investigated and cleared without being taken into custody.[77]

Who were these "dangerous enemy aliens" picked up soon after Pearl Harbor? To qualify as a blacklisted enemy alien, one merely had to be a Japanese language teacher, a priest, a commercial fisherman, a merchant in the export-import trade. One might have received an education in Japan, sent contributions and Red Cross supplies for the Japanese wounded in the China War, or have been one of the toritsuginin, the unpaid subconsular agents who helped illiterate island residents prepare legal papers for the consulate. For others, grounds for arrest were merely leadership in the Japanese community.

> None of the internees was guilty of overt acts against American laws; a few were investigated for espionage, but none for sabotage. In nearly every instance, the internees were judged "on personalities and their utterances, criminal and credit records, and probable nationalistic sympathies."[78]

Some arrestees were locked up in a county jail, the immigration station or an internment camp in Haiku, Maui, awaiting transfer to the Army-administered Sand Island Detention Center across Honolulu Harbor. From there some were sent to War Relocation Authority camps on the mainland; others were transferred to Camp Honouliuli on Oahu.

Hearing boards were appointed on each island to try detainees, and they had considerable procedural latitude. Hearings usually consisted of a summary of FBI evidence and questions about friends and relatives in Japan: whether the detainee had ever visited there or had donated food, clothing or money to that country's war effort. Depending on who was in charge, cases were decided in 15 to 20 minutes, or in three to four days. The boards' recommendations for release, parole or detention were generally upheld by military authorities.[79] Internees paroled before the end of the war had to sign statements releasing the government and all individuals involved from any liability for their detention.[80]

Some detainees felt that they had "pro forma" hearings:

> [The] FBI asked me to go with them to the Department of Immigration for a little while to answer a few questions. When we

reached the Department of Immigration building I was put behind bars for several weeks and no questions were asked of me. We had our meals out in the yard enclosed by walls under armed guards with their rifles drawn. All the time I was there I was not told why I was being held behind bars and neither the FBI nor the Immigration officer asked me any questions. After this I was sent to Sand Island and remained there for six months. It was during my stay at Sand Island [that] the FBI [took] me to the Federal Building where the FBI and military officers question[ed] me. They put their guns on the table in plain view, like a threat. I felt that they were interrogating me as though I were a spy— but I was not. The FBI and military officers told me that since America was at war with Japan and because I was raised in Okinawa, Japan and regardless that I was an American citizen, I was an internee (P.O.W.).[81]

A few weeks prior to December 20, 1942, the government conducted two separate "hearings" at Wailuku, Maui, to determine the fate of the so-called "bad Japs." The officer in charge had already predetermined that we were not good American citizens and he would lock us up until the war was over. The hearings were in reality, merely individual interrogation of suspected "bad Japs." The officer asked several pointed questions which required a yes/no answer. If I answered affirmatively when asked whether I am loyal to the United States, they would accuse me of being a liar. But if I had said no, then I would be thrown in jail. I felt there was no way I could be considered a loyal American.[82]

Conditions and treatment varied among the islands; internees on Maui probably fared best. There, families were allowed to visit and bring in food daily. In contrast, internees at Sand Island on Oahu were treated as criminals or prisoners-of-war until December 20, 1941, when the newly-appointed commander of the Hawaiian Department stated that the Japanese were "detainees" and therefore not governed by military regulations. At first, Sand Island internees were forbidden to communicate with the outside. Incoming letters had to be in English and were heavily censored. Starting in May 1942, newspapers and pencils, pens and paper were allowed in the camp, and family interviews were permitted. For six months internees lived in tents without floorboards until barracks were completed in May 1942. The camp office procured a radio in July, and loudspeakers were installed in each barrack. The loudspeakers not only broadcast music; they also served as receivers to monitor internees' conversations.[83]

Many detainees were eventually released or paroled without restriction, mostly those who had been picked up for breaking curfew or other regulations. The parole policy was colored by military concern for public relations:

> In carry [sic] out the parole policy the release of large numbers at any one time is avoided so as not to create an inference that the military authorities are relaxing their vigilance. Likewise the release of prominent Japanese leaders of known Japanese tendencies is avoided although in the record of many of these cases it appears that no overt acts have been committed by them.[84]

Social shock waves from the sudden pickup and detention of community leaders soon after Pearl Harbor spread beyond the individuals themselves. Families who had once enjoyed prestige and social recognition were suddenly outcasts, avoided by others who thought that any signs of friendship would make them suspect, too. Remaining Issei became reluctant to accept positions of leadership, lest they become suspect to the authorities.[85] To emphasize the distance between themselves and the enemy, 2,400 persons of Japanese descent in Hawaii filed petitions to Anglicize their names in 1942, and decrees for that year totalled more than all name-changes in the previous eight years. On June 5, 1942, more than 1,700 Hawaiian Japanese presented a check to the American government for "bombs on Tokyo."[86]

Despite these estrangements and hardships, it is to the Army's credit that for most of the population in Hawaii it followed the precept of General Emmons: "this is America and we must do things the American Way." His confidence in the people of the territory was reciprocated in innumerable intangible ways, most obviously in the superb record of military service by the Nisei of Hawaii. Hawaii's experience was the mirror image of the West Coast, where the official presumption of disloyalty bore bitter fruit in the alienation of the camps.

The differences between the Hawaiians and their mainland counterparts reflected more than just their treatment since Pearl Harbor. Their dissimilar attitudes appeared most clearly when the two groups were thrown together in the military. Hawaiians felt that West Coast Nisei lacked warmth, were not candid in their personal relationships, and seemed to handle the relocation problem in a weak, passive way. The mainlanders found the Hawaiians uncouth and too ready with their fists.[87] At the same time, the mainlanders envied the Hawaiians' ability "to take what comes their way with a smile." That the men from Hawaii had not spent their lives in an atmosphere of anti-Asian prejudice was reflected in their whole outlook.[88]

Ironically, the *Duncan* case, which reached the Supreme Court after the end of the war, challenged military rule in Hawaii. It also produced a decision that contradicted the *Korematsu* case on the mainland. Two individuals who had been tried in the military provost courts, a civilian shipfitter accused of assaulting Marine guards at the Pearl Harbor Navy Yard in February 1944, and a stockbroker tried for embezzling from a civilian in August 1942, challenged the power of the military to supplant the civil courts.[89] In the sense that the civil courts were replaced by the military, intrusion into normal civil life was greater than on the West Coast, but insofar as military courts operated to find and punish personal guilt, the deviation from the constitutional norm was less than in the exclusion. Hawaii had been attacked, so that upholding military control over civilians on the basis of the war powers of the Constitution should have been more compelling. Justice Black, author of the *Korematsu* opinion, once again wrote the majority opinion. Although in the strictest sense limited to interpreting the power of the governor of Hawaii under the Hawaiian Organic Act which permitted him "in case of rebellion or invasion or imminent danger thereof, when the public safety requires it, [to] suspend the privilege of the writ of habeas corpus, or place the Territory . . . under martial law," Black chose to interpret the statute by examining the historical relation of civil to military power. The Court itself posed the central issue by asking:

> Have the principles and practices developed during the birth and growth of our political institutions been such as to persuade us that Congress intended that loyal civilians in loyal territory should have their daily conduct governed by military orders substituted for criminal laws, and that such civilians should be tried and punished by military tribunals?

No extensive paraphrase is needed to transform this to the central issue of the *Korematsu* case, in which military orders effectively became laws which the courts were not to question if military judgments under the war powers were given extensive deference.

No such deference was afforded the military in Hawaii. There was no talk in *Duncan* of the war powers of the Constitution or emphasis on Congressional authorization of extraordinary measures in wartime. Justice Black followed his question with an historical essay in which he found total military rule the antithesis of the American system of government and held that "martial law" in the statute could not have been intended to authorize supplanting of the civil courts. Since the statute directly spoke of suspending the writ of habeas corpus this seems to be a disingenuous analysis indeed. Black's private remarks to Chief Justice Stone in response to criticism of a draft of the opinion are closer to the mark:

I think the Executive is without Constitutional powers to suspend all legislative enactments in loyal, uninvaded states, to substitute executive edicts for those laws, and to provide for their enforcement by agents chosen by and through tribunals set up by the Executive. . . . In other words, the Constitution, as I understand it, so far as civilians in legal uninvaded territory are concerned, empowers the Executive to "execute" a general code of civil laws, not executive edicts.[90]

This decision in *Duncan v. Kahanamoku* is another lasting and important way in which the experience in Hawaii rebukes events on the West Coast. The case effectively overrules one major predicate of the *Korematsu* decision by showing no deference to military judgment when the control of civilians and civilian institutions in uninvaded territory is at stake. In deciding *Duncan*, the Supreme Court relied on the firm language of a similar case decided at the end of the Civil War, *Ex parte Milligan*: "civil liberty and this kind of martial law cannot endure together; the antagonism is irreconcilable."[91] The same is true of *Duncan* and *Korematsu*.[92]

12

Germans and German Americans

In the first six months of 1942, the United States was engaged in active warfare along the Atlantic Coast with the Germans, who had dispatched submarines to American Atlantic waters, where they patrolled outside harbors and roadsteads. Unconvoyed American ships were torpedoed and destroyed with comparative impunity before minefield defense and antisubmarine warfare became effective several months later. In the last weeks of January 1942, 13 ships were sunk totalling 95,000 gross tons, most of it strategically important tanker tonnage. In February, nearly 60 vessels went down in the North Atlantic and along the American East Coast; more than 100,000 tons were lost. At the same time, the naval war expanded to the east coast of Florida and the Caribbean. March 1942 saw 28 ships totalling more than 150,000 tons sunk along the East Coast and 15 others, more than 90,000 tons, lost in the Gulf of Mexico and the Caribbean. More than half were tankers. The destruction continued through April, May and June as American defenses developed slowly; the peak came in May, when 41 ships were lost in the Gulf.[1]

This devastating warfare often came alarmingly close to shore. Sinkings could be watched from Florida resorts and, on June 15, two American ships were torpedoed in full view of bathers and picnickers at Virginia Beach.[2] The damage done was described by the Navy:

The massacre enjoyed by the U-boats along our Atlantic Coast in 1942 was as much a national disaster as if saboteurs had destroyed half a dozen of our biggest war plants. . . . If a submarine sinks two 6000-ton ships and one 3000-ton tanker, here is a typical account of what we have totally lost; 42 tanks, 8 six-inch Howitzers, 88 twenty-five-pound guns, 40 two-pound guns, 24 armored cars, 50 Bren carriers, 5210 tons of ammunition, 600 rifles, 428 tons of tank supplies, 2000 tons of stores, and 1000 tanks of gasoline. Suppose the three ships had made port and the cargoes were dispersed. In order to knock out the same amount of equipment by air bombing, the enemy would have to make three thousand successful bombing sorties.[3]

Japanese attacks on the West Coast were insignificant by comparison. The few shells lobbed ashore at Goleta, California, and the incendiary balloons floated over the Pacific Northwest amounted to little more than harassment. Yet the far more severe treatment which Japanese Americans as a group received at official hands, and less formally from their fellow citizens, appears to suggest the opposite. The wartime treatment of alien Germans and Italians, as well as the German American experience of the First World War, lends new perspective to the exclusion and detention of the ethnic Japanese.

The less harsh controls faced by German Americans in 1942 did not emerge simply from a more benign view of their intentions. Samuel Eliot Morison, the eminent historian of American naval operations in World War II, firmly believed that disloyal elements along the Atlantic Coast aided German submarine warfare: "The U-boats were undoubtedly helped by enemy agents and clandestine radio transmissions from the United States, as well as by breaking codes."[4] Morison does not support this conclusion with any evidence and, given the lack of corroboration for similar beliefs on the West Coast, one must view it skeptically. Nevertheless, this view surely represents the beliefs of responsible people at the time.

This destructive struggle, with its suggestions of active aid from people on shore, produced no mass exclusion of German aliens or German American citizens from the East Coast. The Justice Department interned East Coast German aliens it thought dangerous, and a small number of German American citizens were individually excluded from coastal areas after review of their personal records. Exclusion or detention of some categories of German aliens was considered, but rejected. Immediately after the Pearl Harbor attack, the FBI picked up Axis nationals whom they suspected, frequently on the basis of membership in suspect organizations.[5] By February 16, 1942, the Justice Department had interned 2,192 Japanese; 1,393 Germans and 264 Italians.[6] For enemy aliens of all nationalities, internment differed markedly from the exclusion program on the West Coast. Hearings on loyalty were held promptly, and release was very likely despite the government's great advantages in the hearing process.

Those arrested were sent to the nearest regional headquarters of the Immigration and Naturalization Service or, when such places were filled, to other temporary sites. Eventually detainees were sent to camps set up during 1941 and managed by the INS, where they received loyalty hearings. Citizens of different professions, including at least one lawyer, sat on each hearing board, whose members served for $1.00 a year plus travel expenses.

Hearings were adversarial. The government was represented by the local United States Attorney's office, and FBI or INS agents generally attended.[7] The detainee was not permitted to have a lawyer present[8] and could not object to questions put to him. He could present through witnesses and affidavits evidence of law-abiding conduct and loyalty to the United States. Hearing boards could recommend release, parole or internment for the duration of the war. Doubts about loyalty were to be resolved in favor of the government. The case record, with the recommendation of the hearing board, was then forwarded to the Attorney General for decision. In reality, the decision of the Alien Enemy Control Unit of the Department of Justice governed.[9]

Other impediments prevented full, fair hearings. Many cases had to proceed through translators; hearing board members were busy and wanted to proceed quickly; sessions frequently lasted until late at night. Fundamentally, in the absence of evidence of particular acts, determining loyalty by interrogation is speculative, and the boards could not overcome that problem. The FBI and the Alien Enemy Control Unit had a running conflict as to how strict a standard should be applied, and the Justice Department obtained removal of hearing officers thought too lenient. By August 1942, the Department of Justice began to recognize that some of its decisions were arbitrary and organized an appeals system for internees. One ground for rehearing was lack of uniformity in treatment between the earlier and later cases.[10] Nevertheless, because the government had unquestioned authority to detain aliens of enemy nationality in time of war, these procedures did represent an effort to provide rough fairness in making individual determinations of loyalty and security risk.

In the spring of 1942 the War Department seriously considered whether the power of Executive Order 9066 should be used to exclude from certain areas all German and Italian aliens or at least some categories of such enemy aliens. Secretary Stimson, in his letter and memorandum of February 20 delegating authority to General DeWitt, had instructed the General to consider and develop plans for excluding German aliens, but to ignore the Italians, at least for the time being.[11] A week earlier, the War Department had asked corps commanders for recommendations on civilian control; it received suggestions for programs which would supposedly provide increased security by excluding large groups of enemy alien residents from extensive stretches of the Pacific and Atlantic coastlines.[12] General DeWitt pressed for a program that would have exempted a number of classes of German and Italian aliens, but would still have removed several thousand Germans and Italians from the West Coast.*[13] There were no serious proposals for the mass movement of categories of American citizens of German and Italian descent, although local commanders sought the power to exclude individual citizens.[14]

The mass movement of Germans and Italians was effectively opposed. With about one million German and Italian aliens in the country, it was quickly recognized that moving such a large group *en masse* presented enormous practical difficulties and economic dislocations.[15] Moreover, exclusion would mean establishing relocation camps, for excluded people would not be accepted in the heartland.[16] In addition, to have detained many Germans who were already refugees from the Nazis would have been bitterly ironic.[17]

But most critical was the public and political perception of the lesser danger presented by Germans and Italians. Within the government, there does not appear to have been much more detailed knowledge about German and Italian individuals than there was about the ethnic Japanese. Writing after the war, the Western Defense Command summed up official ignorance:

> It would be unbelievable to anyone not concerned with intelligence matters that there were not available anywhere prior to Pearl Harbor, a record of German, Italian and Japanese organizations in the United States, with some knowledge of their struc-

---

*In a rare open deviation from the views of his superior, Bendetsen gave his personal recommendation to McCloy; he urged that there be no movement of Italians by groups but only the individual internments that were already being carried out by the Justice Department. Bendetsen wanted to exempt from any move some classes of German aliens in addition to those DeWitt suggested. Memo, Bendetsen to McCloy, May 11, 1942. NARS. RG 107 (CWRIC 287-89).

ture, purposes, and connections with their homelands. The fact
remains that no such lists existed. . . .[18]

In this situation, for the Germans and Italians as for the ethnic Japanese,
public perceptions and their political implications were very important.
The Italians were virtually dismissed as a threat. In February, Stimson
told DeWitt to ignore the Italians for the time being because they
were "potentially less dangerous, as a whole."[19] In May, Archibald
MacLeish, in the Office of Facts and Figures, and Alfred Jaretzki, Jr.,
whom McCloy had brought in to help deal with German and Italian
aliens, proposed to exempt Italians from the restrictions on enemy
aliens.[20] In the fall, after approval by Roosevelt, who dismissed the
Italians as "a lot of opera singers,"[21] Attorney General Biddle announced that they would no longer be considered "aliens of enemy
nationality."[22]

There was greater feeling that there were possibly more sinister
German groups and individuals, but the political weight opposed any
mass movement or detention. In February, when the evacuation of
ethnic Japanese was about to start, Congressman Tolan telegraphed
Biddle about setting up boards to inquire into the individual loyalty
of Germans and Italians.[23] In March, Tolan's Committee published its
findings and recommendations and bluntly dismissed mass movement
of Germans and Italians: "This committee is prepared to say that any
such proposal is out of the question if we intend to win this war."[24]
There was no important Congressional support for such a program,
and the Justice Department also opposed mass evacuation.[25] The President himself told Stimson in early May, when he heard that evacuation
of East Coast Germans and Italians was under consideration, that alien
control was "primarily a civilian matter except of course in the case of
the Japanese mass evacuation on the Pacific Coast." The War Department was to take no action against Germans and Italians on the
East Coast without consulting the President first.[26]

No effective, organized anti-German and anti-Italian agitation
aroused the public as it had against the ethnic Japanese on the West
Coast, and the War Department, although it considered moving some
classes or categories of Germans, was not sufficiently persuaded to
press the President to allow it.[27]

On May 15, Stimson recommended to the President at a Cabinet
meeting that, under the Executive Order, area commanders be allowed
to exclude from militarily sensitive areas particular individuals, but not
classes of German or Italian aliens.[28] Roosevelt approved the plan. On
the West Coast, DeWitt, having first demanded that the War De-

partment absolve him of the consequences of not evacuating entire classes of German and Italian aliens,[29] issued individual exclusion orders to a small number of Germans and Italians.[30] On the East Coast, General Drum followed the same course but also issued orders to dim lights and to exclude all persons, aliens or citizens, from certain military areas which had been narrowly defined to avoid requiring people to relocate.[31] These East Coast orders differ from the Japanese exclusion program because they did not discriminate among American citizens on the basis of ethnicity or parentage.

Very few people suffered individual exclusion. For example, in the Western Defense Command from August 1942 to July 1943, 174 persons, including native-born citizens and enemy aliens, received exclusion orders. Many of those were German-born or Italian-born American citizens. Similar action was taken in the same period by the Eastern and Southern Defense Commands, which barred 59 and 21 persons respectively from coastal areas.[32]

This individualized approach to determining loyalty was followed despite visible, active pro-Nazi operations among German Americans before the outbreak of war. As late as February 20, 1939, the *Deutschamerikanische Volksbund*, popularly and simply known as the Bund, brought more than 20,000 people to Madison Square Garden for a rally to praise Hitler while denouncing Roosevelt and his administration.[33] At that time the Bund was organized by chapters throughout the United States and claimed a membership of more than 200,000.[34] This certainly exaggerated the numbers on which the Bund could rely for active pro-Nazi sympathy, and the Bund itself, full of sound and fury, frequently rang hollow—its leader, Fritz Kuhn, was sent to prison in 1939, convicted of embezzling Bund funds after having led a dissipated life unsuited to his political mission.[35] Nevertheless, at the beginning of the war there were reasonable grounds for anxiety about German-directed sabotage or fifth column activity, substantiated when two groups of German saboteurs landed in New York and Florida from submarines and were arrested in Fall 1942.[36]

Was there a coherent policy behind treating the German aliens and German Americans on the East Coast differently from the Japanese on the West Coast? If one accepted the Western Defense Command's view that ethnic groups remain loyal to their ancestral nation, and further argued that mass measures were necessary only against Japanese Americans either because the loyal could not be distinguished from the disloyal within Asian groups or because urgency did not permit individual review, one would expect a careful official review of all

German Americans in order to detain the disloyal. The government made no such review. The opposing contention would be that German Americans were so fully assimilated that there was no doubt of their undivided loyalty. The prewar history of the Bund makes such an explanation implausible. Equally significant, an analysis of voting patterns shows that, as Roosevelt moved toward an anti-German foreign policy between 1936 and 1940, German American voters shifted away from Roosevelt toward the Republicans.[37] It might also be argued that, with England unconquered, the threat of invasion and coordinated fifth column activity was more remote. But this did not reduce the patent danger of espionage or sabotage on the East Coast, where U-boats were deployed with such devastating effect. The divergent treatment of ethnic Japanese and Germans does not make a logical pattern; one must look elsewhere to understand these events.

Two typical explanations of the divergent treatment of the two ethnic groups have been numbers and political influence.[38] The American population of German descent in 1940 was so large that any major program of exclusion or detention would have been very difficult to execute, with enormous economic and political repercussions. In 1940, 1,237,000 people of German birth lived in the United States, the largest foreign-born ethnic group except for the Italians. Further, if one considered the children of families in which both parents were German-born, the number of Germans in the country reached 5 million and, counting families with one German-born parent, the number rose to 6 million.[39] A population of that size had political muscle; the industrial northeast, the midwest and the northern plains states all had substantial German American voting blocs. Radical measures such as exclusion or detention would have carried a very heavy political cost.

Many believe that the explanation for treating German and Japanese Americans differently lies in nothing so mechanical as numbers or votes, but in visceral reactions of prejudice. While this explanation gives a particularly dark cast to events of 1942, it also holds out hope that as the American people matures, the danger of similarly intolerant actions diminishes. Insofar as reactions to the ethnic Japanese and Germans were influenced by unreasoned, uninformed public perceptions, this reading of history is persuasive, but the history of German Americans over the last eighty years also underscores the importance of war hysteria in 1942.

The German American experience after the United States entered the First World War was far less traumatic and damaging than the Nisei and Issei experience in 1942. Still, it makes clear that the emotional response to war, not racism alone, plays a significant part in the vilification and deprivation of liberty suffered by any ethnic group ancestrally linked to an enemy.

The positions of people of German descent in 1917 and of the Issei and Nisei at the start of the Second World War were much different. In 1917, more than 8 million people in the United States had been born in Germany or had one or both parents born there.[40] Although German Americans were not massively represented politically, their numbers gave them notable political strength and the support of voices outside the ethnic group, such as Senator Robert M. LaFollette of Wisconsin.[41] In fact, in some states, German immigrants were permitted to vote before becoming American citizens.[42] German American sympathy for the fatherland was firmly and publicly expressed during the period of neutrality, when political German ethnic organizations urged an embargo on shipping war materiel to England and France, hoping to prevent war between the United States and Germany.[43] This active support of the German cause occasionally reached the level of sabotaging arms shipments to Europe.[44]

When America went to war in 1917, a steady stream of actions, official and private, were taken against citizens of German descent and resident German aliens. As in 1942, initial fears of sabotage and espionage[45] contributed to a broad range of restrictive government measures. German aliens were excluded from the District of Columbia and kept out of sensitive military areas such as wharves, canals, ships and railroad depots; permission was required to change residence. Several thousand German aliens were interned for minor violations of these regulations.[46] Numerous states disenfranchised aliens with voting rights.[47] In what appears to be a *prima facie* violation of the First Amendment, the German language press was smothered by requiring that it print war news and comment on government actions in English and have them reviewed by the post office.[48] At the start of the war more than 500 German language periodicals were published in the United States; almost half were gone at war's end.[49]

Vigorous and pervasive quasi-governmental groups also pursued citizens of German ancestry. Supported and encouraged by the Attorney General, the American Protective League was organized; its 200,000 untrained members, sworn in as volunteer detectives with badges, set out to investigate spies and saboteurs.[50] No actual spy was ever apprehended by this semi-official network, but it harassed German Americans through thousands of investigations. Informally, immense pressure was brought to bear through Liberty Loan drives and semi-vigilante activity that included one lynching in Illinois.[51]

The history of these attacks in several aspects resembles events of 1942: rumors in the press of sabotage and espionage, stereotypes of the German as an unassimilable, rapacious Hun, and efforts to suppress the institutions—the language and the churches—that were most palpably foreign and perceived as the seedbed of Kaiserism. This history is all the more disturbing because there was no history of extensive anti-German agitation before the war.

The rumors came in from every part of the country:

Allegedly, Germans posing as Bible salesmen tried to stir up the Negroes in the South. In Dayton, the militia guarded the water works against feared acts of German sabotage. German-speaking Red Cross workers in Denver supposedly put glass in bandages and bacteria in medical supplies. Cincinnati's meat packers were rumored to be grinding glass into sausages. In South Dakota, a Mennonite flourmill was closed when a customer reported finding glass chips in the flour.[52]

The stereotypical description of ethnic Germans was well-developed in its viciousness. The American Defense Society, with Theodore Roosevelt as its honorary president, put out a tract attacking the Germans as

the most treacherous, brutal and loathsome nation on earth. . . . The sound of the German language . . . reminds us of the murder of a million helpless old men, unarmed men, women, and children; [and the] driving of about 100,000 young French, Belgian, and Polish women into compulsory prostitution.[53]

Others assailed Germans as barbarous Huns who could never be assimilated into American society.[54]

This war on the domestic front focused first on stamping out the German language. By 1918 approximately half of the states had curtailed or prohibited instruction in German; several, along with dozens of cities and towns, had restricted the freedom of citizens to speak German in public.[55] German churches were investigated and denounced for their supposed allegiance to the German state.[56]

German culture had, of course, seeped more deeply into American life by 1917 than Japanese culture had in 1942, and First World War chauvinism also sought to cleanse the United States of German cultural influence: Bach and Beethoven were banned, German books were burned, German names were changed.[57] Defeating Kaiser Wilhelm, newly-christened the "Beast of Berlin," by denying the citizens of Chicago or Pittsburgh access to Schubert or Goethe obviously promised more emotional release in striking a blow against enemy symbols than thoughtful analysis of how those blows could possibly hurt Germany when they fell on other Americans.

The reaction of many German Americans was not unlike what the Issei and Nisei did. Many ethnic organizations and clubs disappeared or Americanized[58] (though this was not true of the churches, particularly separatist, pacifist sects such as the Mennonites and Hutterites, many of whom left the United States for Canada under the barrage of patriotic oppression[59]), and the loyalty of German Americans had to be proven in the blood of European battlefields.[60] General John J. Pershing, who led American forces in Europe, was himself of German descent, having Anglicized his name from Pfoerschin,[61] but even this counted for little with those who demanded battlefield demonstration of loyalty and reached shocking extremes of demanding military service from the old pacifist sects, who were as adamantly opposed to bearing arms for Germany as for the United States.

This earlier history of vilification hardly clarifies why there was no massive outburst against resident German aliens and German Americans in 1942. Perhaps one scapegoat is enough for a nation's frustrated anger; perhaps assimilation worked to blunt and blur hostilities; perhaps, for other reasons, Americans had come to make distinctions within the German American community between "trustworthy" and "untrustworthy" Germans. In any case, the history of German Americans in 1917 and Japanese Americans in 1942 reveals some basic elements of the country's social structure. We are indeed a nation of immigrants and, of course, virtually every immigrant ethnic group carries some affection for and loyalty to the language, culture and religion of its homeland. The strength of such ties varies depending on whether the reasons for immigration are economic, or spring from persecution due to religion, political views, race or some other factor. Typically, in time ancestral ties are loosened, but in the first few generations they are real and tangible, often more vigorously pursued by a third generation seeking its roots than by an Americanizing second generation. War between the United States and the ancestral country inevitably creates tension for those who, to some degree, wish to maintain loyalty, if not to the political aims, at least to the cultural values and social practices of both countries.

Outside the ethnic group, both world wars have stirred fear and anxiety that the group's loyalty lay with the mother country, not the United States.[62] To some extent Chinese Americans experienced similar reactions during the Korean War.[63] The risks and terrors of war stir deep emotion, and the impulse to act unreflectively is strong—but to do so is to give up one of the basic tenets of our nation by placing ethnic ties above a free choice of citizenship made by the individual. As early as May 1942, after listening to extensive testimony, the Tolan Committee concluded that equating ethnicity with loyalty was unsound: "This testimony has impressed upon us in convincing fashion the fundamental fact that place of birth and technical noncitizenship alone provide no decisive criteria for assessing the alinement [sic] of loyalties in this world-wide conflict."[64] In both world wars we failed to live by those precepts and, through that failure, brought hardship and injustice to loyal citizens and resident aliens.

What remains particularly troubling is that after a quarter century—1917 to 1942—far from demonstrating that we learned from our earlier mistreatment of another ethnic group, we unleashed summary sanctions upon a small ethnic group on a scale unknown in our history; and this course of action was officially sanctioned by the executive with the formal cooperation of the legislature.

The United States has won the loyalty of millions who have chosen to make it their home and country; whatever other basis there may be to suspect disloyalty in wartime, our history shows that ethnic ties to an enemy people are not equivalent to political loyalty to an enemy state. Nevertheless the First World War saw the invasion of First Amendment rights and the development of quasi-governmental groups near vigilantism; World War II brought exclusion and detention with full governmental participation. Both of these invaded rights and liberties which, because they were protected by the Constitution, were afforded the strongest shield available in American law.

Congress, urged by an anxious, angry public, has the power to repeal peacetime prohibitions designed to reinforce those constitutional protections, and the courts can find ways to evade their responsibility. The Supreme Court, striking down the use of martial law in loyal territory at the end of the Civil War, summarized the central issue:

> When peace prevails, and the authority of the government is undisputed, there is no difficulty in preserving the safeguards of liberty; . . . but if society is disturbed by civil commotion—if the passions of men are aroused and the restraints of law weakened, if not disregarded—these safeguards need, and should receive, the watchful care of those intrusted with the guardianship of the Constitution and laws. In no other way can we transmit to posterity unimpaired the blessings of liberty.[65]

13

After Camp

More than forty years have passed since Americans and resident aliens of Japanese ancestry were removed from their homes on the West Coast to the barbed-wire camps of the interior. Forty years fade memories and transform stereotypes. Today, Japanese Americans are not often viewed as unassimilable aliens; since the racial turmoil of the 1960's, indeed, they have been portrayed as the "model minority," a group with high educational and professional achievements, model citizens free of most social pathology who do not agitate or disturb the status quo.[1] Has this once–vilified ethnic group managed to escape at last the effects of its wartime incarceration?

Certainly, Japanese Americans have displayed impressive resilience and fortitude in the face of unique adversity. Entrance and acceptance into the mainstream of American society through the conventional modes of success have been largely accomplished. But success is far from the whole story. Scars, even wounds from exclusion and detention still remain. Relative economic affluence has been gained, but not without high psychic price.

After the release from camp, the Issei and Nisei attempted to rebuild their disrupted lives, more often than not from scratch. Some Issei, then in their late fifties or sixties, never regained lost momentum and stayed impoverished, dependent on their children, for the rest of their lives. Postwar inflation and the labor shortage helped them take up occupations once again. Earnings that approached or exceeded prewar wages provided a morale-boosting sense of accomplishment for the ethnic Japanese—even though their earnings now purchased far less—and the demand for services provided more job opportunities than before the war. The acute postwar housing shortage, however, sometimes forced ethnic Japanese to live in remote areas far from desirable job markets.

Of course, some—the farmers and proprietors—who had most before the war, also lost most. With their financial reserves gone or depleted by the time they were released, many had little or no capital with which to reestablish independent enterprise, particularly with the postwar rise in prices. Most were forced to accept whatever jobs they could find, often menial; others went into businesses that required little start-up capital, such as contract gardening.

It has been argued that evacuation allowed Nisei students to lift their sights beyond the parochial limits of the West Coast and go to eastern and midwestern colleges which opened new doors to advancement for them.[2] Some have contended that evacuation also removed Japanese Americans from low-paying agricultural work, setting them on the road to economic betterment in white collar and professional occupations.[3] But the prewar record of the Nisei indicates that, in a society free of discrimination, Japanese Americans were likely to have advanced rapidly in economic and material terms. The evacuation cannot be characterized as a necessary spur to success.

Both arguments suggest, however, that Japanese Americans should not complain now about setbacks caused by their wartime exile, since they have done very well economically since the war. But a closer look reveals that this "fact" masks other circumstances that make the economic position of Japanese Americans less glittering than it appears.*

---

*A study sponsored by the U.S. Commission on Civil Rights discovered that in San Francisco, Los Angeles, New York and Chicago, the income of ethnic Japanese males with four or more years of college averaged only 83% and Japanese females 53% of that of white males with comparable education residing in the same area. Japanese males who had completed high school to three years of college earned about 83% of the income of white males, and those with less than a high school education earned about 84% that of white males. In Honolulu, however, Japanese males and females with high school and college educations surpassed their white counterparts. Citing a study by Harold H. Wong, the report added that the earnings differential between Japanese and white males in California could not be explained by taking into account such factors as education, labor market experience, United States citizenship, number of years in the United States, vocational training, disa-

More significant than economic loss was the destruction that knew no boundaries between rich and poor—damage to the lives of Issei, Nisei, and even Sansei. In city after city, the Commission heard testimony from former evacuees who for the first time openly expressed pain and anger about evacuation and its aftermath. Many had never articulated their feelings even to their children, or within the ethnic community which shared their experience. It became obvious that a forty-year silence did not mean that bitter memories had dissipated; they had only been buried in a shallow grave.

For Japanese Americans, camp is a point of reference. As one Sansei/Yonsei put it:

> I can go anywhere in the United States today and . . . talk to a Nisei or Japanese American family and after the initial social amenities are taken care of . . . discussions . . . without a doubt . . . will get to the topic of camp. . . . People will ask, "Were you in camp?" And of course I wasn't. And that doesn't end the questions because then they ask, "Were your parents in camp?" And if you tell them what camp your parents were in, and if they were not themselves in that camp, then they would ask if you knew so-and-so who was in that camp.[4]

Despite its painful significance, Japanese American discussions about camp, when they occurred at all, for a long time recounted only the trivial or humorous moments. The Sansei sometimes found this troubling:

> When I first learned of the internment as a youth, I found that it was a difficult matter to discuss with my parents. My perception of them was that they did not speak honestly about the camp experience. Positive aspects were mentioned, if anything at all, but there always seemed to be something that was left out. My feeling was that there was much more to their experience than they wanted to reveal. Their words said one thing, while their hearts were holding something else deep inside.[5]

Dr. Tetsuden Kashima of the University of Washington calls this behavior "social amnesia . . . a group phenomenon in which attempts are made to suppress feelings and memories of particular moments or

---

bility, or labor market area. U.S. Commission on Civil Rights, *Success of Asian Americans: Fact or Fiction?* (Clearinghouse Publication 64, September 1980); Amado Y. Cabezas, "Disadvantaged Employment Status of Asian and Pacific Americans," in *Civil Rights Issues of Asian and Pacific Americans: Myths and Realities* (Paper presented at consultation sponsored by U.S. Commission on Civil Rights, 1979), pp. 440–41.

extended time periods . . . a conscious effort . . . to cover up less than pleasant memories."[6]

Why should these people experience such psychological trauma? They knew they were innocent and, in the opinion of the WRA, the camps had been administered humanely. Dr. Philip Zimbardo, psychology professor at Stanford University, offers insight from his 1971 experiment designed to reveal the psychology of imprisonment:

[W]e populated a mock prison with a group of normal, healthy, young men who had a history of being law-abiding citizens. . . . By a flip of the coin, these college student volunteers were randomly assigned to be inmates or jailers for the projected two-week period of the study. Thus, it was a totally arbitrary decision that determined the fate of the citizen who had done no wrong, but was to be labelled a prisoner and then treated as if he had violated the law of the land.

This Stanford prison experiment had to be terminated in less than one week because it ceased being just a simulation and had taken on all the worst aspects of a real prison. . . . The prisoners were constantly reminded of their loss of freedom and their powerless condition. . . . The sense of helplessness that was evident among the prisoners was reflected not only in their low self-esteem; some of them broke out in psychosomatic rashes . . . and evidenced genuinely disturbed mental functioning. Even though these mock prisoners knew that they had done nothing to deserve the kind of treatment they received, nevertheless, they reported feeling shamed by the surrender of their autonomy to the guards and humbled by a sense of being outcasts, misfits, and transgressors.[7]

The assembly and relocation centers were not prisons in the same sense as Leavenworth or even the minimum-security institutions where Watergate defendants served time. Nonetheless, all had armed guards in sentry towers, and evacuees were not at liberty to come and go as they pleased. As Dr. Zimbardo told the Commission, "My research forces me to conclude 'prison' is any situation wherein one person or group's freedom and liberty are denied by virtue of the arbitrary power of another person or group."[8]

According to Christie W. Kiefer in *Changing Cultures, Changing Lives,* "[P]ersons who have been tormented for some supposed error or deficiency often end up agreeing with the definition of themselves offered by their tormentors and trying to atone for their error."[9] After the bombing of Pearl Harbor, many Issei thought that they, as aliens, might be interned for the duration of the war; but they felt less certain about their children, who, of course, were American citizens by birth.

The Issei, Kiefer found, "felt that they had been deficient in feeling and expressing loyalty to their host country" and are "not inclined to judge the relocation as unfair even when they recall the suffering and loss it brought them."[10] Kiefer added that many Issei had chosen to emigrate, sometimes against the warnings of kin, and had elected to remain in this country after others had left in disgust. They were reluctant to admit that their gamble was a serious mistake. Consequently, "[a]s long as they could see the evacuation as a natural disaster like the typhoons and earthquakes of their homeland, impersonal and therefore blameless, accidental and therefore unavoidable, they would not have to feel the guilt of self-betrayal."[11]

The Nisei's social and psychological response to the wartime experience differed significantly from the Issei's, largely because the Nisei, while acknowledging their ancestral cultural roots, saw themselves first as Americans with rights under the Constitution despite prewar discrimination. Yet their government put them behind barbed wire because of distrust based on their ethnicity. They learned that Constitutional rights were not an individual and personal guarantee if one were an American of Japanese ancestry.

The Nisei adjusted to this assault on their expectations and identity as Americans in a variety of modes which are not mutually exclusive and can change over time. Among the most common are:

• Attempting to deny or avoid the experience and refusing to acknowledge the significance of losses. "Let's forget about it; it is all behind us."[12]

• Losing faith in white America; maintaining a general distrust or hatred toward white society and choosing to associate only with Japanese Americans.[13]

• Turning aggressions inward, as rape victims often do, by blaming themselves for something over which they had little control.[14] Anger is internalized as feelings of guilt, shame, and racial inferiority; and energy is focused on attaining economic success in order to prove that one is not inferior:

> Society has stripped a whole group of people of confidence. We are afraid to speak out. We will try to keep peace at any price. We will not make waves. It makes us uncomfortable to stand out. We want to blend in. We want to be middle America.[15]

• Identifying with the aggressor by refusing to associate with other Japanese Americans and proudly proclaiming ignorance of Japan, its language and culture.[16] This attitude was encouraged by government resettlement policies which stressed assimilation—the WRA admonished former evacuees not to congregate in public, that "no more than three Nisei should walk along the street together and that no more than five should be together in a restaurant," and that it would be wise to avoid living next door to another Japanese American family.[17] Not unusual was the testimony that "when I would see a Japanese American approaching me on the street, I would turn and walk away or dash into a nearby store."[18] This denial of who one was and how one looked bred ethnic hate and, ultimately, self-loathing.

Evacuation dealt a major blow to the family as a social institution. In the camps, Issei lost their roles as family heads and breadwinners. In the messhalls the evening meal, when values and manners were traditionally taught, was no longer a family affair, and lack of privacy even in living quarters made it difficult to discipline children. As a result of WRA policies, Issei, particularly those who could not speak English, could no longer be community leaders. Coming from a culture that values age and respects elders, they found themselves forced prematurely to relinquish their power and status to the younger generation. Even after the war, in many families, a Nisei, not his or her parent, acted as the head.

The scars of wartime incarceration are not borne by the Issei and Nisei alone. It shaped the way in which the Sansei were raised:

> [M]y father [a Nisei] always told us, "Get a good education, for it is something no one could take away from you". . . . He said we should assimilate, for any cultural deviation from the mainstream would only hold us back.[19]

The Nisei told their children, "Don't make waves. Don't stand out. You are different enough anyway." Some would not pass on to their children what they knew about Japanese culture. Some chose not to tell their children of Japanese Americans' wartime suffering, because they felt that ignorance would prevent bitterness and make them better Americans.

The impact of the government's evacuation and resettlement policies went beyond radically altering individual lives; it hastened change in the ethnic communities. The problems of small proprietors in reestablishing themselves were felt widely, since many of their businesses had been located in Japanese districts and depended on ethnic Japanese clientele. Some Japanese proprietors were eventually successful in displacing businesses that had moved in during their absence, but the Japanese districts never quite regained their prewar vitality. The returning Japanese were no longer as geographically concentrated, and the Nisei and Sansei ceased to patronize ethnic stores, preferring to buy from chain stores or other places that offered the best bargains, continuing a process that had begun before World War II.[20]

After the war, ethnic Japanese communities were split by more than geography. The residue of decisions and experiences surrounding the "loyalty" questionnaire is so bitter that, four decades later, an ex-evacuee testified, "[E]ven to this day, there are many amongst us who do not speak about that period for fear that the same harsh feelings might arise up again to the surface."[21] And although it has been many years since they saw prominent community members arrested and interned by the FBI, many remain fearful of taking leadership positions in the ethnic community.[22] The wartime wounds have not entirely healed.

"Before evacuation." "After camp." Words signifying the watershed in the history of Japanese Americans in the United States. Even after four decades, it is the mournful reference point from which these Americans describe changes in their communities, their personal lives, their aspirations. It is the central experience which has shaped the way they see themselves, how they see America, and how they have raised their children.

Appendix

Latin Americans

During World War II the United States expanded its internment program and national security investigations to Latin America on the basis of "military necessity." On the government's invitation, approximately 3,000 residents of Latin America were deported to the United States for internment to secure the Western Hemisphere from internal threats and to supply exchanges for American citizens held by the Axis. Most of these deportees were citizens, or their families, of Japan, Germany and Italy. Although this program was not conducted pursuant to Executive Order 9066, an examination of the extraordinary program of interning aliens from Latin America in the United States completes the account of federal actions to detain and intern civilians of enemy or foreign nationality, particularly those of Japanese ancestry.

What began as a controlled, closely monitored deportation program to detain potentially dangerous diplomatic and consular officials of Axis nations and Axis businessmen grew to include enemy aliens who were teachers, small businessmen, tailors and barbers—mostly people of Japanese ancestry. Over two-thirds, or 2,300, of the Latin American internees deported to the United States were Japanese nationals and their families; over eighty percent came from Peru.[1] About half the Japanese internees were family members, including Nisei, who asked to join their husbands and fathers in camps pending deportation to Japan; family members were classified as "voluntary internees."[2]

Underlying these deportations was fear of Japanese attack in Latin America, particularly at the Panama Canal, which produced suspicion of Latin American Japanese. But a curious wartime triangle trade in Japanese aliens for internment developed, too. Some Latin American countries, particularly Peru, deported Japanese out of cultural prejudice and antagonism based on economic competition; the United States, in turn, sought Latin American Japanese internees to exchange with Japan for American citizens trapped in territories Japan controlled. The same dynamic often affected Germans and Italians.

Deportees from Peru for internment in the United States dominated the Latin American deportation program and thus this discussion centers on them. The history of the Japanese in Peru offers suggestive parallels to West Coast history.

In the late 19th and early 20th centuries, expanding agriculture in Latin America attracted surplus skilled farm labor from Japan; by 1923 almost 20,000 Japanese had settled in Peru alone.[3] During the 1930's, economic depression in Japan and restricted immigration to the United States[4] drew more Japanese to Latin America, where 23,000 entered Brazil in a single year.[5] Worsening economic conditions in Latin America, however, brought discriminatory legislation and business practices aimed at these immigrants.

Japanese in Peru inherited years of prejudice earlier directed against Chinese immigrants. Many Japanese in Latin America had migrated to urban areas where they built close-knit communities, opened small businesses and gained economic independence. The Peruvian Japanese formed ethnic business associations and social organizations, and, although some Japanese married Peruvians and the typical family joined the Roman Catholic church,[6] many kept a love of Japan, nursed feelings of cultural superiority and sent their children to Japan for formal education. In Peru, most Japanese immigrants steadfastly refused Peruvian citizenship. This history fueled Peruvian resentment against them; economic competition, including fears of Japanese farmers and merchants monopolizing fertile land and some service industries, aggravated prejudice. Peru severely restricted Japanese immigration in 1936 and followed up by restricting the right to citizenship of some Peruvian Japanese, including Kibei. In 1940, when about 26,000 Japanese lived in Peru, including 9,000 Nisei,[7] riots broke out. Japanese businesses were destroyed and homes ransacked, and restrictive laws muzzled the Japanese press.

By 1940, the United States had become directly involved with security in Latin America. After the European war erupted in 1939, the government posted FBI agents in United States embassies in Latin America to compile information on Axis nationals and sympathizers.[8] Following Pearl Harbor, the United States immediately moved to secure the Western Hemisphere against dangerous enemy aliens. For the first time, Japanese-owned businesses in Latin America appeared on the United States' Proclaimed List of Blocked Nationals and were thus blacklisted through economic warfare. After a meeting of Western Hemisphere nations early in 1942, the Emergency Advisory Committee for Political Defense was created, composed of representatives from the United States, Argentina, Brazil, Chile, Mexico, Uruguay and Venezuela. The Committee forwarded to Latin American countries recommendations to control subversive activities and to secure the hemisphere, emphasizing internment of Axis nationals.[9] Several Latin American countries, severing ties with the Axis, imposed restrictions against Axis nationals.

Acting on Emergency Advisory Committee recommendations or in response to United States security efforts, sixteen Latin American countries interned at least 8,500 Axis nationals during World War II.[10] Economic and political pressure from the Proclaimed Lists and the Emergency Advisory Committee, coupled with Latin American nations' inability to establish costly security programs, encouraged the United States to accept Latin American enemy aliens for internment. Twelve Latin American countries—Bolivia, Colombia, Costa Rica, the Dominican Republic, Ecuador, El Salvador, Guatemala, Haiti, Honduras, Nicaragua, Panama and Peru—deported some or all of their enemy alien internees to the United States.[11] (Brazil and Venezuela did not.) Once in the United States, the State Department had custody and held internees in camps operated by the Justice Department's Immigration and Naturalization Service (INS).

The model of the Latin American deportation and internment program was developed in Panama. Before the war, the United States had agreed orally and informally with Panamanian officials to intern Japanese nationals during wartime. After the Pearl Harbor attack, Panama declared war on the Axis and froze Japanese assets. Japanese aliens were arrested by Panamanian and American agents for security reasons because they were near the Canal Zone. The War Department instructed the Commanding General of the Caribbean Defense Command to construct an internment camp in Panama for enemy aliens.[12] Panama later agreed to transfer internees to the United States to be traded for Western Hemisphere nationals held in Japan.[13]

In Peru, the State Department aimed to eliminate potential military threats and to integrate Peru's economy and government into the war effort. After war broke out, Peru notified the War Department that the United States could place military installations there; a small military force eventually encamped near the oil fields of northern Peru, and the United States promised $29 million in armaments through Lend-Lease agreements, the largest pledge to a Latin American state.[14] Peru moved quickly against its Japanese residents, whose newspapers, organizations and schools were closed after December 7. Japanese assets were frozen, and the Proclaimed Lists brought hardship to Japanese businesses; some Peruvian Japanese were asked to leave. Before any deportations occurred, almost 500 Japanese registered repatriation requests at the Spanish Embassy, which represented Japan's interests in Peru.[15] This group was among the first to be deported. The initial targets of the American-Peruvian deportation program were enemy alien diplomatic and consular officials and some business representatives of Japan. Peru wished to deport all Japanese and other Axis nationals as well, but the United States recognized its limited need of Latin American Japanese for exchange with Japan; the problems of limited shipping facilities; and the administrative burden of a full-scale enemy alien deportation program. The United States limited the program to deporting officials and "dangerous" enemy aliens.

John K. Emmerson, Third Secretary of the American Embassy in Peru, who had been a language student in Japan and could speak and read Japanese fluently, was assigned to help the Peruvians identify "dangerous" aliens and compile deportation lists.[16] But deportations were in fact planned with little coordination between the United States and Peru, and Peru chose some deportees over others for no apparent reason, although bribery may have been involved. Moreover, the inaccurate portrayal by Peruvian officials of Peruvian Japanese as deceptive and dangerous encouraged the United States to deport and intern not only Japanese nationals, but some Peruvian citizens of Japanese descent.[17]

During early 1942, approximately 1,000 Japanese, 300 Germans and 30 Italians were deported from Peru to the United States, along with about 850 German, Japanese and Italian aliens picked up in Ecuador, Colombia, and Bolivia[18] and an additional 184 men from Panama and Costa Rica.[19] Normal legal proceedings were ignored and none of the Peruvians were issued warrants, granted hearings, or indicted after arrest. On entering the United States, officials of Axis nations were placed in State Department custody and private citizens were sent to INS internment camps in Texas. In most cases passports had been confiscated before landing, and the State Department ordered American consuls in Peru and elsewhere to issue no visas prior to departure.[20] Despite their involuntary arrival, deportees were treated by INS as having illegally entered this country.[21] Thus the deportees became illegal aliens in U.S. custody who were subject to deportation proceedings, i.e., repatriation.

Most of the first group of deportees from Peru were men, primarily diplomatic and consular officials, representatives of Japanese business interests, and private citizens targeted as community leaders and thus "believed to be dangerous." Categorical classifications of some as "believed to be dangerous" enabled the deportation of many private citizens because the United States was unwilling to investigate the need to deport each individual. As John Emmerson later stated: "Lacking incriminating evidence, we established the criteria of leadership and influence in the community to determine those Japanese to be expelled."[22]

By June 1942, many Latin American countries had severed diplomatic relations with the Axis nations. Lend-Lease and trade consignments between the United States and Latin America had strengthened hemispheric unity. But the United States was not confident that Latin America could control subversive activity and thus increased its interest in the deportation and internment program. By this time traffic in the exchange of Japanese and other Axis nationals for American citizens was growing. By early 1942, aided by Swiss and Spanish intermediaries, the United States and Japan had begun negotiating for the exchange of nationals, both officials and private citizens. By July, the United States had deported approximately 1,100 Latin American Japanese and 500 Germans to their home countries.[23] Enemy alien citizens who threatened nothing were uprooted from their homes to be used in the exchange. By August 1942, the State Department estimated that, in addition to the Americans caught as Japan advanced across the southwest Pacific, at least 3,300 Americans were trapped in China and available for exchange with Japan.[24] These considerable numbers increased American interest in receiving Japanese deportees from Latin America. But slow communications, problems in obtaining assurances that repatriates could pass safely through the war zone, shipping shortages, and Justice Department refusal to repatriate an individual against his will, delayed further repatriations for over a year. As a result, "dangerous" enemy aliens were deported to the U.S. at a comfortable pace for both Latin America and the United States, including INS administrators seeking to prevent overcrowding in the camps.

In January 1943, after 200 more Japanese aliens had been deported from Peru, the Justice Department refused a State Department request for the deportation of another 1,000 Latin American Japanese.[25] Unsatisfied with the screening procedures of the American embassy in Peru as well as Peruvian practices in identifying dangerous individuals, the Justice Department sent Raymond Ickes of its Alien Enemy Control Unit to Peru to oversee the selection. Ickes, partially successful in overcoming low-level Peruvian officials' obstructionism and indifference, entertained a novel idea shared by other American officials in Peru and President Prado—to establish internment camps in Peru financed by the United States. The Administration had already requested appropriations to establish an internment camp in Cuba. Moreover, the State Department was reluctant to encourage Peru to breach international law by sending all its Peruvian Japanese from a nonbelligerent state directly to a belligerent one.[26] But the American embassy in Peru vetoed the Peruvian camp idea, distrusting Peruvian officials' ability to intern dangerous individuals—a view supported by Peru's record in the deportation. As Emmerson had reported earlier, "since local police and other officials are susceptible to Japanese bribes, their alertness cannot be depended upon."[27] Indeed, Arthur Shinei Yakabi, a bakery worker deported from Peru, testified: "I was asleep in February 1943 when some Peruvian police came and arrested my employer. My employer pulled a fast one by bribing the police, and offered me as a substitute."[28] In addition, the embassy's view of the danger posed by Peruvian Japanese was changing by the end of summer 1943; Emmerson, now Second Secretary, was confident that the Japanese community no longer constituted a threat to security.[29] The Latin American deportation program continued nevertheless.

In May 1943, the Emergency Advisory Committee adopted a resolution that American republics intern and expel dangerous Axis nationals.[30] Near the end of 1943, the Committee reviewed the Latin American security situation and concluded that direct United States involvement in securing the hemisphere was crucial. Except for Brazil, no Latin American country had initiated security measures compatible with United States standards. The Committee wanted agreements for deportation programs from Chile, Uruguay, Paraguay, Venezuela and Colombia.

The repatriation and exchange program proceeded slowly. In September 1943, over 1,300 Japanese left New York for Japan, over half from Peru, Panama, Costa Rica, Mexico, Nicaragua, Ecuador, Cuba, El Salvador and Guatemala; almost 40 percent of the entire contingent was from Peru.[31]

In the spring of 1944, the State Department realized that no more Axis nationals would be repatriated until the war was over. Nevertheless, from January to October 1944, over 700 Japanese men, women, children and 70 German aliens were deported from Peru to the United States, along with over 130 enemy aliens from Bolivia, Costa Rica and Ecuador.[32] Peru pushed for additional Japanese deportations, but the United States could not commit the shipping and did not want to augment the hundreds of Japanese internees awaiting repatriation. The State Department also decided not to repatriate Axis nationals against their will, realizing that many internees might not want to return to a devastated country. Thus deportation proceedings lagged and the INS internment camps became overcrowded.

Internees at INS camps in Crystal City, Kennedy and Seagoville, Texas, and Missoula, Montana, had two main concerns: having their families join them in the United States and repatriation to Japan. Living conditions at the camps were not unlike those in the war relocation centers. Confinement's bad effects were evident: lack of privacy, family breakdown, listlessness and uncertainty about the future. To safeguard the internees from unhealthy conditions, the camps were inspected routinely by Spain, the International Red Cross, the War Prisoners Aid of the YMCA and the YWCA, the American Friends Service Committee, and the National Catholic Welfare Conference. At the end of the war, approximately 1,400 Latin American Japanese, mostly from Peru, were interned in the United States, awaiting a decision on their destiny. Some wished to return to Latin America, others to Japan. To most it was a choice of the lesser of two evils: they had lost everything in Latin America, but Japan, which they had left to pursue greater economic opportunity, was devastated by the war. A number wanted to remain in the United States and begin anew.

As the end of the war approached in Summer 1945, the United States and other Western Hemisphere nations began to consider the postwar fate of interned Axis nationals. President Truman issued Proclamation 2655 authorizing the United States to deport enemy aliens deemed "to be dangerous to the public peace and safety of the United States."[33] The Latin American Conference on Problems of War and Peace passed a resolution recommending that persons deported for security reasons should be prevented from "further residing in the hemisphere, if such residence would be prejudicial to the future security or welfare of the Americas."[34]

The State and Justice Departments disagreed about security measures to take against interned enemy aliens. The Justice Department wanted to remove internees from its jurisdiction and divorce itself from the deportation and internment program; the State Department wanted to conclude the program by removing all dangerous Axis influences from the hemisphere.[35] As part of its long-term security strategy, in September 1945 the State Department secured a proclamation from President Truman directing the Secretary of State to remove any enemy aliens in the United States from the Western Hemisphere, including those from Latin America, who were illegal aliens and dangerous to hemispheric security.

In December 1945, approximately 800 Peruvian Japanese were voluntarily deported to Japan,[36] but in general the internment ended very slowly and tortuously. The United States sought to return internees who were not classified as dangerous and who refused deportation to Axis countries, to their points of origin in Latin America.[37] But the common hemispheric interests that bred the deportation had dissolved, and the government now had to negotiate about returning internees to Latin America using weak, hastily-written wartime agreements, for the United States had not exacted initial guarantees defining the deportees' postwar fate. For the most part, the Central American and Caribbean countries that had deported enemy aliens to the United States had placed few restrictions on their disposition. Mexico, Colombia and Ecuador had required specific guarantees before releasing enemy aliens to the United States. Peru, Ecuador and El Salvador wanted jurisdiction over internees in order to obtain the return of some German deportees, for many Germans in Latin America, unlike the Japanese, had acquired economic and political influence as well as greater social acceptance. Peru had sought no firm agreement from the United States concerning final destination and wanted to restrict the return of Japanese (but not German) internees. The United States wanted a consistent policy for the Latin American internees and gave Peru the choice of accepting all non-dangerous internees or leaving deportation control to the United States. So negotiations dragged on for the return to Peru of Peruvian Japanese.

Meanwhile, the internees used litigation to block deportation to Axis states. Some German internees filed habeas corpus petitions challenging their detention by the United States, claiming that they were not alien enemies as defined by the Alien Enemy Act of 1798, because they were not natives or citizens of an enemy country. In January 1946, this effort failed when a federal district court ruled that the Latin American internees were "alien enemies" who could legally be detained.[38] After this decision, 513 Japanese (over ninety percent from Peru), 897 Germans and 37 Italians from Latin America in United States internment camps were granted hearings pending deportation to Axis countries.[39] The hearings were a formality leading inevitably to deportation to Axis countries, although most of the remaining Latin American Japanese wished to return to Peru. Voluntary repatriation continued into 1946, with at least 130 Peruvian Japanese returning to Japan by June.[40]

The final destiny of the Latin American Japanese was placed in the hands of the Justice Department after the State Department concluded that insufficient evidence existed to call the remaining Japanese internees dangerous to the Western Hemisphere.[41] The State Department, although willing to proceed with deportations to Japan, hoped the Justice Department would stop deportation proceedings against Peruvian Japanese with families in Peru.[42] The process moved very slowly for those who wanted to remain in the United States or return to Peru. Two Peruvian Japanese, Eigo and Elsa Kudo, remembered their anxious waiting period:

> There were several hearings to persuade these poor internees to leave for Japan. We were one of those who asked, "Why are we illegal aliens when we were brought under armed MPs and processed by the immigration officers upon arrival in New Orleans?" . . . Again and again they repeated, "You are illegal aliens because you have no passports nor visa. . ."[43]

In August 1946, Wayne Collins, an attorney who had often helped Issei and Nisei over the years, arranged for some Peruvian Japanese to be transferred from INS internment camps to a fresh produce processing plant in Seabrook, New Jersey, where Japanese Americans had worked during the exclusion from the West Coast. The internees welcomed Seabrook as an opportunity to escape camp life, restore traditional family life, and earn relatively decent wages while awaiting word of their ultimate fate; at the same time, it must be recognized that conditions at Seabrook were far less attractive than those of ordinary liberated life. Other internees were paroled from the INS camps under sponsorship of American citizens.

To some extent, returning internees to Peru was further complicated during 1946 by a nationalistic pro-Japan underground movement, the Aikoku Doshi-Kai, which sprang up in Peru and South America. Both Peruvian and American officials overestimated the movement's influence, but the United States accepted Peru's reluctance to bring Japanese deportees back into a country inflamed by anti-Japanese sentiment. Peru announced that it would allow only Peruvian citizens of Japanese descent and Japanese related to Peruvian citizens to return,[44] and from May to October 1946, only about 100 Japanese internees went back to Peru.[45] At the same time, almost 600 German nationals were returned to Latin America in the year 1945-46.[46]

At the beginning of 1947, 300 Peruvian Japanese remained in the United States, the majority at Seabrook. Those with family ties in Peru entertained hopes of returning home. Talks between the United States and Peru were stalemated during 1947; negotiations were renewed with the Peruvian government which had come to power in a coup in the winter of 1948–49, but it refused to accept any non-citizens.

In the spring of 1949, exasperated State Department officials concluded that the only solution to the Peruvian Japanese internee problem was to give internees the status of "permanent legally admitted immigrants" who could remain in the United States.[47] Finally, in July 1952, the remaining Japanese Peruvian internees, having resided in the United States for seven years or more, petitioned the Board of Immigration Appeals to reopen hearings to suspend deportation orders, and Congress approved the deportation suspensions in 1953. The wartime deportation and internment program was finally at an end. But, for some, the emotional trauma of the program was endless. Peruvian deportee Ginzo Murono stated: "Some of the people from Peru who were interned with me were separated from their families for many years. In a few cases, the broken families were never reunited."[48]

Historical documents concerning the ethnic Japanese in Latin America are, of course, housed in distant archives, and the Commission has not researched that body of material. Although the need for this extensive, disruptive program has not been definitively reviewed by the Commission, John Emmerson, a well-informed American diplomat in Peru during the program, wrote more than thirty years later: "During my period of service in the embassy, we found no reliable evidence of planned or contemplated acts of sabotage, subversion, or espionage."[49] Whatever justification is offered for this treatment of enemy aliens, many Latin American Japanese never saw their homes again after remaining for many years in a kind of legal no-man's-land. Their history is one of the strange, unhappy, largely forgotten stories of World War II.

Part II

The Aleuts

War and Evacuation in Alaska

About 10,000 years ago migrants from Asia to North America settled on the remote Aleutian Islands. These migrants were the Native Aleuts, who proudly called themselves *Unangan*, "we the people."

The Aleutian Islands form a chain strung across 900 miles from the Alaska Peninsula to the island of Attu, 300 miles from the Kamchatka Peninsula of the Soviet Union. The islands are treeless, blanketed by soft tundra. Northward-flowing tropical air from Japan and frigid, dry air from the Arctic clash there, leaving the islands hidden in fog and swept by violent winds most of the year.

In the 18th century the Aleutian Islands and their 10,000 inhabitants were "discovered" by Russian entrepreneurs. After colonization, the Aleut population was decimated by massacre and disease; when the United States purchased Alaska from the Russians in 1867, only about 2,000 Aleuts remained. The Russians removed several hundred Aleuts to the uninhabited Pribilof Islands of St. Paul and St. George, 200 miles north of the island of Unalaska, to harvest the fur seals that annually migrated there.

By 1867 the aboriginal Aleuts had largely assimilated the western culture of the Russians and were converted to the Russian Orthodox religion. Under American dominance the Aleuts' subsistence economy and aboriginal culture further eroded. The introduction of the American wage-earning economy and educational system, which discouraged traditional Aleut language, art and music, contributed to the attrition.

The irreparable loss of much traditional culture and the tragic demise of the Aleut population was exacerbated by their removal from the Aleutian and Pribilof Islands during World War II. The story of what happened to the Aleuts during the war has, for the most part, remained untold. Like the hard-fought battles of the Aleutian Campaign—the only campaign during World War II to be fought on American soil—it remains a mystery to most Americans, the islands only names in a crossword puzzle. But the Aleuts have never forgotten.

317

In the struggle for naval supremacy the Aleutian Islands were strategically valuable to both the United States and Japan. Beginning in March 1942, United States military intelligence repeatedly warned Alaska defense commanders that Japanese aggression into the Aleutians was imminent. In June 1942 the Japanese launched a swift offensive, bombing Unalaska, invading two other islands and capturing the Aleut villagers on Attu. During this offensive, American military commanders in Alaska ordered the evacuation of Aleuts on the remaining islands to places of relative safety.

The Aleut evacuation and the removal of persons of Japanese ancestry from the West Coast during the same period were separate events—neither caused nor influenced the other. When speaking of the two evacuations, common phrases such as "military necessity" do not hold the same meaning, nor should they. The evacuation from the Aleutian and Pribilof Islands, then under attack, was not a government action influenced by wartime hysteria or fear of sabotage or espionage. Both groups of evacuees suffered economic loss and personal hardship; but the root causes of loss and damage are very different in the two cases.

The evacuation of the Aleuts was a reasonable precaution taken to ensure their safety. But there was a large failure of administration and planning which becomes evident when the central questions are addressed: Why did the military and civilian agencies responsible for Aleut welfare wait until Attu was actually captured before they evacuated the islands? Why were evacuation and relocation policies not formulated by the government departments most knowledgeable about the danger of an enemy attack they expected? And why was the return of the Aleuts to their homes delayed long after the threat of Japanese aggression had passed?

The Aleuts were relocated to abandoned facilities in southeastern Alaska and exposed to a bitter climate and epidemics of disease without adequate protection or medical care. They fell victim to an extraordinarily high death rate, losing many of the elders who sustained their culture. While the Aleuts were in southeastern Alaska, their homes in the Aleutians and Pribilofs were pillaged and ransacked by American military personnel.

In sum, the evacuation of the Aleuts was not planned in a timely or thoughtful manner. The condition of the camps where they were sent was deplorable; their resettlement was slow and inconsiderate.

The official indifference which so many Native American groups have experienced marked the Aleuts as well.

The Aleutian Campaign

As global conflict spread during 1940, U.S. military leaders directed their attention to preventing attacks on our Pacific frontier. The defense of America's western outposts, Alaska, Hawaii and the Panama Canal, were strengthened. Although Alaska was low on the priority list, by June 30, 1940, the Army had committed at least 5,000 troops to its defense.[1]

By the beginning of 1941, America's naval power in the Pacific was weakening relative to Japan's, and the approaching Pacific war increased the strategic value of the Aleutians. The westernmost Aleutian island, Attu, lay only 600 miles from Japan's northern flank in the Kurile Islands. The Boeing plant and Bremerton Navy Yard in Seattle were only eight hours' bomber-flight from the Aleutians. The Aleutians were stepping stones which either the United States or Japan could use offensively. They were also important to the United States as passage points on the shipping route for our Lend-Lease traffic to the Soviet Union.

The Alaska Defense Command (ADC), with Brigadier General Simon B. Buckner in command, was created in February 1941 as part of the recently-formed Western Defense Command to raise Alaska's priority in military operations. Earlier the Navy had established the Alaska Sector under the Thirteenth Naval District commanded by Rear Admiral Charles S. Freeman. Throughout the summer of 1941, garrisoning accelerated. Army facilities were constructed on Unalaska Island to defend the naval installations at Dutch Harbor, and approximately 5,500 troops were brought in.[2] Between June and September 1941, ADC strength tripled.[3]

During the fall of 1941, construction of air bases strategically located at Cold Bay on the Alaska Peninsula and Umnak Island in the Aleutians moved ahead. They were secretly built under the names of fish cannery companies. The Umnak airstrip was particularly essential because it protected Dutch Harbor, which controlled Unimak Strait and passage through the Aleutian chain, linking the Pacific Ocean and the Bering Sea. Strategic use of the Aleutians hinged largely on possession of Dutch Harbor.

Following the Japanese attack on Pearl Harbor, the ADC bolstered the Aleutian bases in preparation for offensives against Japan. Since naval bases in Alaska were still under construction and lacked adequate air support, the ADC was concerned about possible Japanese attack. As the Governor of Alaska, Ernest Gruening, pointed out to Secretary of the Interior Harold L. Ickes:*

> It is well known to the Japanese that the Alaska bases, while designed ultimately to be used offensively, are still far from complete, and that if attacked soon would probably be unable to defend themselves adequately and could therefore be destroyed. . . .
>
> [Dutch Harbor] is the base at which the Japanese can strike most easily and which they will probably select first since it is the most difficult of all to defend.[4]

In mid-March 1942, Army Intelligence reported that a Japanese offensive could be expected at any time.[5] As a result, by the end of April 1942, garrisons in Alaska had doubled to 40,242.[6]

In late April 1942, Colonel Jimmy Doolittle successfully attacked the coast of Japan, dropping bombs on Tokyo Harbor. The stunned Japanese Imperial Staff acted swiftly to secure its newly-acquired possessions and resources in the South Pacific; it believed the destruction of U.S. naval forces was paramount to the further extension of Japanese hegemony in the South Pacific. The Japanese believed, mistakenly, that Doolittle had launched his attack from the Aleutians, so they also acted to protect their exposed northern flank.

On May 5, in an effort to intercept Lend-Lease traffic to Siberia and to cripple U.S. naval forces in the Pacific, Japan authorized the "M I Operation."[7] This two-phase operation involved establishing both defensive and offensive strategic positions in the Pacific. The Japanese planned to attack the Aleutian Islands as a diversion while simultaneously attacking the more strategically valuable Midway Island. They believed U.S. forces would concentrate on defending the Aleutians while Japan's main thrust was directed toward Midway and the destruction of the U.S. fleet that would be trapped between the Aleutians and Midway. Japan would then control strategic Pacific waters from the western Aleutians south to Midway.

The ensuing attack against the U.S. Pacific Fleet was the largest naval operation in Japanese history.[8] Having broken the secret Japanese naval code, the U.S. Navy knew the details of their plan. According to Naval Intelligence reports, an attack force would be launched

---

*Since Alaska was a territory of the United States, the governor was appointed by and reported to the Secretary of the Interior.

from Japan around May 20, and sometime after May 24, the Aleutians and Midway would be attacked.[9] The Commander-in-Chief of the Pacific Fleet, Admiral Chester W. Nimitz, decided not to split his forces and instead dispatched a small nine-ship force to Alaska. On May 25, 1942, Nimitz warned Rear Admiral Robert A. Theobald, Commander of that North Pacific Force, that the "Japanese have completed plans for an amphibious operation to secure an advanced base in the Aleutian Islands. . . ."[10]

Additional intercepted Japanese messages enabled the U.S. to predict even more precisely when the attack would occur: "[B]y 21 May the United States knew fairly accurately what the strength of the [Japanese] Northern Area Force would be and when it would strike, 1 June or shortly thereafter."[11] Poor weather, however, made it impossible to detect the enemy attack force until a Navy patrol plane spotted the Japanese on June 2, 400 miles south of Kiska Island.

On the morning of June 3, 1942, the Japanese bombed Dutch Harbor naval installations and the following day attacked Army facilities at Fort Mears. Nearby Unalaska's air defenses were unable to prevent the enemy attack. Squadrons coming from Cold Bay arrived too late, and the radio communication systems were so inadequate that the secret airfields at Umnak never received word of the Japanese attack. Nevertheless, losses on both sides were minimal. At the same time, the Japanese were suffering decisive defeat at Midway. But the Japanese commander ordered the Aleutian campaign to proceed as planned in order to secure a defensive position in the northern Pacific and to establish bases in preparation for future offensives.[12]

Foggy weather and typically poor radio communications made the roving Japanese fleet impossible to find. On June 7 and 8, while Admiral Theobald was searching for the enemy fleet in the Bering Sea near the Pribilof Islands, the Japanese Northern Force landed approximately 2,500 soldiers on Kiska and Attu, unopposed. Ten U.S. weather crewmen on Kiska were taken prisoner. The following day in Chicagof village on Attu, 42 Aleuts and two non-Aleut Alaska Indian Service employees were captured.

The absence of daily radio reports from Kiska and Attu aroused suspicion that the Japanese had invaded the western Aleutians. This was confirmed on June 10 when the weather cleared enough for an American scouting plane to sight the Japanese occupation forces on Kiska.

Long-distance bombings proved ineffective in dislodging the Japanese, so an airstrip and command post were constructed on Adak

Island in the western Aleutians. Throughout Fall 1942, continuous bombing of enemy installations on Kiska contained the Japanese in a defensive posture. Secret U.S. airfields on Umnak prevented the Japanese from patrolling the waters of the north Pacific from the Aleutians:

> While enemy orders referred to Kiska as "the key position on the northern attacking route against the U.S. in the future," it is fairly evident that the Japanese had no such design and were attempting only to block the American advance.[13]

During the fall, General Buckner garrisoned the islands by landing small forces on Atka and other islands, including St. Paul. To Buckner, the Japanese occupation of Kiska and Attu was the only obstacle to launching an offensive against Japan from the Aleutians. By December 1942, Buckner had 150,000 troops in the Alaskan theatre[14] and, in the following month, Admiral Nimitz ordered the North Pacific Force to clear the islands of Japanese troops.[15]

During the winter of 1943 the North Pacific Force blockaded Attu and Kiska to force Japan to surrender these outposts. The blockade was effective, for the last Japanese supply ship reached Attu in March. Equally devastating, the Japanese had to relinquish air power to the U.S. by the middle of spring; losing more than 1,000 airplanes at Guadalcanal, the Japanese had no replacements for the Aleutian campaign.[16] Finally, Japanese naval supremacy in the north Pacific ended in March after the U.S. won the battle for the Komandorski Islands west of Attu.

Fewer than 10,000 Japanese troops on Kiska and Attu awaited the inevitable attack. On May 11, 1943, the U.S. invaded Attu, and for 19 days waged a successful but bloody battle that cost over 500 American and 2,300 Japanese lives.

In July 1943, the U.S. successfully launched a bombing attack from Adak to Paramushiro on the Kurile Islands, the base of the Japanese Northern Force. The Japanese, facing a weakened northern flank, decided to withdraw their troops from Kiska. In late July, under cover of fog, the Japanese evacuated the island, slipping through the U.S. naval blockade. Almost three weeks later on August 15, 1943, the Navy, Army and Air Force invaded Kiska; heavy fog provided the only resistance. This marked the official end of the Aleutian campaign.

In September 1943, General DeWitt, head of the Western Defense Command, submitted a plan to the Joint Chiefs of Staff for the invasion of Japan by forces based partially on Attu and Kiska. The plan was never used. Also in September, Admiral Nimitz placed the Aleutians in a "Non-Invasion Status"[17] and the Eleventh Air Force was redesignated the Alaska Department and separated from the Western Defense Command, reflecting a lower priority in defense operations. By the end of 1943, Army forces in Alaska were reduced to 113,000 men.

U.S. military combat activity there did not completely cease. Bombing attacks on Paramushiro were launched from Aleutian bases from 1943 to 1945 to keep constant pressure on Japan's northern flank. These attacks tied up one-sixth of Japan's Air Force.[18] By the fall of 1943, however, the threat of Japanese advances and occupation had long since dissipated.[19]

Considering Evacuation

Events between Pearl Harbor and the evacuation from the Aleutian and Pribilof Islands suggest that the government agencies (the Department of the Interior and the military) responsible for protecting the Aleut residents failed to coordinate their activities internally or with each other. Interior officials, despite the growing threat of attack, were unable to agree on the desirability of evacuation and lost valuable planning time. As a result, the military was forced to evacuate the islands without adequate guidance from the Interior Department.

The Interior Department exercised control over policy affecting the Aleuts through three divisions: the Office of Indian Affairs (OIA), the Fish and Wildlife Service (FWS), and the Division of Territories and Island Possessions. On the Aleutian Islands, the OIA's involvement with the Aleuts was limited to education. The OIA established primary schools on the islands, and through its Alaska Indian Service appointed a teacher to the larger villages. The FWS's relationship to the Aleuts was based upon its responsibility to manage the profitable fur seal harvest on the Pribilofs. Since the Aleuts provided the only source of labor for this, the FWS maintained control over the Pribilof Aleuts and assumed responsibility for their education and general welfare. During World War II, the Division of Territories' major concern was to coordinate efforts among the Territorial Government of Alaska, which was under its jurisdiction, and federal war agencies on matters relating to supplying Alaska and evacuating the Aleutians. The military offices that established or carried out policies for civilian evacuation of the islands were the Navy's Alaska Sector under Admiral Freeman, the North Pacific Force under Admiral Theobald, and the Army's Alaska Defense Command under General Buckner.

Fearing Japanese attack, Buckner ordered the evacuation of military dependents from Alaska immediately after Pearl Harbor. Discussions about removing other Aleutian residents were begun by the military and the Interior Department soon thereafter. The Navy Department contacted Paul W. Gordon of the Division of Territories on January 17, 1942, expressing concern for civilians who lived near the military installations at Dutch Harbor:

> It is felt that the evacuation of all white women and children from Unalaska would be to the best interest of the present military situation.[20]

The Army recommended to the Navy that Aleut women and children also be removed in the event of an evacuation, and the Division of Territories relayed this recommendation to Governor Gruening on January 23. The Division concurred with an Army recommendation that "the activities of the Army and Navy connected with evacuation be coordinated with the activities of the Governor's office."[21] The Territorial Governor's office was a logical place to channel information in order to coordinate planning, since it fell under Interior's jurisdiction.

In the absence of Governor Gruening, Acting Territorial Governor E. L. Bartlett called a meeting on March 13, 1942, to discuss plans for evacuation in the event of enemy attack. Representatives of several civilian agencies were present (including Claude Hirst, a junior OIA officer from Juneau), but no military representatives attended the meeting. One conclusion they reached was that

> [N]o general attempt should be made even in the case of actual enemy attack, to evacuate Eskimos or other primitive natives from Alaska. It is felt these people could never adjust themselves to life outside of their present environment, whereas they could "take to the hills" in case of danger and be practically self sufficient for a considerable period.[22]

It was decided that Aleut women and children who lived near Dutch Harbor should be relocated to villages on Unimak Island and on the Alaska Peninsula where they would be "less exposed (to both military and social dangers)."[23] The OIA chose relocation sites after conferring with the Aleuts. Five of the nine possible villages were Aleut villages; in three of these locations living quarters were available in closed fish canneries.

At the meeting, officials recognized the need for further planning to coordinate efforts between the military and civilian branches:

> There is a need for basic thinking and definite decisions on matters of broad policy relating to evacuation, beyond what has been evidenced to date.
> A joint declaration of some kind might be prepared by participating agencies stating evacuation problems and recommending

lines of procedure. This should be addressed to the Army and Navy commands in Alaska and the Governor.[24]

The meeting concluded with a sense of urgency, with agreement that "another meeting of the group (in the very near future) is desirable."[25]

In later discussions, high-ranking OIA and other Interior Department officials remained apprehensive about removing the Aleuts from their homes. They feared that the Aleuts could not adjust easily to a foreign environment. John Collier, Commissioner of the OIA, sent a memorandum to Secretary Ickes on April 10, 1942, calling attention to the OIA's responsibility in establishing plans for Aleuts on the Aleutian Islands. Commissioner Collier pointed out that the Navy said it would not protect villages west of Dutch Harbor, and that Aleuts from the westernmost inhabited islands of Attu and Atka showed no inclination to move.[26]

The OIA faced a difficult situation: it wished neither to evacuate the Aleuts forcibly nor to leave them in a potentially dangerous area. The Aleuts in Unalaska, Collier reported, were willing to be moved eastward.[27] The OIA was relatively free to relocate these people swiftly to the preferred sites chosen at the March 18 meeting. A consensus could not be reached, however, among the military, the OIA and the Governor's office whether *any* Aleuts should be evacuated. As Collier pointed out in the same memorandum to Ickes:

> Our representative at Juneau, Superintendent Hirst, is in favor of evacuation. Governor Gruening is opposed to it on the grounds . . . [that] the dislocation resulting from a forced evacuation would be a greater damage and involve greater risks to the ultimate welfare of the people than the probable risks if they remain where they are. Admiral Freeman . . . has sent us a wire in response to our request for advice which places the responsibility upon us. His wire seems to say that evacuation is desirable but not mandatory. He does say that the Natives are "wholly unprotected from enemy raiders."[28]

Collier warned Ickes that if Dutch Harbor were bombed and Aleut residents of nearby Unalaska were injured, the Interior Department might be criticized. But he cautiously concluded, "I am inclined to leave the Natives where they are, unless the Navy insists that they be moved out."[29] The OIA chose a course which left the Aleuts in their villages; Claude Hirst dissented. It appears that although the Navy had no desire to make the final evacuation decision, the OIA preferred to leave this ultimate responsibility to the Navy. The OIA's position was approved less than a week later by Secretary Ickes, with the stipulation that the Aleuts would be moved if they wished.[30]

Sensing that the coordination of military and civilian operations was not running smoothly, James C. Rettie, Counselor from the Alaska Office of President Roosevelt's National Resources Planning Board, contacted the Director of the Bureau of the Budget, Harold D. Smith, on May 7, 1942, to register his complaints about Alaska's unpreparedness:

> I feel that it is my personal duty . . . to express to you again my grave concern about the present state of affairs in the Territory.
> We shall be worse than fools if we do not anticipate an attack in force against Alaska within the next two months. If nothing is done to remedy the administrative paralysis and lack of clearly defined responsibility now prevailing in Alaska and the inadequate preparations to evacuate civilians, the confusion and loss of life which will follow an attack may easily be worse than it was in Hawaii. The record of inaction, delays, inter-agency squabbles and bickering and lack of proper liaison with the armed forces will be terribly ugly. There will also be the vital question of the need for a unified military command. An outraged public opinion in the United States will rightly insist upon a hard-boiled investigation which might easily shake this administration to its very foundations.
> I therefore plead for the utmost speed and resolution in the issuance of whatever Executive Order the military authorities can and will effectively use to achieve proper coordination between military and civilian activities.[31]

Smith forwarded Rettie's correspondence to Henry L. Stimson, the Secretary of War, but it was not until June 11, 1942, after the Japanese attack, that the President signed Executive Order 9181 to establish the Alaska War Council chaired by the territorial governor with commissioners drawn from civilian agencies. The Council was responsible for maintaining close liaison with the military commanders and for conforming civilian policy to military objectives, "relative to the safety and security of the civilian population of Alaska."[32]

It appears that no coordinated government policy for developing evacuation plans existed, even as the Japanese launched the M I Operation. The day after Dutch Harbor was bombed by the Japanese, Governor Gruening wrote Secretary Ickes. Gruening doubted that an evacuation of Attu and Atka was desirable and tried to dissuade Ickes from forcibly evacuating those islands; moreover, the presence of Japanese vessels in the vicinity would have complicated any evacuation. At this late date, Gruening sought a clear evacuation policy.[33] He pointed out that Admiral Freeman believed that the Japanese might occupy one of the two westernmost islands, endangering the Aleuts there. Freeman had indicated to Gruening that "the Office of Indian Affairs desired this evacuation . . . [and] . . . the Navy had no special wishes or desires in the matter."[34] The OIA appears to have shifted position regarding the desirability of evacuation, and the Navy seems to have declined any decision-making responsibility.

According to Gruening, General Buckner, on the other hand, clearly opposed the evacuation:

> [Buckner] gave me his opinion that it would be a great mistake to evacuate these natives. He said, in effect, that evacuating them was pretty close to destroying them; that they now live under conditions suitable to them; and that if they were removed they would be subject to the deterioration of contact with the white man, would likely fall prey to drink and disease, and probably would never get back to their historic habitat.[35]

Gruening agreed with Buckner as did Superintendent Hirst, who reversed his former position. Gruening went one step further: "[B]efore any decision could be made, a qualified representative of the Office of Indian Affairs [should] proceed to Attu and Atka . . . [to] discuss the matter fully with the natives, and make the appropriate recommendations."[36] Gruening was concerned that the Aleuts understand the full implications of being moved to a strange new environment, although one relatively safe from enemy invasion.

Secretary Ickes responded on June 17, 1942, agreeing with Gruening's recommendation, but ironically noting that:

> [R]ecent events have eliminated this procedure. Attu is now occupied by the enemy, and the Navy is in the process of evacuating the natives of Atka and of the Pribilof Islands. Arrangements are in progress for settling evacuees during whatever period may be necessary in Southeastern Alaska.[37]

Thus began the evacuation of Aleuts from the Aleutian and Pribilof Islands, seemingly without well-developed plans and certainly without a clear policy to define the division of responsibilities between the military and civilian branches of government. The Department of the Interior was unable to reach an internal consensus; the Navy passed decision-making responsibility to Interior; and the Army, despite its knowledge of an inevitable Japanese attack, took a position which they, like the others, would reverse when Japanese invasion became a reality.

Perhaps this unpreparedness can be partially explained by the lack of coordination between the Army and Navy in Alaska. Their headquarters were 300 miles apart, and the exchange of intelligence information was sometimes slow and inaccurate. The commanders of the ADC and the North Pacific Force often clashed because of personality, and this exacerbated difficulties of coordination.[38] Had the Alaska War Council been established earlier, it might have provided an effective focus for military and civilian evacuation planning. By the time the Council was established in June, the ADC and OIA were searching for a place to relocate villagers evacuated from Atka and the Pribilofs.

The Evacuation of Atka and the Pribilof Islands

Following the Japanese bombing of Dutch Harbor, the Navy dispatched the seaplane tender *U.S.S. Gillis* to Atka to search for the elusive Japanese fleet. One of the Navy patrol planes spotted the Japanese invasion force on Kiska, and on June 11, 1942, the Navy launched air raids on Kiska from Nazan Bay on Atka.

The Japanese responded by sending out scouting planes and on June 12, a Japanese reconnaissance plane was sighted over Nazan Bay. At approximately 8:00 p.m., the *Gillis* received orders to evacuate Atka and to apply a scorched-earth policy before leaving.[39] The Commander of the Navy Patrol Wing issued the order to evacuate, to relocate the Atkans to a safe place and to prevent Japanese troops from using the Atkans' housing.[40] The *Gillis* dispatched a unit of sailors to Atka village and evacuated C. Ralph and Ruby Magee, who were employed by the OIA's Alaska Indian Service, she as a schoolteacher and he as a general maintenance man. They were the only people evacuated because, according to the Magees, after eighteen hours of bombing raids on Kiska and sighting a Japanese scout plane, "We had the people move out to their fish camps about three miles from the village, thinking that they might be safer out there in their tents."[41] The Magees were given twenty minutes to pack; then the detail of sailors burned the village, including the Aleut church, leaving only four houses unscathed. The *Gillis* set sail immediately for Dutch Harbor.

Later that evening, most of the Atka Aleuts returned to their burning village. They were spotted by the crew of the seaplane tender *U.S.S. Hulbert* and loaded aboard. The next day the *Hulbert* headed for Nikolski village on Umnak Island, where it eventually dropped off its 62 Aleut passengers to await transportation to Dutch Harbor.[42] On the night of the 13th, Patrol Wing Four reported that a message from Admiral Nimitz revealed that "the Japanese commander in Kiska had directed his aircraft to bomb Nazan Bay. By this time Nazan Bay had been completely evacuated and our forces were safely away."[43] In fact, nineteen Aleuts were stranded at Atka until June 15, when two Navy planes picked them up.

The evacuation of Atka was necessarily hasty, yet the scorched-earth policy might have been implemented more carefully had planning been coordinated properly between the Navy and OIA. The irony was that the Atkans were prepared to evacuate before a Japanese attack, and they could have been given time to take their belongings before the village was destroyed. As the Magees described it:

[Right after Pearl Harbor] we went to tell the villagers that they ought to pack up and be prepared to leave at any time, for we thought that surely the Coast Guard or someone else would come to evacuate us. However, it was not until six months later that we were taken off the island . . . [also] a letter came from the Juneau Alaska Native Service Office in April of 1942 requesting us to talk over with the people the possibility of having to move to some other part of the territory to be safe from any possible aggression by the Japanese. . . . We were to be ready to go at a moment's notice, so all packed up a few belongings to take with us.[44]

After the Japanese attacked Dutch Harbor and captured Attu and Kiska, Interior Department officials anticipated that if the Pribilofs were threatened, those Aleuts would also be evacuated. At the end of May, Admiral Freeman told the FWS that a scorched-earth policy would be used in the Pribilofs if the Japanese attacked, and that sealskins would be included in the destruction.[45] By June 5, the villagers had been warned that an enemy attack was possible, and FWS agents told them what civil defense precautions to take if this came.[46]

The evacuation of the Pribilofs, begun immediately after Atka was evacuated, was executed by the Army with little delay. The Navy's U.S.S. Oriole arrived at St. Paul on June 14, with orders to evacuate the island, but these plans changed when the captain of the vessel learned that the Army's U.S.A.T. Delarof would arrive the following day to evacuate St. Paul and St. George. The villagers were directed to pack their belongings and, two days later on June 16, the 294 Aleuts and 15 non-Aleut FWS employees departed for St. George aboard the Delarof.[47] Carl M. Hoverson, an FWS employee on St. Paul, recalled that "Many personal belongings as well as government property had to be left at the island because of the need for a speedy evacuation."[48]

The Delarof's arrival at St. George was scheduled for June 16, and villagers were notified on the night of June 14 to pack their belongings. Daniel C.R. Benson, an FWS agent and caretaker of St. George, prepared the village:

I was first instructed to prepare the village for destruction first that night by placing a pail of gasoline in each house and building, and a charge of dynamite for each other installation such as storage tanks, light plants, trucks, radio transmitters, receivers, antenna masts, etc. The packing of everybody was to be very simple—absolutely nothing but one suitcase per person and a roll of blankets.[49]

Early in the evening of June 16, 1942, the *Delarof* left St. George. The entire population, 183 Aleuts and 7 non-Aleut FWS employees, was evacuated.[50] Only one person, a radio operator on St. Paul, remained on the Pribilofs. Four signal corpsmen were immediately sent to the islands to set up two radio warning stations and remained in isolation on round-the-clock watch from June to September. As part of the plan to garrison the Aleutians before a U.S. offensive, a small Army force was sent to the Pribilofs on September 19, billeted in the departed villagers' dwellings, and ordered to construct an airstrip.[51]

On June 17, 1942, the *Delarof* arrived at Dutch Harbor with the Pribilof evacuees on board. While the ship was docked, the Army ordered most of the medical supplies and equipment from St. Paul aboard to be transferred to the Army Hospital at Fort Mears. Ward T. Bower, Chief of Alaska Fisheries for FWS, later attempted to reconstruct that incident:

> [W]hen evacuation orders reached St. Paul Island in the previous month, Dr. Berenberg packed eight sealskin barrels with medical supplies and equipment, and packed also the X-ray machine. . . . At Dutch Harbor on June 25, 1942, these eight barrels and one opened package of X-ray film were turned over by Capt. Fred H. Aves, Medical Corps Transport Surgeon of the *USAT Delarof* for use at Fort Mears Hospital . . .[52]

These expensive supplies were scarce and, although the military hospital may have needed them, the Pribilovians were soon to need essential medical care in the relocation camps, but the St. Paul community was not reimbursed, nor were the supplies replaced.

Meanwhile, additional evacuees from Atka and the Pribilofs were creating a food shortage in Unalaska.[53] A decision about permanent relocation had to be made quickly. On June 18, 81 Atkan Aleuts and the Magees were taken aboard the *Delarof* and set sail for an unknown destination.

Conditions aboard the *Delarof* were crowded and unhealthy, for space was inadequate to separate the sick from the well. The first casualty during the Aleuts' evacuation was the infant daughter of Innokenty and Haretina R. Kochutin of St. Paul, who died of pneumonia. Fredrika Martin, a nurse and the wife of a FWS doctor, described the tragedy:

> Since once aboard the ship the St. George doctor felt completely free of responsibility for his islanders and had no personal interest

in any of these patients of his, he could not be coaxed into the disagreeable hold even before all the Aleuts and many non-Aleuts came down after our stay-over at Dutch Harbor with "ship's cold," a serious grippe infection. He did not come to assist even at the birth of a St. George baby or its subsequent death of bronchial pneumonia because of our inability [Dr. Berenberg's and mine] to separate mother and child from other grippe-sufferers, and the mother herself was ill. I think I recall this doctor attending the midnight or after funeral of the poor little mite, such a tiny weighted parcel being let down into the deep waters of the Gulf of Alaska against a shoreline of dramatic peaks and blazing sunset sky.[54]

Six days later, on June 24, the *Delarof* landed at Funter Bay and Killisnoo in southeastern Alaska. While the ship sailed, various divisions within the Department of the Interior frantically sought a place to settle the evacuees.

Deciding on Camp Locations

Planning for relocation sites apparently started on June 15, 1942.[55] As the Pribilofs were evacuated, General Buckner began working directly with the OIA's Superintendent Hirst to choose relocation sites for the Aleuts. The OIA was chiefly responsible, and they determined that Killisnoo Bay village in southeastern Alaska was a potential site for resettlement.[56] Responsibility for settling the Pribilovians was assumed by Edward C. Johnston, Superintendent of the Seal Division of the FWS, who contacted Fisheries Chief Ward Bower on June 15 to discuss available housing.[57] First they tried to secure locations in the Seattle, Washington, area. A large Civilian Conservation Corps (CCC) camp and the Tulalip Indian Reservation were considered, but the CCC camp was occupied and housing at the reservation would have had to be built. Both sites were impractical since time was of the essence; Johnston emphasized that the Pribilovians "must have [a] location within [a] week."[58]

The OIA in Washington, DC, decided that evacuees should stay in Alaska, preferably southeastern Alaska.[59] OIA Assistant Commissioner William Zimmerman contacted Superintendent Hirst on June 16 to report this decision and relay other plans for relocation centers. The evacuation guidelines which had been established at Acting Governor Bartlett's conference in March were followed by a decision that native Alaskans should be evacuated to other parts of Alaska. Apparently the OIA did not wish to relocate the Aleuts to the eastern part of the Aleutian chain or the Alaska Peninsula.

The OIA also decided that Aleuts from the same village should remain together in separate units. Local OIA and FWS officials were asked to choose relocation sites; Assistant Commissioner Zimmerman recommended the use of fish canneries that were either abandoned or vacant during the off-season.[60] The school facilities at Wrangell Institute on Wrangell Island in southeastern Alaska would be a temporary location until such sites were found.

Seattle FWS Representative Donald Hagerty was apparently the Interior official who made final decisions on specific sites. On June 16 Hagerty told Zimmerman that arrangements had been made to house the Atkans at an abandoned fish cannery at Killisnoo on Admiralty Island.[61] The OIA was interested in locations where the Aleuts could support themselves, so job opportunities in nearby canneries made this location attractive.[62] On the same day, Hagerty assigned the Pribilof evacuees to another abandoned cannery at Funter Bay on Admiralty Island in southeastern Alaska.[63] Across Funter Bay from the cannery, abandoned facilities of the Alaska Mining Company were also obtained.[64]

Further Evacuation Along the Chain

Government agencies in Alaska disagreed about the need for further evacuation. By the end of June 1942, the Japanese were only beginning their occupation of the Aleutians and it was not clear whether they were entrenched in an offensive or defensive position. Governor Gruening, as chairman of the Alaska War Council, contacted Secretary Ickes on June 20 and reported that the Council feared the Japanese planned to invade the U.S. mainland, using the Aleutians as a base.[65] General Buckner advised the OIA that no more villages in the Aleutian Islands should be evacuated,[66] but Admiral Freeman felt that other Aleutian villages were in danger.[67] On June 29, 1942, Freeman issued an order "directing the evacuation of all natives from the Aleutian Islands."[68]

In a sweep eastward from Atka to Akutan, the Aleut villages of Nikolski on Umnak Island; Makushin, Biorka, Chernofski and Kashega on Unalaska Island; and Akutan on Akutan Island were evacuated. One week after Freeman issued the order, the first of the remaining villages, Nikolski, was evacuated. Yet Aleut evacuees testified that they were given only a few hours' notice. On July 5, two Navy and Army ships arrived at Nikolski and evacuated the entire village of 70 Aleuts plus Barbara Whitfield (the OIA teacher in the village), her husband Samuel and the non-Aleut foreman of the Aleutian Livestock Company, a sheep ranch on Umnak.

The Aleutian Livestock Company, completely dependent on Aleut labor due to the wartime labor shortage, had been assured by the Alaska Defense Command on May 22, 1942, that "no evacuation had been ordered."[69] It had expected to produce 130,000 pounds of wool during 1942, and the Army thought the company's operation necessary to the war effort. On August 5, 1942, Carlyle Eubank, the company president, protested to the Western Defense command about losing his ranch's work force.[70] Prior to the evacuation, the Navy had telegraphed Nikolski that:

> Nikolski sheep ranchers and four unmarried Aleuts may remain shear sheep inform that they do so at own risk and thereby forfeit government transportation.[71]

The message, however, arrived too late to prevent evacuation of ranch workers, and, stated Eubank, "Under such instructions the natives would not return and we cannot blame our Foreman for not returning."[72] The livestock company later obtained permission from the Army to return to Nikolski, even though the Japanese still occupied Attu and Kiska. That December the foreman came back to the ranch and, for the two following summers, three Aleuts also returned.

The evacuation of the small villages on Unalaska Island and Akutan is not well documented except by personal recollection of the evacuees. According to their testimony, the Nikolski Aleuts—together with villagers from Chernofski, Kashega, and Makushin—departed for southeastern Alaska from Chernofski on the S.S. Columbia, an Alaskan Steamship Company vessel. The OIA reported on August 31 that 72 Aleuts from Nikolski (including the Whitfields), 41 from Akutan, 20 from Kashega, 18 from Biorka, and 9 from Makushin (including one white) had arrived at Wrangell Institute on July 13, 1942.[73] The entire population of these villages was evacuated, Aleut and non-Aleut. The evacuees, who remained at Wrangell Institute for several weeks until the OIA located a place to resettle them, eventually were moved to a CCC camp administered by the OIA at Ward Lake near Ketchikan.

In Unalaska village, confusion and anger spread because of an alleged statement by Assistant Commissioner Zimmerman that the Aleuts in Unalaska had been offered transportation off the island,[74] when in fact they had not. The Mayor of Unalaska, John W. Fletcher, in a telegram to Secretary Ickes on July 7, 1942, urged that transportation to evacuate the Aleuts be made available, claiming that they were "desparate [sic] to be taken out."[75] Fear of Japanese invasion occupied the minds of many Aleuts in Unalaska. Some were able to adjust to new dangers because of the sense of security U.S. military forces brought to the islands, but others took the first opportunity to leave. Philemon Tutiakoff expressed some of these feelings:

[W]e had been notified prior to the bombing [of Dutch Harbor] that we may be evacuated. Naturally, listening to the radio people were alarmed. They became afraid. The most affluent Aleuts and civilians bought their way by Alaska Steamship to places of safety. The Unalaska Aleuts felt that with the presence of the military and the preparations we could see them taking, [we] thought and hoped that the U.S. military would protect us in case of what we all thought was direct assault on the town of Unalaska.[76]

By July 12, 1942, Secretary Ickes had arranged with the Navy to evacuate Unalaskans.[77] A week passed before the Aleuts were evacuated, yet, according to their testimony, the Aleuts were usually given less than twenty-four hours to prepare.

On July 19, 1942, the *S.S. Alaska* docked at Unalaska to evacuate the Aleuts. Commander William N. Updegraf, captain of the Naval station at Dutch Harbor, issued the orders, including the provision that:

All natives, or persons with as much as one eighth (⅛) native blood were compelled to go. . . . Only such portable baggage as the people could carry was permitted. . . . No employee, native or white, of Siems-Drake Puget Sound Company was to be carried.[78]

This order had an obviously unequal effect among Unalaskans. For example, Charles Hope, a white man, remained in Unalaska, while his Aleut wife was required to evacuate.[79]

Although no clear contemporaneous rationale explains why only Aleuts were compelled to leave Unalaska village, several factors suggest partial explanations. The evacuation order may have come literally from Secretary Ickes' request to the Navy to evacuate the *Aleuts* in Unalaska village.[80] Since these evacuees were taken at once to Wrangell Institute, operated by OIA, the evacuation and relocation may have been limited to persons for whom the OIA had some responsibility. According to Fred Geeslin, a former OIA officer, the agency's responsibility and authority extended to persons of one-eighth Native American blood, and its evacuation and relocation efforts would consequently be limited to that group and its own employees.[81] This does not explain, however, why all non-Aleuts residing in the Dutch Harbor-Unalaska area were not evacuated by the military to locations other than OIA evacuation camps. Some non-Aleuts were evacuated from Dutch Harbor after the June bombings. James I. Parsons, a businessman in Dutch

Harbor, and his family were evacuated to Juneau on June 6 by Army order; his facilities were used by the Army to house wounded soldiers.[82]

Many non-Aleuts probably were not evacuated because of the demand for defense construction workers reflected in the specific exemption of Siems-Drake Company employees. Siems-Drake had contracted to handle most of the defense construction work in Alaska for the Navy[83] and, at one point during the war, it employed almost 3,000 civilian construction workers in Dutch Harbor.[84] The shortage of labor was severe. In August 1942, Admiral Freeman complained to General DeWitt that "it has been practically impossible . . . to complete work promptly. At Dutch Harbor, it has been impossible to maintain even the former low level working force."[85] The Navy may have been concerned about the labor shortage and so prevented defense workers from leaving the village. At least one Aleut, John Yatchmanoff, was an employee of the Siems-Drake Company not evacuated for this reason. The order preventing the evacuation of Siems-Drake employees from Unalaska was issued by the Navy even though the workers were not employed by the government, and the Navy's responsibility was limited to processing their applications for work permits.[86]

According to Captain Hobart Copeland, who directed the Unalaska evacuation, some Aleuts protested being moved.[87] Copeland requested permission from Commander Updegraf to compel the Aleuts to go, but Updegraf would not forcibly evacuate them, and Copeland let them stay, thus limiting the impact of Updegraf's expulsion order.

The OIA reported that 111 Unalaskans arrived at Wrangell Institute aboard the S.S. Alaska on July 26, 1942.[88] They remained in Wrangell until late August, when the OIA rented an abandoned cannery at Burnett Inlet on Annette Island in southeastern Alaska.

After the Unalaska evacuation, Admiral Freeman decided that further removal of Aleut villages east of Akutan Island was unnecessary.[89] A total of 881 Aleuts had been evacuated by the military from all Aleut villages west of Unimak Island, including the Pribilofs.[90] The entire population of each village, except Unalaska, was evacuated, including at least 30 non-Aleuts. All but 50 Aleuts were relocated to southeastern Alaska. The remainder were evacuated to the Seattle area by the Army and Navy after the bombing of Dutch Harbor on June 3; ten were hospitalized in the Indian Hospital at Tacoma, Washington;[91] others were military dependents.

Because the evacuation was inadequately planned, the Aleuts lost the personal possessions they reluctantly left behind. Testimony from the evacuees established that in most cases they were given unnecessarily short notice. They were forced to leave behind most personal belongings—including clothing, family albums, musical instruments (a mainstay of Aleut culture), priceless icons of immense religious significance, unique craftwork, boats and essential hunting and fishing equipment. No provision was made by OIA or the military to care for these possessions. They were left unpacked and secured only by locks on the front door or boards nailed across the windows of Aleut homes, vulnerable to theft and the deterioration which followed.

The Attuans' Experience

The story of the Attuans' capture and removal to Japan is perhaps the most tragic of all Aleut experiences during the war. Official failure to warn the Attuans before the Japanese attack about the danger of remaining on the island carried a painful cost: approximately half of the Attuans perished during their captivity.

In May 1942 the Navy attempted to evacuate the islanders. A team of sailors was sent to set up a radio station on Attu, but they failed to land on the island because of adverse weather; the skiffs loaded with radio equipment crashed onshore in the surf. Mike Hodikoff, the Attuan Aleut chief, reached the Navy vessel from shore and, informed of the Japanese threat, was asked if he wanted his people to be evacuated at that time; he declined.[92]

This evacuation offer was not made in a manner that allowed the Attuans to make an informed decision about leaving their island. Governor Gruening had wanted the OIA to discuss these options with the Attuans, and had pointed out to Secretary Ickes on June 4 that "[p]resenting this matter to the . . . Attuites involves something of a problem since it could not be done by a mere radio message. The pros and cons to them [of] so momentous a decision, the possible risks and alternatives, would have to be presented to them understandingly, sympathetically and clearly."[93] Gruening's recommendations to Ickes came too late, and no attempt was ever made by the Interior Department to discuss evacuation possibilities with the Attuans.

When Attu was invaded on June 8, 1942, an Aleut was wounded by Japanese gunfire and the OIA radio operator, Foster Jones, died after being captured. The Japanese began immediately to garrison the island and to construct housing for their troops. Shortly thereafter, the Japanese eased restraints on movement of the Aleuts, who then fished and went about their daily work almost normally. In September 1942, the Japanese changed their Aleutian strategy and decided to abandon Attu (only to return in October).[94] The troops were moved temporarily to Kiska. The Japanese feared the Attuans could reveal military strength and other intelligence secrets to invading American forces, so the 41 Aleuts (one had died in August) were taken to Otaru on Japan's northernmost island of Hokkaido.[95] The non-Aleut schoolteacher, Etta Jones, was taken to Yokohama. Three Attuan evacuees recalled their living conditions in Japan, and reported that they were adequate:

[We] were housed in a large building, supervised by a Japanese policeman, who lived in partitioned rooms in the same building. The Aleuts had no freedom, [and were] held in the same building for the entire war, except the ones who worked in a clay pit near by. The buildings were heated by coal stoves in winter. Hot baths were available whenever the Aleuts wanted them. They slept on the floor on the Japanese standard mats "Tatami" and they had plenty of blankets.[96]

Tuberculosis later spread widely among the Attuans, despite monthly visits to their camp by a doctor who gave routine examinations and inoculations. At one time as many as ten to fifteen Attuans were inpatients at the National Tuberculosis Center in Minamoto-cho,[97] but despite hospitalization many Aleuts died in Japan. The loss of their high-protein diet and fresh food, aggravated by short rations, caused malnutrition and starvation during the last year of their captivity. As the war dragged on, Japan was starved for resources; Japanese troops and the Attuans' guards alike faced shortages.

Half of the Attuans died in Japan and the surviving 21 Aleuts and one newborn baby left Japan in September 1945.[98] Upon reaching Seattle on November 20, the Attuans were informed that they would not be returned to Attu. The reason for this decision is not clear because government documents about their resettlement were destroyed by the OIA in the 1960's.[99] Attu evacuees claim that the government did not allow them to return to Attu because there were too few to sustain a viable community.[100] Instead they were offered transportation to Atka Island. The Atkans and Attuans, however, were traditional rivals, so several Attuans decided against resettling at Atka. To this day, Attu remains uninhabited.

THE EVACUATION CAMPS

Funter Bay

The Aleuts from St. Paul and St. George in the Pribilofs arrived at Funter Bay on Admiralty Island on June 24, 1942. They found the mountains and forests of southeastern Alaska a sharp contrast to the flat, treeless Pribilofs.

The General Living Conditions. Close to 300 Aleuts and FWS personnel from St. Paul found themselves housed at a fish cannery where many buildings, unoccupied for a dozen years, were only used for storage. They were inadequate housing, particularly in winter. Only a few cottages were available to accommodate the many families; most evacuees were forced to live in two dormitory-style buildings where groups of six to thirteen people slept in areas nine or ten feet square. Until fall, many Aleuts had to sleep in relays in these cramped conditions. Lumber to build partitions and walls was scarce, and they hung blankets between families for privacy. Meals for the entire group were prepared and served in a common kitchen and messhall.

The quarters were as rundown as they were cramped:

> The only buildings that are capable of fixing is the two large places where the natives are sleeping. All other houses are absolutely gone from rot. It will be almost impossible to put toilet and bath into any of them except this one we are using as a mess hall and it leaks in thirty places. . . . No brooms, soap or mops or brushes to keep the place suitable for pigs to stay in.[101]

People fell through the rotten wooden floors. A single toilet on the beach just above the low water mark served ninety percent of the evacuees, whose clothes were laundered on the ground or sidewalks.[102] Agent McMillin's first evacuation report to the Superintendent of the Sealing Division ended with these words:

> It seems funny if our government can drop so many people in a place like this then forget about them altogether. . . . If you think that this is any fun, you should be here.[103]

A mile away on the other side of Funter Bay, the 180 Aleuts and FWS employees from St. George had been evacuated to the Admiralty Alaska Gold Mine, also known as the Funter Bay Mine, which had not been worked for several years. The mine was little better than the cannery. One two-story unpartitioned building housed ten families, a total of 46 people. A new mess house was used as a storeroom, canteen and church. Above the messhall, the 26 single men were housed in a low loft accessible only through an outside entrance. The other Aleuts occupied another two-story dormitory similar to the one at the cannery, but the 20 families living there had no heat. In the words of FWS Agent Benson, "The crowded, dark and unheated quarters for the natives are definitely out of the question for the winter."[104] Benson recommended that 32 apartments or two-room cottages be built, with separate facilities for everything except sleeping.

Cookstoves, plumbing fixtures, water tanks and other equipment and supplies proved difficult to procure and, on July 2, on behalf of the evacuees, *Alaska Fishing News* initiated an appeal to canneries and fishermen for all types of gear.[105] Nonetheless, on the same day, Assistant Fishery Supervisor Frank W. Hynes wrote Alaska Fisheries Chief Ward T. Bower:

> We feel that Mr. Johnston has the situation well in hand insofar as the Pribilof natives and whites are concerned and predict that his Funter Bay camp will serve as a model for others to be established later.[106]

By September, apart from local materials, no supplies had arrived.[107]

In early October, the Aleut women of St. Paul submitted a petition protesting their living conditions:

> We the people of this place wants a better place . . . to live. This . . . is no place for a living creature. We drink impure water and then get sick the children's get skin disease even the grown ups are sick from cold.
>
> We ate from the mess house and it is near the toilet only a few yards away. We eat the filth that is flying around.
>
> We got no place to take a bath and no place to wash our clothes or dry them when it rains. We women are always lugging water up stairs and take turns warming it up and the stove is small. We live in a room with our children just enough to turn around in. We used blankets for walls just to live in private. We need clothes and shoes for our children how are we going to clothe them with just a few dollars. Men's are working for $20 a month is nothing to them we used it to see our children eat what they don't get at mess house and then its gone and then we wait for another month to come around.
>
> Why they not take us to a better place to live and work for ourselves and live in a better house. Men and women are very eager to work. When winter come it still would be worse with water all freezed up. . . . Do we have to see our children suffer. We all have rights to speak for ourselves.[108]

The complaints in the petition were discussed with the presenting committee by both Agent McMillin and Superintendent Johnston. In his letter forwarding the petition to Chief Bower, Johnston stated:

> The women were told that under war conditions they could not expect to enjoy the comforts and conditions as they existed on the Pribilof Islands. . . . Analysis of water samples by the Territorial Department of Health indicates the water to be potentially unsafe. . . . Sickness mentioned in the petition is not due to drinking

water. Some of the children have "fish poisoning," which Dr. Smith states is common at this time of the year and will clear up when the salmon runs are over. . . . The toilet which has been in use is over tide water and is farther from living and eating quarters than any on the Pribilofs was. . . . The men are satisfied with the food furnished, but the women do not like the community mess. They refuse to help with the cooking, which is done by the men. . . . The food mentioned in the petition which is bought for the children from the canteen is principally candy.[109]

The superintendent also described what he had done to alleviate the lack of privacy, water, plumbing and laundry facilities, clothing and food.

A year later in Fall 1943, the camps at Funter Bay were visited by numerous government officials, including John Hall of the U.S. Public Health Service, Governor Ernest Gruening, Alaska Attorney General Henry Roden, FWS Director Ira Gabrielson, and Dr. Berneta Block of the Territorial Department of Health. Conditions were little improved. No description is more graphic than the account submitted by Dr. Block after her four-day visit to Funter Bay:

As we entered the first bunkhouse the odor of human excreta and waste was so pungent that I could hardly make the grade. . . . The buildings were in total darkness except for a few candles here and there which I considered distinct fire hazards. . . . [A] mother and as many as three or four children were found in several beds and two or three children in one bunk. . . . The garbage cans were overflowing, human excreta was found next to the doors of the cabins and the drainage boxes into which dishwater and kitchen waste was to be placed were filthy beyond description. . . . I realize that during the first two days we saw the community at its worst. I know that there were very few adults who were well. . . . The water supply is discolored, contaminated and unattractive. . . . [F]acilities for boiling and cooling the water are not readily available. . . . I noticed some lack of the teaching of basic public health fundamentals. Work with such a small group of people who have been wards of the government for a long period of time should have brought better results. It is strange that they could have reverted from a state of thrift and cleanliness on the Islands to the present state of filth, despair, and complete lack of civic pride. I realize, too, that at the time I saw them the community was largely made up of women and children whose husbands were not with them. With proper facilities for leadership, guidance and stimulation . . . the situation could have been quite different.[110]

Assistant Supervisor Hynes made a grim report to his Division Chief, Ward Bower:

[W]e are convinced that unless adequate measures are taken to improve conditions before the arduous winter months begin there is more than a possibility that the death toll from tuberculosis, pneumonia, influenza, and other diseases will so decimate the ranks of the natives that few will survive to return to the islands.[111]

But conditions did not substantially improve at Funter Bay until the winter of 1943–44, a year and a half after the Aleuts had been evacuated.

Medical Care and Education. In Fall 1942, the only full-time medical care at Funter Bay came from a white nurse assisted by an Aleut nurse. They served both the mining and the cannery camps, crossing Funter Bay each day, but doctors were only temporarily assigned to the camp, often remaining for only a few days or weeks. The infirmary at the mining camp was a three-room bungalow; the cannery's was a room twenty feet square. Medical supplies were scarce.

Epidemics raged throughout the Aleuts' stay in southeastern Alaska. The Aleuts suffered from influenza, measles, and pneumonia along with tuberculosis.[112] Twenty-five died in 1943 alone, and it is estimated that at least 40 people died at Funter Bay.

Because of a lack of space and supplies, school began only in January 1943 for children who were not sent to Wrangell Institute, an OIA school. OIA provided no textbooks; later, reading books were loaned, but only $100 was appropriated for supplies. The 55 St. Paul children were taught in the cannery kitchen by teachers who, when weather permitted, crossed the bay to the mining camp to work with the 34 children from St. George. When the cannery crew returned in March, school shut down entirely. Absences due to illness shortened this haphazard school year even further, and the students' progress was negligible. Education in the camps somewhat improved during the second year, when classes were conducted from December until April.

Communication, Transportation and Censorship. These small encampments of evacuees were extremely isolated in their hardship. At Funter Bay, communication with the outside world was limited to a weekly mail service; there was no two-way radio. Timely treatment of the seriously ill was unavailable because the hospital in Juneau had a two-week waiting period for admittance, and prompt response to other emergencies was impossible.

Transportation was whatever arrangements could be made with supply ships or the weekly mailboat. Moreover, Aleuts were required to obtain the FWS agent's permission before they could leave Funter Bay.

In addition, under the First War Powers Act, mail between the Territory of Alaska and the continental U.S., the "Lower 48," was censored. As Hynes acknowledged in 1943:

Censorship has kept the press off our necks thus far but this line of defense is weakening rapidly. A few days ago we were advised by one of the physicians who had inspected the camps . . . that he was preparing a report to the Surgeon General of the United States and also to Secretary Ickes and had no intention of "pulling any punches". He warned that it was only a question of time until some publication, such as Life Magazine, would get hold of the story and play it up, much to the disadvantage of the Service and the Department of Interior as a whole.[113]

Defense Employment, Selective Service and the Fur Seal Industry. The fur seal herd in the Pribilof Islands grows 80% of the world's supply of this luxurious fur.[114] Since 1910, the federal government has fully controlled the harvest of seals and the fur marketing; in 1941, the annual seal slaughter contributed nearly $2.4 million to the U.S. Treasury.[115] The Pribilovian Aleuts were the primary seal harvesters; after evacuation, only 127 seals were taken in 1942, in contrast to over 95,000 in 1941. For the Interior Department, anxious to resume sealing operations in 1943, projected revenue was a major, if not the predominant consideration, in its policy decisions.

The war had created a labor shortage in Alaska and, by the end of June 1942, the U.S. Employment Service was prepared to place a number of Aleut men in suitable jobs.[116] Seal Superintendent Johnston and a few other officials had a different program in mind: they wanted to protect the government's "investment" in the Aleuts and their sealing operation. Assuming that seal harvesting would resume after the war, these officials wished to avoid the inconvenience of locating and collecting Pribilovians scattered to distant parts of Alaska.[117] For this reason the FWS sought to keep the Pribilovians together as a unit and to "pay them a nominal salary to keep them satisfied."[118] Johnston recommended to Bower that:

No individual should be permitted to take his family and leave camp unless he insists on doing so. In that case he should lose all rights as a Pribilof Native and should not be allowed to return to the Pribilofs at any time except as an ordinary visitor.[119]

Bower replied:

[W]e have no definite hold on the Pribilof natives who are evacuated to Funter Bay. With regard to employment elsewhere, the rules concerning these natives can be effective only while they are directly connected with the evacuation camp. While there, they are subject to the jurisdiction, care and support of the Government. If they go away from Funter Bay for a while to engage in other work, there is nothing that we can do to stop them. . . . In my opinion, very few will stay away for any length of time, and when conditions permit them to return to the Pribilof Islands, practically all will be on hand ready and anxious to go. Perhaps experience might give a better appreciation of the excellent care . . . there.[120]

By Fall 1942, Johnston and the local agents stopped trying to keep the Pribilovians at Funter Bay. More than 100 men and their families left, including 27 children who departed for Wrangell Institute.[121]

In addition to losing men to more lucrative employment, the FWS lost other able-bodied sealers to the draft. While on the Pribilofs, the Aleuts had not been registered for Selective Service because the FWS assumed that, as wards of the government, the Aleuts were ineligible for the draft.[122] At Funter Bay the FWS learned differently, and during 1942 all eligible men were registered.[123]

On November 23, 1942, Secretary of the Interior Ickes wrote Secretary of War Stimson urging "that arrangements be made to return the natives and supervisory personnel . . . to the Pribilof Islands next April or May to resume sealing and other operations."[124] At first, the War Department refused Ickes' request,[125] but on January 2, 1943, Stimson notified Ickes that the Pribilof Aleuts and FWS supervisors had been given permission to "return for the sealing season only in order to direct the pruning of the seal herds by military personnel." He added that "[w]ith respect to St. George Island, I have no objection to the return of the natives of that place for rehabilitation."[126]

Few men were available to harvest seals that summer of 1943. By March, seventeen Aleuts had been inducted and another four were subject to immediate induction. The FWS sought four-month furloughs for the draftees and deferments for those not yet inducted. By May, seven of the seventeen servicemen had been granted furloughs, and the other four received deferments for the sealing season.

As plans got under way to resume sealing and to rehabilitate St. George, it was discovered that some Aleuts did not want to return to the islands until the war was over.[127] Superintendent Johnston began to realize that men with good jobs in Juneau might not wish to leave them. He proposed measures to control the situation:

If any workman remains in Juneau or deserts his post during the summer . . . [he] will forfeit any share of the sealing division. Also, I will seriously consider recommending that he be denied return to St. Paul for residence. As St. George is being rehabilitated, any workman who refuses to return this spring will not share in the sealing division and will not be allowed to return at any later date if I can help it. This will include his immediate family (wife and children). Such a man will not receive assistance in any way from the Fish and Wildlife Service at any time and lose all privileges as an island resident.[128]

These recommendations went to Ward Bower,[129] who once again had to direct his subordinates toward a more temperate attitude:

In view of war conditions, the forced evacuation of the islands, and the designation of the area as a war zone, it is scarcely possible or equitable to require complete forfeiture of all rights of return to the Pribilofs. Present conditions just do not warrant such action.[130]

In April, Johnston came up from Seattle to meet with the Pribilovians. The Aleuts wanted better wages and worried about their safety in the Pribilofs that summer. The St. George men asked that their women and children remain at Funter Bay and that the sealers be returned at the end of the season. Johnston conveyed this to Bower as well as a local agent's opinion that all the women wanted to return to St. George.[131] Bower immediately telegraphed back that the "St. George women and children should be left [at] Funter and St. George workmen returned there at end [of] season same as St. Paul workmen."[132] It is not clear who made the decision not to repopulate the island—Bower, the FWS director, or the Secretary of the Interior. In any case, Johnston was relieved:

From the standpoint of safety I am glad the change was made; if we had rehabilitated St. George and afterward a single bomb had been dropped there our whole course of action would have been open to criticism. The men are going up for the sealing season in a much better state of mind now that they do not have to worry about their families.[133]

Despite Chief Bower's moderating words to Superintendent Johnston,[134] testimony before the Commission and informal interviews by Commission staff indicate that the Pribilovian men felt compelled to leave their jobs to harvest the seals; they were told that if they did not, they would never see their homeland again.[135]

When the sealers went up to the Pribilofs that summer, they left behind at Funter Bay 281 women and children and 32 older men. The FWS agents and a doctor accompanied the men, leaving a school-teacher and a storekeeper to manage the camp. Neither had borne such responsibilities before, and they were further hampered by a shortage of men to perform the necessary work. Even worse, a measles epidemic swept Funter Bay that summer—and they had no doctor.

The Aleuts harvested over 117,000 seals during the summer of 1943, a record take which reaped over $1.58 million in fur and seal byproduct sales for the United States Government.[136] The approximately 100 Pribilovian Aleut workers were paid from a pool that gave them close to $1 per skin, and the 13 non-Pribilovian Aleut sealers were paid a salary of $150 per month.[137]

Later in the summer, Bower broached the subject of Johnston's harsh approach with FWS Director Ira Gabrielson, suggesting that some Aleuts might not wish to return to the islands, but would prefer to try their luck in the Lower 48:

> He stated that this was perfectly all right, but that in his opinion most of them had a pretty soft life at the Pribilofs and after working outside for a year or two would be anxious to get back there. . . .
>
> I further said to Dr. Gabrielson that in my opinion it would be of doubtful legality to say to a native of the Pribilof Islands that if he did not go back when we resumed sealing operations, he could never do so. Dr. Gabrielson concurred in this thought.
>
> Dr. Gabrielson said that if some of the natives desired to remain in Alaska or wanted to go to the States to be on their own, they could do so, but of course with the beginning of such departure from our jurisdiction, they would receive no benefits or funds from this Service.[138]

Bower tried to make sure that these views reached Johnston, but he may have been aware of the damage already done. In the end, only a handful of Aleuts remained in Juneau and did not return with the others to the Pribilofs.

Killisnoo

> The people hated this tiny tree-covered island with poor, rocky beaches. There was no place to go hiking, as on large, grassy Atka. Many of the older men became sick and passed on. The younger people became acquainted with the Angoon Indians on Admiralty Island. Drinking became excessive and this led to much trouble. . . . We did our best to keep up the morale.[139]

The 83 Aleuts from Atka were evacuated to Killisnoo Island, three miles from Angoon, opposite the southern tip of Admiralty Island. The closest post office and radio facility was in Angoon, and a weekly boat delivered mail and supplies. The Aleuts arrived on June 25, 1942, with little more than the barest personal possessions. Their new home was a herring cannery which had not been occupied for ten years.

From his ship's stores, Captain Downey of the *Delarof* gave evacuees a four-day supply of food, cooking supplies, a mattress for each adult, and blankets, as he had for the Pribilovians evacuated to Funter Bay. Health officials soon arrived to give inoculations and checkups, and more food and clothing came from Juneau. Killisnoo was managed by schoolteachers employed by the Office of Indian Affairs; Ralph and Ruby Magee accompanied the Atkans to Killisnoo and stayed for a year until they were replaced by Joe and Vivian Kaklen, a native Alaskan non-Aleut couple, followed by Mr. and Mrs. Beebe.[140]

Cabins and houses at the cannery were old and flimsy, but most had stoves and cots or beds.[141] Driftwood to heat the buildings was abundant. A laundry and one bathtub were also available. A small spring yielded very little water, and rain became their major source of supply. There were three privies for more than 80 people. An old messhall was converted into a schoolroom whose desks and benches were built by the best Atkan carpenter, supplies came from Juneau and, in September, school opened. But the winter of 1942 was the coldest in 50 years. Food froze solid and meat was scarce. Many of the older people died.

A doctor and a nurse visited once during the Atkans' three-year stay in southeastern Alaska. The doctor stayed four months, the nurse only two weeks. According to the Atkans, "Dr. Bauer did not ask any questions, but he treated everyone in the camp for V.D. without verification. All that time, the people were not aware that he was treating them for V.D."[142]

After six months at Killisnoo, most of the able-bodied men secured work at Excursion Inlet repairing boats for the government. Others worked near Juneau for the forestry department, on Japonski Island in construction or in the canneries. The young men were drafted. Once the Aleuts obtained employment they no longer received free food and clothing, and the OIA schoolteachers began charging them for items at the store:

> This change did not go over so well with the people. They seemed to think that they should continue to receive the food and clothing free so they could use their money for mail order business and the many drinking parties they felt they owed the Angoon Indians. It was some time before they became reconciled to the change.[143]

Wrangell Institute

Wrangell Institute was the stopover site for Aleuts evacuated from the villages of Nikolski, Akutan, Biorka, Kashega and Makushin until they could be moved to permanent evacuation camps at Ward Lake and Burnett Inlet. The Institute was an OIA boarding school whose principal, George Barrett, was instrumental in selecting the Aleuts' eventual evacuation sites.

For two weeks the Aleuts camped in Army tents on the school grounds. They were given three meals a day, primarily dog salmon, tea and bread. Men and women, young and old, were assigned chores in the Institute's kitchen, laundry and bakery.[144] They also built a barge to transport lumber and other materials to Ward Lake.

Army, Navy and civilian doctors examined the Aleuts; yet, according to one evacuee, they were not treated for tuberculosis, pneumonia, viruses or shock. Head lice were treated, however, and some children and adults were close-cropped, their scalps doused with kerosene to exterminate the parasites.[145]

Wrangell Institute provided sixth through twelfth grades for children covered by the OIA. A former pupil informed the Commission that the school had a capacity of 350 children, but, after evacuation, Aleut children from the camps swelled its ranks to 750. Classrooms were so crowded that eighth graders with the highest grades were skipped to ninth grade. Food remained insufficient, and a year after the influx of new students, the school's health center was still understaffed.[146]

Ward Lake

"My first impression . . . was that of being put in prison."[147]

After their stopover at Wrangell Institute, approximately 200 Aleuts were taken to Ward Lake, sometimes called Ward Cove, an old Civilian Conservation Corps camp eight miles from Ketchikan. Not all were strangers. Some had met while working outside their villages; others had married from one village into another.[148]

The government "officials" at Ward Lake were Barbara and Samuel Whitfield—an OIA schoolteacher and her handyman husband who later left to join the Coast Guard. The Whitfields, who had been stationed with the Aleuts on Nikolski before evacuation, were joined by Fred Geeslin, an OIA resettlement officer.

The CCC camp was nine small cabins and four communal buildings. Each cabin had a small kitchen and a bedroom with two bunk beds. With lumber brought from Wrangell Institute, the Aleuts built additional housing and furniture. Scrap cardboard was used for insulation. Each household was issued a wood burning stove.[149] Shared facilities for the nearly 200 evacuees included an outhouse; a school; a church; and a laundry with a large tin basin, four cold-water faucets and two shower stalls. Water was hauled in buckets from an outside hydrant to each cabin, heated, then taken to the laundry. The village outhouse was a long open trough without seats, and insects were thick, despite the toilet's constant flow of water.[150]

Not everyone lived at the Ward Lake settlement, however. One woman and her family, who thought the Ward Lake houses "shacks," moved into Ketchikan, as did two or three others. Two girls roomed in the Ketchikan hospital where they worked.[151]

Neither the OIA nor any other government agency provided the Aleuts with transportation into town. Taxis could be called but the only telephone was at the OIA school—and the teacher would not let the Aleuts use it.[152] The evacuees were saved from complete isolation by a local entrepreneur, Eugene Wacker, who drove evacuees to Ketchikan for 35 cents each way:

> Now we were able to shop and ride into town to our jobs. . . . He charged us fare between points, but without his consideration and care we would not have done well for jobs and supplies we needed in town.[153]

Wacker also helped the Aleuts find jobs; whenever he heard of an opening,

> [H]e came to our camp to tell us about it and drove those who wanted the job into town. He then would also drive us back to the camp after work. . . . Most of us might have had to go to other communities seeking jobs, but because of him we were near our families at camp. . . . Eugene Wacker did this for the three years we were at Ward Lake.[154]

The men found employment at the canneries and sawmills of Ketchikan, in commercial fishing at Sitka, and in construction at the Army base at Metlakatla.[155] Some were in Alaska Sea Scouts, and during the summers of 1943 and 1944, several went up to work for the Aleutian Livestock Company, a sheep ranch near Nikolski.[156] As at Killisnoo, the Aleuts at Ward Lake no longer received free food and other supplies after the men found work.

Health. Not long after they had come to Ward Lake, the Aleuts were visited by at least one doctor and nurse who found many ill and quarantined those with infectious diseases. Yet, after being diagnosed, the Aleuts say they never received treatment.[157] Generally the OIA schoolteacher, Mrs. Whitfield, acted as the camp's health aide. Harry C. McCain, Ketchikan's Chairman of Police, Health and Sanitation, wrote Governor Gruening on May 19, 1943, that the medical situation was very poor:

[W]e have recently been forced to quarantine their camp in order
. . . to . . . catch up to their venereal disease situation. . . . These
people are also badly honeycombed with tuberculosis, from which
disease a considerable number have died since they were placed
at Ward Cove.[158]

McCain was concerned for the townspeople:

There are a large number of service men in and near Ketchikan
and neither they nor the civilians should be infected with their
diseased conditions. . . . the proprietor of the Totem Lunch in-
quired whether or not she could refuse their patronage for the
reason they were unsanitary and diseased and thus obnoxious to
her regular customers besides requiring an unusual amount of
trouble in sterilizing of their dishes . . . [E]ven the bars would
much prefer not to have their patronage. . . . Therefore we desire
to protest their being kept quartered at Ward Cove and to suggest
they ought to be moved to some suitable location where they
would not have immediate contacts with large numbers of people.[159]

Ketchikan's city council became increasingly involved with the
problem. Barbara Whitfield appealed to the city council on behalf of
the Aleuts, and the Akutan village chief, Mark Petikoff, wrote a letter
to the *Alaska Fishing News* protesting that the Aleuts had been "made
a football;" they demanded "the same treatment as any other group of
citizens" but were "not asking any special favors." It would have been
more useful, he said, to have prevented characters like the whiskey
bootleggers from exploiting the Aleuts in the first place.[160]

Sentiment in Ketchikan grew more sympathetic toward the Aleuts
as some of the townspeople gradually began to recognize the plight of
these war refugees: uprooted from their homes, in less than a year at
Ward Lake, 20 out of less than 200 people had perished and another
half dozen had been sent out for tubercular care. The death rate at
Ward Lake was one of the highest of all the Aleut evacuation camps.

On May 27, 1943, Mayor J.A. Talbot of Ketchikan wrote Superintendent Claude Hirst of the Alaska Indian Service protesting the
poor medical care given the Aleuts. Hirst responded that the Indian
Service had operated a clinic before the city started one and was paying
half the expenses of the city's new clinic. The superintendent also
added that before the war a tuberculosis sanitarium had been recommended for southeastern Alaska and that "we are doing everything
we possibly can with the facilities that have been furnished us."[161]

The Adjustment to Ketchikan. Many Aleuts found the adjustment
to southeastern Alaska difficult, if not fatal:

The older people, especially, said they did not like the trees, which hemmed them in so that they could not see nor breathe freely. . . . Another big complaint was the forced change in economy. Legal restrictions upon hunting and fishing were imposed, and natural food was simply not available . . . The large number of policemen, and their readiness to arrest on the slightest pretext, was also remarked upon more than once. . . . Ridicule, to which the Aleuts were subjected by whites, increased their sensitivity to their status as "natives" and made them more secretive about their customs.[162]

According to Gerald Berreman, an anthropologist who studied Nikolski in the early 1950's:

Not everything in Ward Lake was unpleasant to these people, however. The company of other Aleuts was generally enjoyed. . . . Schooling was also easier to obtain. . . . The most enjoyed aspects . . . were the blessings of western urban society, which money, earned at numerous available jobs, could buy. These were primarily liquor, dancing, and movies.[163]

Nonetheless, Berreman concluded that most villagers were very unhappy:

Everything they were used to was left behind. . . . Money, liquor, and movies were hopeless substitutions for the security of old and familiar ways. . . . Even those who enjoyed "Southeast" welcomed the anticipated return. Those who were offered permanent jobs chose to go back to the old life instead.[164]

Burnett Inlet

The Unalaska evacuees were moved in August 1942 from their temporary quarters at Wrangell Institute to Burnett Inlet, which became their home. They remained at the abandoned cannery on Etolin Island until April 1945. Like Killisnoo and Ward Lake, Burnett Inlet was managed by an OIA schoolteacher and her husband, Edythe J. and Elmer D. Long.

Conditions at Burnett Inlet, although difficult, were not as severe as in the other camps. While the facilities were poor when evacuees arrived, cannery buildings were reconditioned, roughly winterized and converted into small apartments for single people and small families. In addition, four small family houses, a school, teachers' quarters, and a church were built.[165]

In May 1943, Edythe Long wrote that it was "discouraging to . . . hear remarks made to the effect that people are hungry" and that there was "practically no limit to the amount and variety of food furnished these people. . . . With the exception of a few hard to secure items which we divide and ration there has been no limit to the amount of food the evacuees have been issued or allowed to purchase."[166]

As with the evacuees at Killisnoo and Ward Lake, the Aleuts at Burnett Inlet were encouraged to become "as self-sustaining as possible, in accordance with instructions from our Chicago headquarters."[167] While the Aleuts reconditioned some cannery buildings and built others, they were not compensated for their labor beyond "necessary subsistence and other supplies."[168] After the housing was completed, the Aleuts were expected to find jobs and were thereafter charged for supplies.[169]

Health care at Burnett Inlet was poor, but fortunately the death toll was not as high as in other camps. An Aleut midwife delivered babies for mothers who were unable to reach Wrangell in time, and evacuees also sought her help in treating cuts, bruises and illnesses.[170]

One Evacuee's View of Life at Burnett Inlet. Martha Newell was part Aleut and, because she did not wish to accompany her husband when he left for the Lower 48, she was evacuated with the other Aleuts from Unalaska. In March 1943, she wrote her husband, Kenneth, that "[W]e're all anxious to go home. I can't stand thinking of staying another winter, and most of the folks feel the same as there's no work and we are paying for our food,"[171] and "I can't say we are living in good houses. They are all warehouses . . ."[172] She encouraged her husband to write their friend, Congressional Delegate Anthony Dimond.

Kenneth Newell's April letter of complaint to Dimond was promptly brought to the attention of Claude Hirst and Fred Geeslin of the Alaska Indian Service. According to the Indian Service's reply:

> In general the people there [Burnett Inlet] are satisfied and appreciate the efforts being made by the personnel of this office to accommodate them. . . . The complaint of Mrs. Newell is the first to our knowledge. . . . Naturally these people hear of the Pribiloffs [sic] going back, and think they should go back also . . . Even though these evacuees may be receiving less than Japs in concentration camps, as stated by Mrs. Newell, I am sure that the large majority of them are satisfied under the present conditions, and they have expressed that they wish to be self-supporting as they were at their original homes where there are wage earners in their families.[173]

Burnett Inlet schoolteacher Edythe Long also responded to Mrs. Newell's complaints:

> Mrs. Newell has a firm conviction that the more complaints she registers and the more dissatisfaction and discontent she can arouse amongst the evacuees here the sooner the Authorities will be

obliged to move her back to Unalaska. Her entire being is centered on that one purpose—to go back to her home this spring, and it seems she will go to any lengths even of gross misrepresentation to attain this end. She . . . refuses to face the fact that Unalaska is in the war zone and that no women or children can be returned there at present regardless of anyone's views or wishes. She not only complains for herself but goes from house to house spreading discontent . . . Several people have expressed disgust at her unreasonable talk and refuse to listen to her.[174]

Martha Newell died at Burnett Inlet and was returned home to Unalaska for burial.[175]

RETURN TO THE ISLANDS

The Pribilof Islands

After visiting Funter Bay in September 1943, FWS Director Ira Gabrielson was convinced that the Aleuts should be returned to the Pribilofs that fall, and FWS received War Department approval for a return to St. George and tentative approval for St. Paul.[176] But, as local agent McMillin emphasized, there were no furniture and cook stoves on St. George, nor would present supplies last beyond the end of October. He reported that the Aleuts refused to remain under those conditions.[177] He emphatically outlined his views in a telegram to Assistant Superintendent Morton:

> WHOEVER PUSHING FANTASTIC IDEA REHABILITATE PRIBILOFS NOT ACQUAINTED WITH CONDITIONS THIS TIME OF YEAR IN BERING SEA LANDINGS HERE FROM NOW ON VERY UNCERTAIN FOR ANY AMOUNT CARGO WORK AND FOR CONVEYING WOMEN CHILDREN AND SICK PEOPLE STOP CRIMINAL CHARGES SHOULD BE PREFERRED UPON PERSON RESPONSIBLE UNLESS REHABILITATION PLANS DROPPED FOR PRESENT UNTIL SUPPLIES AND EQUIPMENT OBTAINED TO PROPERLY EQUIP STATION.[178]

The FWS officials were surprised:

> YOUR WIRES THIS DATE FIRST INFORMATION REGARDING TRUE CONDITIONS PRIBILOFS.[179]
> WE HAVE ASSUMED ALL ALONG THAT JOHNSTON AND BENSON CONCURRED IN REHABILITATION ST. GEORGE NATIVES THIS FALL AND THAT ONLY QUESTION WAS REGARDING ST. PAUL. THIS OFFICE DOES NOT UNDER-

STAND WHY PLANS FOR ST. GEORGE NEED CHANG-
ING.[180]

FWS Director Gabrielson was reluctant to decide on the Aleuts'
return to the Pribilofs solely on the basis of Agent McMillin's opinion.
Johnston was scheduled to return shortly from a trip to the islands,
and Gabrielson was anxious to learn the superintendent's views before
coming to a final decision.[181] The superintendent, however, arrogated
the authority of his superior; without conferring with Gabrielson, Johnston decided that "neither island would be rehabilitated this fall" and
issued orders to that effect before leaving the Pribilofs.[182]

Despite Johnston's orders to the contrary, however, plans moved
forward to rehabilitate St. George Island partially. One dozen married
and three single men were to remain on the island, where their families
would join them.[183] In the end, the Aleut families "declined their
return" to St. George that fall, and the men on the island finally
departed for Funter Bay on November 11, 1943.[184] The FWS was
forced to prepare for another winter at the evacuation camp, and Chief
Bower wired Gabrielson suggesting that a Public Health nurse and
doctor should be detailed to Funter Bay.[185] It is unclear why the Aleuts
chose not to return then—because of poor health, inadequate supplies
on the island, the lateness of the season and likelihood of poor travel
conditions, or for other reasons. The Commission found no documents
that cast light upon the Aleuts' decision.

By mid-March 1944, arrangements had been made for an Army
transport to return the Pribilovians about May 1, and this time the
plans went ahead. No earlier return was possible because drift ice
surrounded the Pribilofs, and approximately 4,000 tons of supplies and
equipment had to be purchased after appropriations became available.[186]

Funding the Return

As the evacuated Aleuts faced another southeastern Alaskan winter
of continuing decimation from disease, the Interior Department negotiated with the War and Navy Departments for funds and services
to meet the expense of return and rehabilitation. Interior had been
using its Civilian Food Reserve Funds, but it was "very questionable
whether these emergency funds will continue to be available after July
1, 1944, for the care of these Aleut refugees."[187]

On May 23, 1944, the Army, Navy and OIA jointly concluded
that the OIA should administer the resettlement. The Army agreed to
make an initial allotment of $58,000 and the Navy $129,000 to finance

the return and rehabilitation of the islands, with the understanding that both would make subsequent allotments if required. In addition, the Army and Navy were to transfer to the OIA surplus materials and supplies for resettlement.[188]

On August 7, 1944, President Roosevelt approved an allocation of $200,000 from his "Emergency Fund for the President, National Defense, 1942–45" to be used by the Interior Department for rehabilitation of the Aleutian and Pribilof Islands. This sum was for restoration, repair, reconstruction and equipment of public and private buildings and other property, as well as for subsistence of the Aleuts. The allocation included a maximum of $25,000 in aggregate payment of claims for damages suffered by Aleut and white inhabitants, but it excluded claims of commercial or business firms.[189] Because losses were greater than originally anticipated, on July 21, 1945, the OIA requested an additional allotment of $45,000 in order to cover expenses,[190] and a transfer of $51,725 was made from the President's Fund. According to federal budget figures, the actual obligations for "refunds, awards and indemnities" eventually totalled $31,441. For "equipment," "supplies and materials" the total was $177,081.[191]

The Aleutian Islands

Return to the Aleutians proved more difficult than returning to the Pribilofs. In April 1944, Navy and OIA officials met and OIA then authorized the Commander of the Alaska Sector to send the following message to the Chief of Naval Operations:

> In view of impracticability of obtaining school teachers who can act as Bureau of Indian Affairs representatives the difficulty of supplying the villages and impossibility of prevention of intermingling with military personnel they are not desirous of returning Aleuts to the Aleutian Chain.[192]

The OIA officials sent similar messages to their superiors,[193] and proposed moving the Aleuts at Ward Lake to Funter Bay when the Pribilovians had left.

Within the next two weeks, the Alaska Indian Service changed its position. On April 26, B. W. Thoron, Director of the Interior Division of Territories, radiogrammed Governor Gruening seeking his views on the Aleuts' return to the islands that spring. Thoron believed that early resettlement was desirable despite the lack of teachers.[194] Gruening agreed, and stated that the OIA superintendent in Juneau concurred.[195]

Interior assumed that the Aleuts' return was imminent.[196] The status of the village of Unalaska, however, remained unsettled because

of its proximity to Dutch Harbor; accordingly, the OIA was authorized
to defer return by the Unalaskans if no teachers could be found.[197]

On May 13, the War Department directed the Commanding General of the Alaska Department to take necessary action to return the
Aleuts to the islands and rehabilitate their homes. By May 23, the
Army, Navy and Office of Indian Affairs had jointly concluded that the
great variety of local problems meant that OIA's Alaska Indian Service
was best qualified to administer the project. Neither the Army nor the
Navy would undertake any aspect of rehabilitation beyond handling
local relations between Aleuts and military personnel.[198]

Despite apparent agreement, a commitment to move ahead, and
funds to finance rehabilitation, no Aleutian islanders were returned to
the islands that summer, that fall, or at any time during 1944. They
did not leave southeastern Alaska until nearly a year later, April 17,
1945. This delay remains unexplained; it is possible that Lt. General
Delos Emmons wished to reevaluate the situation after replacing Simon
Buckner as commanding general in June 1944. The Commission was
unable to locate any documents beyond those describing the inter-
agency agreement of May 1944 and the Aleuts' arrival on the islands
in April 1945.

RESETTLEMENT

Although the Aleuts were delighted to return to their island homes
after years in southeastern Alaska, they found communities that had
been vandalized and looted by occupying American military forces.
Rehabilitation assessments made for each village only a year after the
Aleuts were evacuated describe disturbingly similar conditions. Reports on Unalaska were typical:

> All buildings were damaged due to lack of normal care and upkeep.
> . . . The furnishings, clothing and personal effects remaining in
> the homes showed, with few exceptions, evidence of weather
> damage and damage by rats. Inspection of contents revealed ex-
> tensive evidence of widespread wanton destruction of property
> and vandalism. Contents of closed packing boxes, trunks and cup-
> boards had been ransacked. Clothing had been scattered over
> floors, trampled and fouled. Dishes, furniture, stoves, radios,
> phonographs, books, and other items had been broken or dam-
> aged. Many items listed on inventories furnished by the occupants
> of the houses were entirely missing. . . . It appears that armed

forces personnel and civilians alike have been responsible for this vandalism and that it occurred over a period of many months.[199]

Perhaps the greatest loss to personal property occurred at the time the Army conducted its clean up of the village in June of 1943. Large numbers of soldiers were in the area at that time removing rubbish and outbuildings and many houses were entered unofficially and souvenirs and other articles were taken.[200]

Many items had been "borrowed" and misplaced:

> Sergie Savaroff said that a new range that he had bought, a coal range—wood range—was gone from his house, a big heavy thing. It was found at an officers' quarters in Umnak; that is about eighty miles north of Nikolski. And his dory that he had left there with an outboard motor—was found in Chernofski, that had been used and not returned.[201]

Many of the Aleuts were forced to camp outdoors at first because their old homes had not yet been repaired and many proved uninhabitable. The Unalaskans were provided with 16 by 20 Army cabanas, two or three for the larger families and "[e]veryone seemed to be contended [sic] with that."[202] Later, it was discovered that the cabanas had to be chained down because of the 90 mph Aleutian winds. Until their village (which had been burned to the ground by the Navy) could be rebuilt, the Atkans lived for a year in Quonset huts shared by as many as nine people in "conditions worse than the camps."[203]

The Aleuts repaired and rebuilt their homes themselves. They received free groceries until their homes were ready. The food, building and repair supplies were procured locally—mostly military surplus, and otherwise purchased primarily from the Northern Commercial Company in Unalaska.[204]

Their losses and resettlement costs were higher than what was originally estimated by the April 1944 survey of evacuated villages. By the time the Aleuts actually returned to the islands, a year had elapsed and very few of the items previously listed as intact could be found in their homes. All household effects and equipment the Aleuts had left behind were missing.[205]

The evacuated Aleuts suffered material losses for which they were never fully recompensed, either in kind or in cash. As devout followers of the Russian Orthodox faith, the Aleuts treasured religious icons brought from czarist Russia and other family heirlooms that represented their greatest spiritual as well as material loss. They were priceless to the Aleuts. Possessions such as houses, furniture, boats and fishing gear were either never replaced or replaced by markedly inferior goods, testified the Aleuts. Some shipments of goods intended for the islands never arrived, they say, speculating that the merchandise was diverted to stores on the mainland. The OIA itself found that its first resettlement officer was not competent to the task of supplying and resettling the Aleuts.[206] His more effective replacement, Fred Geeslin, could not recall filing claims for lost goods or waiting for freight that never arrived, although the deputy United States marshal who eventually took over as resettlement officer testified before the Commission that Geeslin had made a list of items stolen or taken from homes and had turned over a large sheaf of freight bills consigned to various people that had "lost stuff," that "probably five or six" ever received freight, and that OIA had never responded to letters about the loss of freight.[207] Geeslin said that all supplies were purchased locally, and he did not recall any expectation that the Aleuts' personal possessions would be replaced or that some type of monetary compensation would be received.[208]

The federal budget indicates that $31,441 was spent for "refunds, award and indemnities" to Aleut and white evacuees from the Aleutian and Pribilof Islands; $130,719 was spent for "supplies and materials;" and $46,362 for "equipment."[209] The Commission has been unable to recover any further details of these expenditures, the disposition of claims filed, shipping lists, or other documents to verify or disprove the Aleuts' allegations.

World War II Remains Still on Islands. U.S. and Japanese military debris from World War II still litters the Aleutians. Most of it is unsightly; some is hazardous or polluting. Dilapidated military structures such as Quonset huts and hangars, leaky oil and chemical drums, boilers, diesel engines, generators, partially destroyed vehicles, weapon magazines, live munitions and various other pieces of debris are constant, ugly reminders that World War II touched the islands. Large concentrations of debris remain at twelve sites of major military operations or installations during and shortly after World War II; lesser quantities litter sixteen other sites. Ten of the 28 sites are in inhabited areas.[210] On Atka, children used to entertain themselves by placing the powder from unused 50-caliber machinegun shells in empty beer cans and igniting them.[211] As recently as 1979, nine cases of exposed TNT were discovered.[212]

There is so much debris that to remove safety hazards, pollutants and standing structures from areas within existing road networks, i.e., from half the sites, would require approximately 24,260 person-days of direct labor at a total cost of approximately $98 million 1979 dollars. A cleanup limited to hazardous and polluting debris from inhabited areas, ignoring aesthetic considerations, would require 3,272 person-days at a total cost of about $28 million.[213]

EFFECTS OF EVACUATION

Removing the Aleuts from their island homes caused irrevocable change in their way of life. Some may contend that change was inevitable, and that evacuation merely accelerated the process of assimilating "American" culture. Such an argument, however, ignores the way change came about: the Aleuts had their culture snatched from them; they had no choice.

One of the most disturbing consequences of evacuation was the high mortality rate among Aleuts, particularly the elders. Sporadic medical care in the camps no doubt contributed to many deaths. Admittedly, doctors and nurses were no more available in the Aleutians (except Unalaska) than in southeastern Alaska.[214] But the need in "Southeast" was greater. For the Aleuts, often substandard, unsanitary and crowded living conditions deepened the psychological trauma of losing all their possessions after a sudden uprooting and a voyage in the holds of ships. Adaptation to a foreign, heavily-forested environment followed; all these experiences together imposed stresses greater than many people could withstand, and many perished.

The loss of a generation of village elders has had a cultural impact far beyond the grief and pain to their own families. Among those who died were most of the last people on earth who knew the old Aleut ways, how to make the skin boats, traditional clothing or local styles of basketry. The deaths of younger people, in a population with an historically low birth rate, further endangers the Aleuts' survival as a distinct group.

The government's island resettlement policies further eroded the traditional way of life. Not all Aleuts who were evacuated returned to the islands; many had died, some chose greater economic opportunities on the outside, others outmarried. The government, in addition, forbade any return to certain islands. After a wage-earning economy evolved on the islands during the 1900's the Aleuts grew sensitive to industry and government actions that affected employment, education and government expenditures. Economic pressures to locate in areas of broader, more stable economic opportunity prompted substantial migration from smaller to larger villages and beyond the Aleutian chain as well.[215]

Evacuation accelerated these migration patterns and centralized the population. The villages of Makushin, Biorka, Kashega and Chernofski disappeared after the war, their few surviving villagers never returning to those outposts.

Finally, the American military presence on the islands left a heavy mark. Foxes, a cash "crop," and subsistence animals such as seals and caribou, were slaughtered in great numbers as a pastime by bored servicemen and ship crews. Military builders filled in the rich herring-spawning lagoons of Unalaska; pond and tidal-harvest foods were nearly destroyed by oil spills from military vessels.[216] Military debris remains to endanger and pollute many sites.

Through the insult of massive looting and vandalism of their homes and places of worship by American military forces, the Aleuts lost invaluable tangible ties to their past. Houses can eventually be rebuilt and refurnished, but stolen family mementos, heirlooms and religious icons brought from czarist Russia in the early 1800's cannot be recovered.

Removal from their homeland permanently changed nearly every aspect of Aleut life. The many who died in the camps were a huge loss to both family and community which also endangers the future of the Aleuts as a distinct people. Evacuation meant irreversible cultural erosion, destroying their means of pursuing a traditional subsistence way of life. They lost artifacts, but also the ability to recreate them. They lost (or found much reduced) the animals and sea creatures that had been essential to traditional subsistence. The evacuation also destroyed many of the Aleuts' ties to their personal and religious pasts. America, proud of its cultural diversity, thereby lost a distinctive part of itself.

Notes

Parts I and II

NOTE ON ABBREVIATIONS

The Commission's report is based upon hearings, archival research and secondary sources. Some of the more than 750 witnesses composed written testimony to augment their oral statements; other persons submitted written statements but did not testify. Notes therefore cite personal statements and materials under three heads: "testimony" (for oral statements before the Commission), "written testimony" and "unsolicited testimony."

Abbreviations that designate material from major archives and research libraries appear below. The thousands of documents and secondary sources assembled by the Commission required an internal locator system indicated by "CWRIC" followed by a page number. In the Aleut chapter, some CWRIC citations refer to separate files on the war and evacuation in Alaska, cited as "CWRIC AL". At this writing, it is anticipated that, no matter which archive houses Commission files, the locator system will be useful, so it has been included. Other abbreviations include:

Bancroft Library: University of California, Berkeley; collection on Japanese American evacuation and resettlement. To locate individual documents see catalog of this material by Edward N. Barnhart (Berkeley: University of California General Library, 1958).

DOJ: Department of Justice records, Washington, DC; subsequent numbers indicate DOJ files.

FBI: Federal Bureau of Investigation records, Washington, DC.

FDRL: Franklin Delano Roosevelt Library, Hyde Park, NY.

HR: U.S. House of Representatives reports.

LC: Library of Congress, Washington, DC, all divisions.

NARS. RG: National Archives and Records Service, Washington, DC; Record Group.

Sterling Library: Yale University, New Haven, CT; Henry L. Stimson Papers, Manuscript Group No. 465.

1

Before Pearl Harbor

1. For historical background on the pertinent application of the naturalization laws, see *Ozawa* v. *United States*, 260 U.S. 178 (1922); Stefan Thernstrom, ed., *Harvard Encyclopedia of American Ethnic Groups* (Cambridge and London: Belknap Press of Harvard University Press, 1980), pp. 734–48.

2. *In re Ah Yup*, 1 Fed. Cases 223 (Cir. Ct., D. Calif. 1878) (decision of Circuit Judge Sawyer).

3. *Ozawa* v. *United States*, 260 U.S. 178 (1922).

4. At the time of the First World War, it appeared that citizenship was promised to aliens who volunteered to serve in the American military forces; although Japanese aliens volunteered, they were not given citizenship when the courts came to review the law. Bill Hosokawa, *Nisei: The Quiet Americans* (New York: William Morrow & Co., 1969), p. 91; see *In re Charr*, 273 Fed. 207 (W.D. Mo. 1921).

5. Roger Daniels, *The Politics of Prejudice* (Berkeley: University of California Press, 1962), pp. 16–19.

6. In 1849, the Supreme Court decided in the *Passenger Cases* that regulation of immigration was the exclusive domain of the federal government. *Smith* v. *Turner* and *Norris* v. *The City of Boston*, 48 U.S. 282 (1849).

7. Daniels, *Politics of Prejudice*, p. 18.

8. 22 Stat. 58 (May 6, 1882); 27 Stat. 25 (May 5, 1892); 32 Stat. 176 (Apr. 29, 1902).

9. Act to repeal the Chinese Exclusion Acts, to establish quotas, and for other purposes, 57 Stat. 600 (Dec. 17, 1943).

10. William Langer, *An Encyclopedia of World History*, 4th ed. (Boston: Houghton Mifflin, 1968), pp. 815, 919.

11. Daniels, *Politics of Prejudice*, pp. 1–3.

12. *Ibid.*, pp. 2-4.

13. Robert A. Wilson and Bill Hosokawa, *East to America* (New York: William Morrow & Co., 1980), p. 141.

14. Daniels, *Politics of Prejudice*, pp. 3–5.

15. *Ibid.*, pp. 6–7.

16. Wilson and Hosokawa, *East to America*, p. 116.

17. Daniels, *Politics of Prejudice*, p. 1 and Appendix A.

18. Thomas Sowell, *Ethnic America* (New York: Basic Books, Inc., 1981), p. 157; Yasuo Wakatsuki, "Japanese Emigration to the United States, 1866–1924" in *Perspectives in American History*, vol. 12 (1979), p. 465.

19. Daniels, *Politics of Prejudice*, p. 13; see also Leonard Broom and Ruth

Riemer, *Removal and Return* (Berkeley: University of California Press, 1949), p. 7.

20. Carey McWilliams, *Prejudice* (Boston: Little, Brown and Co., 1945), pp. 77–80.

21. Sowell, *Ethnic America*, pp. 155-79.

22. Daniels, *Politics of Prejudice*, p. 1.

23. Bureau of the Census, *Census of Population 1970*, vol. 1, Characteristics of the Population, part 6 (Washington, DC: U.S. Government Printing Office, 1973), p. 86.

24. McWilliams, *Prejudice*, pp. 81-83; see also Jacobus tenBroek, Edward N. Barnhart and Floyd Matson, *Prejudice, War and the Constitution* (Berkeley: University of California Press, 1954), p. 12.

25. McWilliams, *Prejudice*, pp. 77–80.

26. Daniels, *Politics of Prejudice*, pp. 21–22.

27. Remarks quoted from the *San Francisco Examiner* and *San Francisco Chronicle*, both for May 8, 1900, set out in Daniels, *Politics of Prejudice*, p. 21.

28. Daniels, *Politics of Prejudice*, pp. 22–23. This was the beginning of significant labor activity against the Japanese in the United States.

29. Tamotsu Shibutani, *The Derelicts of Company K* (Berkeley: University of California Press, 1978), p. 22.

30. Daniels, *Politics of Prejudice*, pp. 24–27. The resolution asked Congress to limit and diminish the further immigration of Japanese, and set forth ten points against the Japanese which were insulting and inaccurate.

31. *Ibid.*, pp. 27–29.

32. Shibutani, *Derelicts of Company K*, pp. 21–22.

33. Daniels, *Politics of Prejudice*, pp. 27–28. The executive committee of the Socialist Party in California also resolved, in 1906, to oppose Asiatic immigration. Two small organizations, also of laborers, worked with the League: the Anti-Jap Laundry League, and the Anti-Japanese League of Alameda County (a largely fictitious organization). *Ibid.*, pp. 28–30.

34. *Ibid.*, pp. 32–40.

35. *Ibid.*, pp. 34–43; Hosokawa, *Nisei*, p. 89.

36. Daniels, *Politics of Prejudice*, pp. 33–34; Executive Order 589 (March 14, 1907), revoked by Executive Order 10009 (October 18, 1948).

37. tenBroek, *Prejudice, War*, p. 65; see generally Daniels, *Politics of Prejudice*, pp. 50–64.

38. Shibutani, *Derelicts of Company K*, p. 23.

39. Daniels, *Politics of Prejudice*, pp. 61–64, regarding the inefficacy of the Webb-Heney Act; see also tenBroek, *Prejudice, War*, p. 51; McWilliams, *Prejudice*, p. 49.

40. Daniels, *Politics of Prejudice*, pp. 61–64, 79; tenBroek, *Prejudice, War*, pp. 41–42.

41. The Native Sons of the Golden West was an exclusive organization of men born in California, dedicated to preserving the state "as it has always been and God himself intended it shall always be—the White Man's Paradise." Anti-Japanese activity was a focus of the Native Sons for years. The American Legion has a long history of anti-Japanese activity. At its first convention, in

November, 1919, it adopted an anti-Japanese policy. Labor continued to be anti-Japanese, although moving the Japanese from the land, which the policies of some labor groups supported, would most quickly cause cheap labor competition. The California State Grange and the California State Farm Bureau Federation initiated organized anti-Japanese activity in 1920. Their goals were ouster of the Japanese from the state's farmlands, and eventually, their total exclusion. tenBroek, *Prejudice, War*, pp. 32–57; Daniels, *Politics of Prejudice*, pp. 85–87.

42. Shibutani, *Derelicts of Company K*, p. 24.

43. tenBroek, *Prejudice, War*, pp. 59–62.

44. Audrie Girdner and Anne Loftis, *The Great Betrayal: The Evacuation of the Japanese-Americans During World War II* (London: The Macmillan Company, 1969), pp. 92–93.

45. From the Exclusion League's letterhead, cited by Daniels, *Politics of Prejudice*, p. 85.

46. Daniels, *Politics of Prejudice*, p. 88.

47. Girdner and Loftis, *Great Betrayal*, p. 61.

48. Initiative No. 1, Statutes and Amendments to the Codes of California, 1921, p. xxxvii.

49. Daniels, *Politics of Prejudice*, p. 88; see also McWilliams, *Prejudice*, p. 65.

50. Masakazu Iwata, "Summary of *Planted In Good Soil*: Issei Agriculture in the Pacific Coast States," testimony of Japanese American Citizens League National Committee for Redress, Dec. 23, 1981, p. 257. The statistics were:

Year	*Acres held in California by Ethnic Japanese*
1905	62,048
1908	134,057
1918	390,635
1929	328,350

51. Daniels, *Politics of Prejudice*, p. 1.

52. Wilson and Hosokawa, *East to America*, p. 71.

53. *Harvard Encyclopedia of American Ethnic Groups*, p. 563.

54. *Ibid.*, p. 562.

55. Daniels, *Politics of Prejudice*, p. 44.

56. *Ibid.*, pp. 41, 91.

57. *Ibid.*, p. 91.

58. Hosokawa, *Nisei*, p. 45; Girdner and Loftis, *Great Betrayal*, p. 66.

59. tenBroek, *Prejudice, War*, p. 25.

60. Frank F. Chuman, *The Bamboo People: The Law and Japanese Americans* (Del Mar, CA: Publisher's Inc., 1976), p. 111.

61. Bill Hosokawa, *JACL In Quest of Justice* (New York: William Morrow & Co., 1982), p. 105.

62. Morton Grodzins, *Americans Betrayed: Politics and the Japanese Evacuation* (Chicago and London: University of Chicago Press, 1949), p. 11.

63. McWilliams, *Prejudice*, p. 40.

64. Sowell, *Ethnic America*, p. 65.

65. McWilliams, *Prejudice*, pp. 26–29.

66. Daniels, *Politics of Prejudice*, pp. 69, 76–77; tenBroek, *Prejudice, War*, pp. 27, 29–32.

67. Hosokawa, *Nisei*, p. 108.

68. *Ibid.*, p. 108; Girdner and Loftis, *Great Betrayal*, p. 61.

69. See generally Daniels, *Politics of Prejudice*, p. 89; Ruth E. McKee, *Wartime Exile: The Exclusion of the Japanese Americans from the West Coast* (Washington, DC: U.S. Department of the Interior, 1946), pp. 23–29; Wilson and Hosokawa, *East to America*, p. 133.

70. Wilson and Hosokawa, *East to America*, p. 133.

71. tenBroek, *Prejudice, War*, p. 67; McWilliams, *Prejudice*, pp. 90–91.

72. Girdner and Loftis, *Great Betrayal*, pp. 72–73; Wilson and Hosokawa, *East to America*, p. 67.

73. Hosokawa, *Nisei*, pp. 158–59.

74. Shibutani, *Derelicts of Company K*, p. 31; Wilson and Hosokawa, *East to America*, p. 166; Hosokawa, *Nisei*, p. 159.

75. Shibutani, *Derelicts of Company K*, p. 25.

76. Daniel K. Inouye with Lawrence Elliott, *Journey to Washington* (Englewood Cliffs, NJ: Prentice-Hall, 1967), pp. 36–37.

77. Hosokawa, *Nisei*, p. 178.

78. U.S. Department of the Interior, *The Evacuated People: A Quantitative Description* (Washington, DC: U.S. Government Printing Office, 1946), pp. 83–88.

79. Girdner and Loftis, *Great Betrayal*, pp. 45–46.

80. Hosokawa, *Nisei*, pp. 129–30.

81. *Ibid.*, p. 129; Girdner and Loftis, *Great Betrayal*, p. 46.

82. Sowell, *Ethnic America*, p. 170.

83. Hosokawa, *Nisei*, p. 128.

84. Girdner and Loftis, *Great Betrayal*, p. 46.

85. Sowell, *Ethnic America*, p. 157.

86. Wilson and Hosokawa, *East to America*, pp. 60, 111.

87. Girdner and Loftis, *Great Betrayal*, pp. 44–45.

88. Wilson and Hosokawa, *East to America*, pp. 166–87.

89. Broom and Riemer, *Removal and Return*, p. 7.

90. *Idem*.

91. McKee, *Exclusion*, pp. 62–65; Iwata, "Planted in Good Soil," pp. 246–47.

92. McKee, *Exclusion*, p. 8.

93. Daniels, *Politics of Prejudice*, p. 8.

94. McKee, *Exclusion*, p. 65; Iwata, "Planted in Good Soil," p. 247; Sowell, *Ethnic America*, p. 161.

95. Daniels, *Politics of Prejudice*, p. 9.

96. Iwata, "Planted in Good Soil," p. 258.

97. Lon Hatamiya, "Economic Effects of the Second World War Upon Japanese Americans in California," testimony of the Japanese American Citizens League National Committee for Redress, Dec. 23, 1981, p. 161.

98. Daniels, *Politics of Prejudice*, p. 10. *Cf*. Iwata, "Planted in Good Soil,"

p. 254, which states that in 1917 Japanese Americans raised crops worth $55 million, or about 10 percent of the California production.

99. See generally Iwata, "Planted in Good Soil," pp. 267–73.

100. Hosokawa, *Nisei,* pp. 68–69.

101. Iwata, "Planted in Good Soil," p. 258.

102. Grodzins, *Americans Betrayed,* pp. 23, 74–75.

103. Iwata, "Planted in Good Soil," pp. 260–63.

104. Daniels, *Politics of Prejudice,* p. 12; Hatamiya, "Economic Effects," p. 152. *Cf.* McWilliams, *Prejudice,* p. 88, which notes that by 1941, many of these small retail businesses were going bankrupt because of their narrow economic base.

105. Broom and Riemer, *Removal and Return,* pp. 27–31.

106. Hatamiya, "Economic Effects," pp. 152–54; Broom and Riemer, *Removal and Return,* pp. 27–31.

107. Hatamiya, "Economic Effects," p. 162.

108. McKee, *Exclusion,* pp. 92–93.

109. Hatamiya, "Economic Effects," pp. 154–70.

110. Shibutani, *Derelicts of Company K,* p. 26.

111. Hatamiya, "Economic Effects," pp. 161–70.

112. Sowell, *Ethnic America,* pp. 162–70.

113. Sources for this section are Thomas Pettigrew, ed., *The Sociology of Race Relations and Reform* (New York: The Free Press, 1980), p. xvii; J. R. Pole, *The Pursuit of Equality* (Berkeley: University of California Press, 1978), pp. 221–92.

114. *Facts on File,* vol. 2, no. 70 (1942), p. 72.

115. *Missouri ex rel Gaines* v. *Canada,* 305 U.S. 337 (1938).

116. Stimson Diary, Jan. 24, 1942. Sterling Library, Yale University. (CWRIC 19609–10).

2

Executive Order 9066

1. Samuel Eliot Morison, *Oxford History of the American People* (New York: Oxford University Press, 1965), pp. 1001–03. Three other aircraft carriers were at sea, and therefore unaffected. These carriers and their airgroups constituted a striking force far more valuable than the lost battleships. The perception of the destruction, however, did not account for this fact.

2. See, *e.g.*, Notes of Cabinet meetings, Francis Biddle, Attorney General, Dec. 7, 1941. FDRL. Biddle Papers (CWRIC 3790–91).

3. Jeannette Rankin, a pacifist Representative from Montana, voted against the declaration with tears streaming down her face. Francis Biddle, *In Brief Authority* (Garden City, NY: Doubleday & Co. Inc., 1962), pp. 206–07.

4. Morison, *Oxford History of the American People*, p. 1003.

5. James MacGregor Burns, *Roosevelt: The Soldier of Freedom* (New York: Harcourt Brace Jovanovich, 1970), pp. 38–39.

6. J. L. DeWitt, *Final Report: Japanese Evacuation From the West Coast, 1942* (Washington, DC: U.S. Government Printing Office, 1943), p. 34. [hereafter *Final Report*].

7. Brief for the United States, *Korematsu* v. *United States*, No. 22, Oct. Term 1944, pp. 11–12.

8. House Report No. 732, 80th Cong., 1st Sess., reprinted in Hearings before Subcommittee No. 5 of the Committee on the Judiciary, U.S. House of Representatives, 83rd Cong., 2d Sess., on HR 7435 (Serial No. 23), p. 60a.

9. Testimony, John J. McCloy, Washington, DC, Nov. 3, 1981, pp. 45–66; testimony, Karl Bendetsen, Washington, DC, Nov. 2, 1981, p. 32. Like McCloy, Bendetsen believes the evacuation decision was right in the context of the time:

Senator Brooke: One final question. Looking back in hindsight now, do you still think that the decision that was made in 1942 to place the Japanese Americans in camps was the right decision?

Mr. Bendetsen: Viewing it in the circumstances of the time and not from today's time, yes; I think it was. (Testimony, Bendetsen, Washington, DC, Nov. 2, 1981, p. 71).

10. Brief for the United States, *Hirabayashi* v. *United States*, No. 870, Oct. Term 1942, pp. 16–17.

11. Proposal for Coordination of FBI, ONI and MID, June 5, 1940, approved and signed by Louis Johnson, Acting Secretary of War on June 28, 1940. NARS. RG 107 (CWRIC 7362–63); memo, signed by G–2, ONI and FBI, Feb. 9, 1942, approved and signed by Henry L. Stimson, Secretary of

War. NARS. RG 107 (CWRIC 7366–73). This document indicates that ONI and FBI had joint coverage of "Japanese activities."

12. Kenneth Ringle, Jr., "What Did You Do Before The War, Dad?," *Washington Post Magazine,* Dec. 6, 1981; report by Curtis B. Munson, "Japanese on the West Coast," attached to Nov. 7, 1941 memo from John Franklin Carter to the President. FDRL. PSF 106 Stimson (CWRIC 3672–89).

13. Memo, Carter to Roosevelt *re* Munson report, "Japanese on the West Coast," Nov. 7, 1941. The five points certainly suggest that sabotage and espionage by Japanese Americans may occur but conveyed the opinion that there was not very much to fear from the Nisei. The one point that Roosevelt marked for Stimson's attention spoke generally of the fact that key points such as dams and bridges were unguarded and vulnerable. In the text of Munson's report, it was clear that he did not perceive danger from the ethnic Japanese in this situation as much as from the Communists and Nazis, but this may not have been clear if only Carter's brief cover note were read. Memo, FDR to the Secretary of War, Nov. 8, 1941. FDRL. PSF 106 Stimson (CWRIC 3672; 3671).

14. Letter, Stimson to Roosevelt, Feb. 5, 1942. FDRL. PSF 106 Stimson (CWRIC 3670).

15. Report by Curtis B. Munson, "Japanese on the West Coast," attached to memo from Carter to Roosevelt, Nov. 7, 1941. FDRL. PSF 106 Stimson (CWRIC 3673–89).

16. Cover note, Carter to Roosevelt, Dec. 22, 1941, enclosing Munson report of Dec. 20, 1941 (CWRIC 19480–90); cover note, Carter to Roosevelt, Dec. 13, 1941, enclosing Munson update of Jan. 12, 1942 (CWRIC 19495–97); cover note, Carter to Roosevelt, Jan. 28, 1942, enclosing letter with enclosures from Munson (CWRIC 19518–20); memo, Munson to Grace Tully, with enclosures, about Feb. 21, 1942 (CWRIC 19539–50); "Report on Hawaiian Islands," by Munson, attached to memo from Carter to Roosevelt, Dec. 8, 1941. FDRL. PSF Carter (CWRIC 19499–516).

17. Report by Munson, "Report and Suggestions regarding Handling Japanese Question on the Coast," Dec. 20, 1941. FDRL. PSF Carter (CWRIC 19483).

18. *E.g.,* Letter, Bob Alexander to Lloyd Wright, Feb. 18, 1942. FDRL. PSF Carter (CWRIC 19543–46). Nor was the threat limited to coastal areas. German saboteurs landing from submarines had instructions to destroy many inland installations. Letter, Hoover to McIntyre, Secy. to President, with attached memo, June 27, 1942. FDRL. PSF 77 (CWRIC 3691–93).

19. *E.g.,* Memo, Carter to Roosevelt, Jan. 28, 1942. FDRL. PSF Carter (CWRIC 19518).

20. Memo, Lieut. Cmdr. K. D. Ringle to Chief of Naval Operations, Jan. 26, 1942. NARS. RG 107 (CWRIC 275–84). Ringle had three years' study of the Japanese language and people during a tour at the embassy in Tokyo, a year as Assistant District Intelligence Officer in Hawaii; from June 1940 he had directed Naval Intelligence in Los Angeles. Ringle, Report on Japanese Question, Jan. 26, 1942. NARS. RG 107 (CWRIC 277).

21. Ringle, *Washington Post Magazine,* Dec. 6, 1981.

22. Letter, Ringle to Edward N. Barnhart, Mar. 23, 1951 (CWRIC 19567).

23. Ringle, Report on Japanese Question, Jan. 26, 1942. NARS. RG 107 (CWRIC 277).

24. Letter, Ringle to Barnhart, Mar. 23, 1951 (CWRIC 19566).

25. The Proclamation is reproduced at U.S. House of Representatives, Select Committee Investigating National Defense Migration (Tolan Committee), 77th Cong. 2d Sess., 1942, HR Report 2124. Proclamation 2526 applied the promulgated rules and regulations to German aliens; Proclamation 2527 applied them to Italian aliens. Both Proclamation 2526 and 2527 were issued on Dec. 8, 1941.

26. Paul Clark, "Those Other Camps: Japanese Alien Internment during World War II," unpublished manuscript, no date, p. 7, and materials cited (CWRIC 4409).

27. Telegrams, J. Edgar Hoover to All Special Agents in Charge, Dec. 7, 1941. FBI (CWRIC 5826, 5827, 5828); Dec. 8, 1941. FBI (CWRIC 5784–85).

28. Press release, Department of Justice statement of policy, released by Attorney General Francis Biddle, Dec. 10, 1941. FBI (CWRIC 5814–15).

29. Memos, L. L. Laughlin to D. M. Ladd, Dec. 8, 1941. FBI (CWRIC 5781); Francis M. Shea to Hoover, Dec. 10, 1941. FBI (CWRIC 5780).

30. Memo, Lemuel B. Schofield to Edward J. Ennis, Director, Alien Enemy Control Unit, Dec. 10, 1941. FBI (CWRIC 10373).

31. Clark, "Those Other Camps," p. 9, refers to Department of Justice press release, Feb. 16, 1942. (CWRIC 4411).

32. Jacobus tenBroek, Edward N. Barnhart and Floyd W. Matson, *Prejudice, War and the Constitution* (Berkeley: University of California Press, 1954), p. 101.

33. Memo, Hoover to Attorney General, Feb. 2, 1942. FBI (CWRIC 5794–803).

34. Ringle, *Washington Post Magazine*, Dec. 6, 1981.

35. Memo, Hoover to Attorney General, Feb. 2, 1942. FBI (CWRIC 5794–803).

36. Report by Munson, Dec. 20, 1941. FDRL. PSF Carter (CWRIC 19481).

37. Bill Hosokawa, *Nisei: The Quiet Americans* (New York: William Morrow & Co., Inc., 1969), pp. 463–64.

38. Notes of Cabinet meetings, Biddle, Dec. 19, 1941. FDRL. Biddle Papers (CWRIC 3793–94); memo, Hoover to the Attorney General, Dec. 17, 1941:

> With reference to the statement made by the Secretary of Navy to the effect that the Fifth Column activities in Hawaii were exceeded only by the Fifth Column activities in Norway, I wanted to make the suggestion that you might wish to keep in mind the desirability of asking the Secretary of Navy for any specific evidence which he has supporting this statement.
>
> I have already addressed a memorandum to you outlining directly what the scope of the so-called Fifth Column activities in Hawaii has been, and while there no doubt have been agents of the Japanese government active, it is very definitely the opinion of the intelligence officers of the various services in Hawaii that there is no such widespread activity'similar to that

which occurred in Norway. In fact, it is believed a great majority of the population in Hawaii of foreign extraction is law-abiding and is not indulging in any such activities. If the Secretary of Navy has any specific information of the magnitude that he has indicated by his press statement, it might be desirable for you to make inquiry of him for it. FBI (CWRIC 5830).

39. Memo, Carter to Roosevelt. FDRL. PSF Carter (CWRIC 12006).
40. Memo, Hoover to Tolson, Tamm and Ladd, Dec. 8, 1941. FBI (CWRIC 5786).
41. *Honolulu Advertiser,* Dec. 22, 1941, pp. 1, 6 (CWRIC 29567–69).
42. Report by Munson, Dec. 20, 1941. FDRL. PSF Carter (CWRIC 19481–82).
43. Morton Grodzins, *Americans Betrayed* (Chicago: University of Chicago Press, 1949), p. 399.
44. Cover note, Carter to Roosevelt, Dec. 22, 1941; report by Munson, Dec. 20, 1941. FDRL. PSF Carter (CWRIC 19481–90).
45. Report of Roberts Commission, Jan. 23, 1942, contained in Hearings before the Joint Committee on the Investigation of the Pearl Harbor Attack, 79th Cong., Part 39, 1946 (Washington, DC: U.S. Government Printing Office, 1946) [hereafter "Pearl Harbor Investigation"].
46. Pearl Harbor Investigation, Part 39, pp. 12–13.
47. Elting E. Morison, *Turmoil and Tradition* (Boston: Houghton Mifflin Co., 1960), pp. 527–34.
48. Pearl Harbor Investigation, Part 22, p. 86.
49. Report by Munson, Dec. 20, 1941. FDRL. PSF Carter (CWRIC 19483).
50. Pearl Harbor Investigation, Part 23, p. 867 and preceding pages.
51. *Ibid.,* pp. 872–73.
52. Report of the Select Committee Investigating National Defense Migration, HR Report No. 1911, 77th Cong., 2d Sess., March 19, 1942, p. 2.
53. Diary, Stimson, Jan. 20, 1942, p. 3, Sterling Library, Yale University (CWRIC 19598).
54. Pearl Harbor Investigation, Part 23, p. 874.
55. *Ibid.,* pp. 879–80.
56. *Ibid.,* p. 884.
57. *Ibid.,* pp. 642–43, 651.
58. Pearl Harbor Investigation, Part 35, p. 559.
59. Gordon W. Prange, *At Dawn We Slept* (New York: McGraw-Hill Book Co., 1981), pp. 310–12, 650.
60. Carey McWilliams, *Prejudice: Japanese-Americans, Symbol of Racial Intolerance* (Boston: Little, Brown and Co., 1945), pp. 110–11.
61. Diary, Stimson, Jan. 20, 1942, p. 3. Sterling Library, Yale University (CWRIC 19598).
62. Telephone conversation, DeWitt, Gullion and Bendetsen, Feb. 1, 1942. NARS. RG 389 (CWRIC 4316).
63. Memo, Carter to Roosevelt, Dec. 19, 1941. FDRL. PSF Carter (CWRIC 12007).
64. Memo, Hoover to Shea, Dec. 17, 1941. FBI (CWRIC 5777–79).

65. Letter, Ringle to Barnhart, Mar. 23, 1951 (CWRIC 19566).

66. In June 1940, Congress passed the Alien Registration Act (Smith Act), 54 Stat. 670. Registration began under the supervision of the Department of Justice on Aug. 27, 1940. Aliens had to register, be fingerprinted, answer 42 questions and reregister annually. A total of 4,921,452 aliens registered. (Donald R. Perry, "Aliens in the United States," *Annals of the American Academy of Political and Social Science*, vol. 223 [September 1942], pp. 1–9).

67. WDC, *Supplemental Report on Civilian Controls Exercised by the Western Defense Command*, Jan. 1947, pp. 440–41. NARS. RG 338.

68. *Ibid.*, pp. 441–42. In Los Angeles and San Francisco, over $3 million of local commercial and savings accounts were immediately frozen. The amount frozen in Seattle is unknown; the President appointed an Alien Property Custodian in the Department of Justice on Dec. 12, 1941. See Notes on Cabinet Meetings, Biddle, Dec. 12, 1941. FDRL. Biddle Papers (CWRIC 3792).

69. WDC, *Supplemental Report*, pp. 442–43.

70. *Ibid.*, p. 443.

71. Biddle, Notes on Cabinet meetings, Dec. 12, 1941. FDRL. Biddle Papers (CWRIC 3792).

72. Telegram, Marshall to Commanding General, Western Defense Command, Jan. 2, 1942. NARS. RG 338 (CWRIC 3176).

73. Bill Hosokawa, *JACL In Quest of Justice* (New York: William Morrow & Co., 1982), pp. 140–41.

74. *Congressional Record*, p. 9630, 77th Cong., 1st Sess., Dec. 10, 1941.

75. Telegram, Robinett, GHQ Army War College, to G–2 Western Defense Command, Dec. 19, 1941 (CWRIC 3146). See, *e.g.*, memo, Lt. Col. L. R. Forney to Lt. Col. D. A. Stroh, Dec. 22, 1941 (CWRIC 3161); telegram, Lt. Gen. John L. DeWitt to Commanding General of Field Forces, GHQ Army War College, Dec. 22, 1941 (CWRIC 3173); telegram, DeWitt to Adjutant General, Dec. 23, 1941 (CWRIC 3174); telegram, Marshall to DeWitt, Dec. 25, 1941 (CWRIC 3157); telegram, Maj. Gen. E. S. Adams, Adjutant General, to DeWitt, Dec. 25, 1941, suggesting the Secretary of War should consider asking the President to transfer to the War Department the responsibility and authority for control of enemy aliens (CWRIC 3158); telegram, DeWitt to Commanding General of Field Forces, GHQ Army War College, Dec. 26, 1941 (CWRIC 3156). All in NARS. RG 338.

Instructions for arrests of alien enemies were also sought. Those instructions were issued after the first wave of arrests. Memo, Hoover to All Special Agents in Charge, Dec. 27, 1941. FBI (CWRIC 5808–10). Individual determinations about arrest were to be made, with review by the appropriate United States Attorney, then review and decision by the Department of Justice, except where activities of the alien enemies were imminently dangerous.

76. Memo by Forney on conversation with N. J. L. Pieper, FBI, SAC, Jan. 1, 1942 (CWRIC 3167); see also memo, Pieper to DeWitt, containing a telegram from Biddle, Jan. 1, 1942. NARS. RG 338 (CWRIC 1331–32).

77. Memo, Pieper to DeWitt, Jan. 1, 1942. NARS. RG 338 (CWRIC 1331).

78. Telegram, Hoover to James Rowe, Assistant Attorney General, Jan. 7, 1942. NARS. RG 338 (CWRIC 1246–47).

79. Memo, Hoover to Attorney General, Feb. 2, 1942. FBI (CWRIC 5798).

80. Transcription of meeting in DeWitt's office, Jan. 4, 1942. NARS. RG 338 (CWRIC 1250–57).

81. Summary, Rowe to DeWitt, Jan. 4, 1942. NARS. RG 338 (CWRIC 1258–59). As a guideline, the pertinent parts of the memorandum are worth reviewing in their entirety:

This is the summary by Assistant Attorney General ROWE to General DE WITT of a conversation with the Attorney General of the United States, and Mr. ROWE's understanding of what the Department of Justice is prepared to do on questions of Alien Enemy Control referred to him by General DE WITT and his staff. . . .

2. RESTRICTED AREAS.

The Department of Justice tonight will by wire direct the United States Attorneys in the Western Theater of Operations, with particular emphasis on Washington, Oregon, and California, to telephone Major General BENEDICT for recommendations as to what areas should be regarded as restricted. The U.S. Attorney will automatically accept the General's recommendations, and these areas will immediately become restricted areas pending confirmation by the Attorney General. As soon as possible, a press release ordering all enemy aliens to evacuate restricted areas by a certain date and hour will be issued. Any release by the Department of Justice will specifically state that the Attorney General has designated these restricted areas at the specific and urgent request of General DE WITT. The Army will request the Navy to submit its recommendations through General DE WITT. It is believed several days will elapse before the Army will be ready to submit its recommendations.

3. SEARCH WARRANTS.

New forms for search and seizure of prohibited articles in homes controlled by, or inhabited by, alien enemies, are to be received tomorrow morning by FBI teletype. The question of probable cause will be met only by the statement that an alien enemy is resident in such premises. It is Mr. ROWE's understanding that the local United States Attorney's interpretation that more information is necessary to show probable cause is incorrect. The U.S. Attorney will issue a search warrant upon a statement by an FBI Agent that an alien enemy is resident at certain premises. It is not necessary that the Department in Washington be consulted.

4. ALIEN ENEMY REGISTRATION.

The Department feels it can conduct an alien enemy registration in the Western Theater of Operations within a week or ten days. Tomorrow morning by FBI teletype a statement will be sent from Washington outlining a procedure of what the Department is prepared to do. The Department feels it can conduct such a registration, through the local police authorities, much faster than the Army itself. . . .

5. The Department is willing to make spot-raids on alien enemies tomorrow or at any time after the registration, anywhere within the Western Theater of Operations. Mr. ROWE emphasized that such raids must be confined to premises controlled by enemy aliens, or where enemy aliens are resident. In other words, the Department cannot raid a specific locality, cov-

ering every house in that locality, irrespective of whether such houses are inhabited by enemy aliens or citizens. The Attorney General requested Mr. ROWE to make clear to General DE WITT that under no circumstances will the Department of Justice conduct mass raids on alien enemies. It is understood that the term "mass raids" means, eventually a raid on every alien .enemy within the Western Theater of Operations. The Attorney General will oppose such raids and, if overruled by the President, will request the Army to supersede the Department of Justice in the Western Theater of Operations.

See also confirmation of "a more expeditious legal method . . . in connection with the search and seizure of enemy aliens and their property" in letter from Stimson to the President, Feb. 5, 1942. FDRL. PSF Stimson (CWRIC 3670).

82. See, e.g., memo, Pieper to DeWitt, Jan. 1, 1942. NARS. RG 338 (CWRIC 1331). That the Army favored mass raids is reported in a memo, Hoover to Tolson, Tamm and Ladd, Dec. 26, 1941. FBI (CWRIC 5834-37).

83. See, e.g., memo, Pieper to DeWitt, Jan. 22, 1942. NARS. RG 338 (CWRIC 3120).

84. Memo by Forney, conversation with V. Ford Greaves, Federal Communications Commission, Dec. 31, 1941. NARS. RG 338 (CWRIC 3164).

85. Letter, Greaves to DeWitt, Jan. 1, 1942. NARS. RG 338 (CWRIC 8606-07b).

86. Report of conference with General DeWitt, by George Sterling, FCC, Jan. 9, 1942. NARS. RG 173 (CWRIC 8598-602).

87. Memo, Bendetsen to DeWitt, Jan. 3, 1942. NARS. RG 338 (CWRIC 1248).

88. Summary, Rowe to DeWitt, Jan. 4, 1942. NARS. RG 338 (CWRIC 1258-59).

89. Memo summarizing Attorney General's message, Jan. 5, 1942. NARS. RG 338 (CWRIC 1595).

90. See, e.g., memo, W. K. Kilpatrick, Chief of Staff, Pacific Southern Naval Coastal Frontier to DeWitt, Jan. 7, 1942, re "Exclusion of Enemy Aliens from Designated Areas." NARS. RG 338 (CWRIC 3121).

91. Memo, Major C. O. Garver to DeWitt, Jan. 8, 1942. NARS. RG 338 (CWRIC 3122-25).

92. Joseph Stilwell, The Stilwell Papers (New York: W. Sloane Associates, 1948), pp. 5-8.

93. Memo, Hoover to Attorney General, Feb. 1, 1942. DOJ 146-42-012 (CWRIC 10447-56).

94. Memo, Hoover to Tolson, Tamm and Ladd, Dec. 17, 1941. FBI (CWRIC 5831-33).

95. Report by Sterling of conference with DeWitt, Jan. 9, 1942. NARS. RG 173 (CWRIC 8598-602).

96. Diary, Stimson, Feb. 3, 1942, Sterling Library, Yale University (CWRIC 19632).

97. Memo, Munson to Carter, Jan. 12, 1942. FDRL. PSF Carter (CWRIC 19496-97).

98. Ringle, Washington Post Magazine, Dec. 6, 1981.

99. Prange, *At Dawn We Slept*, p. 605; Short stopped at the Presidio in San Francisco on his way home from Hawaii.

100. Grodzins, *Americans Betrayed*, p. 278. (Mayor Fletcher Bowron of Los Angeles reported this remark.)

101. Transcript of meeting in DeWitt's office, Jan. 4, 1942. NARS. RG 338 (CWRIC 1250–57).

102. DeWitt, *Final Report*, p. 34. The 112,000 included, of course, a very substantial number of women and children.

103. Testimony before House Naval Affairs Subcommittee, April 13, 1943. NARS. RG 338 (CWRIC 1725–28).

104. Transcript of conference, DeWitt and newspapermen, April 14, 1943. NARS. RG 338 (CWRIC 26565).

105. Roger Daniels, *Concentration Camps, USA: Japanese-Americans and World War II* (New York: Holt, Rinehart & Winston, 1972), p. 63; tenBroek, *Prejudice, War*, p. 86; Report No. 13, Grodzins in Washington, Oct. 12, 1942. Bancroft Library: A 12.04. (CWRIC 11326–27). The West Coast apparently sustained only two minor Japanese submarine attacks during the war; the first was directed by Kozo Nishino, a submarine commander who in the late 1930's had been taunted by oil rig workers while the tanker he commanded was loading at the Ellwood oilfield near Santa Barbara:

[O]n Feb. 23, 1942 . . . from 7:07 to 7:45 p.m., he directed the shelling of the Ellwood oil fields from his submarine, the *I–17*. Though about 25 shells were fired from a 5.5 inch deck gun, little damage was done. One rig needed a $500 repair job after the shelling, and one man was wounded while trying to defuse an unexploded shell. U.S. planes gave chase . . . but Nishino got away . . . the mainland suffered only one more submarine attack by the Japanese during the war, at Fort Stevens in Oregon. (Irving Wallace *et al.*, "Delayed Revenge," *Parade*, Nov. 21, 1982, p. 18).

106. The atmosphere after Pearl Harbor and its relationship to security on the West Coast is particularly well conveyed by James Rowe, Assistant Attorney General, who opposed exclusion and evacuation and was later interviewed with Dillon Myer by the Earl Warren Oral History Project:

Myer: Everybody got scared.

Rowe: Everybody was. I mean we took an *awful* beating at Pearl Harbor and it caught everybody unawares and then all the news that followed was the Japanese moving, moving, moving. They just had one victory after another.

Myer: They sure did.

Rowe: And the British were not doing well. Hell, the whole world might have come crashing down. And the first requirement of the government was order. Law comes *after* order. (The Earl Warren Oral History Project, *Japanese-American Relocation Reviewed*, vol. 1, 1969, p. 38.)

107. tenBroek, *Prejudice, War*, pp. 78–79.

108. *Ibid.*, p. 79.

109. Grodzins, *Americans Betrayed*, pp. 44–47. In his memoirs at the end of his life, Warren rendered his personal verdict on this part of his history:

I have since deeply regretted the removal order and my own testimony advocating it, because it was not in keeping with our American concept of freedom and the rights of citizens. Whenever I thought of the innocent little children who were torn from home, school friends, and congenial surroundings, I was conscience-stricken. It was wrong to react so impulsively, without positive evidence of disloyalty, even though we felt we had a good motive in the security of our state. It demonstrates the cruelty of war when fear, get-tough military psychology, propaganda, and racial antagonism combine with one's responsibility for public security to produce such acts. I have always believed that I had no prejudice against the Japanese as such except that directly spawned by Pearl Harbor and its aftermath. As district attorney, I had great respect for people of Japanese ancestry, because during my years in that office they created no law enforcement problems. Although we had a sizable Japanese population, neither the young nor the old violated the law. (Earl Warren, *The Memoirs of Chief Justice Earl Warren* [Garden City, NY: Doubleday & Co., Inc., 1977], p. 149.)

110. *Grizzly Bear*, Jan. 1942, reprinted in Morton Grodzins, *Americans Betrayed*, p. 48.

111. Grodzins, *Americans Betrayed*, pp. 49–50.

112. *Ibid.*, pp. 42–43.

113. Resolution of Federal Post No. 97, Dept. of Oregon, American Legion, Portland, OR., reprinted in Hearings before the Select Committee Investigating National Defense Migration, U.S. House of Representatives, 77th Cong., 2d Sess., p. 11389.

114. Grodzins, *Americans Betrayed*, p. 43.

115. Frank J. Taylor, "The People Nobody Wants," *The Saturday Evening Post*, May 9, 1942, p. 66.

116. Grodzins, *Americans Betrayed*, pp. 22–23.

117. William Petersen, *Japanese Americans: Oppression and Success* (New York: Random House, 1971), pp. 77–78. Petersen also points out that as late as September 1942, Carey McWilliams, who before the end of the war wrote a volume entitled *Prejudice* that opposed the exclusion and detention, published an article in *Harper's* suggesting that the exclusion and detention were perhaps all for the best. Norman Thomas was one of the few well-known figures who spoke out against exclusion and detention; he recognized that his position was a lonely one:

In an experience of nearly three decades I have never found it harder to arouse the American public on any important issue than on this. Men and women who know nothing of the facts . . . hotly deny that there are concentration camps. Apparently that is a term to be used only if the guards speak German and carry a whip as well as a rifle. (*Ibid.*, pp. 75–77.)

118. Grodzins, *Americans Betrayed*, pp. 101–03. In 1954, testifying before a Congressional subcommittee considering the Japanese American Evacuation Claims Act, Mayor Bowron summed up the atmosphere of the time and his later judgment on the actions that were taken:

I know of my own knowledge something of the circumstances surrounding the making of the order and the forceful evacuation of the Japanese population of this area, and I know of the hysteria, the wild rumors, the reports, that pervaded the atmosphere and worried a great many of us in responsible positions. We were quite disorganized. Our civil defense organization was not in effect, and with all due respect, the means of making investigations from Federal sources was rather disorganized at times.

There were many rumors floating around, as a result of which, this order of evacuation was made.

I rather hold myself somewhat responsible, with others, for the condition or the representation that possibly brought about that order. I realize that great injustices were done. . . .

Well, personally, I thought it was the right thing to do at the time; in the light of after events, I think it was wrong, now. (Hearings Before Subcommittee No. 5 of the Committee on the Judiciary, House of Representatives, 83rd Cong., 2d Sess., on HR 7435 to amend the Japanese American Evacuation Claims Act of 1948 [1954], pp. 231–32).

119. Grodzins, *Americans Betrayed*, pp. 111–14.

120. *Ibid.*, pp. 92–100.

121. Letter, Leland M. Ford to Stimson, Jan. 16, 1942. NARS. RG 107 (CWRIC 4376); Grodzins, *Americans Betrayed*, pp. 64–65.

122. Grodzins, *Americans Betrayed*, p. 67.

123. Recommendations by Pacific Coast Delegation (U.S. House of Representatives), "Suggested Program" to the President following delegation meeting, Jan. 30, 1942. Bancroft Library. A12.07 (CWRIC 11334).

124. "News and Views by John B. Hughes," radio transcripts, Jan. 5, 6, 7, 9, 15, 19, and 20, 1942 (CWRIC 8707–18).

125. Grodzins, *Americans Betrayed*, pp. 384–86; Alexander H. Leighton, *The Governing of Men* (Princeton: Princeton University Press, 1945), pp. 15–23.

126. tenBroek, *Prejudice, War*, p. 75.

127. Memo by JLD (DeWitt), "Action of Congressional Committee on handling enemy aliens on the West Coast," Jan. 31, 1942. NARS. RG 338 (CWRIC 1321–23). In this memo, DeWitt rejected the suggestion that enemy aliens be interned in Civilian Conservation Corps camps because, in his view, those camps would require troops for guards to the detriment of military functions.

128. Grodzins, *Americans Betrayed*, pp. 241–42.

129. Memo, Hoover to Attorney General, Feb. 2, 1942. FBI (CWRIC 5794, 5796).

130. Testifying before the Commission in 1981, Rowe maintained his position opposing the exclusion, stating that he had never seen any military necessity for it. He also reviewed the performance of the Justice Department in making as strong a case as possible to the President in opposition to the evacuation:

I think we could have done it much better; we were always on the run, I would say; I don't know how you could be on the run and up against the wall at the same time, but that's where we felt we were. The press was after us, Congress was after us, the mail was after us, and we were sort of reacting to all of this.

Now I think in looking back, and we were tired too, we were up all

night, I think we could have done a hell of a lot bettter job, and we didn't
do it. But we were all they had. (Testimony, James Rowe, Washington,
DC, July 14, 1981, p. 72).

Ennis also reviewed his own role and the impact of the evacuation decision
in testifying,

> [N]ow when I look back on it I don't know why I didn't resign, I did
> represent as a member of the Department of Justice, I did represent the
> defendant government in evacuation actions and indeed wrote the briefs,
> argued the cases in the lower courts, and wrote the briefs for the Solicitor
> General for the Supreme Court of the United States. I think I should
> confess that.
>
> But in sum, all I can say for that is that the Constitution not only gives
> great power to the military in time of war, but it appears that it gives
> them power to make very serious mistakes, and I think the only defense
> that can be made of the evacuation in legal terms is that the power to
> control includes the power to control mistakenly and make mistakes as
> great as was made here. (Testimony, Edward Ennis, Washington, DC,
> Nov. 2, 1981, pp. 140–41).

Tom Clark recalled his views and passed judgment on the evacuation decision
in 1976, after he had left the Supreme Court:

> I served during the hectic days during which the ultimate governmental
> policy was formulated . . . I found the final decison for removal of the
> Japanese to be based upon the physical dangers then facing 110,000 people
> of Japanese descent then living in California, Oregon, and Washington.
> I did not expect any sabotage from Japanese residents; there had been
> none in Hawaii where the opportunity was greater; the ONI and FBI had
> a tight oversight of all nationality groups, especially the Japanese. The
> Department of Justice was poised for individual action that would have
> controlled any recalcitrant Japanese, as it had those of German and Italian
> origin who had defied authority. There was little strategic justification for
> the evacuation; these people of Japanese descent, many of them American
> citizens, did not pose a substantial military threat.
>
> As Civilian Coordinator, however, I received hundreds of threatening
> messages against the Japanese community every day. This led to the
> curfew orders promulgated by General DeWitt. . . . The Congress then
> authorized exclusion, and the agitation was such that the Western Defense
> Command decided upon a policy of evacuation. Looking back on it today,
> this was, of course, a mistake. Although the Supreme Court held the
> action constitutional, one must remember that even the Court's judgment
> can be no better than the information on which it is based. In my view,
> the military necessity for the action taken was lacking. (Frank F. Chuman,
> *The Bamboo People* [Del Mar, CA: Publisher's Inc., 1976], preface by
> Tom C. Clark, p. vii).

131. Testimony, Edward Ennis, Washington, DC, Nov. 2, 1981, pp. 139–
41.

132. Telephone conversation, DeWitt, Gullion and Bendetsen, Feb. 1,
1942. NARS. RG 389 (CWRIC 4314–18).

133. The memo presented a number of options including special defense

areas into which ethnic Japanese would be allowed only under special license, special reservations on the West Coast for the ethnic Japanese and curfews. These are close to the conceptual plans that the Justice and the War Departments developed. The memo also argued that the precautionary measures taken should be reasonably adapted to need and that every effort should be made to relieve unnecessary hardship. Memo, Cohen, Cox and Rauh, about Feb. 10, 1942. DOJ 146–13–7–2–0 (CWRIC 12682–89). In writing to the Commission, Rauh remembers the three attorneys pressing for a compromise between the War and Justice Departments which would have involved "curfew and other limited measures." Letter, Rauh to Bernstein, May 21, 1982 (CWRIC 14435–40). The memorandum can fairly be construed to support the legality and propriety of broader measures. Rauh also set out his later views on the evacuation and Cohen's reaction to these events:

> I want to record how deeply Mr. Cohen felt against the evacuation. When I went into his office one night a couple of months later, he showed me a newspaper picture of a little Japanese American boy leaning out the evacuation train window and waving an American flag. Mr. Cohen had tears in his eyes.

I suppose it does not do much good to try and explain historical decisions many years after the event, but I did try this in an essay on civil liberties for the National Jewish Community Relations Advisory Council back in 1969:

> [U]ndoubtedly the cruelest inroad on civil freedom during World War II was the exclusion of the entire population of Japanese ancestry from the Pacific Coast and the detention of most of them in relocation camps. This incredible tragedy resulted, I believe, more from the rigidity of honorable men within the Administration who failed to recognize the need for some post-Pearl-Harbor action to offset Pacific Coast fright of near hysterical proportions (as, for example, the temporary nighttime curfew suggested by some) than from the weakness or venality of the Administration in the face of tremendous military and political pressures.

That was the best I could do then to explain how this tragedy could happen and it is the best I can do now. (*Idem.*)

134. Telephone conversation, DeWitt, Gullion and Bendetsen, Feb. 1, 1942. NARS. RG 389 (CWRIC 4314–18).

135. Telephone conversation, Gullion and Gen. Mark Clark, Feb. 4, 1942. NARS. RG 389 (CWRIC 5936–40).

136. Telephone conversation, DeWitt, Gullion and Bendetsen, Feb. 1, 1942. NARS. RG 389 (CWRIC 4314–18).

137. Telephone conversation, DeWitt and McCloy, Feb. 3, 1942. NARS. RG 107 (CWRIC 135–37) (Gov. Olson); Grodzins, *Americans Betrayed*, pp. 277–78 (Mayor Bowron).

138. Telephone conversation, DeWitt, Gullion and Bendetsen, Feb. 1, 1942. NARS. RG 389 (CWRIC 4314–18).

139. Telephone conversation, Gullion to Clark, Feb. 4, 1942. NARS. RG 389 (CWRIC 5937) ("Yesterday Secretary Stimson, McCloy, Bendetsen and I talked for an hour and a half on the situation and I can tell you that the two

Secretaries are against any mass movement. They are pretty much against it."); Undersecretary of War Patterson apparently supported mass evacuation. McCloy's diary of February 16 records a meeting between McCloy and Patterson in which Patterson "strongly urged immediate and thorough action." Interview of McCloy, Oct. 16, 1942. Bancroft Library. A 5.02 (CWRIC 4491).

140. Diary, Stimson, Feb. 3, 1942. Sterling Library, Yale University (CWRIC 19632). There were, of course, no naturalized Americans of Japanese ancestry; the Nisei were Americans by birth.

141. Telephone conversation, DeWitt and McCloy, Feb. 3, 1942. NARS. RG 107 (CWRIC 131–40).

142. *Ibid*. Given McCloy's concern for the legality of the government's conduct, one must also note the account of the meeting of February 4 between the War Department and the Justice Department which General Gullion gave to General Clark on February 4: "Well, I think McCloy did say this to Biddle— you are putting a Wall Street lawyer in a helluva box, but if it [is] a question of safety of the country, the Constitution of the United States, why the Constitution is just a scrap of paper to me. That is what McCloy said. But they are just a little afraid DeWitt hasn't enough grounds to justify any movements." Telephone conversation, Gullion and Clark, Feb. 4, 1942. NARS. RG 389 (CWRIC 5937). McCloy testified to the Commission that he had not made this statement. (Testimony, John J. McCloy, Washington, DC, Nov. 3, 1981, pp. 17–18, 33–34.)

143. Memo, Strickland to Ladd, Feb. 3, 1942. FBI (CWRIC 5807).

144. Memo, Bureau of Intelligence to Director, Office of Facts and Figures, Feb. 4, 1942; letter, MacLeish to McCloy, Feb. 9, 1942. NARS. RG 107 (CWRIC 124; 117–18).

145. Interview of McCloy, Oct. 16, 1942. Bancroft Library. A5.02 (CWRIC 4491).

146. Memo, Bendetsen to Provost Marshal General, Feb. 4, 1942. NARS. RG 389 (CWRIC 6622–26).

147. Interview of McCloy, Oct. 16, 1942. Bancroft Library. A5.02 (CWRIC 4491).

148. Office of Provost Marshal General proposal, Feb. 5, 1942. NARS. RG 107 (CWRIC 120).

149. Memo, Biddle, "Luncheon Conference with the President," Feb. 7, 1942. FDRL. Biddle Papers (CWRIC 5750).

150. On Feb. 17, 1942, Biddle sent the President an analysis of why the evacuation should not be undertaken. FDRL. PSF Confidential File (CWRIC 5754–55). In fact, that memorandum arrived after the President had told Stimson to go ahead. FDRL. Biddle Papers (CWRIC 5756–58).

151. Diary, Stimson, Feb. 10, 1942. Sterling Library, Yale University. (CWRIC 19649).

152. Memo, Bendetsen to DeWitt, Feb. 10, 1942. NARS. RG 338 (CWRIC 12003–05).

153. Diary, Stimson, Feb. 11, 1942. Sterling Library. Yale University, (CWRIC 19651–52).

154. Walter Lippmann, "The Fifth Column on the Coast," *Washington*

Post, Feb. 12, 1942. NARS. RG 107 (CWRIC 1401). Lippmann's biographer reports the columnist's view of this incident in later life:
In the early 1970s, when Earl Warren publicly recanted, a frail and failing Lippmann kept returning to the issue in conversation. "You know, I still think it was the right thing to do at the time," he told his friend Gilbert Harrison, editor of the *New Republic.* "Not for security reasons, mind you, but because it was necessary to protect the Japanese-Americans from the hysterical mobs on the West Coast." Although he would not admit he had been wrong, neither could he put the issue out of his mind. (Ronald Steel, *Walter Lippmann and The American Century* [Boston: Little, Brown and Co., 1980]), p. 395.

155. Grodzins, *Americans Betrayed,* pp. 92–100.

156. Westbrook Pegler, "Fifth Column problem on Pacific Coast very serious—Japs should be under guard," Feb. 16, 1942. DOJ 146–13–7–2–0 (CWRIC 13333).

157. Manchester E. Boddy, *Japanese in America* (Los Angeles: Manchester E. Boddy, 1921).

158. Telegram, Boddy to Biddle, Feb. 16, 1942; letter, Boddy to Biddle, Feb. 16, 1942. Boddy proposed a "secret defense project" of using the evacuated Japanese to erect a rehabilitation center in a place ten to twelve hours from Los Angeles. NARS. RG 107 (CWRIC 107; 105–06).

159. tenBroek, *Prejudice, War,* pp. 88–89.

160. Recommendations of the Pacific Coast Subcommittee on Alien Enemies and Sabotage (stamped received in the Assistant Secretary's Office, War Department, Feb. 15, 1942). NARS. RG 107 (CWRIC 128); see also letter, Rufus B. Holman to Roosevelt, and attachment, Feb. 13, 1942. NARS. RG 407 (CWRIC 1605–07).

161. Memo, Roosevelt to Secretary of War, Feb. 16, 1942. NARS. RG 407 (CWRIC 1604).

162. Grodzins, *Americans Betrayed,* pp. 73–75.

163. DeWitt, *Final Report,* pp. 33–34.

164. Letter, Biddle to Stimson, Feb. 12, 1942. NARS. RG 407 (CWRIC 5752–53). The letter states in part: "I have no doubt that the Army can legally, at any time, evacuate all persons in a specified territory if such action is deemed essential from a military point of view for the protection and defense of the area."

165. Memo, Biddle to President, Feb. 17, 1942. FDRL. PSF Confidential File (CWRIC 5754–55).

166. Report No. 6, Grodzins in Washington, Sept. 26, 1942. Bancroft Library. A 12.04 (CWRIC 11313–14).

167. Diary, Stimson, Feb. 17, 1942. Sterling Library, Yale University (CWRIC 19684).

168. *Ibid.,* Feb. 18, 1942. (CWRIC 19686–87).

169. Biddle, *In Brief Authority,* p. 219; James Rowe recalls that the Justice Department reviewed the Executive Order and that he hand-carried it to Harold Smith, the Director of the Budget, who in turn presented it to Roosevelt. Interview, James Rowe, Washington, DC, Nov. 23, 1982.

170. Grodzins, *Americans Betrayed,* pp. 187–88.

171. Executive Order No. 9066, Feb. 19, 1942. *Federal Register*, vol. 7 no. 38, Feb. 25, 1942 (CWRIC 4481).

172. Memo, Roosevelt to Stimson, May 5, 1942. NARS. RG 107 (CWRIC 196).

173. Letter, Biddle to Roosevelt, Feb. 20, 1942, and memorandum *re* Executive Order of Feb. 19, 1942. FDRL. OF 4805 (CWRIC 5756–58); compare language of final paragraph quoted with memo by Cohen, Cox and Rauh, "The Japanese Situation on the West Coast," no date. DOJ 146–13–7–2–0 (CWRIC 12682–89).

174. DeWitt, *Final Report*, p. 15.

175. Brief for the United States, *Korematsu* v. *United States*, No. 22, Oct. Term 1944, p. 11, n. 2 (CWRIC 15760):

> The Final Report of General DeWitt (which is dated June 5, 1943, but which was not made public until January 1944), hereinafter cited as Final Report, is relied on in this brief for statistics and other details concerning the actual evacuation and the events that took place subsequent thereto. We have specifically recited in this brief the facts relating to the justification for the evacuation, of which we ask the Court to take judicial notice, and we rely upon the Final Report only to the extent that it relates to such facts.

The Justice Department's internal memoranda dealing with the *Final Report* in the process of preparing the *Korematsu* brief are scathing:

> We are now therefore in possession of substantially incontrovertible evidence that most important statements of fact advanced by General DeWitt to justify the evacuation and detention were incorrect, and furthermore that General DeWitt had cause to know, and in all probability did know, that they were incorrect at the time he embodied them in his final report to General Marshall. (Memo, Burling to Solicitor General, April 13, 1944. DOJ 146–42–7 [CWRIC 5759–64]).

176. Grodzins, *Americans Betrayed*, pp. 134–136; Biddle, *In Brief Authority*, 1962, p. 221.

177. Stetson Conn, Rose C. Engelman and Byron Fairchild, *The United States Army in World War II, The Western Hemisphere: Guarding the United States and Its Outposts* (Washington, DC: Office of the Chief of Military History, United States Army, 1964), p. 147.

178. Grodzins, *Americans Betrayed*, pp. 138–43.

179. tenBroek, *Prejudice, War*, p. 91.

180. Henry L. Stimson and McGeorge Bundy, *On Active Service In Peace and War* (New York: Harper & Brothers, 1947), p. 406. Stimson's brief account of the exclusion and evacuation must be given in full so that his final reckoning of the events can be understood:

> [M]indful of its duty to be prepared for any emergency, the War Department ordered the evacuation of more than a hundred thousand persons of Japanese origin from strategic areas on the west coast. This decision was widely criticized as an unconstitutional invasion of the rights of individuals many of whom were American citizens, but it was eventually approved by the Supreme Court as a legitimate exercise of the war powers of the President. What critics ignored was the situation that led to the

evacuation. Japanese raids on the west coast seemed not only possible but probable in the first months of the war, and it was quite impossible to be sure that the raiders would not receive important help from individuals of Japanese origin. More than that, anti-Japanese feeling on the west coast had reached a level which endangered the lives of all such individuals; incidents of extra-legal violence were increasingly frequent. So, with the President's approval, Stimson ordered and McCloy supervised a general evacuation of Japanese and Japanese Americans from strategic coastal areas, and they believed in 1947 that the eventual result of this evacuation, in the resettlement of a conspicuous minority in many dispersed communities throughout the country, was to produce a distinctly healthier atmosphere for both Japanese and Americans.

It remained a fact that to loyal citizens this forced evacuation was a personal injustice, and Stimson fully appreciated their feelings. He and McCloy were strong advocates of the later formation of combat units of Japanese-American troops; the magnificent record of the 442nd Combat Team justified their advocacy. By their superb courage and devotion to duty, the men of that force won for all Japanese-Americans a clear right to the gratitude and comradeship of their American countrymen. (*Idem.*)

181. Testimony, John J. McCloy, Washington, DC, Nov. 3, 1981, p. 8.

182. Letter, McCloy to Gen. H. A. Drum, Commanding General, Eastern Defense Command, Nov. 16, 1942. NARS. RG 107 (CWRIC 26742–43).

183. Chuman, *Bamboo People*, preface by Tom C. Clark, p. vii.

184. Letter, McCloy to DeWitt, April 8, 1943. NARS. RG 165 (CWRIC 26369–71).

185. Grodzins, *Americans Betrayed*, pp. 152–53.

186. *Ibid.*, pp. 172–73.

187. Brief for the United States, *Hirabayashi* v. *United States*, No. 870, Oct. Term 1942, pp. 10–11 (citations omitted) (CWRIC 14953–54).

188. *Ibid.*, pp. 24–31 (CWRIC 14967–74).

189. tenBroek, *Prejudice, War*, p. 78.

190. Testimony, John J. McCloy, Washington, DC, Nov. 3, 1981, p. 49.

191. Letter, McCloy to Emmons, Nov. 5, 1943. NARS. RG 107 (CWRIC 26605–07). In reviewing the matter forty years later, McCloy told the Commission the wartime decisions should be defended:

My belief and hope is the Commission will conclude, after an objective investigation, that under the circumstances prevailing at the time and with the exigencies of wartime security, the action of the President of the United States and the United States Government in regard to our then Japanese population was reasonably undertaken and thoughtfully and humanely conducted. There has been, in my judgment, at times a spate of quite irresponsible comment to the effect that this wartime move was callous, shameful and induced by racial or punitive motives. It was nothing of the sort.

I know of the decisions that were made, and I think I know who made them, and I think I know generally what the motivation was of those individuals who made them. One fact I would urge the Commission to refer to if any report is made in connection with its examination of the relocation program is the role which the 442nd Combat Team played in establishing once and for all the fundamental loyalty of our Japanese population. . . .

I therefore believe in the interests of all concerned, the Commission would be well advised to conclude that President Roosevelt's wartime action in connection with the relocation of our Japanese-descended population at the outbreak of our war with Japan, was taken and carried out in accordance with the best interests of the country, considering the conditions, exigencies and considerations which then faced the nation. (Testimony, John J. McCloy, Washington, DC, Nov. 3, 1981, pp. 13–14, 16).

3

Exclusion and Evacuation

1. Letter, McCloy to Biddle, Feb. 22, 1942; memo, Bendetsen to McCloy, with attachment, Feb. 22, 1942. NARS. RG 107 (CWRIC 100; 97–99).

2. *Congressonal Record,* March 9, 1942, p. 2071; March 10, 1942, p. 2230.

3. Hearings before the Select Committee Investigating National Defense Migration [hereafter "Tolan Committee"], U.S. House of Representatives, 77th Cong., 2d Sess. (Washington, DC: U.S. Government Printing Office, 1942), p. 11010; Cong. Sparkman expressed the same view, p. 11018.

4. Tolan Committee, p. 11226.

5. *Ibid.,* p. 11181.

6. *Ibid.,* pp. 11141 (Masaoka), 11153 (Tatsuno); but see Louis Goldblatt, Secretary, California State Industrial Union Council, p. 11181.

7. *E.g.,* Tolan Committee, p. 11012.

8. Tolan Committee, pp. 11137 (Masaoka), 11148 (Tani), 11153 (Tatsuno), 11220 (Iiyama and Kumitani), 11240 (Bellquist), 11203 (Chapman), 11207 (Smith), 11178 (Goldblatt).

9. *E.g.,* Tolan Committee, p. 11068.

10. Tolan Committee, pp. 11011–12.

11. *Ibid.,* p. 10974.

12. *Ibid.,* p. 11247.

13. *Ibid.,* pp. 11636–37.

14. *Ibid.,* pp. 10965–70.

15. Francis Biddle, *In Brief Authority* (Garden City, NY: Doubleday & Co., Inc., 1964), p. 207.

16. Cable, Tolan to Biddle, Feb. 28, 1942. NARS. RG 107 (CWRIC 92). Fourth Interim Report of the Select Committee Investigating National Defense Migration, U.S. House of Representatives, 77th Cong., 2d Sess., HR Report No. 2124.

17. *Congressional Record,* March 19, 1942, p. 2726.

18. *Idem.*

19. *Ibid.,* pp. 2729–30.

20. Morton Grodzins provides a comparatively thorough account of what Congressional discussion there was. *Americans Betrayed* (Chicago: University of Chicago Press, 1949), pp. 331–44.

21. *Korematsu* v. *United States,* 323 U.S. 214 (1944).

22. Executive Order 9066, Feb. 19, 1942. 3 CFR, 1938–1943 Comp., pp. 1092–3.

23. Letter and memorandum outline, Stimson to DeWitt, Feb. 20, 1942. NARS. RG 338 (CWRIC 4643–44); NARS. RG 107 (CWRIC 298–304); Roger Daniels, *The Decision to Relocate the Japanese Americans* (New York: J. B. Lippincott, 1975), pp. 116–21.

24. Public Proclamation No. 1, and accompanying material, March 2, 1942. NARS. RG 107 (CWRIC 255–59). The accompanying press release emphasized the military necessity argument: "Military necessity is the sole yardstick by which the Army has selected the military areas announced. Public clamor for evacuation from non-strategic areas and the insistence of local organizations and officials that evacuees not be moved into their communities cannot and will not be considered."

25. J. L. DeWitt, *Final Report, Japanese Evacuation from the West Coast, 1942* (Washington, DC: U.S. Government Printing Office, 1943), pp. 297–98.

26. Public Proclamation No. 1, and accompanying material, March 2, 1942. NARS. RG 107 (CWRIC 255–59).

27. Telephone conversation, Bendetsen and Gufler, Feb. 21,'1942, State Department Records (CWRIC 2806–07).

28. Memo, Hoover to Attorney General, Feb. 27, 1942. NARS. RG 107 (CWRIC 90).

29. Letter, Hosokawa to Secretary of State, Jan. 25, 1942, with attachment, statement by general chairman of JACL Emergency Defense Council of Seattle. NARS. RG 59 (CWRIC 5386–87).

30. Tolan Committee, p. 11061.

31. Memo, Ringle to District Intelligence Officer, March 3, 1942 (CWRIC 19530–34).

32. Tolan Committee, pp. 11020, 11054.

33. Letter, Carville to DeWitt, Feb. 21, 1942; Compton White, a Representative from Idaho, forwarded similar views of the Idaho American Legion to Stimson by letter, March 16, 1942. NARS. RG 338 (CWRIC 767; 5241).

34. Frank J. Taylor, "The People Nobody Wants," *Saturday Evening Post*, May 9, 1942, p. 66; Tolan Committee, p. 11639 (Olson).

35. Tolan Committee, p. 11276.

36. Letter, Knox to Biddle, Feb. 22, 1942. NARS. RG 107 (CWRIC 93).

37. Letter, McCloy to Hopkins, Feb. 21, 1942. NARS. RG 107 (CWRIC 101).

38. DeWitt, *Final Report*, p. 105.

39. *Ibid.*, pp. 107–09.

40. "Net total" is persons who migrated out of the area but did not return to be evacuated with their families, or did not otherwise join families in assembly centers or relocation centers prior to Oct. 31, 1942.

41. DeWitt, *Final Report*, p. 109.

42. *Ibid.*, p. 111. DeWitt estimated that the remaining ten percent probably left before change-of-residence requirements took effect, or simply did not report. An example of a successful voluntary migrant is Ken Matsumoto, National Vice President of the JACL, about whom K. D. Ringle wrote to Milton Eisenhower on April 13, 1942: "He left here [California] ahead of the evacuation order to accept a very good job with the Mayor Jewelry Company, 5th and Vine Streets, Cincinnati, Ohio." NARS. RG 210 (CWRIC 3591).

43. Telegram, McWilliams to Biddle, Feb. 20, 1942; letter, McCloy to Ennis, Feb. 25, 1942. NARS. RG 107 (CWRIC 103; 95).

44. Letter, Collier to Walker, copy to McCloy, March 6, 1942. NARS. RG 107 (CWRIC 79–80).

45. Report of the Select Committee Investigating National Defense Migration, U.S. House of Representatives, 77th Cong., 2d Sess., HR Report No. 1911, pp. 15–19.

46. DeWitt, *Final Report*, p. 78.

47. Recognizing that, from the time the Executive Order was promulgated, some saw that voluntary evacuation could not work, it is not surprising to find that War Department planning for mandatory evacuation began early. On February 26, General Gullion, the Provost Marshal General, wrote to McCloy about the site selection for evacuation centers.ᵃ On March 5, an official in the Judge Advocate General's Office responded to a request from Gullion about legal authority to acquire land by condemnation for use in the resettlement of Japanese citizens and aliens.ᵇ In a memorandum of March 6, 1942, McCloy gave Stimson information for a Cabinet meeting, noting that the public proclamation designating a military area had been issued, and that places were being surveyed where Japanese Americans could be placed: "In the first instance, we will probably put them in tents though the shortage of canvas may affect this."ᶜ McCloy had also asked to have construction expedited so "the Japs" could be moved "as fast as possible."ᵈ Several other documents show early attention to a search for assembly and relocation centers. On March 2, 1942, Charles Burdell, Special Assistant to Attorney General Biddle, wrote Tom Clark that he planned to attend a meeting with county prosecutors in the State of Washington, and that he would ask them to make a survey of all fairgrounds, ballparks, and other camp facilities in each county, and a further survey of trucking facilities. He suggested using the survey results for evacuation of aliens.ᵉ Burdell also noted he was having a similar survey made for the State of Oregon.ᶠ On March 6, Burdell (under Tom Clark's name) forwarded the information about Oregon to Colonel Joseph Conmy of the Army, who seems to have been responsible for some site selection.ᵍ Then on March 7, Tom Clark wrote to Laurence Hewes of the Farm Security Administration in the Department of Agriculture, asking Hewes to develop a list of "all sites available within the limits of the Western Defense Command as resettlement areas where facilities may be established for the persons so evacuated."ʰ Focus was on sites which could be developed within a year and which would support agriculture. Clark noted that two sites had already been selected: Owens River Valley, California, and the Northern Colorado Indian Reservation at Parker, Arizona.ⁱ In short, two weeks after Executive Order 9066 was issued, consideration and planning for a mandatory evacuation and resettlement program was well under way.

ᵃMemo, Gullion to McCloy, Feb. 26, 1942, and attached draft of letter to Morgenthau from Stimson; ᵇMemo, Rand to Provost Marshal General, March 5, 1942; ᶜMemo, McCloy to Stimson, March 6, 1942; ᵈMemo, McCloy to Somervell, March 4, 1942. NARS. RG 107 (CWRIC 390–91, 85–6, 77–78, 87); ᵉLetter, Burdell to Clark, March 2, 1942; ᶠ*Ibid.*; ᵍLetter, Clark (by Burdell) to Conmy, March 6, 1942; ʰLetter, Clark to Hewes, March 7, 1942; ʲIbid. DOJ 146–13–7–2–0 (CWRIC 12147–48, 12149, 12150–51).

48. DeWitt, *Final Report,* p. 151.

49. Memo, telephone conversation, DeWitt and Gullion, March 8, 1942. NARS. RG 338 (CWRIC 2345).

50. Letter, Ford to McCloy, March 12, 1942. NARS. RG 107 (CWRIC 76).

51. Letter, Stimson to Ickes, March 12, 1942. NARS. RG 107 (CWRIC 75).

52. DeWitt, *Final Report,* p. 151.

53. Memo, McCloy to Stimson, March 6, 1942. NARS. RG 107 (CWRIC 77–78).

54. Executive Order 9102. 3 CFR, 1938–1943 Comp., pp. 1123–25.

55. Letter, Roosevelt to Eisenhower, March 18, 1942. FDRL. OF 4849 (CWRIC 3708).

56. Memo to Secretary of the Treasury. FDRL. OF 4849 (CWRIC 3966–67).

57. Executive Order 9102. 3 CRR, 1938–1943 Comp., pp. 1123–25.

58. Ninety-nine Exclusion Orders, each directed to a particular exclusion area, were issued for Military Area No. 1. Jacobus tenBroek, Edward N. Barnhart and Floyd Matson, *Prejudice, War and the Constitution* (Berkeley: University of California Press, 1954), pp. 124–25.

59. *Ibid.,* p. 92.

60. Tolan Committee, p. 11663.

61. Report prepared by Counter Intelligence Section, ONI, "The Japanese Menace on Terminal Island, San Pedro, California," Jan. 18, 1942. NARS. RG 80 (CWRIC 11925–28).

62. Written testimony, Yoshihiko Fujikawa, Los Angeles, Aug. 5, 1981.

63. Ruth E. McKee, *Wartime Exile: The Exclusion of the Japanese Americans from the West Coast* (Washington, DC: U.S. Department of the Interior, 1946), p. 124.

64. Ruth E. McKee, *History of WRA: Pearl Harbor to June 30, 1944,* unpublished manuscript, p. 11.

65. Alexander Leighton, *The Governing of Men* (Princeton: Princeton University Press, 1946), p. 38.

66. Written testimony, Yoshihiko Fujikawa, Los Angeles, Aug. 5, 1981.

67. Tolan Committee, p. 11667.

68. Testimony, Henry Murakami, Los Angeles, Aug. 6, 1981, p. 41.

69. DeWitt, *Final Report,* p. 49.

70. Memo, Bendetsen to Hewes, March 20, 1942. NARS. RG 338 (CWRIC 2087); documents in DeWitt, *Final Report,* Appendix One, pp. 519–21.

71. Report, Rathbone, U.S. Employment Service, June 19, 1942. NARS. RG 338 (CWRIC 2205–08).

72. DeWitt, *Final Report,* p. 91.

73. Telegram, Tolan to Biddle, Feb. 28, 1942. NARS. RG 107 (CWRIC 92).

74. Letter, McCloy to Hopkins, Feb. 21, 1942. NARS. RG 107 (CWRIC 101).

75. Memo, Hopkins to McCloy, Feb. 23, 1946. NARS. RG 107 (CWRIC 96).

76. Memo, Gullion to McCloy, Feb. 26, 1942, and attached draft letter, Stimson to Morgenthau. NARS. RG 107 (CWRIC 390–91).

77. Memo, McCloy to Secretary of War, March 6, 1942. NARS. RG 107 (CWRIC 77–78).

78. Memo, Marshall to DeWitt, May 28, 1942. NARS. RG 107 (CWRIC 2172).

79. Karl Bendetsen, "The Story of the Pacific Coast Japanese Evacuation," address before the Commonwealth Club of San Francisco, May 20, 1942. NARS. RG 338 (CWRIC 1861–68).

80. tenBroek, Prejudice, War, p. 126.

81. Public Proclamation No. 7, June 8, 1942, quoted in tenBroek, Prejudice, War, p. 125.

82. DeWitt, Final Report, pp. 15, 105.

83. Grodzins, Americans Betrayed, pp. 304–05.

84. Ibid., pp. 312–13.

85. DeWitt, Final Report, p. 15.

86. Grodzins, Americans Betrayed, pp. 303–22.

87. tenBroek, Prejudice, War, p. 133.

88. Office of Facts and Figures, the Office for Emergency Management, April 21, 1942, and transmitting letter, Kane to Kimmel, May 13, 1942. NARS. RG 210 (CWRIC 4126–69).

89. Telegram, Federal Council of Churches and Home Missions Council to Biddle, March 3, 1942. NARS. RG 107 (CWRIC 389).

90. Letter, McCloy to Eleanor Roosevelt, March 26, 1942. NARS. RG 107 (CWRIC 70).

91. Tolan Committee, p. 11240.

92. Telegram, Deutsch to Frankfurter, March 28, 1942. NARS. RG 107 (CWRIC 3077).

93. Letter, Frankfurter to McCloy, April 2, 1942. NARS. RG 107 (CWRIC 1740).

94 Bulletin 142, JACL, April 7, 1942. Bancroft Library (CWRIC 11938a–40a).

95. Ex parte Ventura, 44 F. Supp. 520 (W.D. Wash., 1942). Ventura's husband had earlier written the Justice Department in the hope that some exception could be made for his wife, either by making him responsible for her acts or by his volunteering for military service. The request was forwarded to the War Department and must have been refused. Letter, M. S. Ventura to Charles [sic] Biddle, March 14, 1942; Letter, Edward J. Ennis to M. S. Ventura, March 24, 1942 (CWRIC 24540; 24539).

96. On April 20, 1942, Ernest Wakayama and his wife, Toki Wakayama, American citizens, brought habeas corpus cases challenging imprisonment in an assembly center. Before the cases were decided, however, they were dismissed because the Wakayamas decided to seek expatriation to Japan, and their attorney felt that decision would adversely affect their claims. "History of Litigation Involving Western Defense Command." NARS. RG 338 (CWRIC 1628).

97. *United States* v. *Yasui*, 48 F. Supp. 40 (D. Ore. 1942).

98. *United States* v. *Hirabayashi*, 46 F. Supp. 657 (W.D. Wash. 1942).

99. *Hirabayashi* v. *United States*, 320 U.S. 81 (1943); *Yasui* v. *United States*, 320 U.S. 115 (1943).

100. "The Legal Phases of the Exclusion Program and Other Controls Imposed Pursuant to Executive Order No. 9066," p. 13, in *Supplemental Report on Civilian Controls Exercised by the Western Defense Command*. NARS. RG 338. Richard Doi was convicted and sentenced to five months; he did not appeal. "History of Litigation Involving Western Defense Command." NARS. RG 338 (CWRIC 1628). The famous case of Fred Korematsu, an American citizen who attempted to have his facial features surgically changed so that he would not be recognized as an ethnic Japanese and thus be able to remain in California with his non-Japanese fiancee, does not properly fit the category of protest. The appeal of his conviction for violating the exclusion orders was the occasion for the Supreme Court's major review of the constitutionality of the exclusion program and is discussed later.

101. *Ex parte Kanai*, 46 F. Supp. 286 (E.D. Wisc. 1942); see also "History of Litigation Involving Western Defense Command," p. 1. NARS. RG 338 (CWRIC 1627–53).

102. Memo to Watson and attached comments, April 17, 1942. NARS. RG 338 (CWRIC 2193).

103. *Ebel* v. *Drum*, 52 F. Supp. 189 (D. Mass. 1943); *Schueller* v. *Drum*, 51 F. Supp. 383 (E.D. Pa. 1943).

104. 52 F. Supp. 189 at 192 (D. Mass. 1943).

105. 52 F. Supp. 189 at 193 (D. Mass. 1943).

4

Economic Loss

1. 50 U.S.C. App. §1981 *et seq.*
2. 50 U.S.C. App. §1981(a).
3. 1948 U.S. Code Cong. Serv. 2297.
4. Testimony, William Lengacher, Washington, DC, July 14, 1981, pp. 153–54; Department of Justice, unpublished internal report of the Japanese Claims Section on the administration of the Japanese Evacuation Claims Act, undated (circa 1959) and unpaginated (the Commission has numbered the pages 27017–279) [hereafter "DOJ Report"] (CWRIC 27105).
5. DOJ Report (CWRIC 27098–100).
6. Hearings before Subcommittee No. 5 of the Committee on the Judiciary, U.S. House of Representatives, on HR 7435, (83rd Cong., 2d Sess. (1954), Serial No. 23 [hereafter "1954 Hearings"], p. 18a.
7. Leonard Broom and Ruth Riemer, *Removal and Return* (Berkeley: University of California Press, 1949), pp. 202–04. Broom changed his name from "Bloom;" for the sake of consistency, he is referred to here solely by the name of his choice.
8. F. G. Mittelbach, "Concepts and Methods in a Potential Study of Losses Among Japanese American Evacuees in 1942 and Later," paper prepared for the Commission, 1982 (CWRIC 26051–71).
9. 1954 Hearings, p. 42a.
10. Lon Hatamiya, "The Economic Effects of the Second World War Upon Japanese Americans in California," testimony of the Japanese American Citizens League National Committee for Redress, Dec. 23, 1981, p. 168.
11. *Ibid.*, p. 172.
12. *E.g.*, Roger Daniels, *Concentration Camps USA: Japanese Americans and World War II* (New York: Holt, Rinehart & Winston, 1972), p. 168.
13. HR Report No. 1809, 84th Cong., 2d Sess. (1956), p. 5.
14. DOJ Report (CWRIC 27144).
15. HR Report No. 1809, 84th Cong., 2d Sess. (1956).
16. DOJ Report (CWRIC 27278).
17. 50 U.S.C. App. §1984.
18. DOJ Report (CWRIC 27211).
19. *Ibid.* (CWRIC 27160).
20. *Ibid.* (CWRIC 27162).
21. *Claim of George Tsuda*, Adjudications of the Attorney General of the United States, Precedent Decisions Under the Japanese Evacuation Claims Act, 90 (1950).

22. *Claim of Shigemi Orimoto,* Adjudications of the Attorney General of the United States, Precedent Decisions Under the Japanese Evacuation Claims Act, 103 (1950).

23. DOJ Report (CWRIC 27144).

24. Testimony, Mitsuo Usui, Los Angeles, Aug. 5, 1981, p. 26.

25. Testimony, Elsie Hashimoto, Los Angeles, Aug. 5, 1981, p. 139.

26. Testimony, George Matsumoto, San Francisco, Aug. 13, 1981, p. 112.

27. Testimony, Tom Hayase, San Francisco, Aug. 11, 1981, p. 127.

28. U.S. Department of the Interior, *People in Motion: The Postwar Adjustment of the Evacuated Japanese Americans* (Washington, DC: U.S. Government Printing Office, undated [circa 1947]), pp. 57–59.

29. *Ibid.;* Adon Poli, *Japanese Farm Holdings on the Pacific Coast* (Davis, CA: University of California at Davis, College of Agriculture, December 1944) (CWRIC 14405–34).

30. Laurence I. Hewes, Jr., *Final Report of the Participation of the Farm Security Administration in the Evacuation Program of the Wartime Civil Control Administration, Civil Affairs Division, Western Defense Command and Fourth Army, March 15, 1942 through May 31, 1942* [hereafter "Final Report of FSA"] (CWRIC 4540–74).

31. Laurence I. Hewes, Jr., *Supplemental Report of the Participation of the Farm Security Administration in the Evacuation Program of the Wartime Civil Control Administration, Civil Affairs Dvision, Western Defense Command and Fourth Army in Military Area Number 2, June 1, 1942 through August 8, 1942* [hereafter "Supplemental Report of FSA"] (CWRIC 11594–608).

32. Masakazu Iwata, "The Japanese Immigrants in California Agriculture," *Agricultural History,* vol. 36, Jan. 1962, pp. 33–34.

33. Testimony, Mary Tsukamoto, San Francisco, Aug. 12, 1981, p. 79.

34. Testimony, Henry Sakai, Los Angeles, August 4, 1981, p. 234.

35. Written testimony, Clarence Nishizu, Los Angeles, Aug. 4, 1981.

36. Unsolicited testimony, Fred Manaka, Long Beach, CA.

37. Testimony, Jack Fujimoto, Los Angeles, Aug. 5, 1981, p. 60.

38. Testimony, Hiroshi Kamei, Los Angeles, Aug. 6, 1981, p. 243.

39. Testimony, Mike Umeda, San Francisco, Aug. 12, 1981, p. 124.

40. Report of managing secretary of the Western Growers Protective Association, Dec. 1942, reprinted in Morton Grodzins, *Americans Betrayed* (Chicago: University of Chicago Press, 1949), p. 59.

41. Testimony, Vernon Yoshioka, Los Angeles, Aug. 6, 1981, p. 111.

42. Testimony, Heizo Oshima, San Francisco, Aug. 13, 1981, p. 122.

43. *Ibid.,* pp. 120–21.

44. Testimony and written testimony, Mary Ishizuka, Los Angeles, Aug. 5, 1981, p. 231.

45. Testimony and written testimony, Jack Fujimoto, Los Angeles, Aug. 5, 1981, p. 59.

46. Final Report of FSA, pp. 5–6.

47. Memo, James F. van Loben Sels to Tom C. Clark, Coordinator, Enemy Alien Control, WDC, Feb. 23, 1942; letter, Clark to T. M. Bunn, Salinas Valley Exchange, March 12, 1942; letter, Clark to Harold J. Ryan, Agricultural

Resources and Production Committee, Los Angeles County Defense Council, March 10, 1942, DOJ 146–13–7–2–0 (CWRIC 12067; 12078; 12075).

48. Letter, Clark to Ryan, March 10, 1942, DOJ (CWRIC 12075).

49. Letter, Clark to C. D. Nickelsen, County Judge, Hood River, Oregon, March 13, 1942, DOJ (CWRIC 12086).

50. Testimony, Dick Nishi, San Francisco, Aug. 12, 1981, p. 121.

51. Testimony, Ben Yoshioka, Chicago, Sept. 22, 1981, p. 128.

52. Testimony, Shigeo Wakamatsu, Chicago, Sept. 23, 1981, p. 68.

53. Hearings before the Select Committee Investigating National Defense Migration, statement by Emergency Defense Council, Seattle chapter, Japanese American Citizens League; U.S. House of Representatives, 77th Cong., 2d Sess. 1942, p. 11454.

54. Testimony, Shokichi Tokita, Seattle, Sept. 10, 1981, p. 185.

55. Testimony, Shuzo Kato, Seattle, Sept. 9, 1981, p. 199.

56. Testimony, Ben Yoshioka, Chicago, Sept. 22, 1981, pp. 127–28.

57. Testimony, Hosen Oshita, Chicago, Sept. 22, 1981, p. 355.

58. Testimony, Elaine Hayes, Seattle, Sept. 9, 1981, p. 224.

59. Testimony, Kinnosuke Hashimoto, New York, Nov. 23, 1981, p. 123.

60. Unsolicited testimony, George Yoshida, Los Angeles.

61. Testimony, Henry Tanaka, Chicago, Sept, 22, 1981, p. 155.

62. Testimony, Lillian Hayano, Chicago, Sept. 22, 1981, p. 325; Teru Watanabe, Los Angeles, Aug. 6, 1981, p. 246.

63. Unsolicited testimony, George J. Kasai, San Antonio, TX.

64. Testimony, Mutsu Homma, Seattle, Sept. 9, 1981, p. 171.

65. Testimony, William Kika, San Francisco, Aug. 12, 1981, p. 139.

66. Unsolicited testimony, Susumu Myose, Northridge, CA.

67. Unsolicited testimony, Shizuka LaGrange, Seattle, WA.

68. Testimony, Hiroshi Kamei, Los Angeles, Aug. 6, 1981, p. 241.

69. J. L. DeWitt, *Final Report: Japanese Evacuation from the West Coast, 1942* (Washington, DC: U.S. Government Printing Office, 1943), p. 135.

70. *Evacuation Operations, Pacific Coast Military Areas*, The Federal Reserve Bank of San Francisco, Dec. 31, 1942, pp. 17–18.

71. DeWitt, *Final Report*, p. 135.

72. Report of the Select Committee Investigating National Defense Migrations, HR Report No. 1911, 77th Cong., 2d. Sess. (March 19, 1942), pp. 19–20; Cable, Tolan to Biddle, Feb. 28, 1942. NARS. RG 107 (CWRIC 92).

73. DeWitt, *Final Report*, pp. 127–29, 136–38.

74. Report of Select Committee (March 19, 1942), p. 19.

75. Dillon S. Myer, *Uprooted Americans: The Japanese Americans and the War Relocation Authority During World War II* (Tucson, AZ: University of Arizona Press, 1971), p. 253.

76. Dillon S. Myer testimony on Evauction Claims bill, reprinted in Broom and Riemer, *Removal and Return*, p. 129.

77. Poli, *Japanese Farm Holdings*, p. 17.

78. Testimony, Hiroshi Kamei, Los Angeles, Aug. 6, 1981, p. 241.

79. Unsolicited testimony, Henry Yoshitake, Montebello, CA.

80. Testimony, Yasuko Ito, San Francisco, Aug. 13, 1981, p. 52.

81. Unsolicited testimony, Roy Abbey, San Francisco, CA.

82. Testimony, Joe Yamamoto, Los Angeles, Aug. 4, 1981, p. 239.
83. Testimony, John Kimoto, Chicago, Sept, 23, 1981, p. 85.
84. Testimony, Kimiyo Okamoto, San Francisco, Aug. 12, 1981, p. 220.
85. Testimony, Murako Kato, Seattle, Sept. 10, 1981, p. 40.
86. Testimony, Esther Takei Nishio, Los Angeles, Aug. 6, 1981, p. 115.
87. Unsolicited testimony, Henry Hayashino, French Camp, CA.

5

Assembly Centers

1. Testimony, Teru Watanabe, Los Angeles, Aug. 6, 1981, p. 246.
2. Raymond Okamura and Isami Arifuku Waugh, "The Temporary Detention Camps in California," written for the Ethnic Minority Cultural Resources Survey, State of California, manuscript, p. 7. The earlier evacuation of Terminal Island was conducted under separate authority. (CWRIC 26778–800).
3. War Relocation Authority, *The Evacuated People: A Quantitative Description* (Washington, DC: U.S. Government Printing Office, 1946), p. 8. In addition, the WCCA had control of 1,022 persons remaining in institutions in the evacuated area.
4. Okamura and Waugh, "Temporary Detention Camps," p. 10.
5. Dillon S. Myer, *Uprooted Americans: The Japanese Americans and the War Relocation Authority during World War II* (Tucson, AZ: University of Arizona Press, 1971), p. 30.
6. J. L. DeWitt, *Final Report: Japanese Evacuation from the West Coast, 1942* (Washington, DC: U.S. Government Printing Office, 1943), pp. 89–93. Some evacuees recall that they learned where and when to evacuate and what baggage could be carried from posters in the neighborhood rather than from the control station.
7. Testimony, Betty Matsuo, San Francisco, Aug. 11, 1981, p. 273.
8. Monica Sone, *Nisei Daughter* (Seattle and London: University of Washington Press, 1953), p. 166.
9. DeWitt, *Final Report*, p. 100.
10. *Ibid.*, pp. 125–26.
11. Testimony, Grace Nakamura, Los Angeles, Aug. 6, 1981, p. 252.
12. Testimony, Ben Kasubachi, Seattle, Sept. 11, 1981, p. 163.
13. Written testimony, Shigeo Nishimura, Los Angeles, July 23, 1981.
14. Testimony, Grace Nakamura, Los Angeles, Aug. 6, 1981, p. 252.
15. Unsolicited testimony, Leonard Abrams, Philadelphia.
16. Testimony, William Kochiyama, New York, Nov. 23, 1981, p. 97.
17. Okamura and Waugh, "Temporary Detention Camps," p. 8.
18. American National Red Cross, "Report of the American Red Cross Survey of Assembly Centers in California, Oregon, and Washington," August 1942, unpublished manuscript, pp. 18–19. NARS. RG 200 [hereafter "Red Cross Survey of Assembly Centers"].
19. DeWitt, *Final Report*, pp. 152, 158–59.
20. *Ibid.*, pp. 158–59.

21. Testimony, Sally Kazama, Seattle, Sept. 11, 1981, p. 39; DeWitt, *Final Report*, p. 152.

22. DeWitt, *Final Report*, p. 183.

23. *Ibid.*, p. 184.

24. *Ibid.*, pp. 184, 186.

25. Michi Weglyn, *Years of Infamy: The Untold Story of America's Concentration Camps* (New York: William Morrow & Co., 1976), p. 79.

26. Mine Okubo, *Citizen 13660* (New York: Arno Press, 1978 [1946]), p. 63.

27. Testimony, Ken Hayashi, Los Angeles, Aug. 4, 1981, p. 222.

28. Testimony, James M. Goto, M.D., Los Angeles, Aug. 5, 1981, p. 212.

29. Testimony, Toshiko Toku, Seattle, Sept. 10, 1981, p. 39.

30. Testimony, James T. Fujii, Los Angeles, Aug. 6, 1981, p. 80.

31. Testimony, Thomas M. Tajiri, Chicago, Sept. 22, 1981, p. 293.

32. Testimony, Marshall M. Sumida, San Francisco, Aug. 11, 1981, p. 102.

33. Red Cross Survey of Assembly Centers, p. 37.

34. Testimony, Grace Nakamura, Los Angeles, Aug. 6, 1981, p. 253.

35. Okubo, *Citizen 13660*, p. 50.

36. *Ibid.*, pp. 97, 99.

37. Testimony, Peggy Nishimoto Mitchell, Seattle, Sept. 9, 1981, p. 220.

38. Testimony, Kazuko Ige, Chicago, Sept. 22, 1981, p. 313.

39. Testimony, Kinya Noguchi, San Francisco, Aug. 11, 1981, p. 107.

40. Testimony, James M. Goto, M.D., Los Angeles, Aug. 5, 1981, p. 213.

41. Written testimony, Bill Nakagawa, Los Angeles, Aug. 5, 1981.

42. Testimony, Elaine Yoneda, San Francisco, Aug. 12, 1981, p. 46.

43. Okubo, *Citizen 13660*, p. 106.

44. Testimony, George Kawachi, Seattle, Sept. 9, 1981, p. 236.

45. Written testimony, Bill Nakagawa, Los Angeles, Aug. 5, 1981.

46. Sone, *Nisei Daughter*, p. 180.

47. Testimony, Patsy Saiki, Seattle, Sept. 9, 1981, p. 36.

48. Testimony, Peter Ota, Los Angeles, Aug. 6, 1981, p. 98. See testimony, Suzu Kunitani, San Francisco, Aug. 13, 1981, p. 62, for another description of a tuberculosis case. Those whom the WCCA considered too sick to move, who resided in institutions, or who were in prison, received exemptions or deferments until they were able to travel. (DeWitt, *Final Report*, p. 145.)

49. Testimony, Mary Tsukamoto, San Francisco, Aug. 12, 1981, p. 81.

50. Testimony, Mitzi Shio Schectman, Chicago, Sept. 22, 1981, p. 186. Their father eventually joined them at Puyallup and died at Minidoka.

51. DeWitt, *Final Report*, p. 145.

52. Testimony, Sumiko Seo Seki, Los Angeles, Aug. 5, 1981, p. 79.

53. Testimony, Misao Sakamoto, Seattle, Sept. 9, 1981, p. 177.

54. DeWitt, *Final Report*, p. 186. There were apparently some exceptions to the rule. Rachel Kawasaki recalls that her baby's 2:00 a.m. feeding was delivered to her door by jeep. Unsolicited testimony, Rachel Kawasaki, Los Angeles.

55. Unsolicited testimony, Hideo Furukawa, Palo Alto.

56. Weglyn, *Years of Infamy*, p. 82.
57. Testimony, Haru Isaki, Seattle, Sept. 9, 1981, p. 266.
58. Testimony, Sally Kazama, Seattle, Sept. 11, 1981, p. 39.
59. Testimony, Yasuko Ito, San Francisco, Aug. 13, 1981, p. 52.
60. Testimony, Tsuyako Kitashima, San Francisco, Aug. 13, 1981, p. 167.
61. Testimony, Shizuko Tokushige, San Francisco, Aug. 12, 1981, p. 227.
62. Testimony, James M. Goto, M.D., Los Angeles, Aug. 5, 1981, p. 213.
63. Testimony, Masaaki Hironaka, Los Angeles, Aug. 5, 1981, p. 129.
64. Red Cross Survey of Assembly Centers, p. 4.
65. DeWitt, *Final Report*, p. 193.
66. Santa Anita Assembly Center, Arcadia, CA, *Administrative Notice No. 4*, May 12, 1942.
67. DeWitt, *Final Report*, p. 186.
68. Testimony, Tetsu Saito, Los Angeles, Aug. 6, 1981, p. 18.
69. Testimony, Hiroshi Kadokura, Chicago, Sept. 23, 1981, p. 177.
70. Okubo, *Citizen 13660*, p. 86.
71. Letter, Bill Hosokawa to Angus Macbeth, Commission staff, Sept. 14, 1982 (CWRIC 8800-16).
72. Okubo, *Citizen 13660*, p. 78.
73. Testimony, Kinya Noguchi, San Francisco, Aug. 11, 1981, p. 107.
74. Testimony, Misao Sakamoto, Seattle, Sept. 9, 1981, p. 177.
75. DeWitt, *Final Report*, p. 186.
76. *Ibid.*, p. 188.
77. Okubo, *Citizen 13660*, p. 84.
78. Testimony, Masaaki Hironaka, Los Angeles, Aug. 5, 1981, p. 129.
79. "No sharp increase in the number of deaths occurred as a result of the evacuation program." (DeWitt, *Final Report*, p. 190.)
80. *Idem*.
81. Red Cross Survey of Assembly Centers, p. 28.
82. Testimony, Yoshiye Togasaki, M.D., San Francisco, Aug. 11, 1981, p. 227.
83. Unsolicited testimony, George M. Suda, D.D.S., Fresno.
84. Testimony, Kikuo H. Taira, M.D., San Francisco, Aug. 11, 1981, p. 223.
85. Written testimony, Yoshiye Togasaki, M.D., San Francisco, Aug. 11, 1981.
86. Unsolicited testimony, George M. Suda, D.D.S., Fresno.
87. Testimony, Yoshiye Togasaki, M.D., San Francisco, Aug. 11, 1981, p. 227.
88. Testimony, Kikuo H. Taira, M.D., San Francisco, Aug. 11, 1981, p. 223.
89. Testimony, Tom Watanabe, M.D., Los Angeles, Aug. 4, 1981, p. 231.
90. Sone, *Nisei Daughter*, p. 178.
91. Weglyn, *Years of Infamy*, p. 81.
92. DeWitt, *Final Report*, p. 192; testimony, Susumu Sato, Seattle, Sept. 9, 1981, p. 115.
93. Red Cross Survey of Assembly Centers, p. 52.
94. DeWitt, *Final Report*, p. 207.

95. Okubo, *Citizen 13660*, p. 92.
96. Testimony, Frances C. Kitagawa, Los Angeles, Aug. 6, 1981, p. 122.
97. Okubo, *Citizen 13660*, p. 92.
98. DeWitt, *Final Report*, p. 209.
99. Unsolicited testimony, Hiroko Azuma Miyakawa, Matawan, NJ.
100. DeWitt, *Final Report*, p. 208.
101. *Ibid.*, pp. 209–10.
102. Okubo, *Citizen 13660*, p. 88.
103. *Ibid.*, p. 93.
104. Unsolicited testimony, Sachi Kajiwara, Dayton, OH.
105. Okubo, *Citizen 13660*, p. 103.
106. *Ibid.*, p. 105.
107. *Ibid.*, p. 104.
108. DeWitt, *Final Report*, pp. 211–12.
109. *Idem.*
110. Unsolicited testimony, A. Arthur Takemoto, Encinitas, CA.
111. DeWitt, *Final Report*, p. 213.
112. Okubo, *Citizen 13660*, p. 91.
113. DeWitt, *Final Report*, p. 205.
114. Testimony, Masaaki Hironaka, Los Angeles, Aug. 5, 1981, p. 129.
115. Testimony, Yayoi Ono, Los Angeles, Aug. 5, 1981, p. 257.
116. DeWitt, *Final Report*, p. 205.
117. Memo, DeWitt to McCloy, May 2, 1942. NARS. RG 107 (CWRIC 215–17).
118. DeWitt, *Final Report*, pp. 205–06.
119. Testimony, Masaaki Hironaka, Los Angeles, Aug. 5, 1981, p. 130; Weglyn, *Years of Infamy*, p. 81.
120. Testimony, Wilson H. Makabe, San Francisco, Aug. 11, 1981, p. 78.
121. Okubo, *Citizen 13660*, p. 60.
122. DeWitt, *Final Report*, p. 218.
123. Testimony, Lillian Kiyota, San Francisco, Aug. 11, 1981, p. 271.
124. Red Cross Survey of Assembly Centers, p. 22.
125. Minoru Masuda, "Injury and Redress," *Rikka*, vol. 6, no. 3 (Autumn 1979), p. 20; Sone, *Nisei Daughter*, p. 176.
126. Okubo, *Citizen 13660*, p. 59.
127. Testimony, Ruby Okubo, Los Angeles, Aug. 6, 1981, p. 288.
128. DeWitt, *Final Report*, p. 218.
129. Santa Anita Assembly Center, *Regulations*, April 12, 1942.
130. Okubo, *Citizen 13660*, p. 108; Sone, *Nisei Daughter*, p. 187.
131. Testimony, Yoshio Nakamura, Los Angeles, Aug. 6, 1981, p. 249.
132. Okubo, *Citizen 13660*, p. 108.
133. Sone, *Nisei Daughter*, p. 187.
134. DeWitt, *Final Report*, p. 218.
135. Testimony, Sumiko Seo Seki, Los Angeles, Aug. 5, 1981, p. 79.
136. Testimony, Kay Yamashita, Chicago, Sept. 22, 1981, p. 213.
137. Testimony, Thomas M. Tajiri, Chicago, Sept. 22, 1981, p. 294; testimony, Louise Crowley, Seattle, Sept. 9, 1981, p. 69 (Puyallup).

138. Okubo, *Citizen 13660*, p. 79.

139. Unsolicited testimony, Jack Oda, Chicago.

140. Santa Anita Assembly Center, *Administrative Notice No. 5*, May 14, 1942.

6

The Relocation Centers

1. The Manzanar evacuees did not move; Manzanar was transferred by the WCCA to the WRA to become a relocation center on June 1, 1942.

2. Michi Weglyn, *Years of Infamy: The Untold Story of America's Concentration Camps* (New York: William Morrow & Co., 1976), p. 89.

3. Report of the WRA, March 18—June 30, 1942, p. 8. NARS. RG 210. The War Relocation Authority, first under the Office for Emergency Management and later under the U.S. Department of the Interior, issued quarterly reports covering 1942, and thereafter semiannual reports until the agency disbanded in 1946.

4. Report of the WRA, July 1—September 30, 1942, p. 1.

5. Report of the WRA, October 1—December 31, 1942, p. 2.

6. J. L. DeWitt, *Final Report: Japanese Evacuation from the West Coast, 1942* (Washington, DC: U.S. Government Printing Office, 1943), pp. 282–84, 288.

7. *Ibid.*, p. 289.

8. Unsolicited testimony, Chebo Toshitaka Sakaguchi.

9. Testimony, Shizuko S. Tokushige, San Francisco, Aug. 12, 1981, p. 227.

10. Testimony, Henry Sugimoto, New York, Nov. 23, 1981, p. 208; testimony, Hideko Sasaki, Los Angeles, Aug. 6, 1981, p. 134; testimony, Mark Murakami, Seattle, Sept. 9, 1981, p. 38.

11. Testimony, Henry Sugimoto, New York, Nov. 23, 1981, p. 208.

12. Testimony, Dick Nishi, San Francisco, Aug. 12, 1981, p. 121.

13. DeWitt, *Final Report*, p. 289.

14. Unsolicited testimony, George J. Kasai; testimony, Elsie Hashimoto, Los Angeles, Aug. 5, 1981, p. 140; testimony, Shizuko S. Tokushige, San Francisco, Aug. 12, 1981, p. 227; testimony, Kikuo H. Taira, San Francisco, Aug. 11, 1981, p. 225; but see Monica Sone, *Nisei Daughter* (Seattle, WA: University of Washington Press, 1953), p. 190; Mine Okubo, *Citizen 13660* (New York: Arno Press, 1978 [1946]), p. 118.

15. DeWitt, *Final Report*, p. 289.

16. Testimony, Kiyoshi Sonoda, Los Angeles, Aug. 5, 1981, p. 222; testimony, Shizuko S. Tokushige, San Francisco, Aug. 12, 1981, p. 228.

17. Testimony, Dick Nishi, San Francisco, Aug. 12, 1981, p. 121.

18. Unsolicited testimony, George J. Kasai.

19. Testimony, Shizuko S. Tokushige, San Francisco, Aug. 12, 1981, p. 228.

20. Report of the WRA, July 1—September 30, 1942, p. 6.

21. Alexander H. Leighton, *The Governing of Men* (Princeton: Princeton University Press, 1945), pp. 64–66.

22. Executive Order 9102, March 18, 1942. FDRL (CWRIC 6197–99). The WRA, which was established as an agency under the Office for Emergency Management in the Executive Office of the President, was transferred to the Department of the Interior in February 1944.

23. Milton S. Eisenhower, *The President Is Calling* (Garden City, NY: Doubleday & Co., 1974), p. 96. Eisenhower, analyzing the evacuation and detention, concluded that no one was solely responsible because no one could see the "over-all pattern that was emerging." He also concluded:

> The evacuation of Japanese Americans from their homes on the coast to hastily constructed assembly centers and then to inland relocation centers was an inhuman mistake. Thousands of American citizens of Japanese ancestry were stripped of their rights and freedoms and treated almost like enemy prisoners of war. Many lost their homes, their businesses, their savings. For 120,000 Japanese the evacuation was a bad dream come to pass. (Eisenhower, *The President Is Calling*, p. 125).

24. Roger Daniels, *Concentration Camps USA: Japanese Americans and World War II* (New York: Holt, Rinehart & Winston, 1972), p. 91, quoting letter from Eisenhower to Wickard, April 1, 1942.

25. Report of the Select Committee Investigating National Defense Migration, "Preliminary Report and Recommendations of Evacuation of Citizens and Aliens from Military Areas," March 19, 1942, U.S. House of Representatives, 77th Cong., 2d Sess., HR Report No. 1911, p. 17.

26. *Ibid.*, p. 16.

27. *Ibid.*, p. 18.

28. Eisenhower, *The President Is Calling*, p. 117.

29. WDC summary and WRA report of meeting with governors and other officials regarding relocation of Japanese, Salt Lake City, Utah, April 7, 1942. NARS. RG 338 (CWRIC 4188–216).

30. Letter, Mike Masaoka to Eisenhower, April 6, 1942. NARS. RG 210 (CWRIC 3734–51).

31. Eisenhower, *The President Is Calling*, pp. 116–17.

32. The account of the meeting is taken from the WDC summary, above; Eisenhower, *The President Is Calling*, pp. 117–19; and testimony, Karl Bendetsen, Washington, DC, Nov. 2, 1981, p. 40.

33. WDC summary of April 7, 1942 meeting.

34. Eisenhower, *The President Is Calling*, p. 119.

35. Telephone conversation between Bendetsen and Alfred Jaretzki, April 27, 1942. NARS. RG 338 (CWRIC 5226–32).

36. Statement of Philip M. Glick (formerly Solicitor for the War Relocation Authority), Hearings before the Committee on Internal Security, U.S. House of Representatives, 91st Cong., 2d Sess., March 19, 1970, pp. 3045–47. Two exceptions to the decision for confinement were already in progress, student leave and agricultural leave. A later section describes these programs.

37. Eisenhower, *The President Is Calling*, p. 95.

38. *Ibid.*, p. 122.

39. Report of the WRA, March 18—June 30, 1942, p. 6.

40. *Idem.* The War Department had retained an approval right to ensure that "large numbers of evacuees might not be located immediately adjacent to present or proposed military installations or strategically important areas." DeWitt, *Final Report*, p. 248.

41. U.S. Department of the Interior, *WRA: A Story of Human Conservation* (Washington, DC: U.S. Government Printing Office, 1947), p. 20 [hereafter "*WRA Story*"].

42. Report of the WRA, March 18—June 30, 1942, p. 7.

43. *WRA Story*, p. 20.

44. Roger Daniels, *Concentration Camps USA*, p. 96.

45. DeWitt, *Final Report*, p. 263; *WRA Story*, p. 20.

46. Report of the WRA, March 18—June 30, 1942, p. 10.

47. Dorothy S. Thomas and Richard S. Nishimoto, *The Spoilage: Japanese-American Evacuation and Resettlement During World War II* (Berkeley: University of California Press, 1969), p. 28.

48. DeWitt, *Final Report*, p. 264; Report of the WRA, March 18—June 30, 1942, p. 9.

49. DeWitt, *Final Report*, pp. 249–50.

50. *Idem.*

51. DeWitt, *Final Report*, p. 263; Thomas and Nishimoto, *Spoilage*, p. 28.

52. *WRA Story*, p. 22.

53. Letter, Masaoka to Eisenhower, April 6, 1942. NARS. RG 210 (CWRIC 3734–51).

54. *WRA Story*, p. 75.

55. DeWitt, *Final Report*, pp. 248, 264.

56. Unsolicited testimony, George G. Muramoto.

57. Gladys Bell, "Memories of Topaz," unpublished manuscript.

58. Testimony, Elizabeth Nishikawa, Los Angeles, Aug. 4, 1981, p. 210; interview, Aiko Herzig-Yoshinaga, Washington, DC, July 20, 1982.

59. Report of the WRA, March 18—June 30, 1942, p. 12; Thomas and Nishimoto, *Spoilage*, p. 29.

60. Report of the WRA, March 18—June 30, 1942, p. 12; Okubo, *Citizen 13660*, p. 124.

61. Testimony, Elizabeth Nishikawa, Los Angeles, Aug. 4, 1981, p. 209; Report of the WRA, October 1—December 31, 1942, p. 7.

62. Dillon S. Myer, *Uprooted Americans: The Japanese Americans and the War Relocation Authority During World War II* (Tucson, AZ: University of Arizona Press, 1971), p. 31; Report of the WRA, March 18—June 30, 1942, p. 12.

63. DeWitt, *Final Report*, p. 264.

64. Thomas and Nishimoto, *Spoilage*, p. 29; letter, Bill Hosokawa to Angus Macbeth, Commission staff, Sept. 14, 1982 (CWRIC 8800–16).

65. Unsolicited testimony, Susumu Togasaki.

66. "Report on Visit to Japanese Evacuation Camps," undated, cited in Thomas and Nishimoto, *Spoilage*, p. 39.

67. Unsolicited testimony, Dean Meeker, Dane, WI.

68. Thomas and Nishimoto, *Spoilage*, p. 29.

69. *San Francisco Chronicle*, May 26, 1943, quoted in Lillian Baker, *The Concentration Camp Conspiracy* (Glendale, CA: AFHA Publications, 1981), p. 258.

70. Minoru Masuda, "Japanese Americans: Injury and Redress," *Rikka*, vol. 6, no. 3 (Autumn 1979), p. 20.

71. Okubo, *Citizen 13660*, pp. 129–31, 146.

72. Bell, "Memories of Topaz;" testimony, Haru Isaki, Seattle, Sept. 9, 1981, p. 346.

73. Interview, Aiko Herzig-Yoshinaga, Washington, DC, July 20, 1982.

74. Testimony, Ken Hayashi, Los Angeles, Aug. 4, 1981, p. 222.

75. Written testimony, Kikuo H. Taira, San Francisco, Aug. 11, 1981, p. 9.

76. Testimony, Frank M. Kajikawa, Chicago, Sept. 22, 1981, p. 339.

77. Edward H. Spicer, Asael I. Hansen, Katherine Luomala and Marvin K. Opler, *Impounded People: Japanese-Americans in the Relocation Centers* (Tucson, AZ: University of Arizona Press, 1969), p. 66.

78. Report of the WRA, July 1—Sept. 30, 1942, pp. 4–5; unsolicited testimony, Dean Meeker, Dane, WI.

79. Testimony, Shuzo C. Kato, Seattle, Sept. 9, 1981, p. 201.

80. Report of the WRA, July 1—September 30, 1942, p. 4.

81. Thomas and Nishimoto, *Spoilage*, p. 39.

82. *Idem*.

83. Spicer, *Impounded People*, p. 99.

84. Bell, "Memories of Topaz."

85. Testimony, Tom Misawa, San Francisco, Aug. 13, 1981, p. 182.

86. Okubo, *Citizen 13660*, p. 137; *Rikka*, vol. 6, no. 3 (Autumn 1979), p. 20.

87. Written testimony, Noriko S. Bridges, San Francisco, Aug. 11, 1981.

88. Testimony, Henry Sugimoto, New York, Nov. 23, 1981, p. 209; Okubo, *Citizen 13660*, p. 138; Sone, *Nisei Daughter*, pp. 195–96.

89. Sone, *Nisei Daughter*, p. 196; *Rikka*, vol. 6, no. 3 (Autumn 1979), p. 20.

90. Weglyn, *Years of Infamy*, p. 83.

91. Okubo, *Citizen 13660*, pp. 149, 192.

92. Testimony, Tsuyako Shimizu, New York, Nov. 23, 1981, p. 129.

93. Unsolicited testimony, Mary Tonai (Heart Mountain); unsolicited testimony, Olive Ogawa Hall (Poston); testimony, Lillian K. Hayano, Chicago, Sept. 22, 1981, p. 327 (Poston); Okubo, *Citizen 13660*, p. 184 (Topaz).

94. Sone, *Nisei Daughter*, p. 192.

95. Testimony, Eiichi E. Sakauye, San Francisco, Aug. 12, 1981, p. 226.

96. Testimony, George Matsumoto, San Francisco, Aug. 12, 1981, p. 113.

97. Testimony, Kiyo Sato-Viacrucis, San Francisco, Aug. 12, 1981, p. 73.

98. Unsolicited testimony, Ben T. Kawashima.

99. Unsolicited testimony, Sueko Yamasaki Kawamoto; testimony, Tom

Shimasaki, San Francisco, Aug. 11, 1981, p. 117; testimony, Mary F. Odagiri, Los Angeles, Aug. 6, 1981, p. 130.

100. Testimony, Betty Matsuo, San Francisco, Aug. 11, 1981, p. 275.

101. WRA Story, pp. 100–02.

102. Interview, Aiko Herzig-Yoshinaga, Washington, DC, July 20, 1982.

103. Unsolicited testimony, Nobu Kajiwara.

104. Testimony, Yasuko Ito, San Francisco, Aug. 13, 1981, p. 54.

105. WRA Story, p. 102.

106. Testimony, Mamoru Ogata, Los Angeles, Aug. 6, 1981, p. 31; unsolicited testimony, Susumu Togasaki and George J. Kasai.

107. San Francisco Chronicle, May 26, 1943, quoted in Baker, Concentration Camp Conspiracy, p. 259.

108. Report of the WRA, July 1—September 30, 1942, p. 35.

109. Unsolicited testimony, George G. Muramoto.

110. DeWitt, Final Report, p. 186.

111. Report of the WRA, July 1—September 30, 1942, p. 35.

112. Okubo, Citizen 13660, p. 143.

113. WRA Story, p. 102.

114. Ibid., p. 80.

115. Report of the WRA, October 1—December 31, 1942, p. 24.

116. Okubo, Citizen 13660, p. 151; Sone, Nisei Daughter, p. 197.

117. Report of the WRA, October 1—December 31, 1942, p. 8.

118. Idem; Report of the WRA, July 1—September 30, 1942, p. 32; testimony, Tamotsu Tsuchida, San Francisco, Aug. 12, 1981, p. 203; testimony, Harold Ouye, San Francisco, Aug. 12, 1981, p. 85; written testimony, Kiyoshi Sonoda, Los Angeles, Aug. 5, 1981, p. 223.

119. Testimony, Emi Somekawa, Seattle, Sept. 10, 1981, p. 93; Report of the WRA, March 18 - June 30, 1942, p. 29; testimony, Kiyoshi Sonoda, Los Angeles, Aug. 5, 1981, p. 223; Ruth E. McKee, History of WRA: Pearl Harbor to June 30, 1944, unpublished manuscript, 1944, p. 119.

120. Myer, Uprooted Americans, pp. 52–53; McKee, History of WRA, p. 120.

121. Testimony, Miyo Senzaki, Los Angeles, Aug. 5, 1981, p. 154.

122. Testimony, Yoshihiko F. Fujikawa, Los Angeles, Aug. 5, 1981, p. 67.

123. Testimony, Kiyoshi Sonoda, Los Angeles, Aug. 5, 1981, p. 223.

124. Report of the WRA, July 1—Dec. 31, 1943, p. 70.

125. Testimony, Tom Watanabe, Los Angeles, Aug. 4, 1981, p. 231.

126. Testimony, Suzu Kunitani, San Francisco, Aug. 13, 1981, p. 63.

127. Unsolicited testimony, Sachi Kajiwara.

128. Testimony, Tsuye Nozawa, Los Angeles, Aug. 5, 1981, p. 39.

129. Testimony, Yoshiye Togasaki, San Francisco, Aug. 11, 1981, p. 228.

130. Testimony, Elaine Ishikawa Hayes, Seattle, Sept. 9, 1981, p. 223; testimony, Richard Aoki, San Francisco, Aug. 13, 1981, p. 85.

131. Testimony, Samuel T. Shoji, Seattle, Sept. 9, 1981, p. 212.

132. Unsolicited testimony, Rae Ota Yasumura.

133. Report of the WRA, October 1—December 31, 1942, p. 19.

134. Interview, Aiko Herzig-Yoshinaga, Washington, DC, July 20, 1982.

135. Report of the WRA, January 1—June 30, 1943, p. 32.

136. Report of the WRA, October 1—Dec. 31, 1942, p. 7.

137. McKee, *History of WRA*, p. 122.

138. *Ibid.*, pp. 105–07.

139. U.S. Department of the Interior, *The Evacuated People: A Quantitative Description* (Washington, DC: U.S. Government Printing Office, 1946), p. 150.

140. Okubo, *Citizen 13660*, p. 142.

141. Testimony, Peggy Nishimoto Mitchell, Seattle, Sept. 9, 1981, p. 221.

142. Unsolicited testimony, Carolyn Abe Kanaya; Report of the WRA, October 1—December 31, 1942, p. 19.

143. Written testimony, Peggy Nishimoto Mitchell.

144. Testimony, Y. Shiomoto, San Francisco, Aug. 12, 1981, p. 70 (polio); testimony, Alice Okazaki, San Francisco, Aug. 13, 1981, p. 32 (tuberculosis).

145. Report of the WRA, July 1—December 31, 1943, p. 87.

146. Letter, John Rademaker to Frank L. Sweetser, WRA, Sept. 24, 1943. NARS. RG 210 (CWRIC 3211-21).

147. Rita Takahashi Cates, *Comparative Administration and Management of Five War Relocation Authority Camps,* unpublished doctoral dissertation, University of Pittsburgh, September 1980, p. 134.

148. Testimony, Noboru Morimoto, San Francisco, Aug. 13, 1981, p. 144; testimony, Richard Yoshikawa, San Francisco, Aug. 12, 1981, p. 166.

149. Report of the WRA, March 18—June 30, 1942, p. 15.

150. *WRA Story*, p. 76.

151. *Ibid.*, p. 76.

152. *Ibid.*, pp. 78–79.

153. *Ibid.*, pp. 77–79.

154. *Ibid.*, pp. 77, 79–80.

155. *Ibid.*, p. 80.

156. Testimony, Ruth Colburn, San Francisco, Aug. 11, 1981, p. 277.

157. *WRA Story*, pp. 81–82.

158. Testimony, Nellie Sakakihara, San Francisco, Aug. 12, 1981, p. 127; testimony, Soto Yoshida, San Francisco, Aug. 12, 1981, p. 212; testimony, Katsuyo Oekawa, Los Angeles, Aug. 4, 1981, p. 113.

159. Testimony, Tom Hoshiyama, San Francisco, Aug. 13, 1981, p. 49.

160. Testimony, Bert Arata, Chicago, Sept. 23, 1981, p. 174.

161. Testimony, Akira Arai, Chicago, Sept. 22, 1981, p. 428.

162. Report of the WRA, October 1—December 31, 1942, p. 9.

163. Report of the WRA, January 1—June 30, 1943, p. 25; Report of the WRA, October 1—December 31, 1942, pp. 16–17.

164. Report of the WRA, July 1—Dec. 31, 1943, p. 62.

165. *Ibid.*, p. 62.

166. Okubo, *Citizen 13660*, p. 196.

167. Report of the WRA, July 1—December 31, 1943, p. 63.

168. McKee, *History of WRA*, pp. 101–02.

169. Report of the WRA, January 1—June 30, 1943, p. 27.

170. Report of the WRA, July 1—December 31, 1943, p. 67.

171. Report of the WRA, October 1—December 31, 1942, p. 18.

172. Report of the WRA, January 1—June 30, 1943, p. 27.
173. Unsolicited testimony, Susumu Togasaki.
174. Report of the WRA, March 18—June 30, 1942, pp. 24–25.
175. Report of the WRA, October 1—December 31, 1942, p. 20.
176. Report of the WRA, January 1—June 30, 1943, p. 29.
177. Report of the WRA, October 1—December 31, 1942, p. 21.
178. *San Francisco Chronicle,* May 26, 1943, quoted in Baker, *Concentration Camp Conspiracy,* p. 258.
179. Testimony, Kinya Noguchi, San Francisco, Aug. 11, 1981, p. 108.
180. McKee, *History of WRA,* p. 111.
181. Myer, *Uprooted Americans,* p. 49.
182. Report of the WRA, October 1 - December 31, 1942, pp. 14–15.
183. Testimony, Shuzo C. Kato, Seattle, Sept. 9, 1981, p. 201.
184. Testimony, James Hirabayashi, San Francisco, Aug. 11, 1981, p. 261.
185. Report of the WRA, July 1—September 30, 1942, p. 30.
186. Written testimony, Grace Nakamura, Los Angeles, Aug. 6, 1981.
187. McKee, *History of WRA,* p. 112.
188. Report of the WRA, July 1—December 31, 1943, p. 74.
189. Myer, *Uprooted Americans,* p. 51; Unsolicited testimony, Rae Ota Yasumura; testimony, Allan Hida, Chicago, Sept. 22, 1981, p. 124.
190. McKee, *History of WRA,* p. 113; testimony, Hiroshi Kamei, Los Angeles, Sept. 6, 1981, p. 244.
191. Testimony, Bruce Kaji, Los Angeles, Aug. 6, 1981, p. 272.
192. Report of the WRA, October 1—December 31, 1942, p. 15.
193. Myer, *Uprooted Americans,* p. 51.
194. Reports of the WRA, October 1—December 31, 1942, p. 15.
195. Report of the WRA, March 18—June 30, 1942, p. 27; Report of the WRA, July 1—December 31, 1943, p. 75.
196. Testimony, Mary Sugitachi, San Francisco, August 12, 1981, p. 219; Report of the WRA, July 1—September 30, 1942, p. 30.
197. Myer, *Uprooted Americans,* p. 48.
198. Unsolicited testimony, Carolyn Abe Kanaya; written testimony, Mary Sugitachi, San Francisco, Aug. 12, 1981.
199. Unsolicitied testimony, Hiroko Azuma Miyakawa; unsolicited testimony, Roy Mike Hamachi.
200. Weglyn, *Years of Infamy,* p. 92.
201. John Tateishi, "Remembrances of Manzanar," *Rikka,* vol. 6, no. 3 (Autumn 1979), p. 61.
202. McKee, *History, of WRA,* p. 133.
203. Report of the WRA, October 1—December 31, 1942, p. 48.
204. Myer, *Uprooted Americans,* p. 56; *WRA Story,* p. 108.
205. Report of the WRA, October 1—December 31, 1942, p. 48.
206. Okubo, *Citizen 13660,* p. 170.
207. *Ibid.,* p. 171.
208. Written testimony, Mitsuru Sasahara, Los Angeles, July 20, 1981.
209. Report of the WRA, October 1—December 31, 1942, p. 49.
210. Report of the WRA, January 1—June 30, 1943, p. 27.
211. Unsolicited testimony, Kin Ikeda.

212. Written testimony, Mitsuru Sasahara, Los Angeles, Aug. 5, 1981.

213. *Idem*.

214. Bell, "Memories of Topaz," p. 8.

215. Testimony, Ruth Colburn, San Francisco, Aug. 11, 1981, p. 276 *ff*.

216. Report of the WRA, July 1—December 31, 1943, p. 87.

217. Okubo, *Citizen 13660*, pp. 150, 156.

218. *Ibid.*, p. 157; testimony, Tsuyako Shimizu, New York, Nov. 23, 1981, p. 129.

219. *Ibid.*, pp. 182, 187.

220. Report of the WRA, January 1—June 30, 1943, p. 36.

221. Report of the WRA, October 1—December 31, 1942, p. 49.

222. Okubo, *Citizen 13660*, p. 174.

223. Report of the WRA, January 1—June 30, 1943, p. 36.

224. Testimony, Sam Shoji, Seattle, Sept. 9, 1981, p. 277.

225. *WRA Story*, p. 107.

226. Bell, "Memories of Topaz;" Report of the WRA, July 1—September 30, 1942, p. 38.

227. Report of the WRA, October 1—December 31, 1942, p. 27.

228. Report of the WRA, July 1—September 30, 1942, p. 38.

229. McKee, *History of WRA*, p. 135.

230. Report of the WRA, July 1—September 30, 1942, pp. 38–39.

231. Report of the WRA, January 1—June 30, 1943, p. 38.

232. Testimony, Elizabeth Nishikawa, Los Angeles, Aug. 4, 1981, p. 213.

233. *San Francisco Chronicle*, May 26, 1943, quoted in Baker, *Concentration Camp Conspiracy*, p. 258.

234. McKee, *History of WRA*, p. 136.

235. Myer, *Uprooted Americans*, p. 57.

236. McKee, *History of WRA*, p. 138.

237. Myer, *Uprooted Americans*, pp. 38–40.

238. Report of the WRA, July 1—September 30, 1942, p. 23 *ff*.

239. *WRA Story*, pp. 86–87.

240. Myer, *Uprooted Americans*, pp. 39–40.

241. *WRA Story*, p. 90.

242. Myer, *Uprooted Americans*, p. 40.

243. Letter, Hosokawa to Macbeth, Commission staff, Sept. 14, 1982 (CWRIC 8800–16).

244. McKee, *History of WRA*, p. 104; unsolicited testimony, Y. Florence Kubota.

245. Okubo, *Citizen 13660*, p. 155.

246. McKee, *History of WRA*, p. 104.

247. Thomas and Nishimoto, *Spoilage*, p. 27; *San Francisco Chronicle*, May 26, 1943, quoted in Baker, *Concentration Camp Conspiracy*, p. 258.

248. Unsolicited testimony, Suenari Koyasako.

249. Thomas and Nishimoto, *Spoilage*, p. 27.

250. Report by Philip Webster, WRA, August 31—September 2, 1942, quoted in Weglyn, *Years of Infamy*, p. 91; see also testimony, Teru Watanabe, Los Angeles, Aug. 6, 1981, p. 246, shooting at Manzanar.

251. Bell, "Memories of Topaz;" testimony, Vernon Yoshioka, Los Angeles, Aug. 6, 1981, p. 110.

252. Okubo, *Citizen 13660*, p. 180.

253. Testimony, Linda Morimoto, Los Angeles, Aug. 6, 1981, p. 104.

254. McKee, *History of WRA*, p. 105.

255. Testimony, George Takei, Los Angeles, Aug. 4, 1981, p. 201.

256. Myer, *Uprooted Americans*, p. 36.

257. *WRA Story*, p. 93.

258. *San Francisco Chronicle*, May 25, 1943, quoted in Baker, *Concentration Camp Conspiracy*, p. 256.

259. Unsolicited testimony, Harry Y. Ueno, "I was a captive of the U.S. Government."

260. Thomas and Nishimoto, *Spoilage*, p. 40.

261. Report of the WRA, July 1—September 30, 1942, p. 53.

262. *Ibid.*, pp. 58, 60.

263. Cates, *Management of Five Camps*, p. 576.

264. Report of the WRA, July 1—September 30, 1942, pp. 59–60.

265. Letter, Hosokawa to Macbeth, Commission staff, Sept. 14, 1982 (CWRIC 8800–16).

266. Spicer, *Impounded People*, p. 84.

267. Myer, *Uprooted Americans*, p. 60.

268. Cates, *Management of Five Camps*, p. 579.

269. Thomas and Nishimoto, *Spoilage*, p. 45; Myer, *Uprooted Americans*, p. 40; Cates, *Management of Five Camps*, p. 589.

270. Spicer, *Impounded People*, p. 82.

271. *Ibid.*, p. 82.

272. Weglyn, *Years of Infamy*, p. 119; Thomas and Nishimoto, *Spoilage*, p. 73.

273. *WRA Story*, pp. 46–47.

274. Weglyn, *Years of Infamy*, pp. 119–20.

275. Masaoka to Myer, January 14, 1943. NARS. RG 210 (CWRIC 3758).

276. Cates, *Management of Five Camps*, p. 572, quoting Myron E. Gurnea, FBI Report—Survey—Part I, Confidential Report, p. 7. NARS. RG 210.

277. Cates, *Management of Five Camps*, p. 570.

278. Testimony, Elaine Yoneda, San Francisco, Aug. 12, 1981, p. 47.

279. Myer, *Uprooted Americans*, p. 61.

280. Thomas and Nishimoto, *Spoilage*, pp. 43–44; Report of the WRA, July 1—September 30, 1942, pp. 51–54.

281. Testimony, Karl Yoneda, San Francisco, Aug. 11, 1981, pp. 91–92.

282. Unsolicited testimony, Susumu Togasaki, reporting a beating in one section of Poston.

283. Report of the WRA, October 1—December 31, 1942, pp. 31–33.

284. Thomas and Nishimoto, *Spoilage*, p. 46.

285. Report of the WRA, October 1—December 31, 1942, p. 33.

286. *Ibid.*, p. 34.

287. *Ibid.*, p. 36.

288. Thomas and Nishimoto, *Spoilage*, p. 50.

289. Report of the WRA, October 1—December 31, 1942, p. 37.

290. Testimony, Grace Nakamura, Los Angeles, Aug. 6, 1981, p. 253.

291. Thomas and Nishimoto, *Spoilage*, p. 52.

292. McKee, *History of WRA*, pp. 154-55.

293. Unsolicited testimony, Edward Spicer, Chicago, Sept. 1981.

294. Testimony, Peter Suzuki, Chicago, Sept. 23, 1981, pp. 142-44.

295. Unsolicited testimony, Edward Spicer, Chicago, Sept. 1981.

296. Written testimony, Walter Funabiki, San Francisco, Sept. 29, 1981.

297. Eisenhower, *The President Is Calling*, p. 120.

298. McKee, *WRA Story*, p. 30.

299. Eisenhower, *The President Is Calling*, p. 120.

300. Daniels, *Concentration Camps USA*, p. 99.

301. Testimony, Dick Nishi, San Francisco, Aug. 12, 1981, pp. 121-22.

302. Daniels, *Concentration Camps USA*, p. 100.

303. Testimony, Sally Kazama, Seattle, Sept. 11, 1981, p. 52.

304. Testimony, Mary Sakaguchi Oda, Los Angeles, Aug. 4, 1981, p. 97.

305. Report of the WRA, July 1—September 30, 1942, p. 18.

306. Daniels, *Concentration Camps USA*, p. 100.

307. Telephone conversation, DeWitt and Bendetsen, April 4, 1942. NARS. RG 338 (CWRIC 13046).

308 *WRA Story*, p. 31.

309. Daniels, *Concentration Camps USA*, p. 101.

310. Myer, *Uprooted Americans*, pp. 129-30.

311. Weglyn, *Years of Infamy*, p. 98.

312. Report of the WRA, July 1—September 30, 1942, pp. 11-12.

313. Testimony, George Taketa, Chicago, Sept, 22, 1981, p. 269.

314. Testimony, John Takashi Omori, Chicago, Sept. 23, 1981, p. 62.

315. Unsolicited testimony, George Ikeda.

316. Testimony, George Taketa, Chicago, September 22, 1981, p. 270.

317. Weglyn, *Years of Infamy*, p. 100.

318. Written testimony, James Hirabayashi, San Francisco, Aug. 11, 1981, p. 3.

319. Letter, Eisenhower to the President, June 17, 1942. FDRL. OF 4849 (CWRIC 3972).

320. Myer, *Uprooted Americans*, pp. 67-68.

321. tenBroek, *Prejudice, War*, p. 147. WRA Administration Instruction No. 22, July 20, 1942. "Temporary Procedure for Issuance of Permits to Individuals or Single Families to Leave Relocation Centers for Employment Outside Such Centers and the WDC."

322. Myer, *Uprooted Americans*, pp. 132-33.

323. tenBroek, *Prejudice, War*, p. 147. WRA, "Issuance of Leave for Departure from a Relocation Area." 7 Fed. Reg., 7656 (September 26, 1942). These appeared in greater detail in WRA Administrative Instruction No. 22 (Revised), November 6, 1942.

324. Memo, Bendetsen to Commanding General of Western Defense Command, Oct. 3, 1942, NARS. RG 338 (CWRIC 5081).

325. Myer, *Uprooted Americans*, p. 134.

326. *Ibid.*, p. 135.
327. *Ibid.*, pp. 135–38.
328. *WRA Story*, p. 42.
329. Myer, *Uprooted Americans*, p. 138.

7

Loyalty: Leave and Segregation

1. *E.g.*, Eugene Rostow, "The Japanese American Cases—A Disaster," 54 Yale Law Journal 489 (1945).

2. Bill Hosokawa, *Nisei: The Quiet Americans* (New York: William Morrow & Co., 1969), p. 397.

3. For instance, McCloy visited the West Coast in March 1942, and met with Ringle, later writing Biddle that he was "greatly impressed" with Ringle's knowledge. Letter, McCloy to Biddle, March 21, 1942. NARS. RG 107 (CWRIC 12862). He met with the JACL leaders at an emergency National Council meeting called in early March and took the trouble to meet with them socially as well as discussing the Army's program. Bill Hosokawa, *JACL in Quest of Justice* (New York: William Morrow & Co., 1982), pp. 166–67.

4. Ruth E. McKee, *History of WRA: Pearl Harbor to June 30, 1944*, unpublished manuscript, 1949, p. 164.

5. Tamotsu Shibutani, *The Derelicts of Company K* (Berkeley: University of California Press, 1978), p. 49.

6. Memo, DeWitt to Chief of Staff (Marshall), Nov. 20, 1942; memo, DeWitt to McCloy, Nov. 21, 1942; memo, Dedrick to WDC Assistant Chief of Staff, Civil Affairs Division (Bendetsen), Nov. 20, 1942. NARS. RG 107 (CWRIC 5686, 5687, 5680–85).

7. McKee, *History of WRA*, p. 165.

8. *Idem.*

9. Memo, Brigadier General M. G. White, G-1, to McCloy, April 19, 1943. NARS. RG 107 (CWRIC 5665–66).

10. Hosokawa, *Nisei*, p. 397.

11. Memo, McCloy to Eisenhower, May 20, 1943, RG 107, quoted in Roger Daniels, *Concentration Camps USA: Japanese Americans and World War II* (New York: Holt, Rinehart & Winston, 1972), p. 145.

12. Memo, Colonel M. W. Pettigrew to McCloy, Nov. 7, 1942. NARS. RG 107 (CWRIC 13780); memo, Pettigrew to McCloy, Nov. 17, 1942. NARS. RG 407 (CWRIC 13765–70); telephone conversation, DeWitt and McCloy, Jan. 18, 1943. NARS. RG 338 (CWRIC 13210–14).

13. Michi Weglyn, *Years of Infamy: The Untold Story of America's Concentration Camps*, (New York: William Morrow & Co., 1976), footnote 4, p. 305.

14. Edward H. Spicer, Asael T. Hansen, Katherine Luomala and Marvin Opler, *Impounded People: Japanese-Americans in the Relocation Centers* (Tucson, AZ: University of Arizona Press, 1969), p. 142.

15. Dillon S. Myer, *Uprooted Americans: The Japanese Americans and the War Relocation Authority During World War II* (Tucson, AZ: University of Arizona Press, 1971), p. 144.

16. Letter, Mike Masaoka to Stimson, Jan. 15, 1943. NARS. RG 147 (CWRIC 11920).

17. Telephone conversation, McCloy and DeWitt, Jan. 18, 1943. NARS. RG 338 (CWRIC 13210–14).

18. Telephone conversation, DeWitt and McCloy, Jan. 18, 1943. NARS. RG 338 (CWRIC 13210–14); memo, Colonel John J. Bissell to General Strong, Jan. 8, 1943. NARS. RG 319 (CWRIC 14102–03); telephone conversation, Bendetsen and Colonel William P. Scobey, Jan. 18, 1943. NARS. RG 338 (CWRIC 13194–208).

19. Telephone conversation, DeWitt and McCloy, Jan. 18, 1943. NARS. RG 338 (CWRIC 13210–14).

20. Telephone conversation, Bendetsen and Scobey, Jan. 18, 1943. NARS. RG 338 (CWRIC 13194–208).

21. Draft memo to Stimson, Oct. 28, 1942. NARS. RG 407 (CWRIC 13756–60).

22. Memo, Elmer Davis, Director of Office of War Information, to the President, Oct. 2, 1942. NARS. RG 407 (CWRIC 13755).

23. Memo, McCloy to Stimson, Oct. 15, 1942. NARS. RG 107 (CWRIC 13779); draft memo to Stimson, Oct. 28, 1942. NARS. RG 407 (CWRIC 13756–60).

24. Memo, Stimson to Chief of Staff (Marshall), no date. NARS. RG 407 (CWRIC 13753).

25. Thomas D. Murphy, *Ambassadors in Arms: The Story of Hawaii's 100th Battalion* (Honolulu: University of Hawaii Press, 1954), pp. 109–10.

26. *Idem.*

27. Testimony, John J. McCloy, Washington, DC, Nov. 3, 1981, p. 25. The War Department position stands in sharp contrast to that of the Navy. Responding to Davis's memo, Navy Secretary Knox not only did not agree with Davis's suggestion but also suggested that everyone's time could be better spent handling the "problem" of Japanese sympathizers in Hawaii; letter, Knox to the President, Oct. 17, 1942. NARS. RG 107 (CWRIC 565).

28. Memo for the record, Office of Provost Marshal General, Jan. 9, 1943. NARS. RG 210 (CWRIC 12795–97).

29. *Idem.*

30. *Idem.*

31. Memo, DeWitt to Marshall, Jan. 27, 1943. NARS. RG 107 (CWRIC 5114–23).

32. Telephone conversation, Bendetsen and Captain John M. Hall, Jan. 19, 1943. NARS. RG 338 (CWRIC 13183).

33. Report of the War Relocation Authority, Jan. 1-June 30, 1943, p. 9 [hereafter "Report of the WRA"]. The War Relocation Authority, first under the Office for Emergency Management and later under the U.S. Department of the Interior, issued quarterly reports covering 1942, and thereafter semi-annual reports until the agency disbanded in 1946.

34. Myer, *Uprooted Americans*, p. 72.

35. Memo, DeWitt to Marshall, Jan. 27, 1943, NARS. RG 107 (CWRIC 5114–23).

36. Press release, War Department, Jan. 28, 1943. NARS. RG 338 (CWRIC 8339–40).

37. Letter, the President to Stimson, Feb. 1, 1943. NARS. RG 338 (CWRIC 8338).

38. Report of the WRA, January 1-June 30, 1943, p. 9.

39. Question No. 28, DSS Form 304A (1–23–43), "Statement of United States Citizen of Japanese Ancestry," in *History of the Japanese Program*, prepared by the Japanese American Branch, Office of the Provost Marshal General. NARS. RG 338 (CWRIC 2959–62).

40. Report of the WRA, Jan. 1-June 30, 1943, p. 14.

41. Testimony, Grace Nakamura, Los Angeles, Aug. 6, 1981, p. 254.

42. U.S. Department of the Interior, *WRA: A Story of Human Conservation* (Washington, DC: U.S. Government Printing Office, 1956), p. 56 [hereafter "*WRA Story*"].

43. Dorothy S. Thomas and Richard S. Nishimoto, *The Spoilage: Japanese-American Evacuation and Resettlement During World War II* (Berkeley: University of California Press, 1969), pp. 60–61.

44. Testimony, Carnegie Ouye, San Francisco, Aug. 12, 1981, p. 68.

45. Memo, Hartwell C. Davis, 13th Naval District, to Director of Naval Intelligence, March 30, 1943. NARS. RG 210 (CWRIC 1785–87).

46. Myer, *Uprooted Americans*, p. 73.

47. Weglyn, *Years of Infamy*, p. 138.

48. *Ibid.*, p. 141.

49. Testimony, Minoru Mochizuki, Chicago, Sept. 23, 1981, pp. 87–88.

50. Robert A. Wilson and Bill Hosokawa, *East to America: A History of the Japanese in the United States* (New York: William Morrow & Co., 1980), p. 228.

51. Testimony, Ben Takeshita, San Francisco, Aug 11, 1981, pp. 219–20.

52. Michi Weglyn, *Years of Infamy*, p. 138.

53. Testimony, Mary S. Oda, Los Angeles, Aug. 4, 1981, p. 98.

54. Testimony, Harold Ouye, San Francisco, Aug. 12, 1981, p. 85.

55. Spicer, *Impounded People*, p. 146.

56. See Thomas and Nishimoto, *Spoilage*, pp. 72–82, for a full discussion of registration at Tule Lake.

57. Testimony, Frank Kageta, San Francisco, Aug. 13, 1981, p. 15.

58. Spicer, *Impounded People*, p. 148.

59. Myer, *Uprooted Americans*, p. 73.

60. Report of the WRA, Jan. 1-June 30, 1943, p. 10.

61. Memo, Dedrick to McCloy and Bendetsen, Nov. 20, 1942. NARS. RG 107 (CWRIC 5680–85).

62. McKee, *History of WRA*, p. 167.

63. Report of the WRA, January 1-June 30, 1943, p. 10.

64. U. S. Department of the Interior, *The Evacuated People: A Quantitative Description*, (Washington, DC: U.S. Government Printing Office, 1946), p. 165.

65. WDC, *Supplemental Report on Civilian Controls Exercised by Western Defense Command*, Jan. 1947, p. 32. NARS. RG 338.

66. Spicer, *Impounded People*, p. 152.

67. Myer, *Uprooted Americans*, p. 73; Hosokawa, *Nisei*, p. 365.

68. Testimony, Chiyoji Iwao, San Francisco, Aug. 12, 1981, pp. 111–12.

69. Testimony, Albert Nakai, San Francisco, Aug. 12, 1981, pp. 140–41.

70. Testimony, Arthur T. Morimitsu, Chicago, Sept. 23, 1981, p. 50.

71. Testimony, Ben Takeshita, San Francisco, Aug. 11, 1981, p. 219.

72. Testimony, Harry Taketa, Chicago, Sept. 22, 1981, p. 272.

73. Murphy, *Ambassadors in Arms*, p. 111.

74. All of the material on the research project is taken from WDC, *Supplemental Report on Civilian Controls Exercised by Western Defense Command*, Jan. 1947, pp. 188–417 and recommendations (last) page, which is unnumbered. NARS. RG 338.

75. *Ibid.*, p. 229.

76. *Ibid.*, p. 281.

77. *Ibid.*, recommendations (last) page.

78. *Ibid.*, pp. 682–84.

79. Memo, DeWitt to Marshall, Jan. 27, 1943. NARS. RG 107 (CWRIC 5114–23).

80. *Idem.*

81. *Idem.*

82. Jacobus tenBroek, Edward N. Barnhart and Floyd W. Matson, *Prejudice, War, and the Constitution: Causes and Consequences of the Evacuation of the Japanese Americans in World War II* (Berkeley: University of California Press, 1954), pp. 153–57.

83. *WRA Story*, p. 59.

84. WDC, *Supplemental Report*, p. 152.

85. Report of the WRA, Jan. 1-June 30, 1943, p. 15.

86. *Ibid.*, p. 16.

87. Myer, *Uprooted Americans*, pp. 138–39.

88. tenBroek, *Prejudice, War*, pp. 151–52.

89. *Ibid.*, p. 153.

90. Memo, John P. Frank, Office of the Under Secretary of the Interior, to Ickes, Secretary of the Interior, no date. NARS. (CWRIC 8776–78).

91. tenBroek, *Prejudice, War*, p. 153.

92. *Idem.*

93. Telegram, Mayor Fiorello LaGuardia to Abe Fortas, Under Secretary of the Interior, April 11, 1944. NARS. RG 48 (CWRIC 6371).

94. Letter, LaGuardia to Ickes, April 21, 1944. NARS. RG 48 (CWRIC 6372).

95. Letter, Dillon S. Myer to the Attorney General, Feb. 1, 1944. DOJ 146–42–26 (CWRIC 9524–26).

96. Myer, *Uprooted Americans*, p. 140.

97. Dorothy S. Thomas, *The Salvage: Japanese American Evacuation and Resettlement* (Berkeley: University of California Press, 1952), p. 111.

98. *Ibid.*, pp. 116–17.

99. U.S. Department of the Interior, *People in Motion: The Postwar*

Adjustment of the Evacuated Japanese Americans (Washington, DC: U.S. Government Printing Office, 1947), p. 7.

100. Testimony, Kinnosuke Hashimoto, New York, Nov. 23, 1981, p. 124; testimony, Chiyoko K. Sasaki, Los Angeles, Aug. 6, 1981, p. 91.

101. Testimony, Hideko Sasaki, Los Angeles, Aug. 6, 1981, p. 136.

102. Testimony, Shizu Sue Lofton, Chicago, Sept. 22, 1981, p. 316.

103. Testimony, Kinnosuke Hashimoto, New York, Nov. 23, 1981, pp. 123–24; testimony, Miyo Senzaki, Los Angeles, Aug. 5, 1981, p. 156; testimony, Mary Fumiko Kurihara, Los Angeles, Aug. 4, 1981, p. 104; testimony, Tatsu Hori, San Francisco, Aug. 12, 1981, pp. 136–38; testimony, Fuki Abe, San Francisco, Aug. 12, 1981, p. 133; testimony, Tom Nakao, Seattle, Sept. 9, 1981, p. 249.

104. Testimony, William Kika, San Francisco, Aug. 12, 1981, p. 139.

105. Testimony, Minoru Tamaki, San Francisco, Aug. 13, 1981, p. 186.

106. Testimony, Mitzi Shio Schectman, Chicago, Sept. 22, 1981, pp. 188–89.

107. McKee, *History of WRA*, p. 197.

108. Testimony, May Ichida, Chicago, Sept. 22, 1981, p. 281.

109. Testimony, Kiyoshi Sonoda, Los Angeles, Aug. 5, 1981, p. 225; testimony, Marian Kadomatsu, Los Angeles, Aug. 6, 1981, p. 283; unsolicited testimony, Mary Smeltzer, LaVerne, CA.

110. Thomas, *Salvage*, p. 109.

111. Myer, *Uprooted Americans*, p. 140.

112. U.S. Department of the Interior, *People in Motion*, p. 48.

113. *Ibid.*, pp. 146–47.

114. *Ibid.*, p. 48.

115. Testimony, Kazutoshi Mayeda, Chicago, Sept. 22, 1981, pp. 299–300.

116. U.S. Department of the Interior, *People in Motion*, p. 81.

117. Testimony, Mamoru Ogata, Los Angeles, Aug. 6, 1981, p. 32; testimony, Charles Nagao, New York, Nov. 23, 1981, pp. 38–39; testimony, Ginzo Murono, New York, Nov. 23, 1981, pp. 31–32.

118. U.S. Department of the Interior, *People in Motion*, p. 147.

119. *Ibid.*, p. 237.

120. Memo, DeWitt to Chief of Staff (Marshall), Aug. 23, 1942. NARS. RG 107 (CWRIC 930–31).

121. Memo, DeWitt to Chief of Staff, Sept. 8, 1942; memo, Bendetsen to DeWitt, Oct. 9, 1942; memo, DeWitt to Chief of Staff, Nov. 23, 1942. NARS. RG 338 (CWRIC 12932; 12929; 5070–72).

122. Letter, McCloy to Myer, Oct. 30, 1942. NARS. RG 107 (CWRIC 904–05).

123. Letter, McCloy to DeWitt, Nov. 24, 1942. NARS. RG 338 (CWRIC 12934); letter, McCloy to E. M. Rowalt, Acting Director, WRA, Nov. 25, 1942. NARS. RG 107 (CWRIC 4492).

124. Letter, DeWitt to McCloy, with attachment, Dec. 15, 1942. NARS. RG 338 (CWRIC 12942–82).

125. Letter, Myer to Stimson, June 8, 1943. NARS. RG 338 (CWRIC 1286–92).

126. Myer, *Uprooted Americans*, p. 71.
127. *Ibid.*, p. 75.
128. *Ibid.*, pp. 75–76.
129. *WRA Story*, p. 63.
130. Myer, *Uprooted Americans*, p. 76; tenBroek, *Prejudice, War*, p. 161.
131. tenBroek, *Prejudice, War*, p. 161.
132. Weglyn, *Years of Infamy*, pp. 157–58.
133. Thomas and Nishimoto, *Spoilage*, pp. 104–06.
134. Spicer, *Impounded People*, pp. 178–79.
135. U.S. Department of the Interior, *Evacuated People*, p. 169.
136. Thomas and Nishimoto, *Spoilage*, pp. 109–10.
137. *Ibid.*, pp. 121–30.
138. Myer, *Uprooted Americans*, p. 79.
139. Thomas and Nishimoto, *Spoilage*, pp. 142–46.
140. Unsolicited testimony, deposition of Tokio Yamane.
141. Thomas and Nishimoto, *Spoilage*, p. 150.
142. *Ibid.*, p. 147.
143. Testimony, Bebe Reschke, Los Angeles, Aug. 6, 1981, pp. 61–62.

8

Ending the Exclusion

1. The early University of California study of the wartime experience of the Nikkei produced four volumes which follow this pattern. *Americans Betrayed* by Morton Grodzins and *Prejudice, War, and the Constitution* by tenBroek, Barnhart and Matson emphasize the history which produced the Executive Order, while *The Salvage* by Dorothy S. Thomas and *The Spoilage* by Thomas and Richard S. Nishimoto deal with the camp experience and its impact on evacuees. Roger Daniels, a major historian of the Japanese Americans in the Second World War, uses these two themes as the major division in his bibliography to *Concentration Camps USA*, the most comprehensive of his books on the period.

2. DeWitt, *Final Report: Japanese Evacuation from the West Coast, 1942* (Washington, DC: U.S. Government Printing Office, 1943), p. 34.

3. WDC, *Supplemental Report on Civilian Controls Exercised by Western Defense Command*, January 1947. NARS. RG 338. The opening sentence of the first chapter of the *Supplemental Report* sets out the thesis and philosophical foundation of the work: "The acts reported in this chapter are presented as evidence in support of the main thesis that it was impossible, as well as impracticable, to separate the dangerous from the non-dangerous members of the Japanese population."

The volume was designed to answer those who were critical of the measures taken in the "dark days" of 1942, to provide the War Department with a complete defense for the exclusion, evacuation and detention if there were further litigation or Congress attempted to place limitations on the wartime power of the military. (*Ibid.*, pp. 1–2).

4. *E.g.*, Letter, McCloy to DeWitt, April 8, 1943. NARS. RG 165 (CWRIC 26369–71). McCloy has informed the Commission that this letter accurately reflected his views during the war. Letter, McCloy to Macbeth, Commission staff, Oct. 18, 1982. (CWRIC 29637–38).

5. Report of the Select Committee Investigating National Defense Migration, U.S. House of Representatives 77th Cong., 2d Sess. HR Report No. 1911, p. 17:

> To date the committee has been unable to secure from anyone charged with responsibility a clear-cut statement of the status of the Japanese evacuees, alien or citizens, after they pass through the reception center.
>
> To date the committee has encountered a general disposition to treat the Japanese, whether citizen or alien, as a group, and to subject even the citizens to a scrutiny not applied to the alien German and Italian. The

evacuation order of General DeWitt, for example, places greater restrictions upon the residence of Japanese citizens than upon German and Italian aliens. It is not clear whether this means that plans exist, either in the Army or in the civilian agencies now assisting the Army, for the segregation of all Japanese for the duration of the war.

6. Telephone conversation, McCloy and Bendetsen, April 19, 1943. NARS. RG 338 (CWRIC 24067).

7. Telephone conversation, DeWitt and Gullion, Jan. 14, 1943. NARS. RG 338 (CWRIC 8218).

8. Cable, DeWitt to Marshall, Jan. 18, 1943. NARS. RG 338 (CWRIC 13209).

9. Telephone conversation, McCloy and DeWitt, Jan. 18, 1943. NARS. RG 338 (CWRIC 13210).

10. Telephone conversation, Bendetsen and Hall, Jan. 19, 1943. NARS. RG 338 (CWRIC 13189).

11. Ibid. (CWRIC 13183, 13189).

12. Memorandum, DeWitt to Marshall, Jan. 27, 1943. NARS. RG 107 (CWRIC 5114–23).

13. Telephone conversation, McCloy and DeWitt, Jan. 18, 1943. NARS. RG 338 (CWRIC 13210–14).

14. Telephone conversation, Bendetsen and Braun, Jan. 22, 1943. NARS. RG 338 (CWRIC 13163–64).

15. Memorandum, Stimson to Marshall, undated. NARS. RG 407 (CWRIC 13753).

16. Telephone conversation, Bendetsen and Hall, Jan. 19, 1943. NARS. RG 338 (CWRIC 13186, 13190).

17. Ibid. (CWRIC 13185–86).

18. Telephone conversation, McCloy and DeWitt, Jan. 18, 1943. NARS. RG 338 (CWRIC 13210–14).

19. Telephone conversation, Bendetsen and Hall, Jan. 19, 1943. NARS. RG 338 (CWRIC 13187–88).

20. Letter, Myer to McCloy, Jan. 15, 1943. NARS. RG 107 (CWRIC 531–32).

21. Letter, McCloy to DeWitt, Feb. 11, 1943. NARS. RG 107 (CWRIC 527–28). DeWitt responded, "I have a feeling that [the letter] was not prepared or signed by you. Its style and signature tends [sic] to confirm this feeling." Letter, DeWitt to McCloy, Feb. 15, 1943. NARS. RG 107 (CWRIC 526).

22. "Return of United States Soldiers of Japanese Ancestry to the Evacuated Areas." NARS. RG 338 (CWRIC 14663–14701); WDC, Supplemental Report on Civilian Controls Exercised by Western Defense Command, January 1947, NARS. RG 338, pp. 454–62.

23. Letter, McCloy to DeWitt, April 8, 1943. NARS. RG 165 (CWRIC 26369–71).

24. DeWitt, testimony before House Naval Affairs Committee, April 13, 1943. NARS. RG 338 (CWRIC 14698–99).

25. Morton Grodzins, Americans Betrayed (Chicago: University of Chicago Press, 1949), p. 62; DeWitt, testimony before House Naval Affairs Committee, April 13, 1943. NARS. RG 338 (CWRIC 14699–700).

26. Transcript of conference, DeWitt and newspapermen, April 14, 1943. NARS. RG 338 (CWRIC 26565).

27. Telephone conversation, McCloy and Bendetsen, April 19, 1943. NARS. RG 338 (CWRIC 24066).

28. Telephone conversation, Bendetsen and Barnett, April 29, 1943. NARS. RG 338 (CWRIC 24075).

29. Telephone conversation, McCloy and Bendetsen, April 19, 1943. NARS. RG 338 (CWRIC 24066–71).

30. Telephone conversation, Bendetsen and Barnett, April 29, 1943, NARS. RG 338 (CWRIC 24075–79).

31. Telegram, DeWitt to Barnett, April 27, 1943. NARS. RG 338 (CWRIC 24074).

32. Telephone conversation, DeWitt and Bendetsen, June 17, 1943. NARS. RG 338 (CWRIC 24134); Theodore E. Smith, statement, June 29, 1943. NARS. RG 338 (CWRIC 24141); Smith's statement reads in its entirety: "I certify that this date I witnessed the destruction by burning of the galley proofs, galley papers, drafts and memorandums [sic] of the original report of the Japanese Evacuation." DeWitt was not entirely successful; the Commission located a copy of the original April report in the National Archives, RG 338.

33. Memo, Bendetsen to DeWitt, May 3, 1943. NARS. RG 338 (CWRIC 24080).

34. Telephone conversation, Bendetsen and Barnett, April 29, 1943. NARS. RG 338 (CWRIC 24076–78).

35. Letter, Ickes to McCloy, July 5, 1943. NARS. RG 107 (CWRIC 14011b); letter, McCloy to Ickes, July 14, 1943. NARS. RG 107 (CWRIC 14011a).

36. Memorandum, McCloy to McNarney, May 28, 1943. NARS. RG 107 (CWRIC 19386–87).

37. Radiogram, Emmons to McCloy, Sept. 14, 1943. NARS. RG 338 (CWRIC 26541); paraphrase of confidential radiogram, McCloy to Emmons, Sept. 15, 1943. NARS. RG 338 (CWRIC 5058).

38. Letter, Myer to Stimson, March 11, 1943. NARS. RG 338 (CWRIC 1272–82).

39. Telephone conversation, Bendetsen and Barnett, April 29, 1943. NARS. RG 338 (CWRIC 24076a).

40. Letter, Stimson to Myer, May 10, 1943. NARS. RG 107 (CWRIC 14075–77).

41. Carey McWilliams, *Prejudice* (Boston: Little, Brown and Co., 1945), p. 243.

42. McWilliams, *Prejudice*, pp. 231–73.

43. *Ibid.*, p. 247.

44. *Ibid.*, pp. 248–49.

45. Dillon S. Myer, *Uprooted Americans: The Japanese Americans and the War Relocation Authority during World War II* (Tucson, AZ: University of Arizona Press, 1971), pp. 93–94; letter with attachment, Chandler to Hoover, April 8, 1943. FBI (CWRIC 17195–98).

46. For a more complete list of restrictive measures, see McWilliams, *Prejudice*, pp. 250–51.

47. *San Francisco Chronicle,* April 17, 1943; *Los Angeles Times,* April 22, 1943.

48. McWilliams, *Prejudice,* pp. 251–52.

49. Myer, *Uprooted Americans,* p. 96.

50. Pacific Coast Committee on American Principles and Fair Play, statement, June 15, 1943. (CWRIC 5858–59).

51. Myer, *Uprooted Americans,* pp. 96–97.

52. McWilliams, *Prejudice,* p. 254.

53. Statement of Dillon S. Myer before the House Committee on Un-American Activities, July 6, 1943, quoted in Myer, *Uprooted Americans,* p. 99.

54. Myer, *Uprooted Americans,* p. 100.

55. McWilliams, *Prejudice,* p. 256.

56. *Washington Post,* April 15, 1943.

57. Press release, July 17, 1943. NARS. RG 210 (CWRIC 26040–42). The release stated that it had been prepared at the President's request by the War Department and the WRA; it masked the division within the Department: "[T]he War Department and the Commanding General of the Western Defense Command have been in close and continuing consultation and agreement on all matters relating to evacuation and security of the West Coast areas." In preparing the statement, McCloy told Bendetsen that Roosevelt had directed that no statement should be made suggesting that the ethnic Japanese would not go back to the coast before the end of the war. The President's direction was not for attribution. Telephone conversation, McCloy and Bendetsen, July 10, 1943. NARS. RG 107 (CWRIC 19417–22). The Commission has not been able to determine whether Roosevelt also knew that the top civilian officials of the War Department no longer believed there was military justification for excluding loyal Japanese Americans from the West Coast.

58. Letter, Warren to DeWitt, with enclosures, July 7, 1943. NARS. RG 338 (CWRIC 26087–89); letter, DeWitt to Warren, July 10, 1943. NARS. RG 338 (CWRIC 26090).

59. Letter, McCloy to Emmons, Nov. 5, 1943. NARS. RG 107 (CWRIC 808–10).

60. Letter, Emmons to McCloy, Nov. 10, 1943. NARS. RG 107 (CWRIC 806–07).

61. Memorandum, Biddle to FDR, Dec. 30, 1943. FDRL. OF 4849 (CWRIC 3721–24).

62. Memorandum, FDR to Rosenman, Jan. 5, 1944. FDRL. OF 4849 (CWRIC 3978).

63. E.O. 9423, 3 C.F.R., pp. 302–03, Feb. 16, 1944. (CWRIC 6200–01).

64. Francis Biddle Papers: Cabinet Meetings, January 1944—May 1945, Summary of Cabinet Meeting of May 26, 1944. FDRL (CWRIC 3794).

65. Letter, Ickes to Roosevelt, June 2, 1944. FDRL. OF 4849 (CWRIC 3719–20).

After the Interior Department became responsible for the WRA program, Secretary Ickes issued a statement on April 13, 1944, making plain his view that the major task of WRA was relocation, and that hate and prejudice on the part of the American public was an unacceptable way to greet relocation. Press release, Secretary of the Interior, April 13, 1944, DOJ 146–13–7–2–0. (CWRIC 12719–22). Ickes specifically did not discuss relocation to the West Coast, but his description of the problem as largely a local one for the people in California, Washington and Oregon, strongly suggests his view that evacuees should be returned to those states. He was firm in his stand against prejudice.

66. Memorandum, Stettinius to FDR, June 9, 1944. FDRL. OF 4849 (CWRIC 3716).

67. Memorandum, FDR to the Acting Secretary of State and the Secretary of the Interior, June 12, 1944. FDRL. OF 4849 (CWRIC 3717–18).

68. Letter, Bonesteel to McCloy, July 3, 1944. NARS. RG 107 (CWRIC 780).

69. Letter, Bonesteel to McCloy, July 31, 1944. NARS. RG 338 (CWRIC 437–38).

70. Memorandum, Burling to Ennis, July 18, 1944. DOJ 146–42–107 (CWRIC 10389).

71. Memorandum, King to Chief of Staff, U.S. Army, Sept. 28, 1944. NARS. RG 107 (CWRIC 614).

72. *Supplemental Report on Civilian Controls Exercised by Western Defense Command*, Jan. 1947. NARS. RG 338, pp. 511–20; Jacobus tenBroek, Edward N. Barnhart and Floyd W. Matson, *Prejudice, War and The Constitution* (Berkeley: University of California Press, 1954), pp. 171–72.

73. tenBroek, *Prejudice, War*, pp. 157–59. In addition, members of the soldier's immediate family could travel in his company, and cleared evacuees could pass through an exclusion zone en route to Hawaii. Travel limited to seven travel corridors between relocation centers in the exclusion zone and outside cities could be without escort. Other travel had to be escorted, with the cost borne by the evacuee. (*Idem.*)

74. *Idem.*

75. *Shiramizu* v. *Bonesteel*, No. 494474 (Sup. Ct. L.A. County, CA); letter, Bonesteel to McCloy, July 31, 1944. NARS. RG 338 (CWRIC 437–38).

76. *Ochikubo* v. *Bonesteel*, No. 3834–PH (S.D. Cal.).

77. *Ex parte Endo*, 323 U.S. 283 (1944).

78. Memo, Greer to Commanding General, SCS, WDC, July 19, 1944. NARS. RG 338 (CWRIC 2355–58).

79. See, e.g., memo, Ennis to Carr, July 14, 1944, DOJ 146–42–107. (CWRIC 9802); memo, Fahy to McCloy, Aug. 4, 1944. DOJ 146–42–107. (CWRIC 9804–09).

80. Letter, Bonesteel to McCloy, July 31, 1944. NARS. RG 338 (CWRIC 437–38).

81. Memo, Fahy to McCloy, Aug. 4, 1944. DOJ 146–42–107 (CWRIC 9807–08).

82. *Ibid.*, (CWRIC 9804–09).

83. Transcript of judge's remarks at hearing on Oct. 2, 1944 in *Ochikubo* v. *Bonesteel*, sent by Carr to Wechsler by letter, Oct. 18, 1944. DOJ 146–42–107. (CWRIC 9849–54). The United States had also filed a detailed affidavit setting forth what effect sabotage and espionage could have on the defensive and offensive military efforts of the United States. The affidavit does not make an argument that exclusion is impelled by military necessity.

84. Memo, Bonesteel to Chief of Staff, Aug. 8, 1944. NARS. RG 338 (CWRIC 768–75).

85. Memo, Bonesteel to Chief of Staff, Sept. 19, 1944. NARS. RG 338 (CWRIC 2676–78).

86. Memo, Bonesteel to Chief of Staff, Sept. 21, 1944. NARS. RG 107 (CWRIC 671–74).

87. Letter, McCloy to Bonesteel, Oct. 31, 1944. NARS. RG 107 (CWRIC 668).

88. Letter, McCloy to Forrestal, Dec. 19, 1944. NARS. RG 107 (CWRIC 612–13).

89. Letter, Biddle to McCloy, Nov. 20, 1944. NARS. RG 107 (CWRIC 661).

90. Roosevelt Presidential Press and Radio Conferences, No. 982 (Nov. 21, 1944), FDR Complete Press Conferences, vol. 24, pp. 246–47. FDRL (CWRIC 3597–98).

91. Memo, Myer to Fortas, Dec. 9, 1944. NARS. RG 48 (CWRIC 6409–12).

92. Letter, Wechsler to McCloy, Nov. 28, 1944. NARS. RG 107 (CWRIC 653).

93. Letter, Gerhardt to Myer, Dec. 11, 1944. NARS. RG 107 (CWRIC 634–35).

94. Memo, Wilbur to the Chief of Staff, Dec. 9, 1944. NARS. RG 107 (CWRIC 641–42).

95. Letter, Gerhardt to Myer, Dec. 11, 1944. NARS. RG 107 (CWRIC 634–35).

96. Memo, Wilbur to Chief of Staff, Dec. 9, 1944. NARS. RG 107 (CWRIC 641–42).

97. Memo, Stimson to FDR, Dec. 13, 1944. NARS. RG 107 (CWRIC 9622–28).

98. Note, Stimson to Tully, Dec. 13, 1944. NARS. RG 107 (CWRIC 620).

99. Memo, Bogue to Gerhardt, Dec. 14, 1944. NARS. RG 107 (CWRIC 621).

100. Letter, Ryan to Myer, Dec. 15, 1944. NARS. RG 107 (CWRIC 619).

101. Letter, Solicitor General to Chief Justice, Dec. 16, 1944. DOJ 146–42–26 (CWRIC 9630–31).

102. Public Proclamation No. 21, Dec. 17, 1944. DOJ 146–42–26 (CWRIC 9611–14).

103. "For Release 1700 EWT," Dec. 17, 1944. DOJ 146–42–26 (CWRIC 9613–16).

104. "For Release 1400 PWT," Dec. 17, 1944. DOJ 146–42–26 (CWRIC 9619–21).

105. Memorandum, Ickes to the Staff of the WRA, Dec. 19, 1944. NARS. RG 48 (CWRIC 6406).

106. *Korematsu* v. *United States,* 323 U.S. 214 (1944); *Ex parte Endo,* 323 U.S. 283 (1944).

107. Eugene Rostow, "The Japanese American Cases—A Disaster," 54 Yale Law Journal 489, 520 (1945) (footnotes omitted).

108. *Duncan* v. *Kahanamoku,* 327 U.S. 304 (1946); see analysis in Chapter 11, *Hawaii,* pp. 280–82.

109. *Fullilove* v. *Klutznick,* 448 U.S. 448, 507 (1980) (Justice Powell concurring).

110. *Bolling* v. *Sharp,* 347 U.S. 497 (1954).

111. *Youngstown Sheet and Tube Co.* v. *Sawyer,* 343 U.S. 579 (1952).

112. In his autobiography, Justice Douglas commented on the decisions and his own later view of the cases:

> Was it constitutional to evacuate only citizens of Japanese ancestry? That was an issue hotly contested both in the curfew case (*Hirabayashi* v. *United States,* 320 U.S. 81) and in the evacuation case (*Korematsu* v. *United States,* 323 U.S. 214).
>
> The Pentagon's argument was that if the Japanese army landed in areas thickly populated by Americans of Japanese ancestry, the opportunity for sabotage and confusion would be great. By doffing their uniforms they would be indistinguishable from the other thousands of people of like color and stature. It was not much of an argument, but it swayed a majority of the Court, including myself. The severe bite of the military evacuation order was not in a requirement to move out but in the requirement to move out of the West Coast and move into concentration camps in the interior. Locking up the evacuees after they had been removed had no military justification. I wrote a concurring opinion, which I never published, agreeing to the evacuation but not to evacuation *via* the concentration camps. My Brethren, especially Black and Frankfurter, urged me strongly not to publish. "The issue of detention is not here," they said. "And the Court never decides a constitutional question not present." The latter was of course not true, as John Marshall's famous *Marbury* v. *Madison* (5 U.S. 137) shows. Technically, however, the question of detention was not presented to us. Yet evacuation via detention camps was before us, and I have always regretted that I bowed to my elders and withdrew my opinion.
>
> On the same day that we decided the evacuation case we held that there was no authority to detain a citizen, absent evidence of a crime (*Ex parte Endo,* 323 U.S. 283). Meanwhile, however, grave injustices had been committed. Fine American citizens had been robbed of their properties by racists—crimes that might not have happened if the Court had not followed the Pentagon so literally. The evacuation case, like the flag-salute case, was ever on my conscience. Murphy and Rutledge, dissenting, had been right. (William O. Douglas, *The Court Years: 1939–1975* [New York: Random House, 1980], pp. 279–80.)

113. Memo, Myer to Secretary of the Interior, March 31, 1945. NARS. RG 48 (CWRIC 6264–67).

114. Letter, Grunert to McCloy, Jan. 29, 1945. NARS. RG 107 (CWRIC 312–13).

115. Letter, Pratt to McCloy, Feb. 3, 1945. NARS. RG 107 (CWRIC 593–96).

116. Letter, Pratt to Lewis, Dec. 18, 1944. NARS. RG 338 (CWRIC

12995–96). McCloy shared this view. Minutes, Committee of Three (State/ War/Navy), Jan. 8, 1945. NARS. RG 107 (CWRIC 14156–58).

117. See, e.g., Letter, Baldwin, American Civil Liberties Union, to Ickes, April 19, 1945. NARS. RG 48 (CWRIC 6385); letter, Fortas to Besig, ACLU, Sept. 10, 1945. NARS. RG 48 (CWRIC 6379); memo, Fortas to Secretary of the Interior, July 18, 1945, and attached memo, Myer to the Secretary, July 7, 1945. NARS. RG 48 (CWRIC 6380–83); see also letter, Wechsler to Fortas, May 16, 1945, and reply, Fortas to Wechsler, May 17, 1945. NARS. RG 48 (CWRIC 6259–61).

118. Letter, Ickes to May, April 2, 1945. NARS. RG 210 (CWRIC 19452–54).

119. Letter, Assistant Secretary of the Interior Chapman to Attorney General Clark, March 1, 1946. NARS. RG 210 (CWRIC 1971–72).

120. U.S. Department of the Interior, *People in Motion* (Washington, DC: U.S. Government Printing Office, 1947), p. 198.

121. Myer, *Uprooted Americans*, pp. 194–95.

122. Testimony, Yasuko A. Ito, San Francisco, Aug. 13, 1981, p. 54.

123. Unsolicited testimony, Harue Ozaki; unsolicited testimony, Sumie Koide.

124. Testimony, Paul Nagano, Seattle, Sept. 9, 1981, p. 120.

125. Testimony, Toaru Ishiyama, Chicago, Sept. 22, 1981, p. 202.

126. Testimony, Mitzi Shio Schectman, Chicago, Sept. 22, 1981, p. 188; testimony, Toshimi William Kumagai, San Francisco, Aug. 12, 1981, p. 215; testimony, James Shizuru, San Francisco, Aug. 13, 1981, pp. 83–84; testimony, Kimiyo Okamoto, San Francisco, Aug. 12, 1981, p. 223.

127. U.S. Department of the Interior, *People in Motion*, p. 10.

128. *Idem.*

129. Testimony, Dick Nishi, San Francisco, Aug. 12, 1981, p. 122; unsolicited testimony, Dave Tatsuno.

130. U.S. Department of the Interior, *People in Motion*, p. 47.

131. Testimony, Kinnosuke Hashimoto, New York, Nov. 23, 1981, p. 124; testimony, Ayako Uyeda, Seattle, Sept. 10, 1981, p. 34.

132. Testimony, Frances C. Kitagawa, Los Angeles, Aug. 6, 1981, p. 124; testimony, Murako Kato, Seattle, Sept. 10, 1981, p. 40.

133. Testimony, Kiku Funabiki, San Francisco, Aug. 12, 1981, p. 63; testimony, Heizo Oshima, San Francisco, Aug. 13, 1981, p. 122; testimony, Alice Okazaki, San Francisco, Aug. 13, 1981, p. 33; testimony, Nellie Sakakihara, San Francisco, Aug. 12, 1981, p. 128; testimony, Matsui Mori, Los Angeles, Aug. 6, 1981, p. 279.

134. Testimony, George Matsuoka, San Francisco, Aug. 12, 1981, p. 120; testimony, Emiko Shinagawa, San Francisco, Aug. 13, 1981, p. 107.

135. Unsolicited testimony, Kin Ikeda.

136. Testimony, Toshimi William Kumagai, San Francisco, Aug. 12, 1981, p. 215; testimony, George Hagiwara, San Francisco, Aug. 11, 1981, p. 115; written testimony, Noriko Sawada Bridges, San Francisco, Aug. 11, 1981; testimony, Mary Fusako Odagiri, Los Angeles, Aug. 6, 1981, p. 131; testimony, Mitsuru Sasahara, Los Angeles, Aug. 5, 1981, p. 89; testimony, Peggy Nishimoto Mitchell, Seattle, Sept. 9, 1981, p. 222.

137. U.S. Department of the Interior, *People in Motion*, p. 166.

138. Testimony, Sam Shoji, Seattle, Sept. 9, 1981, p. 208; testimony, Mitsuye Tono Kamada, New York, Nov. 23, 1981, p. 53.

139. Unsolicited testimony, Y. Florence Kubota; unsolicited testimony, A. Arthur Takemoto.

140. Testimony, Marian Matsuko Kadomatsu, Los Angeles, Aug. 6, 1981, p. 286.

141. Testimony, John J. Saito, Los Angeles, Aug. 6, 1981, p. 102.

142. Myer, *Uprooted Americans*, p. 198; testimony, Lawrence Shikuma, San Francisco, Aug. 13, 1981, p. 124.

143. U.S. Department of the Interior, *People in Motion*, p. 62.

144. Testimony, Yoshiaki Sako, Seattle, Sept. 10, 1981, p. 30; testimony, Yoshihiko Tanabe, Seattle, Sept. 11, 1981, p. 74; testimony, Robert T. Mizukami, Seattle, Sept. 10, 1981, p. 13; testimony, Arthur G. Barnett, Seattle, Sept. 9, 1981, p. 67; testimony, Lawrence Shikuma, San Francisco, Aug. 13, 1981, p. 124.

145. Testimony, Betty Matsuo, San Francisco, Aug. 11, 1981, p. 275; unsolicited testimony, Shizuka Taniguchi LaGrange; testimony, Thomas Takemura, Seattle, Sept. 9, 1981, p. 97; testimony, Louise Crowley, Seattle, Sept. 9, 1981, pp. 70–72; testimony, Fuki O. Abe, San Francisco, Aug. 12, 1981, p. 133.

146. Testimony, Kiyoo Yamashita, Los Angeles, Aug. 6, 1981, p. 24; testimony, Chiyo Tomihiro, Chicago, Sept. 22, 1981, p. 132; testimony, Kimiyo Okamoto, San Francisco, Aug. 12, 1981, p. 221; testimony, Fred Ross, Seattle, Sept. 11, 1981, p. 71; unsolicited testimony, Nobu Kajiwara; testimony, Dan Ono, San Francisco, Aug. 12, 1981, pp. 237–38; testimony, Sumie Itami Bartz, Seattle, Sept. 11, 1981, pp. 11–12.

147. U.S. Department of the Interior, *People in Motion*, p. 63.

148. *Ibid.*, p. 62.

149. Testimony, Henry Sakai, Los Angeles, Aug. 4, 1981, p. 234; testimony, H. Roy Setsuda, Chicago, Sept. 22, 1981, p. 363.

150. Testimony, Ikuo Komatsu, Chicago, Sept. 22, 1981, p. 208; testimony, Kiyo Sato-Viacrucis, San Francisco, Aug. 12, 1981, pp. 71–76.

151. Testimony, Soto Yoshida, San Francisco, Aug. 12, 1981, p. 212; unsolicited testimony, Susumu Togasaki.

152. Roger Daniels, *Concentration Camps USA: Japanese Americans and World War II* (New York: Holt, Rinehart & Winston, 1972), pp. 162–63.

9

Protest and Disaffection

1. Elmer Davis to FDR, Oct. 2, 1942. NARS. RG 407 (CWRIC 13755).

2. Roger Daniels, *Concentration Camps USA: Japanese Americans and World War II* (New York: Holt, Rinehart & Winston, 1972), p. 123.

3. *Idem*.

4. *Idem*.

5. Selective Service System, Local Board Memorandum No. 179 (Amended Jan. 14, 1944). NARS. RG 147 (CWRIC 11788).

6. U.S. Department of the Interior, *The Evacuated People: A Quantitative Description* (Washington, DC: U.S. Government Printing Office, 1946), p. 128.

7. *Idem*.

8. Tamotsu Shibutani, *The Derelicts of Company K* (Berkeley: University of California Press, 1978), p. 61.

9. *Idem*.

10. U.S. Department of the Interior, *Evacuated People*, p. 128.

11. Michi Weglyn, *Years of Infamy: The Untold Story of America's Concentration Camps* (New York: William Morrow & Co., 1976), p. 303.

12. Testimony, Edward Ennis, Washington, DC, Nov. 2, 1981, p. 139.

13. Dorothy S. Thomas and Richard S. Nishimoto, *The Spoilage: Japanese American Evacuation and Resettlement During World War II* (Berkeley and Los Angeles: University of California Press, 1946), pp. 286–88.

14. Unsolicited testimony, Tokio Yamane.

15. Weglyn, *Years of Infamy*, pp. 203–04.

16. Thomas and Nishimoto, *Spoilage*, pp. 291–302.

17. Jacobus tenBroek, Edward N. Barnhart, and Floyd W. Matson, *Prejudice, War and the Constitution* (Berkeley: University of California Press, 1954), p. 175.

18. *Ibid.*, p. 176.

19. Frank Chuman, *The Bamboo People: The Law and Japanese Americans* (Del Mar, CA: Publisher's Inc., 1976), p. 268; testimony, Edward Ennis, Washington, DC, Nov. 2, 1981, p. 136.

20. tenBroek, *Prejudice, War*, p. 176.

21. *Idem*.

22. Thomas and Nishimoto, *Spoilage*, pp. 303–06.

23. *Ibid.*, pp. 261–74.

24. *Ibid.*, p. 307.

25. *Ibid.*, p. 308.

26. *Ibid.*, p. 312.

27. *Ibid.*, p. 313.

28. Written testimony, Taeko Sakai Okamura, San Francisco, Aug. 13, 1981, p. 4.

29. Testimony, Kinya Noguchi, San Francisco, Aug. 11, 1981, p. 111.

30. Written testimony, Albert Yoshitaka Nakai, San Francisco, Aug. 12, 1981, p. 4.

31. Thomas and Nishimoto, *Spoilage*, pp. 325–26.

32. *Ibid.*, p. 324.

33. *Ibid.*, p. 333.

34. *Ibid.*, p. 335.

35. *Ibid.*, p. 347.

36. *Ibid.*, p. 338.

37. *Ibid.*, p. 340.

38. *Ibid.*, p. 350.

39. *Ibid.*, p. 342.

40. Chuman, *Bamboo People*, p. 268.

41. Testimony, Edward Ennis, Washington, DC, Nov. 2, 1981, p. 162.

42. Thomas and Nishimoto, *Spoilage*, pp. 347–48.

43. *Ibid.*, p. 357.

44. Weglyn, *Years of Infamy*, p. 244; Thomas and Nishimoto, *Spoilage*, p. 357.

45. Weglyn, *Years of Infamy*, p. 246.

46. *Ibid.*, p. 252.

47. *Ibid.*, p. 255.

48. *Ibid.*, p. 258.

49. *Ibid.*, p. 260; *Abo* v. *Clark*, 77 F. Supp. 806 (1948).

50. *Ibid.*, p. 262; *Abo* v. *Clark*, 186 F. 2d 766 (9th Cir. 1950), *cert. denied*, 342 U.S. 832 (1951).

51. *Ibid.*, p. 265.

52. U.S. Department of the Interior, *Evacuated People*, p. 157.

53. DeWitt, *Final Report*, p. 324.

54. U.S. Department of the Interior, *Evacuated People*, p. 157.

55. Weglyn, *Years of Infamy*, p. 154.

56. U.S. Department of the Interior, *Evacuated People*, p. 157.

57. Weglyn, *Years of Infamy*, pp. 136–47.

58. U.S. Department of the Interior, *Evacuated People*, p. 157.

59. Thomas and Nishimoto, *Spoilage*, p. 232.

60. U.S. Department of the Interior, *Evacuated People*, p. 196.

61. tenBroek, *Prejudice, War*, p. 181.

10

Military Service

1. S. I. Hayakawa, *Through the Communication Barrier* (New York: Harper & Row, 1979), pp. 136–37.

2. Selective Service System, Special Groups, Special Monograph no. 10, vol. 1 (Washington, DC: U.S. Department of the Army), p. 142 (CWRIC 29640).

3. Joseph D. Harrington, *Yankee Samurai: The Secret Role of Nisei in America's Pacific Victory* (Detroit: Pettigrew Enterprises Inc., 1979), p. 19; Bill Hosokawa, *Nisei, The Quiet Americans* (New York: William Morrow & Co., 1969), pp. 394–95.

4. Military Intelligence Service Language School, *The MISLS Album* (San Francisco: MISLS, 1946), p. 9; Hosokawa, *Nisei*, p. 397.

5. Hosokawa, *Nisei*, p. 396.

6. *Ibid.*, p. 397.

7. Harrington, *Yankee Samurai*, p. 93.

8. MISLS, *Album*, p. 11.

9. Hosokawa, *Nisei*, pp. 397–98.

10. Testimony, Mark Murakami, Seattle, Sept. 9, 1981, p. 39.

11. Harrington, *Yankee Samurai*, p. 108.

12. MISLS, *Album*, pp. 104–05.

13. Hosokawa, *Nisei*, p. 398.

14. Harrington, *Yankee Samurai*, p. 112.

15. Hosokawa, *Nisei*, p. 398.

16. Harrington, *Yankee Samurai*, p. 66.

17. MISLS, *Album*, pp. 104–05.

18. Hosokawa, *Nisei*, p. 398.

19. MISLS, *Album*, pp. 104–05; Hosokawa, *Nisei*, p. 398.

20. Testimony, Arthur T. Morimitsu, Chicago, Sept. 23, 1981, p. 51.

21. Hosokawa, *Nisei*, p. 399; Harrington, *Yankee Samurai*, p. 355.

22. Testimony, Arthur T. Morimitsu, Chicago, Sept. 23, 1981, p. 51.

23. See Chapter 11, *Hawaii*.

24. Thomas D. Murphy, *Ambassadors in Arms: The Story of Hawaii's 100th Battalion* (Honolulu: University of Hawaii Press, 1954), pp. 58, 69.

25. *Ibid.*, pp. 81–96, 119.

26. Letter, Hosokawa to Macbeth, Commission staff, Sept. 14, 1982 (CWRIC 8800–16).

27. Chester Tanaka, *Go For Broke: A Pictorial History of the Japanese American 100th Infantry Battalion and 442d Regimental Combat Team* (Richmond, CA: Go For Broke, Inc., 1982), p. 37.

28. Murphy, *Ambassadors In Arms*, p. 175.

29. Ruth E. McKee, *History of WRA: Pearl Harbor to June 30, 1944,* unpublished manuscript, 1944, p. 168; Tanaka, *Go For Broke*, p. 49; see generally Murphy, *Ambassadors in Arms*, pp. 123–76, for a full account of the campaign.

30. Testimony, Warren Fencl, Chicago, Sept. 23, 1981, p. 36.

31. Tanaka, *Go For Broke*, pp. 47–51.

32. Tanaka, *Go For Broke*, p. 65.

33. U.S. Department of the Interior, *People in Motion: The Postwar Adjustment of the Evacuated Japanese Americans* (Washington, DC: U.S. Government Printing Office, 1947), p. 18.

34. Tanaka, *Go For Broke*, p. 73.

35. Hosokawa, *Nisei*, p. 405.

36. Report of the Seventh Army, quoted in Hosokawa, *Nisei*, p. 405.

37. Hosokawa, *Nisei*, p. 405.

38. Tanaka, *Go For Broke*, pp. 90–101.

39. Hosokawa, *Nisei*, p. 405.

40. Tanaka, *Go For Broke*, p. 103.

41. See Murphy, *Ambassadors In Arms*, pp. 225–44, for a full account of the Vosges Mountains campaign.

42. Testimony, Sam Ozaki, Chicago, Sept. 22, 1981, pp. 342–43.

43. Murphy, *Ambassadors In Arms*, p. 257.

44. Tanaka, *Go For Broke*, pp. 119–27.

45. Tamotsu Shibutani, *The Derelicts of Company K* (Berkeley: University of California Press, 1978), p. 84.

46. Tanaka, *Go For Broke*, pp. 136, 140.

47. Hosokawa, *Nisei*, pp. 409–10.

48. Testimony, Masato Nakagawa, Chicago, Sept. 23, 1981, p. 48.

49. Selective Service System, Special Groups, Special Monograph no. 10, vol. 1, pp. 141–42.

50. Hosokawa, *Nisei*, pp. 418–20.

51. *Ibid.,* pp. 420–21.

52. Letter, Hosokawa to Macbeth, Commission staff, Sept. 14, 1982 (CWRIC 8800–16).

53. Tanaka, *Go For Broke*, pp. 162–64.

54. Testimony, Mitsuo Usui, Los Angeles, Aug. 5, 1981, p 28.

55. Tanaka, *Go For Broke*, p. 168.

56. Murphy, *Ambassadors in Arms*, pp. 274–76.

57. U.S. Department of the Interior, *People In Motion*, p. 19.

58. *Ibid.,* pp. 23–24.

59. *Ibid.,* p. 18.

11

Hawaii

1. William Petersen, *Japanese Americans* (New York: Random House, 1971), p. 59.

2. Tamotsu Shibutani, *The Derelicts of Company K* (Berkeley: University of California Press, 1978), p. 21.

3. The G-2 staff in Hawaii "stated repeatedly to the [Western Defense Command] staff members that there was no problem in judging whether or not a person of Japanese ancestry was dangerous or non-dangerous; for all one had to do was sit and talk to the man for fifteen minutes and the [sic] would be no question in one's mind." WDC, *Supplemental Report on Civilian Controls Exercised by Western Defense Command*, Jan. 1947, pp. 174–75. NARS. RG 338.

4. Robert Wilson and Bill Hosokawa, *East to America* (New York: William Morrow & Co., 1980), p. 27.

5. *Ibid.*, pp. 140–52.

6. Report, C. H. Coggins, "The Japanese in Hawaii," undated. NARS. RG 80 (CWRIC 6964–84); Bureau of the Census, *Census of Population 1940*, vol. 3, Characteristics of the Population, part 1 (Washington, DC: U.S. Government Printing Office, 1943), pp. 585–601.

7. Wilson and Hosokawa, *East to America*, p. 153.

8. Brief for United States, *Duncan v. Kahanamoku*, No. 14, Oct. Term 1945 (CWRIC 12166–75).

9. Stetson Conn, Rose C. Engelman and Byron Fairchild, *The United States Army in World War II, The Western Hemisphere: Guarding the United States and its Outposts* (Washington, DC: Office of the Chief of Military History, Department of the Army, 1964), p. 199. [hereafter *"Guarding"*].

10. Memo, District Intelligence Officer, Fourteenth Naval District to District Intelligence Officer, Third Naval District, Feb. 9, 1942, reprinted in Hearings before the Joint Committee on the Investigation of the Pearl Harbor Attack, 79th Cong. (Washington, DC: U.S. Government Printing Office, 1946), Part 35, pp. 337–38 [hereafter "Pearl Harbor Investigation"].

11. See Chapter 2, *Executive Order 9066*.

12. Pearl Harbor Investigation, Part 39, p. 120.

13. Diary, Stimson, Jan. 20, 1942. Sterling Library, Yale University (CWRIC 19596–98).

14. On the tiny isolated Hawaiian Island of Niihau where news of the Pearl Harbor bombing had not yet arrived, a crippled Japanese plane crashed on its return from the successful attack. A Hawaiian discovered the pilot and

confiscated his weapons and papers. Ishimatsu Shintani, an Issei, and Yoshio Harada, a Nisei, acted as interpreters; the latter spent a short time privately with the pilot. After the meeting, Harada freed the pilot, helped him set up two machine guns in the village, and threatened to kill everyone unless the military papers were produced. In an unguarded moment six days later, two Hawaiians taken hostage jumped the pair. The pilot was killed and Harada fatally shot himself. Gwenfread Allen, *Hawaii's War Years* (Westport, CT.: Greenwood Press, 1971 [1950]), pp. 44–46.

15. Notes of Cabinet meeting, Biddle, Dec. 19, 1941. FDRL. Biddle Papers (CWRIC 3793).

16. *Honolulu Advertiser*, Dec. 22, 1941, pp. 1 and 6 (CWRIC 29567–69).

17. Ruth E. McKee, *History of WRA—Pearl Harbor to June 30, 1944*, unpublished manuscript, 1944, p. 165; Shibutani, *Derelicts of Company K*, p. 38.

18. Shibutani, *Derelicts of Company K*, p. 38.

19. McKee, *History of WRA*, p. 165.

20. *Ibid.*, p. 164.

21. Shibutani, *Derelicts of Company K*, p. 35.

22. McKee, *History of WRA*, p. 165.

23. Allen, *War Years*, p. 167.

24. *Ibid.*, pp. 141–42.

25. *Ibid.*, p. 396.

26. Conn, *Guarding*, p. 200.

27. Allen, *War Years*, pp. 141, 146–48, 402.

28. *Ibid.*, p. 120. The ID registration project was suggested in June 1941 by the Office of Civilian Defense to enable identification of persons killed in an attack. Plans had progressed so far that by 1:30 p.m. on December 7, the first ID cards were printed. By the end of the war, registration records and cards had been consulted 300,000 times by police and security agencies.

29. *Ibid.*, p. 92.

30. *Ibid.*, pp. 172–73.

The commission tried only eight cases during its four years of existence. Among them were three cases of murder, one of which resulted in the death sentence, later commuted to imprisonment. In that case, the defendant was represented by an officer who had no legal training, although the prosecution was in the hands of a trained attorney. The five commissioners were not lawyers, and in its study of the trial, the Department of Interior noted that the commissioners had not been told the distinction between first and second degree murder, even though the evidence strongly suggested the lesser charge.

The three Honolulu provost courts tried nearly 19,000 cases by the end of the first half of 1942. Trials were generally held on the same day as the arrest. Typically, "After the defendent had made his plea, all witnesses stood in a semicircle before the judge and were each peremptorily questioned by him. When the judge felt that he had sufficient evidence, he rendered an immediate decision, imposed sentence, and proceeded to the next case. The defendent could make a statement on his own behalf, but his allotment of time was frequently limited. He had little opportunity to cross-examine witnesses.

He could obtain a lawyer, although some judges indicated in open court that they did not desire attorneys to participate in the trials."

31. Brief for the United States, *Duncan* v. *Kahanamoku,* No. 14,Oct. Term 1945 (CWRIC 12166–75).

32. Allen, *War Years,* p. 174; Diary, Harold I. Ickes, Feb. 1, 1942. Ickes Collection, LC, Microfilm reel 5/12, p. 6303 (CWRIC 6583).

33. Brief for the United States, *Duncan* v. *Kahanamoku,* No. 14, Oct. Term 1945 (CWRIC 12166–75).

34. Diary, Ickes, Oct. 25, 1942. LC, Microfilm reel 2/12, p. 7561 (CWRIC 6584).

35. Brief for the United States, *Duncan* v. *Kahanamoku,* No. 14, Oct. Term 1945 (CWRIC 12166–75).

36. Conn, *Guarding,* p. 208.

37. *Ibid.,* pp. 208–09.

Immediately after the attack on Pearl Harbor, the Army had requested the authority to evacuate the families of servicemen to the mainland at government expense. It later expanded the request to include other civilian women and children who wanted to evacuate as well as tourists stranded on Oahu when the war broke out. Beyond removing civilians from a vulnerable Oahu, evacuation eased the housing shortage and left fewer mouths to feed. (Conn, *Guarding,* p. 202).

38. *Ibid.,* p. 209.

39. *Idem.*

40. Memo, Chief of Staff to U.S. Joint Chiefs of Staff, Feb. 12, 1942. FDRL. PSF Confidential File (CWRIC 3664–65).

41. Conn, *Guarding,* p. 210.

42. *Ibid.,* pp. 210–11.

43. Memo, Dwight D. Eisenhower to McCloy, April 3, 1942. NARS. RG 107 (CWRIC 586–87).

44. Memo, McCloy to Eisenhower, March 28, 1942. NARS. RG 107 (CWRIC 588–89).

45. *Idem.*

46. Diary, Stimson, April 7, 1942. Sterling Library, Yale University (CWRIC 19763).

47. Diary, Stimson, April 15 and 24, 1942. Sterling Library, Yale University (CWRIC 19764–66).

48. Memo, Knox to FDR, April 20, 1942. NARS. RG 107 (CWRIC 582).

49. Cabinet meeting notes, Stimson, April 24, 1942. Sterling Library, Yale University (CWRIC 19731).

50. Diary, Stimson, April 28, 1942. Sterling Library, Yale University (CWRIC 19767).

51. Memo, King and Marshall to FDR, July 15, 1942. FDRL. PSF Safe File (CWRIC 3815–16).

52. Letter, Emmons to McCloy, April 29, 1942. NARS. RG 107 (CWRIC 579–80).

53. Conn, *Guarding,* pp. 211–12.

54. Memo, J. R. Deane to McCloy, July 17, 1942. NARS. RG 107 (CWRIC 572).

55. Letter, Knox to FDR, Oct. 17, 1942. NARS. RG 107 (CWRIC 565).
56. Conn, *Guarding*, p. 212.
57. Telephone conversation, Bendetsen and Hall, Oct. 5, 1942. NARS. RG 338 (CWRIC 8202–06).
58. Letter, Knox to FDR, Oct. 17, 1942. NARS. RG 107 (CWRIC 565).
59. Letter, Stimson to FDR, Oct. 29, 1942. NARS. RG 107 (CWRIC 566).
60. Letter, Emmons to Stimson, Nov. 2, 1942. NARS. RG 107 (CWRIC 562).
61. Memo, FDR to Stimson and Marshall, Nov. 2, 1942. NARS. RG 107 (CWRIC 563).
62. Memo, McFadden to Bendetsen, Nov. 19, 1942. NARS. RG 338 (CWRIC 8200–01).
63. Memo, Blake to Officer in Charge, Dec. 1, 1942. NARS. RG 210 (CWRIC 29548–53).
64. Hawaiian Report, Edwin G. Arnold to Myer, Dec. 16, 1943. NARS. RG 210 (CWRIC 29554–60).
65. Allen, *War Years*, p. 397.
66. Memo, Hall to McCloy, Dec. 30, 1942. NARS. RG 107 (CWRIC 554–56).
67. Letter, Stimson to Hull, March 30, 1943. NARS. RG 59 (CWRIC 12792).
68. Letter, Myer to McCloy, Feb. 27, 1943. NARS. RG 107 (CWRIC 551–52). Some typical responses to loyalty question no. 28 were:
"I cannot answer until I find out why I was evacuated to the mainland."
"I was interned for 14 months, and if they can give me the reason for interning me, then I can decide."
"Previous to my detention my sincere frame of mind was loyalty to serve the USA in all emergency, namely armed forces, in active combat duty or to protect the country in which I inherited the constitutional rights, to defend USA from any or all attacks by foreign or domestic enemy activities. However, I was greatly angered because of detaining me as an enemy alien, in spite of the fact my status of orderly and law abiding citizen had been established without cause, reason or any other charge, as yet unknown to me, I greatly regret, however, wish to refrain from answering the above questions."
"It is difficult for me to answer questions 27 and 28 because I was interned at Sand Island, I swore allegiance to the USA but the FBI said that I was not a true American citizen and was forced to say no."
"During my period of 10 months in the concentration camp, I swore many times to the allegiance of these United States, but was not recognized by the government. When I was up before a Hearing Board, I was denied the privileges of a citizen, and at the present time, it is very difficult for me to answer these questions. This all happened before I was concentrated in the camp during an investigation held by the government." NARS. RG 210 (CWRIC 29561–62).
69. Conn, *Guarding*, p. 214.

70. WDC, *Supplemental Report on Civilian Controls Exercised by Western Defense Command,* Jan. 1947, p. 172. NARS. RG 338.

71. Keiho (Yasutaro) Soga, *Tessaku Seikatsu* (Honolulu: Hawaii Times Ltd., 1948). Selected excerpts transl. by Library of Congress (CWRIC 14865–82).

72. WDC, *Supplemental Report on Civilian Controls Exercised by Western Defense Command,* Jan. 1947, p. 173. NARS. RG 338.

73. Allen, *War Years,* p. 141.

74. Letter, Ickes to Stimson, Feb. 14, 1945. NARS. RG 210 (CWRIC 29563–64).

75. Letter, Stimson to Ickes, May 2, 1945. NARS. RG 210 (CWRIC 29565–66).

76. Allen, *War Years,* pp. 140–41.

77. *Ibid.,* p. 134.

78. *Idem.*

79. *Ibid.,* p. 135. The boards were allowed considerable latitude, and the hearings were informal and similar to those conducted on the West Coast. Accounts vary, however, with regard to the composition of the boards. Although Allen describes them as civilian, a number of internees indicate that they were composed of military officers.

80. *Ibid.,* p. 137.

81. Unsolicited testimony, Mitsunobu Miyahira.

82. Unsolicited testimony, Kwantoku Goya.

83. Soga, *Tessaku Seikatsu.*

84. Radio, Richardson to McCloy, Feb. 11, 1944. NARS. RG 107 (CWRIC 542).

85. Andrew W. Lind, *Hawaii Japanese: An Experiment in Democracy* (Princeton: Princeton University Press, 1946), pp. 74, 104.

86. Allen, *War Years,* p. 399.

87. Shibutani, *Derelicts of Company K,* pp. 82–83.

88. Thomas D. Murphy, *Ambassadors in Arms* (Honolulu: University of Hawaii Press, 1954), pp. 114–15.

89. *Duncan v. Kahanamoku,* 327 U.S. 304 (1946).

90. Letter, Black to Stone, Jan. 18, 1946. LC, Hugo Black Papers (CWRIC 12597–99).

91. *Ex parte Milligan,* 71 U.S. 2,124 (1866).

92. For an analysis which reconciles *Duncan* and *Korematsu,* see Charles Fairman, "The Supreme Court on Military Jurisdiction: Martial Rule in Hawaii and the Yamashita Case," 59 Harv. L. Rev. 833 (1946). Fairman sees the distinction between the cases in the fact that in Hawaii the military government "did not recognize adequately that the civil government should rightly have continued to preside over all matters which the public defense did not require to be placed under direct military control, nor did it take into proper account the basic principle that the commander's authority over civil affairs is limited to measures of demonstrable necessity." (p. 858) Fairman extensively analyzes

the facts and record in *Duncan* but makes no close examination of the facts in *Korematsu*. It is, of course, the Commission's conclusion after studying the factual record that no showing of "demonstrable necessity" could have been made.

12

Germans and German Americans

1. Samuel Eliot Morison, *The Battle of the Atlantic* (Boston: Little, Brown & Co., 1961), pp. 131–45.

2. *Ibid.*, p. 157.

3. *Training Manual* prepared by Airasdevlant Naval Air Station, Quonset Point, Rhode Island, quoted in Morison, *Battle*, pp. 127–28.

4. Morison, *Battle*, p. 128.

5. Peter B. Sheridan, "The Internment of German and Italian Aliens Compared with the Internment of Japanese Aliens in the United States during World War II: A Brief History and Analysis," staff paper, Congressional Research Service, Library of Congress, Nov. 24, 1980, pp. 1–2 (CWRIC 25886–904).

6. U.S. Department of Justice news release, Feb. 16, 1942, quoted in Paul Clark, "Those Other Camps: Japanese Alien Internment During World War II," unpublished manuscript, no date, p. 9 (CWRIC 4403–55).

7. Clark, "Those Other Camps," p. 13 (CWRIC 4415).

8. The exclusion of lawyers was designed to save time and to put the procedure on a common-sense basis. Francis Biddle, *In Brief Authority* (Garden City, NY: Doubleday & Co., Inc., 1962), p. 208.

9. Testimony, Edward J. Ennis, Washington, DC, Nov. 2, 1981, p. 181.

10. Clark, "Those Other Camps," pp. 14–18 (CWRIC 4416–20).

11. Letter and memorandum outline, Stimson to DeWitt, Feb. 20, 1942. NARS. RG 338 (CWRIC 4643–44); NARS. RG 107 (CWRIC 298–304).

12. Stetson Conn, Rose C. Engelman and Byron Fairchild, *The United States Army in World War II, The Western Hemisphere: Guarding the United States and Its Outposts* (Washington, DC: Office of the Chief of Military History, United States Army, 1964), p. 144 [hereafter *Guarding*].

13. Memo, Bendetsen to McCloy, May 10, 1942. NARS. RG 338 (CWRIC 290–94).

14. Conn, *Guarding*, p. 145; Jacobus tenBroek, Edward N. Barnhart and Floyd W. Matson, *Prejudice, War and the Constitution* (Berkeley: University of California Press, 1954), pp. 103–05.

15. Memo, Alfred Jaretzki to Colonel Ralph Tate, June 4, 1942. NARS. RG 107 (CWRIC 6697–99).

16. Telephone conversation, Jaretzki to Bendetsen, April 27, 1942. NARS. RG 338 (CWRIC 5226–32).

17. Memo, Jaretzki to McCloy, May 21, 1942. NARS. RG 107 (CWRIC 171–74).

18. Western Defense Command, *Supplemental Report on Civil Controls Exercised by the Western Defense Command*, Jan. 1947, p. 859. NARS. RG 338.

19. Memo, Stimson to DeWitt, Feb. 20, 1942. NARS. RG 107 (CWRIC 4643–44).

20. Memo, Jaretzki to McCloy, May 21, 1942. NARS. RG 107 (CWRIC 171–74).

21. Biddle, *In Brief Authority*, p. 207.

22. Title 28—Judicial Administration, Chapter I, Part 30, Travel and Other Conduct of Aliens of Enemy Nationalities, amendment effective date Oct. 19, 1942. NARS. RG 338 (CWRIC 851–52).

23. Telegram, Tolan to Biddle, Feb. 28, 1942. NARS. RG 107 (CWRIC 92).

24. Report of the Select Committee Investigating National Defense Migration, U.S. House of Representatives, 77th Cong., 2d Sess., HR Report No. 1911, p. 24 [hereafter "Tolan Committee, Report No. 1911"].

25. Memo, Biddle to Roosevelt, April 9, 1942, cited in Conn, *Guarding*, p. 145.

26. Memo, Roosevelt to Stimson, May 5, 1942. NARS. RG 107 (CWRIC 196).

27. *Idem*. Roosevelt had instructed Stimson that no action under Executive Order 9066 was to be taken on the East Coast without prior discussion with the President.

28. Memo, Stimson to Roosevelt, May 14, 1942. NARS. RG 107 (CWRIC 197); notes of Cabinet meetings, May 15, 1942. FDRL. Biddle Papers (CWRIC 3796).

29. Conn, *Guarding*, p. 146.

30. *Idem;* testimony, Angelo deGuttadauro, New York, Nov. 23, 1981, p. 106.

31. Tolan Committee, Report No. 1911, pp. 35–36.

32. Edward M. Barnhart, "The Individual Exclusion of Japanese Americans in World War II," *Pacific Historical Review*, vol. 29 (May 1960), p. 113.

33. Richard O'Connor, *The German-Americans, An Informal History* (Boston: Little, Brown & Co., 1968), p. 449.

34. LaVern J. Rippley, *The German-Americans* (Boston: Twayne Publishers, 1976), p. 204.

35. O'Connor, *The German-Americans*, pp. 445–52; Rippley, *The German-Americans*, pp. 205–06.

36. Rippley, *The German-Americans*, p. 207.

37. *Ibid.*, p. 211; see Stephan Thernstrom, ed., *Harvard Encyclopedia of American Ethnic Groups* (Cambridge and London: Belknap Press of Harvard University Press, 1980), p. 810: "Much of the vaunted midwestern isolationism of the 1930s and 1940s can be explained by German American votes against involvement in a war against Germany."

38. *E.g.*, O'Connor, *The German-Americans*, pp. 376–77.

39. Rippley, *The German-Americans*, p. 209.

40. O'Connor, *The German-Americans*, p. 377.

41. Rippley, *The German-Americans*, p. 185; Frederick C. Leubke, *Bonds*

of Loyalty: German-Americans and World War I (DeKalb, IL: Northern Illinois University Press, 1974), pp. 208–10; O'Connor, *The German-Americans,* pp. 408–11.

42. *Harvard Encyclopedia of American Ethnic Groups,* pp. 740–41.

43. Rippley, *The German-Americans,* pp. 180–83; O'Connor, *The German-Americans,* pp. 388–91; Leubke, *Bonds of Loyalty,* p. 122.

44. Rippley, *The German-Americans,* p. 184; O'Connor, *The German-Americans,* pp. 402–04.

45. Leubke, *Bonds of Loyalty,* p. 210; Rippley, *The German-Americans,* pp. 185–86.

46. Leubke, *Bonds of Loyalty,* pp. 255–56.

47. *Ibid.,* p. 255.

48. *Ibid.,* pp. 241–42.

49. *Ibid.,* p. 271.

50. *Ibid.,* p. 210.

51. *Ibid.,* pp. 273–81; Rippley, *The German-Americans,* p. 186.

52. Rippley, *The German-Americans,* p. 186.

53. Leubke, *Bonds of Loyalty,* p. 216.

54. O'Connor, *The German-Americans,* p. 392; Rippley, *The German-Americans,* pp. 186–87.

55. Leubke, *Bonds of Loyalty,* p. 252.

56. *Ibid.,* pp. 285–86.

57. Rippley, *The German-Americans,* p. 186.

58. Leubke, *Bonds of Loyalty,* p. 270.

59. *Ibid.,* pp. 289–90.

60. O'Connor, *The German-Americans,* pp. 416, 421–28.

61. *Ibid.,* p. 427.

62. In a government inquiry after the war, the intelligence services acknowledged how myopic this view had been:

In connection with subversive welfare [sic], during the last war, I would like to make this observation. In the fall of 1941 and the winter of 1942, we expected that subversive elements would be found mainly in the alien population. To our amazement by 1943 we discovered such was not the case at all. Most aliens were scared to death. So most of our disloyal individuals were old-line families in this country. That was amazing to us, and we had to face the facts and recognize it.

Hearings before War Department Civilian Defense Board, Dec. 5, 1946, Report of War Department Civil Defense Board, an. I, p. 81, quoted in Conn, *Guarding,* p. 145.

63. *Harvard Encyclopedia of American Ethnic Groups,* pp. 685–86.

64. Fourth Interim Report of the Select Committee Investigating National Defense Migration, U.S. House of Representatives, 77th Cong., 2d Sess., HR Report No. 2124, p. 25.

65. *Ex parte Milligan,* 71 U.S. 2, 123–24 (1866).

13

After Camp

1. William Petersen, "Success Story, Japanese-American Style," *New York Times Magazine,* Jan. 9, 1966, pp. 20–21ff.; "Success Story: Outwhiting the Whites," *Newsweek,* June 21, 1971, p. 24.

2. Testimony, Senator S. I. Hayakawa, Los Angeles, Aug. 4, 1981, p. 15.

3. Written testimony, Lon Hatamiya, "Economic Effects of the Second World War upon Japanese Americans in California," prepared for the Japanese American Citizens League National Committee on Redress, Dec. 22, 1981, pp. 215–17.

4. Testimony, Warren Tadashi Furutani, Los Angeles, Aug. 5, 1981, p. 167.

5. Testimony, Michael Yoshii, San Francisco, Aug. 11, 1981, p. 246.

6. Testimony, Tetsuden Kashima, Seattle, Sept. 11, 1981, p. 102.

7. Testimony, Philip Zimbardo, San Francisco, Aug. 11, 1981, p. 147.

8. *Idem.*

9. Christie W. Kiefer, *Changing Cultures, Changing Lives* (San Francisco: Jossey-Bass Publishers, 1974), p. 65.

10. *Idem.*

11. *Ibid.,* p. 66.

12. See, e.g., testimony, Toaru Ishiyama, Chicago, Sept. 22, 1981, p. 200; testimony, Edward Himeno, Los Angeles, Aug. 6, 1981, p. 69; testimony, Tetsuden Kashima, Seattle, Sept. 11, 1981, p. 103.

13. See, e.g., testimony, James Okutsu, San Francisco, Aug. 11, 1981, p. 243.

14. See, e.g., Kiefer, *Changing Cultures,* p. 65; testimony, Philip Zimbardo, San Francisco, Aug. 11, 1981, p. 147; testimony, James Okutsu, San Francisco, Aug. 11, 1981, p. 242; testimony, Toaru Ishiyama, Chicago, Sept. 22, 1981, p. 202.

15. Testimony, Kiyo Sato-Viacrucis, San Francisco, Aug. 12, 1981, p. 75.

16. See, e.g., testimony, James Okutsu, San Francisco, Aug. 11, 1981, p. 243.

17. Edward H. Spicer, Asael T. Hansen, Katherine Luomala and Marvin K. Opler, *Impounded People: Japanese-Americans in the Relocation Centers* (Tucson, AZ: University of Arizona Press, 1969), p. 282; testimony, Henry Tanaka, Chicago, Sept. 22, 1981, p. 156.

18. Testimony, Henry Tanaka, Chicago, Sept. 22, 1981, p. 156.

19. Testimony, Karen Umemoto, San Francisco, Aug. 12, 1981, p. 149.

20. Cheryl L. Cole, *A History of the Japanese Community in Sacramento,*

1883–1972: Organizations, Businesses, and Generational Response to Majority Domination and Stereotypes (San Francisco: R & E Associates, 1974), p. 72.

21. Testimony, Ben Takeshita, San Francisco, Aug 11, 1981, p. 219.

22. Testimony, David T. Nakagawa, San Francisco, Aug. 12, 1981, p. 188.

Appendix: Latin Americans

1. Edward N. Barnhart, "Japanese Internees from Peru," *Pacific Historical Review*, vol. 31, no. 2 (May 1962), pp. 169–78.

2. U.S. Department of Justice, *Annual Reports for Fiscal Years 1943–46* (Washington, DC: U.S. Department of Justice, 1944–47), (CWRIC 14641).

3. C. Harvey Gardiner, *Pawns in a Triangle of Hate: The Peruvian Japanese and the United States* (Seattle: University of Washington Press, 1981), p. 4.

4. Stephan Thernstrom, ed., *Harvard Encyclopedia of American Ethnic Groups* (Cambridge and London: The Belknap Press of Harvard University Press, 1980), p. 563.

5. Gardiner, *Pawns*, p. 6.

6. U.S. Department of State, *The Japanese in Peru*, report attributed to John K. Emmerson, 1943. NARS. RG 59 (CWRIC 29645–99), p. 45.

7. John K. Emmerson, *The Japanese Thread* (New York: Holt, Rinehart & Winston, 1978), p. 131.

8. Barnhart, "Japanese Internees," p. 172.

9. Emmerson, *Japanese Thread*, p. 126.

10. Barnhart, "Japanese Internees," p. 172.

11. *Idem*.

12. Telegram, U.S. Department of State to U.S. Ambassador to Panama, Dec. 12, 1941. NARS. RG 59 (CWRIC 6944).

13. Gardiner *Pawns*, p. 14; telegram, U.S. Embassy in Panama to Secretary of State, May 18, 1942. NARS. RG 59 (CWRIC 6944).

14. Gardiner, *Pawns*, pp. 20–21.

15. *Ibid.*, p. 25.

16. *Ibid.*, p. 22; Emmerson, *Japanese Thread*, p. 140.

17. Attorney General Francis Biddle and Under Secretary of State Sumner Welles had previously agreed that interning citizens of Latin American states among the internees brought from Panama and Costa Rica posed no legal problem. (Gardiner, *Pawns*, pp. 21–24.)

18. *Ibid.*, pp. 25–46.

19. *Ibid.*, p. 58.

20. *Ibid.*, p. 29.

21. Barnhart, "Japanese Internees," p. 173.

22. Emmerson, *Japanese Thread*, p. 143.

23. Gardiner, *Pawns*, pp. 31, 48.

24. *Ibid.*, p. 56.

25. *Ibid.*, p. 67.

26. A September 8, 1942, State Department memorandum shows that State was concerned "whether any effort should be made to influence Peru to breach the international law provisions," and that after a decision was made on this issue, "then a decision can be reached as to whether the United States will undertake the wholesale removal of all Japanese from Peru over a period of time." Memorandum, Hanley, September 8, 1942. NARS. RG 59 (CWRIC 6943).

27. Letter, Emmerson to U.S. Ambassador to Peru, April 18, 1942. NARS. RG 59 (CWRIC 5648–49).

28. Testimony, Arthur Shinei Yakabi, New York, Nov. 23, 1981, p. 33.

29. Emmerson, *Japanese Thread*, p. 147.

30. Gardiner, *Pawns*, p. 17.

31. *Ibid.*, p. 84.

32. *Ibid.*, pp. 88–107.

33. 3 CFR, 1943–1948 Comp., p. 57.

34. Emmerson, *Japanese Thread*, p. 149.

35. Gardiner, *Pawns*, p. 114.

36. *Ibid.*, p. 124.

37. Barnhart, "Japanese Internees," p. 174.

38. Gardiner, *Pawns*, p. 133; one German internee, von Heymann, won a reversal in the Second Circuit Court of Appeals, *United States* v. *Watkins*, 159 F.2d 650 (2d Cir. 1947).

39. Gardiner, *Pawns*, p. 134.

40. *Ibid.*, p. 130.

41. Barnhart, "Japanese Internees," pp. 174–75.

42. Gardiner, *Pawns*, pp. 142–43.

43. Written testimony, Eigo and Elsa Kudo, Chicago, Sept. 22, 1981.

44. Barnhart, "Japanese Internees," p. 174.

45. Gardiner, *Pawns*, pp. 153–57.

46. Barnhart, "Japanese Internees," p. 174.

47. Gardiner, *Pawns*, p. 168.

48. Testimony, Ginzo Murono, New York, Nov. 23, 1981, p. 32.

49. Emmerson, *Japanese Thread*, p. 148.

The Aleuts: War and Evacuation in Alaska

1. Stetson Conn, Rose C. Engelman and Byron Fairchild, *The United States Army in World War II, The Western Hemisphere: Guarding the United States and Its Outposts* (Washington, DC: Office of the Chief of Military History, United States Army, 1964), p. 230. [hereafter *Guarding*].

2. *Ibid.*, p. 237.

3. *Ibid.*, p. 238.

4. Memo, Ernest Gruening to Harold L. Ickes, Feb. 14, 1942. NARS. RG 126 (CWRIC AL6160–64).

5. Conn, *Guarding*, p. 259.

6. *Ibid.*, p. 255.

7. Brian Wynne Garfield. *The Thousand Mile War* (Garden City, NY: Doubleday & Co., Inc., 1969), p. 7.

8. *Ibid.*, p. 4.

9. *Ibid.*, p. 12.

10. *Ibid.*, p. 14.

11. Conn, *Guarding*, p. 260.

12. Western Defense Command, *Final Report of Reduction and Occupation of Attu from the Combat Intelligence Point of View*, Foreword, August 9, 1943 [hereafter WDC, *Final Report Attu*], in John C. Kirtland and David F. Coffin, Jr., *The Relocation and Internment of the Aleuts During World War II*, vol. 1: *The Military Situation* (Anchorage, AK: Aleutian-Pribilof Islands Association, Inc., 1981), p. 172 [hereafter *Military*].

13. Conn, *Guarding*, p. 274.

14. Garfield, *Thousand Mile War*, p. 150.

15. *Ibid.*, p. 165.

16. *Ibid.*, p. 168.

17. *Ibid.*, p. 291.

18. *Ibid.*, p. 279.

19. The Western Defense Command reported on Aug. 9, 1943, that Japan "never exhibited any particular determination to improve the Attu and Kiska bases and was dilatory in the construction of proper facilities for the basing of land-based aircraft; coupled with the lack of enemy naval strength in the Aleutians area, [this] leads to the assumption that the enemy has not given the Aleutians theatre a very high priority. The conclusion can also be drawn that he lacked the necessary equipment, material, planes and naval forces required to adequately exploit his holdings in the Aleutians." (Typographical errors in the passage have been corrected.) (WDC, *Final Report Attu*, p. 172).

A Naval Intelligence report, dated Dec. 15, 1944, concludes that the Japanese threat to the entire western United States was removed by late Fall 1944, and that the end of the defensive position of the U.S. in the Aleutians coincided with the end of the Aleutian Campaign in August 1943. Advanced Intelligence Center of the North Pacific Area, *Aleutian Campaign: A Brief Historical Outline to and Including the Occupation of Kiska, August 1943*, Dec. 15, 1944, p. 111. NARS. RG 313 (CWRIC AL101).

20. Memo, Scheurmann of Navy Department to Paul W. Gordon, Jan. 16, 1942. NARS. RG 126 (CWRIC AL6168).

21. Memo, Gordon to Ernest Gruening, Jan. 23, 1942. NARS. RG 126 (CWRIC AL6170).

22. Minutes, Acting Governor of Alaska E. L. Bartlett's Evacuation Planning Meeting, March 13, 1942. Evidence submitted by John C. Kirtland for the Aleutian/Pribilof Islands Association at public hearing of the Commission in Anchorage, Alaska, Sept. 15, 1981; John C. Kirtland and David F. Coffin, Jr., *The Relocation and Internment of the Aleuts during World War II*, vol. 2: *The Evacuation* (Anchorage, AK: Aleutian/Pribilof Islands Association, Inc., 1981), pp. 1–3 [hereafter *Evacuation*].

23. *Idem.*

24. *Idem.*

25. *Idem.*

26. Memo, John Collier to Harold L. Ickes, April 10, 1942, in Kirtland, *Evacuation*, p. 4.

27. *Idem.*

28. *Idem.*

29. *Idem.*

30. *Idem.* Secretary Ickes' response is recorded on this memorandum and dated April 15, 1942: "I concur unless they want to move."

31. Letter, James C. Rettie to Harold D. Smith, May 7, 1942. NARS. RG 407 (CWRIC AL102).

32. Executive Order 9181, "Administration of the Federal Government Services in Alaska," June 11, 1942. 3 CFR 1167–69, 1938–1943 Comp.

33. Letter, Gruening to Ickes, June 4, 1942. NARS. RG 126 (CWRIC AL6149–50).

34. *Idem.*

35. *Idem.*

36. *Idem.*

37. Letter, Ickes to Gruening, June 17, 1942. NARS. RG 126 (CWRIC AL6153).

38. Conn, *Guarding*, pp. 266–67.

39. War Diary, *USS Gillis*, May 23 to June 30, 1942, in Kirtland, *Evacuation*, p. 33.

40. *Idem.*

41. C. Ralph and Ruby J. Magee, "Our Atka Experience 1940–1942," in Kirtland, *Evacuation*, pp. 13–17.

42. War Diary, *USS Hulbert*, June 1 to 30, 1942, in Kirtland, *Evacuation*, pp. 30–32.

43. War Diary, Navy Patrol Wing Four, May 27 to June 30, 1942, in Kirtland, *Evacuation*, pp. 27–29.

44. Magee, "Atka Experience," in Kirtland, *Evacuation*, pp. 13–17.

45. Letter, Edward C. Johnston to Ward T. Bower, May 28, 1942, in Kirtland, *Military*, p. 90.

46. Carl M. Hoverson, "Public Notice: St. Paul Village," June 5, 1942, in Kirtland, *Military*, p. 87.

47. Passenger List, *USAT Delarof,* June 16, 1942, in Kirtland, *Evacuation,* pp. 43–57.

48. Letter, Hoverson to Johnston, June 27, 1942. Indian Claims Commission Dockets No. 352 and 369 (CWRIC AL203) [hereafter ICC Exhibit].

49. Letter, Daniel C. R. Benson to Johnston, July 8, 1942, in Kirtland, *Evacuation*, pp. 9–11.

50. Passenger List, *USAT Delarof,* in Kirtland, *Evacuation,* pp. 43–57.

51. Conn, *Guarding,* p. 272.

52. Letter, Bower to F. G. Morton, Dec. 30, 1943, in John C. Kirtland and David F. Coffin, Jr., *The Relocation and Internment of the Aleuts during World War II,* vol. 4: *Repatriation and Resettlement,* pp. 130–32 [hereafter *Resettlement*].

53. Telegram, Margaret Quinn to Claude M. Hirst, June 16, 1942, in Kirtland, *Evacuation,* p. 73.

54. Letter, Fredrika Martin, March 1965, in Kirtland, *Evacuation,* pp. 25–26.

55. Telegram, Donald T. Hagerty to William Zimmerman, June 15, 1942. NARS. RG 126 (CWRIC AL6159).

56. *Idem.*

57. Telegram, Johnston to Bower, June 15, 1942, in Kirtland, *Evacuation,* p. 72.

58. *Idem.*

59. Telegram, Zimmerman to Hirst, June 16, 1942. NARS. RG 126 (CWRIC AL6157–58).

60. *Idem.*

61. Telegram, Hagerty to Zimmerman, June 16, 1942. NARS. RG 126 (CWRIC AL6156).

62. *Idem;* Telegram, Bower to Johnston, June 17, 1942; letter, Hirst to Gruening, June 29, 1942, both in Kirtland, *Evacuation,* pp. 83–84, 162–67.

63. Radio message, Hagerty to Commissioner of OIA, June 17, 1942. NARS. RG 126 (CWRIC AL6154); lease between P. E. Harris and Company and the United States Government, June 16, 1942, in Kirtland, *Evacuation,* pp. 130–33.

64. Telegram, Johnston to Hirst, July 16, 1942; letter, Hirst to Gruening, June 29, 1942, both in Kirtland, *Evacuation,* pp. 134, 162–67.

65. Telegram, Gruening to Ickes, June 20, 1942, in Kirtland, *Military,* p. 85.

66. Message, Hirst to Hagerty, June 24, 1942. NARS. RG 126 (CWRIC AL6146).

67. Admiral Freeman and General DeWitt had agreed earlier, on June 18, 1942, that: "In order to prevent their capture by the Japanese, the natives of the Pribiloff [sic] Islands, Atka and a few other Aleutian Islands were evacuated to places of comparative safety." Western Defense Command, *History of the Western Defense Command: March 17, 1941 to September 30, 1945* (Washington, DC: Office of the Chief of Military History, Department of the Army, Historical Manuscript File, Reel no. 192), p. 15 (CWRIC AL6582).

68. Letter, Captain Hobart W. Copeland to Commanding General, APO, Seattle, Washington, Jan. 17, 1944. NARS. RG 75 (CWRIC AL6305–06).

69. Letter, Carlyle C. Eubank to Colonel B. I. Reed, Adjutant General, Western Defense Command, Aug. 5, 1942. NARS. RG 338 (CWRIC AL6552–54).

70. *Idem*.

71. *Idem*.

72. *Idem*.

73. Memo, Zimmerman to Oscar Chapman, Assistant Secretary of Interior, Aug. 31, 1942, in Kirtland, *Evacuation*, pp. 40–41.

74. Telegram, John W. Fletcher to Ickes, July 7, 1942. NARS. RG 126 (CWRIC AL6145).

75. *Idem*.

76. Testimony, Philemon Tutiakoff, Unalaska, AK, Sept. 17, 1981, p. 8.

77. Letter, James V. Forrestal to Ickes, July 12, 1942, in Kirtland, *Evacuation*, p. 67.

78. Letter, Copeland to Commanding General, APO, Seattle, Washington, Jan. 17, 1944. NARS. RG 75 (CWRIC AL6305–06).

79. Testimony, John C. Kirtland, Anchorage, Sept. 15, 1981, p. 27.

80. Letter, Ickes to Forrestal, July 9, 1942, in Kirtland, *Evacuation*, p. 65.

81. Telephone conversation, Commission staff and Fred Geeslin, May 25, 1982 (CWRIC AL104).

82. Letter, James I. Parsons to Office of the Governor of Alaska, no date. NARS. M.939 Papers of Alaska Territorial Governor Ernest Gruening, Reel 291 (CWRIC AL105).

83. Memo, Colonel Karl R. Bendetsen to Captain Young, July 1, 1942. NARS. RG 338 (CWRIC AL6562); memo, Colonel Irwin Clawson to Colonel William A. Boekel, July 5, 1942. NARS. RG 338 (CWRIC AL6563–65).

84. Testimony, Verne Robinson, Unalaska, AK, Sept. 17, 1981, p. 61.

85. Memo, Freeman to DeWitt, Aug. 29, 1942. NARS. RG 338 (CWRIC AL6559–60).

86. Memo, Clawson to Boekel, July 5, 1942. NARS. RG 338 (CWRIC AL6563–65).

By late 1942, however, the Navy was removing its contract workers and the Army had concluded that: "There is nothing requiring work of more civilians than there is now [sic] at Dutch Harbor. . . . More civilians coming in would only make the problem more complicated even if they do not actually cause trouble. . . . Civilians are almost entirely dependent on Army for medical treatment and supply but seldom are controlled by Army." Radio incoming (paraphrase) from Alaska Defense Command Fort Richardson to Commanding General, Western Defense Command and Fourth Army, Dec. 6, 1942. NARS. RG 338 (CWRIC AL151).

87. Letter, Copeland to Commanding General, APO, Seattle, Washington, Jan. 17, 1944. NARS. RG 75 (CWRIC AL6305–06).

88. Memo, Zimmerman to Chapman, Aug. 31, 1942, in Kirtland, *Evacuation*, pp. 40–41.

89. *Idem*.

90. *Idem*.

91. *Idem*.

92. *Alaska Geographic*, ed. Lael Morgan, "The Aleutians," vol. 7, no. 3 (Anchorage, 1980), p. 139; interview, Commissioner Hugh G. Mitchell and Admiral James S. Russell (Ret.), Sept., 1981 (CWRIC AL107); telephone conversations, Commission staff and Lael Morgan, Jan. 8, 1982; James S. Russell, Jan. 8, 1982; Boyd A. Omang, Jan. 12, 1982 (CWRIC AL108).

93. Letter, Gruening to Ickes, June 4, 1942. NARS. RG 126 (CWRIC AL6149).

94. WDC, *Final Report Attu*.

95. "Preliminary Report Concerning the 1942 Japanese Invasion and Occupation of Attu and the Subsequent Removal of Attuans to Japan 1942–1945," Dec. 19, 1978, in Kirtland, *Military*, pp. 109, 125.

96. Letter, William C. House to Commission staff, Jan. 21, 1982, "Reunion between William C. House, Steve Hodikoff, Innokenty and Willie Golodoff," May 20, 1979 (CWRIC AL106).

97. Kirtland, *Military*, p. 125.

98. *Ibid.*, p. 127.

99. Letter, Seattle National Records Center to Commission staff, Jan. 1982.

100. Testimony, Parascovia Wright and Innokenty Golodoff, Anchorage, Sept. 15, 1981, pp. 137–38.

101. Letter, Lee C. McMillin to Johnston, July 11, 1942, in John C. Kirtland and David F. Coffin, Jr., *The Relocation and Internment of the Aleuts during World War II*, vol. 3: *Conditions at the Camp* (Anchorage, AK: Aleutian/ Pribilof Islands Association, Inc., 1981), pp. 8–9 [hereafter *Conditions*].

102. Letter, McMillin to Johnston, Aug. 5, 1942. Indian Claims Commission Dockets No. 352 and 369.

103. Letter, McMillin to Johnston, July 11, 1942, in Kirtland, *Conditions*, pp. 8–9.

104. Letter, Benson to Johnston, July 6, 1942, in Kirtland, *Evacuation*, pp. 174–76.

105. Telegram, Logan to Johnston, July 2, 1942, in Kirtland, *Evacuation*, p. 180.

106. Letter, Frank W. Hynes to Ward T. Bower, July 2, 1942, in Kirtland, *Evacuation*, p. 182.

107. Letter, McMillin to Everett Smith, Sept. 11, 1942, in Kirtland, *Conditions*, p. 126.

108. Letter, Johnston to Bower, Oct. 10, 1942, with petition by Aleut women. ICC Exhibit 529.

109. *Idem*.

110. Report by N. Berneta Block, Oct. 2–6, 1943, in Kirtland, *Conditions*, pp. 34–37.

111. Letter, Hynes to Bower, Oct. 28, 1943, in Kirtland, *Conditions*, pp. 40–42.

112. Letter, Kirtland to Senator Ted Stevens, May 6, 1980; N. Berneta Block, "Report of Trip to Funter Bay," Oct. 2–6, 1943, both in Hearings before the Committee on Governmental Affairs, United States Senate, 96th Cong. 2d Sess., on S. 1647, March 18, 1980, pp. 233–34, 238–41.

113. Letter, Hynes to Bower, Oct. 28, 1943, in Kirtland, *Conditions*, pp. 40–42.

114. Harold L. Ickes, *Annual Report of the Secretary of the Interior for the Fiscal Year Ended June 30, 1946* (Washington, DC: U.S. Government Printing Office, 1946), p. 303.

115. Ernest H. Gruening, *Annual Report of the Governor of Alaska to the Secretary of the Interior for Fiscal Year Ended June 30, 1942* (Washington, DC: U.S. Government Printing Office, 1942), p. 15.

116. Letter, R. E. Barnes to Johnston, June 29, 1942, in Kirtland, *Conditions*, pp. 115–17.

117. Letter, Johnston to Barnes, July 7, 1942, in Kirtland, *Conditions*, pp. 122–23.

118. Letter, McMillin to Johnston, July 1, 1942, in Kirtland, *Conditions*, pp. 120–21.

119. Letter, Johnston to Bower, July 15, 1942. ICC Exhibit 526.

120. Letter, Bower to Johnston, July 31, 1942, in Kirtland, *Evacuation*, pp. 110–12.

121. Letter, Johnston to G. Donald Gibbons, Nov. 2, 1942, in Kirtland, *Conditions*, pp. 127–29.

122. Letter, McMillin to Johnston, July 11, 1942, in Kirtland, *Conditions*, pp. 8–9.

123. Memo, Bess E. O'Neill to Captain Collins, Sept. 25, 1942, in Kirtland, *Conditions*, p. 135.

124. Letter, Ickes to Stimson, Nov. 23, 1942, in John C. Kirtland and David F. Coffin, Jr., *The Relocation and Internment of the Aleuts during World War II*, vol. 4: *Repatriation and Resettlement* (Anchorage, AK: Aleutian/Pribilof Islands Association, Inc., 1981), p. 2 [hereafter *Resettlement*].

125. Letter, Stimson to Ickes, Dec. 4, 1942, in Kirtland, *Resettlement*, p. 8.

126. Letter, Stimson to Ickes, Jan. 2, 1943, in Kirtland, *Resettlement*, p. 12.

127. Letter, McMillin to Johnston, Mar. 6, 1943, in John C. Kirtland and David F. Coffin, Jr., *The Relocation and Internment of the Aleuts during World War II*, vol. 5: *Sealing Operations* (Anchorage, AK: Aleutian/Pribilof Islands Association, Inc., 1981), p. 30 [hereafter *Sealing*].

128. Letter, Johnston to McMillin, Mar. 17, 1943. ICC Exhibit.

129. Letter, Johnston to Bower, Mar. 19, 1943, in Kirtland, *Resettlement*, pp. 169–70.

130. Letter, Bower to Johnston, Mar. 30, 1943, in Kirtland, *Resettlement*, pp. 171–72.

131. Letter, Johnston to Bower, April 27, 1943. ICC Exhibit 545.

132. Telegram, Bower to Morton, April 29, 1943, in Kirtland, *Sealing*, p. 44.

133. Letter, Johnston to Bower, May 5, 1943. ICC Exhibit.

134. Letter, Bower to Johnston, March 30, 1943, in Kirtland, *Resettlement*, pp. 171–72.

135. See testimony, Stefan A. Lekanof, St. Paul, AK, Sept. 19, 1981, p. 36. In 1945, Johnston repeated his adherence to Bower's official policy, but the views he expressed to McMillin and Bower make it altogether likely that the official position was not consistently presented to the Pribilovians.

136. Ernest H. Gruening, *Annual Report of the Governor of Alaska to the Secretary of the Interior for the Fiscal Year Ended June 30, 1944* (Washington, DC: U.S. Government Printing Office, 1944), p. 13.

137. Telegram, Geeslin to George T. Barrett, April 25, 1943, in Kirtland, *Sealing*, p. 43.

138. Letter, Bower to Morton, July 17, 1943, in Kirtland, *Resettlement*, pp. 173–74.

139. Magee, "Atka Experience," in Kirtland, *Evacuation*, pp. 13–17.

140. Letter, Sally Swetzof for Atka Village Council to Donna Fujioka, Commission staff, Feb. 23, 1982 (CWRIC 29700–03).

141. Letter, Hirst to Gruening, June 29, 1942, in Kirtland, *Evacuation*, pp. 162–67.

142. Letter, Swetzof to Fujioka, Feb. 23, 1982. (CWRIC 29700–03).

143. Magee, "Atka Experience," in Kirtland, *Evacuation*, pp. 13–17.

144. Testimony, Lavera Dushkin and Leonty Savaroff, Unalaska, AK, Sept. 17, 1981, pp. 29, 14.

145. Testimony, Lavera Dushkin, Unalaska, AK, Sept. 17, 1981, p. 29.

146. Testimony, Gertrude Svarny, Unalaska, AK, Sept. 17, 1981, p. 80.

147. Testimony, Dorofey Chercasen, Unalaska, AK, Sept. 17, 1981, p. 21.

148. Gerald D. Berreman, *A Contemporary Study of Nikolski: An Aleutian Village*, unpublished master's thesis in anthropology, University of Oregon, Eugene, June 1953, p. 255.

149. Testimony, Lavera Dushkin, Unalaska, AK, Sept. 17, 1981, p. 30; testimony, William Ermeloff, Unalaska, AK, Sept. 17, 1981, p. 34.

150. Testimony, Lavera Dushkin, Unalaska, AK, Sept. 17, 1981, pp. 29–30.

151. Berreman, *Nikolski*, p. 255.

152. Testimony, Dorofey Chercasen, Unalaska, AK, Sept. 17, 1981, p. 22.

153. *Idem.*

154. *Idem.*

155. Dorofey Chercasen and Paul Merculief, "Military Evacuation of Nikolski Village during the Second World War, 1941–1945" (Prepared for the Aleutian/Pribilof Islands Association), in Kirtland, *Conditions*, pp 67–72.

156. Berreman, *Nikolski*, p. 265.

157. Testimony, Father Paul Merculief for the Nikolski Corporation, Unalaska, AK, Sept. 17, 1981, p. 46.

158. Letter, Harry G. McCain to Gruening, May 19, 1943. NARS. RG 75/33 (CWRIC AL6324–25).

159. *Idem*.

160. Mark Petikoff, letter to the editor, *Alaska Fishing News*, May 21, 1943, p. 5. NARS. RG 75/33 (CWRIC AL6329).

161. Letter, Hirst to J. A. Talbot, June 5, 1943. NARS. RG 75/33 (CWRIC AL6321–22).

162. Berreman, *Nikolski*, pp. 256–57.

163. *Ibid.*, pp. 257–58.

164. *Ibid.*, p. 259.

165. Letter, Geeslin to Anthony J. Dimond, April 24, 1943. NARS. RG 75/33 (CWRIC AL6351–52).

166. Letter, Edythe J. Long to Fred R. Geeslin, May 6, 1943. NARS. RG 75/33 (CWRIC 6346–48).

167. Letter, Geeslin to Dimond, April 24, 1943. NARS. RG 75/33 (CWRIC AL6351–52).

168. *Idem*.

169. *Idem*.

170. Testimony of Lillie McGarvey, Anchorage, AK, Sept. 15, 1981, p. 152.

171. Letter, Martha Newell to Kenneth Newell, March 18, 1943. NARS. RG 75/33 (CWRIC AL5357).

172. Letter, Martha Newell to Kenneth Newell, March 26, 1943. NARS. RG 75/33 (CWRIC AL6356).

173. Letter, Geeslin to Cong. Del. Dimond, April 24, 1943. NARS. RG 75/33 (CWRIC AL6351–52).

174. Letter, Long to Geeslin, May 6, 1943. NARS. RG 75/33 (CWRIC AL6346–48).

175. List compiled by the Aleutian/Pribilof Islands Association, Inc., in Kirtland, *Conditions*, p. 108.

176. Telegram, Charles E. Jackson to Morton, Sept. 8, 1943, in Kirtland, *Resettlement*, p. 14.

177. Telegram, McMillin to Morton, Sept. 20, 1943; telegram, Morton to Bower, Sept. 20, 1943, both in Kirtland, *Resettlement*, p. 16.

178. Telegram, McMillin to Morton, Sept. 20, 1943; telegram, Morton to Bower, Sept. 20, 1943, both in Kirtland, *Resettlement*, p. 18.

179. Telegram, Morton to McMillin, Sept. 21, 1943, in Kirtland, *Resettlement*, p. 22.

180. Telegram, Bower to Morton, Sept. 21, 1943, in Kirtland, *Resettlement*, p. 21.

181. *Idem*.

182. Telegram, McMillin to Morton, Sept. 22, 1943, in Kirtland, *Resettlement*, pp. 25–26.

183. Letter, Morton to Homer J. Merriott, Oct. 7, 1943, in Kirtland, *Resettlement*, pp. 28–29.

184. Telegram, Bower to Johnston, Nov. 3, 1943. ICC Exhibit.

185. *Idem*.

186. Letter, Johnston to Hans Floe, March 17, 1944, in Kirtland, *Resettlement*, p. 168.

187. Memorandum, Thoron to Chapman, Oct. 19, 1943. NARS. RG 126 (CWRIC AL6137).

188. Memorandum for the record, June 10, 1944, in Kirtland, *Resettlement*, p. 153; see also pp. 152, 155, 157.

189. Letter, Knox to Ickes, Aug. 30, 1944, in Kirtland, *Resettlement*, p. 190.

190. Letter, Don C. Foster to William A. Brophy, Jan. 29, 1946, in Kirtland, *Resettlement*, pp. 238–43.

191. *The Budget of the U.S. Government for the Fiscal Year Ending June 30, 1947* (Washington, DC: U.S. Government Printing Office, 1946), p. 393, and *The Budget of the U.S. Government for the Fiscal Year Ending June 30, 1948* (Washington, DC: U.S. Government Printing Office, 1947), p. 461.

192. Radio message, COMNORPAC to CNO, April 13, 1944, in Kirtland, *Resettlement*, p. 52.

193. Letter, Zimmerman to Thoron, April 12, 1944. NARS. RG 126 (CWRIC AL6167).

194. Radio message, Thoron to Gruening, April 26, 1944. NARS. RG 126 (CWRIC AL6134).

195. Radio message, Gruening to Thoron, April 28, 1944, in Kirtland, *Resettlement*, p. 55.

196. Letter, Michael W. Straus to Forrestal, May 6, 1944. NARS. RG 126 (CWRIC AL 6166); letter, Straus to Stimson, May 6, 1944, in Kirtland, *Resettlement*, p. 56.

197. *Idem*.

198. Letter, Buckner to Secretary of War and Secretary of Navy, May 23, 1944, in Kirtland, *Resettlement*, p. 152.

199. Report on Unalaska Community (no date). NARS. RG 75 (CWRIC AL6307–08).

200. Memo, Fort Mears military police to Commanding General, Seattle, Jan. 12, 1944. NARS. RG 75 (CWRIC AL6290–01).

201. Testimony, Father Paul Merculief for the Nikolski Corporation, Unalaska, AK, Sept. 17, 1981, p. 47.

202. Testimony, Verne Robinson, Unalaska, AK, Sept. 17, 1981, p. 57.

203. Unsolicited testimony, deposition of Teresa Snigaroff Gardner Doty.

204. Telephone conversation, Geeslin and Commission staff, May 25, 1982 (CWRIC AL104).

205. Letter, Foster to Brophy, Jan. 29, 1946, in Kirtland, *Resettlement*, pp. 238–43.

206. *Idem*.

207. Testimony, Verne Robinson, Unalaska, AK, Sept. 17, 1981, pp. 56–57.

208. Telephone conversation, Geeslin and Commission staff, May 25, 1982 (CWRIC AL104).

209. *The Budget of the U.S. Government for the Fiscal Year Ending June 30, 1947* (Washington, DC: U.S. Government Printing Office, 1946), p. 393,

and *The Budget of the U.S. Government for the Fiscal Year Ending June 30, 1948* (Washington, DC: U.S. Government Printing Office, 1947), p. 461.

210. Tetra Tech, Inc., Department of the Army, Corps of Engineers, *Working Draft Environmental Impact Statement for World War II Debris Removal and Clean Up, Aleutian Islands and Lower Alaska Peninsula, Alaska,* Aug. 15, 1979, pp. 206–07 (CWRIC 29704–34).

211. Testimony, Henry Dirks, Anchorage, Sept. 15, 1981, p. 131.

212. Testimony, Alice Petrivelli, Anchorage, Sept. 15, 1981, p. 123.

213. Tetra Tech, Inc., *Debris Removal Alaska*.

214. Telephone conversation, Geeslin and Commission staff, May 25, 1982 (CWRIC AL104).

215. Dorothy Jones, *Patterns of Village Growth and Decline in the Aleutians,* Paper No. 11 (Fairbanks, AK: Institute of Social, Economic and Government Research, University of Alaska, Fairbanks, October 1973), pp. 1–4.

216. Testimony, Lillie McGarvey, Anchorage, Sept. 15, 1981, p. 140; and *Alaska Geographic,* ed. Lael Morgan, "The Aleutians," vol. 7, no. 3, 1980, p. 161.

Part III

Recommendations

Recommendations

In 1980 Congress established a bipartisan Commission on Wartime Relocation and Internment of Civilians, and directed it to:

1. review the facts and circumstances surrounding Executive Order Numbered 9066, issued February 19, 1942, and the impact of such Executive Order on American citizens and permanent resident aliens.

2. review directives of United States military forces requiring the relocation and, in some cases, detention in internment camps of American citizens, including Aleut civilians, and permanent resident. aliens of the Aleutian and Pribilof Islands; and

3. recommend appropriate remedies.

The Commission fulfilled the first two mandates by submitting to Congress in February 1983 a unanimous report, *Personal Justice Denied*, which extensively reviews the history and circumstances of the fateful decisions to exclude, remove and then to detain Japanese Americans and Japanese resident aliens from the West Coast, as well as the treatment of Aleuts during World War

II. * The remedies which the Commission recommends in this second and final part of its report are based upon the conclusions of that report as well as upon further studies done for the Commission, particularly an analysis of the economic impact of exclusion and detention.

In considering recommendations, the Congress and the nation therefore must bear in mind the Commission's basic factual findings about the wartime treatment of American citizens of Japanese ancestry and resident Japanese aliens, as well as of the people of the Aleutian Islands. A brief review of the major findings of *Personal Justice Denied* is followed by the Commission's recommendations.

I. AMERICAN CITIZENS OF JAPANESE ANCESTRY AND RESIDENT JAPANESE ALIENS

On February 19, 1942, ten weeks after the Pearl Harbor attack, President Franklin D. Roosevelt signed Executive Order 9066, empowering the Secretary of War and the military commanders to whom he delegated authority to exclude any and all persons, citizens and aliens, from designated areas in order to secure national defense objectives against sabotage, espionage and fifth column activity. Shortly thereafter, on the alleged basis of military necessity, all American citizens of Japanese descent and all Japanese resident aliens were excluded from the West Coast. A small number — 5,000 to 10,000 — were removed from the West Coast and placed in "relocation centers" — bleak barrack camps in desolate areas of the Western states, guarded by military police.

---

*Publisher's note: In the original publication, the recommendations appeared in a separate volume with the title *Part 2: Recommendations*.

People sent to relocation centers were permitted to leave only after a loyalty review on terms set, in consultation with the military, by the War Relocation Authority, the civilian agency that ran the camps. During the course of the war, approximately 35,000 evacuees were allowed to leave the camps to join the Army, attend college outside the West Coast or take whatever private employment might be available to them. When the exclusion of Japanese Americans and resident aliens from the West Coast was ended in December 1944, about 85,000 people remained in government custody.

This policy of exclusion, removal and detention was carried out without individual review, and prolonged exclusion continued without adequate regard to evacuees' demonstrated loyalty to the United States. Congress, fully aware of the policy of removal and detention, supported it by enacting a federal statute which made criminal the violation of orders issued pursuant to Executive Order 9066. The United States Supreme Court also upheld exclusion in the context of war, but struck down the detention of loyal American citizens on the ground that this did not rest on statutory authority. All this was done despite the fact that no documented acts of espionage, sabotage or fifth column activity were shown to have been committed by any identifiable American citizen of Japanese ancestry or resident Japanese alien on the West Coast. *

Officials took far more individualized, selective action against enemy aliens of other nationalities. No mass exclusion or detention, in any part of the country, was ordered against American citizens of German or Italian descent. The ethnic Japanese suffered a unique injustice during these years.

The Commission has examined the central events which created this history, especially the decisions that proved to be turning points in the flow of events.

The federal government contended that its decision to exclude ethnic Japanese from the West Coast was justified by "military necessity." Careful review of the facts by the Commission has not revealed any security or military threat from the West Coast ethnic Japanese in 1942. The record does not support the claim that military necessity justified the exclusion of the ethnic Japanese from

*Recent press reports take issue with this conclusion by the Commission; this is addressed separately in an addendum to another Commission volume, *Papers for the Commission*.

the West Coast, with the consequent loss of property and personal liberty.

The decision to detain followed indirectly from the alleged military necessity for exclusion. No one offered a direct military justification for detention; the War Relocation Authority adopted detention primarily in reaction to the vocal popular feeling that people whom the government considered too great a threat to remain at liberty on the West Coast should not live freely elsewhere. The WRA contended that the initial detention in relocation centers was necessary for the evacuees' safety, and that controls on departure would assure that the ethnic Japanese escaped mistreatment by other Americans when they left the camps. It follows, however, from the Commission's conclusion that no military necessity justified the exclusion that there was no basis for this detention.

In early 1943, the government proposed to end detention, but not exclusion, through a loyalty review program designed to open the gates of the camps for the loyal, particularly those who volunteered to join the Army. This program represented a compromise between those who believed exclusion was no longer necessary and those who would prolong it. It gave some ethnic Japanese an opportunity to demonstrate loyalty to the United States most graphically — on the battlefield. Particularly after detention, such means of proving loyalty should not have been necessary. Yet distinguished service of Japanese Americans both in Europe and the Pacific had a profound impact in fostering postwar acceptance of the ethnic Japanese in America. It opened the gates of the camps and began to reestablish normal life for some people. But it did not grant the presumption of loyalty to all American citizens of Japanese descent. With no apparent rationale or justification, the loyalty review program failed to end exclusion from the West Coast of those who were found loyal.

By the spring of 1943, the highest civilian and military officials of the War Department had concluded that, after the loyalty review, military requirements no longer justified excluding American citizens of Japanese descent or resident aliens from the West Coast. The exclusion was imposed through orders based on the Secretary of War's authority; nevertheless, the War Department did not act to lift the ban. The extent to which these views were communicated to the White House is unclear, but twelve months later, in May 1944, a recommendation to end exclusion was put before the President at a Cabinet meeting. Nevertheless, exclusion ended only after the Presidential election in November 1944. No plausible reason connected to wartime security supports this delay in allowing the ethnic Japanese to return to their homes, jobs and businesses — although the delay meant, as a practical matter, that most evacuees continued to be confined in relocation camps for an additional eighteen months.

In sum, Executive Order 9066 was not justified by military necessity, and the decisions that followed from it — exclusion, detention, the ending of detention and the ending of exclusion — were not founded upon military considerations. The broad historical causes that shaped these decisions were race prejudice, war hysteria and a failure of political leadership. Widespread ignorance about Americans of Japanese descent contributed to a policy conceived in haste and executed in an atmosphere of fear and anger at Japan. A grave personal injustice was done to the American citizens and resident aliens of Japanese ancestry who, without individual review or any probative evidence against them, were excluded, removed and detained by the United States during World War II.

The excluded people suffered enormous damages and losses, both material and intangible. To the disastrous loss of farms, businesses and homes must be added the disruption for many years of careers and professional lives, as well as the long-term loss of income, earnings and opportunity. Japanese American participation in the postwar boom was delayed and damaged by the losses of valuable land and growing enterprises on the West Coast which they sustained in 1942. An analysis of the economic losses suffered as a consequence of the exclusion and detention was performed for the Commission, Congress having extended the Commission's life in large measure to permit such a study. It is estimated that, as a result of the exclusion and detention, in 1945 dollars the ethnic Japanese lost between $108 and $164 million in income and between $41 and $206 million in property for which no compensation was made after the war under the terms of the Japanese-American Evacuation Claims Act. Adjusting these figures to account for inflation alone, the total losses of income and property fall between $810 million and $2 billion in 1983 dollars. It has not been possible to calculate the effects upon human capital of lost education, job training and the like.

Less tangibly, the ethnic Japanese suffered the injury of unjustified stigma that marked the excluded. There were physical illnesses and injuries directly related to detention, but the deprivation of liberty is no less injurious because it wounds the spirit rather than the body. Evacuation and relocation brought psychological pain, and the weakening of a traditionally strong family structure under pressure of separation and camp conditions. No price can be placed on these deprivations.

These facts present the Commission with a complex problem of great magnitude to which there is no ready or satisfactory answer. No amount of money can fully compensate the excluded people for their losses and sufferings. Two and a half years behind the barbed-wire of a relocation camp, branded potentially disloyal because of one's ethnicity alone — these injustices cannot neatly be translated into dollars and cents. Some find such an attempt in itself a means of minimizing the enormity of these events in a constitutional republic. History cannot be undone; anything we do now must inevitably be an expression of regret and an affirmation of our better values as a nation, not an accounting which balances or erases the events of the war. That is now beyond anyone's power.

It is well within our power, however, to provide remedies for violations of our own laws and principles. This is one important reason for the several forms of redress recommended below. Another is that our nation's ability to honor democratic values even in times of stress depends largely upon our collective memory of lapses from our constitutional commitment to liberty and due process. Nations that forget or ignore injustices are more likely to repeat them.

The governmental decisions of 1942 were not the work of a few men driven by animus, but decisions supported or accepted by public servants from nearly every part of the political spectrum. Nor did sustained or vocal opposition come from the American public. The wartime events produced an unjust result that visited great suffering upon an entire group of citizens, and upon resident aliens whom the Constitution also protects. While we do not analogize these events to the Holocaust — for the detention camps were not death camps — this is hardly cause for comfort in a democracy, even forty years later.

The belief that we Americans are exceptional often threatens our freedom by allowing us to look complacently at evil-doing elsewhere and to insist that "It can't happen here." Recalling the events of exclusion and detention, ensuring that later generations of Americans know this history, is critical immunization against infection by the virus of prejudice and the emotion of wartime struggle. "It did happen here" is a message that must be transmitted, not as an exercise in self-laceration but as an admonition for the future. Among our strengths as a nation is our willingness to acknowledge imperfection as well as to struggle for a more just society. It is in a spirit of continuing that struggle that the Commission recommends several forms of redress.

In proposing remedial measures, the Commission makes its recommendations in light of a history of postwar actions by federal, state and local governments to recognize and partially to redress the wrongs that were done:

• In 1948, Congress passed the Japanese-American Evacuation Claims Act; this gave persons of Japanese ancestry the right to claim from the government real and personal property losses that occurred as a consequence of the exclusion and evacuation. The Act did not allow claims for lost income or for pain and suffering. Approximately $37 million was paid in claims, an amount far below what would have been full and fair compensation for actual economic losses. Awards were low because elaborate proof of loss was required, and incentives for settling claims below their full value were built into the Act.

• In 1972, the Social Security Act was amended so that Japanese Americans over the age of eighteen would be deemed to have earned and contributed to the Social Security system during their detention.

• In 1978, the federal civil service retirement provisions were amended to allow the Japanese Americans civil service retirement credit for time spent in detention after the age of eighteen.

• In four instances, former government employees have received a measure of compensation. In 1982, the State of California enacted a statute permitting the few thousand Japanese Americans in the civil service, who were dismissed or who resigned during the war because of their Japanese ethnicity, to claim $5,000 as reparation. In late 1982, the Los Angeles County Board of Supervisors enacted a similar program for the Japanese Americans it employed in 1942. San Francisco and the State of Washington recently passed statutes providing similar relief to former employees who were excluded.

Each measure acknowledges to some degree the wrongs inflicted during the war upon the ethnic Japanese. None can fully compensate or, indeed, make the group whole again.

The Commission makes the following recommendations for remedies in several forms as an act of national apology.

1. The Commission recommends that Congress pass a joint resolution, to be signed by the President, which recognizes that a grave injustice was done and offers the apologies of the nation for the acts of exclusion, removal and detention.

2. The Commission recommends that the President pardon those who were convicted of violating the statutes imposing a curfew on American citizens on the basis of their ethnicity and requiring the ethnic Japanese to leave designated areas of the West Coast or to report to assembly centers. The Commission further recommends that the Department of Justice review other wartime convictions of the ethnic Japanese and recommend to the President that he pardon those whose offenses were grounded in a refusal to accept treatment that discriminated among citizens on the basis of race or ethnicity. Both recommendations are made without prejudice to cases currently before the courts.

3. The Commission recommends that Congress direct the Executive agencies to which Japanese Americans* may apply for the restitution of positions, status or entitlements lost in whole or in part because of acts or events between December 1941 and 1945 to review such applications with liberality, giving full consideration to the historical findings of this Commission. For example, the responsible divisions of the Department of Defense should be instructed to review cases of less than honorable discharge of Japanese Americans from the armed services during World War II over which disputes remain, and the Secretary of Health and Human Services should be directed to instruct the Commissioner of Social

---

*This recommendation and those that follow apply to all ethnic Japanese excluded or detained during World War II without regard to the explicit legal authority under which the government acted.

Security to review any remaining complaints of inequity in entitlements due to the wartime detention.

4. The Commission recommends that Congress demonstrate official recognition of the injustice done to American citizens of Japanese ancestry and Japanese resident aliens during the Second World War, and that it recognize the nation's need to make redress for these events, by appropriating monies to establish a special foundation.

The Commissioners all believe a fund for educational and humanitarian purposes related to the wartime events is appropriate, and all agree that no fund would be sufficient to make whole again the lives damaged by the exclusion and detention. The Commissioners agree that such a fund appropriately addresses an injustice suffered by an entire ethnic group, as distinguished from individual deprivations.

Such a fund should sponsor research and public educational activities so that the events which were the subject of this inquiry will be remembered, and so that the causes and circumstances of this and similar events may be illuminated and understood. A nation which wishes to remain just to its citizens must not forget its lapses. The recommended foundation might appropriately fund comparative studies of similar civil liberties abuses or of the effect upon particular groups of racial prejudice embodied by government action in times of national stress; for example, the fund's public educational activity might include preparing and distributing the Commission's findings about these events to textbook publishers, educators and libraries.

5. The Commissioners, with the exception of Congressman Lungren, recommend that Congress establish a fund which will provide personal redress to those who were excluded, as well as serve the purposes set out in Recommendation 4. Appropriations of $1.5 billion should be made to the fund over a reasonable period to be determined by Congress. This fund should be used, first, to provide a one-time per capita compensatory payment of $20,000 to each of the approximately 60,000 surviving persons excluded from their places of residence pursuant to Executive Order 9066[1]. The

---

[1]Commissioner William M. Marutani formally renounces any monetary recompense either direct or indirect.

burden should be on the government to locate survivors, without requiring any application for payment, and payments should be made to the oldest survivors first. After per capita payments, the remainder of the fund should be used for the public educational purposes discussed in Recommendation 4 as well as for the general welfare of the Japanese American community. This should be accomplished by grants for purposes such as aid to the elderly and scholarships for education, weighing, where appropriate, the effect of the exclusion and detention on the descendants of those who were detained. Individual payments in compensation for loss or damage should not be made.

The fund should be administered by a Board, the majority of whose members are Americans of Japanese descent appointed by the President and confirmed by the Senate. The compensation of members of the Board should be limited to their expenses and per diem payments at accepted governmental rates.

II.   THE ALEUTS[2]

When the Japanese attacked and captured the two westernmost Aleutian islands, Kiska and Attu, the military evacuated the Aleuts from the Pribilofs and from many islands in the Aleutian chain. This action was justified as a measure to protect civilians in an active theatre of war. The Commission found no persuasive showing that evacuation of the Aleuts was motivated by racism or that it was undertaken for any reason but their safety. The evacuation of the Aleuts was a rational wartime measure taken to safeguard them.

Following the evacuation, however, the approximately 900 evacuated Aleuts suffered at the hands of the government in two distinct ways. First, no plan had been developed to care for them by the civilian agencies in the Department of the Interior which had responsibility for Aleut interests. As a result, they were transported to southeastern Alaska and housed in camps set up typically at abandoned gold mines or canneries. Conditions varied among camps, but housing, sanitation and eating conditions in most were

[2]Commissioner Joan Z. Bernstein recuses herself from participation in recommending remedies for the Aleuts because of a potential conflict of interest involving representation by the law firm of which she is a member.

deplorable. Medical care was inadequate; illness and disease were widespread. While exact numbers are not available, it appears that approximately ten percent of the Aleut evacuees died during the two to three years they spent in the camps.

This treatment clearly failed to meet the government's responsibility to those under its care.

Second, on returning to their villages, the Aleuts found that many houses and churches had been vandalized by the U.S. military. Houses, churches, furniture, boats and fishing gear were missing, damaged or destroyed. Devout followers of the Russian Orthodox faith, the Aleuts had treasured religious icons from czarist Russia and other family heirlooms; now gone, they were a significant loss spiritually as well as materially. Insofar as the government attempted to make good some of these losses, it typically replaced Aleut possessions with inferior goods, and the losses were never remedied adequately.

The Fifth Amendment commits the government to compensating for property it takes. Appropriate, full compensation clearly has not been made in the case of the Aleuts.

In addition, the island of Attu, now used at least in part by the Coast Guard, was never returned to the Aleuts after the Second World War. There also remain in the Aleutians large quantities of wartime debris, much of it hazardous. A great deal, but not all, of this material rests on federally-owned land.

No effective system of records exists by which to estimate Aleut property losses exactly; certainly there is no readily available means of putting a dollar value upon the suffering and death brought to Aleuts in the camps. The Commissioners agree that a claims procedure would not be an effective method of compensation. Therefore, the sums included in the Commission's recommendations were chosen to recognize fundamental justice as the Commissioners perceive it on the basis of the testimony and evidence before them. The recommended amounts do not reflect a precise balancing of actual losses; this is now, after many years, a practical impossibility.

1. The Commissioners, with Congressman Lungren dissenting, recommend that Congress establish a fund for the beneficial use of the Aleuts in the amount of $5 million. The principal and interest of the fund should be spent for community and individual purposes that would be compensatory for the losses and injuries Aleuts suffered as a result of the evacuation. These injuries, as *Personal Justice Denied* describes, include lasting disruption of traditional Aleut means of subsistence and, with it, the weakening of their cultural tradition. The Commissioners therefore foresee entirely appropriate expenditures from the proposed fund for community educational, cultural or historical rebuilding in addition to medical or social services.

2. The Commissioners, with Congressman Lungren dissenting, recommend that Congress appropriate funds and direct a payment of $5,000 per capita to each of the few hundred surviving Aleuts who were evacuated from the Aleutian or Pribilof Islands by the federal government during World War II.

3. The Commission recommends that Congress appropriate funds and direct the relevant government agency to rebuild and restore the churches damaged or destroyed in the Aleutian Islands in the course of World War II; preference in employment should be given to Aleuts in performing the work of rebuilding and restoring these buildings, which were community centers as well as houses of worship.

4. The Commission recommends that Congress appropriate adequate funds through the public works budget for the Army Corps of Engineers to clear away the debris that remains from World War II in and around populated areas of the Aleutian Islands.

5. The Commission recommends that Congress declare Attu to be native land and that Attu be conveyed to the Aleuts through their native corporation upon condition that the native corporation is able to negotiate an agreement with the Coast Guard which will allow that service to continue essential functions on the island.

Finally, the Commission recommends that a permanent collection be established and funded in the National Archives to house and make available for research the collection of government and private documents, personal testimony and other materials which the Commission amassed during its inquiry.

The Commission believes that, for reasons of redressing the personal injustice done to thousands of Americans and resident alien Japanese, and to the Aleuts—and for compelling reasons of preserving a truthful sense of our own history and the lessons we can learn from it—these recommendations should be enacted by the Congress. In the late 1930's W. H. Auden wrote lines that express our present need to acknowledge and to make amends:

> We are left alone with our day, and the time is short and
>
> History to the defeated
>
> May say Alas but cannot help or pardon.

It is our belief that, though history cannot be unmade, it is well within our power to offer help, and to acknowledge error.

Part IV

Papers for the Commission

Addendum to Personal Justice Denied

There have been recent reports in the press[1] which point out that the Commission's report, *Personal Justice Denied*, does not make reference to the multi-volume Department of Defense publication, *The "Magic" Background of Pearl Harbor*.[2] Those volumes contain Japanese diplomatic cables of 1941 which American cryptanalysts deciphered, a small number of which refer to Japan's intelligence efforts in the United States. There is a penumbra to the articles which suggests that if the Commission had been aware that Japan had an intelligence network in this country which involved any American citizens of Japanese ancestry or resident Japanese aliens, it would have reached different conclusions and opinions about Executive Order 9066.

In fact, review of the "Magic" cables does not alter the Commission's position. Rather, it confirms the views expressed by the Commission. *Personal Justice Denied* devoted several pages to analyzing the American intelligence views of Japan's espionage, sabotage, and fifth column capabilities on the West Coast in late 1941 and 1942.[3] Several relevant points were made in that discussion. First, the intelligence sources reviewed assumed that Japan had a modest number of intelligence agents and perhaps potential saboteurs on the West Coast in 1942. Second, people familiar with the intelligence activities of Japan believed that the Japanese intelligence network employed many who

471

were not ethnic Japanese. Third, the intelligence experts believed that any threat of sabotage, espionage or fifth column activity was limited and controllable and did not justify mass exclusion of the ethnic Japanese from the West Coast.[4] Nothing in the "Magic" cables contradicts these basic points.

What the "Magic" cables show is an effort by Japan to develop an intelligence capability in the United States made up of both non-ethnic Japanese and ethnic Japanese. In fact, in sending instructions about who should be used in such an effort, the cables first emphasize groups *other* than the Issei and Nisei:

> (5) Utilization of U.S. citizens of foreign extractions (other than Japanese), aliens (other than Japanese), communists, Negroes, labor union members, and anti-Semites, in carrying out the investigations described in the preceding paragraph would undoubtedly bear the best results.
>
> These men, moreover, should have access to governmental establishments, (laboratories?), governmental organizations of various characters, factories, and transportation facilities.
>
> (6) Utilization of our "Second Generations" and our resident nationals. (In view of the fact that if there is any slip in this phase, our people in the U.S. will be subjected to considerable persecution, and the utmost caution must be exercised).[5]

Among the more than 4,000 "Magic" cables in 1941, only a very small number reflect the collection of intelligence which was not clearly public information or data obtainable by legal observation. The limited number of cables which include sensitive information frequently do not make clear the source of the information, and those that do refer to both persons who were not ethnic Japanese as well as ethnic Japanese. This is shown by what is probably the most complete report from the United States describing Japan's intelligence-gathering effort, a cable of May 9, 1941 from Los Angeles; the cable also demonstrates the difficulty of determining how much, if any, of the information collection was secret or illegal:

> We are doing everything in our power to establish outside contacts in connection with our efforts to gather intelligence material. In this regard, we have decided to make use of white persons and Negroes, through Japanese persons whom we can't trust completely. (It not only would be very difficult to hire U.S. (military?) experts for this work at the present time, but the expenses would be exceedingly high.) We shall, furthermore, maintain close connections with the Japanese Association, the Chamber of Commerce, and the newspapers.

With regard to airplane manufacturing plans and other military establishments in other parts, we plan to establish very close relations with various organizations and in strict secrecy have them keep these military establishments under close surveillance. Through such means, we hope to be able to obtain accurate and detailed intelligence reports. We have already established contacts with absolutely reliable Japanese in the San Pedro and San Diego area, who will keep a close watch on all shipments of airplanes and other war materials, and report the amounts and destination of such shipments. The same steps have been taken with regard to traffic across the U.S.-Mexico border.

We shall maintain connection with our second generations who are at present in the (U.S.) Army, to keep us informed of various developments in the Army. We also have connections with our second generations working in airplane plants for intelligence purposes.

With regard to the Navy, we are cooperating with our Naval Attache's office, and are submitting reports as accurately and as speedily as possible.

We are having Nakazawa investigate and summarize information gathered through first hand and newspaper reports, with regard to military movements, labor disputes, communistic activities and other similar matters. With regard to anti-Jewish movements, we are having investigations made by both prominent Americans and Japanese who are connected with the movie industry which is centered in this area. We have already established connections with very influential Negroes to keep us informed with regard to the Negro movement.[6]

This cable also illustrates the further problem that it is very difficult to distinguish puffery from truth in the "Magic" documents—certainly later cables do not show the transmission of information which would have given Japan knowledge of anything but a very small part of the items listed in this cable. Of course, information could be transmitted by methods other than "Magic" codes, but there is considerable room to doubt that any program of this sort was fulfilled.

Next, there is no indication in the "Magic" cables of a sabotage or fifth column organization.[7] The likelihood of sabotage and fifth column aid in case of attack were, of course, major arguments advanced in support of the exclusion.

As to the intelligence network being identifiable and controllable, the "Magic" volumes end with the Pearl Harbor attack and do not report whether Japanese agents were picked up by the FBI immediately after December 7th. But an occasional indication is available. One of the few persons with a Japanese name mentioned in the cables in connection with covert activities is one Iwasaki, who had been in touch with William Dudley Pelley, leader of the Silver Shirts, a fascist organization in the United States.[8] The records of the Western Defense Command show that it became fully familiar with Iwasaki's relation to the Silver Shirts and knew that he had returned to Japan before the outbreak of war.[9] Evidence of this sort tends to corroborate the views that intelligence experts, such as Lieutenant Commander Ringle of the Office of Naval Intelligence, expressed in 1942.

The startling news would have been to discover that Japan had no intelligence capability on the West Coast before Pearl Harbor. What has been found in the "Magic" cables only reaffirms the conclusions and opinions the Commission reached in its report.

One reason that the documents were not located and reviewed is that there is no clear evidence that they played any part in the decision to issue Executive Order 9066 or to pursue the policy of exclusion and detention of the West Coast ethnic Japanese. The Commission did not locate references to the "Magic" cables in the extensive documents of the time which deal with exclusion and detention. Within the War Department the impetus for the Executive Order came primarily from General DeWitt on the West Coast, and he was not on the distribution list for "Magic" material.[10] From May to November, 1941, President Roosevelt did not see the "Magic" cables,[11] so that it is a matter of speculation how, if at all, the minor cables dealing with intelligence in the United States were reported to him by those who summarized the cables orally. It is equally difficult to tell what, if any, part of the cable traffic was known to those not on the distribution.

No one who was in the War Department in 1941 and on the distribution for "Magic" information is alive today, so that one cannot demonstrate whether or not these cables had any influence on their thinking when the issue of exclusion was raised. The person still alive who was closest to those who saw the "Magic" cables is John J. McCloy; he testified before the Commission about the basis of the War Department's request for the Executive Order, and in discussing espionage and sabotage made no argument that intelligence from Japanese sources played any part in the decision:

> MR. MACBETH: First, is it your memory that there were no known cases of actual sabotage from Japanese aliens or Japanese American citizens on the West Coast prior to the signing of the Executive Order?
>
> MR. McCLOY: I can't say—I don't know whether there were or whether there weren't. There were rumors that there was vio-

lence and some espionage, that everybody was reporting in that there were signals from the Coast and they were close enough to watch the convoys. Whether it was espionage or not, I can't say. But this wasn't such a motivating factor with us, the possibility was there, and I think the soldiers who were military minded always had—they weren't saying that they wanted—they wanted to try to eliminate as far as possible all potential sabotage or espionage after the attack, and I don't know that they had any records at that time; I didn't know of any record of any convictions; there were suspicions and rumors but that's as far as I can go.

MR. MACBETH: Would it be fair then to say that the decision was made not on the basis of actual events of sabotage or espionage known to the War Department, but on the fear of possible future actions, is that right?

MR. McCLOY: Yes. Except, of course, the Pearl Harbor attack itself.[12]

In sum, the "Magic" cables confirm the basic analysis presented by the Commission.

Much has been made of the sentence in *Personal Justice Denied* which states that "not a single documented act of espionage, sabotage or fifth column activity was committed by an American citizen of Japanese ancestry or by a resident Japanese alien on the West Coast." This statement stands. The "Magic" cables do not identify individuals in those groups who committed demonstrable acts of espionage, sabotage or fifth column activity.

Since it is always possible that such an identification might one day be made, it is worth underscoring that espionage or sabotage by a small group does not justify excluding and detaining the entire ethnic group to which they belong. During World War II the following Caucasians were convicted of espionage on the mainland: William A. Schuler, Dr. Otto Willumeit, Gerhard Kunze, Rev. Kurt B. Molzahn, Nicholine Buonapane, Frederick V. Williams, David W. Ryder, Igor Stepanoff, Arthur C. Read, Mrs. Valvalee Dickinson, John Farnsworth, Harry A. Thompson, Frederick H. Wright, John C. LeClair, Joseph H. Smyth, Walker G. Matheson, Ralph Townsend, and Mimo de Guzman.[13] Such evidence provides no good argument for excluding all German Americans or English Americans from the coasts and detaining them in the interior. Equally, there was no good argument for excluding and detaining the Japanese Americans.

Angus MacBeth
June 1983

NOTES

1. "1941 Cables Boasted of Japanese-American Spying," *New York Times*, May 22, 1983; "U.S. Knew of Japanese-American Spies," *The Washington Times*, May 31, 1983.

2. Department of Defense, *The "Magic" Background of Pearl Harbor*, Washington, D.C.: U.S. Government Printing Office, 1977. The eight volumes of this publication digest and reproduce cables sent in the highest grades of the cryptographic system of the Japanese Foreign Office which American crypt-analysts had broken by the fall of 1940. The information derived from this source was designated "Magic" by the United States. The volumes contain approximately 4,200 cables dated from February to December 1941. They are of primary interest in the context of the discussions between Secretary of State Cordell Hull and Ambassador Kichisaburo Nomura.

3. *Personal Justice Denied*, pp. 51–60.

4. Although not cited in *Personal Justice Denied*, this last point was also made in testimony before the Commission by an official Department of Defense witness, Fred Beck, the Executive of the Historical Services Division, United States Army, Center of Military History: "Although military and domestic intelligence agencies paid special attention to the Kibei, that group of Japanese that returned to Japan for an education, no intelligence service made plans for mass evacuation of Japanese population before the war, and all of them resisted that idea after Pearl Harbor." Washington, July 14, 1981, p. 158.

5. *The "Magic" Background*, vol. 1, pp. A-76 to A-77.

6. *The "Magic" Background*, vol. 1, pp. A-99.

7. In fact, the cables suggest the opposite. The following cable was sent from San Francisco to Tokyo on February 10, 1941:

> 1. Seeing how Japanese-American relations have lately become so strained, pronounced unrest has been noted among Japanese dwelling in the United States. Now, considering the fact that there is a shortage of Japanese ships and considering the position, I think that our agencies in the United States ought to take suitable measures to instruct Japanese societies and organizations of all sorts to put the minds of these second generationers and their native parents at rest, and whether there is a war between the United States and Japan or not, have them stay where they are with as much tranquility as possible.
>
> 2. Of course, we will try to get but a necessarily small number of Japanese citizens registered in Japan as well as their families, but we will have to study the psychology of the vast majority of the Japanese citizens in this country as well as of the second generation and do our best to keep them from getting excited and feeling uneasy. Therefore, I think that we ought to be careful to instruct everyone in responsible positions, as well as Japanese newspaper correspondents, to help us in this task. *The "Magic" Background*, vol. 1, p. A-106.

8. *The "Magic" Background*, vol. II, Appendix, pp. A-178 to A-179.

9. Western Defense Command, *Supplemental Report on Civilian Con-*

trols Exercised by the Western Command, Appendix II, Tab C. NARS. RG 338 [CWRIC 25858].

10. Army Security Agency, "Signal Intelligence Disclosures in the Pearl Harbor Investigation" (1947); Ronald Lewin, *The American Magic*, London: Penguin Books, Ltd., 1983, p. 67. Distribution of "Magic" information was limited to the Secretary of War, the Army Chief of Staff, the Director of Military Intelligence, the Secretary of the Navy, the Chief of Naval Operations, the Chief of the Navy's War Plans Division, the Director of Naval Intelligence, the Secretary of State and the President.

11. Ruth R. Harris, "The 'Magic' Leak of 1941 and Japanese-American Relations," *Pacific Historical Review*, vol. 50, p. 77 (1981).

12. Washington, D.C., Nov. 3, 1981, pp. 45–46.

13. Jacobus tenBroek, Edward N. Barnhart and Floyd Matson, *Prejudice, War and the Constitution*, Berkeley: University of California Press, 1954, p. 393.

ADDITIONAL VIEWS OF CONGRESSMAN DANIEL E. LUNGREN

Having chosen to present additional views, some might conclude that I in some way find fault with the basic conclusions of the Commission on Wartime Relocation and Internment of Civilians. I do not. The history of the period leaves little room for doubt that a grave injustice was committed when the United States government chose to intern the nearly 120,000 Americans of Japanese ancestry living on the west coast. The decision was wrong.

Furthermore, I would concur with the finding of the commission that the implementation of Executive Order 9066 was largely a result of "race prejudice, war hysteria and a failure of political leadership."

I am concerned, however, that the information contained in the Department of Defense publication, *The "Magic" Background of Pearl Harbor*, has not been considered to be as significant as the facts suggest it should be.

For us as a commission to deny that the decoded Japanese cables compiled in the "Magic" volumes did not influence the decisions made by America's leaders, tends to undercut the credibility of our historical pursuit.

Although history now shows that the Japanese government was not successful in its efforts, the cables clearly indicate that there were verifiable and overt attempts made by the Japanese government to organize Japanese-Americans into various categories and recruit them for espionage activities.

After considering the weight of the evidence, it seems inconceivable that these classified cables did not play at least a limited role in the decisions that were made. This is especially true, since it seems certain that the Secretary of War, the Army Chief of Staff, the Director of Military Intelligence, the Secretary of the Navy, the Chief of Naval Operations, the Chief of the Navy's War Plans Division, the Director of Naval Intelligence, the Secretary of State, and the President all had knowledge of the contents of the cables dealing with Japanese espionage activities.

Furthermore, there is little reason to believe that these cables were considered to be anything but genuine. Japan, at that time, had a highly professional diplomatic corps. One should also remember that at this time the Japanese government was developing a reputation as an effective military aggressor. As American historian Samuel Eliot Morison points out: "Never in modern history has there been so quick and valuable a series of conquests; even Hitler's were inferior." This leads to the conclusion that those responsible for the military decisions in the United States would have considered the cables to be very credible.

As vice-chairman of the commission and one who is committed to examining all facets of the events that transpired, I believe that it would be inappropriate for the commission to ignore the probability that the cables played some small role in the decisions which ultimately affected the Japanese-Americans. Indeed, we as a commission should encourage further deliberation on this issue as Congress begins to address the subject.

Finally, while the conclusions of the commission still stand, some statements in the body of the commission report may need to be revised. Again, I would emphasize that the intelligence information now being discussed changes only slightly the relative weight distributed among the three identified causes of the proclamation and implementation of Executive Order 9066—i.e., "race prejudice, war hysteria and a failure of political leadership"—and contributes to the commission's ongoing goal of maintaining historical accuracy.

Index

Abbey, Roy: 393
Abe, Fuki O.: 415, 425
Abrams, Leonard: 136
Aikoku Doshi-Kai: 313
Alaska, S.S.: 334, 335
Alaska Defense Command (ADC): 319–20, 323, 327–28, 333
Alaska Department: 323, 354
Alaska Fishing News: 339, 349
Alaska Indian Service: 323, 328, 349, 351, 354
Alaska Sector: 319, 323, 354
Alaska War Council: 326–28, 332
Alaskan evacuation: 18–19, 318; Akutan Island, 332, 333; Aleut history: 317; Aleutian campaign: 319–23, 328; Atka Island: 328–29; Attu Island invasion: 336–37; Burnett Inlet camp: 335, 350–52; camp site selection: 331; decision for: 323–28; effects of: 357–59; Funter Bay camp: 20–21, 337–45; Killisnoo camp: 345–46; Pribilof Islands: 329–31, 352–54; resettlement: 22, 352–57; summary: 18–23; Umnak Island: 332–33; Unalaska Island: 332–35; Unimak Island, 324, 335; Ward Lake camp: 347–50; Wrangell Institute: 346–47
Aleutian Livestock Company: 333
Aleuts. *See* Alaskan evacuation
Alien Control Authority: 104
Alien Enemy Act of 1798: 54, 312
Alien Enemy Control Unit: 285, 309
Alien land laws: 34, 37
Alien Property Custodian: 61, 131
Amache relocation center. *See* Granada, CO, relocation center
American Civil Liberties Union (ACLU): 69, 247
American Defense Society: 291
American Federation of Labor: 32

American Friends Service Committee: 171, 181, 311
American Friends Society: 173
American Legion: 4, 34, 37, 68, 69, 224
American Loyalty League: 41
American Protective League: 290
Anderson, Rep. John Z.: 70
Anti-Jap Laundry League: 34
Anti-Japanese prejudice: birthrate fear: 38; cultural factors: 38–42; economic factors: 42–44; Hawaii: 16, 261; history of: 28–36; Pearl Harbor and: 28, 67–72, 91; racial factors: 44–46; resettlement and: 203–04, 224–25; summary: 4–6; yellow peril fear: 37–38
Aoki, Richard: 404
Arai, Akira: 405
Arata, Bert: 405
Army, U.S.: Alaskan role: 319, 322–24, 327, 329–33, 335, 347, 353–55; assembly center role: 105–07, 130, 144, 146, 147; enemy alien policies: 62–65; evacuation role: 94, 101, 103, 105, 107, 109; exclusion decision and: 8, 67; Hawaiian role: 16–17, 264–68, 270, 280; loyalty program role: 190, 191; Nisei service: 17, 186–91, 254–59; relocation center role: 156, 175, 247; segregation center role: 211. *See also* Western Defense Command
Army Intelligence: 64, 190, 254, 264, 320
Army Map Service: 259
Arrests: 54–55, 60, 108, 261, 278, 285
Arthur, Pres. Chester A.: 29
Asiatic Exclusion League. *See* California Joint Immigration Committee; Japanese Exclusion League

Assembly centers: administration of: 107; arrival at: 135–37; clothing: 143; education: 144–45; employment: 146; family separation: 140–41; food: 141–42; housing: 137–40; medical care: 143–44; publications: 146; recreation: 145; religious activities: 145; sanitation: 142–43; security: 147–48; self-government: 146; sites: xii, 105–06, 137, 138
Aves, Capt. Fred H.: 330

Bainbridge Island, WA, evacuation: 109
Barnett, Arthur G.: 425
Barrett, George: 346
Bartlett, E. L.: 324, 331
Bartz, Sumie I.: 425
Bell, Gladys: 158, 160
Bellquist, Eric C.: 113
Bendetsen, Col. Karl R.: 65, 198, 227, 286n; end of exclusion and: 214–19, 223; evacuation role: 101, 106, 109, 111; exclusion decision and: 50, 74, 75, 77–78, 84; relocation role: 154–55
Benson, Daniel C. R.: 329–30, 338–39, 352
Berreman, Gerald: 349–50
Biddle, Francis: 18, 49, 107, 130; citizenship renunciation policy: 248; end of exclusion and: 227–28, 233; enemy alien policy: 54–55, 62, 74; evacuation and: 78–79, 81, 83–85, 103, 104, 107, 110; exclusion decision and: 9, 56, 64, 69, 73, 74, 78–79, 81, 83–86; German-Italian exclusion policy: 287
Bismarck, ND, internment camp: xii, 109
Black, Justice Hugo L.: 236, 281–82
Black Dragons: 53–54, 178
Bloch, Rear Adm. Claude C.: 272
Block, Berneta: 340
Bloom, Leonard. See Broom, Leonard
Board of Immigration Appeals: 314
Boddy, Manchester: 80–81

Bonesteel, Gen. C. H.: 229–32
Bower, Ward T.: 330, 331, 339, 340, 342, 344–45, 353
Bowron, Mayor Fletcher: 5, 69, 376–77
Braun, Mr.: 217
Bridges, Noriko S.: 403, 424
British Intelligence: 53
Broom, Leonard: 119–20, 393
Buckner, Brig. Gen. Simon B.: 319, 322, 323, 327, 331, 332, 355
Buddhism: 40
Budget Bureau: 107, 326
Bund: 288, 289
Burdell, Charles: 387
Bureau of Indian Affairs. See Office of Indian Affairs
Burling, J. L.: 77, 230
Burnett Inlet, AK, evacuation camp: 335, 350–51
Butte Camp. See Gila River, AZ, relocation center

California Farm Bureau Federation: 69, 365
California Joint Immigration Committee: 4, 34, 36, 67–68, 91, 96
California Real Estate Association: 35
California State Department of Agriculture: 70
California State Federation of Labor: 4, 34
California State Grange: 4, 34, 365
California State Personnel Board: 70
Camp Harmony. See Puyallup, WA, assembly center
Canal Camp. See Gila River, AZ, relocation center
Caribbean Defense Command: 307
Carr, Gov. Ralph L.: 102–03, 155
Carter, John Franklin: 51–53, 56
Carville, Gov. E. P.: 102
Cates, Rita: 165
Censorship: 61, 95, 174, 267, 279, 342
Census Bureau: 104–05n
Central Utah relocation center. See Topaz, UT, relocation center
Chamber of Commerce: 35

Chandler, Sen. A. B.: 208, 224
Chercasen, Dorofey: 449
Chinese Exclusion Act of 1882: 29, 30, 32
Chinese Exclusion Convention: 32
Citizenship: 114–15, 206; Asian naturalization ban: 29; dual: 39, 71, 90; renunciation: 247–51
Civilian Food Reserve Funds: 353
Clark, Lieut. Gen. Mark W.: 257
Clark, Justice Tom C.: 18, 73, 84, 89, 105n, 126, 378–79, 387
Clothing: Aleut evacuation camps: 339, 345–46; assembly centers: 143; relocation centers: 163
Coffee, Rep. John M.: 48n
Cohen, Benjamin: 73, 85, 379
Colburn, Ruth: 405, 407
Collier, John: 104, 325
Collins, Wayne: 247, 250, 251, 313
Colorado River relocation center. See Poston, AZ, relocation center
Columbia, S.S.: 333
Commission on Wartime Relocation and Internment of Civilians: 1, 3–4, 10, 16, 27, 50, 121, 138, 195, 297, 298, 362
Community Analysis Section: 180
Compensation: 118–21, 357
Congress, U. S.: censorship action: 61; citizenship renunciation law: 248; deportation suspension: 314; end of exclusion and: 224–27; exclusion action: 3, 95–99; exclusion decision and: 70–71, 81–82, 84; German-Italian exclusion action: 287; immigration laws: 29, 32, 33, 36; relocation action: 224–27, 240. See also Tolan Committee
Conmy, Col. Joseph: 387
Conn, Stetson: 88
Contraband: 7, 54, 62, 88, 147–48, 175
Copeland, Capt. Hobart: 335
Cosmopolitan: 37
Costello, Rep. John M.: 95, 226
Cox, Oscar: 73, 85
Crowley, Louise: 424

Crystal City, TX, internment camp: xii, 311
Curfew: 101, 113–15, 129, 147, 267

Danaher, Sen. John A.: 99
Daniels, Roger: 33, 391
Davis, Elmer: 188–89, 246
Dedrick, Calvert: 105n
DeGuttadauro, Angelo: 437
Delarof, U.S.A.T.: 329–31, 345
Denson relocation center: See Jerome, AR, relocation center
Deportation. See Latin American deportation program; Repatriation
Detention: decision for: 9–10, 70–72, 155; effects of: 10–12, 240–43, 280, 297–301; end to: 12–15, 183, 185–90; enemy aliens: 61, 71, 72, 109, 264, 284–85; German-Italian Americans: 264, 284–86; Hawaii: 264, 270–72, 276–82; Latin American deportees: 305–14; loyalty hearings: 285; segregation program: 15, 206–12. See also Internment camps; Loyalty review program; Relocation centers
Deutsch, Monroe: 113
Deutschamerikanische Volksbund: 288, 289
DeWitt, Lieut. Gen. John L.: 64, 89, 92, 102, 322, 335; assembly centers and: 105–06, 130, 146; evacuation and: 93, 100–01, 105–07, 109, 111, 115; end of exclusion and: 15, 215–18, 220–25, 227; exclusion decision and: 6–9, 50, 59, 62–63, 65–66, 72, 74–77, 80, 82–83, 91, 95, 213–14; exclusion report: 7, 86–90, 98n, 103–04, 106–07, 111–12, 130, 213–14, 222–23, 237–38; German-Italian exclusion and: 286–88; loyalty review and: 13, 191, 201, 215–18; segregation program: 206–07
Dies Committee on Un-American Activities: 225, 226
Dimond, Cong. Del. Anthony: 351
Dirks, Henry: 452

Disturbances: assembly centers: 147–48; relocation centers: 178–80; segregation camp: 209–11, 249
Division of Territories and Island Possessions: 323, 324, 354
Doi, Richard: 390
Doolittle, Col. Jimmy: 320
Doty, Teresa S. G.: 451
Douglas, Justice William O.: 18, 239
Draft. See Military service
Drum, Gen. Hugh E.: 288
Duncan v. Kahanamoku: 238, 281–82
Dushkin, Lavera: 449

Eastern Defense Command: 240, 288
Ebel, Maximilian: 115, 116
Economic loss: 94, 108–10, 117, 121–22, 296; agriculture: 122–27; Aleuts: 22–23, 335–36, 355–57; automobiles: 129–30; businesses: 127–29; caretaker management and: 133; compensation for: 118–21, 357; fishing: 109, 124; property disposal: 130–32; white collar workers: 129
Education: Aleut evacuation camps: 341, 346; assembly centers: 144–45; college leave: 180–81; Japanese language schools: 39–40, 68, 261; pre-war level: 43–44; relocation centers: 170–72, 180–81; return to Japan: 40; school segregation: 33
Eisenhower, Milton: 18, 107, 183, 186, 271; center management policy: 157, 166, 181, 186; leave policy: 181; Nisei military service and: 188, 189; resettlement policy: 10, 152–55, 165
Eleventh Air Force. See Alaska Department
Elliot, Rep. Alfred J.: 70
Emergency Advisory Committee for Political Defense: 306–07, 310
Emmerson, John K.: 308–10, 314
Emmons, Gen. Delos: Alaska command: 355; Hawaii command: 17, 56, 187, 256, 268–74, 276; Nisei military service and: 187, 256; West Coast command: 224, 227, 230–31, 262

Employment: Aleuts: 324–48, 350; assembly centers: 146; post-Pearl Harbor: 70, 71, 97; pre-war: 42–44, 122–23; relocation centers: 165–69, 181–82; resettlement period: 205–06, 241, 242, 295–96; segregation camp: 209
Endo, Ex parte: 231, 235, 239–40
Endo, Mitsuye: 231
Enemy aliens: 59–67, 69, 70, 73–74, 101, 109, 111, 264, 266–67, 284, 285, 287
Ennis, Edward: 379, 426, 436; evacuation role: 104; exclusion decision and: 73, 77, 84, 85, 378; renunciation program and: 247, 250
Ermeloff, William: 449
Espionage. See Subversive activities
Eubank, Carlyle: 333
Evacuation: claims settlement: 118–21, 357; economic effects of: 121–33, 296; effects of: 295–301; German and Italian Americans: 101, 286, 287; Hawaii: 264–65, 268–77; legal challenges: 113–16; mandatory: 94, 104–12, 273; military area designation: 100–01; public reaction: 102–03, 112–13; voluntary: 9, 76, 93–94, 101–04, 111, 112, 273, 277. See also Alaskan evacuation; Assembly centers; Executive Order 9066; Relocation centers
Evacuation camps (Aleut): adjustment to: 349–51; education: 341, 346, 347; employment: 21, 342–48, 350; living conditions: 20, 338–41, 345–47, 350; medical care: 20–21, 330, 341, 345–51; outside access: 341–42, 345, 347–48; sites: 324, 331–32, 335
Evacuation Claims Act. See Japanese American Evacuation Claims Act
"Evacuation of Japanese and Other Subversive Persons from the Pacific Coast": 82
Exclusion. See Executive Order 9066
Exclusion orders: exemptions: 115, 230–31; German and Italian Amer-

icans: 288; instructions: 111*f* (Fig. C); issuance: 109–11; legal challenges: 113–16; prohibited area map: 111*f* (Fig. B); rescission of: 235–36; sample of: 111*f* (Fig. A)

Executive Order 9066: 18; Commission review: 1–2; decision making climate: 8–9; effects of: 10–12; end to: 15–16, 232–36; enemy alien policies and: 60–67; enforcement power: 3, 113–16, 95–99; formulation of: 72–86; German-Italian application: 285–88; Hawaiian authority: 16–17, 273; implementation of: 9–10, 99–112, 287–88; issuance: 2, 27, 49–50; justification for: 6–8, 85–92; legal challenges: 113–16, 231, 236–39; loyalty determination issue: 213–28, 288–89; pressure for: 4–6, 67–72, 77, 81–82; reaction to: 93–95; resettlement and: 227–32; security risk issue: 51–60; summary: 2–3

Executive Order 9102: 107, 152

Executive Order 9181: 326

Executive Order 9423: 228

Expatriation: 209, 251–52, 275

Fair Employment Practices Commission: 46

Family separation: 94, 108, 140–41, 242, 250, 277, 314

Farm Security Administration: 131

Federal Bureau of Investigation (FBI): 77, 101, 129; arrests: 54–55, 108, 278–79, 284, 285; assembly center role: 147; confiscation activities: 7, 62, 88; exclusion decision and: 8, 55; intelligence activities: 51, 54, 57–58, 74, 264, 306; loyalty program role: 190; relocation center role: 176, 179, 183

Federal Communications Commission (FCC): 7, 62–63, 65, 88

Federal Council of Churches: 113

Federal Reserve: Bank: 110, 120, 130, 131; Board: 111

Federal Security Agency: 102

Fencl, Warren: 256

Field, Henry: 104–05*n*

Final Report: Japanese Evacuation from the West Coast, 1942: 7, 86–90, 98*n*, 103–04, 106–07, 111–12, 130, 213–14, 222–23, 237–38

First War Powers Act: 342

Fish and Wildlife Service (FWS): 19, 323, 329, 331, 332, 342–45, 352–53

Fletcher, John W.: 333

Food: Aleut evacuation camps: 338, 345–48, 350; assembly centers: 141–42; relocation centers: 162–63, 176

Ford, Rep. Leland: 70, 84, 106, 159

Fortas, Justice Abe: 203

442nd Regimental Combat Team: 13, 188, 189, 191, 215, 253, 256–60

Frankfurter, Justice Felix: 113

Freeman, Adm. Charles S.: 63–64, 319, 323, 325–27, 329, 332, 335

Fresno, CA, assembly center: xii, 138, 143, 144

Fujii, James T.: 396

Fujikawa, Yoshihiko F.: 108–09, 388, 404

Fujimoto, Jack: 124, 392

Funabiki, Kiku: 424

Funabiki, Walter: 409

Funter Bay, AK, evacuation camp: 20–21, 332, 337–45

Furukawa, Hideo: 396

Furutani, Warren T.: 439

Gabrielson, Ira: 340, 345, 352, 353

Garver, Maj. Carter: 63–64

Gearhart, Rep. Bertram: 61

Geeslin, Fred: 334, 347, 351, 356–57, 451, 452

Gentlemen's Agreement: 34–36, 263

German Americans: 3, 59, 66, 112; arrests: 54, 55; exclusion: 85, 100, 101, 115–16, 285–89, 292–93; Hawaii: 59, 264, 266–67; internment: 264, 284–85; Latin American deportees: 305, 308, 310, 312, 313;

military service: 193; World War I experience: 7, 17–18, 289–92
Germany: 283–84
Gila River, AZ, relocation center: xii, 156, 157, 160, 168, 176
Gillis, U. S. S.: 328
Golodoff, Innokenty: 447
Gordon, Paul W.: 324
Goto, James M.: 140, 396, 397
Goya, Kwantoku: 434
Granada, CO, relocation center: xii, 157, 165, 251
Grant, Madison: 37–38
Greaves, V. Ford: 63
Green, Gen. Thomas H.: 268
Grizzly Bear: 68
Grodzins, Morton: 8, 90, 112, 392
Grower-Shipper Vegetable Association: 69
Gruening, Gov. Ernest: 320, 324–27, 332, 336, 340, 348, 354
Gullion, Gen. Allen W.: 74–75, 77, 78, 84, 106, 215, 387

Habeas corpus: 16, 113–15, 262, 263, 312
Hagerty, Donald: 332
Hagiwara, George: 424
Haiku, HA, internment camp: 278–79
Hall, John: 340
Hall, Capt. John M.: 216, 218, 219
Hall, Olive O.: 403
Hamachi, Roy M.: 406
Harada, Yoshio: 431
Harassment: pre-exclusion: 7, 88–89; relocation centers: 151, 181, 182; resettlement period: 205, 206, 242, 259–60
Hashimoto, Elsie: 392, 400
Hashimoto, Kinnosuke: 393, 415, 424
Hatamiya, Lon: 119–20, 366, 367, 439
Hawaii: 16–17, 261–62; evacuation decision: 264–65, 268–74; evacuation program: 274–77; internment program: 278–82; Japanese immigration: 30, 262–63; martial law: 263–64, 266–68, 281–82; Nisei mil-

itary service: 197, 256, 265–66; security problem: 263–66
Hawaii Defense Act: 263
Hawaii National Guard: 187, 256
Hawaii Territorial Guard: 265–66
Hawaiian Department: 264–66, 270, 273, 274, 276, 279
Hawaiian Organic Act: 263, 281
Hawaiian Provisional Infantry Battalion: 265
Hayakawa, Sen. S. I.: 253, 439
Hayano, Lillian: 393, 403
Hayase, Tom: 392
Hayashi, Ken: 396, 403
Hayashino, Henry: 394
Hayes, Elaine I.: 393, 404
Hayes, Pres. Rutherford B.: 29
Hearst publications: 37, 71, 166, 227
Heart Mountain, WY, relocation center: xii, 156, 157, 159, 161, 168, 174, 246
Herzig-Yoshinaga, Aiko: 401, 403, 404
Hewes, Laurence: 387
Hida, Allan: 406
Himeno, Edward: 439
Hirabayashi, Gordon: 115
Hirabayashi, James: 406, 409
Hirabayashi v. *United States*: 6–8, 86, 91
Hironaka, Masaaki: 397, 398
Hirst, Claude: 324, 325, 327, 331, 349, 351
Hodikoff, Mike: 336
Home Missions Council: 113
Homma, Mutsu: 129
Hoover, J. Edgar: 55, 60, 62, 64–65, 72–74, 101
Hope, Charles: 334
Hopkins, Harry: 103, 110
Hori, Tatsu: 415
Hoshiyama, Tom: 405
Hosokawa, Bill: 397, 402, 407, 408, 428
House Naval Affairs Committee: 224–25
House Select Committee Investigating National Defense Migration. *See* Tolan Committee

Housing: Aleut evacuation camps: 338–40; assembly centers: 345–47, 350; internment camps: 279; relocation centers: 158–62, 350; resettlement period: 204–05, 241–42, 296; segregation camp: 209
Houston Press: 260
Hoverson, Carl M.: 329
Hughes, John B.: 71
Hulbert, U.S.S.: 328
Hunt relocation center. *See* Minidoka, ID, relocation center
Hynes, Frank W.: 339–42

Ichida, May: 205, 415
Ickes, Harold: 223, 236; Aleut evacuation and: 320, 325–27, 332–34, 336; end of exclusion and: 228, 229, 240; Hawaii and: 268, 277
Ickes, Raymond: 309–10
Ige, Kazuko: 140
Ikeda, George: 409
Ikeda, Kin: 406, 424
Immigration: 28–33, 262–63, 306
Immigration and Naturalization Service (INS): 285, 307–10
Inman, State Sen. J. M.: 36
Inouye, Sen. Daniels: 39–40, 259
Intelligence activities: 8, 51–60, 64–65, 264
Interior Department: Aleut evacuation role: 320, 323–27, 329, 331–34, 336, 342–44, 353, 354; Hawaiian role: 268, 277; resettlement role: 104, 228, 240, 277. *See also* War Relocation Authority
Internal Revenue Service: 118
International Film Service Corp.: 37
Internment. *See* Detention
Internment camps: xii, 179, 250, 276–77, 284–85, 307, 309, 311, 313
Irwin, Wallace: 37
Isaki, Haru: 397, 403
Ishiyama, Toaru: 424, 439
Ishizuka, Mary: 125–26
Isolation camps: xii, 179–80

Italian Americans: 3, 8, 54, 55, 66, 85, 98, 100, 101, 193, 264, 266–67, 284, 305, 308, 312
Ito, Yasuko A.: 393, 397, 404, 424
Iwao, Chiyoji: 414
Iwata, Masakazu: 365, 367, 392
Izac, Rep. Ed V.: 222

Jackson, Justice Robert H.: 49
Japan: Aleutian campaign: 320–23, 328, 336–37; dual citizenship: 39; emigration restrictions: 33–34; exchange of nationals: 309; fear of: 37–38; military activities: 5, 47–48, 284
Japanese American Joint Board (JAJB): 190, 197, 198, 201–02, 231
Japanese American Citizens League (JACL): 41, 96, 101–02, 113, 118–19, 154, 157, 178, 188, 208, 246, 365–67, 391, 439
Japanese American Evacuation Claims Act: 12, 50, 118–21
Japanese Association: 39, 41, 61
Japanese Exclusion League: 32–34, 36. *See also* California Joint Immigration Committee
Jaretzki, Alfred, Jr.: 287
Jerome, AR, relocation center: xii, 157, 165, 276
Johnston, Edward C.: 331, 339–40, 342–45, 352
Joint Chiefs of Staff: 270, 322
Joint Immigration Committee. *See* California Joint Immigration Committee
Jones, Etta: 336
Jones, Foster: 336
Jus sanguinis principle: 39
Justice Department: 5, 49, 70, 95, 103, 106–08, 130; citizenship renunciation program: 248, 250; end of exclusion and: 227–28, 231, 234, 235, 240; enemy alien arrests: 54–55, 62, 284, 285; exclusion decision and: 55, 72–75, 78–79, 83–86, 90–91; German American exclusion and: 284–85, 287; Hawaii exclusion and: 272,

276–77; internment: xii, 179, 250, 276–77, 284–85, 307, 309, 311, 313; Latin American deportation program role: 307, 309, 311, 313; legal cases: 50, 87–88, 90–91, 115; resettlement claims: 118, 120–21; restricted areas: 63, 72–74, 100, 101. *See also* Federal Bureau of Investigation; Immigration and Naturalization Service

Kadokura, Hiroshi: 397
Kadomatsu, Marian M.: 415, 425
Kageta, Frank: 194–95
Kaji, Bruce: 406
Kajikawa, Frank M.: 403
Kajiwara, Nobu: 404, 425
Kajiwara, Sachi: 145, 404
Kaklen, Joe: 346
Kaklen, Vivian: 346
Kamada, Mitsuye T.: 425
Kamei, Hiroshi: 124, 393
Kanai, Lincoln: 115
Kanaya, Carolyn A.: 405, 406
Kasai, George J.: 393, 400, 404
Kashima, Tetsuden: 297–98, 439
Kasubachi, Ben: 395
Kato, Murako: 394, 424
Kato, Shuzo C.: 393, 403, 406
Kawachi, George: 396
Kawamoto, Sueko Y.: 403
Kawasaki, Rachel: 396
Kawashima, Ben T.: 403
Kazama, Sally: 396, 397, 409
Kenjinkais: 41
Kennedy, TX, internment camp: 311
Kibei: 7, 31n, 40, 178, 206–08, 249, 254, 275, 278, 306
Kiefer, Christie W.: 298–99
Kika, William: 393, 415
Killisnoo, AK, evacuation camp: 332, 345–46
Kimmel, Adm. Husband E.: 65
Kimoto, John: 394
King, Adm. E. J.: 230, 272
Kirtland, John C.: 446
Kitagawa, Frances C.: 144, 424

Kitashima, Tsuyako: 397
Kiyota, Lillian: 398
Knox, Frank: 49; evacuation role: 103, 108; exclusion decision and: 5, 55–57; Hawaii exclusion and: 55–56, 264, 269, 272, 273
Kochiyama, William: 136
Kochutin, Haretina R.: 330
Kochutin, Innokenty: 330
Koide, Sumie: 424
Komatsu, Ikuo: 425
Korematsu, Fred: 236, 390
Korematsu v. United States: 236–39, 281, 282, 382
Koyasako, Suenari: 407
Kubota, Y. Florence: 425
Kudo, Eigo: 313
Kudo, Elsa: 313
Kuehn, Bernard J. O.: 59
Kuhn, Fritz: 288
Kumagai, Toshimi W.: 424
Kunitani, Suzu: 396, 404
Kurihara, Mary F.: 415
Kyne, Peter B.: 37

LaFollette, Sen. Robert M.: 290
LaGrange, Shizuka T.: 393, 425
LaGuardia, Mayor Fiorello: 203
Land ownership: 34, 35, 42, 154, 225
Latin American Conference on Problems of War and Peace: 311
Latin American deportation program: 305–14
Lea, Rep. Clarence: 81
Lea, Homer: 79
Leave programs: Aleut evacuation camps: 342; assembly centers: 146; relocation centers: 177, 178, 180–84, 190
Leighton, Alexander H.: 151–52
Lekanof, Stefan A.: 449
Lengacher, William: 391
Leupp, AZ, isolation camp: xii, 179–80
Lippmann, Walter: 80, 83, 84
Lofton, Shizu S.: 415
Long, Edythe J.: 350, 351

Long, Elmer D.: 350
Los Angeles County Asiatic Association: 35
Los Angeles County Board of Supervisors: 70
Los Angeles Times: 225
Loyalty review program: development of: 13, 187–90; effects of: 211–12, 245, 251, 301; non-Japanese: 285; opposition to: 203–04, 215–19; registration: 13–15, 191–97, 251, 276; rehearings: 208; review process: 197–204

M I Operation: 320
MacArthur, Gen. Douglas: 48
McCain, Harry C.: 348–49
McClatchy, V. S.: 36, 44
McCloy, John J.: 49, 216, 383–84; end of exclusion and: 15, 92, 214–15, 220–24, 229, 230, 232, 233; evacuation role: 103, 104, 107, 110, 113, 387; exclusion decision and: 8–9, 50, 74–78, 84, 89; German-Italian exclusion and: 287; Hawaii exclusion and: 270–73; loyalty review and: 13, 217; Nisei military service and: 13, 186–89; segregation program and: 206, 208
McGarvey, Lillie: 452
MacLeish, Archibald: 46, 77, 287
McLemore, Henry: 71–72
McMillin, Lee C.: 338, 339, 352
McNarney, Lieut. Gen. Joseph T.: 189
McWilliams, Carey: 104
Magee, C. Ralph: 328–30, 346
Magee, Ruby: 328–30, 346
Makabe, Wilson H.: 398
Manaka, Fred: 392
Manzanar, CA: assembly center: 106, 138–39, 143, 144, 146; relocation center: xii, 156–58, 160, 164, 168, 173–75, 179–80, 182
Marine Corps: 255
Marshall, Gen. George C.: 206; end of exclusion and: 15, 215, 220, 223,

232; Hawaii exclusion and: 272; Nisei combat team and: 13, 189, 215, 256
Martial law: 16, 238, 262–63, 266–68, 280–82
Martin, Fredrika: 330–31
Maryknoll Mission: 101
Marysville, CA, assembly center: xii, 138, 146
Masaoka, Mike: 154, 157, 178
Masuda, Mary: 259
Matsumoto, George: 392, 403
Matsumoto, Ken: 386
Matsuo, Betty: 395, 404, 425
Matsuoka, George: 424
Maw, Gov. Herbert: 155
May, Rep. Andrew: 240
Mayeda, Kazutoshi: 415
Mayer, AZ, assembly center: xii, 106, 138
Mayfield, Irving: 58–59
Medical care: Aleut evacuation camps: 341, 345–51; assembly centers: 143–44; relocation centers: 163–65
Meeker, Dean: 159, 403
Merced, CA, assembly center: xii, 138, 144
Merculief, Paul: 449, 451
Merrill's Marauders: 259
Military areas: 77, 80, 100–01, 103, 107, 110–12
Military intelligence. *See* Army Intelligence; Naval Intelligence
Military Intelligence Service Language School (MISLS): 188, 253–56
Military service: 61, 253–54, 259–60; Aleuts: 343, 346; draft: 187–89, 191, 193, 195, 246–47; Hawaiians: 17, 187, 197, 256–57, 265–66; intelligence language school: 254–56; Nisei combat team: 13, 188, 189, 191, 215, 253, 256–60; Nisei exclusion and: 66, 220–22, 225
Milligan, Ex parte: 282
Minidoka, ID, relocation center: xii, 156, 157, 159–61, 165, 170, 174, 194, 251
Misawa, Tom: 403

Missoula, MT, internment camp: xii, 311
Mitchell, Peggy N.: 140, 405, 425
Miyahira, Mitsunobu: 434
Miyakawa, Hiroko A.: 398, 406
Mizukami, Robert T.: 425
Moab, UT, isolation camp: xii, 179
Mochizuki, Minoru: 413
Morgan, Lael: 447
Mori, Matsui: 424
Morimitsu, Arthur T.: 255, 414, 428
Morimoto, Linda: 408
Morimoto, Noboru: 405
Morison, Samuel Eliot: 284
Morton, F. G.: 352
Mott, Rep. James Wheaton: 222
Munemori, Pfc. Sadao: 258
Munson, Curtis B.: 52–53, 56–57, 60
Murakami, Henry: 109
Murakami, Mark: 254, 400
Muramoto, George G.: 401, 404
Murono, Ginzo: 314, 415
Murphy, Justice Frank: 237
Myer, Dillon: 131, 226, 228; end of exclusion and: 224, 234–35, 240; Hawaii evacuation and: 276; leave program: 203–04, 240; loyalty program: 195; Nisei military service and: 188; resettlement policy: 183–84, 186; segregation program: 207–09
Myose, Susumu: 393

Nagano, Paul: 424
Nagao, Charles: 415
Nakagawa, Bill: 396
Nakagawa, David T.: 440
Nakagawa, Masato: 258
Nakai, Albert Y.: 414, 427
Nakamura, Grace: 136, 395, 396, 406, 409, 413
Nakamura, Yoshio: 398
Nakao, Tom: 415
National Catholic Welfare Conference: 311
National Resources Planning Board: 326

National Student Relocation Council: 181
Nationality Act of 1940: 100n
Native Daughters of the Golden West: 4, 34, 68
Native Sons of the Golden West: 4, 34, 68, 364–65
Naturalization: 29, 31, 33
Naturalization Act of 1790: 28–29
Naval Intelligence: 8, 53–54, 60, 190, 193, 264, 320
Navy, U. S.: 168, 255; Alaskan evacuation: 319, 323–25, 327–29, 332–36, 347, 353, 354; Aleutian campaign: 319–23; end of exclusion and: 230; Hawaii exclusion and: 270
Navy Department: 49, 51; Aleut evacuation role: 324, 353; exclusion decision and: 5, 55–57; Hawaii exclusion and: 55–56, 264, 269, 272, 273; West Coast evacuation role: 103, 108
Neustadt, Richard: 102
Newell, Kenneth: 351
Newell, Martha: 351
Newell relocation center. See Tule Lake, CA
Nikolski Corporation: 449, 451
Nimitz, Adm. Chester W.: 321, 322, 328
Nishi, Dick: 393, 400, 409, 424
Nishikawa, Elizabeth: 401, 407
Nishimura, Shigeo: 395
Nishino, Kozo: 375
Nishio, Esther T.: 394
Nishizu, Clarence: 123–24
Noguchi, Kinya: 396, 397, 406, 427
North Pacific Force: 321–23
Northern California Civil Liberties Union: 69
Northern Colorado Indian Reservation, AZ: 106
Nozawa, Tsuye: 404

Ochikubo v. Bonesteel: 231
Oda, Jack: 399
Oda, Mary S.: 409, 413

Odagiri, Mary F.: 404, 424
Oekawa, Katsuyo: 405
Office for Emergency Management: 112
Office of Facts and Figures: 77, 112, 287
Office of Indian Affairs (OIA): 19, 104, 323–25, 327–29, 331–37, 341, 346–50, 353–54, 356
Office of Internal Security: 266
Office of Strategic Services (OSS): 259
Office of the Alien Property Custodian. See Alien Property Custodian
Office of War Information (OWI): 188–89, 259
Ogata, Mamoru: 404, 415
Okamoto, Kimiyo: 133, 424, 425
Okamura, Taeko: 248
Okazaki, Alice: 405, 424
Okubo, Mine: 175–76
Okubo, Ruby: 398
Okutsu, James: 439
Olson, Gov. Culbert: 5, 70, 76, 98
Omang, Boyd A.: 447
Omori, John T.: 409
100th Infantry Battalion: 253, 256, 265
Ono, Dan: 425
Ono, Yayoi: 146
Oriental Exclusion Act of 1924: 37
Oriole, U.S.S.: 329
Oshima, Heizo: 125, 392, 424
Oshita, Hosen: 393
Ota, Peter: 140
Otsuka, Sgt. George: 260
Ouye, Carnegie: 413
Ouye, Harold: 404, 413
Ozaki, Harue: 424
Ozaki, Sam: 258

Pacific Coast Committee on American Principles and Fair Play: 184, 225–26
Panama: 307
Panay: 37
Parsons, James I.: 335
Passing of the Great Race: 37

"Patria": 37
Patterson, Robert: 84, 380
Pegler, Westbrook: 80, 83
Perry, Commodore Matthew: 29–30
Pershing, Gen. John J.: 292
Peru: 305–14
Petikoff, Mark: 349
Petrivelli, Alice: 452
Phelan, Mayor James D.: 32
Pickett, Clarence: 181
Pinedale, CA, assembly center: xii, 106, 138, 140, 143
Poindexter, Joseph B.: 268
Pomona, CA, assembly center: xii, 138, 148
Portland, OR, assembly center: xii, 106, 137–39, 182
Poston, AZ, relocation center: 151, 156, 157, 161, 165, 168, 174, 178, 246
Powell, Justice Lewis: 239
Prado, Pres. Manuel: 310
Pratt, Maj. Gen. Henry C.: 240
Presidential Proclamation No. 2525: 54
Presidential Proclamation No. 2627: 268
Presidential Proclamation No. 2655: 311
Press: 6, 32, 56, 67–69, 71, 77, 80, 225–27
Pribilof Islands. See Alaskan evacuation
Privacy: 140, 160, 338
Proclaimed List of Blocked Nationals: 306, 307
Proclamations. See Presidential Proclamations; Public Proclamations
Progressive Citizens' League: 41
Prohibited areas. See Military areas; Restricted areas
Property protection: 103, 104, 110–11, 121–22, 130–31, 336
Protective custody rationale: 7, 88–89
Public Health Service: 143, 340
Public Proclamation No. 1: 100–01, 103

Public Proclamation No. 4: 103, 107
Public Proclamation No. 6: 111
Public Proclamation No. 7: 111
Public Proclamation No. 21: 235–36, 240
Publications: assembly centers: 146; relocation centers: 173–74
Puyallup, WA, assembly center: xii, 137–40, 142, 144, 147–48

Quartermaster Corps: 259

Racial discrimination: 44–46, 239. *See also* Anti–Japanese prejudice
Randolph, A. Philip: 46
Rasmussen, Capt. Kai: 254
Rathbone, Tom G.: 109–10
Rauh, Joseph: 73, 85, 379
Recreation: assembly centers: 145; relocation centers: 172–73
Red Cross: 137–39, 142, 144, 147, 311
Religious activities: assembly centers: 145; relocation centers: 173
Relocation centers: administration of: 107, 152, 157–58; arrival at: 149, 151–52; closing: 240; clothing: 163; disturbances: 178–80; education: 170–72, 180–81; employment: 165–69, 181–82; food: 162–63, 176; Hawaiians in: 276, 277; housing: 158–62; leave: 177, 178, 180–84, 190, 203; loyalty registration: 191–97; medical care: 163–65; problems: 176–78; publications: 173–74; recreation: 172–73; religious activities: 173; resettlement from: 183–84, 203–06; security: 174–76; self–government: 174, 177; sites: xii, 156–57
Renunciation program: 247–51
Repatriation: 209, 251–52, 275–77, 309–12
Resegregationists: 248–49
Resettlement: Aleuts: 337, 352–59; Hawaiians: 277; Latin American deportees: 312–14; West Coast: 183–84, 203–06, 229–30, 232, 240–43
Restricted areas: 63, 72, 77, 101

Reschke, Bebe: 416
Rettie, James C.: 326
Reynolds, Sen. Robert: 95
Riemer, Ruth: 119, 393
Ringle, Lieut. Cmdr. K. D.: 53–54, 60, 65
Rising Tide of Color Against White World Supremacy: 38
Rivers relocation center. *See* Gila River, AZ, relocation center
Roberts, Justice Owen J.: 57, 59, 264, 265
Roberts Commission: 57–58, 264, 265
Robinson, Verne: 446, 451
Rocky Shimpo: 246
Roden, Henry: 340
Rohwer, AR, relocation center: xii, 157, 162
Roosevelt, Eleanor: 113
Roosevelt, Pres. Franklin D.: 46–48; Alaska and: 326, 353; Cabinet: 49; end of exclusion and: 15, 215, 227–29, 233–35; enemy alien actions: 54, 62; exclusion decision: 2, 6, 8, 9, 27, 49, 51–53, 70–71, 78–79, 81–83, 85; German–Italian exclusion policy: 287; Hawaii and: 268, 270–74; Nisei military service and: 189, 191; relocation and: 104n, 107, 152, 156, 183, 228
Roosevelt, Pres. Theodore: 33, 291
Root, Elihu: 33
Ross, Fred: 425
Rostow, Eugene: 237–38
Rowe, James: 65, 73, 74, 77, 78, 84, 85, 377–78, 381
Russell, Adm. James S.: 447
Ryan, Col. William: 235

Sabotage. *See* Subversive activities
Sacramento, CA, assembly center: xii, 106, 138
Saiki, Patsy: 396
Saito, John J.: 241–42
Saito, Tetsu: 397
Sakaguchi, Chebo T.: 400
Sakai, Henry: 123, 425
Sakakida, Richard: 255

Sakakihara, Nellie: 405, 424
Sakamoto, Misao: 396, 397
Sakauye, Eiichi E.: 403
Sako, Yoshiaki: 425
Salinas, CA, assembly center: xii, 138
San Francisco Chronicle: 32, 174, 225
San Francisco School Board: 33
Sand Island, HA, detention center: 275, 278, 279
Sanitation: Aleut evacuation camps: 338–40; assembly centers: 142–43
Santa Anita, CA, assembly center: xii, 138, 139, 141, 142, 144, 146–48
Santa Fe, NM, internment camp: xii
Sasahara, Mitsuru: 406, 407, 425
Sasaki, Chiyoko K.: 415
Sasaki, Hideko: 400, 415
Sato, Susumu: 397
Sato–Viacrucis, Kiyo: 403, 425, 439
Saturday Evening Post: 37, 69
Savaroff, Leonty: 449
Savaroff, Sergei: 355
Schectman, Mitzi S.: 396, 415, 424
Schueller, Olga: 115
Scobey, Col. William P.: 188
Seabrook Farms, NJ: 206, 313
Seagoville, TX, internment camp: 311
Search and seizure: 62. See also Contraband
Security: assembly centers: 147–48; relocation centers: 174–76; segregation camp: 208
Segregation program: 15, 206–12, 234, 247–51
Seki, Sumiko S.: 396, 398
Select Committee Investigating National Defense Migration. See Tolan Committee
Selective Service: 186–88, 193, 246, 343
Self–government: assembly centers: 146; relocation centers: 174, 177
Senzaki, Miyo: 404, 415
Setsuda, H. Roy: 425
"Shadows of the West": 37
Shikuma, Lawrence: 425
Shimasaki, Tom: 403–04
Shimizu, Tsuyako: 403, 407
Shinagawa, Emiko: 424

Shintani, Ishimatsu: 431
Shinto: 40, 173
Shiomoto, Y.: 405
Shiramizu v. Bonesteel: 231
Shivers, Robert L.: 57–58, 60
Shizuru, James: 424
Shoji, Samuel T.: 404, 407, 425
Short, Gen. Walter C.: 56, 57, 65, 262
Siems–Drake Company: 335
Smeltzer, Mary: 415
Smith, Harold D.: 326
Somekawa, Emi: 404
Sone, Monica: 161
Sonoda, Kiyoshi: 400, 404, 415
Southern Defense Command: 288
Spain: 247, 309, 311
Spicer, Edward: 180, 409
Sproul, Robert G.: 181, 226
Stainback, Ingram M.: 268
State Department: 307–14
Stephens, Gov. William: 38
Stettinius, Edward, Jr.: 228–29
Stilwell, Maj. Gen. Joseph W.: 64, 260
Stimson, Henry L.: 18, 46, 49, 66, 83, 99–100, 189; Aleut evacuation and: 326, 343; end of exclusion and: 15, 215, 217, 220, 222–24, 228, 235; evacuation role: 100, 106, 186, 187; exclusion decision and: 6, 8–9, 59, 74, 75, 79–80, 82, 84–85, 89, 187, 382–83; German–Italian exclusion and: 285–87; Hawaii exclusion and: 264, 270–74, 276; loyalty review program: 13, 217; Nisei military service and: 189, 191; segregation program: 208
Stockton, CA, assembly center: xii, 138, 145
Stoddard, Lothrop: 37–38
Stone, Justice Harlan F.: 235, 282
Subversive activities: 5, 8, 38, 51–60, 63, 65, 66, 95–96, 264, 272, 278, 288
Suda, George M.: 397
Sugimoto, Henry: 400, 403
Sugitachi, Mary: 406
Sumida, Marshall M.: 396

Supreme Court, U.S.: exclusion cases: 3, 49–50, 86–88, 99, 115, 236–40; martial law cases: 238–39, 281–82, 293; naturalization case: 29; racial discrimination cases: 44, 45
Suzuki, Peter: 180
Svarny, Gertrude: 449
Swanson, Virginia: 113
Swetzof, Sally: 449

Taft, Sen. Robert A.: 99
Taira, Kikuo H.: 397, 400, 403
Tajiri, Thomas M.: 396, 398
Takei, George: 176
Takemoto, A. Arthur: 398, 425
Takemura, Thomas: 425
Takeshita, Ben: 413, 414, 440
Taketa, George: 409
Taketa, Harry: 414
Talbot, J. A.: 349
Tamaki, Minoru: 415
Tanabe, Yoshihiko: 425
Tanaka, Henry: 393, 439
Tanforan, CA, assembly center: xii, 136, 138, 140, 141, 144–48
Tatsuno, Dave: 424
Taylor, Angus: 58, 60, 272, 276
Terminal Island, CA, evacuation: 69, 108–09
Theobald, Rear Adm. Robert A.: 321, 323
Thomas, Rep. J. Parnell: 225
Thomas, Norman: 376
Thoron, B. W.: 354
Togasaki, Susumu: 168–69, 402, 404, 408, 425
Togasaki, Yoshiye: 143, 397, 404
Tokita, Shokichi: 127
Toku, Toshiko: 396
Tokushige, Shizuko S.: 397, 400
Tolan, Rep. John H.: 95, 110, 287
Tolan Committee: 86–87n, 95–99, 102, 104, 113, 130, 131, 153, 214, 287, 293
Toland, John: 104–05n
Tomihiro, Chiyo: 425
Tonai, Mary: 403
Topaz, UT, relocation center: 157–61, 164, 165, 173, 175

Townshend, Harold H.: 226
Treasury Department: 61, 110–11
Truman, Harry S.: 258, 260, 311
Tsuchida, Tamotsu: 404
Tsukamoto, Mary: 123, 396
Tulare, CA, assembly center: xii, 138, 144, 147
Tule Lake, CA: relocation center: xii, 156–57, 159, 164, 168, 170–71, 174, 176, 180, 194–95; segregation center: 15, 208–11, 234, 240, 245, 247–51
Tully, Grace: 104–05n
Turlock, CA, assembly center: xii, 138
Tutiakoff, Philemon: 334

U. S. Commission on Civil Rights: 296–97n
U. S. Employment Service: 109, 182, 342
Ueno, Harry Y.: 408
Umeda, Mike: 392
Umemoto, Karen: 439
United Citizens Federation: 85
Updegraf, Cmdr. William N.: 334, 335
Usui, Mitsuo: 259–60, 392
Uyeda, Ayako: 424

Valor of Ignorance: 79
Varsity Victory Volunteers: 266
Ventura, Ex parte: 113–14, 389
Ventura, Mary: 113
Vigilantism: 7, 89
Violence. See Disturbances; Harassment

Wacker, Eugene: 348
WACs: 259
Wakamatsu, Shigeo: 127
Wakayama, Ernest: 389
Wakayama, Toki: 389
Wallgren, Sen. Monrad C.: 240
War Department: 27, 49, 51, 52, 254, 260; Aleut evacuation role: 343, 352–54; end of exclusion and: 15, 213–

24, 228, 230, 232, 234, 240; enemy alien policies: 62; evacuation role, 9, 93, 95, 106, 107, 111; exclusion decision and: 5, 59, 66–67, 70–80, 82, 84–90; German-Italian exclusion policy: 285–87; Hawaii and: 17, 262, 268–74, 276, 277; Latin American deportation role: 307; loyalty review program: 13, 186, 187, 189, 191, 195, 197, 198, 218–20; Nisei military service and: 13, 220, 246, 253, 260; relocation centers and: 156, 158; segregation program: 206–08
War Plans Division: 270
War Prisoners Aid: 311
War Relocation Authority (WRA): 131, 260; center administration: 12, 144, 157–58, 160, 162–70, 173, 175–78, 180, 182; citizenship renunciation program: 248; disturbances and: 178–80, 248, 250; end of exclusion and: 224–26, 228, 234–36, 240, 241; establishment of: 107, 152; Hawaii evacuation role: 275–77; isolation camps: 179–80; leave program: 12, 185, 202–04; loyalty review role: 2, 13, 186, 190–92, 195, 197, 202–04, 276; Nisei military service and: 246; repatriation and: 251–52; resettlement policy: 10, 153–55, 183–84, 186, 205, 299–300; segregation program: 206–08; site selection: 156–57
Ward Lake, AK, evacuation camp: 347–50
Warren, Chief Justice Earl: 5, 68, 70, 77, 80, 90, 96–98, 102, 227, 375–76
Wartime Civil Control Administration (WCCA): 103, 107, 109, 126, 136–38, 140–46, 251
Washington Post: 226–27
Watanabe, Teru: 393, 395, 407
Watanabe, Tom: 397, 404
Webb, U. S.: 68
Webb-Heney Act: 34
Weckerling, Lieut. Col. John: 254
Western Defense Command (WDC): 175; Alaskan role: 323, 333; end of

exclusion and: 15, 214–24, 227, 229–30, 234, 235, 240; enemy alien policies: 62; evacuation role: 9, 93, 100, 103, 105n, 107; exclusion decision and: 64–65, 72; exclusion justification: 213–14; German-Italian exclusion and: 286–88; leave program: 180–81; loyalty review role: 13, 186, 190, 191, 195, 198–201; segregation program: 206–07. See also DeWitt, Gen. John L.; Wartime Civil Control Administration
Western Growers Protective Association: 69, 124–25
Whitfield, Barbara: 332–33, 347–49
Whitfield, Samuel: 332–33, 347
Wilkinson, Admiral: 272
Willoughby, Gen. Charles: 256
Wilson, Admiral: 272
Wilson, Pres. Woodrow: 34
Wong, Harold H.: 296n
Wrangell Institute: 333–35, 341, 343, 346–47
Wright, Parascovia: 447

Yakabi, Arthur S.: 310
Yamane, Tokio: 210, 247
Yamamoto, Joe: 132
Yamashita, Kay: 398
Yamashita, Kiyoo: 425
Yasui, Minoru: 114
Yasumura, Rae O.: 404, 406
Yatchmanoff, John: 335
"Yellow peril": 37–38
YMCA: 173, 311
Yoneda, Elaine: 140, 408
Yoshida, George: 128–29
Yoshida, Soto: 405, 425
Yoshii, Michael: 439
Yoshikawa, Richard: 405
Yoshioka, Ben: 393
Yoshioka, Vernon: 392, 408
Yoshitake, Henry: 393
YWCA: 173, 311

Zimbardo, Philip: 298, 439
Zimmerman, William: 331–32

☆U.S. GOVERNMENT PRINTING OFFICE 1983 392-960